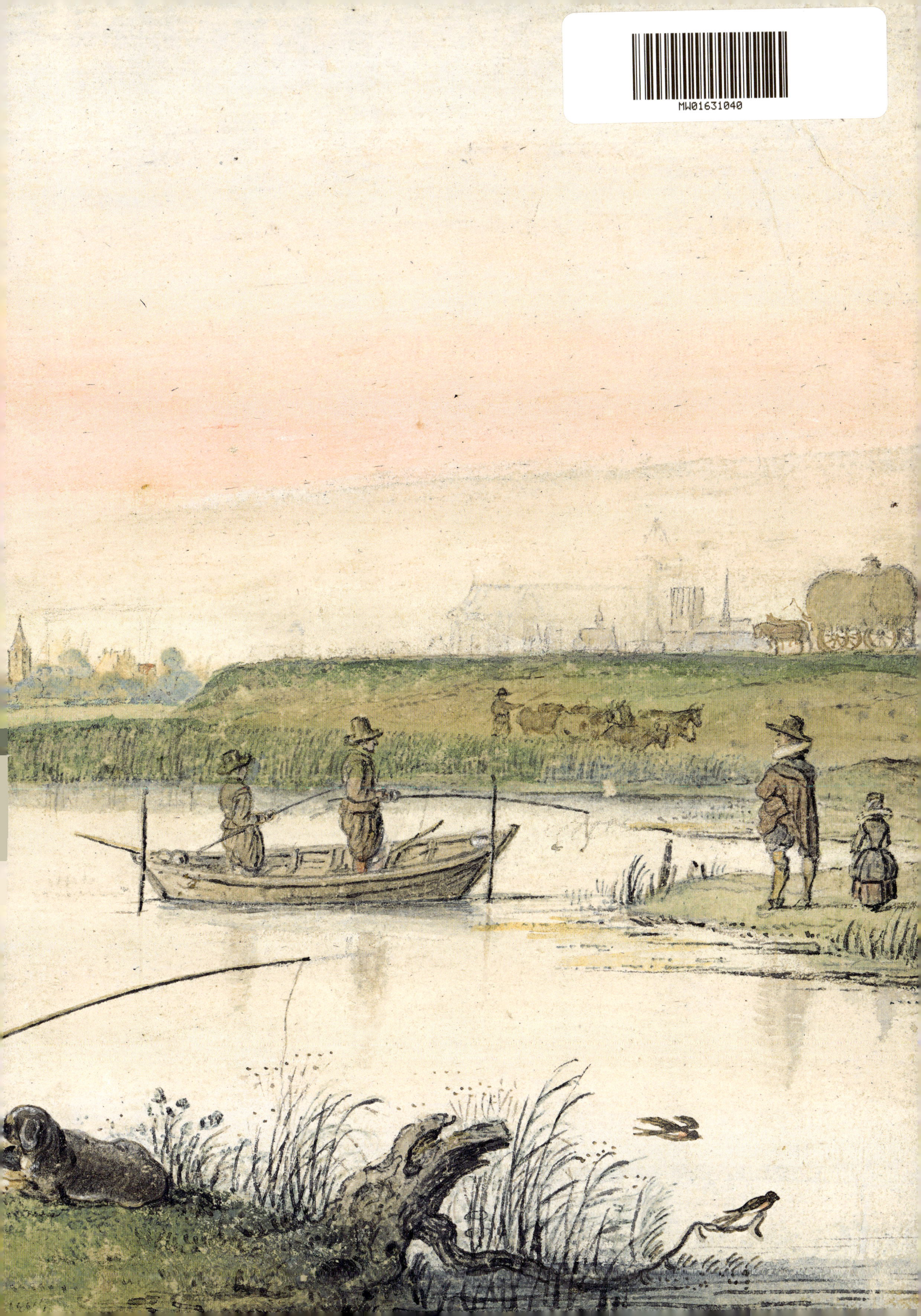

Far and Away DRAWINGS FROM THE CLEMENT C. MOORE COLLECTION

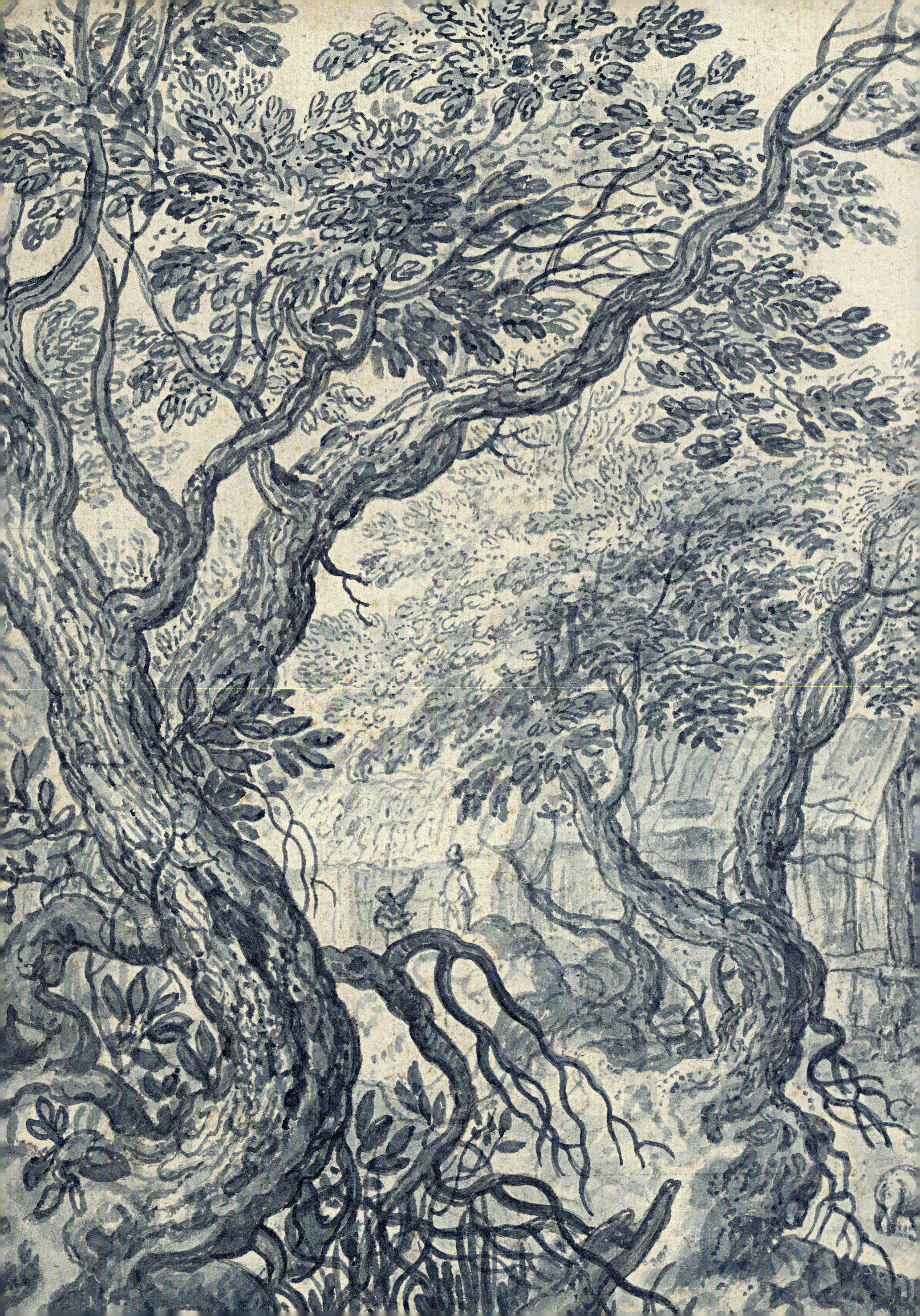

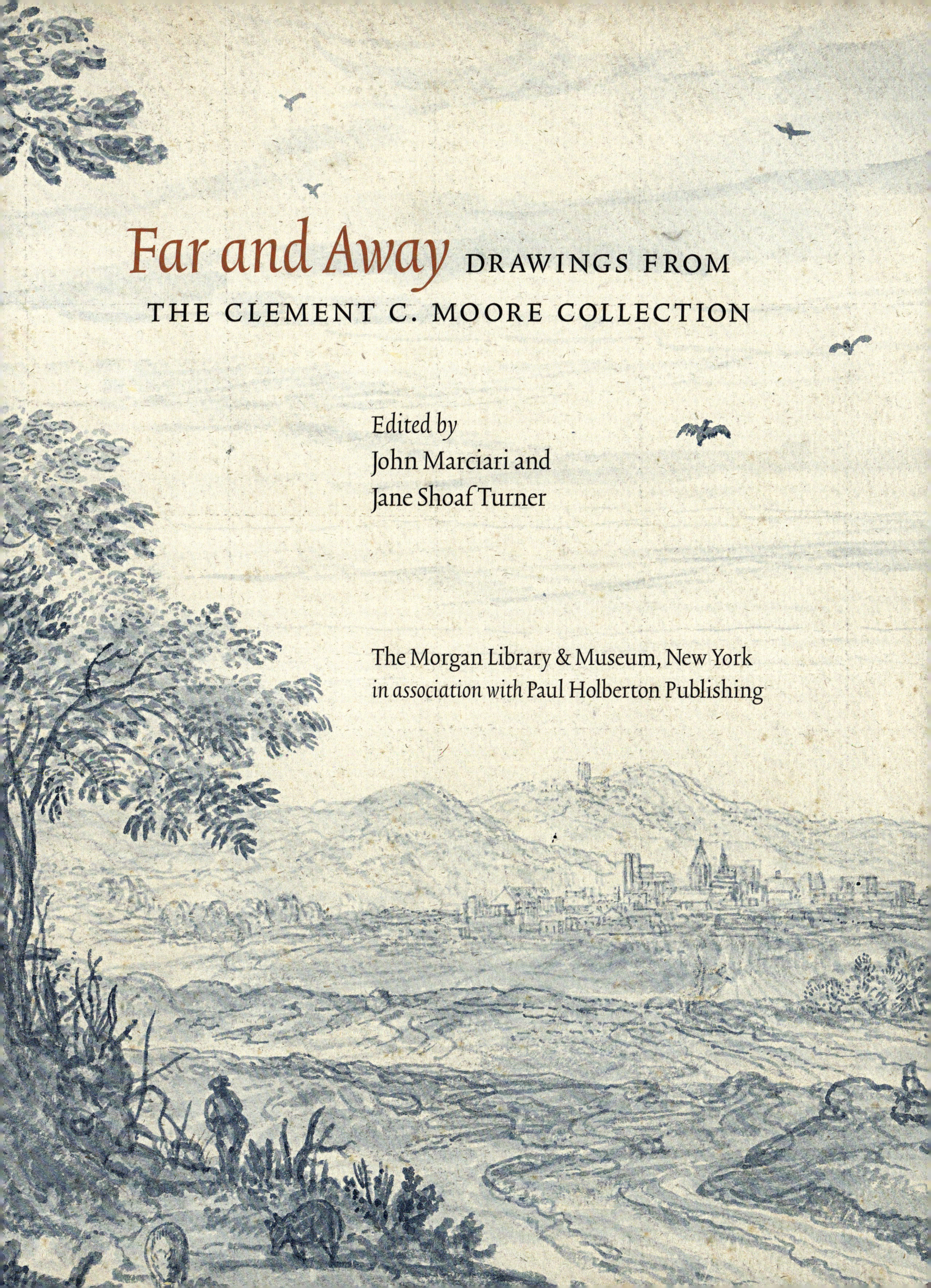

Far and Away DRAWINGS FROM THE CLEMENT C. MOORE COLLECTION

Edited by
John Marciari and
Jane Shoaf Turner

The Morgan Library & Museum, New York
in association with Paul Holberton Publishing

Published to accompany an exhibition at
the Morgan Library & Museum, New York,
28 June–22 September 2024

Far and Away: Drawings from the Clement C. Moore Collection is supported by the Lucy Ricciardi Family Exhibition Fund and the Wolfgang Ratjen Stiftung, Liechtenstein. Additional support is provided by Diane A. Nixon, Karen B. Cohen, Robert Dance, Elizabeth and Jean-Marie Eveillard, and George S. Abrams, Esq. The exhibition is a program of the Morgan Drawing Institute.

Published in 2024 by the Morgan Library & Museum and Paul Holberton Publishing

The Morgan Library & Museum
225 Madison Avenue
New York, NY 10016
www.themorgan.org

Paul Holberton Publishing, London
www.paulholberton.com

FOR THE MORGAN LIBRARY & MUSEUM

Karen Banks, Publications Manager
Yuri Chong, Assistant Editor
Marilyn Palmeri, Imaging & Rights Director
Eva Soos, Imaging & Rights Manager
Janny Chiu, Photographer
Min Tian, Special Projects Assistant
Mary Beth Soya, Imaging & Rights Intern

Designed by Laura Parker
Edited by Sarah Kane
Printed in Verona by 4-Flying Srl trading as E-Graphic

A CIP catalogue record for this book is available from the Library of Congress.

Cover illustration: Detail of no. 61; frontispiece: Detail of no. 15; p. 5: Detail of no. 52; p. 6: Detail of no. 81; p. 9: Detail of no. 46; p. 10: Detail of no. 76; p. 13: Detail of no. 7; p. 14: Detail of no. 1; pp. 28–29: Detail of no. 67; endpapers: Detail of cat. 18

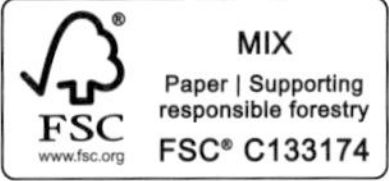

IMAGE CREDITS

The following credits, which are keyed to page numbers unless otherwise indicated, apply to photographic reproductions and the institutional ownership of works illustrated. Every effort has been made to trace copyright owners and photographers. The Morgan apologizes for any unintentional omissions and would be pleased to add an acknowledgment in future editions.

INSTITUTIONAL CREDITS

Alamy Stock Photo/Ken Felepchuk: 204; © Albertina, Wien: 142; Anglesey Abbey © National Trust: 119; © Archivo Fotográfico Museo Nacional del Prado: 176; ART Collection/Alamy Stock Photo: 207; © Art in Flanders/Bridgeman Images: 114; © Ashmolean Museum, University of Oxford: 65, 184, 229–30, 238; Photograph provided by Auction House Schwab, Mannheim, Germany: 108; The Baltimore Museum of Art: Garrett Collection, BMA 1946.112.1842: 38 (fig.4.1), BMA 1946.112.1847: 38 (fig. 4.2); © Barber Institute of Fine Arts/© The Henry Barber Trust, The Barber Institute of Fine Arts, University of Birmingham/Bridgeman Images: 140; Bassenge Auctions, Berlin: 186 (fig. 59.1); Bayerische Staatsgemäldesammlungen-Alte Pinakothek München: 64 (fig. 13.4); © Beaux-Arts de Paris, Dist. RMN-Grand Palais/Art Resource, NY: 111 (fig. 31.1), 210 (fig. 69.2); bpk Bildagentur/Herzog Anton Ulrich-Museum, Braunschweig, Germany/Art Resource, NY: 188 (fig. 60.1), 221; bpk Bildagentur/Klassik Stiftung, Weimar, Germany/Art Resource, NY: 162 (fig. 50.2), 192; bpk Bildagentur/Kupferstichkabinett/Staatliche Kunstsammlungen, Dresden, Germany/Art Resource, NY: 138 (fig. 41.2); bpk Bildagentur/Kupferstichkabinett/Staatliche Museen, Berlin, Germany/Art Resource, NY: 78, 134 (fig. 39.4); © The Trustees of the British Museum: 55, 90, 132 (fig. 38.2), 172, 190, 193; Photograph © Christie's Images/Bridgeman Images: 168; Cooper Hewitt, Smithsonian Design Museum, Museum purchase through gift of various donors, accession number 1901-39-161: 32; Photo © The Courtauld/Bridgeman Images: 132 (fig. 38.3), 138 (fig. 41.1); © Dulwich Picture Gallery/Bridgeman Images: 74 (fig. 17.2), 240; Harvard Art Museums/Fogg Museum, Bequest of Charles A. Loeser, Photo © President and Fellows of Harvard College, 1932.335: 94 (fig. 26.2); Huis Van Gijn, bequest of Mr. Simon van Gijn, 1922: 202 (figs. 66.1–2); © Kröller-Müller Museum: 224; Kunstpalast - LVR-ZMB – ARTOTHEK: 144; The Metropolitan Museum of Art, New York, Purchase, Louis V. Bell, Harris Brisbane Dick, Fletcher, and Rogers Funds and Joseph Pulitzer Bequest, Frits and Rita Markus Fund, several members of The Chairman's Council and Mr. and Mrs. Mark Fisch Gifts, 2013, 2013.645: 50; The Metropolitan Museum of Art, New York, Fletcher and Frits and Rita Markus Funds, 2013, 2013.144: 167; The Morgan Library & Museum: I, 215: 188 (fig. 60.2), III, 145, 152, III, 170: 98 (fig. 27.2), III, 186a: 145, IV, 168, 88, RvR 115: 133; © Museum of Fine Arts and Lace, Alençon (France): 173; The Museum of the Lubomirski Princes at the Ossoliński National Institute, Wrocław: 136; National Galleries of Scotland. David Laing Bequest to the Royal Scottish Academy on loan 1974: 162 (fig. 50.1); National Museum, Stockholm, Acquisition transferred 1866 from Kongl. Museum, Dutch Drawings in Swedish Public Collections, Inv. No. NMH 2166/1863: 208; Philadelphia Museum of Art, The Muriel and Philip Berman Gift, acquired from the John S. Phillips bequest of 1876 to the Pennsylvania Academy of the Fine Arts, with funds contributed by Muriel and Philip Berman, gifts (by exchange) of Lisa Norris Elkins, Bryant W. Langston, Samuel S. White 3rd and Vera White, with additional funds contributed by John Howard McFadden, Jr., Thomas Skelton Harrison, and the Philip H. and A.S.W. Rosenbach Foundation, 1985, Accession Number: 1985-52-3265: 34; The Portland Collection, Harley Gallery, Welbeck Estate, Nottinghamshire/Bridgeman Images: 105; Rijksmuseum, Amsterdam, Gift of C. Hofstede de Groot, The Hague: 180; 20, 23, 30, 44, 48, 60, 70, 82, 84 (fig. 21.2), 84 (fig. 21.1), 98 (fig. 27.1), 102, 106, 120, 122, 124, 134 (fig. 39.3), 134 (fig. 39.2), 154, 164, 170, 174, 186 (fig. 59.2), 210 (fig. 69.1), on loan from the City of Amsterdam: 218; Museum purchase, 1951, Collection of The John and Mable Ringling, Museum of Art, the State Art Museum of Florida, a division of Florida State University, SN654: 178; Scala/Art Resource, NY: 130; Photograph Courtesy of Sotheby's, Inc. ©: 74 (fig. 17.1), 160; © Tate/Tate Images: 232; Photograph courtesy of Teylers Museum: 72, 201 (fig. 65.1); Universitaire Bibliotheken Leiden: 62 (fig. 13.2); © Victoria and Albert Museum, London: 86.

PHOTOGRAPHER CREDITS

Jörg P. Anders: 78; 134 (fig. 39.4); Herbert Boswank: 138 (fig. 41.2); Martin P. Bühler: 24; Janny Chiu: front and back covers; 2–3, 5–6, 9–10, 13–14, 19, 21, 28–29, 31, 33, 35, 37, 41–43, 45, 49, 51, 53–54, 57, 59, 61, 63, 67, 69, 71, 75, 77, 79, 81, 85, 87, 89, 91, 93, 95, 97, 99, 101, 103, 107, 109, 113, 115, 117–18, 121, 123, 125–26, 129, 131, 135, 137, 139, 141, 143, 147, 149–151, 153, 157, 159, 161, 163, 165–66, 169, 171, 175, 177, 179, 183, 185, 187, 188 (fig. 60.2), 189, 191, 195, 197, 199–201, 203, 205, 209, 211, 214–15, 217, 219, 223, 227, 231, 233, 235, 237, 239, 241–42, 245; Steven H. Crossot: 88, 98 (fig. 27.2), 145, 152; Pascal Faligot: 76; Ken Felepchuk: 204; Matt Flynn: 32; Patrick Goetelen, Geneva: 56; Rik Klein Gotink: 224; Graham S. Haber: 133; Annette Hiller: 144; Mitro Hood: 38; Dr. Camilla Pietrabissa: 158; Jacob Schou-Hansen: 156 (fig. 47.2); Hans Thorwid: 208; Richard Valencia: 22, 134 (fig. 38.3); Graeme Yule: 162 (fig. 50.1); Martijn Zegel: 72.

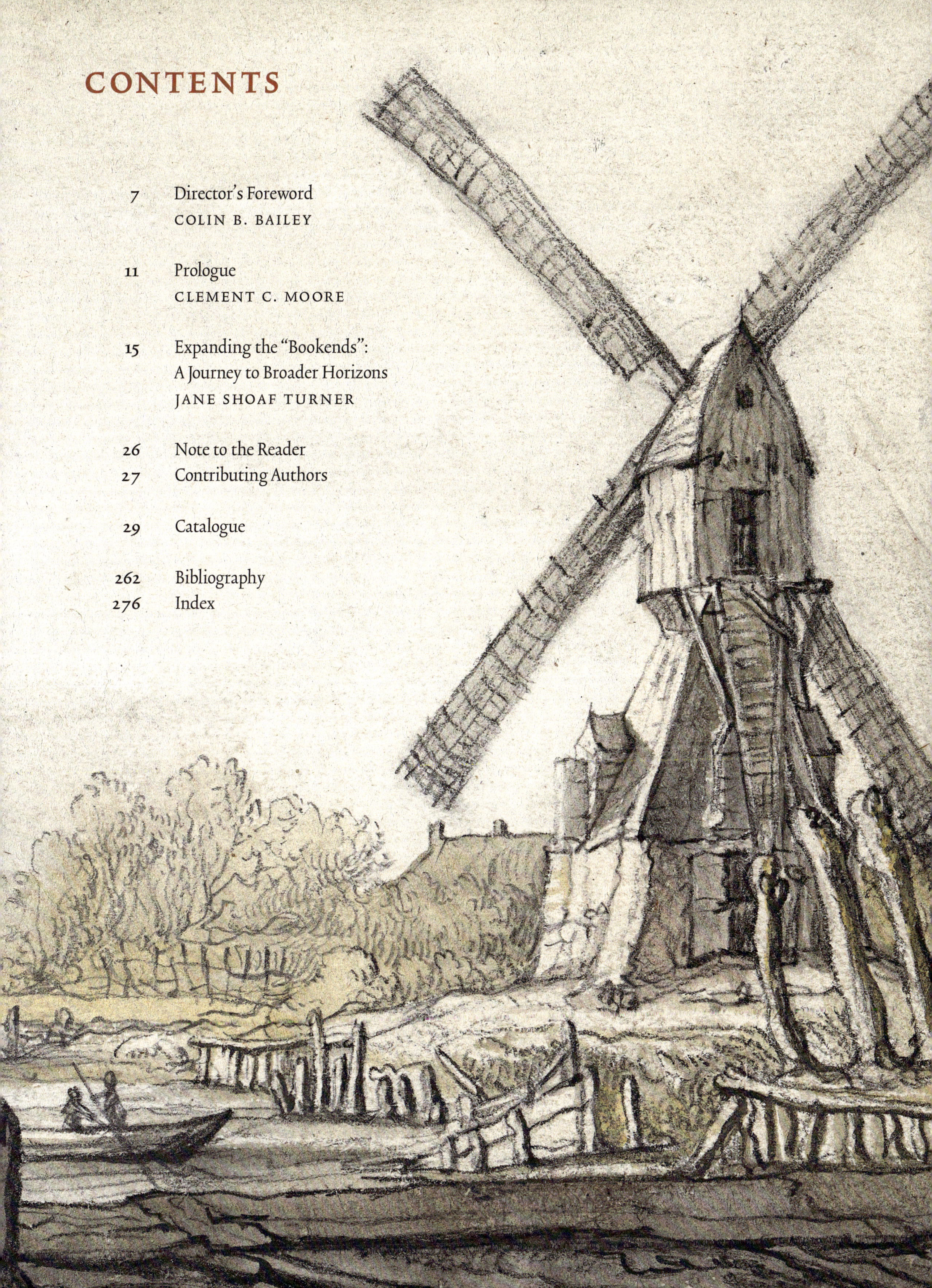

CONTENTS

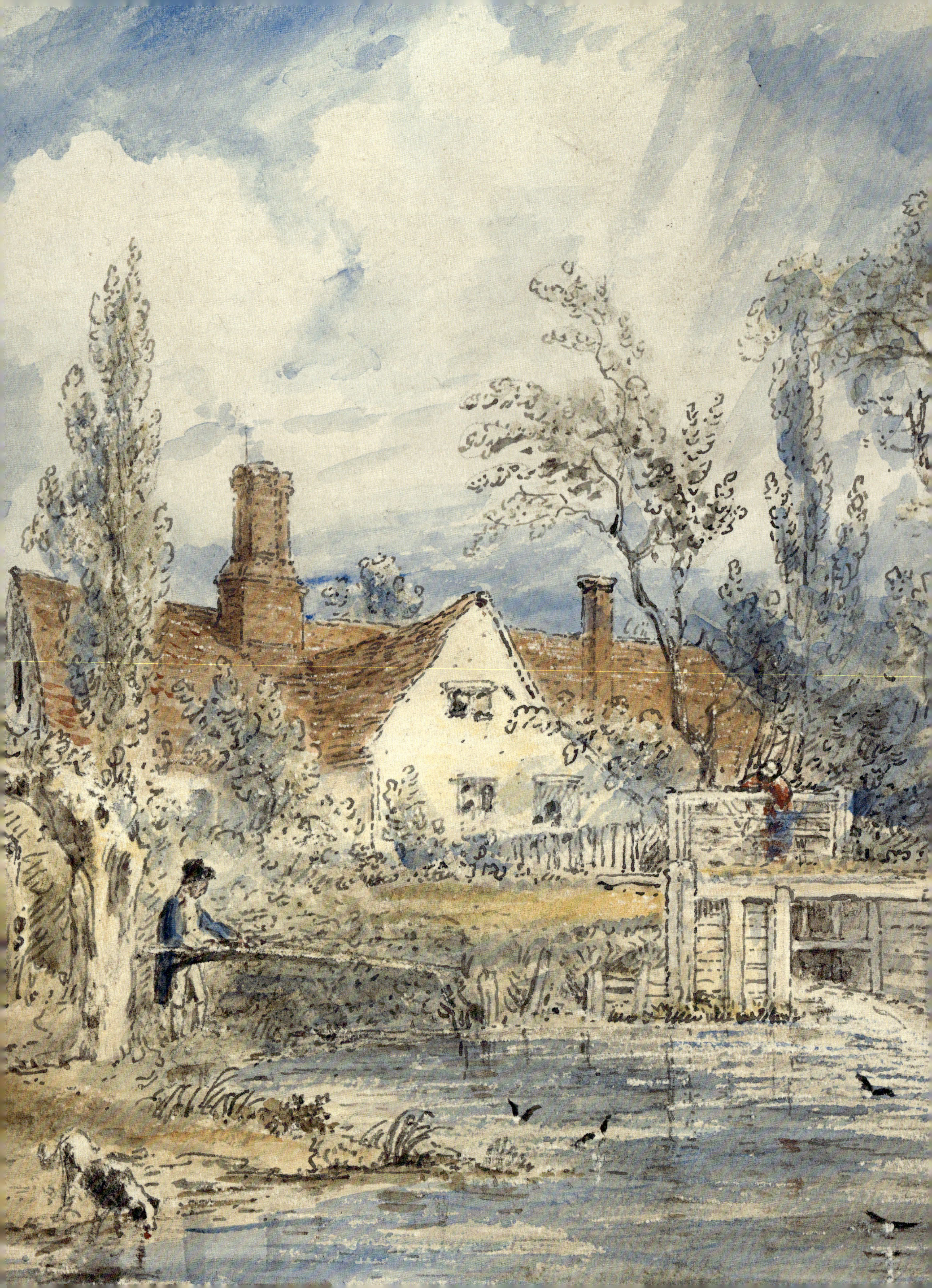

DIRECTOR'S FOREWORD

Colin B. Bailey

Clement C. Moore—or Chips as he is universally known—first became involved with the Morgan in the mid-1990s after striking up a friendship with then-Director, Charles E. Pierce, Jr. He joined the museum's Association of Fellows in 1998 and became increasingly involved with the institution as he met and became fast friends with Jane Turner, who was completing her scholarly catalogue of the Morgan's Dutch drawings. Chips also worked closely with the leaders of the drawings department, first William M. Griswold (1995–2001) and interim head Egbert Haverkamp-Begemann (2001–3), and at greater length with Rhoda Eitel-Porter (2003–10). More recently, he has worked collaboratively with Linda Wolk-Simon (2011–13), who oversaw the first exhibition from his collection, and, since 2014, with John Marciari, who is the curator of the current exhibition and co-editor of this volume along with Jane Turner.

As Chips's connections to the Morgan continued to develop, he supported new endeavors. To help train future generations of drawings scholars and curators, he established the Moore Curatorial Fellowship at the Morgan in 2004. Over the past twenty years this fellowship has supported the professional development of eleven emerging scholars of drawings, and the Moore Fellows continue to play a key role in the department's robust program of exhibitions and publications. Chips's close ties to the Morgan also led to his appointment as a Trustee of the Morgan Library & Museum in 2005; he has been a Vice President of the Board since 2014. But beyond our walls, Chips's involvement with the larger world of collectors, dealers, and scholars devoted to works on paper has inspired him to play a larger role in the field. In 2005, he also joined the Board of Directors of the journal *Master Drawings*, serving as Treasurer beginning in 2007 and becoming President in 2015. In these leadership roles, Chips has always looked forward, anticipating new directions in scholarship and institutional outreach while maintaining the highest standards of excellence and connoisseurship.

All the while, his collecting has continued at a steady pace. The exhibition devoted to his collection in 2012, *Rembrandt's World*, featured more than seventy-five drawings by Rembrandt and his contemporaries. The exhibition marked a pivotal moment for Chips as he shared his private passion with the public and colleagues alike, including a scholars' day full of energetic dialogue and insight. While the 2012 exhibition focused on drawings made in the Dutch Republic—particularly in the seventeenth century—Chips's horizons continued to broaden, and, as Jane Turner's introductory essay to this catalogue explains, the collection has grown to include works made not only by the Dutch abroad, but also by British, Flemish, French, and Italian artists who influenced, or were influenced by, the Dutch. Always a thoughtful, self-aware collector, in recent years Chips has become an elder statesman of sorts in the world of drawings, being honored by *Master Drawings* with a Festschrift volume in 2022, and in 2023 speaking about his collection in events at Master Drawings week here in New York and during a conference held at Amsterdam's Rijksmuseum.

The acquisitions of the past decade and, especially, Chips and Liz Moore's promised gift of their entire collection of drawings have inspired this second exhibition, on the occasion of the Morgan's centennial year, in which we celebrate the collections that form the Morgan's varied holdings. The main exhibition includes around eighty works, chosen to reflect the breadth, depth, and superlative quality of the collection as a whole. I am also delighted that Chips has agreed to share a selection of modern American drawings from his collection, which will be on view in the Morgan's Thaw Case on our Lower Level during the run of the exhibition. The Morgan's dynamic collection continues to evolve through major gifts such as these.

I am grateful above all to the editors of this volume: John Marciari, Charles W. Engelhard Curator and Department Head, Drawings and Prints, and Curatorial Chair, and Jane Turner, former Head of the Rijksprentenkabinet, Amsterdam. In working closely with Chips and the seventeen other experts who wrote for this volume, they have shepherded this project to completion. On behalf of us all, I extend my thanks to this catalogue's many authors, who have graciously shared their expertise and enthusiasm. Many of the authors number among Chips's friends in the drawings world: indeed, this catalogue is also something of an *album amicorum*. Among the authors are two former assistant curators in the Morgan's drawings department with whom Chips worked particularly closely: Ilona van Tuinen, Head of the Rijksprentenkabinet, and Austėja Mackelaitė, Curator of Drawings at the Rijksmuseum, as well as former Morgan Drawing Institute Fellow Robert Fucci, a Lecturer at the University of Amsterdam. Another author is a former Moore Fellow, Elizabeth Nogrady, who recently took up the curatorship of the Leiden Collection in New York.

Thanks are also due to John Marciari's colleagues in the drawings department, especially Sarah W. Mallory, Annette and Oscar de la Renta Assistant Curator, and Jennifer Tonkovich,

Eugene and Clare Thaw Curator, with the support of Daniel Tsai, the Frank Strasser Administrator. I know they are especially grateful for the meticulous efforts of Esther Levy, the Zukerman Departmental Assistant, and Catherine Lammersen, an academic year intern in 2022–23, in the organization of this volume. The contributions of Reba Fishman Snyder, Walter and Constance Burke Paper Conservator, and Rebecca Pollak, Associate Paper Conservator, of the Thaw Conservation Center, who examined and documented the drawings, were essential to the preparation of the catalogue and exhibition.

For producing this beautiful catalogue, we thank publisher Paul Holberton and designer Laura Parker, along with the Morgan's Publications Manager, Karen Banks. We are indebted to Sarah Kane for her thoughtful editing and the Morgan's Editor, Ryan Newbanks, and Assistant Editor, Yuri Chong, for their efficient support. The efforts of Marilyn Palmeri, Director of Imaging and Rights, Eva Soos, Manager of Imaging and Rights, and Janny Chiu, Photographer, have yielded a beautifully illustrated tome that brings to life these often complex and delicate works.

This catalogue accompanies an exhibition of the Moore collection at the Morgan. We are grateful to the museum's Director of Exhibition and Collection Management, Elizabeth Abbarno, who has overseen the many movements of the Moore drawings in preparation for the show. I extend my thanks to her colleagues Anne Reilly-Manalo and Erika Hernandez Lomas, for their assistance with logistics, and to Walsh Hansen for safely and elegantly installing the drawings.

Far and Away: Drawings from the Clement C. Moore Collection is supported by the Lucy Ricciardi Family Exhibition Fund and the Wolfgang Ratjen Stiftung, Liechtenstein. Additional support is provided by Diane A. Nixon, Karen B. Cohen, Robert Dance, Elizabeth and Jean-Marie Eveillard, and George S. Abrams, Esq. The exhibition is a program of the Morgan Drawing Institute.

I reserve far and away my deepest gratitude and thanks to Chips and Liz Moore, who have done so much to enrich not only the Morgan's collections, but also the activities of the drawings department and the field of drawing more broadly. Their generosity is boundless and their trust in the Morgan inspiring.

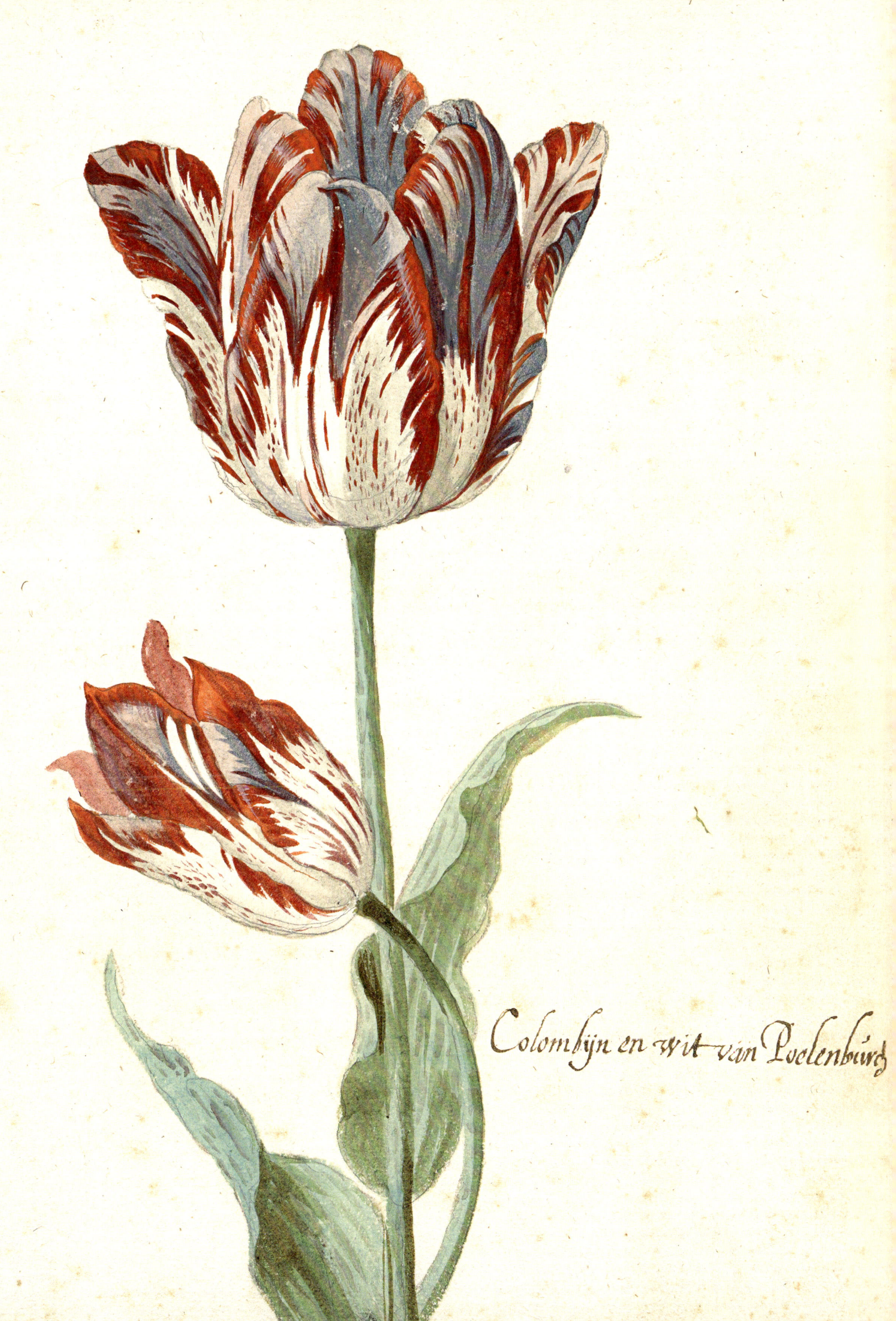
Colombijn en wit van Poelenburch

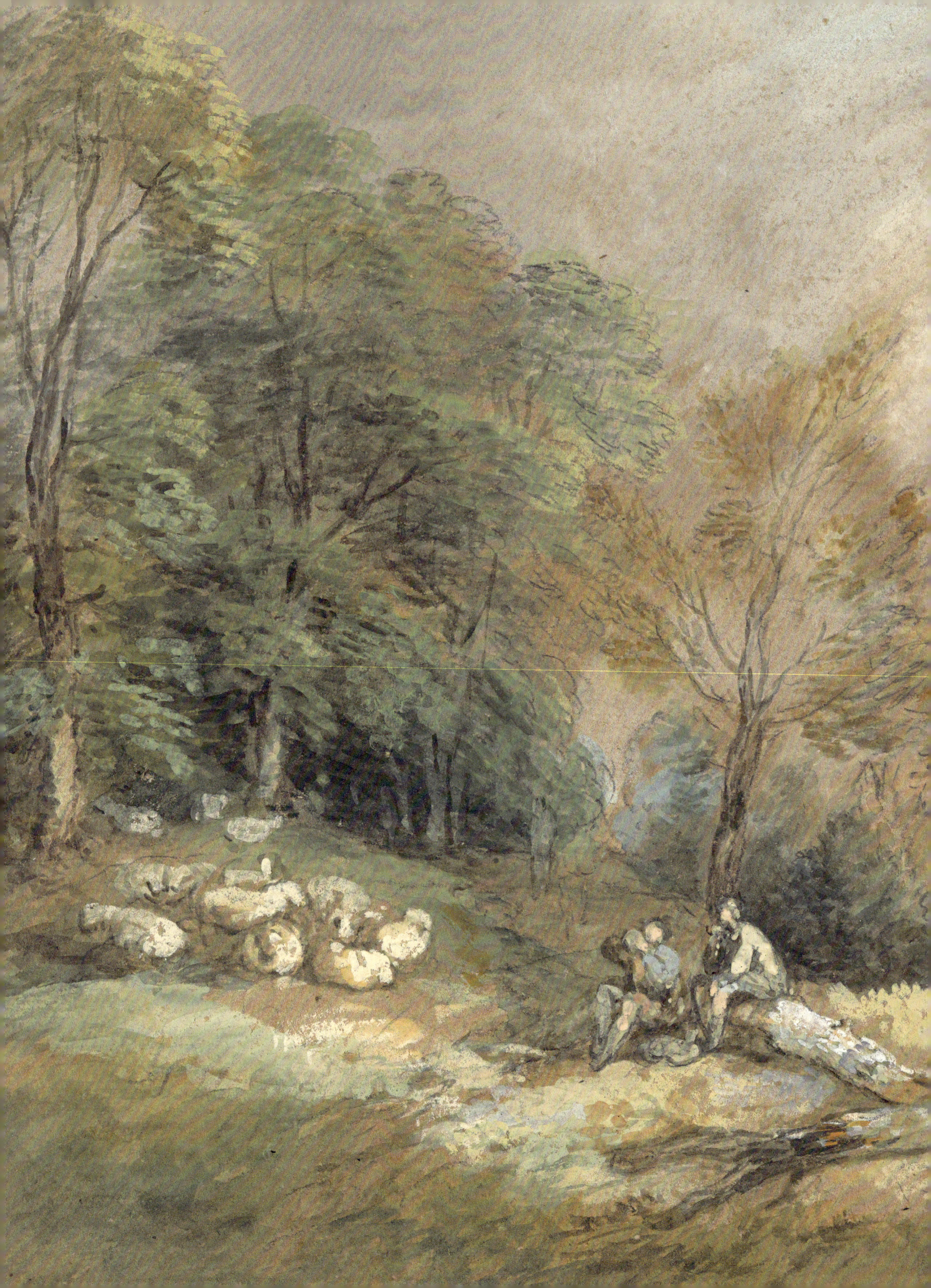

PROLOGUE

Clement C. Moore

More often than not, words of appreciation are added to the end of a catalogue essay. In this case, though, it is fitting to begin by expressing my deepest gratitude to Colin Bailey, Director of the Morgan Library & Museum, and to John Marciari, Charles W. Engelhard Curator, Head of the Department of Drawings and Prints, and Curatorial Chair. It was their decision to show this collection on the hundredth anniversary of the Morgan. In addition, they have pulled together some of the finest scholars to write catalogue entries. I am proud to have so many friends represented here, and equally proud to be associated with this excellent institution.

One more personal note: two sets of eyes are always better when looking at drawings. The extra pair belonging to my great friend Jane Turner has given each of us so much pleasure when parsing out a motif and then writing up that picture in an entry. Athena, or some other god, was clearly smiling when Jane came into my life.

In the spring of 2023, my wife Liz and I visited Amsterdam for the unprecedented exhibition of paintings by Johannes Vermeer. At the same time, that museum sponsored a symposium on drawings, scheduled by the Rijksmuseum's Curator of Drawings and Prints, Ilona van Tuinen, and her husband, Rob Fucci, who teaches at the University of Amsterdam. It was a two-day event where many, mostly young scholars presented papers on subjects important to their studies. At the last moment, Ilona asked me to be the final participant in a conversation from the perspective of a private collector.

One of Ilona's topics centered around the question, "How do you just know when you like a drawing, when it speaks to you, or when it doesn't (even when others around you love it)?" I bluffed my way through with an answer that focused on looking at a lot of drawings over the years, on knowing your taste, on trusting your intuition; but, inside, I felt the answer had eluded me. It wasn't until the next day, relaxing on the ride home, that the answer became clear. Actually, it had been in front of us all the time. I had been recounting stories about the images in the collection: portraits, landscapes, seascapes, and even history subjects. The answer to Ilona's insightful question lay in the stories these artists were trying to tell us.

If the story was easily apparent, most often in the subject matter, but perhaps elsewhere, such as the drawing's technique, its paper, the importance or rarity of the maker, the condition, perhaps even the provenance: any of these would be a deciding factor. Some very good artists tell pretty much the same story over again, so once such an artist is represented in the collection, I don't feel compelled to add another sheet by the same hand. Sometimes the story is hidden, but I feel I'll find it over time. Condition is critical, of course, though perfection is less important to me than it once was. These sheets have lived their own lives for the past 400 years. A spot of oil might mean the drawing was used by its maker in his studio. I am a pushover for a good red chalk drawing (and who isn't?), so when one comes to my attention it is tough not to go for it.

A private collection is driven by its owner's taste. In my case, I started quite narrowly, but over the years I have expanded my vision of what works. The real addiction as an amateur lies in the thrill of research, in gaining knowledge on many unfamiliar subjects.

With Dutch and Flemish drawings, I began with a fascination for images where land and water come together. The collection is much broader now and has moved farther afield. There are drawings by Dutch artists who traveled abroad—to Italy, England, and northern Europe. There are drawings by artists who were influenced by their Dutch predecessors. There is even a drawing or two by artists who may have influenced their later Netherlandish counterparts.

Some of the stories are universal. Take the birth of a child in Jordaens's *Birth of St. John the Baptist* (no. 27). What could be more important than this scene where a gaggle of women coo over a newborn, a dog yapping, while the father stands away from the group looking in? Or a couple of young boys fishing on a summer evening depicted by Avercamp (no. 18). This is what boys do; I did it when I was their age. Or an old woman, near the end of her life, who is in great pain, and seeking solace, as captured by Rembrandt (no. 39).

Not all stories are this obvious, though. Peter Lely's enigmatic study of an English gentleman (no. 49) presents the image of a young, effete, and slightly arrogant patrician. At one point I thought he might be the Duke of Richmond, but the identity of the sitter has escaped all of us who examined the portrait.

Other works are modest and quiet in their tone, but with brilliant technique that beguiles the viewer. The two Gainsboroughs (nos. 76 and 77) were created for the artist's own pleasure, I am told. Profoundly influenced by Ruisdael, he drew shepherds sitting in a lovely wood watching their contented flock, and a group of travelers by a campfire at sunset. The first is done in opaque watercolor while the other is largely in chalk. Both are superb examples of the artist's craft.

In a similar vein, the red chalk drawing by Abraham Bloemaert (no. 10), who is a favorite of mine, was done to show the rear of his model's head with her hair braided and piled up. Why would he do this if he was painting her face? Perhaps he had to know how it would look on paper.

Sometimes the story lies purely in the way a line is drawn. The *View of Diemen* (no. 41) uses very little ink to express this riverscape. Whoever the artist, he learned his craft very well from his master, Rembrandt. Conversely, Lieven Cruyl's drawing of the construction of the Pont Royal over the Seine (no. 67) is a mass of lines, but each one is important. Horses attached to a turnstile bring power to a series of cogs that turn paddles which pump water from the caissons. Workers pull timbers into place, while others bring more wood to the project. This is a masterful drawing.

A couple of years ago, another "exhibition of the decade" was put together by the Isabella Stewart Gardner Museum. Liz and I visited the collection of six paintings by Titian created for King Philip of Spain. Mrs. Gardner owned the great *Rape of Europa*, which we knew, while we must have seen a number of the others in their respective museums. Bloemaert's version of *Danaë* (no. 11), Titian's first painting in the series, has been in the collection for some time. And when my friend Herbert Kasper's drawings came up for auction, I was able to acquire his Goltzius of *Callisto's Pregnancy Revealed to Diana* (no. 7). Kasper favored Mannerist drawings, which were not generally to my taste, but this was a Goltzius, and a scene taken from Titian's *poesie*. This is an excellent example of how my taste as a collector has expanded over time.

Other examples would be the addition of the Guercino (no. 23), the Claude (no. 33), and the Campagnola (no. 1) drawings. In Rome, Claude Lorrain was close to a Dutch group called the Bamboccianti. They learned from him (and maybe he from them as well). To my eye the Guercino, once owned by Peter Lely, closely resembles the style of early Dutch landscape draftsmen, particularly Esaias van de Velde. And the Campagnola, which came from a friend's collection, is so lovely and influential, still on its Mariette mount, I would find any reason I could to make it fit.

Two drawings by Poelenburch are included in the selection for this exhibition (nos. 29 and 30). One is a studio drawing in red chalk of bathers, useful for many of his paintings. Not only a red chalk drawing, it is of a subject that has been painted often over the centuries—that of bathers. How could I pass it up? The other is a brilliant drawing of that glorious Italian light reflected in a scene again where water and land meet. If an artist can draw something as sophisticated and subtle as this gentle light reflecting off water, then his or her story is worth knowing. Furthermore, the signature on the verso of no. 29 confirms that this series of drawings is by Poelenburch.

The French artist Jacques Callot (no. 24) came to my attention because of an exhibition devoted to Rembrandt's drawings and prints at the Denver Art Museum. It was through that exhibition that I learned of Callot's influence on Rembrandt. This little drawing of working men is comparable to prints Rembrandt might have owned.

Drawings from nature are important to us. The two companion drawings of the blue morpho by Pieter Holsteyn the Younger (no. 47a, b) show different aspects of the butterfly: the first with its wings extended and the second with wings closed and at rest. While hiking in Costa Rica, Liz and I saw this magnificent butterfly with its cobalt-blue wings reflecting sunlight. I showed our naturalist guide these images on my phone. She was intrigued because she sensed they had been drawn from life (by an artist from the seventeenth century who never visited the Americas). Something about the way the butterfly stood on its legs told her this.

Lastly, the impressive seascape by Willem van de Velde (no. 45b) showing the *Visit of Charles II to the Rebuilt "Tiger" at Woolwich* came to auction after having belonged to members of the Morgan family. The drawing does not actually show the vessel in the title, strange as that may be. When the 12th Duke of Northumberland sold his extensive collection of naval drawings by the Van de Veldes, however, tucked amongst the lots was an image of the *Tiger* (no. 45a), which we also acquired. These are a fitting coda to my own story and thus a good place to end.

For Liz and me these drawings are more than a collection. They are an entry point into living history. Several represent some of the greatest emotions we will experience as humans. Many record the pride and joy of a newly forming society by depicting what those prolific, brilliant Dutch artists saw as significant. To the two of us these drawings transcend time, and we believe they always will.

My enormous thanks to all my friends and colleagues who contributed their time and effort to making this catalogue successful. Nineteen different scholars from various backgrounds wrote entries. Added to these essayists are editors, designers, and photographers. Sadly, brevity prevents each of them from being acknowledged more extensively here. Despite that constraint, each has been thanked privately for their splendid contributions. Without them, this catalogue could not have come into being.

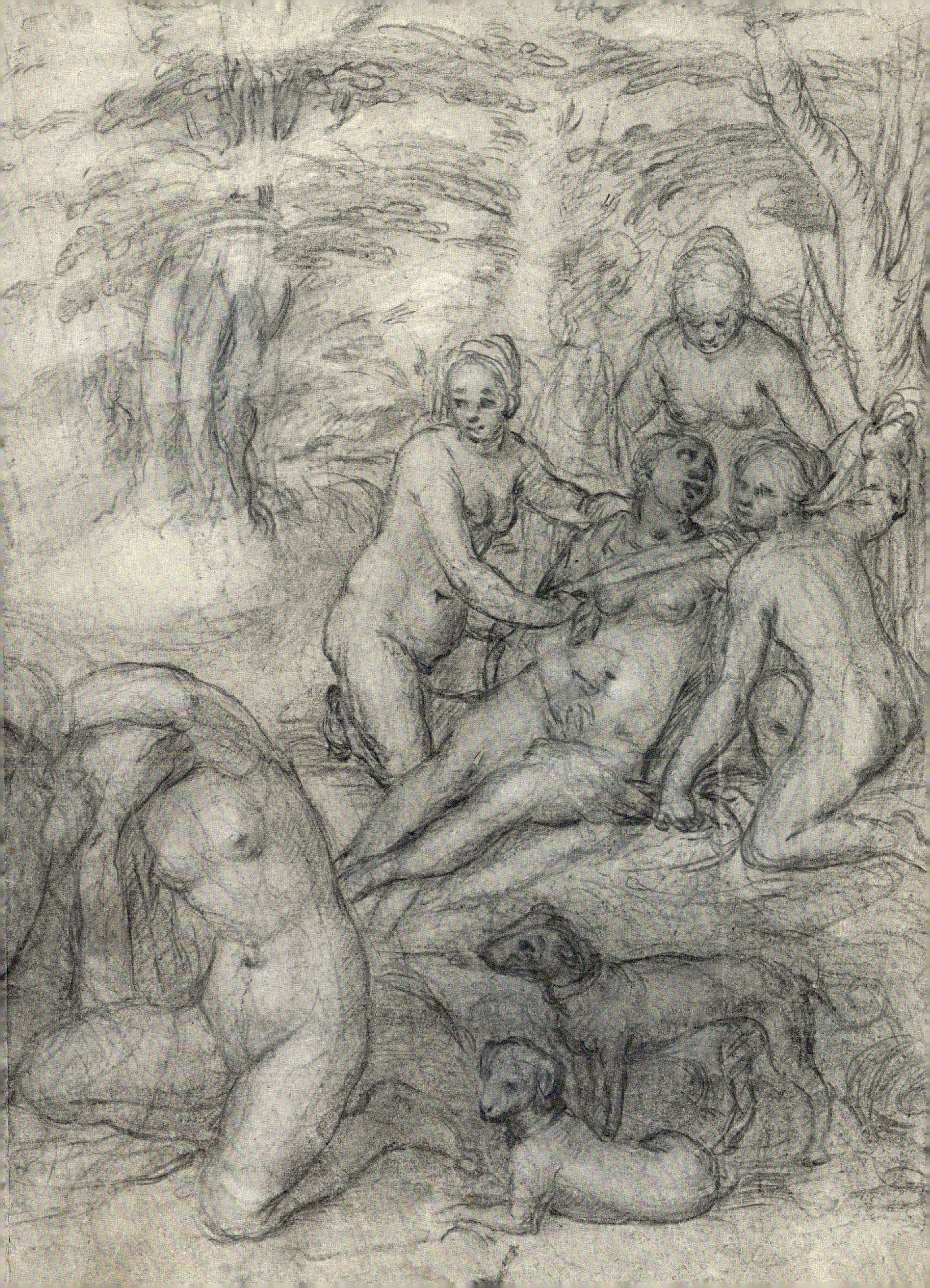

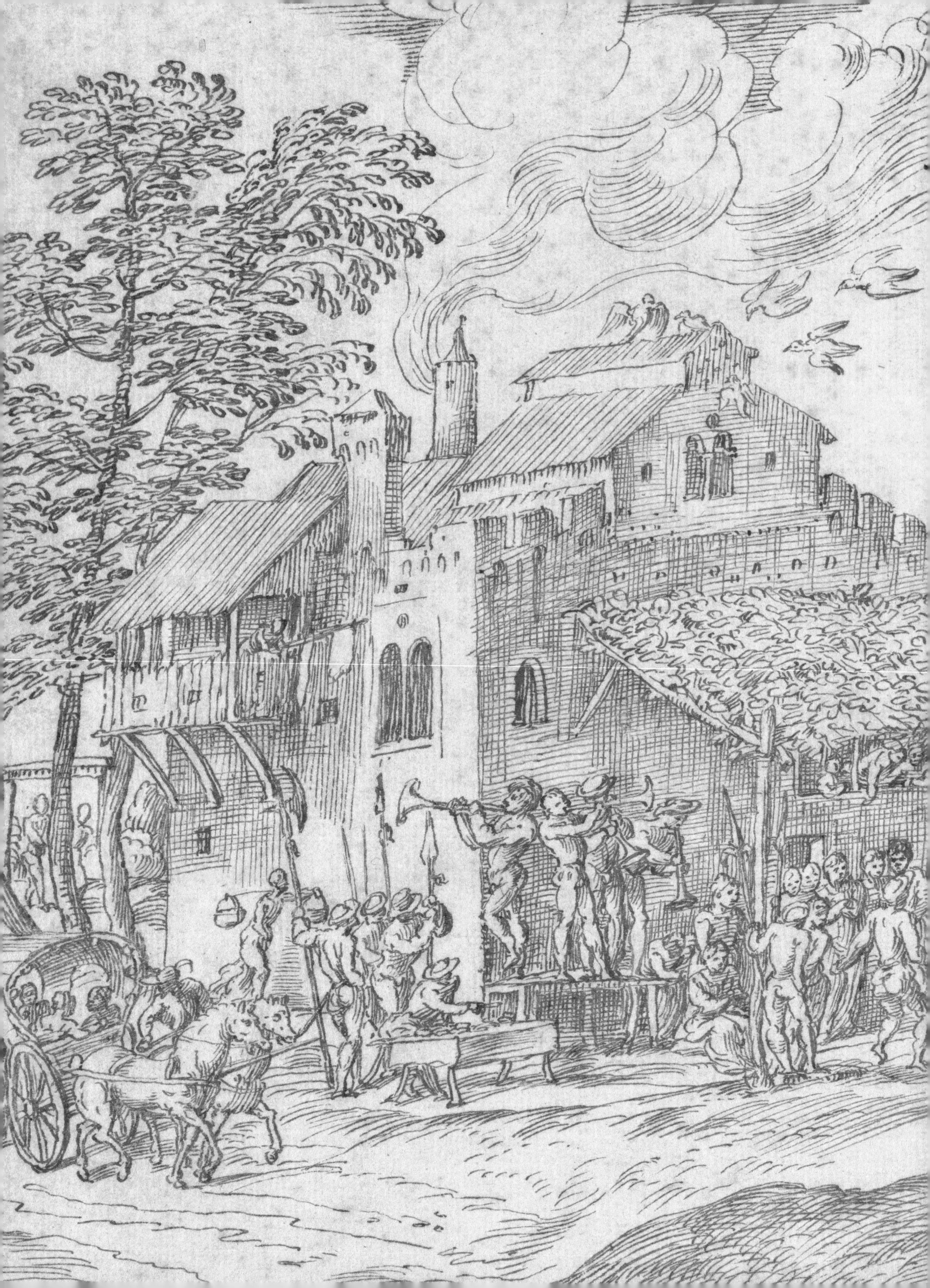

EXPANDING THE "BOOKENDS": A JOURNEY TO BROADER HORIZONS

Jane Shoaf Turner

The introduction to the exhibition catalogue *Rembrandt's World: Dutch Drawings from the Clement C. Moore Collection* (shown at the Morgan in early 2012) includes an overview of the *kunstbeschouwing*, the eighteenth- and early nineteenth-century Dutch tradition of private evening "art showings." At such events, amateurs sat at candlelit tables and examined loose drawings, sharing their passions as collectors while smoking Gouda pipes, sipping wine, and eating cookies. Those events anticipated the kind of intense, private study sessions that Chips Moore and I enjoyed while preparing the catalogue. Until those sessions, he had not often spoken about his drawings. Collecting had been a deeply personal but essentially *private* passion.

Much has changed in the intervening dozen years. With increasing regularity, Chips has publicly shared his knowledge, enthusiasm, and stories, beginning with the decision to offer his drawings to visitors to the 2012 exhibition, and continuing with his address at the opening of the same exhibition at the Teylers Museum, Haarlem, in 2013. His conversation with Jennifer Tonkovich and fellow collector George Abrams at the "Talking Drawings" panel during the Master Drawings New York week in January 2023 (fig. 1) was followed by a similar discussion with Ilona van Tuinen before an audience at the Peck Drawings Symposium at the Rijksmuseum in June 2023. Additionally, he has been an engaging host to a growing number of scholars—including most of this catalogue's authors—who have studied his drawings in his New York apartment or at his farm in Maryland.

The shift from "private" to "public" persona is not the only change. To quote from Chips's discussion with Jennifer Tonkovich, his collecting activities can be defined as a pair of "bookends." The space between bookends supporting a row of favorite books expands or contracts as the preferred tomes change over time.

Chips's "bookends"—his collecting horizons, so to speak—have certainly spread farther apart. They no longer buttress a drawings collection comprised solely of examples by Dutch artists made in their native land—the focus of the 2012 exhibition. If, twelve years ago, it was hoped there would be a follow-up show featuring drawings by Flemish artists and by Dutchmen outside their home turf, that now seems a relatively tame ambition. The present selection does, of course, include works by Dutch and Flemish artists made during travels in Italy (nos. 29, 31, 35, 48, 55), England (nos. 42, 43, 45, 49, 61), and France (nos. 57, 67). Also represented are artists who settled abroad permanently: Jan van der Straet (no. 2), known as Johannes Stradanus or Giovanni Stradano once in Italy at the court of the Medici; Sir Peter Lely (no. 49), who became a naturalized British subject and an important court painter in England; Jan Siberechts (no. 61), enticed to England in 1672 or 1673 by George Villiers, 2nd Duke of Buckingham; Willem van de Velde the Elder (no. 45a,b) and his son Willem the Younger, who switched allegiance during the Anglo-Dutch wars to receive an annual salary from English king Charles II;

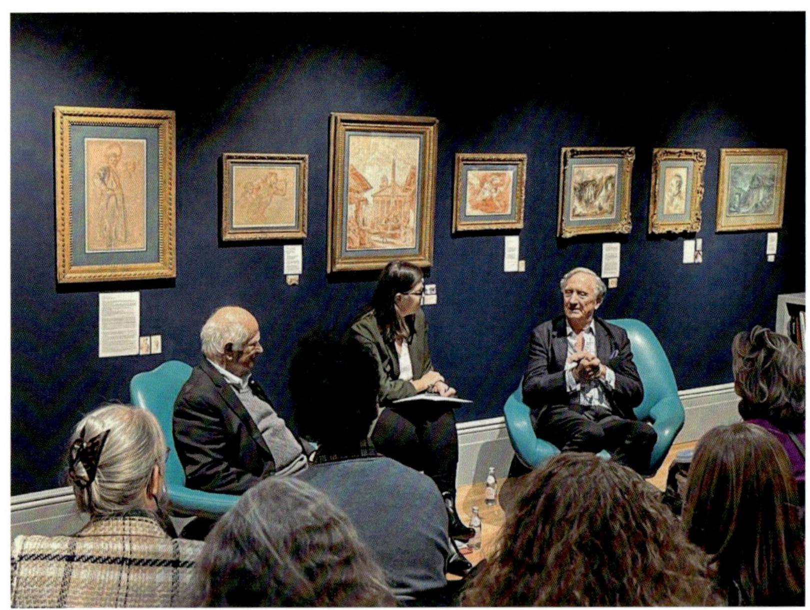

1 Chips Moore in conversation with Jennifer Tonkovich and George Abrams, "Collector Conversations: Talking Drawings" panel, Nicholas Hall Fine Art, New York, 21 January 2023.

and Johanna Helena Herolt (no. 73), who followed in the footsteps of her mother and sister, relocating permanently to Dutch Suriname in 1711. More significantly, alongside such examples of Netherlanders "on the move" are works in the Moore collection by native draftsmen from Italy (nos. 1, 23), France (nos. 24, 33), and, above all, Britain (nos. 75–77, 79–81).

That there is always, however, a connection with Chips's first love corresponds to the literary device also known as "bookending." This powerful storytelling technique takes a central narrative (e.g., drawing in the seventeenth-century Northern Netherlands) and "wraps" it—begins and ends it—with one or more separate short stories. The short story is entirely different from the main narrative, yet supports the overall piece.

And so it is with "bookending" in the Moore collection. Rembrandt—a favorite artist—was inspired, especially in early drawings (e.g., no. 37), by the linear style of prints by Frenchman Jacques Callot. Why not, then, add a sheet of chalk figure studies by Callot himself (no. 24)? Likewise, we know thanks to drawn copies by Rembrandt (e.g., fig. 2)[1] that he was attracted to works on paper by sixteenth-century Venetian artists, hence the acquisition of a pen-and-ink landscape drawing by Domenico Campagnola (no. 1), executed a century before the Dutchman spent hours sketching the countryside to fend off bouts of depression following the death of his beloved wife, Saskia.

If Rembrandt looked back a hundred years to Venetian models, the opposite was true of artists and collectors in Great Britain in the eighteenth and early nineteenth centuries. They turned their sights back to the Netherlands, especially to works from the so-called Golden Age. After a law was passed in 1694 during the reign of William and Mary, Dutch art was allowed for the first time to be imported for auction in Britain.[2] The following century witnessed a profound shift in taste among British collectors, with works by seventeenth-century Dutch artists supplanting Italian and French paintings acquired during the Grand Tour. The popularity of Dutch art then naturally influenced the work of living British artists, especially landscapists such as Alexander Cozens (no. 75), Thomas Gainsborough (nos. 76–77), and John Constable (nos. 80–81).

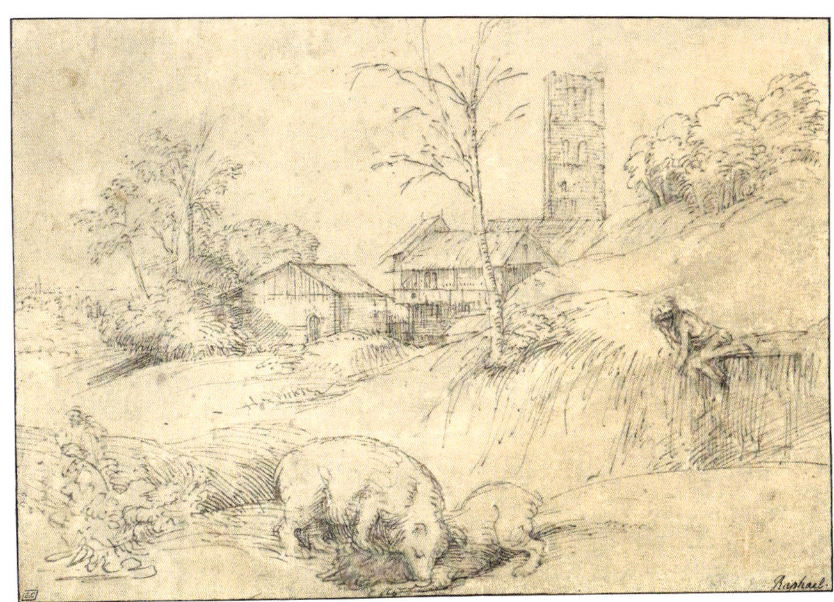

2 Rembrandt (after Titian), *Landscape with a Bear Fighting with a Goat*, ca. 1650. Frits Lugt Collection, Fondation Custodia, Paris.

Given the expanded geographical boundaries defined by this show's "bookends," it is worth exploring the challenges and perils faced by seventeenth- and eighteenth-century Dutch and Flemish draftsmen and women as they journeyed both near and far and away from the comfort zone of their studios.[3] Some fled wars and religious persecution; others acted as spies. Often, like Chips, they simply wanted to broaden their horizons and went in search of opportunities, rich patrons, warmer climates, or exotic subject matter.

LOCAL TRAVEL

The Republic of the Seven United Netherlands—like its successor, the present-day Netherlands—was a small country, roughly 16,000 square miles (i.e., not much larger than Chips's beloved state of Maryland). Artists could thus get around easily, on foot or by horseback (no. 51), by packmule, sailboat, or ferry (no. 42). They could travel along a canal in a barge known as a *trekschuit*, full of gossiping passengers every bit as tedious as what led to the introduction of "quiet cars" on modern trains. Drawn by horsepower or manpower, a *trekschuit* (literally a "tow-boat") was used for centuries to transport less well-to-do passengers between Dutch cities (fig. 3).[4] The earliest *trekschuit* route was introduced in 1632 between Amsterdam and Haarlem and carried up to thirty passengers. Within three and a half decades, an evening service was introduced alongside six to eight daily services. The speed was about four and a half miles per hour—faster than walking—and more comfortable than stagecoach. The journey between Haarlem and Leiden took about four hours, and in the nineteenth century it cost between 16 and 21 stuivers (half a euro in today's money); that sounds like a bargain, but it equated to an average workman's daily wage.

Since the canals served as the city's sewers, the smell in summer could be horrendous. As noted by a nineteenth-century traveler:

> There is something nauseating about the motion of the barge that makes your most fascinating book tedious, . . . but the barges are filled, above all, with the most dismal sort of prattling genius. . . . The barge chatter regularly consists

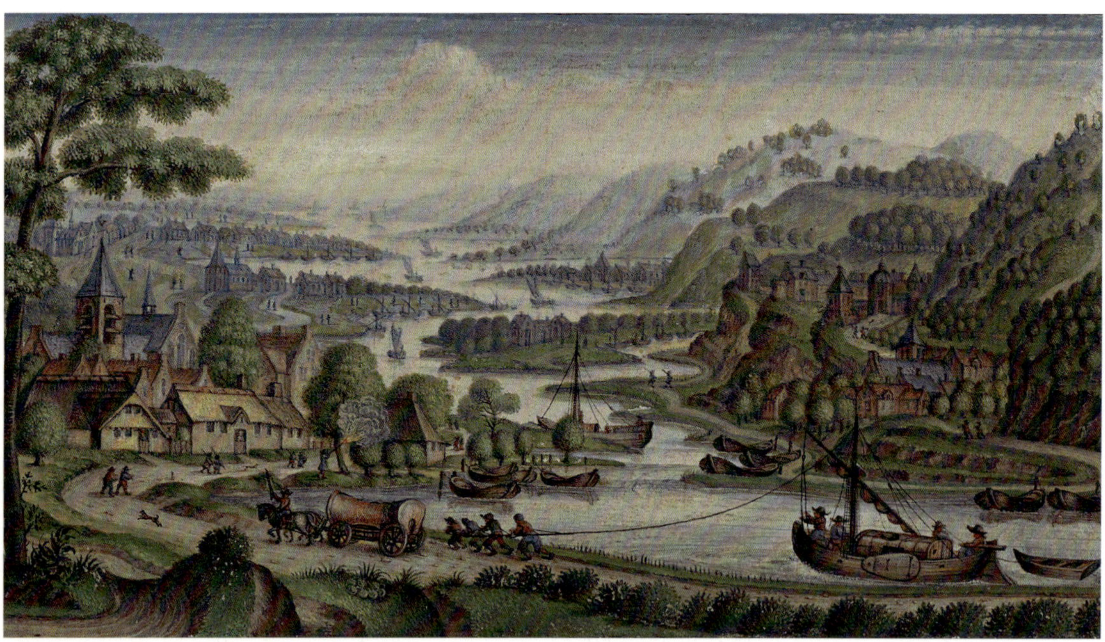

3 Jacob Berents, *Extensive River Landscape with Travelers Pulling a "Trekschuit,"* ca. 1700. John and Marine van Vlissingen Art Foundation.

> of the same ingredients. . . . Barge anecdotes are utterly unbearable. . . . I do not believe that anybody ever had a single clever thought in a *trekschuit*. On the contrary: the deckhouse is the true domain of all possible prejudices, . . . the breeding ground for all manner of ugly, base weaknesses. There are examples of people who by traveling too much in *trekschuiten* have become craven, creeping, miserly, stubborn, and a plain ol' pain in the neck.[5]

Imagine if they'd had cell phones! The same nineteenth-century writer described the stagecoach as

> . . . a jolting, confined, rumbling, filthy, draughty, hard, wobbly box, a kind of large rattling coffin on four wheels; in one there is no room for our thighs, in another no room for our knees; we disembark from one with frozen toes, and from the other with a stiff neck; we ride until we are sick, we ride until our heads ache, we ride ourselves silly, going mad from the whirring in our ears and the clattering at our feet; and all the time we anxiously wonder, while our bowels are being shaken up, whether it would be preferable to emerge dead or alive![6]

VENTURING FURTHER AFIELD

Moving beyond the borders of the Northern and Southern Netherlands, artists regularly crossed the Channel to England, went north to Scandinavia, south to France, and across the Alps to Italy. The travels through France of Lambert Doomer and Willem Schellinks in 1646 are well documented, thanks not only to surviving drawings, but to a detailed travel diary kept by Schellinks.[7] Doomer sailed via the Isle of Wight to Nantes, where his two brothers were then living; Schellinks departed by ship from the Dutch island of Texel on 7 April. Ten days later, he was in the village of Den Helder on the Dutch coast; conditions must have still been wintery though it was April, for they found four ships run aground in ice; a week later he complained of a violent tempest that lasted two or three days (fig. 4).

4 Hendrick Avercamp, *Shipwreck in a Storm* (detail), ca. 1630 (no. 19).

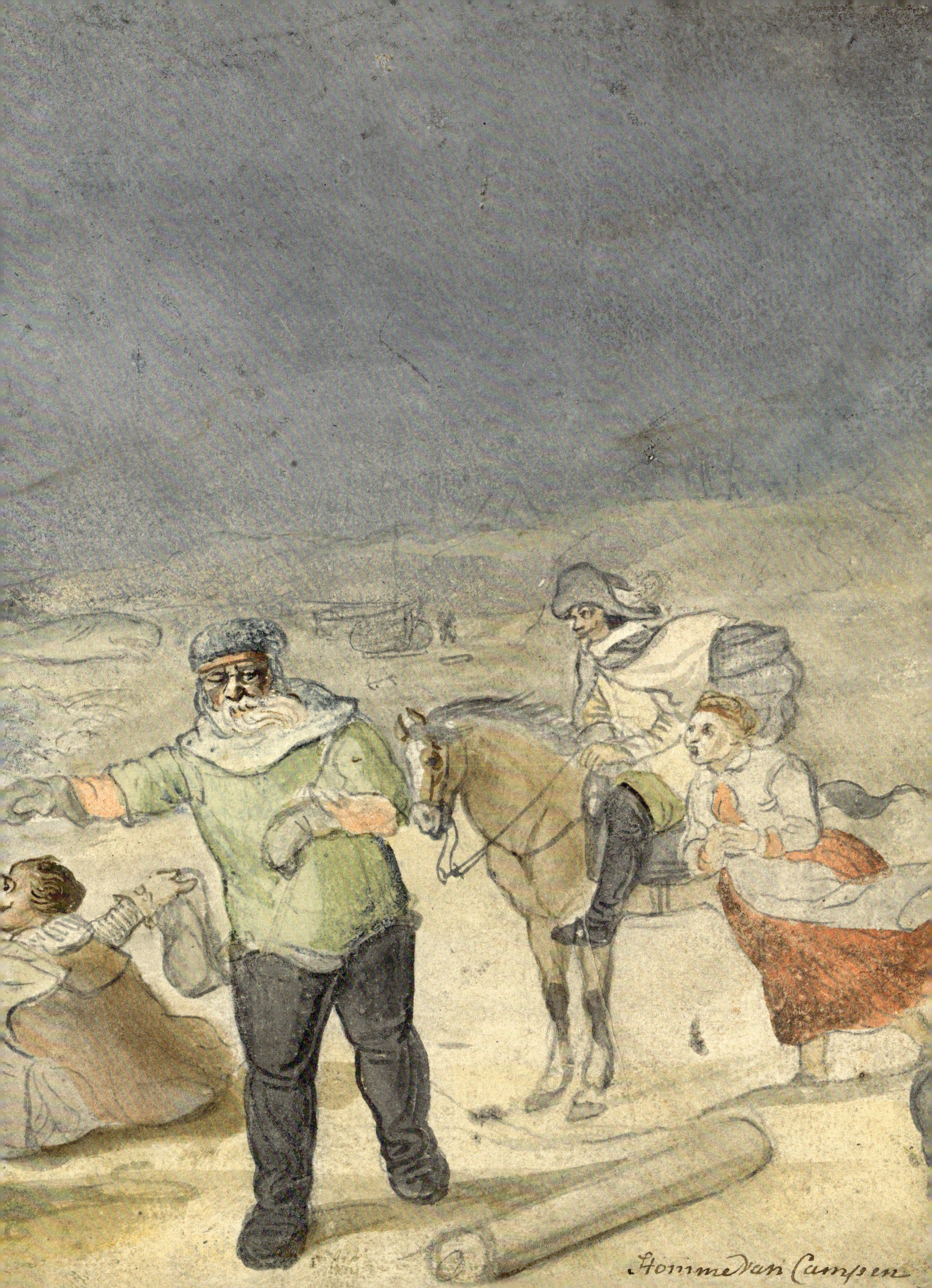
Stomme van Campen

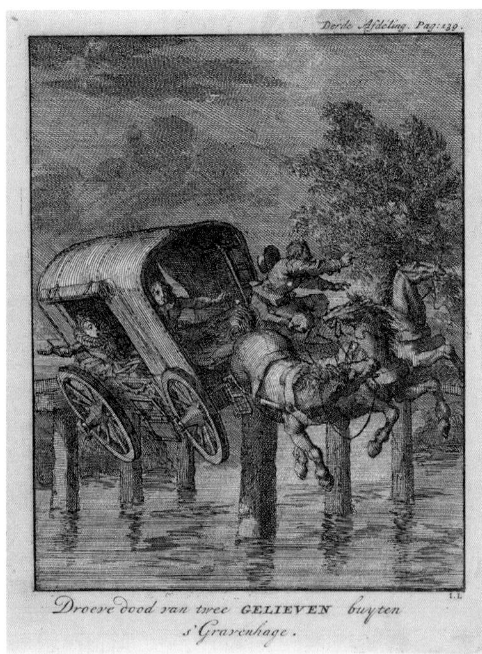

5 Jan Luyken, *Fatal Accident with a Stagecoach*, ca. 1699. Rijksprentenkabinet, Amsterdam.

On 17 May Schellinks arrived in Nantes, suffering from a severe fever, attributable to "the long sea journey, marine air, and poor provisions on board."[8] After he recovered and sent his reluctant brother (ailing from "gales") back to the Netherlands, he and Doomer departed by stagecoach on 3 July and spent a month visiting châteaux and towns along the Loire. During a second month, again traveling by coach, they moved from Paris to Rouen, then to Le Havre. Over the course of twelve weeks (eighty-three days), they covered over 600 miles, at an average of just over seven miles per day. Among the drawings of French locations by Doomer is the *View of Paris as Seen from Montmartre* (no. 57), one of many finished replicas of sketches from that 1646 trip. In his diary, Schellinks complained of the high cost of rooms in Rouen, but he wished to stay there an extra day or so because the price of lodgings in the port city of Le Havre was even worse ("they know how to take advantage of tourist strangers"). This led to a major conflict with Doomer, anxious not to miss the boat from Le Havre. Schellinks's "obstinate" travel companion—as he described Doomer—stormed off, leaving Schellinks without cash for his return journey.

There is no diary to document the activities of Flemish artist Jan Siberechts in England (no. 61). However, his experience probably matched the first-hand tales of woe in the diary of Schellinks, whose party, by then including the young Jacques Thierry II (for whom he was acting as mentor or bear leader), had barely landed in England when trouble began (fig. 5):[9] "After driving a while, our coach overturned, fortunately without anybody being hurt, but . . . Master Jacques twisted his foot and sprained his ankle, so that he could not stand on it for seven or eight weeks and had to be carried everywhere."[10] The next day was no better: "We went on, the road became bad . . . and our coach broke down, and we all got off, except Master Thierry, who could not stand nor walk because of his sprained ankle."

The lad's injury led them to travel from Gravesend to Dover by boat, first via the Thames, then by sea. Schellinks wryly noted: "[T]his should have been a very pleasant journey, but the sea and the weather decided otherwise." After spending an anxious and drenched night, they finally reached Margate. A further leg of their journey, this time on horseback (fig. 6), transpired no better: "On the 28th four of us rode on horseback to the Downs, keeping to the high land near the sea, a very pleasant road. During a hard gallop my horse stumbled and fell forward to its knees, and I, being unprepared, was unseated and shot over the horse's head; it was a great miracle that I did not break my neck."

The many Dutch draftsmen who set off for Italy in pursuit of its soft, golden light faced much the same bureaucracy as today's post-COVID tourists:

> [A] passport was an essential document, as was a health certificate. There were strict controls at borders and ports. Money was another problem; the traveler always had to have the right currency. . . . Finding shelter for the night was no problem for people travelling with a carrier [read, a modern tour group], but others had to look for accommodation themselves. . . . [At their lodgings] they had to state their nationality, religion, age, and social status, and sign a visitors' book.[11]

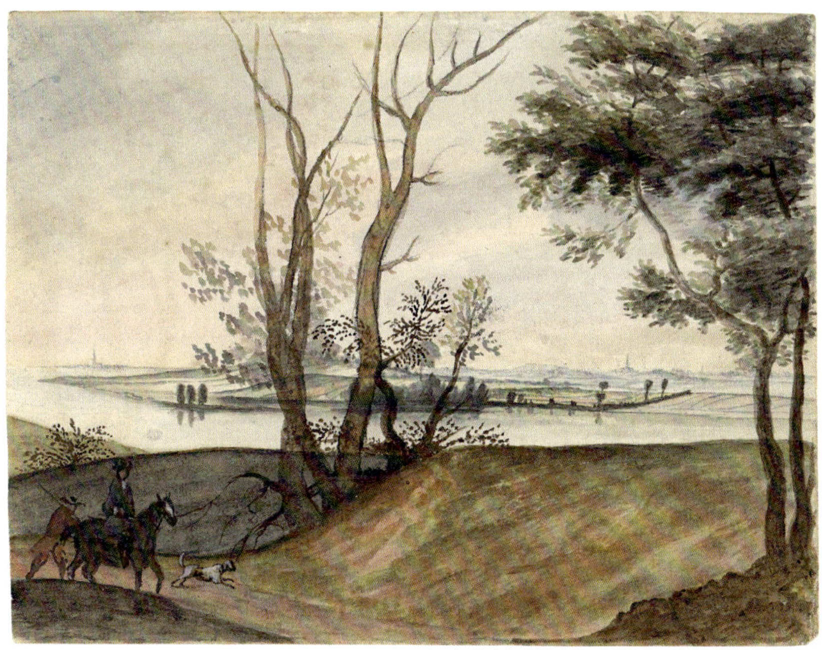

6 Jan Siberechts, *Horseman along a River in England*, after 1672 (no. 61, verso).

There were two main routes from the Netherlands to Italy: one went by boat to Normandy, then by land to Paris, south to the Loire, to Lyon, then by boat down the Rhône to the Mediterranean. The other popular route was via Germany along the Rhine to Basel and then across the Alps to Milan or through Austria via Innsbruck to Venice. To appreciate the awesomeness—and perilous dangers—of such alpine routes, we turn to the seventeenth-century travel journal of artist Vincent Laurensz van der Vinne, who in 1652 headed to Italy with fellow artists Guillam Dubois and Dirck Helmbreeker. Van der Vinne began to report on their journey only when it got difficult in the Swiss Alps:

> The mountains [are] indeed at times so steep that a section cannot be crossed and the rider has to dismount and lead his horse himself. The ground is rocky and inflicts damage, so that unless driven by desire one would desist from clambering over it, but in the ascending and descending one sees the most astounding landscapes of forests, cliffs, lakes, rivers, brooks, and vistas.[12]

Another risk faced by Dutch artists traveling to Italy was the threat of ambush by banditti. Shortly after Van der Vinne's description of alpine mountains, he was kidnapped by rebels in the Swiss Peasant War, who suspected him of being an enemy spy. He was brutally strip-searched, and, though he managed to escape and return to Basel, ultimately he abandoned all hopes of making it to Italy.

Dutch artists arriving in Venice by boat, such as Thomas Wijck (no. 48), were often subject to quarantine, a practice that began in the fourteenth century to protect coastal Italian cities from plague. Ships arriving in Venice from infected ports had to sit at anchor for forty days before landing. The term "quarantine" is derived from the Italian words *quaranta giorni* (forty days).

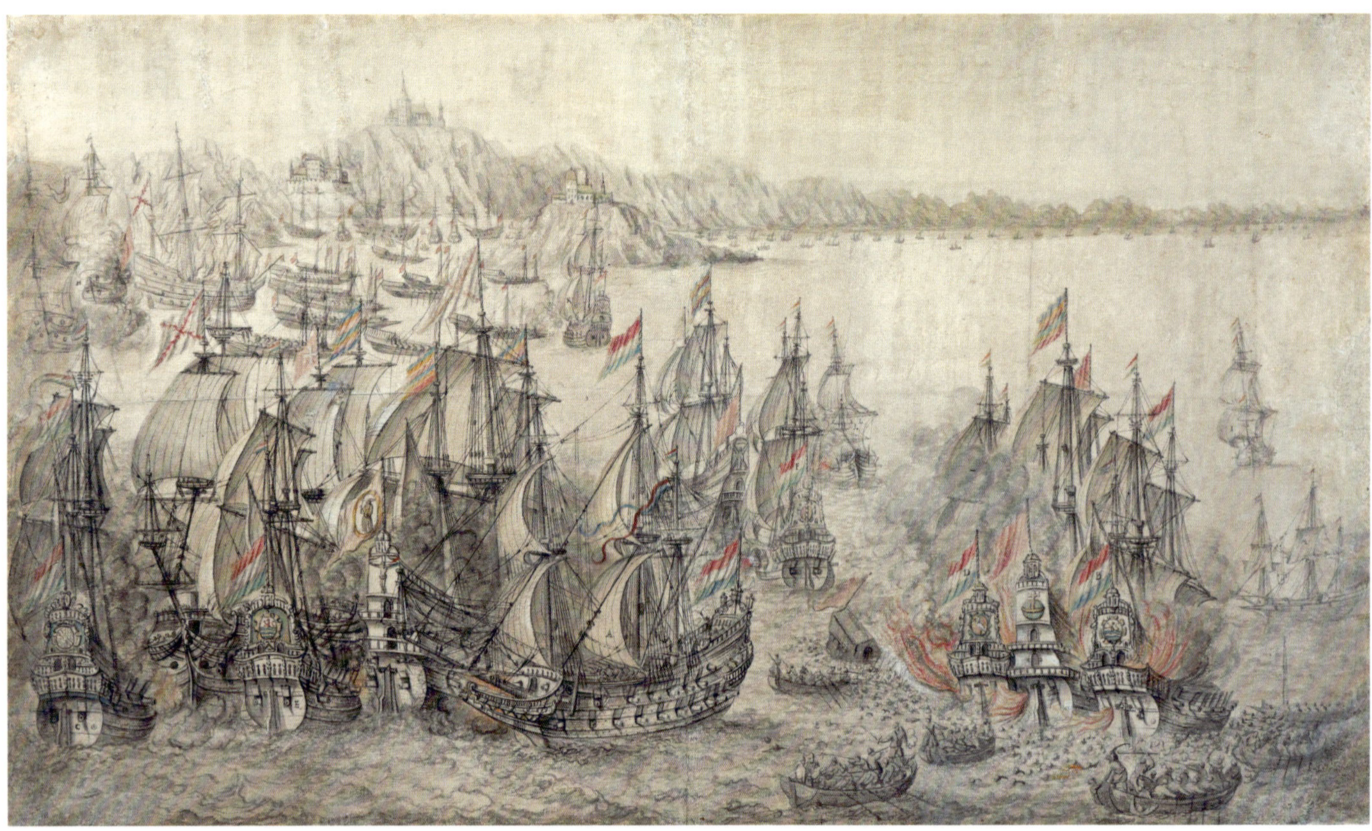

7 Johannes Vinckboons, *Sea Battle between Dutch and Portuguese Fleets off the Coast of Goa in 1638*, ca. 1665. Clement C. Moore Collection.

BEYOND CONTINENTAL EUROPE

Travel throughout Western Europe was only the beginning for Dutch artists. In the late sixteenth century and the early seventeenth, Dutch merchants—often competing with the Portuguese, Spanish, or English—began to conduct trade on far-flung shores (fig. 7).[13] The establishment of the Dutch East India Company (known by its Dutch acronym VOC) in 1602 and the West India Company (WIC) in 1621, the latter active in West Africa and in North and South America, resulted in a dramatic expansion of maritime trade and travel. The Dutch sailed to the Arctic Circle in search of a northern route to China; to Asia, via South Africa, in search of spices, porcelain, and silk; to West Africa in search of ivory, gold, pepper, and enslaved peoples; to the Caribbean for salt; and to Brazil for sugar. Along the way, in 1626 they purchased the island of Manhattan from Native Americans for a mere $24 worth of trading goods.

The first Dutch ships sailed for the "Spice Islands" in the East Indies in 1598. This was two years after a failed attempt to reach Asia via the Arctic Circle, where seventeen sailors became trapped by ice at the Russian island of Nova Zembla. The crew spent nine months of the long arctic winter on the island, where remains of their camp were discovered in the nineteenth century.[14] What sort of merchandise was brought along to trade in China? Extraordinarily, the goods included piles of contemporary Dutch prints by such artists as Jacques de Gheyn (nos. 8–9). The sheets, found frozen in solid bricks of ice, were later painstakingly separated by Rijksmuseum conservators (e.g., fig. 8).[15]

Like many European colonial powers, the Dutch monopolized trade through pirating, privateering or just plain strong-arm tactics. The WIC, notionally set up as a "trade" organization, was more interested in plundering Spanish ships

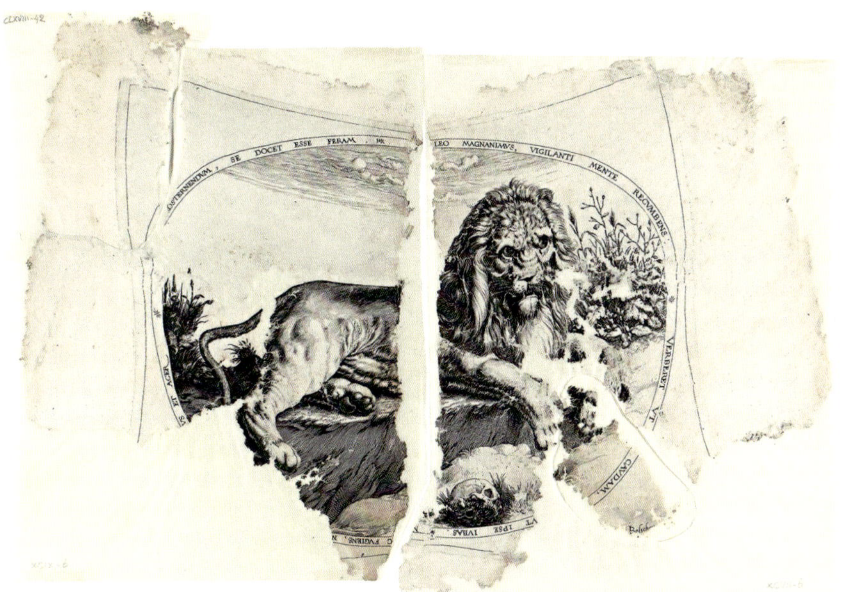

8 Jacques de Gheyn, *The Lion*, 1580–96. Rijksmuseum, Amsterdam.

carrying treasure from the New World. Their first attempt at piracy, in 1626, failed, but the following year one of its admirals captured the fleet in Cuba. The booty of silver, worth over 11.5 million guilders, was so enormous, it took eight days to load it onto thirty-one warships. On the other side of the globe, Jan Pietersz Coen, the governor-general of Batavia on the island of Java in Indonesia, the main destination of the VOC ships, brutally killed, expelled, or sold into slavery some 15,000 inhabitants of the island of Banda. Their crime? They had dared to conduct illicit trade in mace and nutmeg with third parties.

Perhaps not surprisingly, there are few visual records of the conditions under which crews or passengers on VOC or WIC ships traveled such distances. According to an account of the voyage of the ship *Welcome* that sailed with William Penn in August 1682 from Deal, England, to Pennsylvania: "There was very little light or air, and no bathrooms. . . . [A]fter standing in barrels for a while, [water] was neither pleasant nor safe to drink. Everyone, even the children, drank beer instead. . . . [O]n some voyages as many as half the passengers died before they reached their destination."[16] An even more poignant mid-eighteenth-century description of a trans-Atlantic crossing from Germany to Philadelphia paints a horrific picture of a journey that could vary from 47 to 138 days:

> [D]uring the voyage there is on board . . . terrible misery, stench, fumes, horror, vomiting, many kinds of seasickness, fever, dysentery, headache, heat, constipation, boils, scurvy, cancer, mouth rot, and the like, all of which come from old and sharply-salted food and meat, also from very bad and foul water, so that many die miserably. . . . No one can have an idea of the sufferings which women in confinement have to bear with their innocent children on board these ships . . . many a mother is cast into the water with her child as soon as she is dead. . . . Children from one to seven years rarely survive the voyage; . . . I witnessed such misery in no less than thirty-two children in our ship, all of whom were thrown into the sea. The parents grieve all the more since their children find no resting place in the earth, but are devoured by the monsters of the sea.[17]

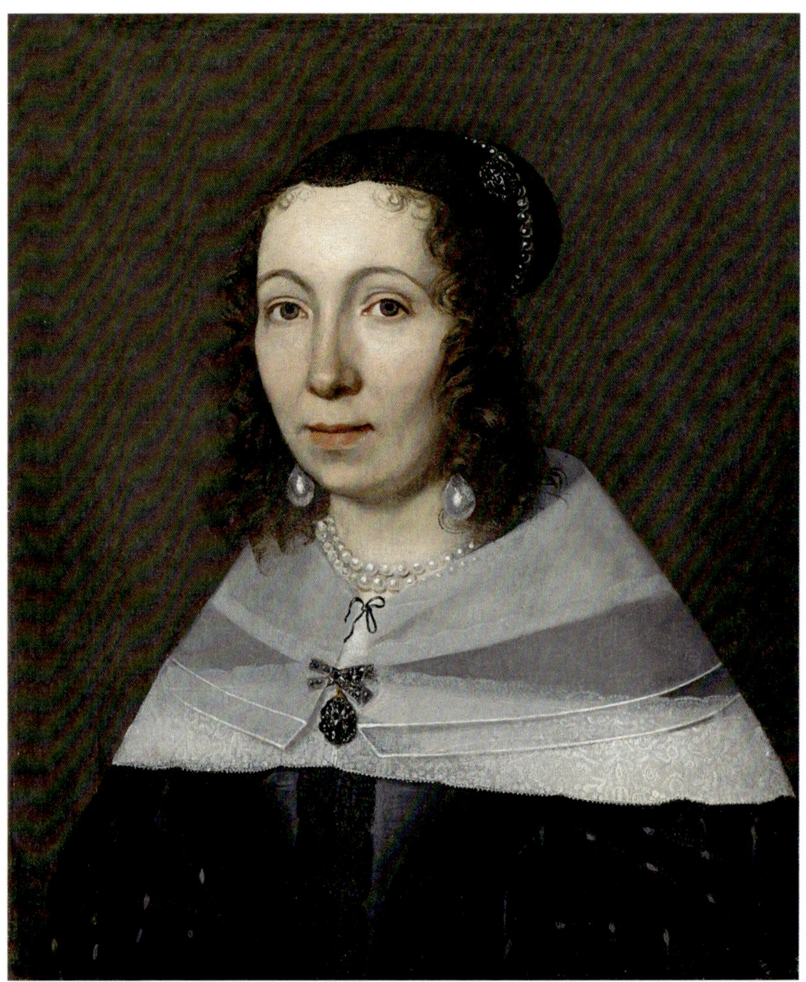

9 Jacob Marrel (?), *Portrait of Maria Sibylla Merian*, 1679. Kunstmuseum, Basel.

Given such conditions, can we ever fully appreciate the extraordinary courage and curiosity that led a fifty-two-year-old divorcée, Maria Sibylla Merian (fig. 9),[18] and her daughter Dorothea Maria Graff to self-finance a ten-week journey sailing halfway around the world to Suriname in 1699, a trip made by Dorothea's sister, Johanna Herolt, a dozen years later? Merian aimed to spend five years recording Suriname's tropical insects and animals. After twenty-one months, however, she became ill (possibly with malaria) and returned to the Netherlands, where she published *Metamorphosis insectorum Surinamensium* (no. 70). She condemned the Dutch merchants in Suriname for their treatment of enslaved people, one of whom assisted her in her research. She also lamented their resistance to plant or export anything other than sugar.

We can but marvel at the fortitude of this pioneering woman, who, ahead of her time and unconstrained by the cultural "bookends" of her era, traveled far and away from her native land.

NOTES

1 Figure 2: Pen and brown ink, 203 x 294 mm; Frits Lugt Collection, Fondation Custodia, Paris, inv. 6584; see Schatborn 2010, no. 16.

2 For the market and taste for Dutch art in Great Britain between 1694 and 1760, see Meadows 1988 and Chong 1987b.

3 Much of the remaining portions of this essay are based on an unpublished keynote lecture I presented at the opening of the exhibition *Crossroads: Drawing the Dutch Landscape* at Harvard Art Museums on 23 May 2022, which incorporated material from Schapelhouman 2015: 8–14.

4 Figure 3: Opaque watercolor on vellum, 94 x 163 mm; John and Marine van Vlissingen Art Foundation, inv. 2004/24; see Shoaf Turner and Te Rijdt 2015, 158, no. 67.

5 See Schapelhouman 2015, 11–12. (Eng. trans. of all original Dutch quotations included in this essay from Schapelhouman 2015 are by Kist & Kilian, Amsterdam.) The account was by Nicolaas Beets (1814–1903), who, writing in 1837 under the pseudonym of Hildebrand, penned the hilarious essay "Varen en rijden" ("Sailing and riding"); for which see Hildebrand (ed. Van den Berg et al. 1998), 1: 106–7: "Dan is er iets weeheidaanbrengends in de beweging der schuit, dat uw belangrijkst boek vervelend maakt . . . maar vooral is er in de trekschuiten een praatgenius van een ellendig soort. De schuitpraatjes bestaan geregeld uit dezelfde ingrediënten. . . . Schuitanecdoten zijn volkomen onverdragelijk; . . . Ik geloof niet dat iemand ooit ééne geestige gedachte gehad heeft in een trekschuit. Integendeel: de roef is de ware atmosfeer voor alle mogelijke vooroordelen, de geschikte bewaarplaats van alle verouderde begrippen, de kweekschool van allerlei leelijke, lage gebreken. Daar zijn voorbeelden van menschen, die door te veel in trekschuiten te varen, lafhartig, kruipend, gierig, koppig en kwelgeesten zijn geworden."

6 See Schapelhouman 2015, 12. For the original, see Hildebrand (ed. Van den Berg et al. 1998), 1: 111: "Maar velen uwer collegae zetten ons in een schokkende, nauwe, dreunende, vuile, tochtige, harde, tuitelige doos, een soort van groote rammelende builkist op vier wielen; in de eene, hebben wij geen plaats voor onze dijen, in de andere, geen ruimte voor onze knieën; uit deze komen wij met bevroren teenen, uit gene met een stijven nek; wij rijden ons ziek, wij rijden ons hoofdpijn, wij rijden ons dóór, wij meenen gek te worden van het gesnor aan onze ooren en 't gedender aan onze voeten; en dikwijls denken wij er, onder het dooreenwerpen onzer ingewanden, met bekommering aan, wat gelukkiger zijn zou, dood of levend er uit te komen!"

7 Willem Schellinks's *Dagh-Register*, MS, Kongelige Bibliotek, Copenhagen, NKS 370 40. The RKD owns a photocopy of this manuscript and an (incomplete) transcription. Another copy is in the Bodleian Library, probably written by Jaques Thierry II (1648–1709), son of the merchant and ship owner Jaques Thierry (1604–1677), who paid Schellinks to escort his son on a Grand Tour through England.

8 The portions of Schellinks's diary from his travels in France are published by Alsteens and Buijs 2008, 346–437; for the quoted passage, ibid., 355.

9 Figure 5: Etching, 198 x 151 mm; Rijksprentenkabinet, Amsterdam, inv. RP-P-OB-44.770.

10 The English portions of Schellinks's diary in England were edited and transcribed by Maurice Exwood and H.L. Lehmann; for the three quotations from this segment of the diary, see Schellinks (ed. Exwood and Lehmann 1993), 33–35.

11 Schatborn 2001, 20.

12 See Schapelhouman 2015, 10. The quotation is from Van der Vinne (ed. Sliggers 1979), 95: "Van daer al over en tusschen 'tgeberchte, ja somtijts soo steijl dat een peert ruijter die niet berijden kan, maer moet van sijn paert klimmen en leijden tselve daer over. Er is een steen achtighe gront, quaet om te gebruijken, soo dat indien de lust niet aen en porde, men soude het over klouteren staken maer men siet int klimmen en dalen de vreemste lantschappen van bosschen, rotsen, meren, revieren, beeken en verschieten, die 'toogh soude konnen bedencken."

13 Figure 7: Pen and black ink, gray wash, and watercolor over black chalk, 438 x 760 mm. Clement C. Moore Collection.

14 The finds are now preserved in the Rijksmuseum, Amsterdam; see De Hond and Mostert 2013.

15 Figure 8: Engraving, 385 x 556 mm; Rijksmuseum, Amsterdam, inv. NG-NM-9486-1-2.

16 See https://www.calebpuseyhouse.com/the-voyage-of-the-welcome.html. For further accounts, see Dobson 2008.

17 The quotation is from *Gottlieb Mittelberger's Journey to Pennsylvania in the Year 1750 and Return to Germany in the Year 1754* (Philadelphia, 1898), for which see https://history.hanover.edu/courses/excerpts/144mittelberger.html.

18 Figure 9: Oil on canvas, 59 x 50.5 cm; Kunstmuseum, Basel, inv. 436.

NOTE TO THE READER

Catalogue entries are organized according to the birth date of the artist.

Many artists are known by a variety of name variants. For Dutch, Flemish, and Netherlandish artists, we follow the forms used by the RKD – Netherlands Institute for Art History (www.rkd.nl); for others, we follow the *Grove Dictionary of Art*, now part of Oxford Art Online (www.oxfordartonline.com).

Life dates of artists and other historical figures have been omitted from the running text but can be found in the Index.

Media descriptions are deliberately brief, with focus on the materials used for the drawing rather than techniques. Unless otherwise noted, the support for drawings is white or off-white rag laid paper. Measurements are given in millimeters, maximum height before maximum width.

The References field of each entry attempts to include all substantive discussions but not necessarily every mention in print. When a drawing is discussed under an attribution different from that in the current catalogue, that has been indicated in parentheses following the page or catalogue number reference.

Watermarks are briefly described with references to the following standard handbooks, the full references for which are found in the Bibliography: Briquet 1966, Churchill 1935, Heawood 1950, Laurentius and Laurentius 2007 and 2008, Piccard 1961–97, and Tschudin 1958.

A number of standard abbreviations are used throughout the catalogue, including the following, for which full references are found in the Bibliography:

B.
See Bartsch 1801–21

Hollstein
Hollstein numbers when given in the text refer to the 60 volumes of Hollstein 1949–2004. New Hollstein volumes, with commentary by modern scholars, are indicated by references to individual volumes according to the names of those scholars (e.g., Mielke 2015)

L.
Lugt numbers when given in the Provenance refer to the two published volumes of collector's marks (Lugt 1921 and Lugt 1956) as well the updated online catalogue available at www.marquesdecollections.fr

RKD
RKD – Netherlands Institute for Art History, The Hague, usually referring to material on the website www.rkd.nl

A number of drawings are identified in this catalogue and elsewhere as belonging to the Baymeath Art Trust (BAT), or as having been gifts or partial gifts to the Morgan Library & Museum from the Baymeath Art Trust. The BAT was established by Clement C. Moore. The works therein have been placed on deposit at the Morgan from the time of their acquisition, with the intention that they would eventually become gifts to the institution.

CONTRIBUTING AUTHORS

SA Susan Anderson, Curatorial Research Associate, Harvard Art Museums, and Curator, Maida and George Abrams Collection

RF Robert Fucci, Lecturer, History of Art, University of Amsterdam

AM Austėja Mackelaitė, Curator of Drawings, Rijksmuseum

SWM Sarah W. Mallory, Annette and Oscar de la Renta Assistant Curator, Drawings and Prints, Morgan Library & Museum

JJM John Marciari, Charles W. Engelhard Curator, Department Head of Drawings and Prints, and Curatorial Chair, Morgan Library & Museum

EN Elizabeth Nogrady, Curator, The Leiden Collection

MCP Michiel Plomp, former Chief Curator of Art Collections, Teylers Museum

MR Marleen Ram, Curator of Art Collections, Teylers Museum

WWR William Robinson, Maida and George Abrams Curator of Drawings, emeritus, Harvard Art Museums/Fogg Museum

GMGR Gregory Rubinstein, Head of Old Master and Early British Drawings, Sotheby's

JSS Joanna Sheers Seidenstein, Assistant Curator, Drawings and Prints, The Metropolitan Museum of Art

LvS Leonore van Sloten, Senior Curator, Rembrandthuis Museum

AS Annemarie Stefes, independent art historian currently working for the Wallraf-Richartz-Museum & Fondation Corboud, Cologne

MvS Maud van Suylen, Curator of Drawings, Rijksmuseum

JT Jennifer Tonkovich, Eugene and Clare Thaw Curator, Drawings and Prints, Morgan Library & Museum

IvT Ilona van Tuinen, Head of the Rijksprentenkabinet, Rijksmuseum

JST Jane Shoaf Turner, Editor, *Master Drawings*, and former Head of the Rijksprentenkabinet, Rijksmuseum

TW Thomas Williams, author and art dealer, London

JY Jonny Yarker, Director, Lowell Libson and Jonny Yarker Ltd.

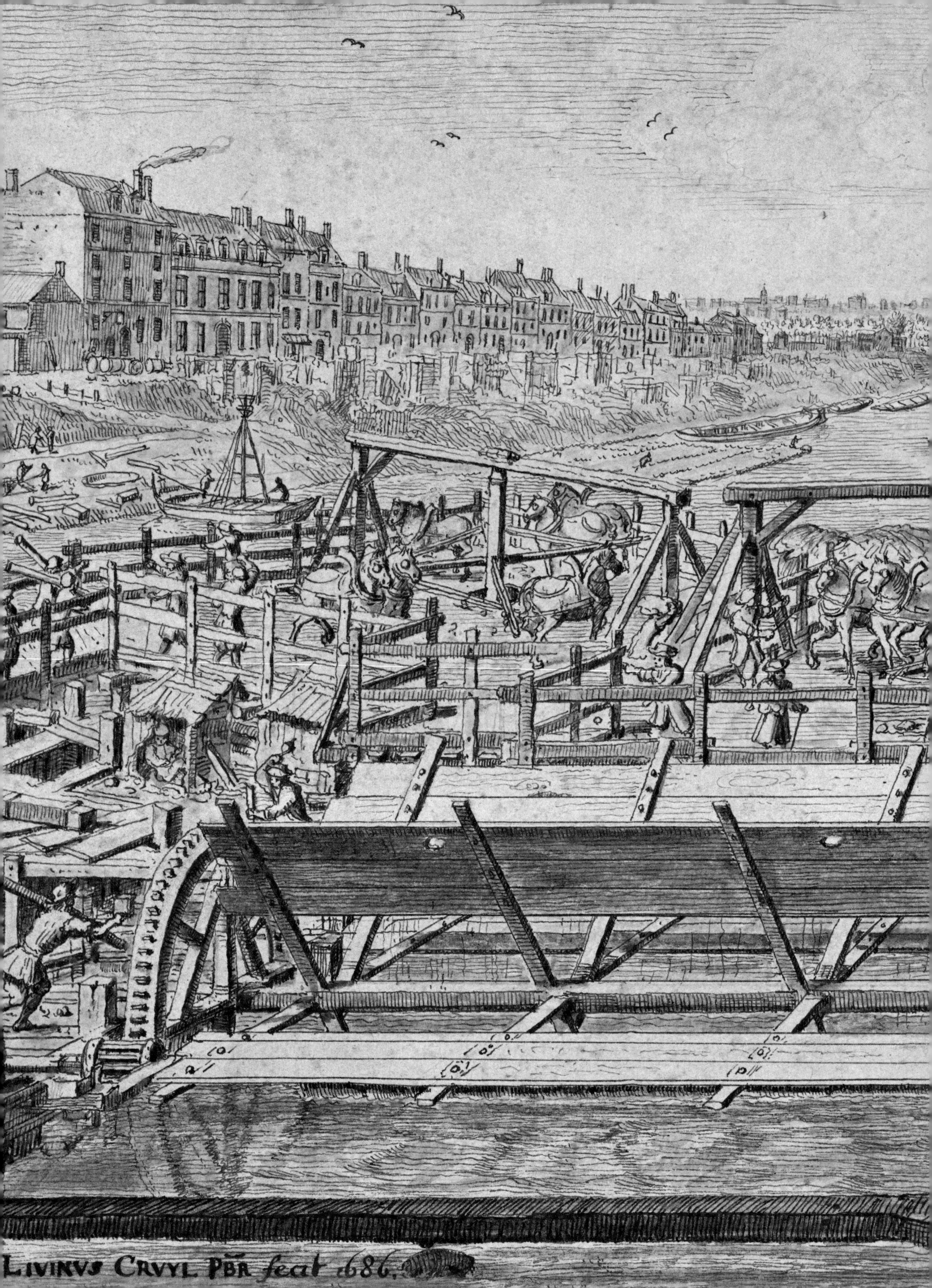
LIVINUS CRUYL PBR fecit 1686

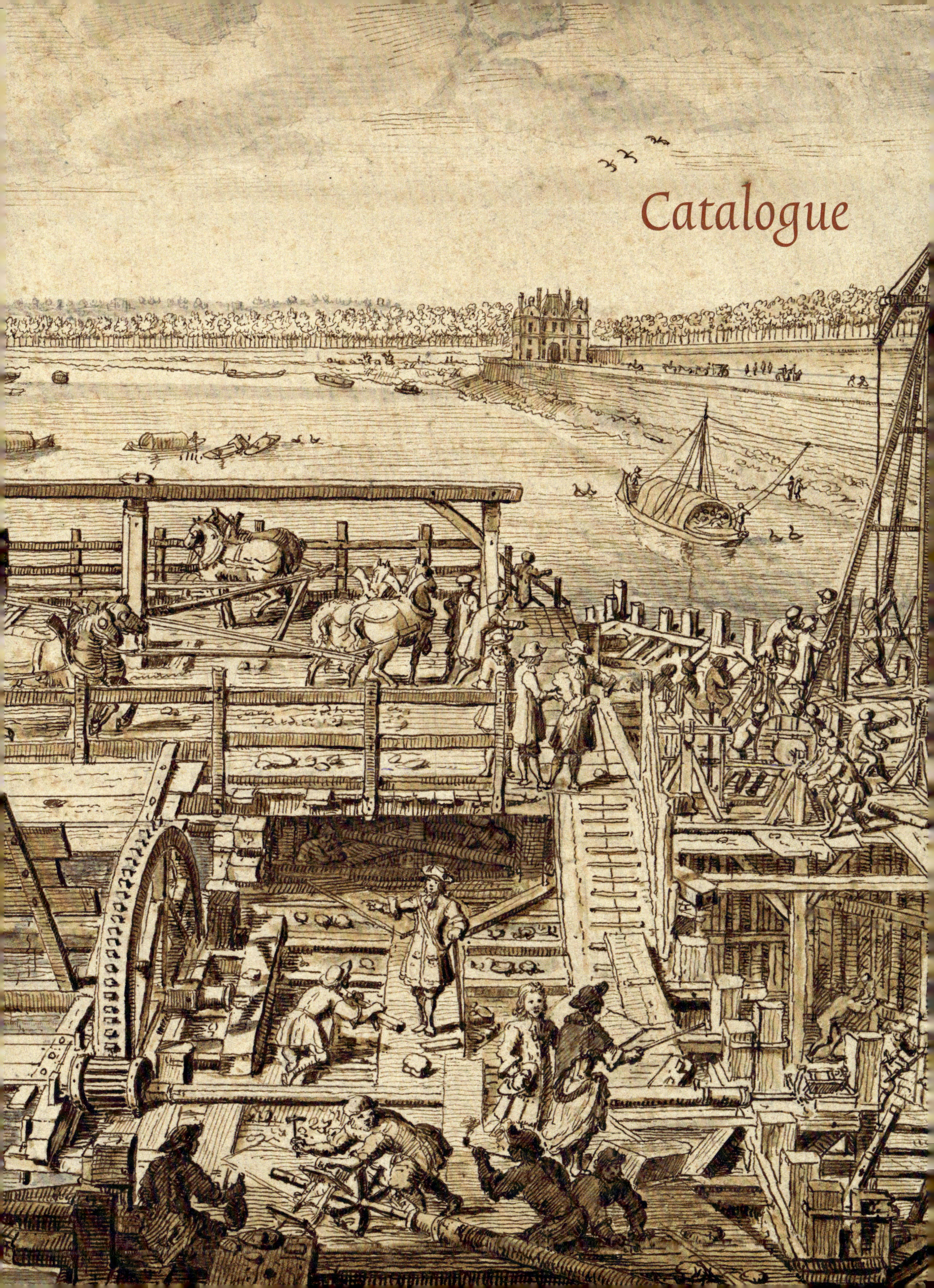

Catalogue

DOMENICO CAMPAGNOLA

Venice ca. 1500–1564 Padua

1

Landscape with a Village Festival, ca. 1550

Pen and brown ink
239 x 380 mm

INSCRIPTIONS Verso, lower center, in black chalk: 0314/91

PROVENANCE Unidentified collector (L. 2508, recto, lower center); probably Pierre Crozat (1665–1740), Paris (no mark; see L. 3612);[1] Pierre-Jean Mariette (1694–1774), Paris (L. 2097, recto, lower right); his sale, F. Basan, Paris, 11 November 1775–30 January 1776, part of lot 257, to Charles-Philippe Campion, Abbé de Tersan (1737–1819), Paris; Jean-Baptiste Séroux d'Agincourt (1730–1814), Paris (no mark; see L. 3643), to 1790; Willem Anne Lestevenon (1750–1830), Paris, probably 1790–1805;[2] from whom acquired by Jean-Baptiste-Florentin-Gabriel de Meyran, Marquis de Lagoy (1764–1829), Aix-en-Provence (L. 1710, recto, lower right); his sale, C.P. Pieri-Bénard, Paris, 17–19 April 1834, lot 62; Savile Gallery, London, 1930; Durlacher Brothers, New York, 1937; where purchased by Joseph V. Reed, Sr. (1902–1973), West Falls Church, VA; by descent to Adrian P. Reed (1931–1999), Centreville, MD; by descent to his widow, Nancy Jane Reed; from whom acquired by Clement C. Moore, 2018

SELECT REFERENCES Savile 1930, no. 6; Durlacher 1937, no. 4; Walker 1941, appendix 21, no. 132; Paris 1967, 51; Eidelberg 1995, 134, n. 35; Rosenberg and Prat 1996, 1: 402–3, under no. 252; Te Rijdt 2003, 29, 273; Py 2015, 397; Plomp and Sonnabend 2016, under no. 34; Nickel 2017, 1: 283–84, no. 175; Rosenberg 2019, 1: no. I260

Promised gift of Clement C. and Elizabeth Y. Moore

This recently rediscovered sheet is a lively and typical example of the landscape drawings of Domenico Campagnola. Pastoral subjects were one of the great developments in Venetian art of the early sixteenth century. Building upon the models of Giorgione, of his adoptive father Giulio Campagnola, and especially of Titian (as seen both in Titian's drawings and the woodcuts made after his designs), Campagnola became a specialist of such landscape art, producing scores of drawings and woodcuts like the present work, with distant mountains, views of towns and rustic buildings, sinuous paths, riverscapes, and ruins, all animated with long, rhythmic lines especially in the foregrounds and the turbulent skies. Such works had an outsized impact on later landscape artists. Campagnola's onetime pupil Girolamo Muziano would carry the style to Rome and would there impart it to followers such as Matthijs Bril (see no. 6). Northern artists active in the Veneto—Pauwels Franck (Paolo Fiammingo) or Lodewijk Toeput (Pozzoserrato), for example—would also have direct contact with Campagnola, but equally, through the broad dissemination of his drawings and prints, Campagnola would have an influence on many more, including Hieronymous Cock, Pieter Bruegel the Elder, Hendrick Goltzius, and others.

The interest in Campagnola's landscapes was also strong in eighteenth-century France. Pierre Crozat acquired many of his Italian drawings during his time in Italy early in the century, most of which eventually passed (like the present sheet) to Pierre-Jean Mariette: this example retains Mariette's familiar blue mount. While they were owned by Crozat, moreover, many of Campagnola's landscapes were copied by Jean-Antoine Watteau, including the *Village Festival*. Watteau's original has been lost, but a counterproof is in the Rijksprentenkabinet (fig. 1.1).[3] The frequent discussions of that drawing have made regular reference to Campagnola's model, unseen since its sale in 1937 but rediscovered by Chips Moore in 2018, still with the family who had purchased it eighty years earlier.

Campagnola here depicts a lively rural festival, where under a pergola figures dance to the music of the horn players at left; the arriving wagons appear to be filled with women, perhaps bringing them from the town in the distance

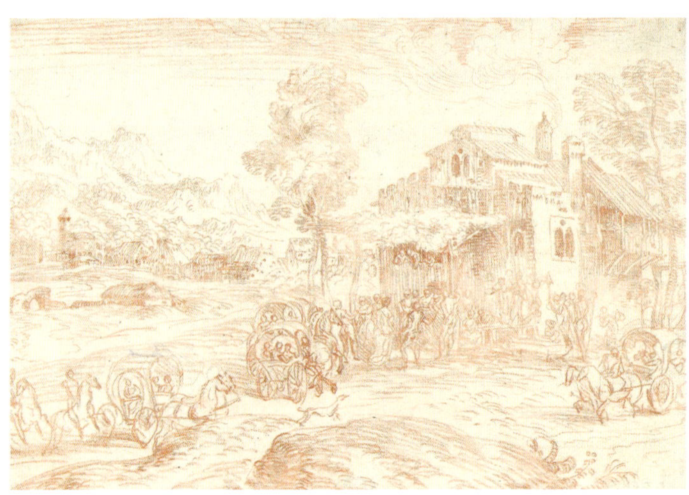

1.1 Jean-Antoine Watteau (after Domenico Campagnola), *Landscape with a Village Festival*, ca. 1714–15. Rijksprentenkabinet, Amsterdam.

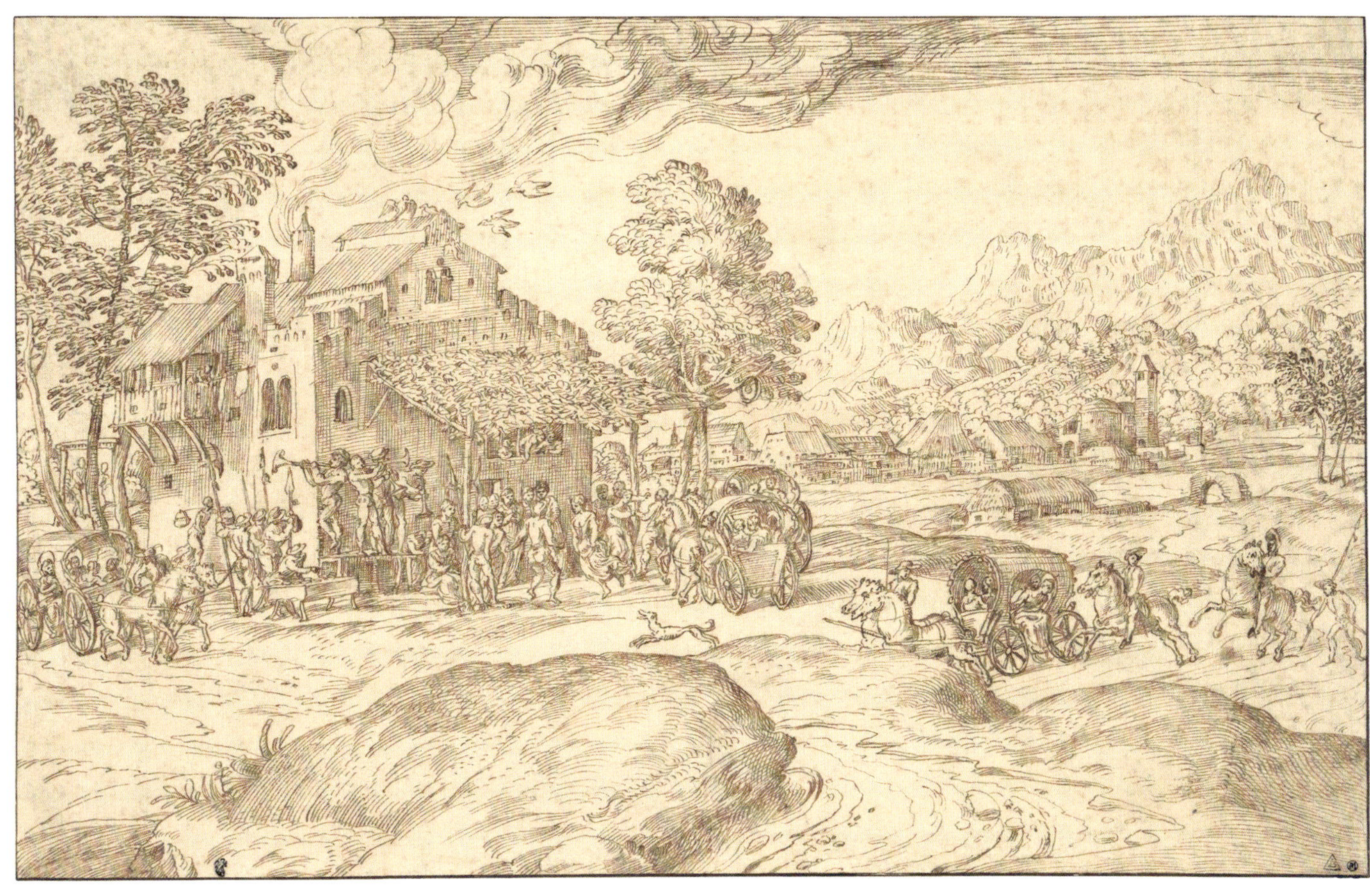

to accompany the soldiers and other men already present. The setting itself is interesting, the sort of semi-fortified farming estate house once more regularly found in the Venetian countryside. These came to be replaced by Palladian villas in the second half of the sixteenth century and few earlier examples remain; the fifteenth-century Villa Querini Stampalia in Pressana is, however, typologically akin to the building in Campagnola's drawing. JJM

JAN VAN DER STRAET, *known as* JOHANNES STRADANUS

Bruges 1523–1605 Florence

2

The Return of Cincinnatus to Rome, ca. 1590–1600

Pen and brown ink and wash, and black chalk, with white opaque watercolor
193 x 265 mm

INSCRIPTIONS Verso of mount, center, in graphite: *Stradanus del*, and in pen and brown ink: *Strada Delineavit fiorenze*. In transmitted light, an inscription on the original sheet is partly visible along the lower edge, but it has not been deciphered.

PROVENANCE Possibly Dr. Karl Gröber (1885–1945), Munich; Weinmüller, Munich, 28 October 1953, lot 749; Wynne Jeudwine (1920–1984), London, by 1963; Bonhams, New York, 27 January 2006, lot 160; Jean-Luc Baroni, London; from whom acquired by Clement C. Moore, 2006

SELECT REFERENCES Jeudwine 1963, no. 35; Baroni Vannucci 1997, no. 186; Ongpin 2006, no. 9

Promised gift of Clement C. and Elizabeth Y. Moore

Born in Bruges, Jan van der Straet trained under Pieter Aertsen in Antwerp but then left the Netherlands and traveled south, stopping in Lyon and Venice but arriving in Florence by 1546. Initially a painter and a tapestry designer, Stradanus was increasingly active as a print designer from the 1570s onward, sending designs especially to the Antwerp publisher Philips Galle. Connecting the artistic and literary world of Italy with the printmaking and publishing centers in the north, Stradanus and his works would provide impetus for many Dutch and Flemish artists to travel to Italy.[1]

The Moore drawing represents the story of Lucius Quinctius Cincinnatus. A patrician statesman during the early Roman Republic, Cincinnatus had retired from politics to work on his farm outside Rome. When the city was threatened by the forces of the Aequi, however, the Senate decided to recall Cincinnatus, nominating him as dictator and sending messengers to inform him. Most depictions of the scene show the messengers arriving at the farm and addressing Cincinnatus as he guides his plow, but, in Stradanus's original conception, we instead see Cincinnatus returning to Rome, still carrying his farming implements as he arrives at the Senate. A fantastic view of the city is in the distance, with recognizable monuments including the Pantheon, Column of Trajan, and Torre delle Milizie—all built many centuries after Cincinnatus's life.

Following his typical practice, Stradanus began the design process with a quick sketch (fig. 2.1),[2] one of many such studies from his sketchbooks or albums found today mainly at the Cooper Hewitt but also at the Morgan and elsewhere. Both the sketch and the Moore drawing were mistakenly identified by Baroni Vannucci as depicting the story of Odysseus and the Lastrygonians because of the inscription on the Cooper Hewitt sketch ("L'estrigones"),[3] though the inscription clearly refers instead to the naval scene in the upper half of the sheet, showing the rocks hurled by the giants at Odysseus's fleet. The Odysseus sketch is one of a series of drawings—both small sketches like that at Cooper Hewitt and larger, more finished drawings at Museum Boijmans Van Beuningen, the Courtauld, and elsewhere—that were intended to be illustrations for an edition of Homer planned by Stradanus's Florentine associate Luigi Alamanni but never realized before the scholar's death in 1603.[4]

The Cincinnatus drawings are likely close in time to the Odysseus series sketched out on the same sheets and thus would date to the final decade of Stradanus's career. While akin to other print designs by Stradanus, however, the intended function of the Cincinnatus drawings is not clear. Because Cincinnatus renounced power and returned to his farm after securing the safety of Rome, he became a model for civic virtue and temperance; accordingly, the drawing could have been for a set of illustrations depicting virtues rather than for a history of Rome. In support of this, it might be noted that another of the Odysseus sketches at Cooper Hewitt has on the lower half of the sheet a depiction of Titus Sabinus and his dog, an image of faithfulness.[5] Yet, if other drawings relating to a planned set of virtues survive, they have not yet been identified, and Dorine van Sasse van Ysselt suggests instead that the Titus Sabinus drawing, like the similar *Fidelity of the Eagle of the Girl from Sestos* at Cooper Hewitt, was for a possible extension of Stradanus's *Venationes* series.[6] The Cincinnatus story would have no place there, and Stradanus's intention for the design thus remains a mystery. JJM

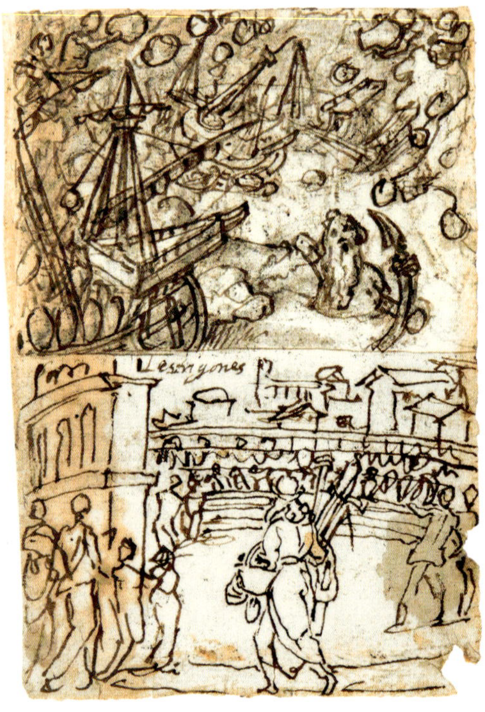

2.1 Jan van der Straet, *Odysseus's Fleet Destroyed by the Lastrygonians and Cincinnatus Called to the Dictatorship of Rome*, ca. 1590–1600. Cooper Hewitt Smithsonian Design Museum, New York.

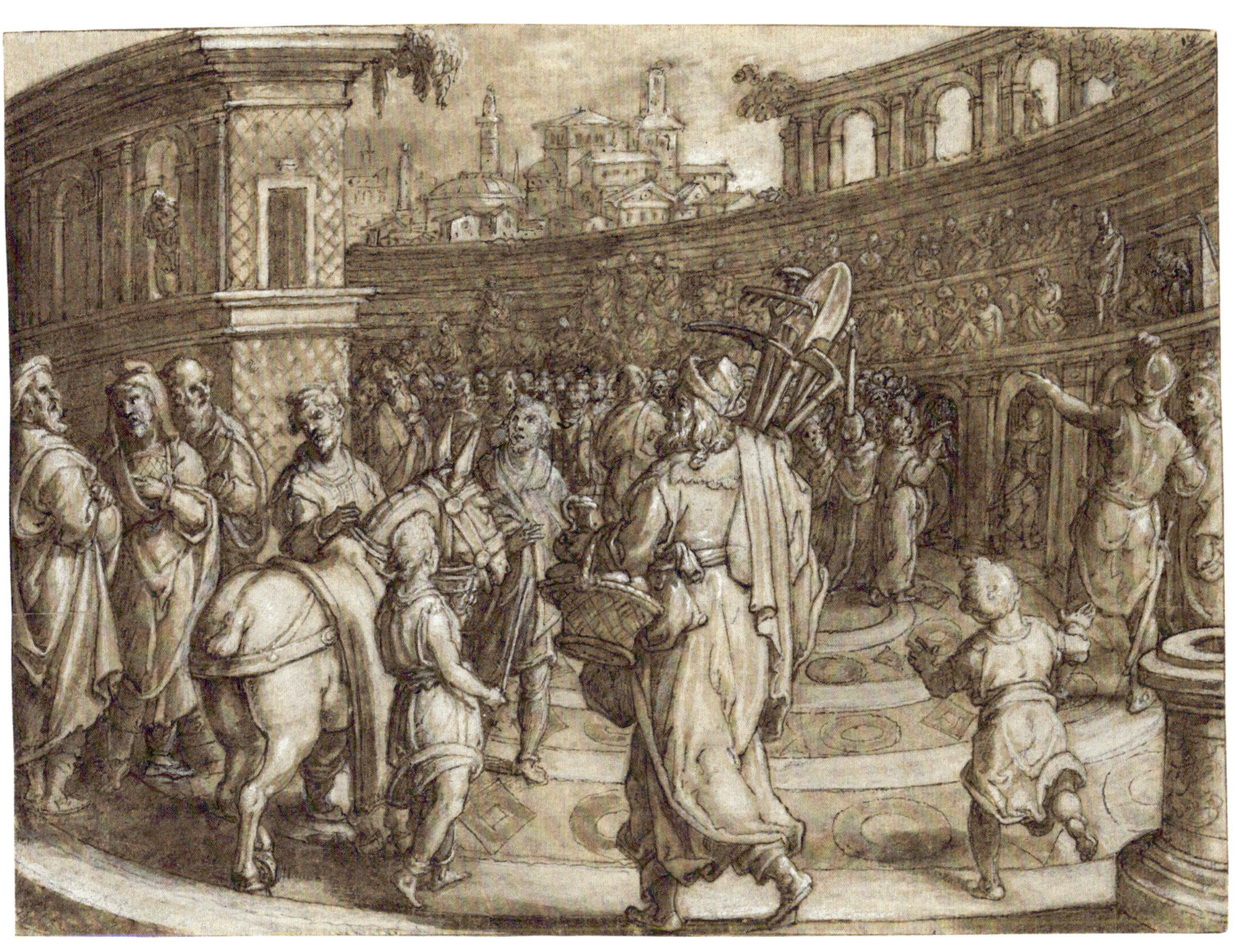

DIRCK BARENDSZ

Amsterdam 1534–1592 Amsterdam

3

Ecce Homo, ca. 1581–87

Oil on paper
252 x 206 mm

INSCRIPTIONS Recto, lower right, signed with monogram: Th.B; verso, upper right, in graphite: 24718; verso, lower center, in graphite: M232; verso of mount, lower right, in pen and brown ink: *Theodorus. Bernard.* and, in a different hand: *. . . d'un Album disposé par Charles Quint. Maitre de Pint.* [?]

PROVENANCE Private collection, France, by 1759; private collection, France, ca. 1851; Pierre Berge & Associés, Paris, 21 March 2007, lot 10; Nicolaas Teeuwisse, Berlin; from whom acquired by Clement C. Moore for the Baymeath Art Trust, 2008

SELECT REFERENCES Teeuwisse 2008, no. 1

Promised gift of Clement C. and Elizabeth Y. Moore, through the Baymeath Art Trust

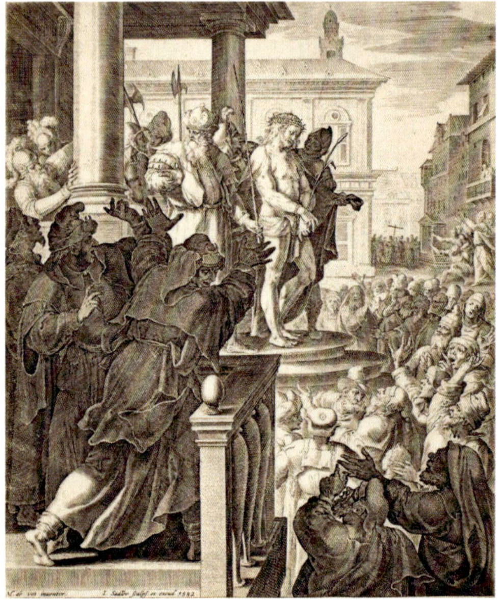

3.1 Hans Sadeler (after Maerten de Vos), *Ecce Homo*, 1582. Philadelphia Museum of Art.

Dirck Barendsz was recognized by contemporaries, including Karel van Mander, as having played a major role in the introduction of modern Italian style into Dutch art, a manner learned from his seven years in Titian's workshop around 1555–62.[1] The impact of this Venetian period is clear in Barendsz's greatest surviving painting, the *Life of the Virgin* triptych in the Sint-Janskerk at Gouda, but also in his drawings, especially the series of monochrome oil sketches that includes the *Ecce Homo*.[2]

The great connoisseur Pierre-Jean Mariette recorded in his manuscript *Abecedario* that he had seen a series of forty sketches apparently intended as models for prints. Mariette admired the drawings and associated them with Barendsz, but mistakenly attributed them to Hans Sadeler, who made engravings after several. The works remained together until the mid-nineteenth century, when the group was offered to the Louvre.[3] They then disappeared until the mid-1970s, when they began to be sold at French auctions; this led to their initial publication, by Jacques Foucart and Pierre Rosenberg, who recognized the drawings as those mentioned by Mariette and who argued conclusively for their attribution to Barendsz.[4] To date, twenty-seven of the forty have emerged, with the *Ecce Homo* the most recent to reappear.[5]

Although an oil sketch would hardly seem the medium best suited for translation into engraving, the drawings do appear to have been models for a print series, even if only a few were translated into prints by Sadeler.[6] The prints are undated, but other Barendsz designs engraved by Sadeler are dated between 1581 and 1587. It seems likely that these are from the same moment, and also that the drawings were made around that time. Sadeler may have abandoned the series when he moved to Munich in 1588.

The oil sketch technique of these works itself has been alternately linked to similar drawings by northern artists, including Joachim Beuckelaer or Anthonie Blocklandt, or to Venetian examples. (Although the most obvious Venetian oil sketches by Domenico Tintoretto and Palma Giovane postdate Barendsz's stay in Venice, he may have been inspired by some of Andrea Schiavone's drawings, which were done precisely during Barendsz's time there.[7]) Alternately, perhaps they are simply an experiment of Barendsz's own. Even if made two decades after returning from Italy, however, the sketches reveal his deep appreciation of Venetian models, not only in their flickering, painterly chiaroscuro—so reminiscent of Titian and Tintoretto—but also, in the case of the *Ecce Homo*, in the church of the background. This recalls Andrea Palladio's facade for San Francesco della Vigna but does not copy it and may be an experiment in Palladian design by the learned Barendsz, who in other instances borrowed from Sebastiano Serlio.[8]

Finally, a comparison must be drawn between Barendsz's *Ecce Homo* and a version by Maerten de Vos, engraved by Hans Sadeler in 1582 (fig. 3.1).[9] Both set the scene in a modern Italian cityscape, with Christ exposed to a seething crowd; both have dramatic foreground figures in shadow, whose gesturing hands stand out against the brighter background. Given the common link to Sadeler, the similarities can hardly be coincidental, but the relationship between the two designers (who were in Venice at the same time in the 1550s) remains to be explored further.[10] JJM

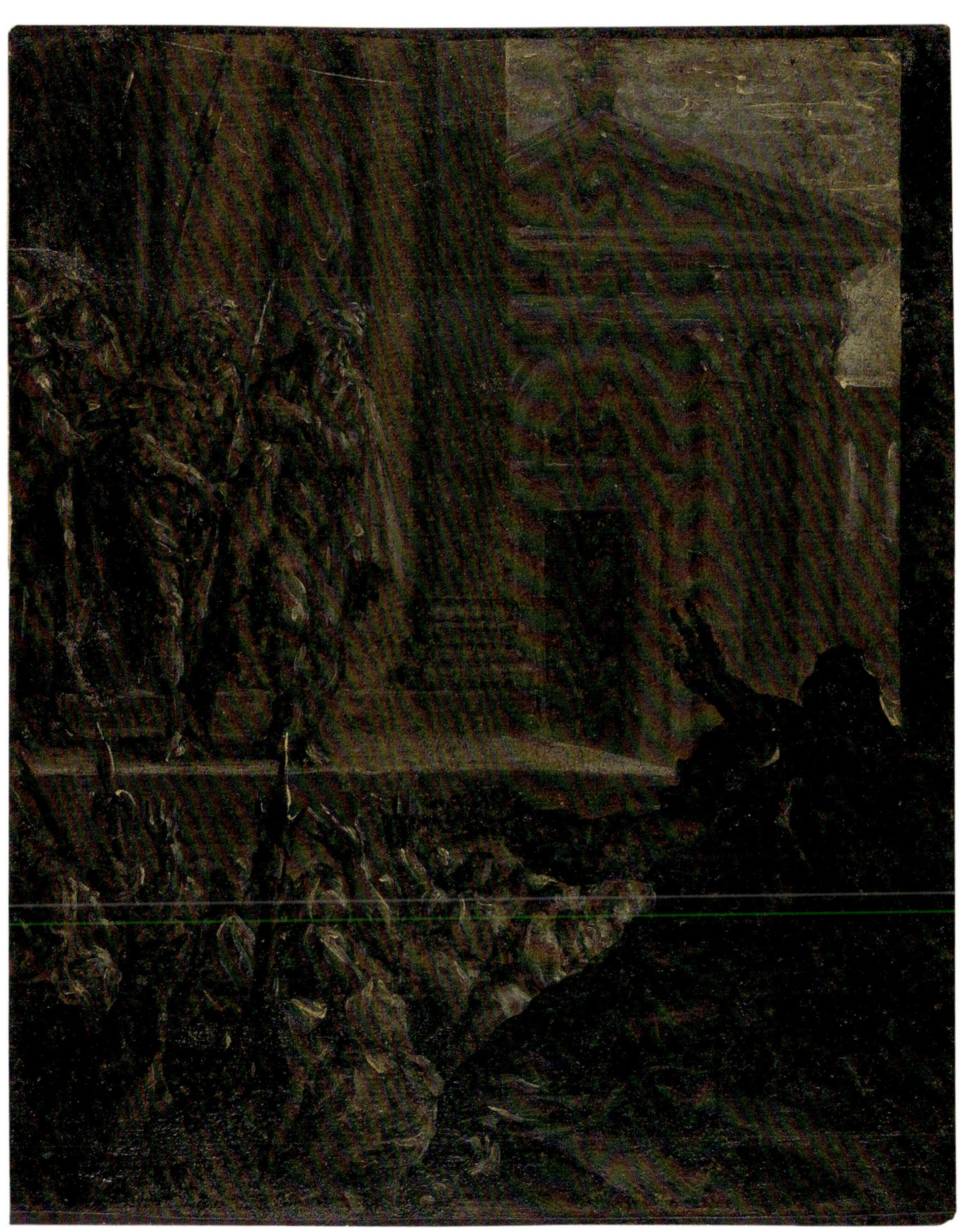

HANS BOL

Mechelen 1534–1593 Amsterdam

4a,b

Bear Hunt (a) and *Wolf Hunt* (b), 1582

Pen and brown ink, with brown and gray wash, over traces of black chalk

(a) 68 x 219 mm; (b) 75 x 207 mm

INSCRIPTIONS (a) Recto, lower center, in pen and brown ink: *Hans boL*; verso, left, in pen and brown ink: 148; verso of mount, lower right: HBol 1582; label with the printed number 471; (b) verso of mount, lower right: HBol 1582; label with the printed number 473

PROVENANCE Alfred von Wurzbach-Tannenberg (1845–1915), Vienna (L. 2587, verso, lower left); Gilhofer & Ranschburg, Lucerne, 28 June 1934, lots 44 and 45; private collection, France;[1] Eric Caudron, Paris, 19 March 2014, lot 22; Galerie Nathalie Motte Masselink, Paris; from whom acquired by Clement C. Moore, 2014

SELECT REFERENCES Mielke 2015, part II: 164–65, under nos. 281 and 286

Promised gift of Clement C. and Elizabeth Y. Moore

Across the horizontal expanse of each of these diminutive sheets, the dramatic action of a hunt unfolds. Human and animal bodies run, lunge, tangle, and flail. Drapery billows in the melee. The wide format of the drawings encourages the eye to wander, gradually taking in their abundant detail: wolves tussling with domesticated canines (the former distinguished by their bushier tails), a dog biting a bear's rump, a shepherd running after his imperiled flock, hunters hiding in trees, and a dead animal hanging from a branch.

These precisely rendered sheets are two of the six surviving drawings Hans Bol made for an extensive series of forty-seven printed hunting and fishing scenes issued in 1582 by Antwerp publisher Philips Galle.[2] Bol was an important transitional figure in the development of the landscape genre in the Netherlands, beginning his career as an etcher and designer of prints in his native Mechelen, in the south, before fleeing, in 1584, to the north, where he would eventually settle in Amsterdam and focus on the production of finished drawings for the market. The present works, from his Mechelen period, demonstrate Bol's affinity for complex multifigure scenes—whether hunts, peasant kermesses, or biblical and mythological episodes—in extensive landscape settings. They also exhibit the artist's lively handling of the pen and characteristic inclusion of distant townscapes, which these drawings situate the violent activity in the foreground away from, but in proximity to, civic life.

Cut by Adriaen Collaert and other members of Galle's workshop, the prints (figs. 4.1 and 4.2)[3] found a ready market among urban buyers, for whom hunting would have resonated as a pastime.[4] Bol's series, including more than twenty species of animals and depictions of indigenous hunting practices in the Americas, might also have attracted the attention of those interested in natural history and the customs of people around the world.[5]

Apart from the many tapestry and stained-glass cycles and painted *spalliere* and cassone panels in which hunting had long featured as a subject, printed precedents for Bol's works include a series of hunting scenes engraved by Virgil Solis and four sets of prints designed by Bol's older contemporary, Johannes Stradanus. While Bol's series included novel depictions of very specific local fishing practices,[6] bear and wolf hunts were well-established artistic subjects, with one or both figuring in Solis's and Stradanus's series, among the latter a large suite of forty-four engravings published by Philips Galle in 1578–80 that included two bear hunts and two wolf hunts.[7]

For his wolf and bear hunts, Bol borrowed and reimagined various motifs from Stradanus. Combining these elements with imagery of his own invention and imbuing them with greater naturalism, the younger artist succeeded in creating fresh treatments. Bol's wolf hunt, for example, integrates into one scene the hunting methods that the elder artist parceled out into two separate prints in the 1578–80 series: hunting *par force*, with dogs and pikes—generally associated with the nobility[8]—and trapping. Bol enunciates the class distinctions between the figures engaged in these two pursuits, particularly with the elaborately costumed figure on horseback and the simply dressed farmer tending to the dead wolf hanging in a noose trap in the tree at far left. This contrast is even more pronounced in the bear hunt, in which the rider and the man lying on the ground wear armor. The latter drawing also takes its cue from one of Stradanus's 1578–80

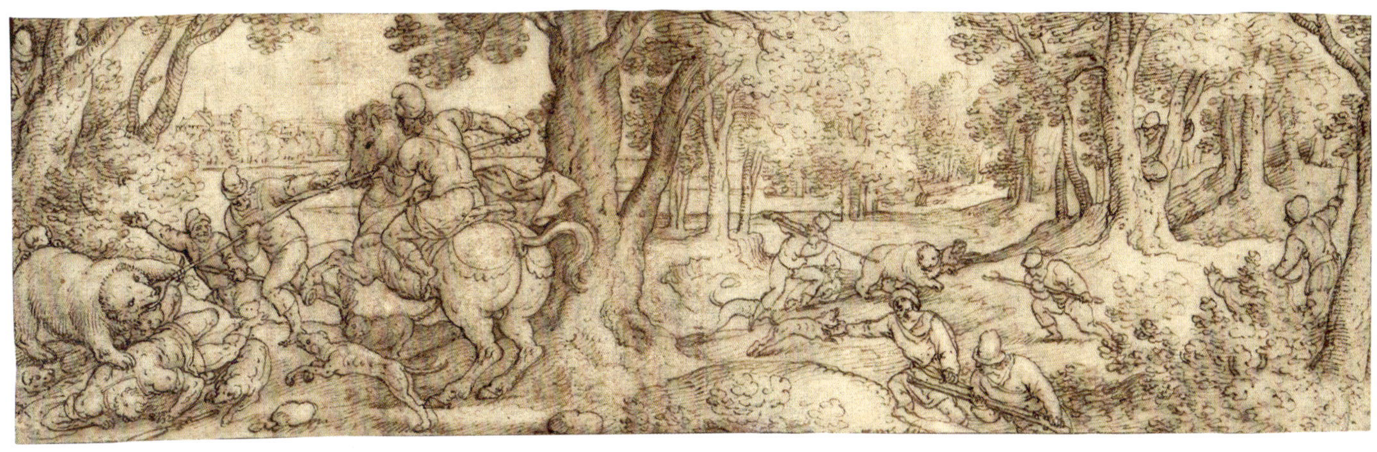

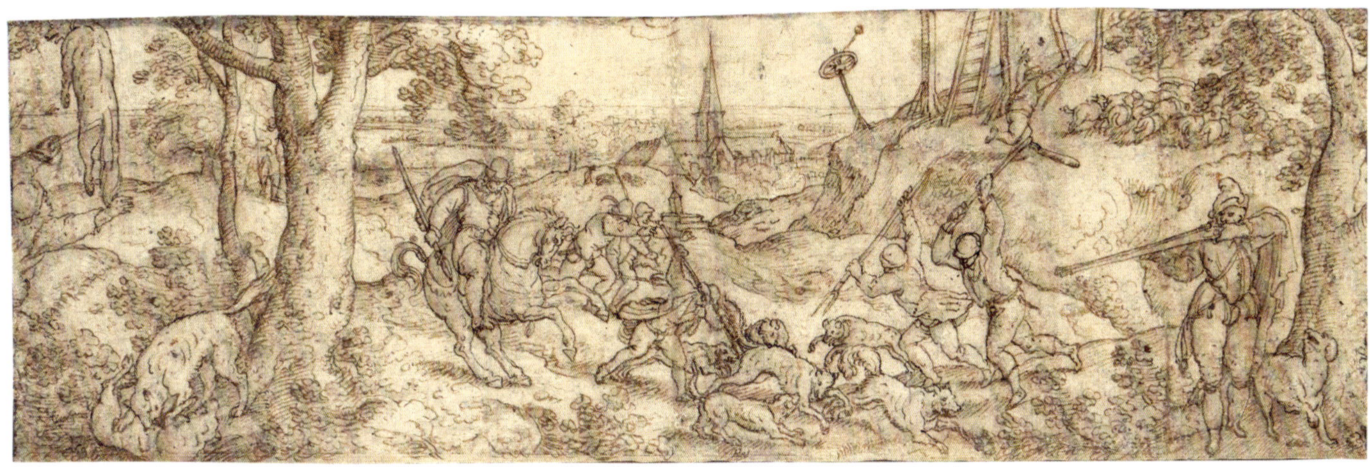

4.1 Adriaen Collaert (after Hans Bol), *Bear Hunt*, plate 9 from the series *Venationis, piscationis, et avcvpii typi* (Hunting, Fishing, and Fowling Scenes), 1582. Garrett Collection, Baltimore Museum of Art.

4.2 Adriaen Collaert (after Hans Bol), *Wolf Hunt*, plate 4 from the series *Venationis, piscationis, et avcvpii typi* (Hunting, Fishing, and Fowling Scenes), 1582. Garrett Collection, Baltimore Museum of Art.

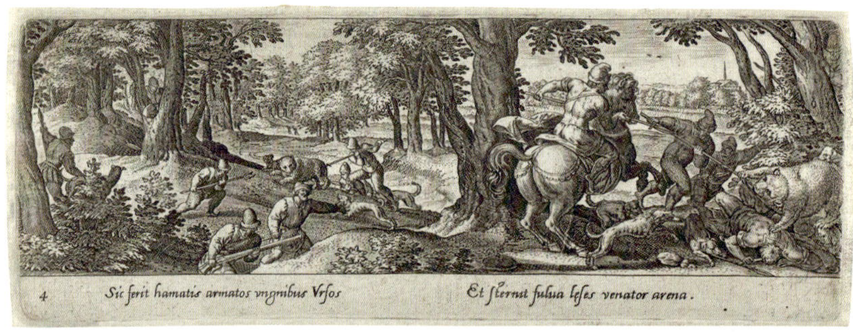

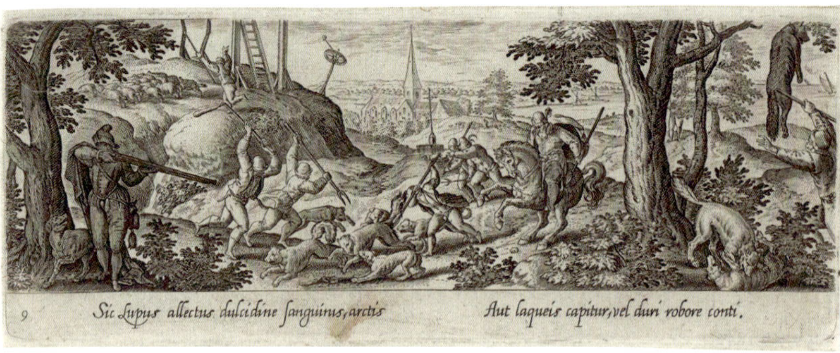

prints, in which a similar encounter between hunters, dogs, and bear appears at lower left. In turn, Bol's composition, specifically the armor worn by the two hunters, seems to have informed a later bear hunt by Stradanus published ca. 1596, also by Galle.[9]

A curious detail in the background of Bol's wolf hunt is the breaking wheel (or Catherine wheel), a torture device used in public executions. Its presence strongly suggests that the wooden posts adjacent to it are the supports of a gallows. These motifs, which reappear in the series—in the *Rabbit Hunt* and *Fox Hunt with Fire*[10]—may serve to locate the scenes on the outskirts of town, where gallows fields were generally found.[11] Plausibly here they also, in combination with the prominent church in the background, possess some allegorical significance in the vein of Pieter Bruegel the Elder's similar motifs in his 1562 *Triumph of Death* (Museo Nacional del Prado, Madrid). In that painting, many of the skeletons carry long pikes; in the foreground two work together to trap a group of people in a net, while on the cliffs beyond them, another, accompanied by two dogs, chases a naked man as if he were wild game.

Both drawings are enlivened with a vivid sense of motion that underscores the precarity of the hunters' efforts and heightens the sense of danger. In the bear hunt, a man lying face-down on the ground is mauled by an enormous bear who seems entirely unperturbed by the hunting dogs and who takes control with his mouth and his claw of the spear pointed at him, seemingly knocking its wielder off balance.[12] Similarly, in the other drawing, two wolves hurtle toward the picture plane, outrunning and potentially escaping the hunting dogs at their tails. At far left, a third wolf clearly bests the domesticated canine with whom he tussles.

Bol's compositions had a long afterlife, inspiring many later artists, among them David Vinckboons, who designed a series of hunting scenes published in 1612.[13] More broadly, the distinctive format of Bol's drawings and the related prints became popular for landscape drawings and prints among the next generation, particularly Esaias van de Velde and Jan van de Velde II. **JSS**

JACOB SAVERY

Kortrijk 1565/67–1603 Amsterdam

5

The Month of May, 1595

Brush and blue ink and wash with white opaque watercolor; framing lines in brown ink and incidental marks in red chalk

210 x 310 mm

WATERMARK Basilisk (dragon) threatening a church or house with Basel crozier, similar to Tschudin 292 (Basel, 1600), Briquet 1383 (Basel, 1585), and Piccard 33482 (Neuenburg, Baden, 1592)

INSCRIPTIONS Recto, lower left, in blue watercolor: *SAVERY 95*; recto, lower center, in blue watercolor: *Maius*

PROVENANCE Possibly Paul Mantz (1821–1895), Paris; private collection, Belgium, ca. 1900–ca. 2010; art market, Brussels; private collection, France; Nicolas Schwed, Paris;[1] from whom acquired by Clement C. Moore for the Baymeath Art Trust, 2016

Promised gift of Clement C. and Elizabeth Y. Moore, through the Baymeath Art Trust

Jacob Savery studied in Antwerp in the early 1580s with the landscapist Hans Bol (see no. 4a, b). He left Antwerp and settled in Haarlem by 1585, joining the guild there in 1587. In 1591 he became a citizen of Amsterdam, where he remained until his death in 1603.

Savery produced oil paintings, drawings, prints, and small, detailed landscapes in opaque watercolor, a type developed by Bol. His early work, from the 1580s to the middle of the 1590s, clearly shows his debt to his teacher's example. In the later 1590s he produced pen-and-ink landscapes in a technique that emulated drawings by Pieter Bruegel the Elder. Some of these, inscribed with a plausible imitation of Bruegel's signature and dates from 1559–62, appear to be deliberate forgeries intended to pass as original works by Bruegel and were generally accepted as such until the 1980s.[2]

The Moore drawing belongs to a series representing the months of the year. The suite presumably comprised twelve compositions, of which ten are known today. All are landscapes with numerous figures, executed in the same media on sheets of similar dimensions, and identically signed and dated "SAVERY 95." Two have been in the collection of the Ashmolean Museum, University of Oxford, since 1834, and another was acquired by Frits Lugt in 1954 and bequeathed by him to the Fondation Custodia, Paris.[3] Seven more appeared on the Paris art market in 2015. In addition to the present sheet, two from that group are in the J. Paul Getty Museum, Los Angeles, and four in private collections.[4] Drawings illustrating the months of April and July are missing and possibly lost. The sheets that came to light in 2015 include a bottom margin of about one centimeter in which the artist inscribed the name of the month represented. The margins and titles have been trimmed from the Lugt and Ashmolean drawings.

Renaissance images of the months derived from a medieval tradition of seasonal activities depicted in the calendar pages of books of hours and other contexts.

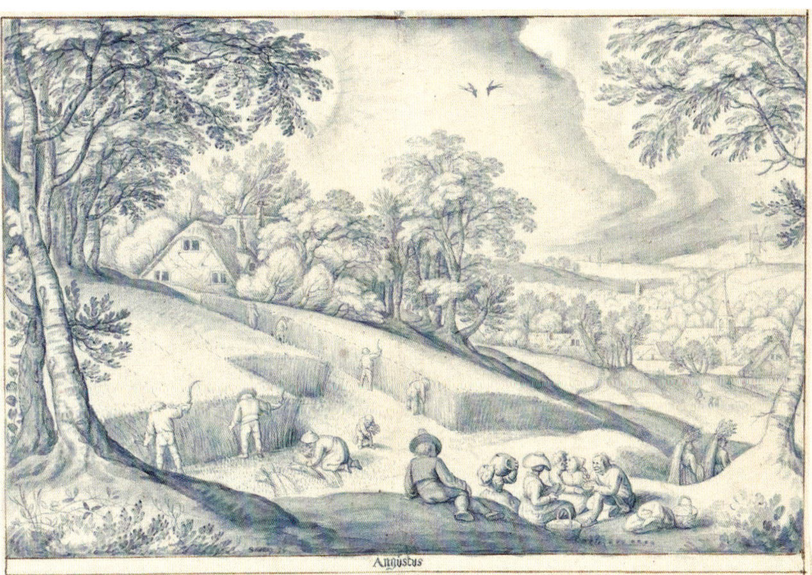

5.1 Jacob Savery, *The Month of August*, 1595. J. Paul Getty Museum, Los Angeles.

Most illustrated the months with appropriate agricultural labors—for example, sheepshearing for June or the grain harvest for August, as Savery represented those months in other sheets in this series (fig. 5.1).[5] That this tradition continued through the sixteenth century is attested not only by Savery's series but also by a set of months designed by Bol and engraved ca. 1581 by Adriaen Collaert, with which Savery's compositions share numerous similarities.[6] In the Moore drawing, he followed iconographic precedent by showing May as a time of rejuvenation and leisure in nature. Hunters depart for the chase while courting couples make music, feast, stroll on the grounds of a castle, and glide across a pond in a pleasure boat festooned with fragrant boughs.

Savery drew all the works in the series with a brush and blue ink and wash prepared with indigo, a pigment extracted from the indigo plant and imported from South Asia or Africa. A few inconspicuous highlights were added in opaque white watercolor.[7] Blue transparent watercolor emerged as a popular drawing medium in the Netherlands in the last third of the sixteenth century. It was used, in combination with other media, by landscapists such as Jan Breughel the Elder and by figural artists, including Johannes Stradanus, among many others.[8] It rarely served, as here and in the work by Isaak Major in this exhibition (no. 15), as the primary medium of the drawing. WWR

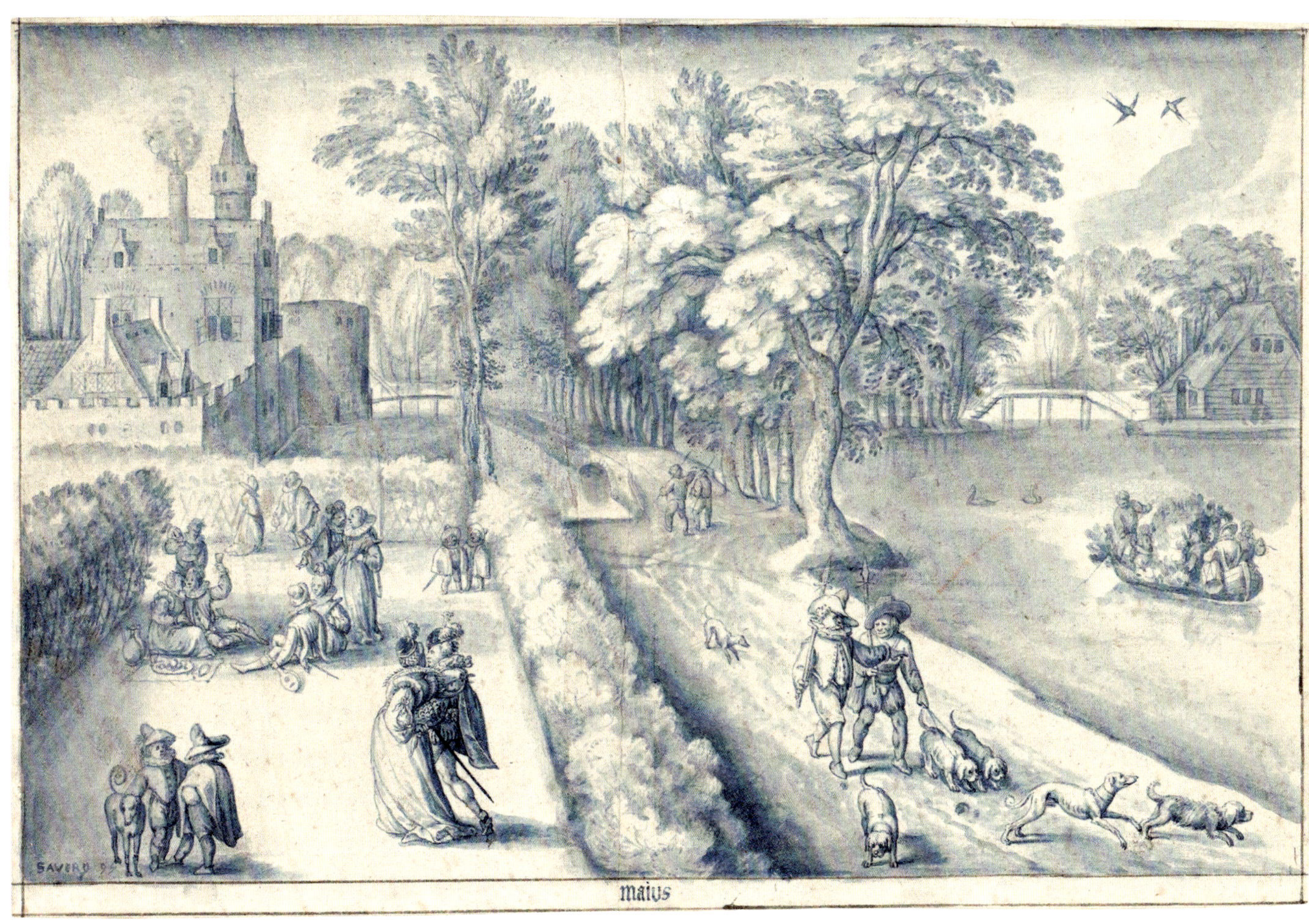
maius

MATTHIJS BRIL

Antwerp ca. 1550–1583 Rome

6

Landscape with a House by a Lake, ca. 1575–83

Pen and brown ink, over black chalk
240 x 193 mm

WATERMARK Eagle with wings spread

INSCRIPTIONS Recto, lower right, in pen and brown ink: *Paul Bril.*; verso, in pen and brown ink: *Mattens Brill*; recto of mount, lower center, in pen and black ink: *Paul Bril.*

PROVENANCE Hill-Stone, New York; from whom acquired by Clement C. Moore, 2008

Promised gift of Clement C. and Elizabeth Y. Moore

Born in Antwerp probably in 1550, Matthijs Bril was the son of a painter, also named Matthijs, about whom little is known. He presumably received artistic training from his father, but, like so many of his countrymen, undertook a journey to Italy while still a young man. The pattern of northern artists traveling south was already well established, and Bril was likely aware that Antwerp printers routinely published designs sent by Johannes Stradanus (see no. 2) and other northerners in Italy. By 1575, Bril was in Rome, at work in the Sala Ducale of the Vatican Palace. He was identified from the start as a landscape specialist and thus found ready work on the decorative schemes of the Vatican Palace, especially after Girolamo Muziano—who had himself once been known as "the youth of the landscapes"—assumed supervision of the project. By August 1582, Bril had married and seemingly planned to settle in Rome, but less than a year later he died. He had nonetheless a substantial legacy, for his younger brother Paul arrived in 1582, adopted Matthijs's mode of depicting landscapes (see fig. 6.1, for example, a landscape by Paul Bril also in the Moore collection),[1] and enjoyed a successful career until his own death more than forty years later; the Brils would have a major impact on the development of landscape painting in Rome and farther afield.[2]

Matthijs and Paul Bril also developed a distinctive style of landscape drawing that was equally influential, especially among northern artists, not least because Paul allowed visiting artists access to his and his brother's drawings, which were readily copied and carried back home.[3] Matthijs essentially drew in two modes: a topographically accurate style akin to that of many northerners, but also an imaginative, fantastic manner.[4] The present drawing has all the typical characteristics of the latter: a large tree dominates the foreground, rising high above the horizon but growing precariously from rocks on the ground; steep slopes lead to an isolated, rustic building, which as so often in Matthijs's drawings is set on an island and must be reached by boat or by a perilous footbridge. The organization of the scene, allowing the viewer two different visual paths into the composition, is typical of the artist, as is the style and technique. Matthijs began the work with a black chalk sketch that is now only partly visible (for example in the uninked trees above the house) before employing a variety of pen lines and hatching to create tonal variations. Unlike Paul, Matthijs did not usually employ wash, adopting instead a dense network of lines.

The origins of this landscape style are somewhat disputed. It has been suggested that Matthijs could have been inspired by some of Pieter Bruegel's similar drawings,[5] but it seems equally—or more—plausible to suggest that, like so many artists who arrived in Rome, he adopted local conventions. His topographic drawings, that is, employ penwork comparable to that of many northern artists, but the fantasy landscapes are distinctly akin to drawings by Muziano.[6] This is hardly surprising, for Muziano was not only the papal painter and Matthijs's supervisor at the Vatican but also the head of the Accademia di San Luca from the time of its foundation in 1577;[7] he was in the late 1570s the most successful artist in Rome, and thus an obvious model for emulation.[8] JJM

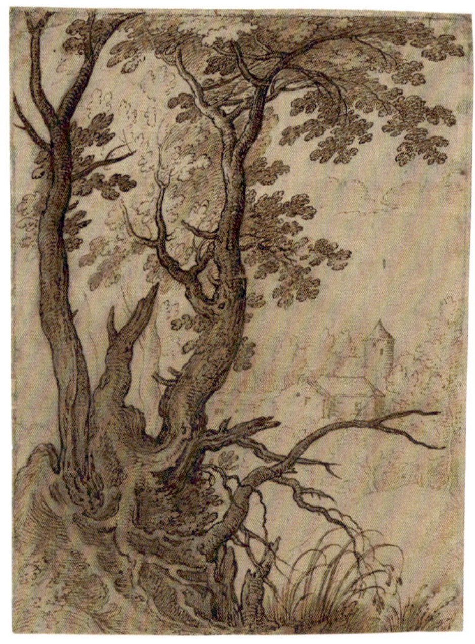

6.1 Paul Bril, *A Tree with Gnarled Roots, with Rural Dwellings in the Background*, ca. 1590–1600. Clement C. Moore Collection.

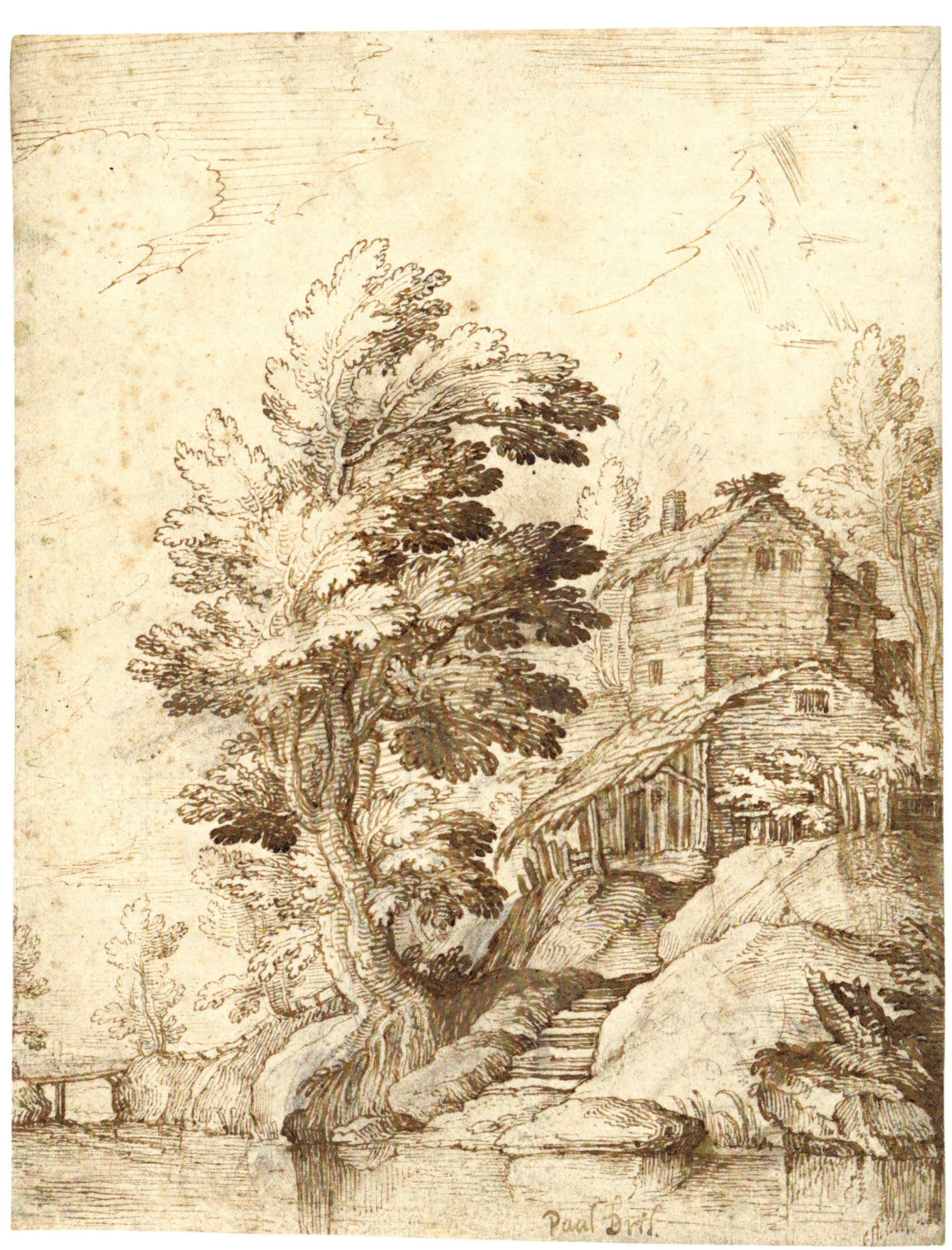
Paul Bril

HENDRICK GOLTZIUS

Brüggen 1558–1617 Haarlem

7

Callisto's Pregnancy Revealed to Diana, ca. 1600

Black and white chalk, with traces of blue and pink chalk
389 x 511 mm

WATERMARK Strasbourg lily

INSCRIPTIONS Recto, lower left, in black chalk: *19* or *9*

PROVENANCE Evert Jan Thomassen à Thuessink van der Hoop van Slochteren (1875–1952), Fraeylemaborg; Beyers, Utrecht, 6 October 1971, part of lot 675; Hans van Leeuwen (1911–2010), Amsterdam (no mark; see L. 2799a and 5935); Christie's, Amsterdam, 24 November 1992, lot 86; Pfeiffer collection; W.M. Brady & Co., New York, from whom acquired by Herbert Kasper (1926–2020), New York, 2004; his sale, Christie's, New York, 14 October 2021, lot 4; where acquired by Clement C. Moore

SELECT REFERENCES Schatborn 1975, 142–44; Frerichs and Schatborn 1975, no. 44; Utrecht 1978, no. 48; Bremen 1979, no. 46; Fribourg et al. 1982, no. 33; Verhagen, Van Heusden, and Kolks 1987, no. 29; Reznicek 1993, no. K 108a; Sluijter 2000a, 302, n. 88; Bernheimer 2001, 8–9; Griswold et al. 2011, no. 36; Nichols 2013, 159, under no. A-43

Promised gift of Clement C. and Elizabeth Y. Moore

In the 1604 biography of his friend Hendrick Goltzius, Karel van Mander celebrated that artist as the master of effortless delineation. As described by the writer, there was no one else who could be "so sure and quick at drawing a figure, and even an entire history offhand without making a sketch, completed with the pen in one go so perfectly and precisely and with such great liveliness."[1] While many of Goltzius's surviving drawings support this description—including a swiftly rendered *Portrait of a Smiling Boy*, also in the Moore collection[2]—the present work, like a number of other sheets from around 1600, showcases a different side of his artistic persona. The thick contours produced by tracing and retracing the outlines of the figures, the crossings out, the multiple pentimenti, and the layering of black, white, and colored chalks result in an elaborate, heavily worked image, simultaneously displaying Goltzius's prowess and attesting to the difficulty of creating such complex multifigure narratives.

The drawing also reflects the artist's deep engagement with subjects from Ovid's *Metamorphoses*, which began in the 1580s and culminated between 1588 and 1590 when he produced more than fifty designs for illustrations of the Roman poet's text.[3] While the discovery of Callisto's pregnancy was not among the pivotal episodes in that work—in fact, the scene had been omitted from most illustrated sixteenth- and early seventeenth-century Dutch editions of the *Metamorphoses*—it came to occupy an important place in prints, drawings, and paintings by Goltzius and his contemporaries.[4] The *Diana and Callisto* (ca. 1556–59) by Titian—a painting conceived as part of the renowned *poesie* series, commissioned by King Philip II of Spain—is the reason behind the explosion of this previously minor subject in the Netherlands at the turn of the seventeenth century.[5] After 1566, when Cornelis Cort made an engraving of a later version of the composition, Titian's iconography began widely circulating in Italy and beyond (fig. 7.1).[6]

In Cort's print, Diana, the stern-faced goddess of the hunt, points her hand at the Arcadian nymph Callisto, who writhes and flails her arms as her clothes are torn off by three of Diana's attendants. The nymph's exposed swollen belly reveals that she is pregnant—a consequence of an earlier episode in the story, in which Callisto was raped by Jupiter. Since the nymphs are committed to chastity, this revelation leads to Callisto's banishment from Diana's band of followers.

As argued by Eric Jan Sluijter, Cort's print after Titian "allowed Goltzius to emulate both an invention by this famous master and the print by a famous engraver, an opportunity he seems to have eagerly seized."[7] Indeed, Goltzius retained many features of Titian's composition, combining the moment of Callisto's disrobing with Diana's condemnation of the nymph and reusing some of the poses for the nude figures. At the same time, significant changes were introduced. The artist transferred the vertical scene to a horizontal format, which resulted in a greater distance between the Diana and the Callisto groups, thus reducing the narrative tension. Following a compositional strategy that harkened back to his earlier Mannerist period, Goltzius placed the main scene in the middle ground and introduced a group of three undressing nymphs in the center foreground.[8] Other changes were more subtle, yet equally impactful. Note, for instance, that the artist eliminated all signs of struggle between Callisto and the women disrobing her against her will, which substantially affected the tenor of the scene.

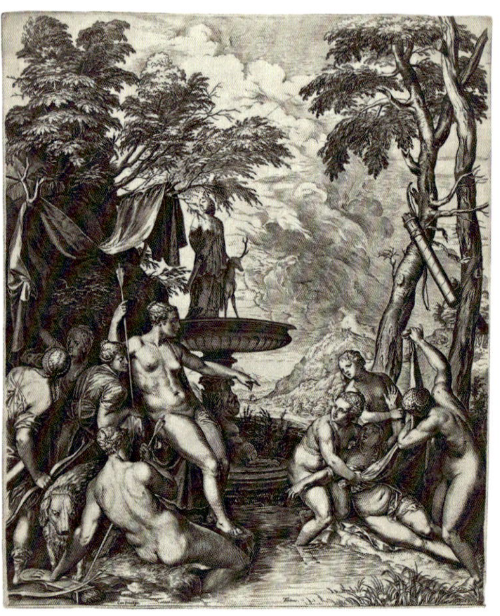

7.1 Cornelis Cort (after Titian), *Diana Discovering Callisto's Pregnancy*, 1566. Rijksprentenkabinet, Amsterdam.

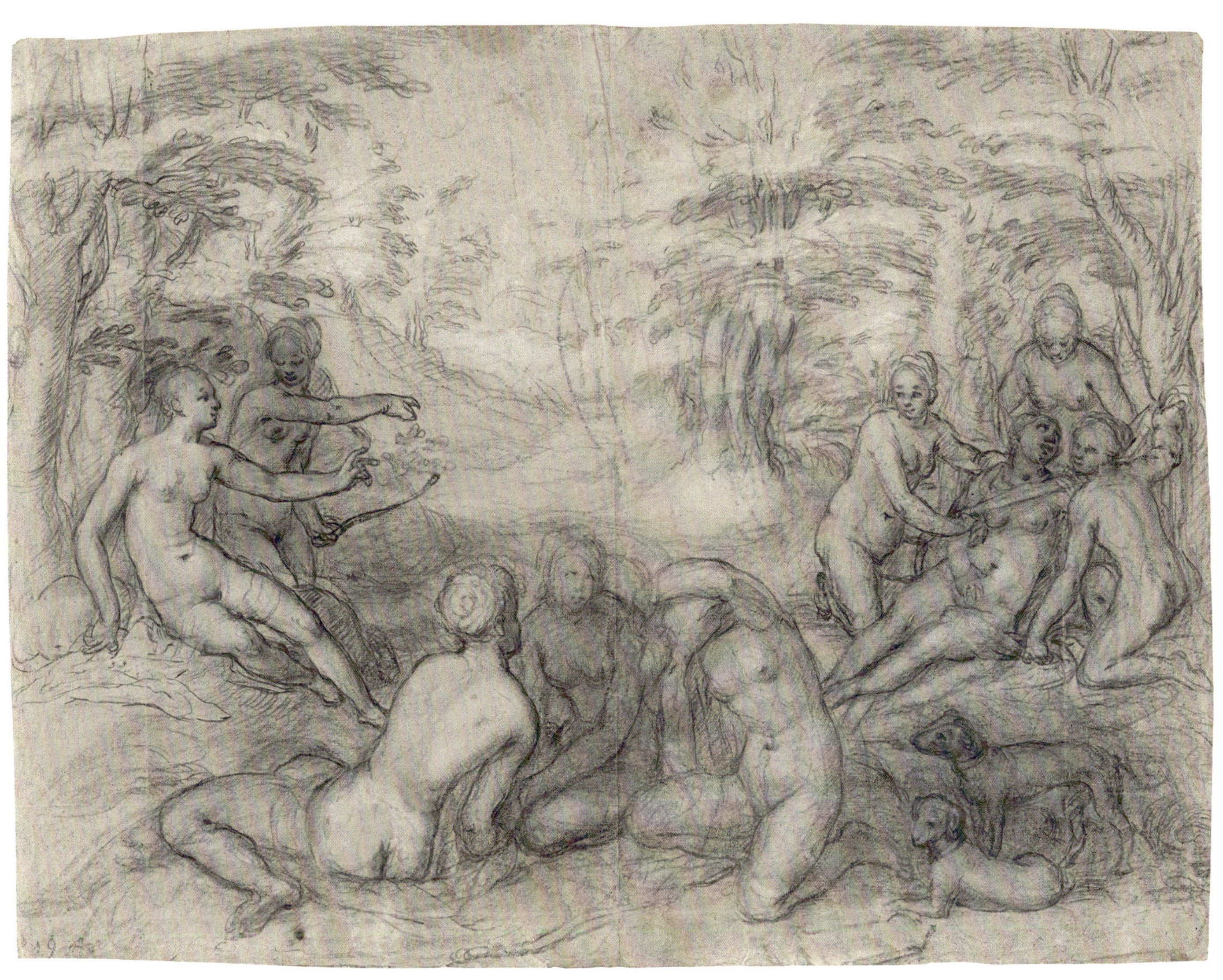

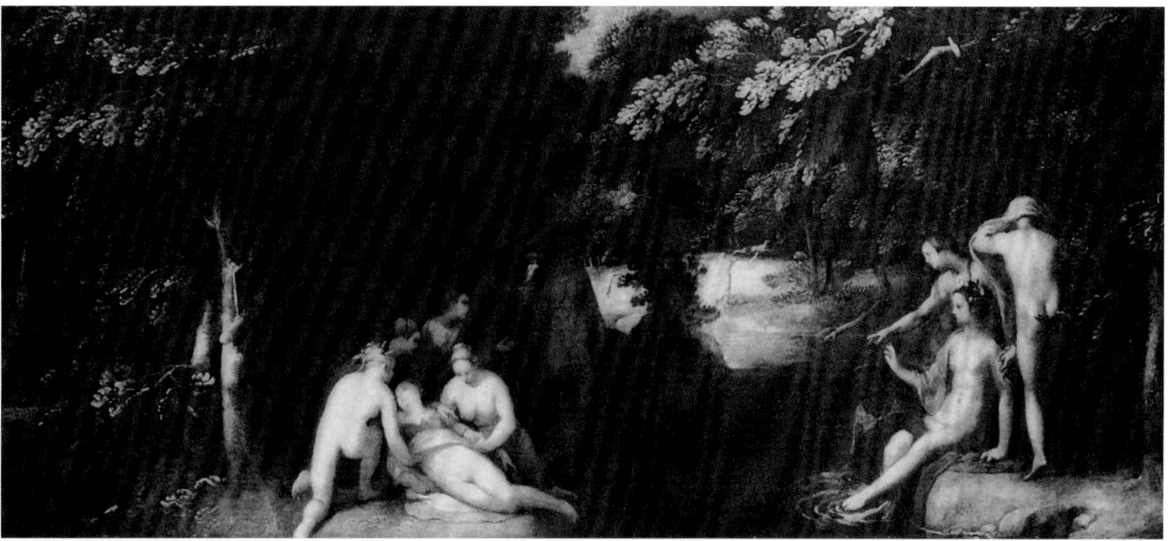

7.2 Cornelis Cornelisz van Haarlem, *Diana Discovering Callisto's Pregnancy*, ca. 1600. Present whereabouts unknown.

Since the discovery of the drawing in 1975, art historians have puzzled over the question of its function. Because of the popularity of the subject in prints by Goltzius and his circle, it had been suggested that the drawing could have been created as a design for an engraving, while its large size has led to conjectures that the sheet could have served as a preparatory study for a tapestry or a painting.[9] With regard to the latter, it can be noted that the painting that bears the closest relationship to the present drawing was executed not by Goltzius himself but by Cornelis Cornelisz van Haarlem, his close associate (fig. 7.2).[10] In that work, as in the Moore drawing, Diana and her nymphs are located within a verdant forest landscape. While the placement of the two groups is reversed, their poses—especially the positions of Diana and Callisto—are very close. Since the painting and the drawing are dated around the same time, it remains unclear whether Cornelisz van Haarlem was relying on a drawing by Goltzius to make his piece, or if Goltzius drew inspiration from the painted work of his friend and colleague.

It is also possible that the artist conceived the sheet as a preparatory study for an autonomous drawing. Starting around 1600, Goltzius created a number of such works, often focusing on mythological subjects. A grisaille pen drawing in the collection of the Rijksprentenkabinet depicts the *Birth of Adonis*, another episode from Ovid's *Metamorphoses*.[11] The sheet is close in size to the Moore drawing and, as a surviving study in the Kunstsammlungen der Veste Coburg shows, was developed with the help of preparatory studies in chalk.[12] It might therefore offer a good indication of the end result that Goltzius had in mind when making the present work. AM

JACQUES DE GHEYN II

Antwerp 1565–1629 The Hague

8

Studies of a Clergyman, Christ at the Column, and Other Figures, ca. 1600–1610

Pen and brown ink, over black chalk
264 x 236 mm

INSCRIPTIONS Verso, upper center, in red chalk: G 1057; verso, lower right, in graphite: 204 (encircled); below that, in graphite: 241

PROVENANCE Prince Wladimir Nikolaevitch Argoutinsky-Dolgoroukoff (1874–1941), Paris (L. 2602d); his sale, R.W.P. de Vries, Amsterdam, 27 March 1925, lot 129 (to "De Vries"); Louis Godefroy (1885–1934), Paris, by 1928; Franz W. Koenigs (1881–1941), Cologne and Haarlem (no mark; see L. 1023a); by descent to the private collectors from whom acquired through Johan Bosch van Rosenthal, Art Consult, Amsterdam, by Clement C. Moore, 2014

SELECT REFERENCES Godefroy 1928, no. 53; Van Regteren Altena 1983, 2: no. 496

Promised gift of Clement C. and Elizabeth Y. Moore

Endlessly one's eyes could wander over this sheet between the individual motifs depicted by Jacques de Gheyn II in a seemingly effortless flow of lines in pen and brown ink. From the heavily cloaked monk at right to the figure of Christ bound to a pillar at left, these virtuoso sketches combine ideas that the artist might have encountered in everyday life with those that sprang from his imagination. In not knowing on which motif to focus next, the viewer is continually surprised and pleased when studying the Moore drawing—and it seems as if De Gheyn deliberately anticipated this phenomenon.

The choice of motifs and how to bring them together on this sheet were made rather consciously by the draftsman. The preliminary notations in black chalk used for the boyish head staring at us at left, as well as the woman merging into a tree, support this theory, indicating a more thorough approach than would have resulted from spontaneous sketching. Notable, too, is that for the two men at the upper right, De Gheyn reverted to an earlier compositional drawing, *Job on a Dunghill, Tried by His Friends* in the collection of the Yale University Art Gallery, New Haven, in which they appear among a group of figures in the background.[1] Moreover, the drawing features a subtle, though probably well thought-out *mise en page*, one that is characterized by three full-length figural elements on the lower half of the page, "crowned" by details of heads at the top.

Similarly composed sheets are preserved in a number of collections, including the Rijksprentenkabinet, Amsterdam (fig. 8.1),[2] the Metropolitan Museum of Art, New York,[3] and the Hessisches Landesmuseum, Darmstadt.[4] They share the presence of more than one motif, taken from both reality as well as imagination, and an equal and deliberate distribution of such motifs on the paper. Unlike sheets by De Gheyn showing several studies after the same model or body parts, these drawings combine the two principles that, according to Karel van Mander, were necessary in order to understand all the reasons of Art, that is "veel nae t'leven, en met eenen uyt den gheest te doen" (a great deal both from life and at the same time from imagination).[5] De Gheyn mastered this approach to drawing like no other, as Van Mander emphasized in his biography and is also abundantly clear from the many drawings in De Gheyn's oeuvre depicting natural history subjects as well as witchcraft.

J.Q. van Regteren Altena was the first to suggest that these so-called "study sheets," in their design and execution, were created as finished works of art in the tradition of model book sheets and didactic sketchbooks, such as those made by Abraham Bloemaert (no. 10).[6] Rather than for workshop use, the general consensus today, according to Holm Bevers and William W. Robinson, is that De Gheyn presumably made these for sale or gift.[7] Through De Gheyn's connections established at the time of his stay in the university city of Leiden and later in the political climate of The Hague, he might have had contact with patrons who would have commissioned or bought such drawings. After all, it is known that a small circle of friends and connoisseurs, among them Rembrandt, owned examples.[8] The question arises whether these drawings and their apparently arbitrary juxtaposition of individual motifs had a higher purpose, such as provoking conversation. In any case, their owners must surely have derived pleasure from looking at them and, where possible, from identifying their sources.

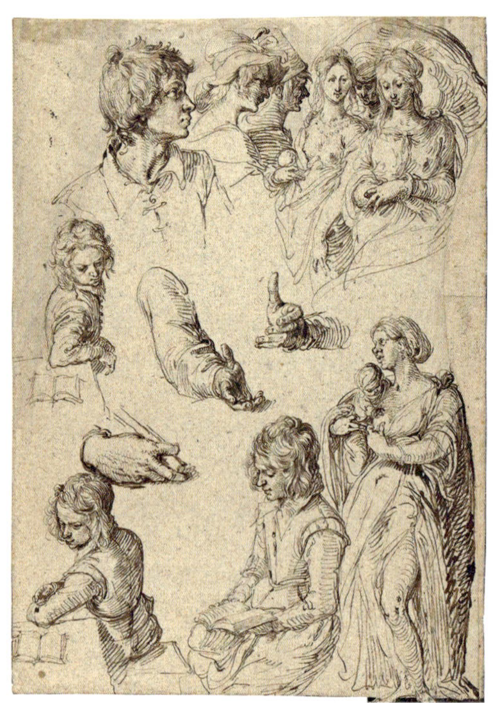

8.1 Jacques de Gheyn II, *Studies of Hands and Figures*, 1604. Rijksprentenkabinet, Amsterdam.

For instance, past owners might have discussed the identity of the woman at the center of this sheet undergoing a gradual transformation into a tree. Such a figure usually evokes the myth of Apollo and Daphne as recounted in Ovid's *Metamorphoses*. However, in that story the two central characters are generally depicted together, as Apollo witnesses Daphne turning into a laurel tree with her limbs sprouting into branches. In the Moore sketch, by contrast, she stands by herself, incorporated into the robust tree trunk with its thick bark. Therefore, the tale illustrated by De Gheyn is presumably another one, namely that of Lotis. In Ovid's *Fasti*, the nymph Lotis is woken up by the braying of a donkey and thus escapes Priapus's attempt to assault her by transforming into a lotus tree. The narrative continues when Dryope plucks a blossom from Lotis's tree, resulting in her own transformation into a dark poplar. Iconographical conundrums of this sort, and their investigation, would provide continual appeal to the interests of the owner of a sheet like this. MvS

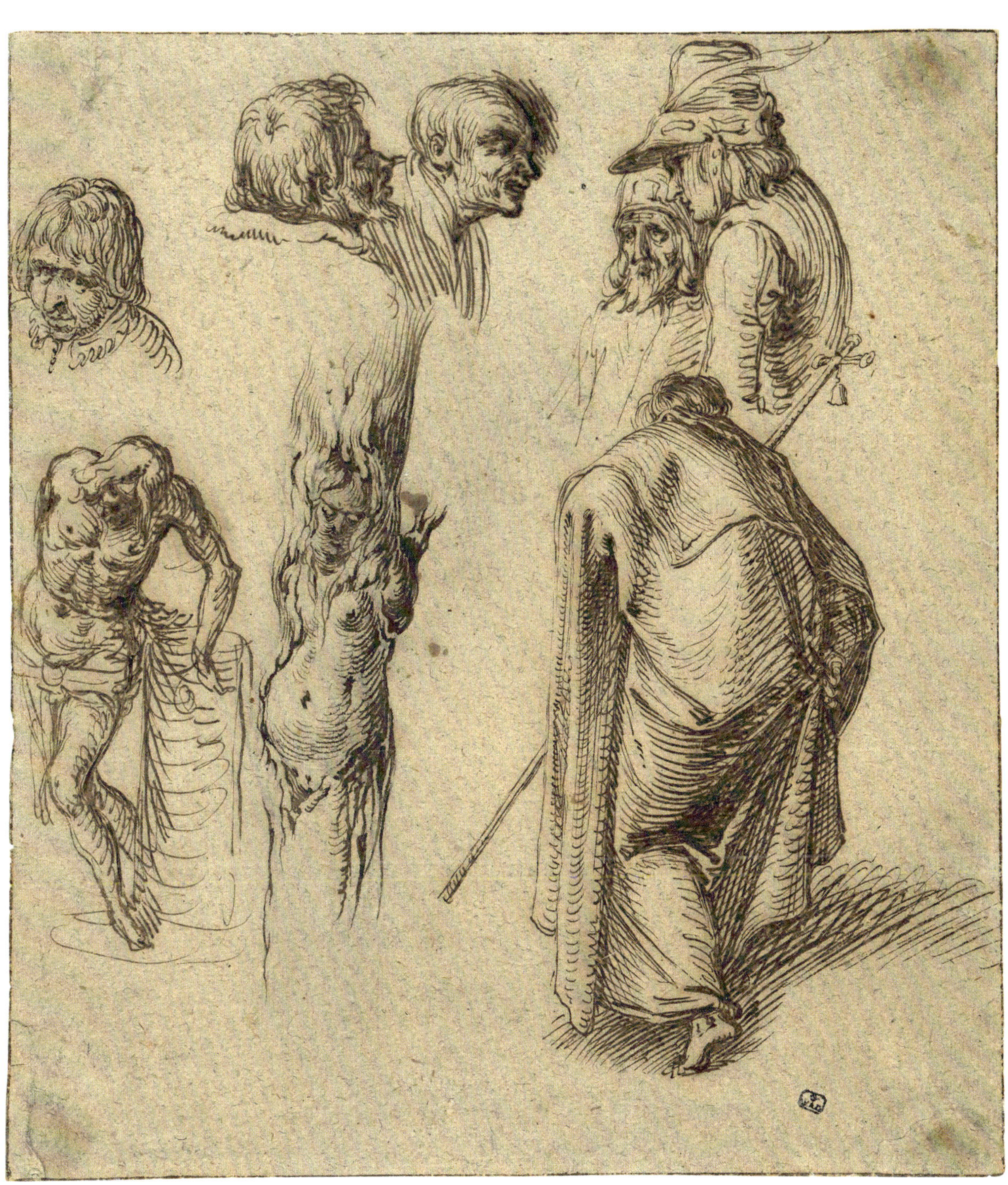

JACQUES DE GHEYN II

Antwerp 1565–1629 The Hague

9a,b

A Soldier Visited by Father Time (a) and *A Soldier Accompanied by Envy* (b), ca. 1620

Pen and brown ink, over black chalk
Each 84 x 78 mm

WATERMARK (a) Hunting horn within a shield, similar to Laurentius and Laurentius 2007, no. 587 (Sluijs, 1619)

PROVENANCE Private collection, the Netherlands; Onno van Seggelen Fine Arts, Rotterdam; from whom acquired by Clement C. Moore, 2020

Promised gift of Clement C. and Elizabeth Y. Moore

That Jacques de Gheyn II was knowledgeable about the handling of military weapons and a soldier's readiness for battle is clear from the more than one hundred designs by him for various drills represented in the manual *Wapenhandelinghe* published in 1606.[1] The armored soldier depicted in each of this pair of drawings, however, is in no state to take action or handle a weapon, as he is focused on dealing with unwanted company. In one of the Moore drawings, the figure is seated on a barrel and visited by Father Time, who confronts him with his remaining lifespan; in the other sheet, the reclining soldier gazes rather bewilderedly ahead, supported by the figure of Envy (*Invidia*), eating her heart.

Both representations relate to themes often depicted by De Gheyn. Around 1596, the artist drew the figure of Envy for a series of Vices and Virtues published by Zacharias Dolendo.[2] Closely linked to this personification is the subject of witchcraft, which De Gheyn treated in various works. His interest in the theme of the transience of life is reflected, for example, in the painted *Vanitas Still Life* (1603) kept in the Metropolitan Museum of Art, New York,[3] and in the terrifying drawing of *A Woman and Death* in the Rijksprentenkabinet, Amsterdam.[4] Yet, the context of the allegorical drawings under discussion seems to be more mocking in tone.

That it is most likely one and the same soldier depicted in both sheets is evident from the figure's helmet and distinctive mustache. With his full armor, it might even have been De Gheyn's intention to depict the god Mars. It is quite possible that he was rendered with other allegorical figures in now-lost drawings, and that these two sheets belong to a larger set. The artist's intentions nonetheless remain unclear. Such a series might have been preparatory for prints, yet neither drawing betrays any sign of indentation for transfer to a copper plate.

A striking comparison can be drawn between the Moore drawing and a larger drawing by De Gheyn, the *Sheet with Two Figural Compositions and Studies of Helmets and Arms* (ca. 1620–29), in the Metropolitan Museum of Art, New York (fig. 9.1).[5] At the lower left are two figures, each apparently holding the staff of the god of medicine, Asclepius. The figure in the foreground wearing a toga may represent the god. Although he looks defeated and leans forward, his pose is similar to that of the soldier with Father Time in the Moore drawing, seated on a barrel with his foot resting on a ball. The figures in both compositions are placed against an empty plane on the left, perhaps representing a wall, used to frame the vignette.

In the last decade of De Gheyn's career, not only did the artist often work on a similar small, square format (often around 100–150 mm),[6] but also, his penwork became looser. Having abandoned the distinctively Mannerist and accurate pen strokes derived from his training with Hendrick Goltzius, his handling of the pen became freer and more rapid. For the soldier visited by Father Time, the hatching is firm, with thick overlapping pen lines, in contrast to the short, nervous dashes used, for example, to depict the sand in the hourglass. The rendering of the figure of Envy seems to have been done in an even more casual manner, with less dense crosshatching. Beneath the pen lines in both, traces of initial outlines in black chalk are visible, as was typical of De Gheyn's working method (see also no. 8). MvS

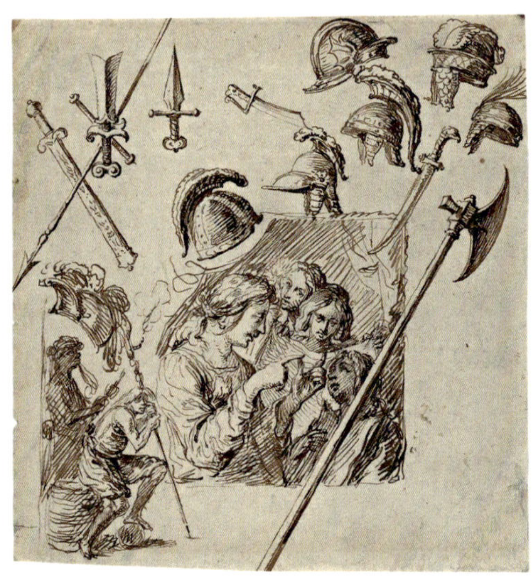

9.1 Jacques de Gheyn II, *Sheet with Two Figural Compositions and Studies of Helmets and Arms*, ca. 1620–29. Metropolitan Museum of Art, New York.

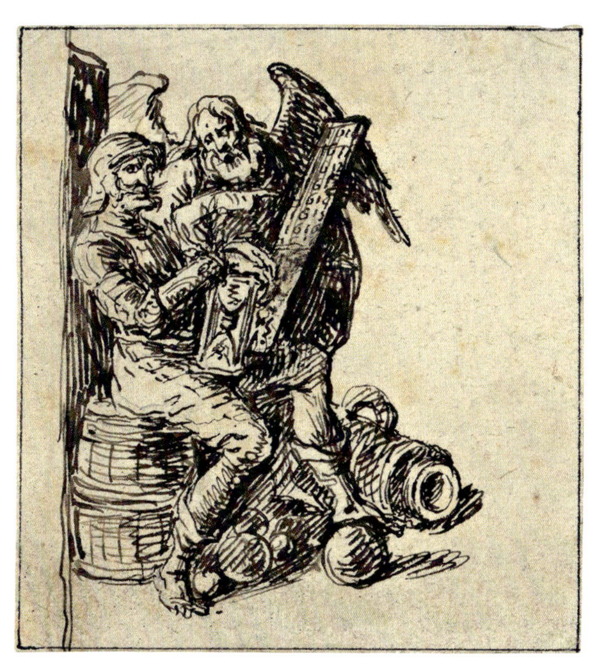

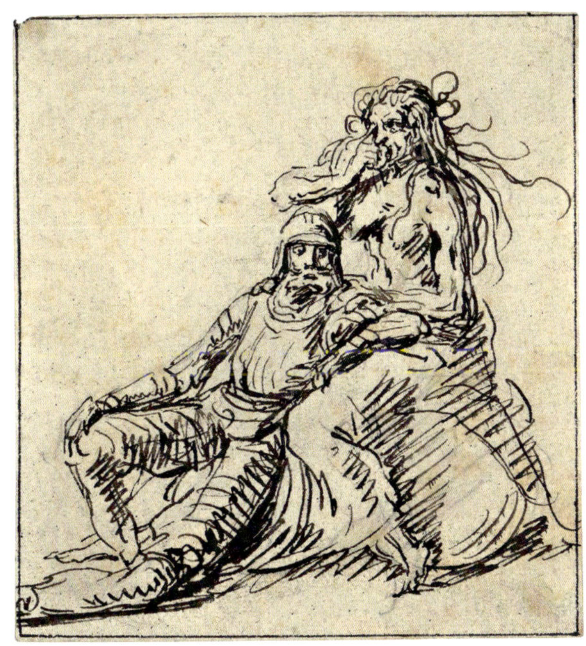

ABRAHAM BLOEMAERT

Gorinchem 1566–1651 Utrecht

10

Head Studies (recto); *Figure Studies* (verso), ca. 1591–1605

Red chalk, with pen and brown ink and opaque white watercolor (recto); red chalk, with pen and brown ink (verso)
158 x 165 mm

WATERMARK Fragment at bottom: three balls, bishop's hat

INSCRIPTIONS Recto, upper right, in brown ink, *58*; verso, upper right, in brown ink: *60*

PROVENANCE André Giroux (1801–1879), Paris (no mark; see L. 5838); his sale, Delestre and Lair-Dubreuil, Paris, 18–19 April 1904, as part of lot 175; possibly Gaston Verdé-Delisle (1862–1928), Paris; thence by descent within the Verdé-Delisle family; their sale, Claude Aguttes, Neuilly-sur-Seine, 27 March 2012, lot 16; P. & D. Colnaghi and Co., London, 2014; from whom acquired by Clement C. Moore, 2014

SELECT REFERENCES Bolten 2017, 69, 90, 114–15, nos. A26 and A52

Promised gift of Clement C. and Elizabeth Y. Moore

Studies like this, with several corporeal forms arranged loosely on a single page, played a key role in the working process and legacy of Utrecht artist Abraham Bloemaert. The Moore sheet features multiple heads, all of which share a similar countenance but are turned at slightly different angles. They display diverse hairstyles and headgear ranging from a modest headscarf to intricate braids. In the lower left of the recto, the heads are cut from another piece of paper affixed on the sheet, blending almost seamlessly with the other visages. On the verso are less developed versions of two similar heads, a detail of the same braided coiffure, and two hands holding a piece of cloth with an additional form—perhaps a figure—sketched between them.

A highly skilled, prolific draftsman, Bloemaert reveals his deft handling of materials in the present work through the mingling of media used. Red chalk predominates, applied with varied pressure to create graceful, undulating lines; basket-weave hatching defines the contours of the figures' necks and cheeks, lending them a sculptural heft. Atop the chalk is ink, selectively employed, to define the elaborate braids of the figure at upper left of the recto, while touches of white create highlights that give further dimension to the forms.

As is typical of Bloemaert's study sheets, this drawing was not made in preparation for a specific painting or print, yet the individual motifs can be related to other works in his oeuvre. Like many of his predecessors and peers, Bloemaert mined his own study drawings—ranging from isolated facial features, to heads, to full-length figures—in the process of formulating new compositions for prints and paintings.[1] Such a stock of studies could serve repeatedly as a precious, enduring resource for his artistic production. The figures in the present sheet could be applied alternately to a goddess reclining in a landscape, a woman toiling with farm tools, or a saint at prayer. More specifically, in this instance, the hands on the verso resemble those in the 1605 engraving of *Veronica Holding the Sudarium* by Jacob Matham after Bloemaert.[2]

Subsequently, this sheet and others like it laid the foundation for the dissemination of Bloemaert's imagery through reproductive prints. As indicated by the subject matter, medium, and numbers "58" and "60" in the upper corners, this drawing belongs to the so-called "Giroux album," the group of (now dispersed) studies by Bloemaert that sold in 1904 at the Paris auction of the collection of the nineteenth-century artist André Giroux.[3] This group can be viewed as a precursor to the "Cambridge album," another set of studies by Bloemaert now at the Fitzwilliam Museum, Cambridge, which served as models for the book of prints engraved and published by his son Frederick between 1651 and 1656;[4] later editions included that published by Nicolaes Visscher II beginning around 1680, and another in association with Bernard Picart (who rearranged the prints) with its popular moniker, the *Tekenboek*, in 1740.[5] With such models circulating through prints, generations of professional artists, amateurs, and art lovers were able to absorb his imagery piece by piece, enjoying the pleasure of viewing and learning from a career's worth of study drawings gathered together without explanatory text. Useful as these prints may have been in securing Bloemaert's legacy as a draftsman, however, it is actual working drawings like the present sheet that reveal the singular prowess of a draftsman who spent a lifetime relentlessly capturing and compiling life's fleeting moments. EN

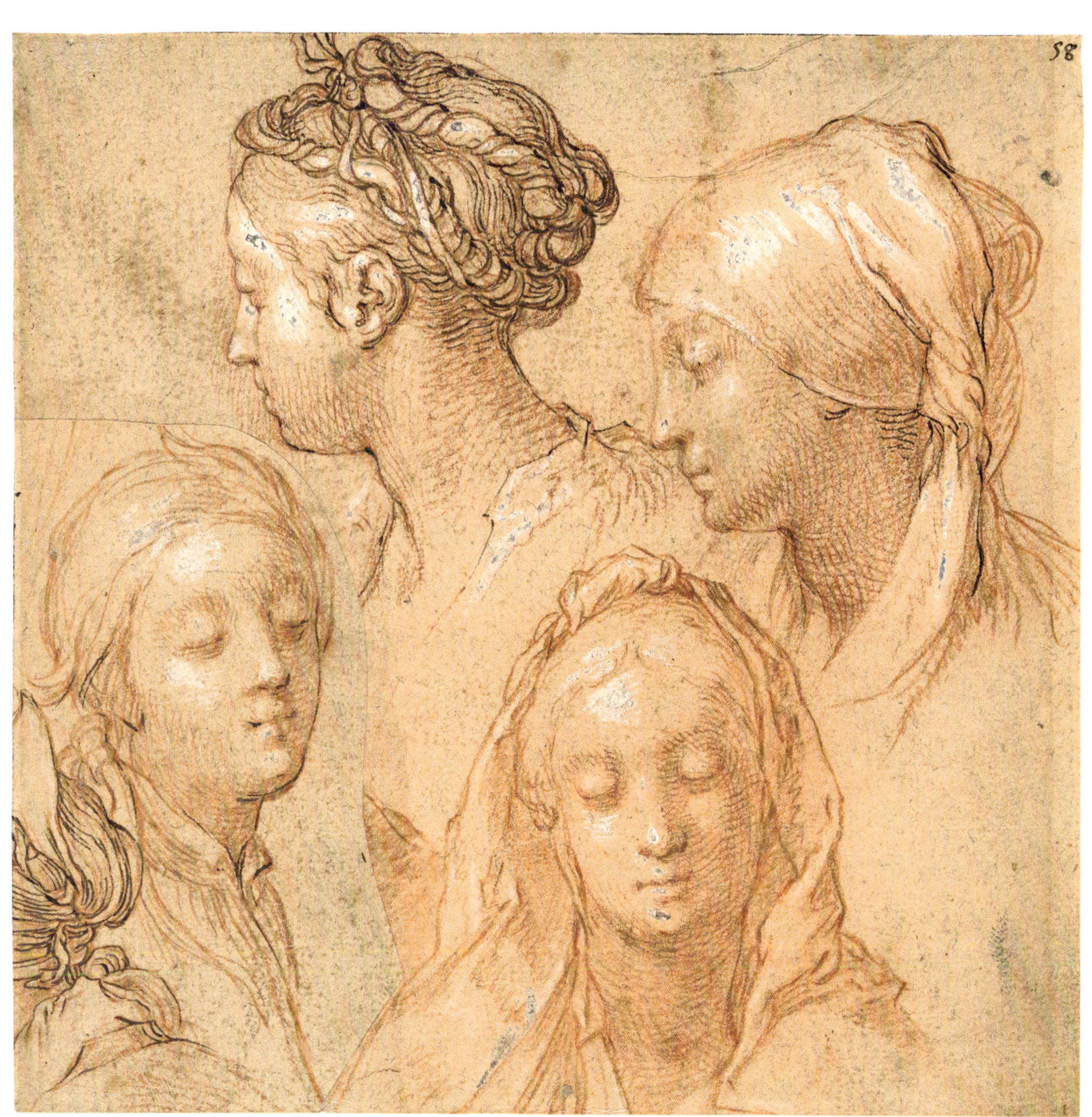

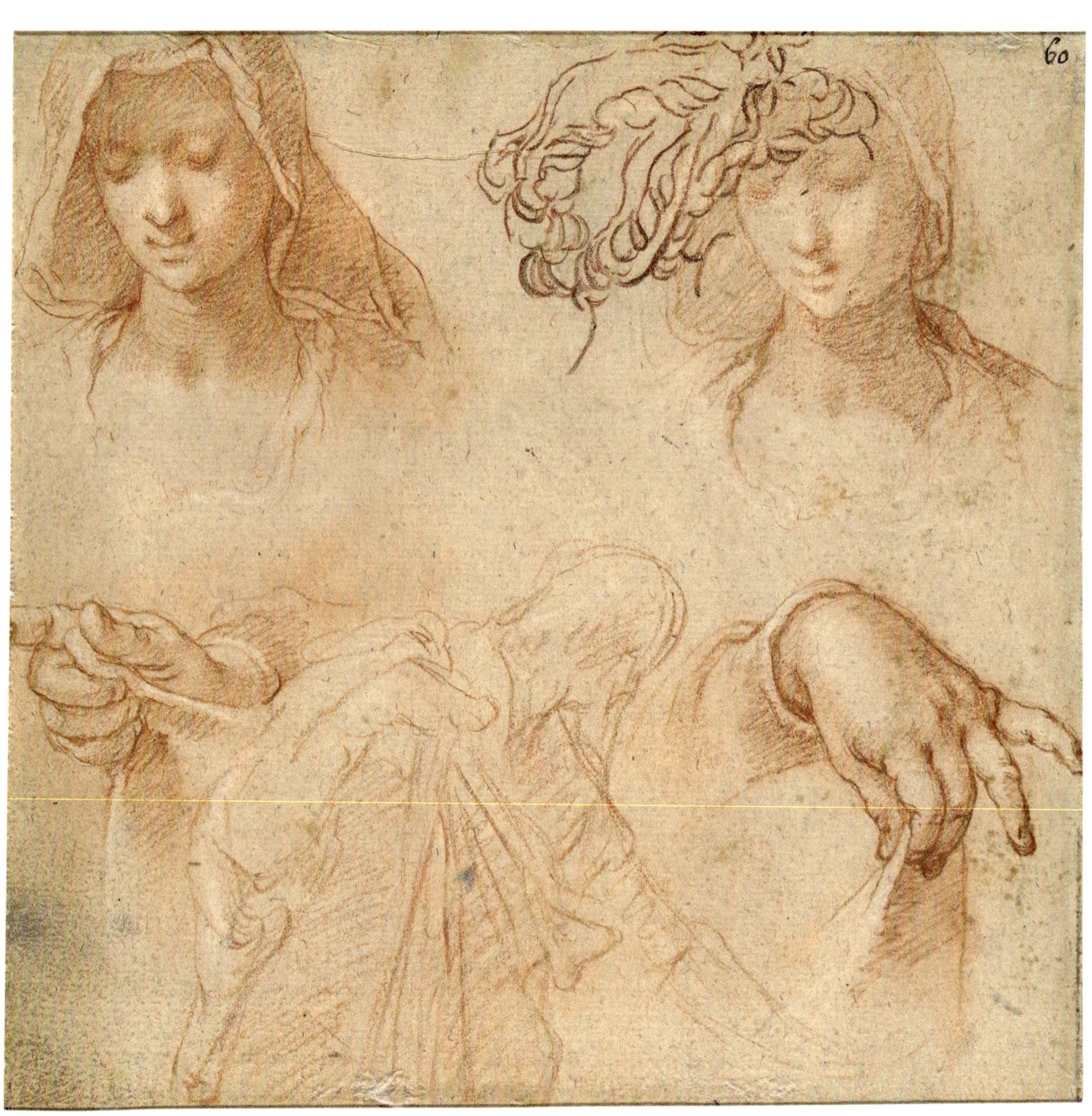

ABRAHAM BLOEMAERT

Gorinchem 1566–1651 Utrecht

11

Danaë Receiving the Golden Rain, ca. 1610

Pen and brown ink and wash, with white opaque watercolor and red watercolor, over black chalk, on beige paper; contours incised for transfer
184 x 252 mm

WATERMARK Illegible fragment

INSCRIPTIONS Verso, center, in brown ink (upside down): *A Blomart*; to the left of this (correct orientation), in graphite: 5—0; just below center (turned 90° to the right), in graphite: *S6*; along left edge (turned 90° to the left), in graphite: 5; and at upper right, in blue crayon: 20 (encircled)

PROVENANCE Possibly Kunst & Auktionshaus, Berlin, 13 April 1935, lot 473 ("Bloemaert. Danae auf dem Ruhebett. Handzeichnung"); private collection, Germany; Kunsthandel Thomas le Claire, Hamburg; from whom acquired by Clement C. Moore, 2007

SELECT REFERENCES Bolten 2007, 1: 176, under no. 493, 2: 223; Widerkehr 2007, part 2: 95, under no. 188; Shoaf Turner 2012, no. 6; Strasser 2013, 72, under no. 24, n. 6; Bolten 2017, 45–46, no. 493b

Promised gift of Clement C. and Elizabeth Y. Moore

This is Bloemaert's finished and indented *modello* for the engraving, in reverse (fig. 11.1), made in 1610 by Jacob Matham, the stepson of Hendrick Goltzius (see nos. 7, 14).[1] Excluding the depth of the legend on the bottom of the print, the images are virtually the same size, and the stylus indentations—throughout the sheet and not (as once claimed) just on the figures—match exactly. There is thus no need to posit a lost preparatory drawing, as have Bolten and others. This was confirmed in 2014, when Morgan conservators and curators used a specialized digital photographic technique known as Reflectance Transformation Imaging (RTI) to uncover and publish online the physical evidence of the process by which Jacob Matham marked up the drawing and transformed it into a print.[2]

In the engraving, Matham made only minor adjustments, such as adding the crowned head of Jupiter blowing a shower of gold coins from clouds at the top of the composition and representing the figure of Danaë with her eyes half closed, as if she were about to drift off to sleep. Yet even with her eyes open, as in the drawing, the blushing maiden seems oblivious to the shower of coins pouring into the drapery held aloft by her servant. According to Greek legend, the coins were the disguise adopted by Jupiter to gain entrance to the bedchamber of Danaë, the beautiful daughter of King Acrisius of Argos and Eurydice. She had been locked away in a fortified tower by her father to prevent her from bearing a male child, since an oracle consulted by Acrisius had foretold that he would be killed by his daughter's son. Danaë became impregnated by Jupiter's shower of coins and bore Perseus, who many years later accidentally struck the aging Acrisius with his javelin, thus fulfilling the prophecy.

The late Jaap Bolten identified what he considered to be an earlier preparatory study for the composition in the Kunstsammlung der Universität Göttingen.[3] There is a nearly identical version in the Special Collections of the

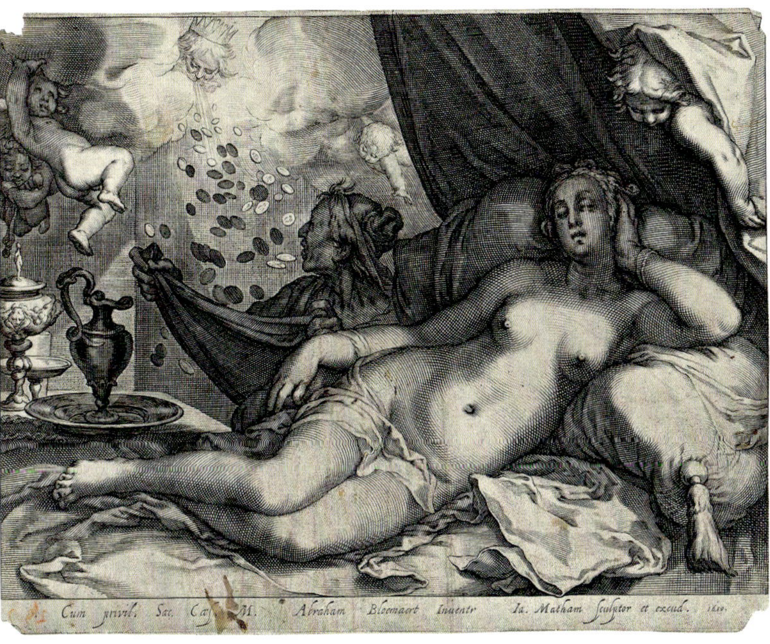

11.1 Jacob Matham (after Abraham Bloemaert), *Danaë Receiving the Golden Rain*, 1610. British Museum, London.

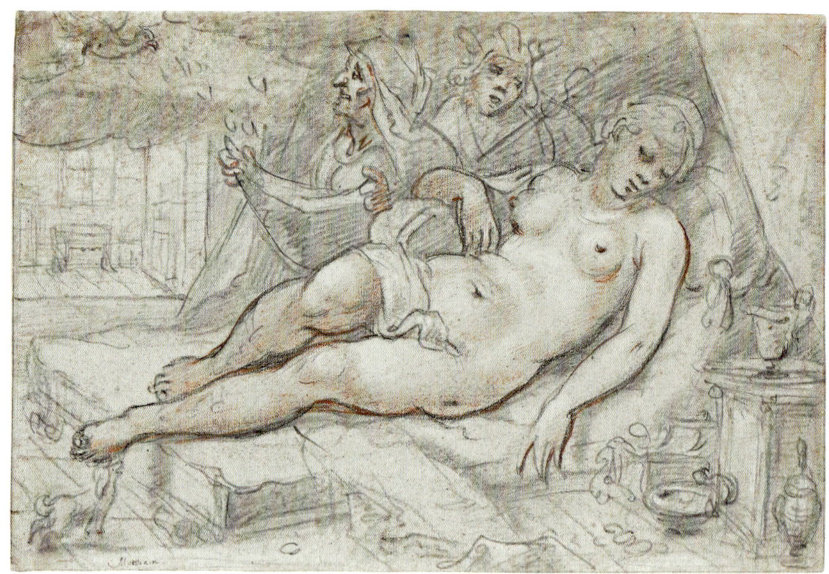

11.2 Jacob Matham, *Danaë Receiving the Golden Rain*, ca. 1603. Collection of Jean Bonna, Geneva.

Universiteitsbibliotheek Leiden.[4] In these pen drawings, Danaë's body is in roughly the same position, though with her head thrown back and her right arm fully extended. Likewise, the arm of the maid is held out and her head tilted up: she looks toward an eagle (rather than coins) blown from the mouth of Jupiter. The god's crowned head is exactly the same as in the final print, but the motif of the eagle (his attribute) was eliminated in both the present drawing and the engraving.

Mythological stories such as this offered an acceptable vehicle for the depiction of female nudes by sixteenth- and seventeenth-century artists—especially at the turn of the seventeenth century, when Dutch artists, increasingly interested in the accurate depiction of their surroundings, produced some of the earliest female nude studies from life. Perhaps we will never know whether Bloemaert had access to Goltzius's sensuous chalk drawings of female nudes, such as the overtly erotic *Recumbent Female Nude* of 1594, now in an American private collection,[5] but the subject and composition of the present drawing show his direct indebtedness to, among other sources, Goltzius's painting of the same theme dated 1603, now in the Los Angeles County Museum of Art.[6] Matham's own drawing of the subject, in the collection of Jean Bonna, Geneva (fig. 11.2),[7] is also clearly dependent on the Goltzius painting, as is evident from Danaë's bent right arm, but the figure of the maid more closely resembles the present work. JST

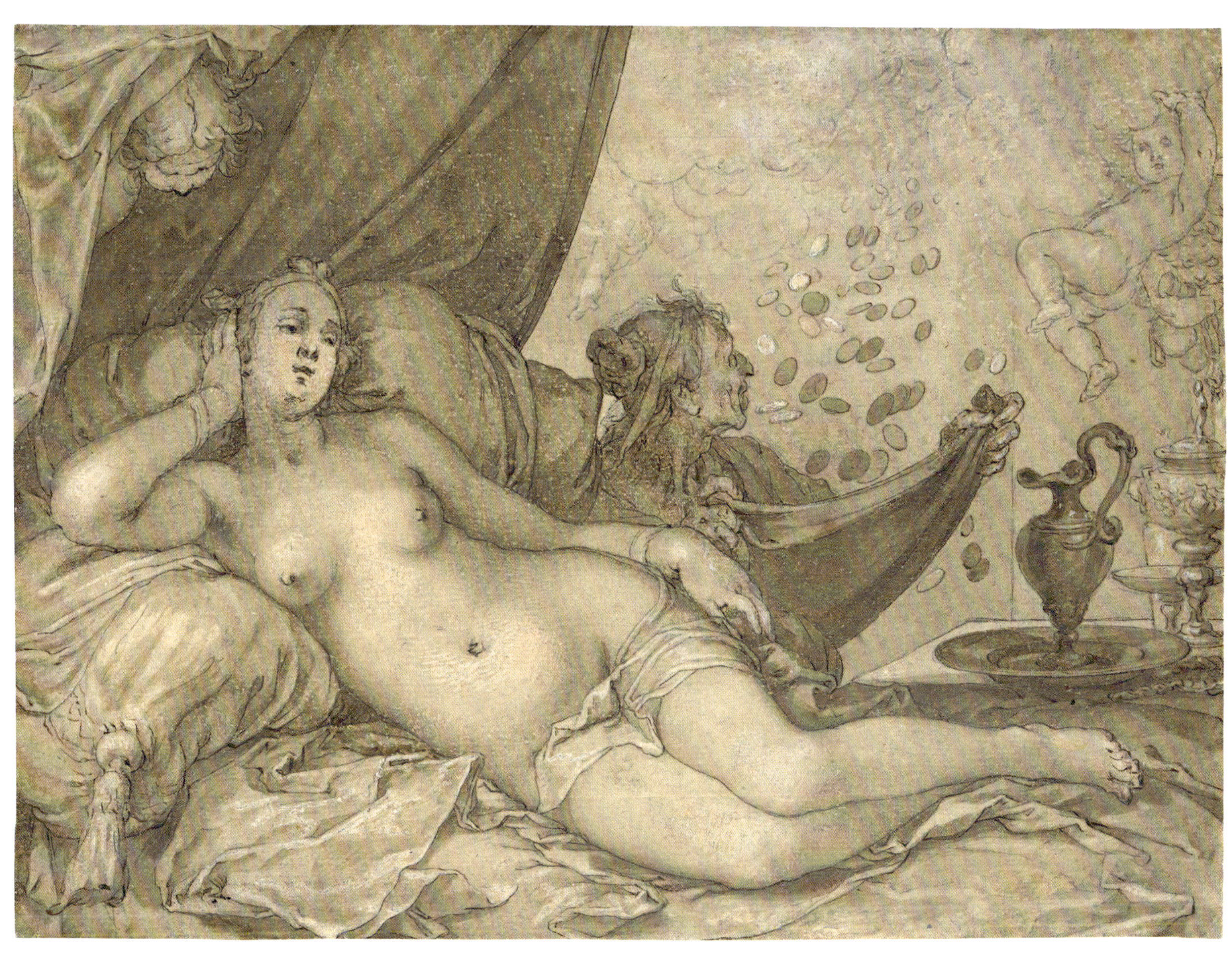

HENDRIK VROOM

Haarlem ca. 1566–1640 Haarlem

12

A Beach Scene with Fishermen Bringing in Their Catch (recto); *A Ship Riding the Waves in a Stormy Sea* (verso), ca. 1620–39

Pen and brown ink
121 x 280 mm

WATERMARK Coat of arms with a French lily, similar to Hinterding 2006, 2: 204, no. C.d.a (FLC 1286) and 3: 434 (1639); Laurentius and Laurentius 2007, nos. 437 (1622), 438 (1630)

PROVENANCE Private collection, the Netherlands; Onno van Seggelen Fine Arts, Rotterdam; from whom acquired by Clement C. Moore, 2018

Promised gift of Clement C. and Elizabeth Y. Moore

Born into a family of artists, Hendrik Vroom developed into the most prominent marine artist in the Northern Netherlands around 1600. He was of great influence on the next generation of marine painters, such as Cornelis Claesz van Wieringen and Jan Porcellis. According to Van Mander, Vroom was a well-traveled man, undertaking trips to Spain, Italy, France, and Portugal in the late 1580s.[1] Because of his experiences at sea, he developed great insight into accurately depicting ships with all their details. In addition, he was one of the first artists to represent the hustle and bustle of activities on the beach, including fishing, a theme loved by Dutch artists well into the nineteenth century.

The present sheet is a rare drawn example of this subject, focusing only on human activities on the beach. Men carry the freshly caught fish onto the shore, where it would be loaded into large baskets. In the Dutch Republic, especially in Haarlem, where Vroom settled in 1592, women played an important role in fishing. Here they seem merely to be supervising the loading of the baskets, but often they carried the fish freshly caught by their husbands all the way from the beach at Zandvoort, through the dunes, to the city center to sell at the market. On the way back, after a long day's work, they would get a drink at De Stinkende Emmer (The Smelly Bucket), an inn that owed its name to the empty, stinking buckets left outside.

The oblong drawing was probably part of a larger, double-sided sheet with two full compositional sketches, comparable to two sheets, one now in the Rijksprentenkabinet, Amsterdam,[2] the other in the Frits Lugt Collection, Fondation Custodia, Paris (fig. 12.1).[3] A former owner of that drawing must have separated the upper and lower compositions, cutting through the sketch on the verso, which represents a ship with billowing sails in a stormy sea. Given its sketchier nature and the use of a slightly broader pen, George Keyes and Frits Lugt questioned the attribution of the Paris sheet to Vroom.[4] There seems, however, to be no fundamental difference from other securely attributed drawings, such as the 1625 dated *Ships in a Storm* in Yale University Art Gallery, New Haven,[5] as was argued by Karel Boon, who convincingly reassigned the Paris work to Vroom.[6]

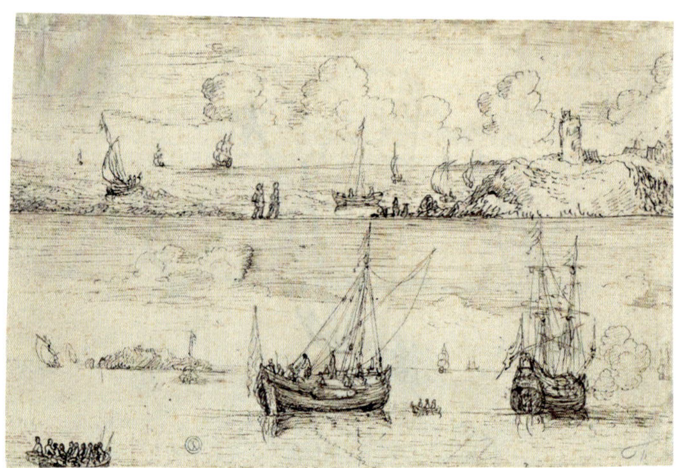

12.1 Hendrik Vroom, *Two Compositional Sketches of Shipping off a Dutch Coast* (verso), ca. 1620–39. Frits Lugt Collection, Fondation Custodia, Paris.

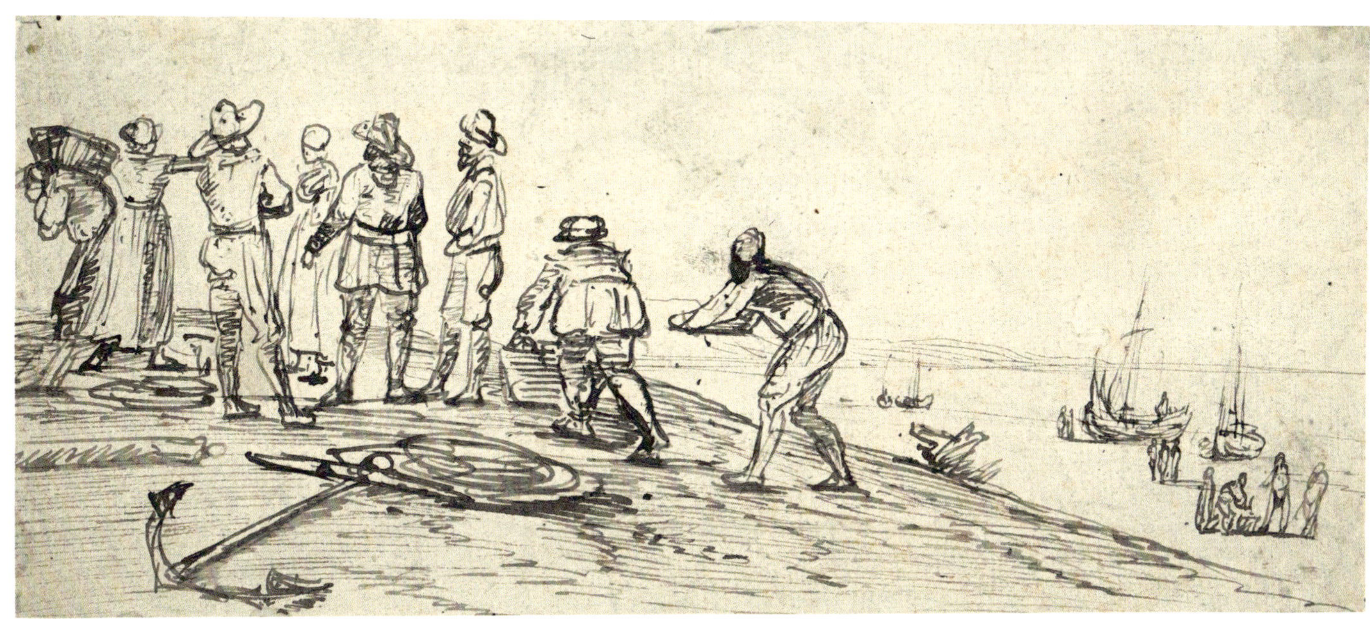

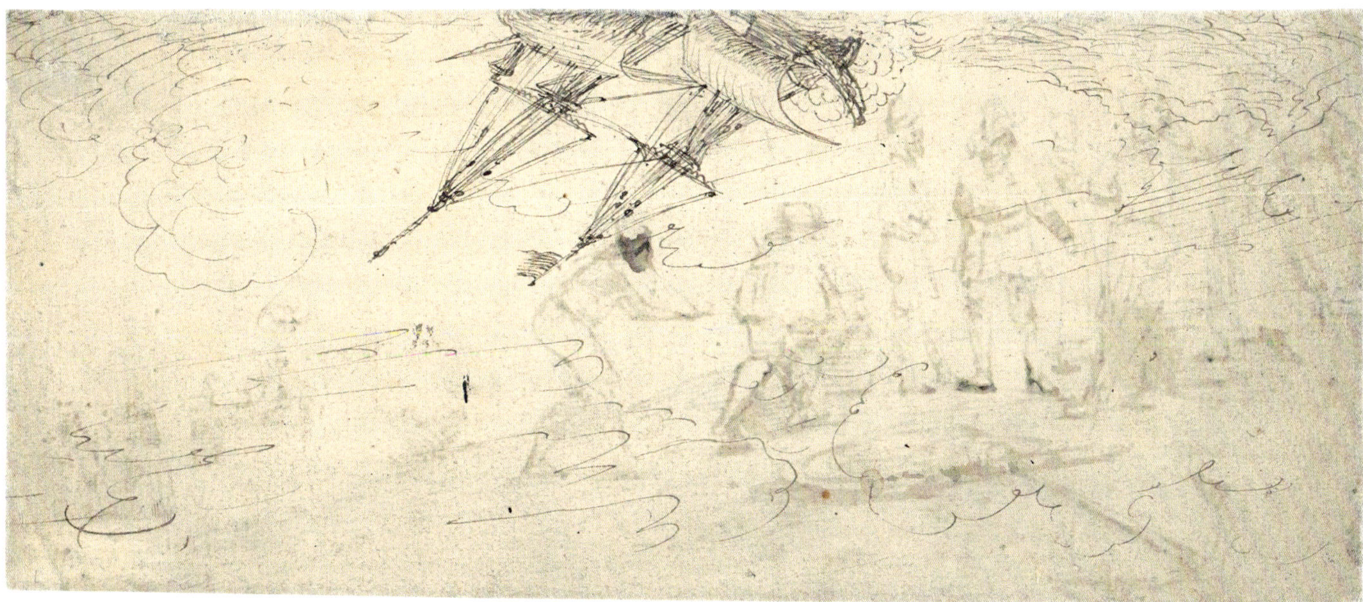

A broad pen, perhaps a reed pen, was also used for the drawing on the recto of the Moore sheet. Vroom employed this medium throughout his career. It can already be found, in combination with a finer quill pen, in his earliest known drawings, a group of French landscapes executed after his return to the Netherlands in 1589.[7] The present sheet probably dates from the 1620s or 1630s, comparable to the Amsterdam drawing mentioned above.[8] MR

JAN BREUGHEL THE ELDER

Brussels 1568–1625 Antwerp

13a,b

Studies of Elegant Figures, Three Monks, and a Priest Taking the Waters at Spa (a) and *Study of Elegant Figures Taking the Waters at Spa* (b, recto); *Studies of Six Figures* (b, verso), 1612

Pen and brown ink, with brown and gray wash, over traces of black chalk; framing line in brown ink (recto of both sheets); pen and brown ink (verso of 13b)
(a) 118 x 178 mm; (b) 110 x 178 mm

INSCRIPTIONS (a) Recto, lower left, in point of brush and brown wash: B; verso of the original Glomy mount (which combines nos. 13a and 13b), upper left, in graphite: *100* (*20*) C. *Du Gardin*; (b) verso, upper left center, in brown ink: *groon sattyn* ("green satin"); verso, lower right, in black chalk: D

PROVENANCE Jean-Baptiste Glomy (1711–1786), Paris (L. 1119, on mount); Sir Louis du Pan Mallet (1864–1936), British ambassador to the Ottoman Empire; Christie's, London, 6 July 2004, one of a pair in lot 163; where acquired by Clement C. Moore

SELECT REFERENCES Klinge 2005, 142, under no. 26; Gerszi and Wood Ruby 2019, no. 60

Promised gift of Clement C. and Elizabeth Y. Moore

Compared to the many independent Dutch landscapes and nature studies that make up the bulk of the Moore drawings collection, few other works in this exhibition served as many different purposes as this pair of sketches from life by Jan Breughel the Elder. The two study sheets, one of them double-sided, have been together at least since the eighteenth century when they were mounted in a single mat by the famous Parisian restorer, collector, and dealer Jean-Baptiste Glomy, whose embossed dry stamp initial "G" appears at the lower right corner of the white border.

Thanks to a large, two-plate etching by Guilliam van Nieulandt II, *Large View of Spa with Two Mineral Springs* (fig. 13.1),[1] after a lost drawing by Breughel,[2] we know exactly where the Moore pair of sketches were made: the Belgian town of Spa, southeast of Liège, whose name became eponymous with sites of natural thermal baths, as well as with a modern brand of sparkling and flat mineral water. The Latin title on Van Nieulandt's print (*VICUS SPADANUS AMOENISSIMUS ET SALUBERRIMUS*) translates as: "The Village of Spa, Most Pleasant and Good for One's Health." Breughel's visit to the popular tourist destination, renowned for its supposed curative properties, is further documented by his drawing of Spa dated 22 August 1612 in the Frits Lugt Collection, Fondation Custodia, Paris.[3] His visit there may well have overlapped with that of Italian artist Remigio Cantagallina, who was traveling through the Southern Netherlands in 1612–13.[4]

The medallion vignettes depicting two of Spa's four main mineral springs in the lower corners of Van Nieulandt's etching incorporate figural motifs from the Moore sketches and two other sheets—one in the Special Collections, Universiteitsbibliotheek Leiden (fig. 13.2),[5] and the other in the Bibliothèque Royale de Belgique, Brussels (fig. 13.3).[6] The vignette on the left represents the Sauvenière spring and includes figures from the group at center left of no. 13a (the head of a woman offering water, and the little boy trying to peer over the shoulders of the

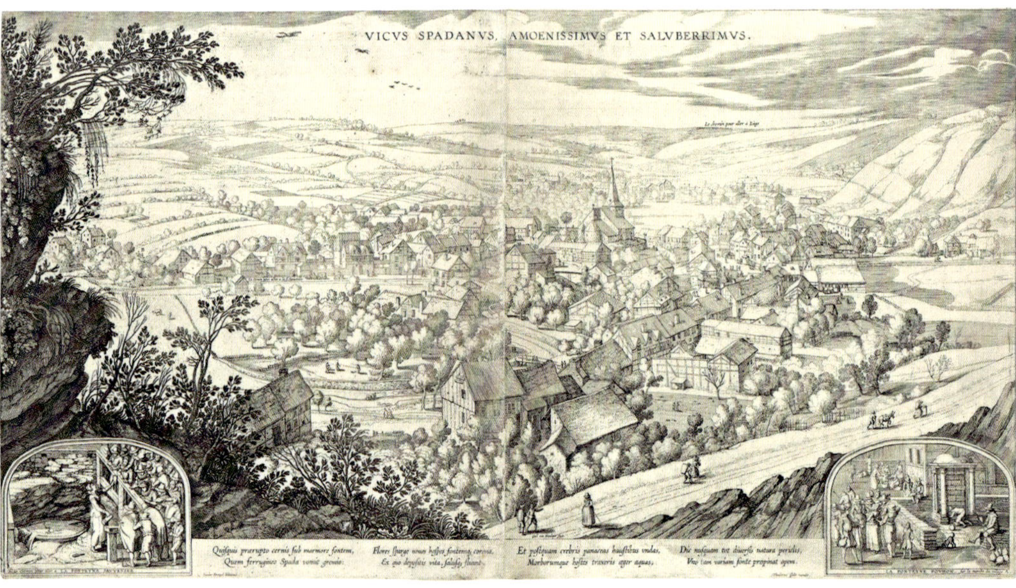

13.1 Guilliam van Nieulandt II (after Jan Breughel the Elder), *Large View of Spa with Two Mineral Springs*, ca. 1612. Rijksprentenkabinet, Amsterdam.

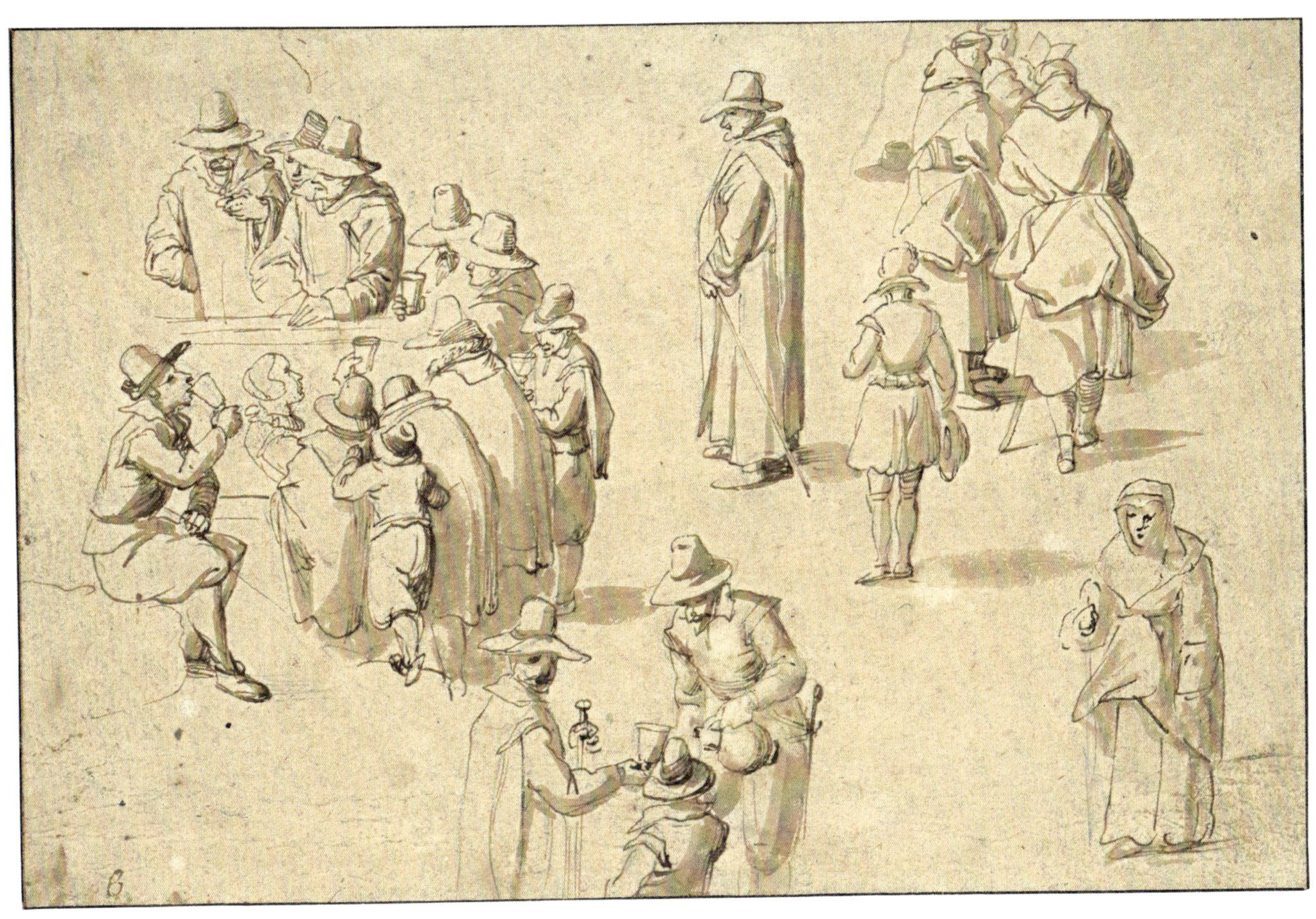

13.2 Jan Breughel the Elder, *Visitors to the Sauvenière Fountain at Spa*, 1612. Special Collections, Universiteitsbibliotheek Leiden.

13.3 Jan Breughel the Elder, *Visitors to the Pouhon Fountain at Spa*, 1612. Bibliothèque Royale de Belgique, Brussels.

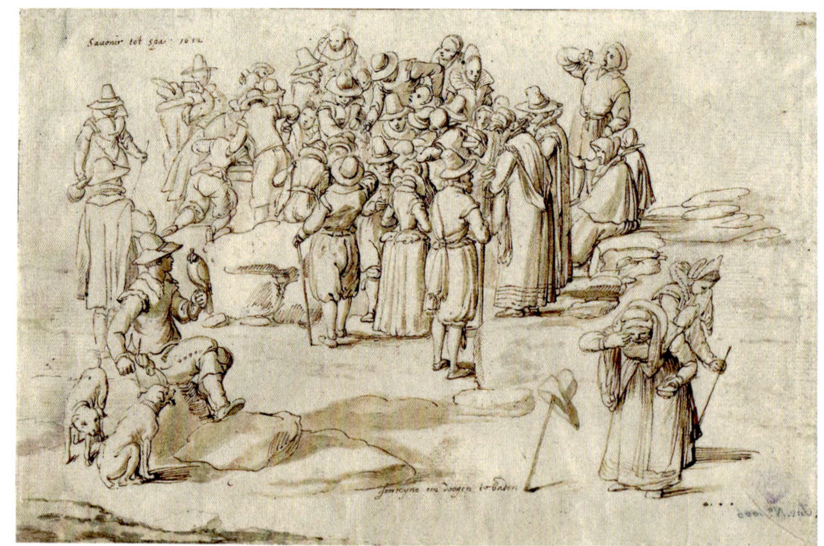

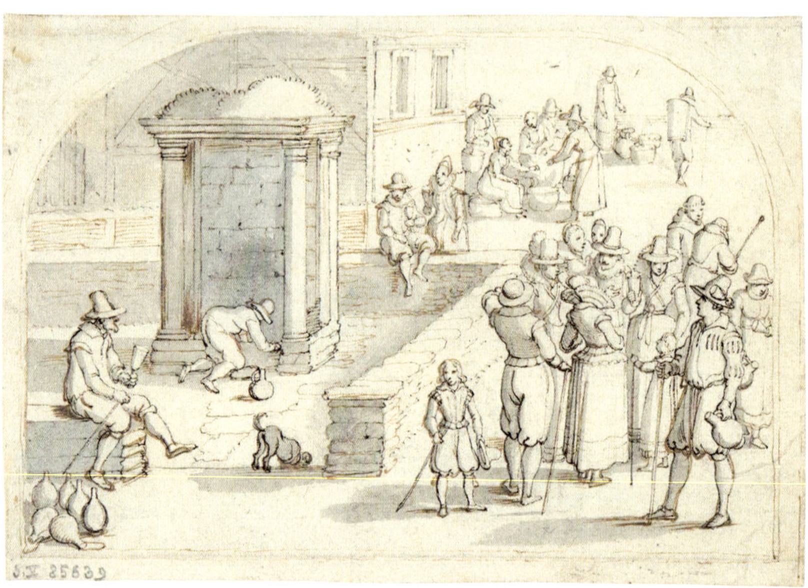

two cloaked figures with their backs to the viewer), as well as the figure of a man holding a glass up to his mouth from the upper right of the Leiden sketch. At lower right of the etching is the Pouhon fountain, which incorporates the figure of a man with a walking stick and his back to the viewer at the center of the Leiden sketch, and from the recto of no. 13b several of the female figures at left and the little boy holding his hat and sword from the upper right. The Brussels drawing is a finished study, in reverse, corresponding in all details with the Pouhon vignette.

Although sheets of figure studies by Breughel are relatively rare, many more must once have existed in a stock repertory kept for future use. The three Moore sketches not only spontaneously captured the lively, colorful array of young and old subjects taking the waters at Spa on a hot day in August 1612, they continued to fulfill functions in the artist's studio for years to come. Dating from the same year as Van Nieulandt's etching of Spa is Breughel's painting of a *Village Scene* in the Alte Pinakothek, Munich (fig. 13.4),[7] which depicts at lower center the group of seven figures from the left of the recto of no. 13b, alongside a man seen from behind with a sword and his arms akimbo taken from the verso of the same sheet, replacing the

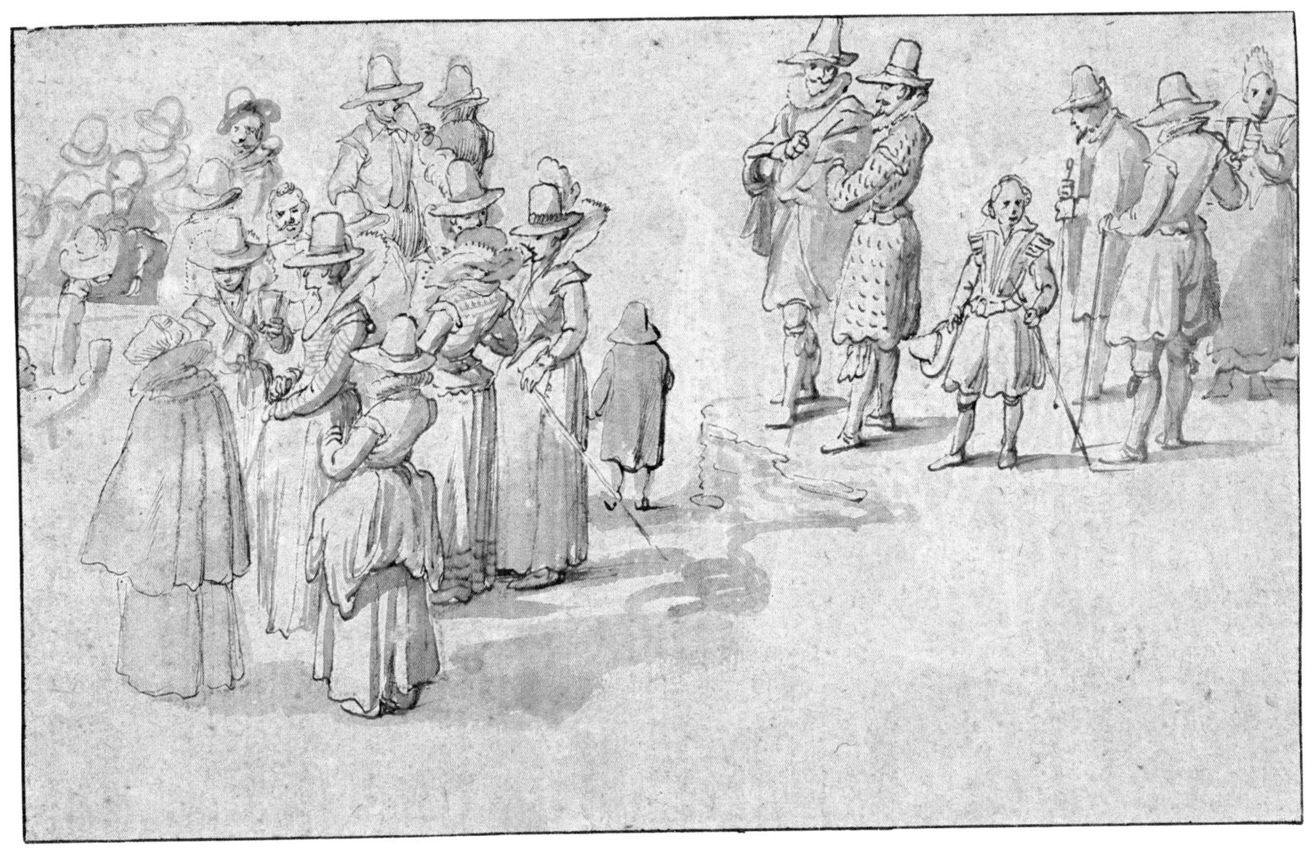

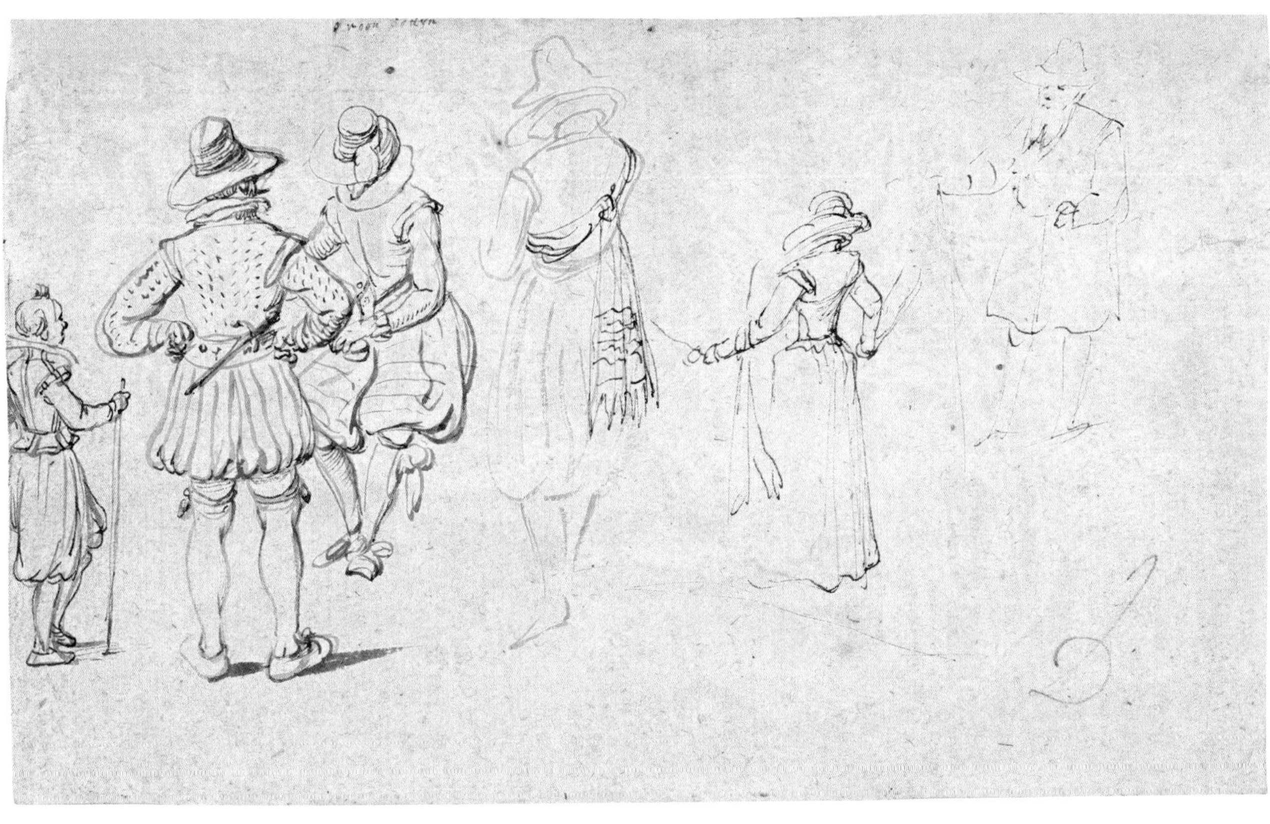

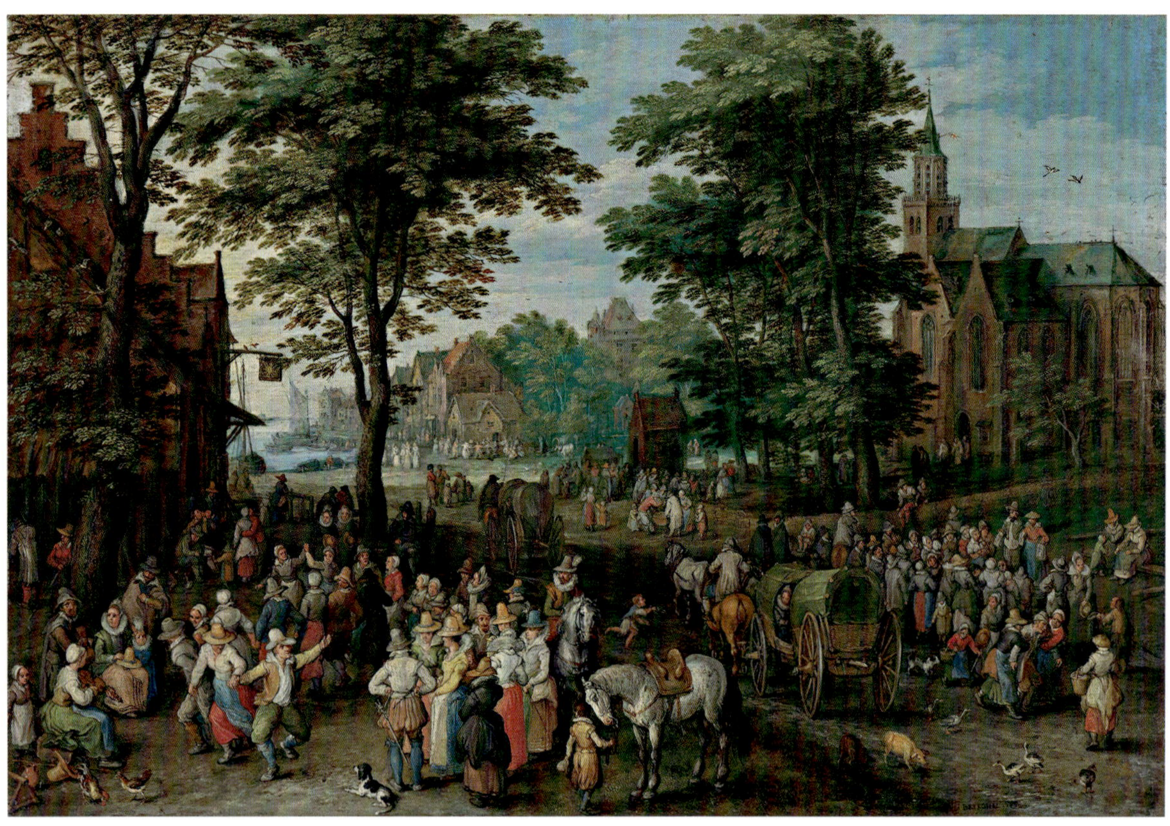

13.4 Jan Breughel the Elder, *Village Scene*, 1612. Alte Pinakothek, Munich.

woman in a cape at the edge of the group of seven. The four women at the center of that same group, joined this time by the shawled woman to their left and an adaption of the man seen from behind with arms akimbo from the verso, reappear in the *Village Kermis in Schelle with a Self-Portrait* (1614), in the Kunsthistorisches Museum, Vienna.[8] In that painting, the man with the sword is dressed in green, perhaps satin, as alluded to in the inscription above him in the Moore sketch. A painting from 1613 or 1617 (the final digit is unclear), *Village Landscape with Figures Preparing to Depart* in the Harold Samuel Collection belonging to the City of London Corporation and on display at the Mansion House,[9] features at lower center the three figures on the right edge of that group of seven (a man and two women).[10] The motif of the sword-wielding man with his arms akimbo seems to have been a favorite, for he recurs some six to ten years later at lower center, accompanied by a whippet, in the *Wedding Banquet* (1623) in the Museo Nacional del Prado, Madrid.[11] **JST**

JACOB MATHAM

Haarlem 1571–1631 Haarlem

14

A Couple Embracing in a Landscape, ca. 1610–30

Pen and brown ink on vellum
192 x 298 mm

INSCRIPTIONS Recto, lower right, signed, in pen and brown ink: *Iac. Matham Fecit*; verso, lower right, in graphite: *Matham*; verso, upper edge, in graphite: *LMBI J1961*; verso, lower center, in graphite: *10*

PROVENANCE (Possibly) Max, Freiherr von Eelking (1813–1878), Meiningen; (possibly) his sale, J.M. Heberle, Cologne, 4 June 1902, lot 321; John Postle Heseltine (1843–1929), London (no mark; see L. 1507–8); his sale, Frederik Muller, Amsterdam, 27–28 May 1913, lot 144; Richard Ederheimer (1892–1959), New York (no mark; see L. 1711), by 1913; his sale, Anderson Galleries, Inc., New York, 9 April 1919, lot 28 (presumably bought in); his sale, Anderson Galleries, Inc., New York, 6 November 1924, lot 28; Lady Anne Babington (1908–1964), Fakenham, Norfolk; her sale, Christie's, London, 11 December 1962, lot 143 (to "Weitzner"); (probably) Julius H. Weitzner (1896–1986), London and New York, 1962; Thomas Williams Fine Art, London; from whom acquired by Clement C. Moore, 2012

Promised gift of Clement C. and Elizabeth Y. Moore

This heady and visceral scene of love, music, drink, and dance is the work of Haarlem artist Jacob Matham.[1] Though perhaps best known as a printmaker in the studio of his stepfather Hendrick Goltzius, Matham also produced a number of meticulously rendered drawings like this one. Dominating the composition is a couple embracing at left, ensconced in drapery that does little to obscure their lovemaking. Nearby, an alert dog stands sentry. Surrounding them is the natural beauty of trees, rolling hills, and soaring birds punctuated by man-made luxury objects such as jewelry, a finely wrought pitcher, and a fantastical fountain. Behind the pair, vignettes of merriment occupy the landscape, including dancing figures, musicians, and revelers gathered around a table.

Details found in this sheet—in particular the ornamental girdle across the chest of the woman (a type often worn by Venus in prints by Matham and his circle) and the presence of a winged cupid at center—evoke an antique, mythological past even as the precise subject remains elusive.[2] The classical elements combined with themes of passionate decadence link the drawing to the aesthetic of European courtly circles, namely the imagery of Bartholomaeus Spranger made at the court of Rudolf II in Prague. Matham knew intimately the work of Spranger, a favorite source for Goltzius's innovative prints of the 1580s and after whom Matham himself made multiple engravings, even after Spranger's death in 1611.[3] Relatedly, this amalgamation of myth and love shows a connection to Italian models, not surprising given Matham's ongoing and evolving relationship to art from Italy over the course of his career. Early on he was exposed to Italian imagery through Goltzius, and he engraved images after Italian artists, such as the *Christ Raising the Only Son of the Widow in Naïn* after Federico Zuccaro, based on a drawing acquired by Goltzius while in Italy in 1590/91.[4] Later, from 1593 to 1597, Matham traveled himself to Venice and Rome, where he produced

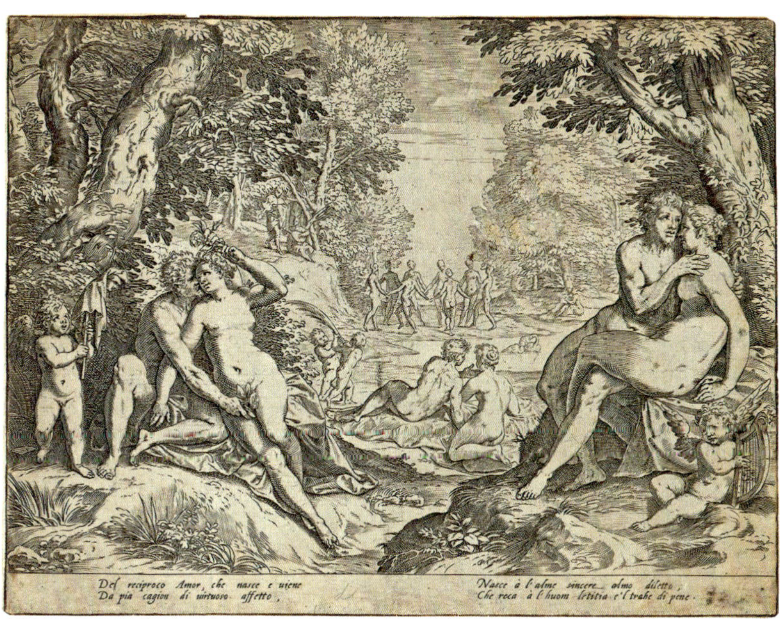

14.1 Agostino Carracci (after Pauwels Franck), *Reciproco Amore*, ca. 1589–95. Ashmolean Museum, Oxford.

reproductive prints and drawings after paintings by Italian artists, a practice he continued upon his return to Haarlem.[5]

The drawing in the Moore collection holds a particular resemblance to a print from around 1589–95 by Agostino Carracci after a painting entitled *Reciproco Amore* (Reciprocal Love) likely by Pauwels Franck, the Flemish artist also known as Paolo Fiammingo, who worked in Venice (fig. 14.1).[6] The print and Matham's drawing share multiple elements, including larger figures embracing in the foreground, a hilly landscape with trees, musicians on a hillside, and a circle of figures with cupid at center. Some components from the drawing and print—namely the lovers, musicians, and crowded table—appear compressed and reoriented in a vertical oval format for Matham's engraving *A God and Goddess Embracing*, from around 1600 to 1605.[7]

The present sheet was created with ink, a medium with which Matham experimented at different points in his career to create pen works that skillfully imitate engraving—a type of drawing known as a *Federkunststuck*, which was brought to its dizzying apogee by Matham's stepfather, Goltzius.[8] This example features an impressive combination of hatching and stippling that disguises the lack of forgiveness in the technique. The manner in which some motifs, particularly the dog, appear to lie atop rather than in the composition suggests that the work may date to shortly before Matham's death. At that time, he was experimenting with smaller pen works, including a sheet dated 1630, now in the Musée des Beaux-Arts et d'Archéologie, Besançon, which features several very similar, overly discreet, whippet-like dogs in profile.[9] Whatever the precise circumstances of its creation, the drawing's prominent signature at lower right shows that Matham clearly asserted his role as creator: he angled his signature "Iac. Matham Fecit" into the base of the fountain, creating the illusion that it was not written in ink, but carved into stone. EN

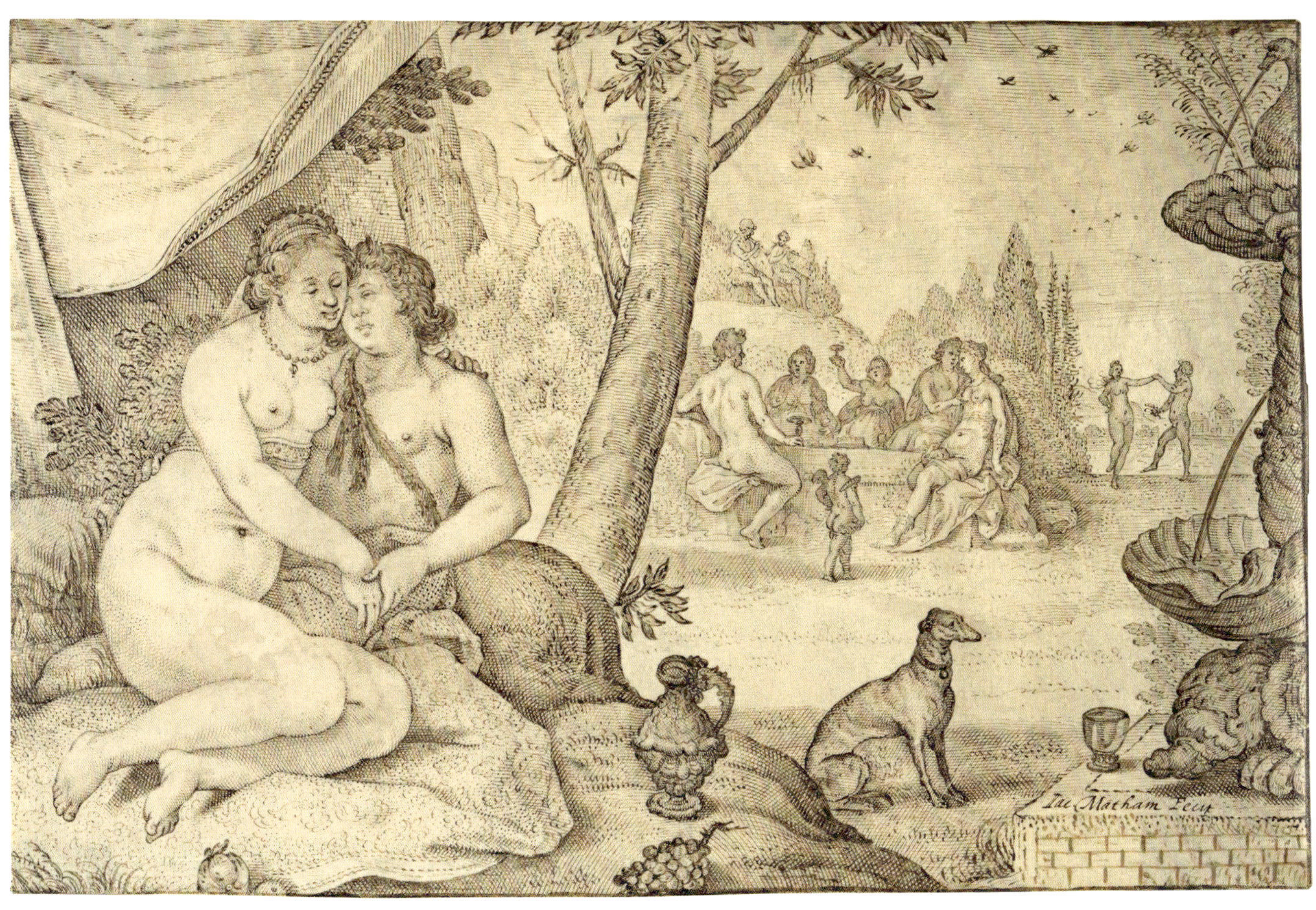
Iac Matham Fecit

ISAAK MAJOR

Frankfurt am Main ca. 1576–after 1642 Vienna

15

Figures in a Wooded Landscape with a City in the Distance, ca. 1620–30

Point of brush and blue ink, over black chalk, squared in black chalk; traces of framing lines in black chalk and pen and brown ink
239 x 365 mm

INSCRIPTIONS Recto, upper right, in pen and brown ink: *40*; verso, upper center, in graphite: *16*.

PROVENANCE Possibly James Bretherton (1730–1806), London; possibly his sale, Christie's, London, 31 January 1799 sqq., as part of lot 48b (as Paul Bril); John Thane (1748–1818), London (L. 1544, recto, lower center);[1] his sale, Jones, London, 25–26 March 1819, as part of lot 26 (as Paul Bril); unidentified collector (L. 2823, recto, lower right); Prof. Einar Perman (1893–1976), Stockholm, by 1953;[2] Sotheby's, New York, 28 January 2016, lot 215; where acquired by Clement C. Moore

SELECT REFERENCES Stockholm 1953, no. 80 (as Flemish master); Perman 1962, no. 135 (as Flemish master)

Promised gift of Clement C. and Elizabeth Y. Moore

Nestled among winding trees is a wooden cottage, overlooking a mountainous landscape with a city by the water in the distance. In the foreground, pigs root through the earth as they are being watched by a herdsman. A little farther up the hill, two men are absorbed in conversation.

This drawing belongs to a stylistically coherent group of fantastical landscape drawings meticulously drawn with the tip of the brush and blue ink. Names of artists associated with this group in the past include Paul Bril, Joos de Momper, Jacob and Roelant Savery, Pieter Stevens, and Jan Siberechts. In 1979, however, Joaneath Spicer convincingly attributed them to Isaak Major, based on the similarities between the drawings and Major's graphic work.[3]

In the most recent publication on this group, Freyda Spira lists ten drawings.[4] To this, a significant number of eleven sheets can now be added, including the Moore drawing, which brings the total to twenty-one landscape drawings in brush and blue ink by Major.[5] The artist seems to have worked primarily on two different sizes of paper: larger sheets of about 235 x 360 mm and smaller sheets of about 135 x 210 mm.[6] The larger sheets match the measurements of Major's series of nine landscape etchings, posthumously published by Jeremias Wolff in Augsburg.[7] Two of these drawings can be directly related to this print series.[8] The present sheet, which is squared for transfer, is not.

It has been suggested that the drawings were made as models for a projected series of prints that was never completed.[9] Another, more likely possibility is that the drawn landscape series was produced as an independent work of art. This is supported not only by the remarkable execution in blue ink, but also by the old numbering system that can be found in the upper right corner of the majority of the larger drawings.[10] The numbers run from 4 to 144, so it can be assumed that Major's drawn oeuvre must have been a great deal larger. Perhaps these sheets were once part of an album with landscape drawings compiled by the artist.

Major's landscapes recall the drawings that Roelant Savery made during his 1606–7 trip to the Tirol Mountains, commissioned by Emperor Rudolf II.[11] These drawings were bound in an album that later ended up in the possession of Rembrandt. Major, who is believed to have been a pupil of Savery and Aegidius Sadeler II at the Prague court, must have known these drawings and used them as a source of inspiration. MR

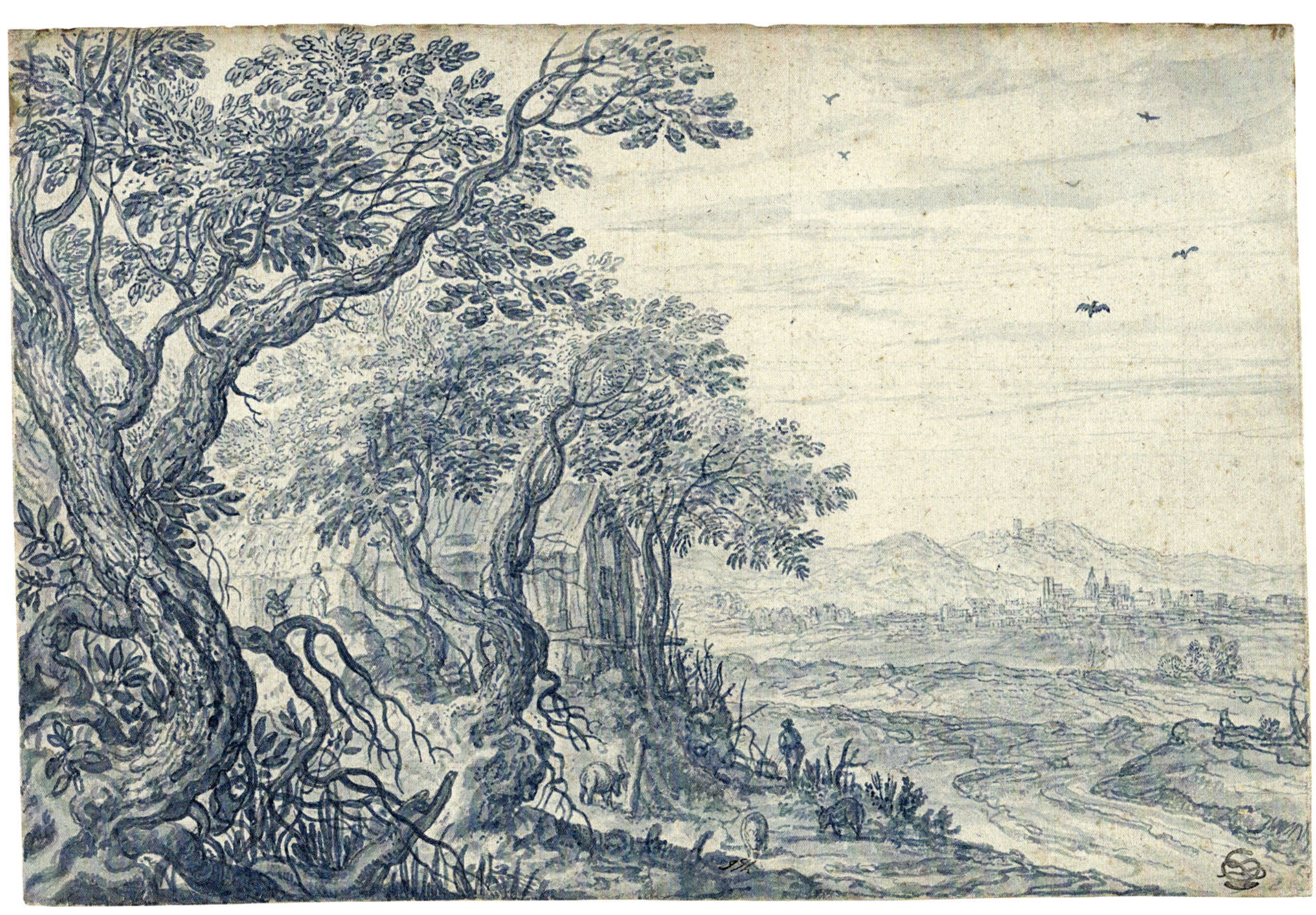

DAVID VINCKBOONS

Mechelen 1576–ca. 1632 Amsterdam

16

The Entry of Christ into Jerusalem, ca. 1610

Pen and brown ink, with gray, brown, and blue wash and white opaque watercolor, over traces of black chalk; traces of framing line in black chalk
318 x 450 mm

INSCRIPTIONS Recto, lower right, in pen and brown ink: *Vinckeboons*; verso, center, in pen and brown ink: 4; verso, lower right, graphite: 010644

PROVENANCE Gottfried Winkler (1731–1795), Leipzig (according to 1839 Spengler sale cat.); Johann Conrad Spengler (1767–1839), Copenhagen (no mark; see L. 1434); his sale, Imp. Luno, Copenhagen, 8 October 1839, lot 1579; Heinrich Wilhelm Campe (1770–1862), Leipzig (L. 1391, lower left); his sale, C.G. Boerner, Leipzig, 25 April 1921, lot 188; A. Deiker, Braunfels; private collection, Canada; Sotheby Mak van Waay, Amsterdam, 2 November 1987, lot 23; Thomas le Claire Kunsthandel, Hamburg, 1989; private collection, Germany; Thomas le Claire Kunsthandel, Hamburg; from whom acquired by Clement C. Moore, 2014

SELECT REFERENCES Wurzbach 1906–11, 2: 791, under Bolswert, no. 3; Kassel 1930, no. 241; Hollstein, 3: 73, under no. 14; Hollstein, 37: 35, under Schelte A. Bolswert; Ertz and Nitze-Ertz 2016, no. Z128; Bleyerveld and Veldman 2016, 237, under no. 231

Promised gift of Clement C. and Elizabeth Y. Moore

Throngs of people joyously wave palm fronds and spread their cloaks before Christ as he rides a donkey into Jerusalem. The city's profile rises in the distance. Recounted in all four Gospels of the New Testament and commemorated by Christians annually on Palm Sunday, this biblical episode was eminently well suited to the artistic interests of David Vinckboons. Born in Flanders, Vinckboons moved to the Northern Netherlands as a child and spent his career in Amsterdam, producing paintings, autonomous drawings, and an extraordinary number of print designs, the large majority of which depict figures in lush, wooded landscapes. Not only does the subject of Christ's triumphant entry into Jerusalem call for a panoply of human figures within a Mediterranean landscape filled with trees, it is a story in which characters interact with their natural surroundings: the tax collector Zacchaeus—pictured at far right in the present work—climbs a tree to get a better view of Christ, and members of the crowd harvest their fronds from a nearby field[1]—implied here by the small figure emerging from the grove with a bundle of branches over his shoulder in the left mid-ground.

This large sheet is closely related to an engraving in the same orientation by Schelte Adamsz Bolswert, which cites Vinckboons as the designer (fig. 16.1).[2] Various differences between the two, along with the pentimenti and overall searching quality of the drawing, suggest that it represents an early stage in Vinckboons's development of the composition, and that Bolswert's engraving therefore reproduces a more finished version that is now lost.[3] It is probable that the orientation of this lost work was reversed, as the engraver's prints, whether after dedicated print designs or reproducing finished paintings, generally inverted their models. Notably, a drawing in reverse orientation by Vinckboons now in the Teylers Museum in Haarlem (fig. 16.2)[4] shares with Bolswert's engraving, though on a much smaller scale, precisely the details that differ in the Moore sheet: Christ appears in strict profile, and the figure in the tree crouches rather than extends his body upward; in the foreground, a youth runs, carrying palm fronds, and a

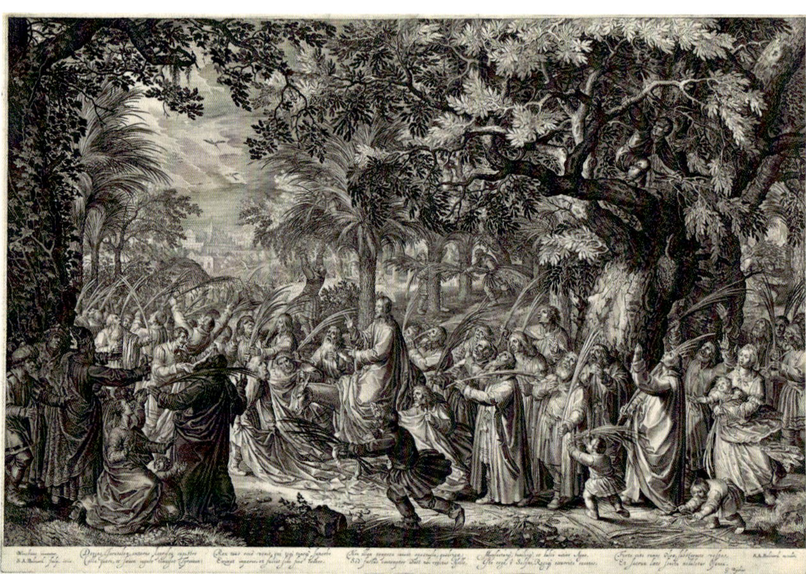

16.1 Schelte Adamsz Bolswert (after David Vinckboons), *The Entry of Christ into Jerusalem*, 1612. Rijksprentenkabinet, Amsterdam.

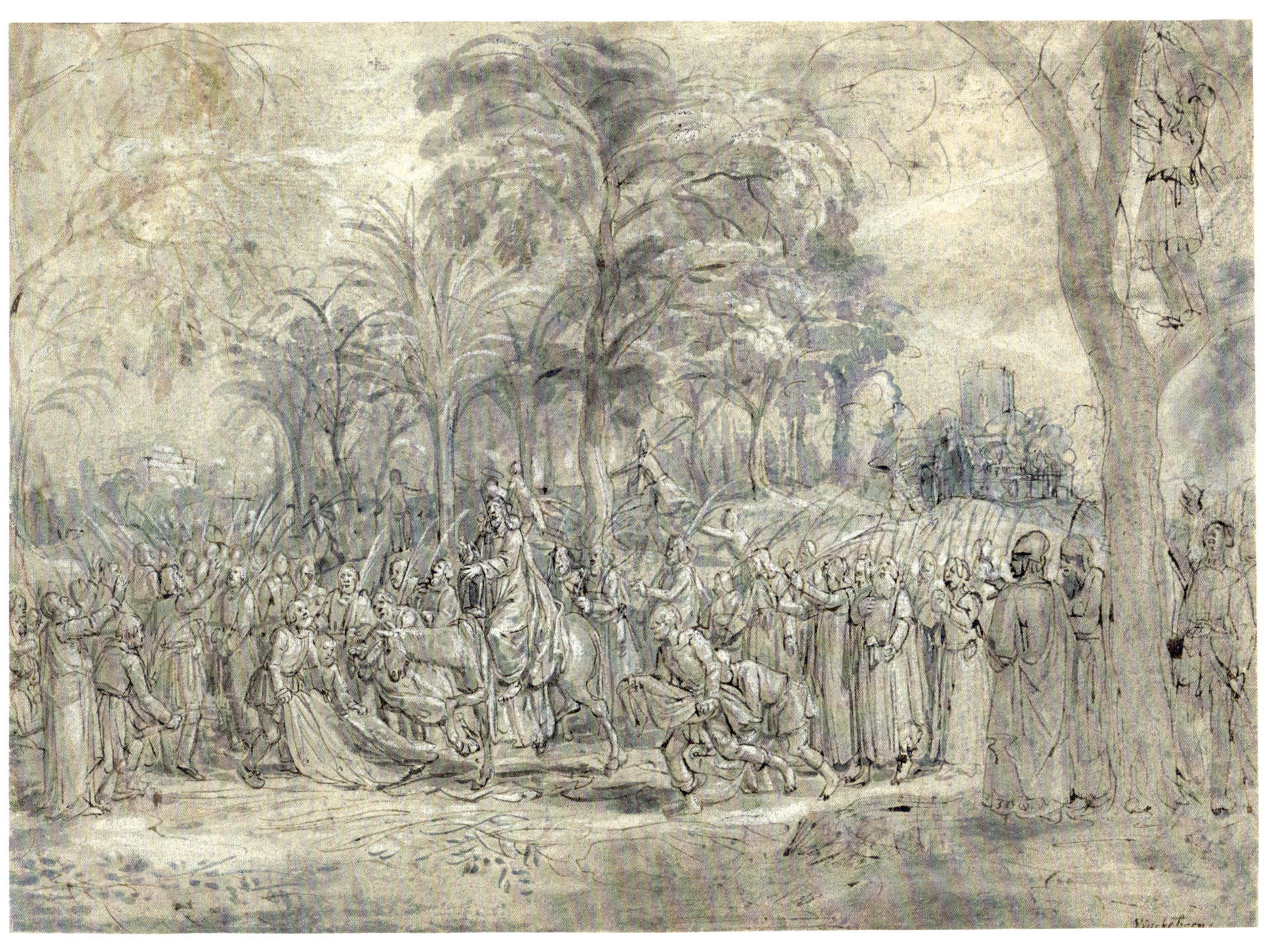

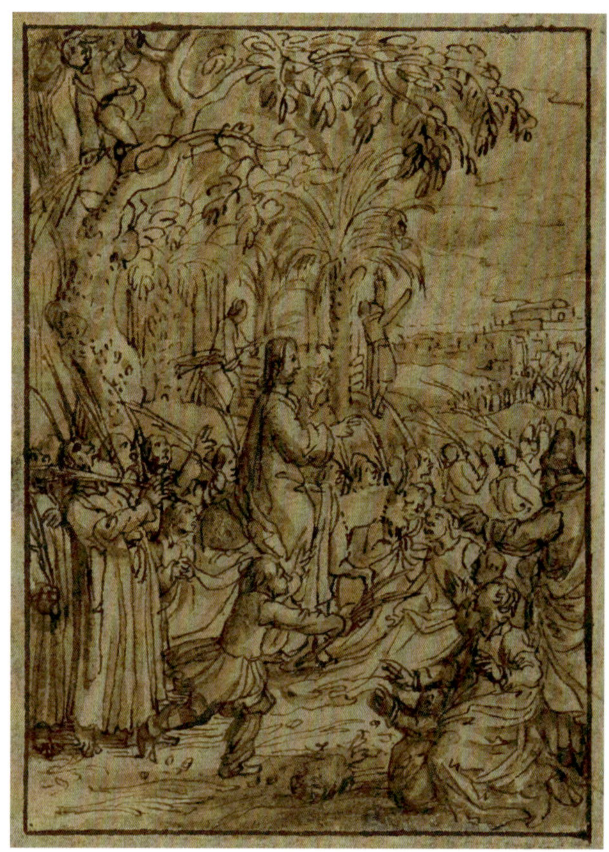

16.2 David Vinckboons, *The Entry of Christ into Jerusalem*, ca. 1611. Teylers Museum, Haarlem.

mother and child kneel and raise their arms in awe; and in the middle distance a figure actively pulls down branches from a tree. Thought to date to the same period (ca. 1611), the Teylers work belongs to a group of drawings depicting episodes in the life of Christ; although no corresponding prints are known, all of the surviving sheets are incised for transfer, strongly suggesting that they were intended as print designs and may well have been engraved.[5] This drawing most likely reflects the changes Vinckboons made in a now-lost final design recorded in Bolswert's print. It is plausible, however, that the engraver referred directly to the Teylers sheet for these details, while the Moore drawing established the overall composition, scale, and play of light and shadow.

Regardless of their precise relationships to the print, the Moore and Teylers drawings together show Vinckboons thinking through the biblical text and devising solutions to depict the story with the utmost liveliness. The present work exhibits Vinckboons's characteristic integration of pen and ink with pale washes of gray and blue and ample touches of white opaque watercolor—a technique favored by many Flemish-born artists of the period. Deft flecks of the pen detail the smiling faces of the worshippers and the skeptical expressions of the two figures in the right foreground, probably Pharisees, while the cool tones of the blue and gray in combination with the opaque white suggest an almost glistening light. **JSS**

PETER PAUL RUBENS

Siegen 1577–1640 Antwerp

17

St. Lambert, ca. 1630–33

Pen and brown ink and wash, and black chalk, laid down
295 x 163 mm

WATERMARK Standing angel facing front, similar to Briquet 677 (1572/1630) or 678 (1594/1624)

INSCRIPTIONS Recto, lower right, in pen and brown ink (somewhat effaced): P.P.R.

PROVENANCE Galerie Fischer, Lucerne, 2 June 1945, lot 232; Sotheby's, London, 9 July 2008, lot 20; Jean-Luc Baroni, London; from whom acquired by Clement C. Moore, 2017

SELECT REFERENCES Van Tuinen 2018, 21–22; Logan 2018

Promised gift of Clement C. and Elizabeth Y. Moore

This drawing first appeared on the market in 1945 at Galerie Fischer in Lucerne, Switzerland, where it was catalogued as a study of St. Norbert by Rubens. Overlooked by scholars, it remained unpublished and disappeared from the public eye. In 2008, the work reemerged at Sotheby's in London, where it was catalogued as Rubens, only this time with the correct identification of the subject matter: St. Lambert.[1] After having been acquired by Chips Moore in 2017, it was included in the 2018 exhibition *Power and Grace* at the Morgan Library & Museum and published for the first time in the accompanying catalogue.[2]

St. Lambert (ca. 638–ca. 705), bishop of Maastricht, was sojourning in Liège when he was brutally murdered during his evening prayers. The site of his death, at the heart of today's city of Liège, became the location for the great Gothic cathedral of Saint-Lambert, which was destroyed at the end of the eighteenth century. Despite his fame in the city where he died, St. Lambert remains a local, little-known saint, mostly venerated today in the few churches dedicated to him in the nearby Dutch provinces of Limburg and Noord-Brabant.

St. Lambert is depicted as a monumental standing figure, reading from the open book in his proper left hand and holding a crozier in the right. The saint towers over two of his killers lying lifeless at his feet, while the presence of a third body is suggested at the right. During Rubens's lifetime, there was no significant pictorial tradition of St. Lambert to speak of, and certainly not in the widely available medium of prints. Interestingly, this representation of St. Lambert with his book, crozier, and killers at his feet echoes that of sixteenth-century wooden sculptures produced in and around Liège.[3] This might suggest that the artist had first-hand contact with the local tradition in that city and perhaps even made this drawing in preparation for a commission there. Notable in this regard is that Rubens made several visits, albeit diplomatic, to Maastricht and Liège between 1632 and 1633.

It has so far proven impossible to connect the drawing to any known commission or project. As a result, it is equally difficult to identify what the project's medium might have been. An argument in favor of a sculpture is the strong visual link with an oil sketch by Rubens from ca. 1622–23 depicting a similarly monumental, frontal St. Norbert (fig. 17.1),[4] which was preparatory for an alabaster sculpture executed by Hans van Mildert.[5] But it is also conceivable that the drawing was a study for a side panel of an altarpiece. A striking example from earlier in Rubens's career is the majestic St. Amandus in an oil sketch from ca. 1610, which was preparatory for one of the outer wings of Rubens's *Raising of the Cross Triptych* for the Sint-Walburgiskerk, Antwerp (fig. 17.2).[6] St. Lambert and St. Amandus share several formal similarities, including their facial types, long beards, and general gravitas.

There is no doubt that the *St. Lambert* fits comfortably within the visual language of Rubens's oeuvre. It is therefore all the more puzzling that it is hard to find other drawings by him that closely resemble this one in style and technique. Rubens tended to work either in ink (pen and wash) or chalk. On rare occasions he did combine those media, though with the black chalk generally serving as the underdrawing, rather than being broadly applied over the pen and wash as here.[7] There are a few exceptions in which the black chalk and the pen are assigned

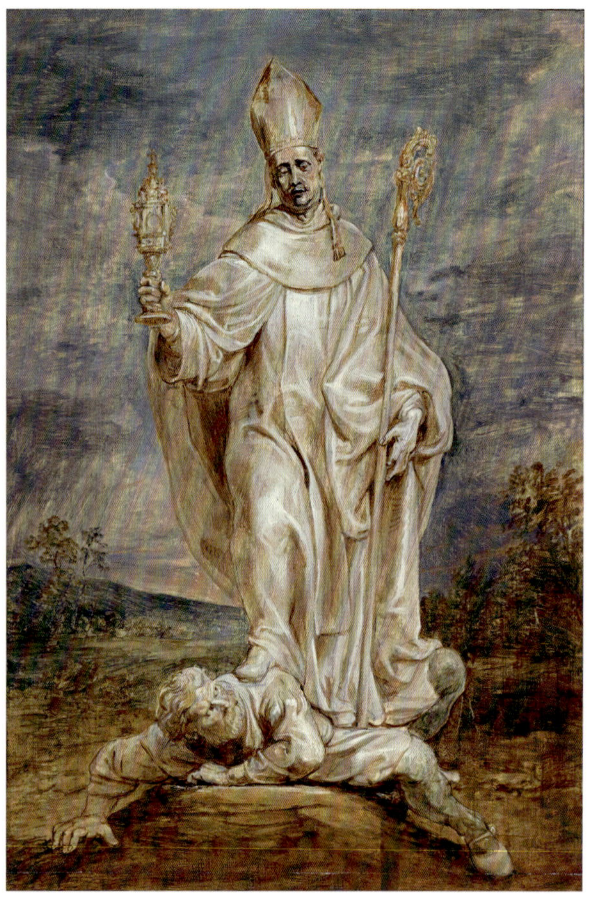

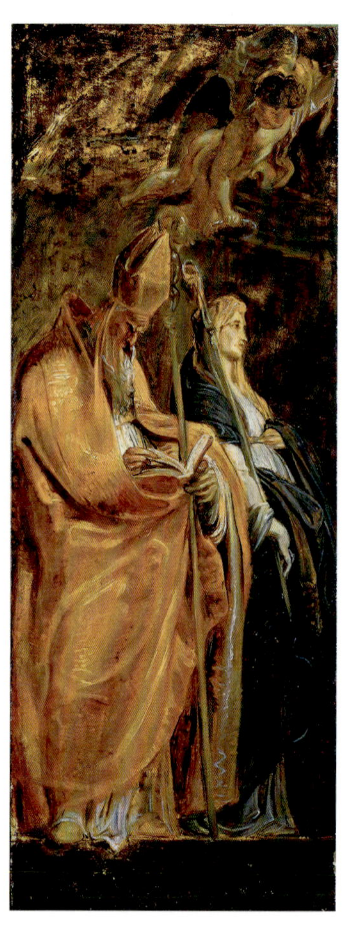

17.1 Peter Paul Rubens, *St. Norbert Overcoming Tanchelm*, ca. 1622–23. Private collection.

17.2 Peter Paul Rubens, *SS. Amandus and Walburga*, ca. 1610. Dulwich Picture Gallery, London.

an equal role, for example a drawing depicting *Venus Admonishing the Fettered Cupid* from ca. 1633–35 and a 1631 frontispiece design for the works of Ludovicus Blosius.[8] However, the former drawing contains no wash, and in the latter the black chalk serves to enhance or add to the existing contour lines. In the present drawing, the black chalk serves almost as a mid-tone to the saturated dark brown washes, unusual for Rubens. As for the penwork, the fine, swift pen lines in the *St. Lambert* are applied with ease and skill. There are some brilliant passages, such as the foreshortened crozier (very similar to that in the *St. Norbert* oil sketch), the foreshortened heads of the murderers in the foreground, and the few squiggly yet perfectly placed lines describing the saint's face. But these line types are also hard to find in the rest of Rubens's oeuvre. These considerations give room for pause.[9] Whereas we cannot exclude the possibility that this is a rare, more experimental drawing by Rubens, we should also consider the option that it was executed by a gifted artist close to him, likely around 1630. IvT

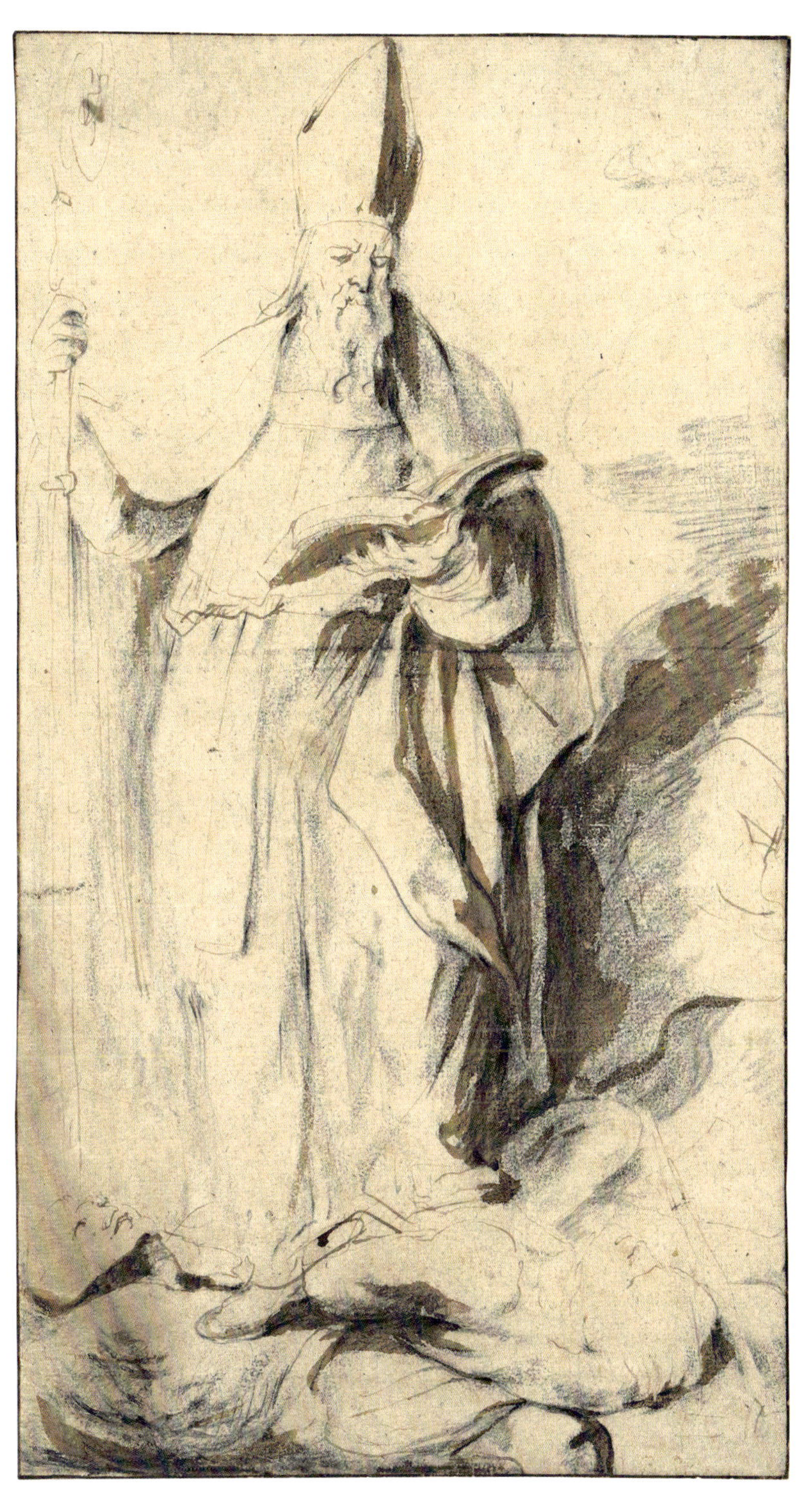

HENDRICK AVERCAMP

Amsterdam 1585–1634 Kampen

18

Fishermen on a Riverbank with the Town of Kampen in the Distance, ca. 1615–20

Brush and pen and brown and black ink, with watercolor and opaque watercolor, over traces of black chalk, on paper prepared with a white lead ground;[1] framing line in black ink
178 x 272 mm

WATERMARK Eagle above three balls, similar to Heawood 1248 (Holland, 1618)

INSCRIPTIONS Recto, lower left, signed with monogram, in brush and black ink: *AH* (in ligature); verso, upper left, in graphite: *A19* (inv. no. from Duits probate notebook); verso, lower left, in graphite: *779*; below that, in an eighteenth-century hand, in brown ink: 1151; and below that, in graphite: *Averkamp*

PROVENANCE Possibly Eduard Cichorius (1819–1907), Leipzig and Dresden;[2] Oskar Huldschinsky (1845/47–1931), Berlin; his sale, Paul Graupe, Berlin, 3 November 1931, lot 4 (with lot 3, *River Landscape near Ouderkerk*, a similar watercolor by Avercamp dated 1622, 19 x 29 cm, to "Mensing, Amsterdam"); Frederik Muller & Co., Amsterdam; from whom purchased by Charles E. Duits (1882–1969), London (no mark; see L. 533a), 2 April 1955; thence by descent; acquired through Thomas Williams Fine Art, London, by Clement C. Moore, 2007

SELECT REFERENCES Göpel 1931; Welcker 1933, no. T 548; Welcker (ed. Hensbroek-van der Poel 1979), no. T 548; Nihom-Nijstad 1983, 7–8, under no. 4; Van Hasselt and Van Berge-Gerbaud 1989, 3, under no. 1; Buvelot and Buijs 2002, 47–48 and 194, under no. 2; Williams 2008, no. 12; Shoaf Turner 2012, no. 17; Lee 2022, 38

Promised gift of Clement C. and Elizabeth Y. Moore

This finished, independent watercolor is an exceptional work by an artist better known for his winter landscapes with numerous figures enjoying the ice. If relatively rare in theme, it is nevertheless typical of Avercamp in its combination of low horizon and panoramic viewpoint with an intense interest in color and anecdotal detail. The artist conveyed not only a sense of season—spring (to judge from the buds on the tree on the left)—but a sense of time. The sky is blushed with pink, streaked against the warm golden glow of a late sunset. As every serious angler knows, mornings and evenings are the best time of day to catch fish, that is, when they come to the surface to feed. It cannot be early morning, for at upper right is a wagon full of hay heading home after a long day of harvesting.[3]

An old copy of the present drawing in the Schlossmuseum, Weimar,[4] shows that the sheet was once broader and was trimmed on the right side. The copy includes two women seated farther along the riverbank from the well-dressed man and little girl, as well as another figure and child silhouetted on the dike in front of the road with the hay wagon. These figures also appear in an autograph painted version of the composition in the Frits Lugt Collection, Fondation Custodia, Paris (fig. 18.1), datable ca. 1620–25.[5] This is an unusual instance of Avercamp having made a painted version of one of his finished watercolors. Subtle differences in the height of the crown of the men's hats (taller in this watercolor, shallower in the painting) indicate an interval of some five to ten years between the two works.[6] In the later, painted version, Avercamp reduced the overall scale of the figures in relation to the setting and made other minor changes. From left to right, he replaced the budding tree with a hoist; removed the trap in the water behind the standing figure with a bucket suspended on a fishing rod;[7] added trees in full leaf, transforming it into a summer scene;[8] inserted a gallows with corpses of a man and a woman (a morbid but recurrent motif of the artist); drastically reduced the size of the sailboat and shifted it to the background near the gallows; eliminated the foreground stump; and replaced the herder and cattle with a duck hunter. **JST**

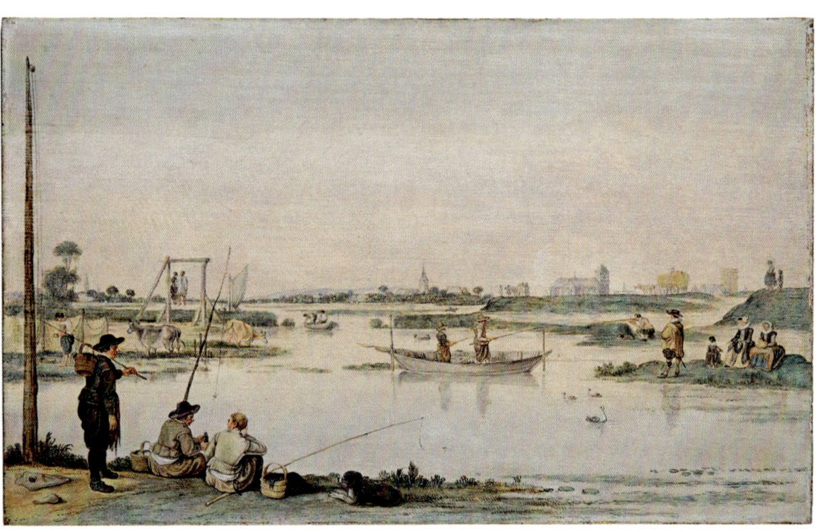

18.1 Hendrick Avercamp, *River Landscape near Kampen*, ca. 1620–25. Frits Lugt Collection, Fondation Custodia, Paris.

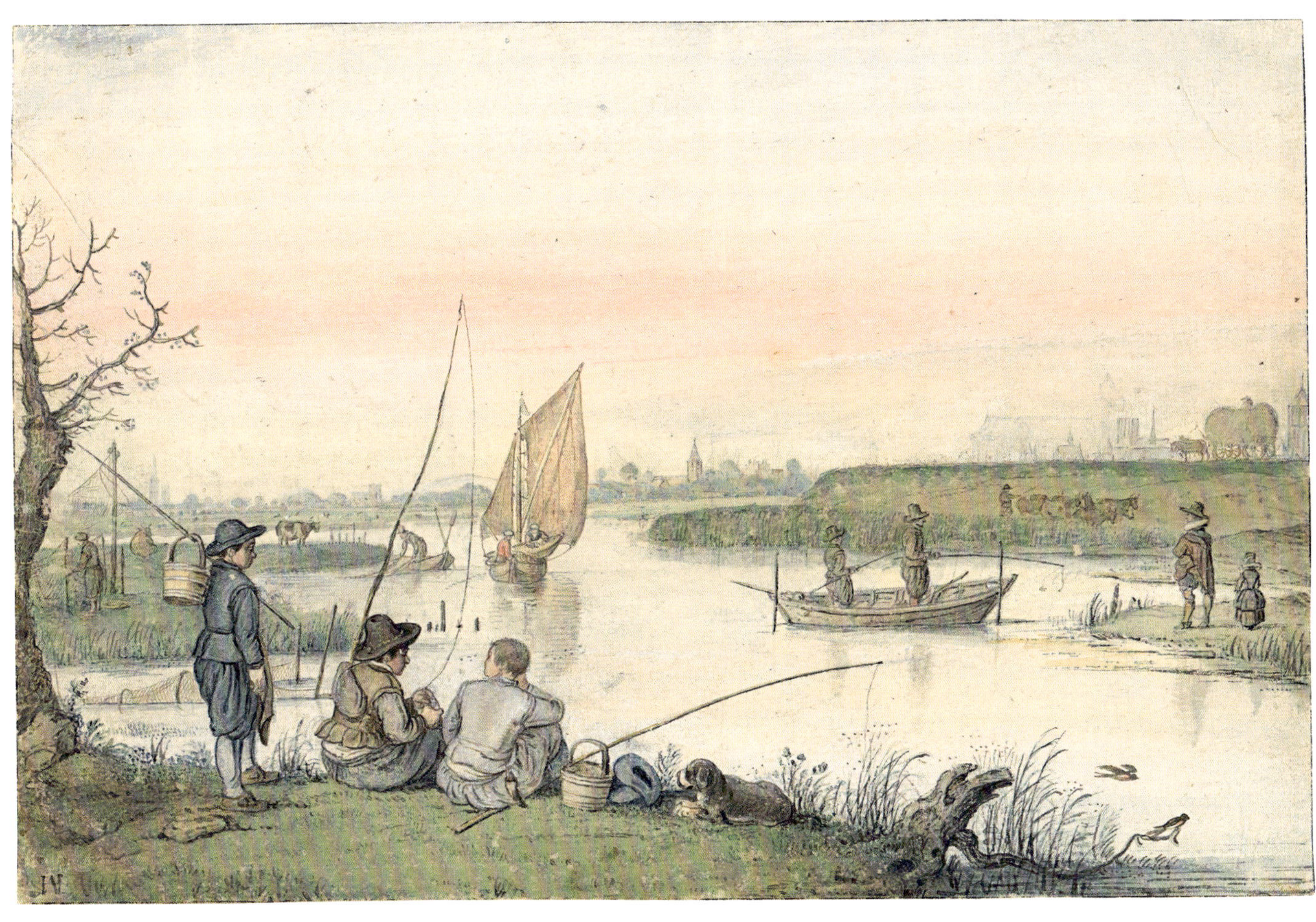

HENDRICK AVERCAMP

Amsterdam 1585–1634 Kampen

19

Shipwreck in a Storm, ca. 1630

Point of brush and gray ink, with watercolor and opaque watercolor, over graphite; framing line in brown ink
162 x 288 mm

INSCRIPTIONS Recto, lower right, in brown ink: *Stomme van Campen*; verso, lower center, in black chalk: *Hend Avercamp bijgenaemtd Stomme van Kampe*

PROVENANCE Possibly Constantine Phipps, 1st Baron Mulgrave (1722–1775), New Ross, Co. Wexford; Frank Wilson, London; from whom acquired by Johan Quirijn van Regteren Altena (1899–1980), Amsterdam (no mark; see L. 4617), with 118 others, 21 August 1930 (according to his inventory book, no. 895); by descent to his heirs; their sale, Christie's, London, 8–10 July 2014, lot 40; where acquired by Clement C. Moore

SELECT REFERENCES Giltaij 1976, no. 8; Welcker (ed. Hensbroek-van der Poel 1979), no. T 31.1

Promised gift of Clement C. and Elizabeth Y. Moore

If a prevalent early thematic focus among the landscapes and seascapes in the Moore collection was the meeting of land and water—the nexus where, to use the collector's own words, "nature is most interesting"[1]—the present sheet and a few others in this exhibition (e.g., nos. 45 and 58) reflect a slightly different type of confrontation, what one might call the "meeting of man and nature."

The history of the Netherlands is inextricably linked to the sea. Roughly a third of the country consists of polders up to 6 or 7 meters below sea level (from land reclamation that began in the fourteenth century). The relationship between the Dutch and water has thus always been one of confrontation, management, and respect—centuries before global warming and rising sea levels threatened to make the country disappear into the North Sea.

The vulnerability of the Dutch to the sea is exemplified by this watercolor, a complete contrast to the serene calm that pervades Avercamp's scene of fishermen at sunset (no. 18). As is true of an equally rare watercolor of a storm scene by Avercamp in the Kupferstichkabinett, Berlin (fig. 19.1),[2] the artist here applied broad, rough streaks of blue-gray to suggest heavy rain sweeping across the beach. The clothing of the figures is buffeted by strong winds. The ships in the Berlin drawing are clearly battling the elements, but in the Moore drawing the situation has taken a more ominous turn. A desperate group of onlookers watch from the beach as a ship founders in the waves and a lifeboat with survivors (perhaps added as an afterthought) makes its perilous way to the shore.

In the center background (above the arm of the man in a green tunic) is another casualty of the storm—a beached whale. There were at least forty instances of stranded whales on Dutch coasts between 1521 and the end of the seventeenth century.[3] Such sights were perceived by locals as signs of God's power and as omens of impending doom—viz, the potential shipwreck at left.[4] To cite another example, in 1599 a pamphlet described the Spanish invasion of the region around Cleves in August of 1598 as having been presaged by the beaching

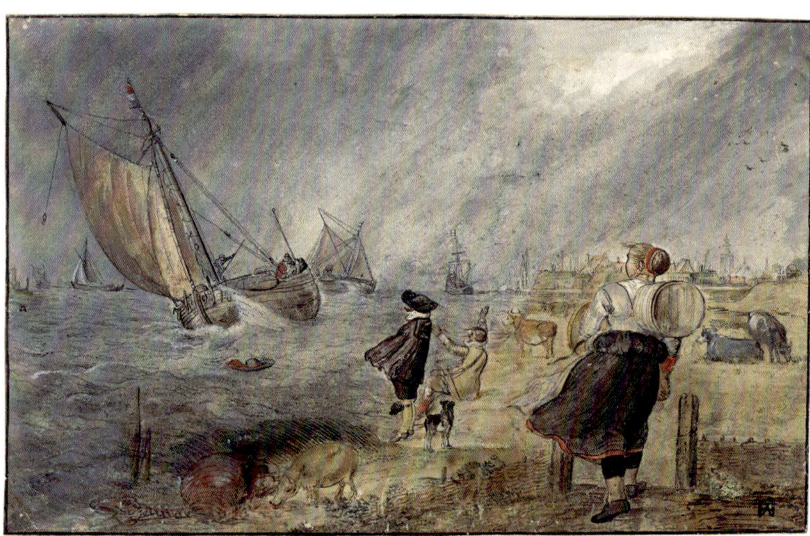

19.1 Hendrick Avercamp, *Seashore during a Storm with Figures*, ca. 1630. Kupferstichkabinett, Berlin.

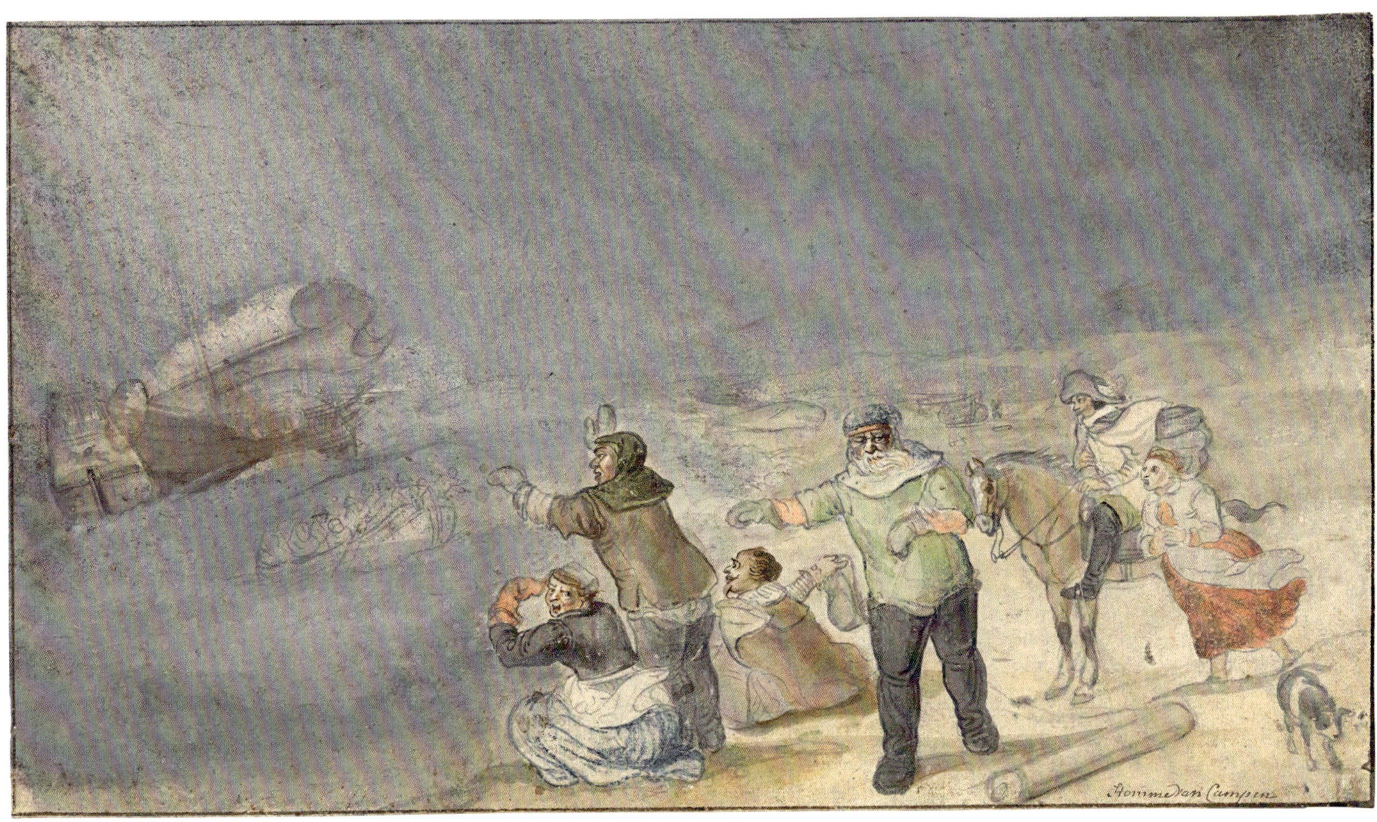

of a whale near Berkhey, between Scheveningen and Katwijk, on 3 February[5]—an event famously recorded by Hendrick Goltzius in a drawing in the Teylers Museum, Haarlem,[6] engraved the same year by his stepson Jacob Matham.[7] Other contemporary depictions of beached whales include a drawing in the Kupferstichkabinett, Berlin, made on 21 January 1617 by Willem Buytewech,[8] which he later etched;[9] the same event was recorded by Esaias van de Velde in a painting in the New Bedford Whaling Museum, New Bedford, MA.[10] The legend on an engraving of 1602 by Jan Saenredam, *Stranded Whale near Beverwijck*,[11] linked that particular occasion, which occurred on 19 December 1601, with several disasters that year: the ongoing siege of Ostend by Archduke Albert's army; two solar and three lunar eclipses; an earthquake; and a severe outbreak of plague. **JST**

CLAES JANSZ VISSCHER

Amsterdam 1586/87–1652 Amsterdam

20

A Farm on the Road between Haarlem and Leiden with Travelers in the Foreground (recto); *The Church at Rijnsaterwoude* (verso), 1607

Pen and brown ink; framing lines in brown ink (recto); pen and brown ink, with graphite (verso)
142 x 189 mm

WATERMARK Fragment of a flowerpot

INSCRIPTIONS Recto, upper center, in the artist's hand, in pen and brown ink: *1607 buyten haerlem aen de wech na / Leyden*; lower center, possibly in a later hand, in pen and brown ink: *21*; verso, lower center, in the artist's hand, in pen and brown ink: *1607*; verso, center right, in pen and brown ink: *A*; verso, upper left, in pen and gray ink: *Rynsater / woude*; verso, upper left, in a modern hand, in graphite: *Rijnland*

PROVENANCE Jhr. Mr. Willem Adriaan Beelaerts van Blokland (1883–1935), The Hague (no mark; see L. 4471); thence by descent; acquired through Johan Bosch van Rosenthal, Art Consult, Amsterdam, by Clement C. Moore, 2016

SELECT REFERENCES Simon 1958, nos. 36 and 37; Niemeyer 1958, 74–79; Schapelhouman and Schatborn 1998, 181, under no. 391, nn. 2 and 4

Promised gift of Clement C. and Elizabeth Y. Moore

Tree branches sway, leaves rustle, and a horse leaps before our eyes. This implied motion is mirrored by the energetic, rapid flecks and loops of the pen. Such immediacy—of motifs and execution—yields the sensation that we look over the artist's shoulder, watching him as he hurries to capture the fleeting world around him. Surely drawn, at least in large part, in the outdoors and from direct observation, a practice widely promoted in the period, this work focuses emphatically on the here and now. Such an approach would become the dominant mode of landscape representation in seventeenth-century Dutch art, largely thanks to the pivotal efforts of draftsman, printmaker, and publisher Claes Jansz Visscher.

Dated by the artist on both the recto and the verso, this double-sided sheet belongs to a group of drawings that Visscher made in 1607 and 1608, possibly once forming the leaves of a sketchbook.[1] These works depict landscape views in and around the Dutch cities of Haarlem, Leiden, and Amsterdam, and several of them served as models for prints, including some of the etchings in Visscher's well-known series of ca. 1612, *Plaisante plaetsen* (Pleasant Places), representing a dozen sites in the vicinity of Haarlem.[2] Inspired by the revolutionary Small Landscapes series of 1559–61, copies of which Visscher would also issue in 1612, his landscapes share with these important and unusual sixteenth-century precursors their distinctly local subject matter and their low vantage points and horizon lines, the latter largely obscured by buildings such that there is only a minimal view into the distance. Visscher's works, in direct contrast to most sixteenth-century landscapes, encourage us not to contemplate the macrocosm, but rather to home in on a slice of life in a Dutch village.

The present sheet was not among the drawings that Visscher reproduced in print, but the recto can be connected to the Pleasant Places series in light of the locale it depicts—as identified by the artist in the inscription at top—and specific motifs that reappear in some of the etchings. Most significantly, the man and woman in the foreground of the recto anticipate the well-dressed couples that appear in *On the Road to Leiden* and in *Pot's Inn* (fig. 20.1).[3] Rendered in the drawing with the same rapidity and seemingly with the same formulation of ink as the rest of the composition—if with thicker, heavier lines as befit a foreground *repoussoir*—these figures are likely inventions on Visscher's part, perhaps drawn on the spot or added later in the studio.[4] Either way, their inclusion here represents a significant moment in Visscher's development of the Pleasant Places series. Reiterated as strolling couples in the etchings, such figures arguably function as stand-ins for the viewers of the prints whom Visscher addresses on the series title page: "for the enjoyment of art lovers who do not have time to travel far." Their presence serves to transport the viewer to the site depicted, affirming the experience of armchair travel that the works afford. Moreover, several of the prints echo the drawing in the placement of figures in shadow in the immediate foreground, facing toward the landscape—precursors to the *Rückenfigur* of German Romanticism.[5] Featured prominently in the foreground of two of the etchings, including *Pot's Inn*, is a draftsman at work, suggesting now quite overtly that we look over the artist's shoulder as he observes and records the scene at hand.

The verso, identified in an inscription not by Visscher but in another period hand as a view of Rijnsaterwoude, a small village in South Holland, more than

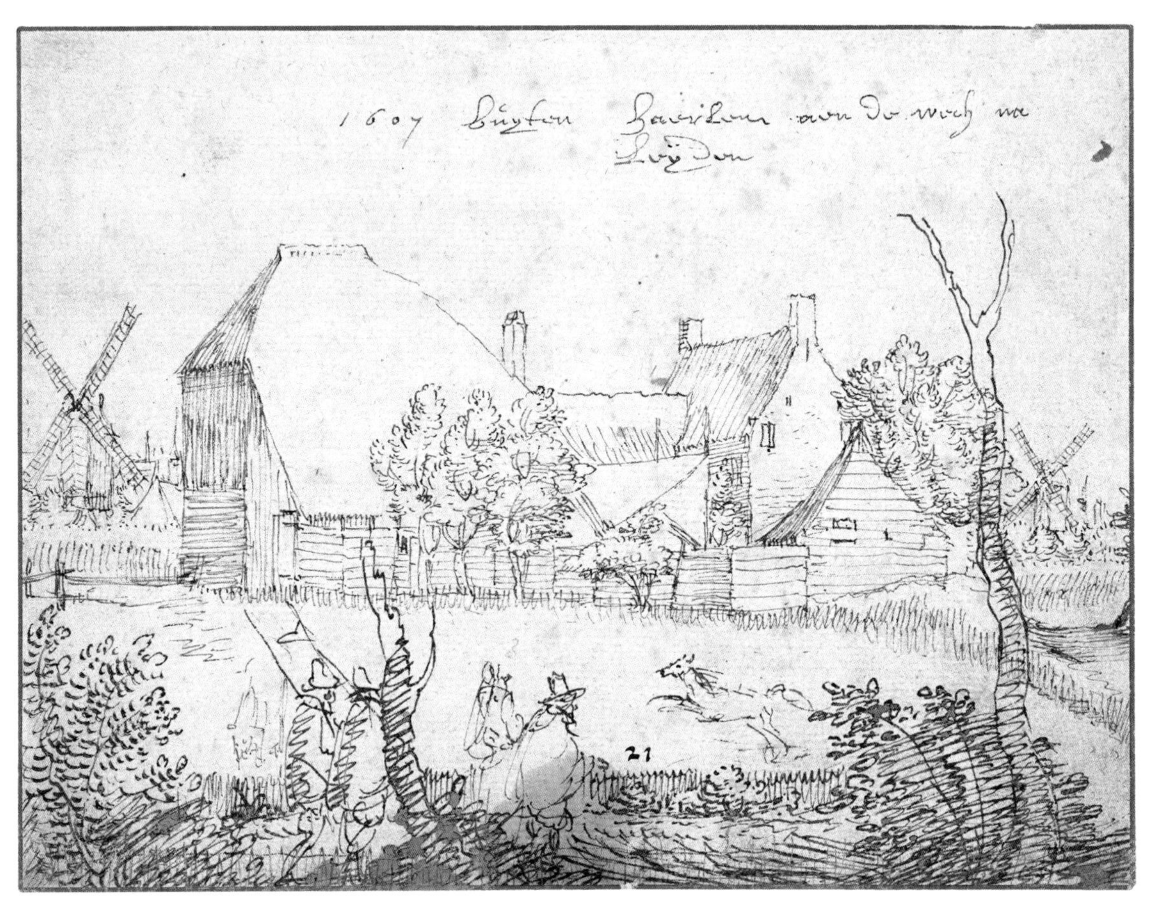
1607
21

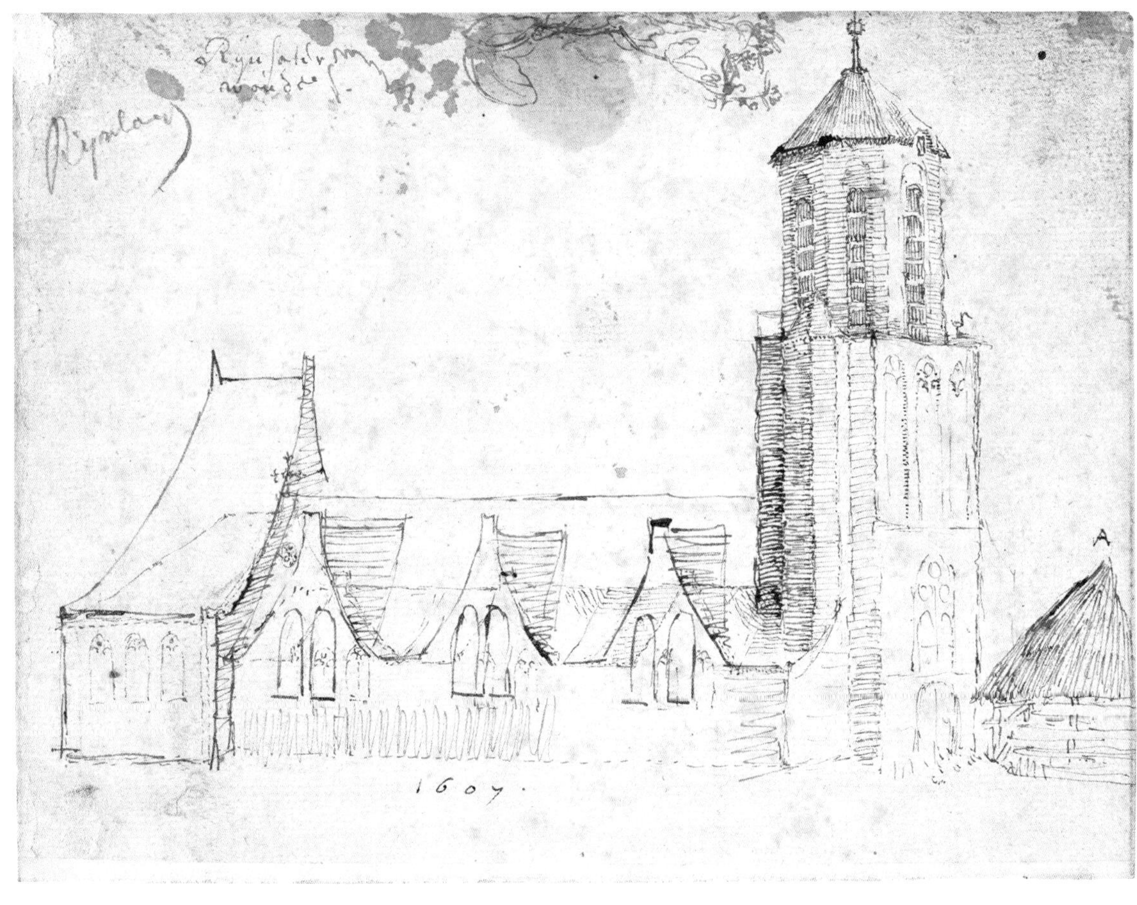
A
1607.

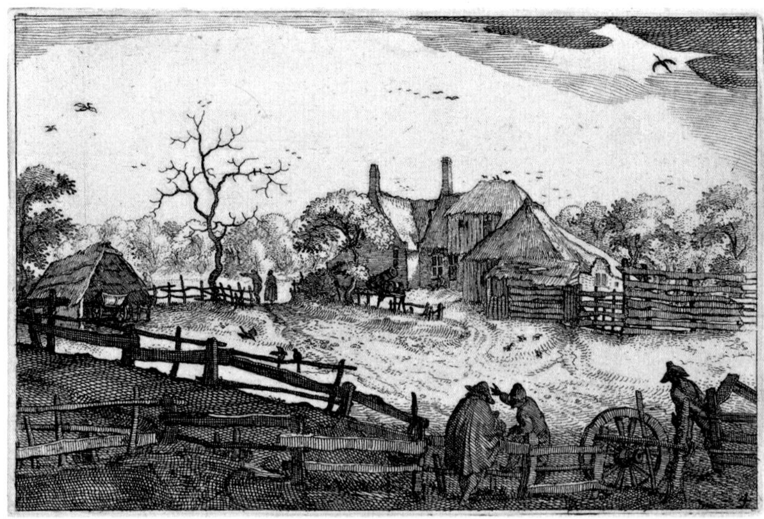

20.1 Claes Jansz Visscher, *Pot's Inn*, plate 4 of *Plaisante plaetsen*, ca. 1612. Rijksprentenkabinet, Amsterdam.

15 kilometers northeast of Leiden, relates to no realized etching but may also have been drawn with a possible print project in mind. It depicts the Woudse Dom, a sixteenth-century church that still stands today in partially rebuilt and restored form. With his characteristically lively handling, Visscher recorded the key architectural and decorative details of the building, employing short horizontal strokes as a shorthand for the tower's brickwork. To the right of the tower is a small thatch-roofed structure and, directly above it, a clearly rendered "A." Such letters do not appear in Visscher's printed landscapes, but were common in topographical prints of the period, in which they, in combination with keys, served to identify specific sites. Alternatively, as suggested by other drawings by Visscher with similar inscriptions, the artist may have devised such notations for his own purposes, perhaps as a way of keeping track of specific motifs he intended to reuse.[6]

At the top edge of the verso, rotated 90 degrees and in a warmer brown ink, is a partial sketch of a plant. A similarly focused study of flora appears on the verso of another drawing in the 1607–8 group (Maida and George Abrams Collection, Boston).[7] These sketches show Visscher making full use of his paper to record the world around him in all its many forms. Although the drawings themselves were not intended for an audience, their survival allows us still today to feel as though we wander with the artist and bear witness to the careful observation—and imagination—that went into his creations. JSS

ESAIAS VAN DE VELDE

Amsterdam 1587–1630 The Hague

21

Summer Landscape with Reapers, ca. 1629

Black chalk, with gray and brown washes; additions (perhaps made later) in opaque gray wash
263 x 187 mm

WATERMARK Shield, similar to Churchill 264 (seventeenth century), possibly representing the Arms of Burgundy and Austria, center

INSCRIPTIONS Verso, lower left, in pen and brown ink: N905.; verso, lower left, in gray ink: *Esaias . v.d. Velde.*; verso, lower left, in graphite: S.F.; verso, upper left, in blue pencil: No. 481

PROVENANCE Jhr. Johann Goll van Franckenstein (1722–1785), Amsterdam (L. 2987, verso, lower left, with his numbering in brown ink: N905.); private collection, France; Sotheby's, Amsterdam, 12 November 1996, lot 69 (bought in); Bob P. Haboldt & Co., New York; from whom acquired by Clement C. Moore, 1998

SELECT REFERENCES Bradley 2006, 101

Promised gift of Clement C. and Elizabeth Y. Moore

Seasonal imagery was popular among contemporary Dutch and Flemish landscape specialists, especially scenes set in farmland or villages that offered a distinct contrast with the typically urban lives of artists and their audiences.[1] Commonly falling into cycles of four images depicting the seasons, or twelve of the months, drawings such as this, showing farmers reaping and gathering grain, could represent Summer, or more specifically August, when grain harvesting generally took place.[2] No other drawings by Esaias van de Velde, however, match this one in terms of having a similar size, format, and seasonal subject matter. If it was once part of a series, then the others are missing.

What does survive from Van de Velde's hand is a complete set (although long ago broken up) of twelve smaller-format drawings of the Twelve Months dated 1629.[3] These comprise one of the earliest sets of drawings of the Twelve Months by a Dutch artist, though several print series of the theme had already been in circulation, such as those by the artist's cousin Jan van de Velde II.[4] Of particular interest from Esaias's 1629 series of drawings is a scene representing the month of August in the Rijksprentenkabinet, which is remarkably similar in composition and format, although the present sheet is twice its size (fig. 21.1).[5] In both, men actively swing their short scythes with one hand while securing the stalks of grain with a tool called a mat-hook in the other. Reinforcing the gender norms of the era, Esaias shows the women either gathering the already-cut grain lying on the ground, or (in the case of the present work) bringing supplies and refreshments. He anonymizes the figures somewhat, creating an idealized air that resonates with the universal and ageless nature of the activity itself. As the Latin caption under one of Jan van de Velde's printed depictions of August reads: "You reign, Ceres, divine, famous, / charged with ample crops by the heavenly Jupiter. / What we sow and what was sown you favor, / Look how you bend the blond-ripened ears of grain!"[6] The appeal to a mythological god in this address seems to reflect an urge, also apparent in the image itself, to seek timelessness in the face of a changing world.

An innovative aspect of this sheet, shared by the 1629 series, is its vertical format. Like most artists at the time, Esaias employed a horizontal format for the vast majority of his landscape subjects. Here, he creatively addresses the challenge by lending the sky and trees greater weight, while still managing to build a fluid series of receding ground zones using the figure groups, rows of grain, and in the background the trees and house. The convincing perspectival arrangement of elements within the composition (or *ordonnantie*, as contemporary theorists such as Karel van Mander called it) was always one of Van de Velde's primary concerns in his landscape imagery. He also innovated in his technique. Van de Velde was one of the first landscape artists to make regular use of black chalk instead of pen and ink, a practice he used increasingly after his move to The Hague in 1618.[7] In his later works such as this one, he deftly combined it with subtly applied washes, softening volumetric forms and increasing the overall tonal range. One of his motivations for using a larger sheet here would have been the greater freedom in exploring these effects. It compares favorably, for example, with the aforementioned smaller version, which is necessarily more cursory in touch and style.

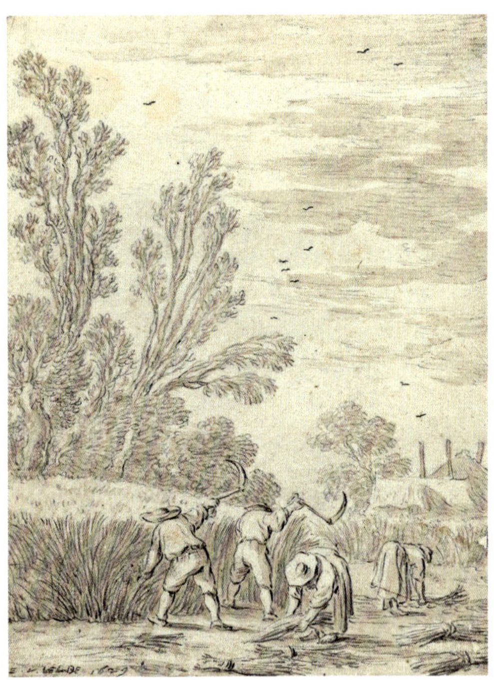

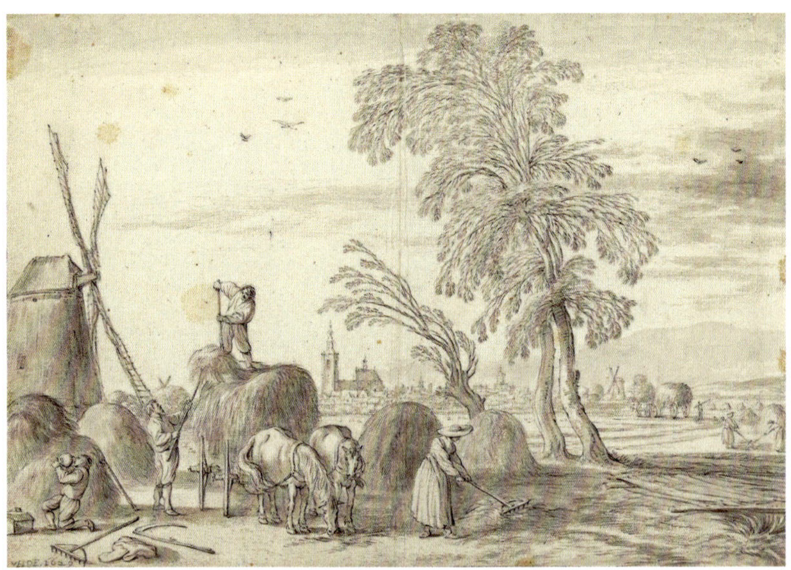

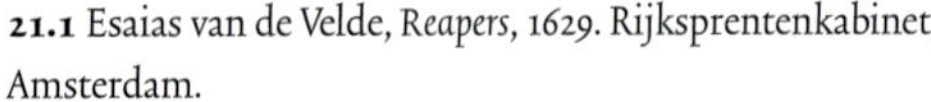

21.1 Esaias van de Velde, *Reapers*, 1629. Rijksprentenkabinet, Amsterdam.

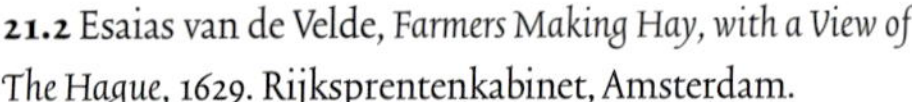

21.2 Esaias van de Velde, *Farmers Making Hay, with a View of The Hague*, 1629. Rijksprentenkabinet, Amsterdam.

It is impossible to say whether this drawing was made before or after the 1629 series, but it has long been presumed, rightly, to date around the same time. This can be confirmed by an exact watermark match found between this sheet and another one dated 1629 in the Rijksprentenkabinet, *Farmers Making Hay, with a View of The Hague* (fig. 21.2).[8] Worth noting is that this latter sheet is twice the size of the present one (and therefore four times the size of the smaller version), suggesting that Esaias had a large-format ream of paper that he might divide in halves or quarters to make smaller works, a practice that also makes sense when working in series. The lack of known companions for the present drawing, however, makes it just as likely, if not more so, that it was always meant to stand as an independent work, similarly concerned with the cyclic nature of time and the transience it implies. **RF**

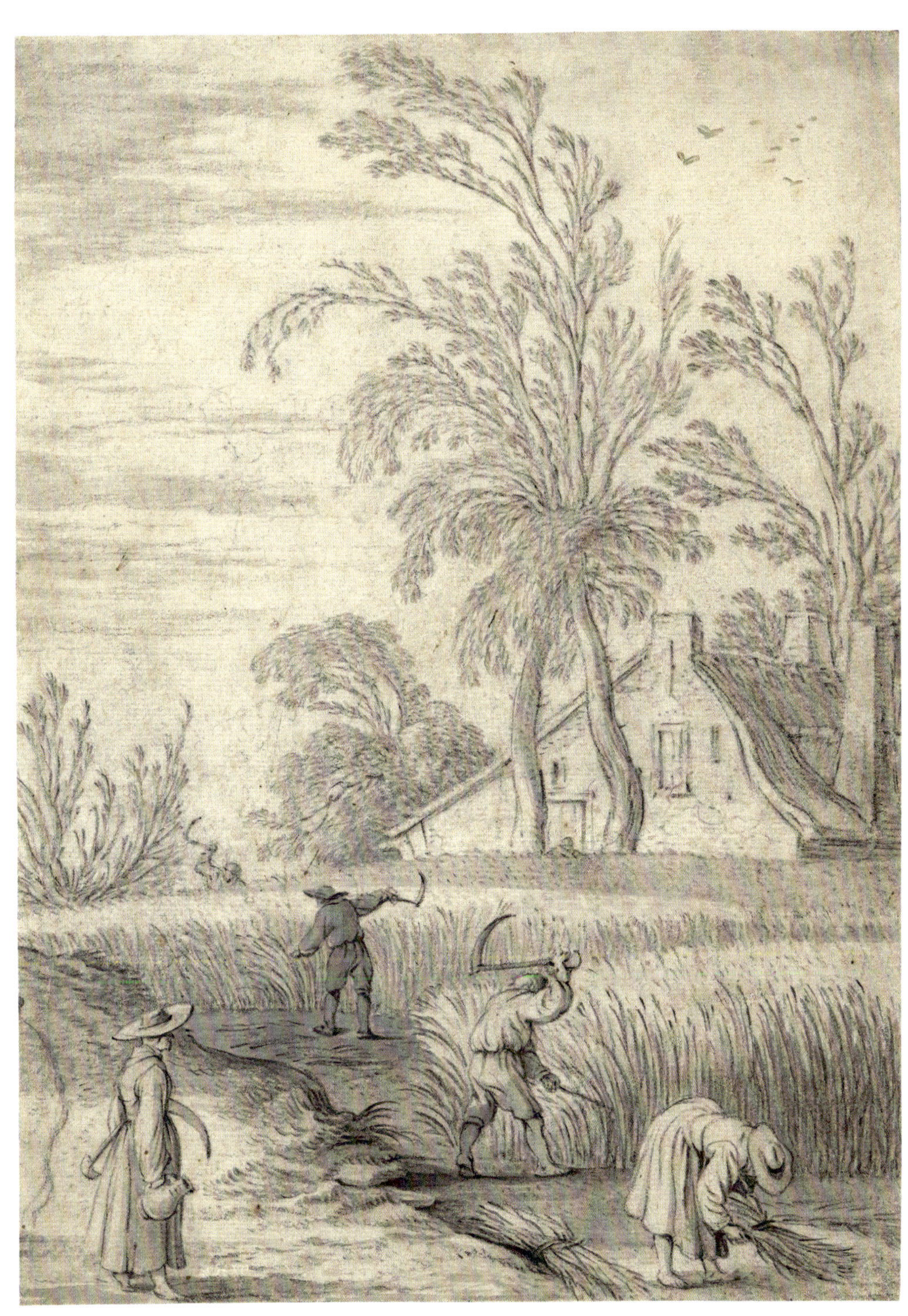

CORNELIS HENDRICKSZ VROOM

Danzig (?) 1590/92–1661 Haarlem

22

Hills beyond a River or Lake, with a Large Tree in the Foreground, 1620s

Pen and two shades of brown ink, with brown wash; framing line in brown ink

201 x 313 mm

INSCRIPTIONS Verso, lower left, in graphite: *Claes v Beresteyn fec. / (Stichter van het Hofje)*

PROVENANCE Frederik Muller, Amsterdam, 20–21 November 1882, lot 7 (from anonymous owner, as Claes van Beresteyn); Carl Schöffer (1841–1915), Amsterdam (no mark; see L. 3009); his sale, Frederik Muller, Amsterdam, 30–31 May 1893, lot 18 (as Claes van Beresteyn, bought in); his subsequent sale, R.W.P. de Vries, Amsterdam, 8–10 May 1900, lot 17 (as Claes van Beresteyn; to "Poortenaar"); Jhr. Dr. Eltjo Aldegondus van Beresteyn (1876–1948), The Hague (two Van Beresteyn family collector's marks on verso, neither in Lugt: one circular stamp left of center in black ink, with text *FAMILIE-ARCHIEF VAN BERESTEYN* around the perimeter of the crest, with a boar sejant erect in the center; the second stamp in red ink also with a boar sejant erect at center); Mrs. P. van Marle-van Beresteyn, Wassenaar; Sotheby's, Amsterdam, 2 November 2004, lot 59; where acquired by Clement C. Moore

SELECT REFERENCES Gerson 1940, no. B 15 (as Claes van Beresteyn, though reminiscent of the work of Cornelis Vroom); Keyes 1975, 1: 72–73, 2: no. D 37 and 178 (under no. P 11), 212 (under no. D 3, erroneously referred to as D 36 rather than D 37; as ca. 1625), 183 (under no. P 20), 188 (under no. P 27), 224 (under no. D 22); Shoaf Turner 2012, no. 20

Promised gift of Clement C. and Elizabeth Y. Moore

Of the many qualities needed to form a successful private collection, the one that is most often overlooked is patience. With a draftsman as rare as Vroom, it would have been all too tempting to snatch up the first example that came along. But the collector waited. His patience was well rewarded when he ultimately managed to secure this sheet, described by George Keyes in his monograph on the artist as "one of Vroom's most beautiful and impressive drawings . . . a triumph of realistic perception fired by imagination."[1] Vroom's delicately rendered views, especially prized by collectors of seventeenth-century Dutch landscapes, comprise countless dots and dashes combined to create a highly impressionistic effect of shimmering light reflected on water and through clusters of dappled leaves.

Drawings such as the present sheet and related hilly landscapes, for example *Path by Woods and Field* in the Victoria and Albert Museum, London (fig. 22.1),[2] and *Hilly Landscape with a Stone Bridge* in the Rijksprentenkabinet, Amsterdam,[3] all datable to the 1620s, are often assumed to represent serene views of the English countryside,[4] a proposal that will seem utterly convincing to anyone who has traveled along the Thames Valley in parts of rural Kent, Sussex, or Surrey. Yet Vroom's presumed 1627–28 sojourn in England has been thrown into doubt. It is now thought that the references to "Vroom" and "Young Vroom" in English documents dated March 1627 and November 1628 (always without a given name) may be to Cornelis's younger brother, Frederick Vroom, a marine and landscape painter. As noted by Irene van Thiel-Stroman on the basis of a detailed study of the documents, it looks as if Frederick went abroad while Cornelis may have remained in Haarlem[5]—where, it might be added, he would have come in close contact with this style of penmanship in landscape drawings by such artists as Goltzius, De Gheyn, and Willem Buytewech. Cornelis was certainly in Haarlem in 1629. Frederick's absence around this same time is implied in various notarial documents dated between 1631 and 1633 concerning an earlier bitter family dispute. Cornelis and Frederick's mother and father, the marine painter Hendrik

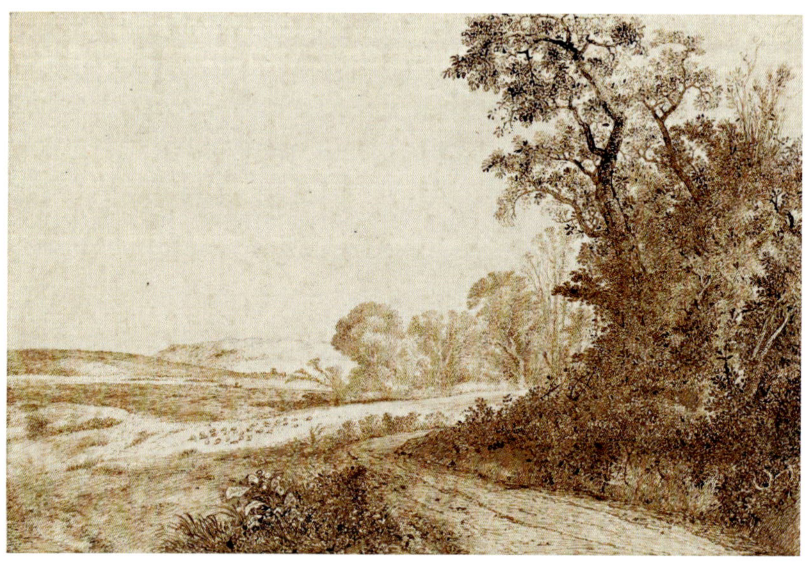

22.1 Cornelis Hendricksz Vroom, *Path by Woods and Field*, 1620s. Victoria and Albert Museum, London.

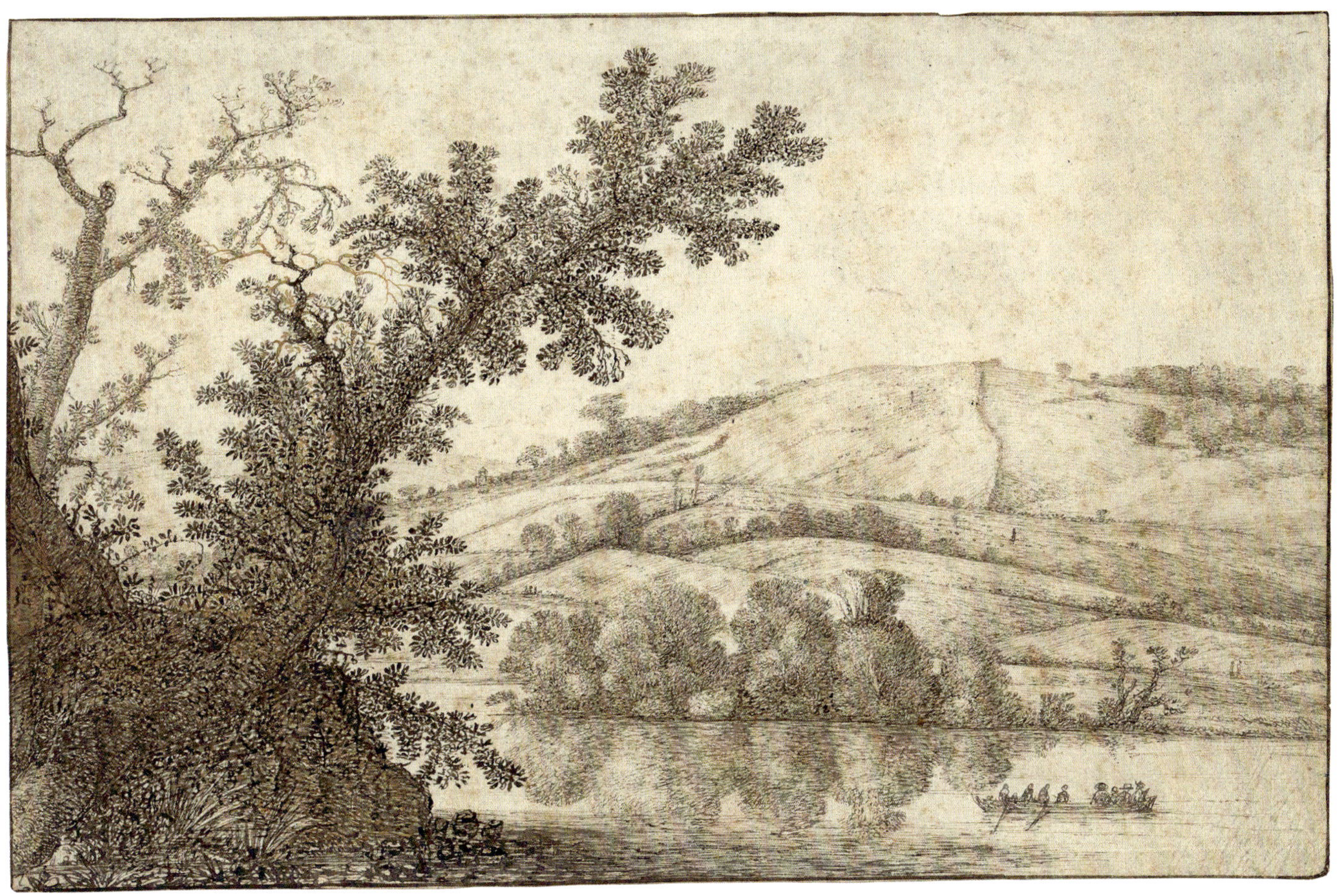

Vroom, were staunch Catholics. They had fiercely disapproved of their daughter Cornelia's wish to marry a Calvinist, Cornelis Adriaensz Backer, who later served as alderman and mayor of Haarlem. Cornelis Vroom took his sister's side. Frederick "on his return" (the documents never state from where) sided with his parents. Cornelis later accused his brother of "fueling" the family feud. When the pregnant Cornelia was banished from the family home by her mother and Frederick, Cornelis helped her flee to Beverwijk. The couple eventually married in December 1630, and Cornelis lived with the Backers for some time before he was eventually reconciled with his parents.

If not a depiction of the English countryside, as previously suggested, the present drawing and other views like it might represent scenery in one of the southern or eastern provinces of the Netherlands, such as Limburg.[6] **JST**

GIOVANNI FRANCESCO BARBIERI, *called* GUERCINO

Ferrara 1591–1666 Bologna

23

Landscape with a River and a Man Crossing a Bridge, ca. 1620–25

Pen and brown ink
146 x 300 mm

INSCRIPTIONS Recto, lower right, in pen and brown ink: *WE* (written mark of William Esdaile, L. 2617); verso, upper center, in graphite: *Guerchino 1591–1666*; verso, upper center, in pen and brown ink: *del Cent...* and *5—7—*; verso, center, in pen and brown ink, in the hand of William Esdaile: *Formerly in Sr Peter Lely's collection* and *Ottley's coll^n 1804 WE P8N38+*; verso, lower center, in pen and black ink: *Guerchino.8.1.*

PROVENANCE Sir Peter Lely (1618–1680), London (L. 2091, lower right); William Young Ottley (1771–1836), London (no mark; see L. 2664);[1] William Esdaile (1758–1837), London (L. 2617, recto, lower right, and verso, lower center); probably his sale, Christie's, London, 18 June 1840, probably lot 268 ("Buildings on a river"); private collection, France; Galerie Didier Aaron, Paris and New York; from whom acquired by Clement C. Moore, 2018

Promised gift of Clement C. and Elizabeth Y. Moore

Among the most admired and eagerly collected artists of the Italian seventeenth century, Guercino sent paintings from Cento and Bologna in central Italy to patrons as far away as Madrid, Paris, and London. Most of his drawings, however, were considered to be the working materials of the studio and were not sold or given away by the artist. Inherited by his nephews Benedetto and Cesare Gennari, the drawings largely remained in the Casa Gennari until the eighteenth century, when they were eagerly purchased especially by English collectors including John Bouverie and Richard Dalton, the latter of whom was responsible for the more than 800 drawings by Guercino and his workshop now in the Royal Collection Trust at Windsor Castle.

One notable group of drawings did begin to circulate during the seventeenth century, in the decade following Guercino's death. In the early 1670s, Benedetto Gennari worked in Paris and while there had Jean Pesne produce a set of etchings copying a group of landscape drawings by Guercino; when Gennari moved to England a few years later, he sold these drawings to William Cavendish, later the 1st Duke of Devonshire. Benedetto was also likely the source for the drawings by Guercino that were owned by the artist-collector Peter Lely, given that the two artists would have come into contact at the English court. These included the present sheet as well as another in the Morgan's collection.[2]

Although the Pesne etchings and the Devonshire drawings helped create a demand for landscape drawings like the Moore sheet, most of Guercino's landscape sketches seem to have remained in his workshop during his lifetime and were thus presumably drawn for his own enjoyment. They continue an Italian tradition of pen landscapes that can be traced back to the work of Titian and Domenico Campagnola (see no. 1), but which in the workshop of the Carracci family also began to narrow its horizons to focus on more intimate riverine scenes. Guercino was likely aware of the Campagnola and Carracci drawings, and perhaps also northern European prints,[3] though in the end he brought his own distinctive penwork to bear on the genre. With a boat on a river, a small footbridge, and

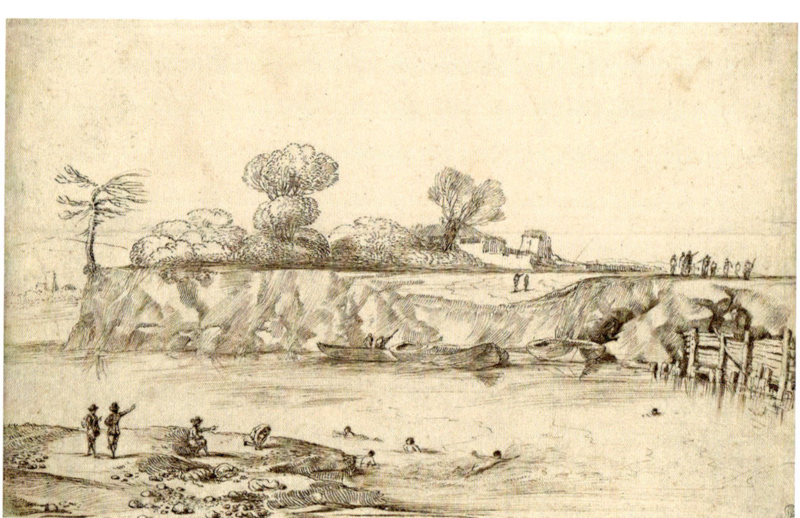

23.1 Guercino, *River Landscape with Bathers*, ca. 1630–35. Morgan Library & Museum, New York.

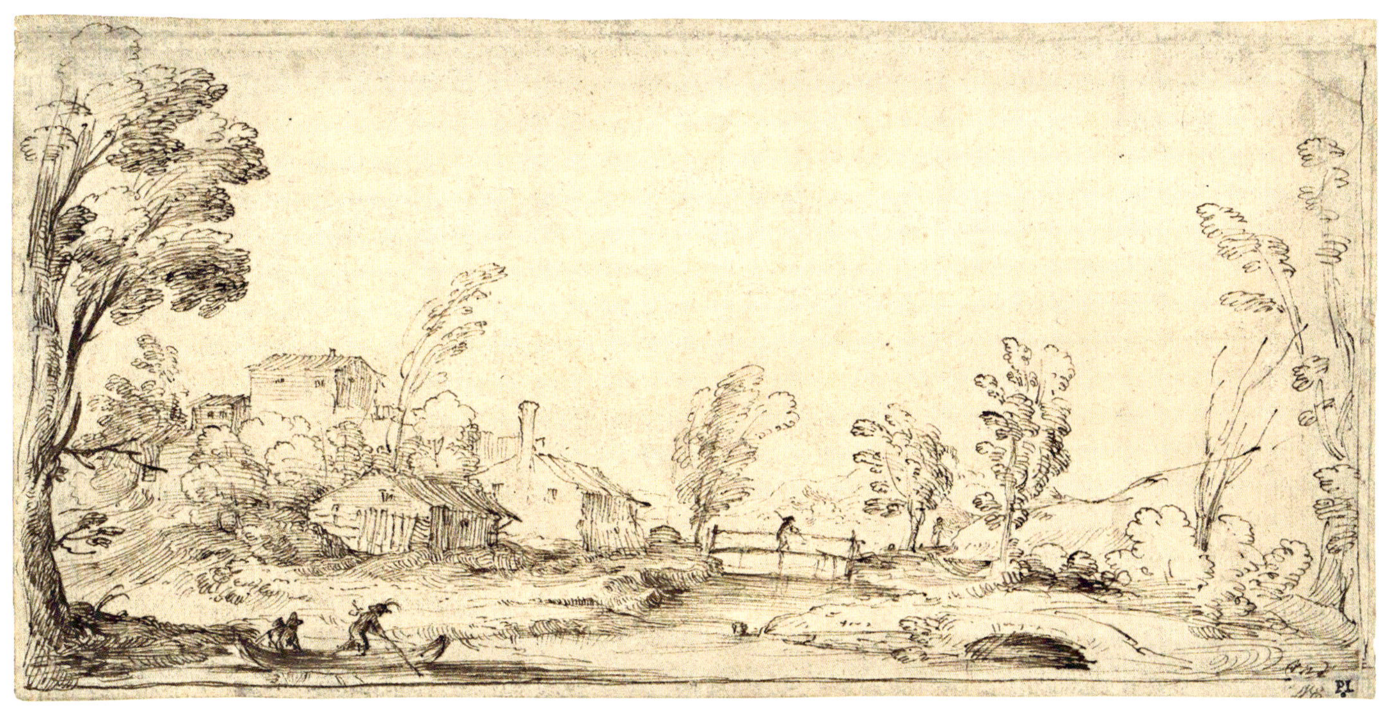

rustic buildings set among trees, this airy sketch captures country life on a bright summer or autumn day.

The dating of Guercino's landscapes has proven a famously difficult exercise, with few securely dated sheets offering firm points of comparison.[4] Nicholas Turner has suggested that the Moore drawing could date to as early as ca. 1615, comparing it to a more finished sheet in the Uffizi and to Guercino's painted landscapes for Casa Pannini in his native Cento; David Stone has also suggested an early date for the sheet.[5] For the present author, however, the Moore drawing lacks the slightly naïve spirit of the early Uffizi landscape drawing and the Cento paintings, and it seems closer to Guercino's landscapes done during and after his Roman sojourn of 1621–23. Another landscape at the Uffizi, with an inscribed date of 1626, provides one point of comparison,[6] but the penwork and conception are not far from other works, for example the *River Landscape with Bathers* at the Morgan (fig. 23.1), that are usually dated to the early 1630s.[7] A bit more freely conceived and less rigidly structured than most of the examples usually placed in the 1630s, the Moore *Landscape with a River* might best be dated to the early- to mid-1620s. With regard to the subject, Prisco Bagni has suggested that scenes such as these might be based on features of the landscape around Cento,[8] though even those that echo elements of the local surroundings were probably drawn in the studio on the basis of remembered motifs. JJM

JACQUES CALLOT

Nancy 1592–1635 Nancy

24

Study of a Peddler with His "Hutte," a Hunter Carrying a Gun, and a Young Man with a Walking Stick, ca. 1620

Black chalk
74 x 188 mm

INSCRIPTIONS Verso, center, in graphite: 3; verso, lower right, in graphite (upside down): 4

PROVENANCE Jean-Denis Lempereur (1701–1779), Paris (L. 1740, recto, lower right, partly effaced); possibly his sale, Boileau et Joullain, Paris, 24 May 1773 sqq., as part of lot 696; Gaston Delestre (1913–1969), Paris; Tajan, Paris, 16 May 2013, lot 49; W.M. Brady & Co., New York; from whom acquired by Clement C. Moore, 2019

Promised gift of Clement C. and Elizabeth Y. Moore

Although Callot may be best remembered for his amusing commedia dell'arte performers, unsettling portrayals of hunchbacks, and complex depictions of courtly events, he also was renowned for his keen observation of ordinary life. While at the ducal court of Cosimo II de' Medici in Florence from 1612 until 1621, Callot took an interest in the city's residents, including those at the social margins who solicited support outside the city's churches, in piazzas, and on the street. Callot's depictions formed the basis of his print series *Les Gueux* (The Beggars). Instead of mocking or moralizing about the life of the urban indigent, Callot's depictions reveal a measure of compassion. He portrayed the elderly swaddled in layers against the cold; injured veterans soliciting alms with an open hat, mug, or upturned palm; and women with children to feed. The Beggars appeared in 1622 and fed Rembrandt's lively interest in the vulnerable among Leiden's populace (see no. 37). Callot's observations extended to a wide range of citizens and tradespeople, and his prints chronicling events in Florence contain a full range of humanity.

This sheet with its quick, incisive studies of three men is likely part of the research that contributed to Callot's most important Florentine engraving, *The Fair at Impruneta* of 1620. Outdoor fairs allowed seventeenth-century artists to feature a diverse crowd in an expansive landscape. For Callot, it was the chance to create a panoramic view rich with incident cataloguing the many activities animating the fairgrounds at Impruneta, a market town south of Florence. Jacques Lieure noted that Callot visited the Impruneta fair in October 1619 for the feast of St. Luke. There, the artist filled a sketchbook, now in the Uffizi, with fifty-five studies in red and black chalk documenting the bustling crowd, in preparation for a print with around 1,300 figures.[1] This practice of drawing figures engaged in workday activities was not restricted to his visit to the fair, and motifs such as those on the present sheet reflect his ongoing gathering of characters and poses.

More horizontal in format than the Uffizi sketchbook pages, the present sheet accommodates three distinct figures. As with the paired figures on many of the

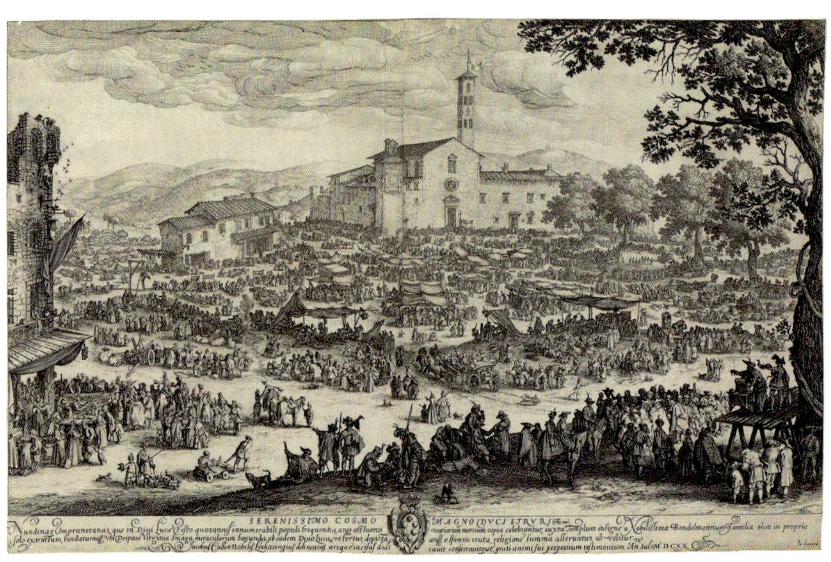

24.1 Jacques Callot, *The Fair at Impruneta*, ca. 1620. British Museum, London.

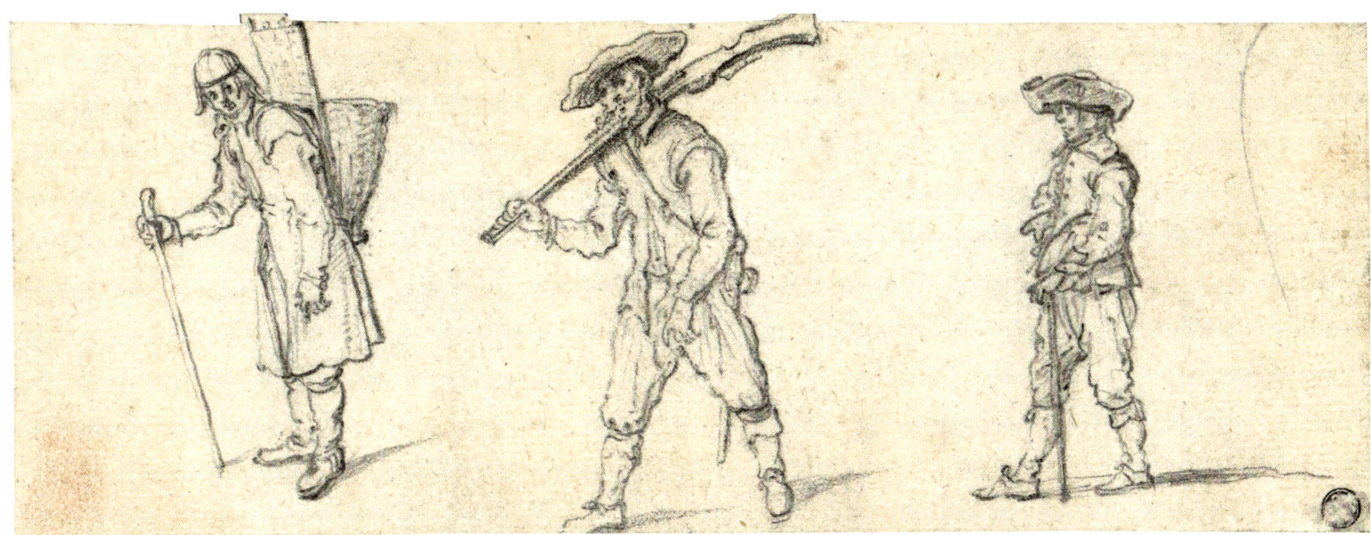

Uffizi pages, Callot has situated each figure at a slightly different point, with the figure at far right on a smaller scale than the others. At left, the itinerant peddler, with his walking stick and distinctive *hutte*, a basket-like pack often used for carrying bread, was a common feature at fairs among the roving merchants selling wares. His long hair peeks out from under a simple cap. At center, a hunter or soldier wearing a large-brimmed hat, a sword at his side, and carrying a long gun walks vigorously. The alert glances of the peddler and hunter remind us that the artist was likely observing passersby, capturing their pose or attitude quickly, as they noted his activity. The third figure, a young man observed at a greater distance, stands alert, his hand resting on a walking stick, striding in profile and unaware of the artist. Technical examination reveals that the contours of this figure were incised, indicating that it was transferred to another support. Characters similar to the first and third on this sheet appear in the background of *The Fair at Impruneta* among the vast crowd (fig. 24.1).[2]

Some of Callot's earliest drawings, small figures deftly drawn in black chalk, contain wispy, mannered bodies jotted down so swiftly they resemble abbreviated thoughts. Gradually his figures developed convincing volume and naturalistic movement. By the time he began using the Uffizi sketchbook, around 1619, Callot was an expert in conjuring believable figures on a small scale. This sheet reveals his knack for moving beyond stock figures to capture the particular nature of individuals, a specificity of form and movement that remains a marvel to those who look closely at Callot's prints. JT

GERRIT VAN HONTHORST

Utrecht 1592–1656 Utrecht

25

A Woman at an Embroidery Frame (recto), *Aristotle and Phyllis* (verso), ca. 1630–40

Black chalk, pen and brown ink, and white chalk (recto); black and white chalk (verso)

250 x 224 mm

WATERMARK Possible monogram "CH" or "GH"; this mark is found on other drawings from the same set, including the *Pastoral Scene of a Man and a Woman, Presumed Portraits of Frederick V and Elizabeth Stuart of Bohemia* discussed further below (see n. 1)

INSCRIPTIONS Verso, lower left, in black chalk: *n° 18*

PROVENANCE Private collection, Belgium, since ca. 1900; Nicolas Schwed, Paris; from whom acquired by Clement C. Moore, 2014

SELECT REFERENCES Bréton, Jouslin de Noray, and Schwed 2014, no. 12; Koldeweij 2017, 73–74

Promised gift of Clement C. and Elizabeth Y. Moore

Gerrit van Honthorst enjoyed a successful but notably peripatetic career. First trained by Abraham Bloemaert in his native Utrecht, Honthorst traveled to Italy around 1610 or 1615 and remained there until 1620. He worked for major patrons, including Vincenzo Giustiniani, Scipione Borghese, and Cosimo II de' Medici, painting both cabinet pictures and public altarpieces in a tenebrist style that earned him the nickname "Gherardo delle Notti" (Gerrit of the Night-Pieces). He returned to Utrecht in 1620 and married, but even as he settled down he began to attract further international attention. He was called to England in 1628 to work for Charles I and the Duke of Buckingham, for whom he continued to paint even after returning to the Netherlands. Honthorst's Caravaggism waned as he concentrated on courtly portraiture for patrons including Frederick V, King of Bohemia, and his queen, Elizabeth Stuart; Christian IV, King of Denmark; and Prince Frederick Henry and Amalia van Solms.

Roughly seventy drawings by Honthorst survive, nearly half of which—including the present sheet—came to light only in 2014.[1] This large corpus has rightly drawn attention, and Honthorst is sometimes said to be the only Caravaggesque artist who used drawing as a regular part of his practice, though in fact most did employ drawings, at least for compositional sketches if not for academic figure drawings.[2] Indeed, apart from a few head studies, a copy after Caravaggio's *Crucifixion of St. Peter*,[3] and one academic figure study done in Rome,[4] Honthorst's drawings are compositional studies akin to the present sheet, invariably sketched in black chalk, then sometimes refined with pen, white heightening, and/or wash. Few of these match his finished paintings exactly, though many seem like initial thoughts for specific commissions.

The Moore drawing is described in the 2014 catalogue as "A Young Woman Drawing," but, as also recognized by Anna Koldeweij, the object on the table is not an easel, but rather an embroidery frame, the loose strings for which are held in the young woman's proper left hand.[5] (This explains why the angled surface is essentially transparent, allowing a view of the body of the youth behind the table.) Like drawing, embroidery was a skill in which young women were instructed, and the study is one of several that depict the activities of the children of Honthorst's royal patrons. Koldeweij suggests that the Moore drawing shows Sophia van de Palts, the youngest daughter of Frederick V and Elizabeth Stuart, but this is uncertain, since she was not born until 1630 and most of the drawings in this set date from the late 1620s to the early 1640s. Given the fact that the woman in the drawing would seem to be in her teens, it seems equally possible that the sitter could be her older sister, Elisabeth van de Palts, who was born in 1618.

The verso of the sheet (fig. 25.1) depicts Aristotle and Phyllis.[6] In this cautionary tale, Aristotle warns his pupil Alexander the Great not to be too distracted by the charms of his mistress Phyllis. She took her revenge by seducing Aristotle and demanding that the besotted philosopher allow her to ride him like a horse, having arranged for Alexander to witness his tutor's humiliation. The motif was a popular one in medieval and Renaissance art, but seventeenth-century depictions are rare.[7] No painting of the subject by Honthorst is known, but he could have experimented with the theme around the time that he painted the similar story of Phryne tempting Xenocrates in the mid-1620s.[8] JJM

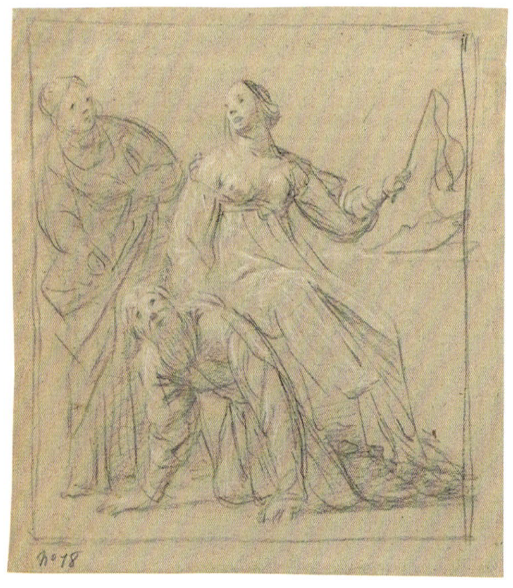

25.1 Gerrit van Honthorst, *Aristotle and Phyllis*, ca. 1623–25. Verso of no. 25.

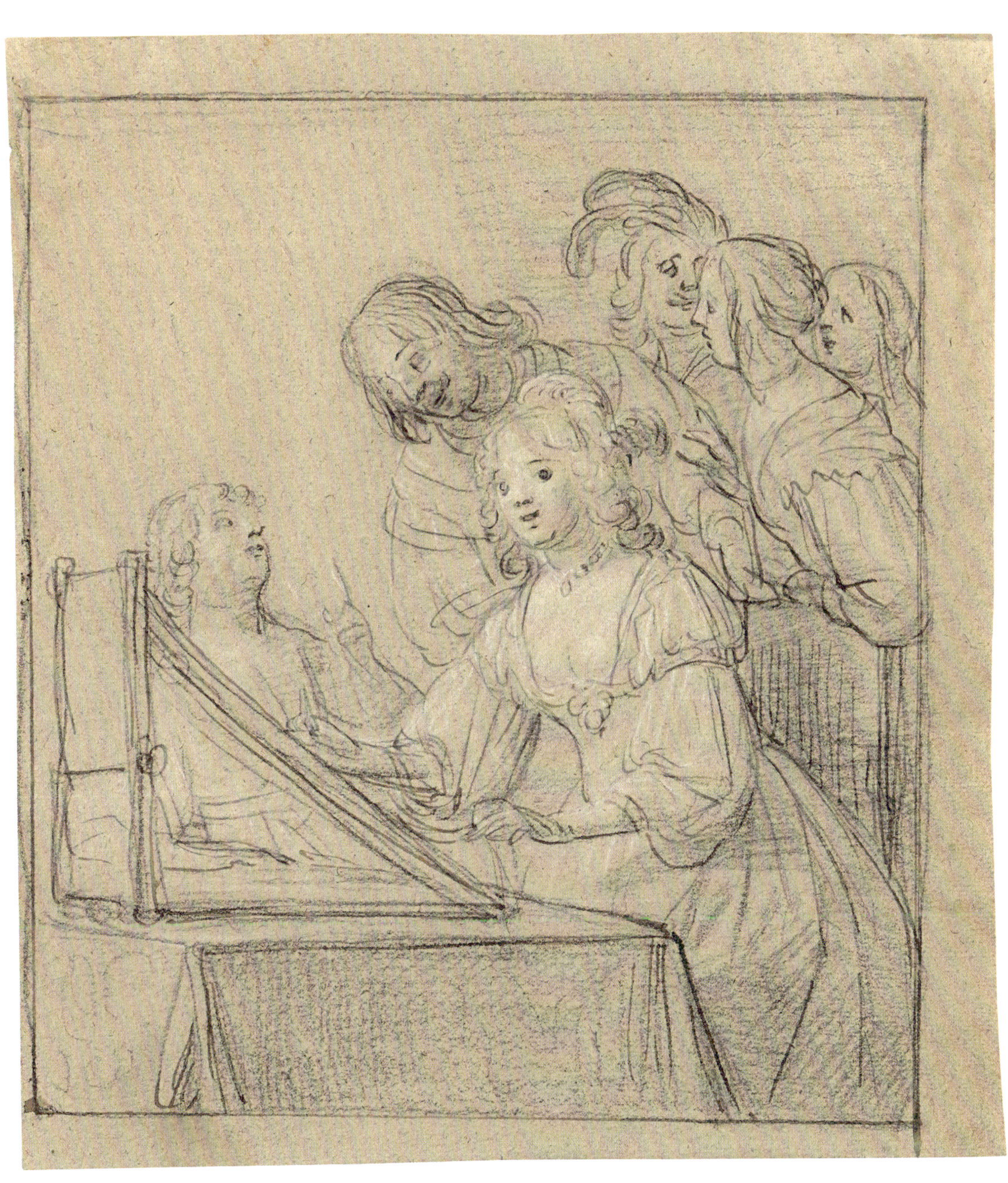

JACOB JORDAENS

Antwerp 1593–1678 Antwerp

26

Mercury Standing, Seen from Behind, ca. 1620

Red and black chalk, with brown wash, red watercolor, and white and brown opaque watercolor
464 x 283 mm

WATERMARK Post horn within a shield, surmounted by a crown, over "4" and "WR"; the watermark is of a type found in paper produced in the Low Countries throughout the seventeenth century, with similar examples including Heawood 2654 (no location, 1616), 2715 (Amsterdam, 1668), 2722 (Leiden, 1665), and 2723 (Amsterdam, 1671)

INSCRIPTIONS Recto, lower right, in pen and brown ink: *Rubens*; recto, upper left, in red chalk: C

PROVENANCE Hôtel Drouot, Paris, 4 May 1933, lot 87; Hôtel Drouot, Paris, 4 February 1972; Galerie Claude Aubry, Paris, 1974; Jacques Petit-Hory (1929–1992), Paris (no mark; see L. 4138), by 1978; Hôtel Drouot, Audap-Godeau-Solanet, Paris, 26 June 1987, lot 123; Christie's, Amsterdam, 25 November 1992, lot 542; Tajan, Paris, 7 April 1995, lot 94; Bert Quadvlieg, the Netherlands; his sale, Hampel, Munich, 4 December 2009, lot 25 (bought in); the drawing remained with Bert Quadvlieg until 2018; Jean-Luc Baroni, 2018–19; from whom acquired by Clement C. Moore and the Morgan, 2019

SELECT REFERENCES Chantelou 1972, 17; D'Hulst 1974, 1: no. A53; Held 1978, 726; D'Hulst 1980, 363; Oursel 1981, 82; Chaldecott and Marty de Cambiaire 2019, no. 7; Bailey et al. 2024, 13–14

Morgan Library & Museum, Partial gift of Clement C. Moore II and partial purchase on the Acquisitions Fund, inv. 2019.103

Most likely dating to around 1620, when Jacob Jordaens was associated with Rubens's Antwerp workshop, this large-scale drawing offers a number of puzzles at first glance: it is a view from behind of a figure wearing the helmet and winged sandals of Mercury; yet, the figure is clearly a woman and has the carnal quality of a life study. At the same time, she is also shown standing on a round base, like a sculpture. The figure relates, in fact, to an ivory statuette designed by Rubens and kept in the artist's studio, where it was described in the inventory drawn up after the artist's death; the work is now at the State Hermitage Museum (fig. 26.1).[1] Seen from behind, the Mercury in Jordaens's drawing is depicted on a round pedestal, in a pose identical to that of the statuette, and is of roughly the same size. However, the distinctly female anatomy and the fleshy quality of the figure in the drawing makes it appear that Jordaens did not simply aim to produce a drawing of the statuette but, instead, arranged a female model in a pose inspired by the ivory Mercury. This relates to the well-established Flemish workshop practice of drawing from live models who were studied in poses derived from sculpture, drawings, or paintings. The Morgan's masterful *Seated Male Youth* by Rubens is another example of the practice, in which the pose of the male model was clearly based on Girolamo Muziano's *Penitent St. Jerome*, a drawing that Rubens owned;[2] Rubens's several drawings of a *Nude Youth in the Pose of the Spinario* offer further demonstration.[3] What is more, the ivory statuette of Mercury was paired with one of Venus, and the young Jordaens seems to be playing a complex game of merging the two works. The sensual handling of the flesh seems to be further inspired by drawings made by Rubens in connection with the statuettes, such as the *Venus Seen*

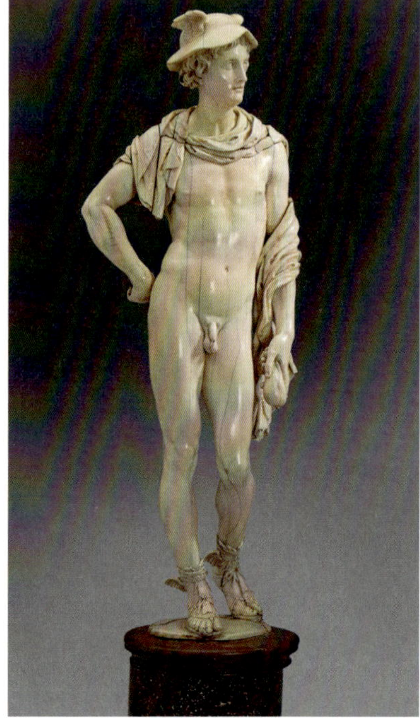

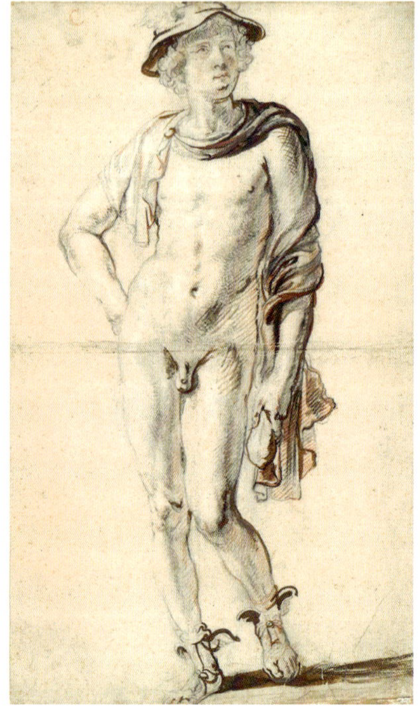

26.1 Flemish School, *Mercury*, ca. 1620 (?). State Hermitage Museum, St. Petersburg.

26.2 Jacob Jordaens, *Mercury*, ca. 1620. Harvard University Art Museums, Cambridge (MA).

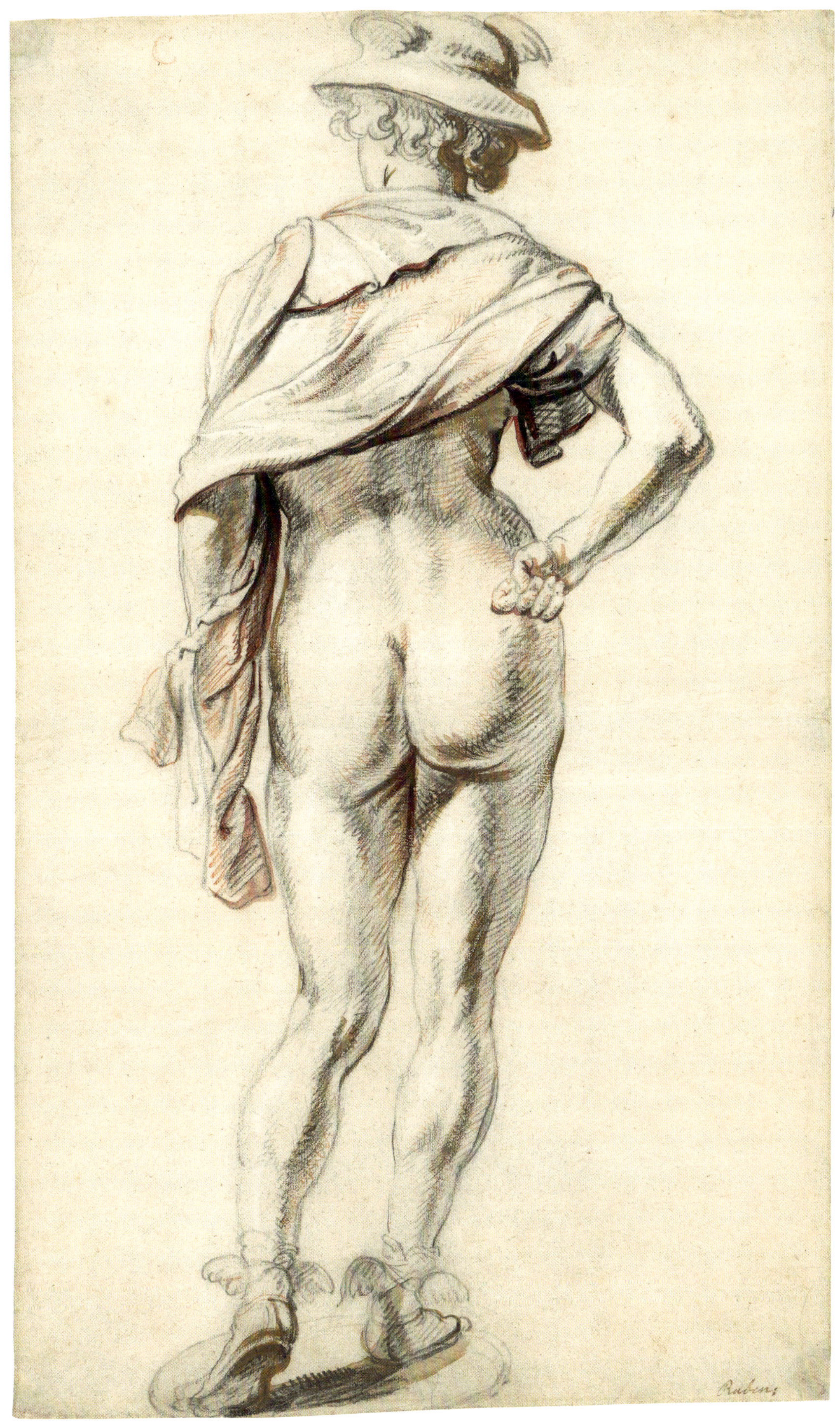
Rubens

from Behind at the Louvre.[4] Jordaens, however, makes the figure entirely his own through the creation of a complex system of hatching in black and red chalks and the addition of vibrant washes and opaque watercolor.[5] First emerging during his years in Rubens's workshop, this technique became a distinguishing feature of his draftsmanship for the rest of his career, seen for example in his brightly colored compositional studies (see no. 27) as well as his portrait drawings.[6] The pristine condition of the *Mercury* also allows us to appreciate the highly sensitive light effects achieved through the use of reserve paper and the addition of white opaque watercolor, creating the impression of a surface that simultaneously evokes both ivory and human flesh.

A companion piece to the *Mercury Seen from Behind*, depicting the same statuette in a frontal view, is at Harvard (fig. 26.2).[7] This matches the Morgan drawing in technique and size, and the two studies were surely done at the same time, although the Harvard study is a far more conventional copy of the male prototype. Further drawings of the statuette, by other members of Rubens's studio, are also known, including a sheet in the Statens Museum for Kunst, Copenhagen, previously attributed to Georg Petel.[8] There, the figure is adapted to include the rooster at his feet and a caduceus, such that it is again perhaps not a literal copy after the statuette, but rather another drawing playing with the exercise of having a model pose to match the sculpture.

These drawings did not, however, merely serve as ends in themselves, but remained part of the working material of the studio. Rubens reused the sculpture and the related drawings as the basis for his own painting of Mercury from the mid-1630s, now in the Museo Nacional del Prado,[9] and Jordaens must have retained his drawing when he left Rubens's workshop and set up his own, for the figure is echoed in a much later *Mercury and Argus* produced by his studio.[10] JJM

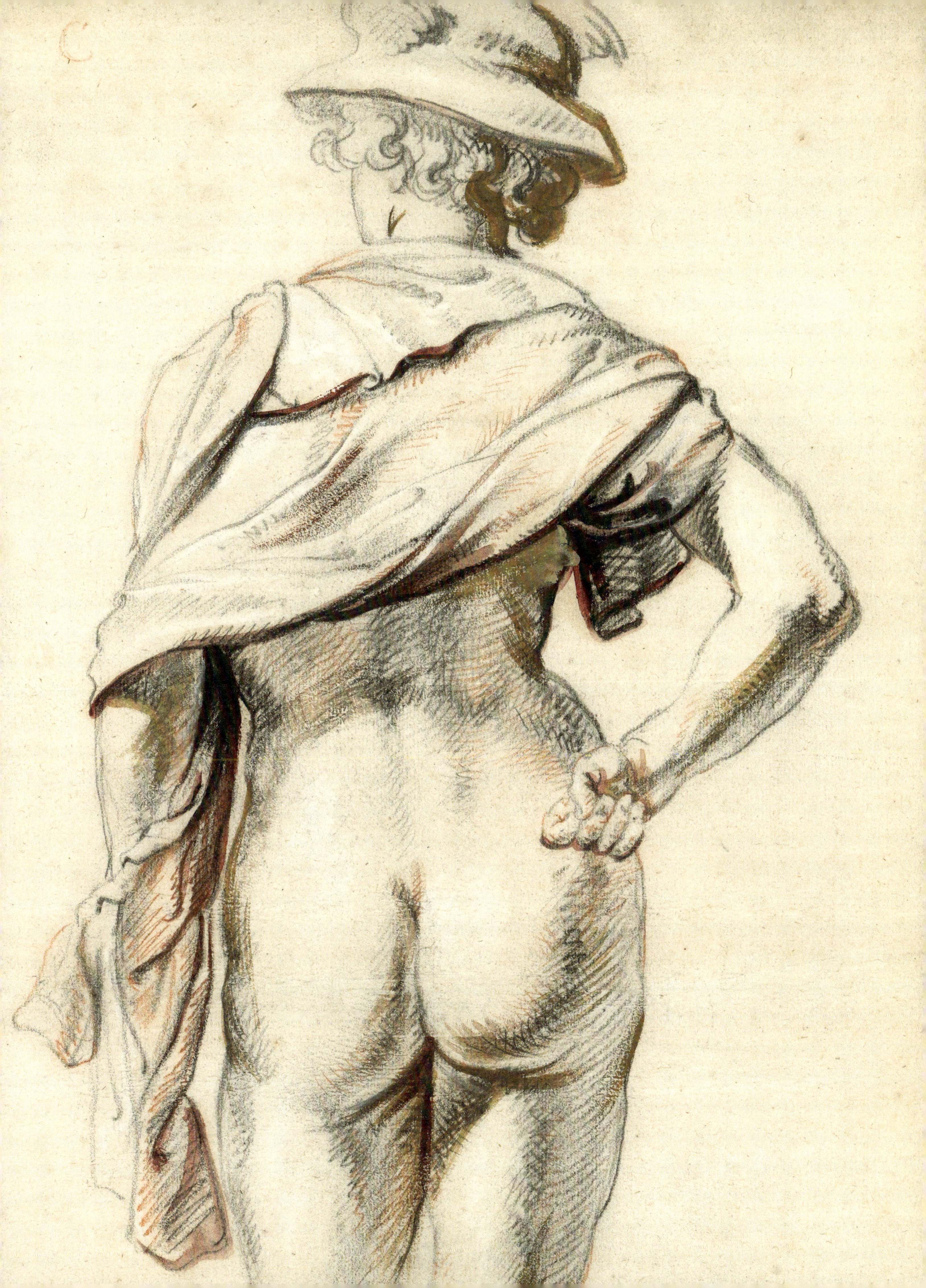

JACOB JORDAENS

Antwerp 1593–1678 Antwerp

27

The Birth of St. John the Baptist, ca. 1660–65

Black, red, and white chalk, with pen and brown ink, red chalk wash, black/gray and blue wash, on paper consisting of three parts, joined at the left, laid down
395 x 286 mm

INSCRIPTIONS Recto, lower center of tertiary support, in pen and brown ink: *Jordans*; verso, center left, in graphite: *2063* and lower right: *7440*; verso, upper left, in pen and ink: Bb N° 48

PROVENANCE Sir Francis Ferrand Foljambe (1750–1814), Osberton Hall, Scofton, near Worksop, Nottinghamshire; thence by decent; C.G. Boerner, New York and Düsseldorf; from whom acquired by Clement C. Moore, 2013

SELECT REFERENCES Van Tuinen 2018, 26, 32, n. 61

Promised gift of Clement C. and Elizabeth Y. Moore

The episode of the birth of St. John the Baptist is recounted in the Gospel of St. Luke. The priest Zacharias and his wife Elizabeth were an older couple who had remained childless. One day, while Zacharias was burning incense in the temple, the archangel Gabriel visited him and announced that Elizabeth would bear a son, who was to be named John. Zacharias, dumbfounded, expressed disbelief and, as a result, lost his ability to speak (Luke 1:5–20). After the baby's birth, Zacharias wrote on his tablet: "His name is John." His speech immediately returned (Luke 1:57–64).

In this beautifully balanced composition in hues of red, gray, and a touch of light blue, Jordaens, one of the three giants of seventeenth-century Flemish art together with Rubens and Van Dyck, depicted Zacharias clutching his tablet at the far left of this charming maternity scene. His left hand is pressed against his left cheek as a visual reminder of his loss of speech. Elizabeth is sitting upright in a red canopy bed under an oculus dome. While one woman is handing her a bowl of sustenance, in the central foreground a group of five other women is preparing the infant's bath, of whom the bespectacled eldest is gazing intently at the chubby newborn. With his usual penchant for drama, Jordaens depicted the other four women in the midst of a dynamic exchange in which all attention is directed at the young woman reaching for the big vessel in the right foreground, who is, in a sense, about to baptize the Baptist. At the same time, Jordaens's brilliant use of the reserve of the paper in the clothing and skin tones creates a subtle luminosity and the illusion that the child is emanating light.

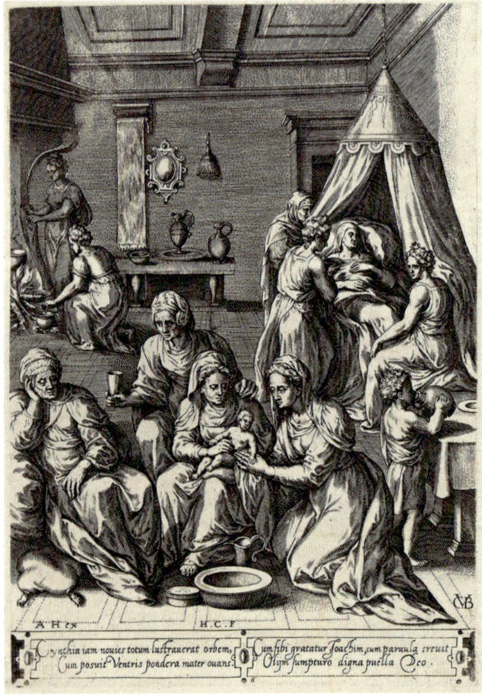

27.1 Hans Collaert the Elder (after Crispijn van den Broeck), *The Birth of the Virgin*, 1576. Rijksprentenkabinet, Amsterdam.

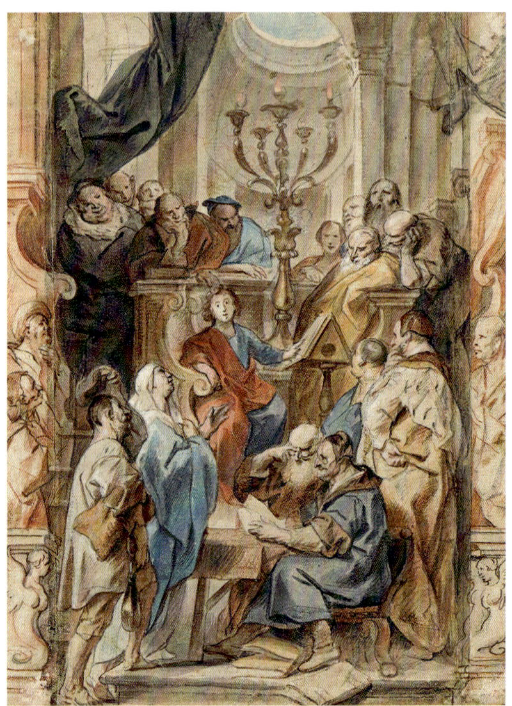

27.2 Jacob Jordaens, *Christ among the Doctors*, ca. 1663. Morgan Library & Museum, New York.

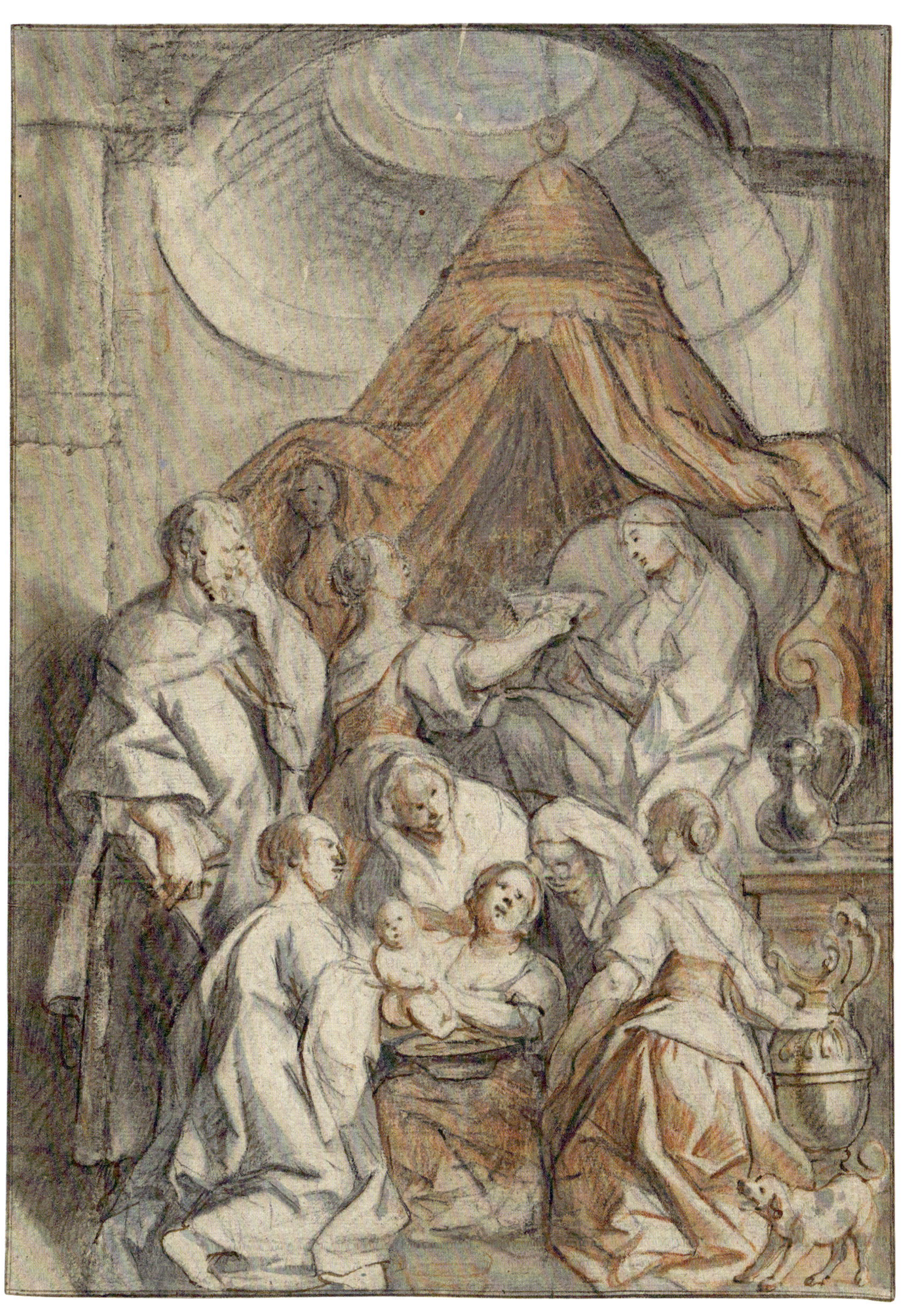

In 2013, this drawing, then entirely unknown, appeared with the gallery C.G. Boerner, where it was catalogued as *The Birth of the Virgin*.[1] After acquiring the work, however, Clement Moore recognized the correct subject matter based on the presence of Zacharias.[2] Boerner's initial identification is understandable, because in the rich pictorial tradition there are many similarities between the two birth scenes.[3] In fact, an important visual source for Jordaens appears to have been a sixteenth-century print of the Birth of the Virgin—not John the Baptist—executed by Hans Collaert the Elder after the Antwerp artist Crispijn van den Broeck (fig. 27.1).[4] Even though the print is more densely populated, the general compositional division between the care for the new mother in the background and that for the newborn in the foreground, a recurring iconographical construct, is similar. Especially striking in this particular print is the similar, tent-like canopy hanging from a chain suspended from the ceiling.

It is likely that Jordaens executed the Moore drawing in preparation for a painting or part of an altarpiece, perhaps in a chapel or church dedicated to St. John, but no related work is known. Like the majority of Jordaens's drawings, this sheet is not dated. The relatively sober palette and confident, angular contour lines point to a date in the latter part of his career, probably somewhere in the 1660s, Jordaens's last active decade. A date around 1660–65 seems plausible, given that Jordaens experimented with the motif of the oculus dome around this time, as in two studies for *Christ among the Doctors* of ca. 1663, one of which is at the Morgan Library & Museum (fig. 27.2).[5]

There has yet to emerge a thorough analysis of Jordaens's highly idiosyncratic tendency of cutting and pasting pieces of paper together as part of his artistic practice. In this case, he joined two narrow vertical pieces of paper at the left.[6] Since the media on the added strips of paper are consistent with the rest of the drawing and since one of the additions runs through the back of key figure Zacharias, it is likely that Jordaens had already prepared the sheet in this way before he started drawing.[7] **IvT**

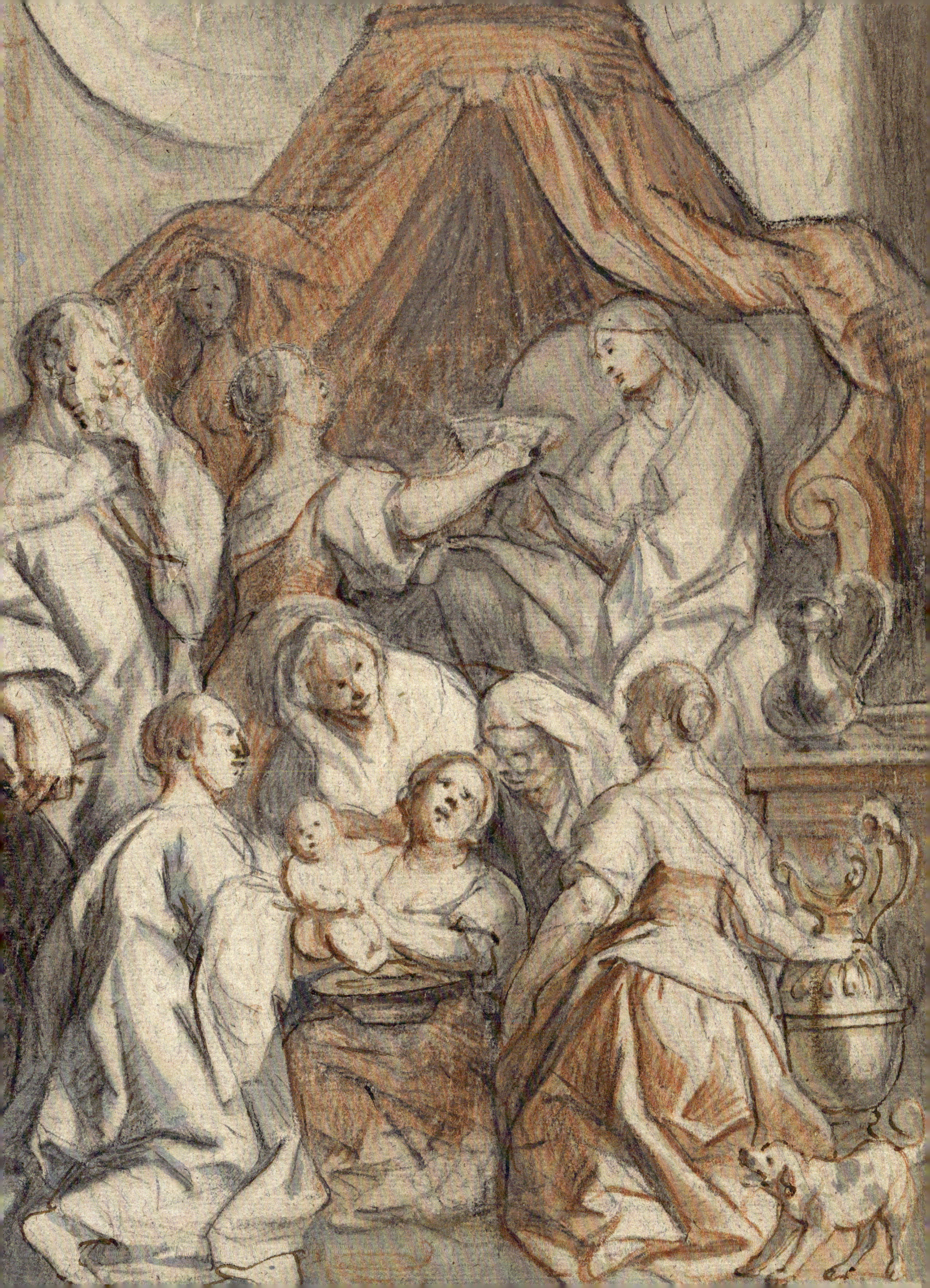

JAN VAN DE VELDE II

Rotterdam or Delft 1593–1641 Enkhuizen

28

A View of the Ruin of the Huis ter Kleef, near Haarlem, ca. 1615

Pen and brown ink, over black chalk
178 x 285 mm

WATERMARK Crowned coat of arms with the Golden Fleece

PROVENANCE Acquired on the English art market by a private collection, ca. 1967–68; thence by descent; Christie's, London, 5 July 2021, lot 33; where acquired by Clement C. Moore

SELECT REFERENCES Fucci 2022a, 11–12

Promised gift of Clement C. and Elizabeth Y. Moore

This is one of the most significant drawings by Jan van de Velde to emerge in recent years, coming to light at auction in 2021. The composition was already known through a drawing in the Kupferstichkabinett, Berlin, long suspected to be a copy, its status further confirmed by the appearance of the original.[1] The work depicts the ruins of the Huis ter Kleef, an important castle just north of Haarlem that was destroyed during the Dutch Revolt after the Spanish successfully besieged the city in 1572–73.[2] With an intriguing twist, the artist added mountains in the background, ones that simply do not exist in the province of Holland. With his conflation of real and imaginary elements, Jan van de Velde reveals an interesting facet of his lifelong engagement with ruins. He sometimes cast them as sites of memory, reflective of traumatic wartime events from the not-too-distant past, but he also used ruins, as here, to create evocative images in a different aesthetic register, ones dislocated from time and specific place.[3]

The Huis ter Kleef played a dark role during the siege since it served as the headquarters for the commander of the Spanish army, Don Fadrique. When the city finally fell in July 1573, he ordered the execution of nearly the entire garrison of around 2,000 men, a notoriously bloody act that proved as infamous as the massacres the same army had carried out in Mechelen, Zutphen, and Naarden the year before. The Spanish destroyed the Huis ter Kleef before the main army left the area so it could not be used by Dutch forces to recapture the city. The fantastical nature of Van de Velde's background might seem surprising given the gravitas that was conferred on the ruin by contemporary Haarlemers. The minister Samuel Ampzing, for example, wrote verses for a captioned print of the ruin for his 1628 history of Haarlem, stating in no uncertain terms his odium for the Spanish.[4] After noting that it served as Don Fadrique's camp, he goes on to say: "Who founded it nobody knows for certain / But how it was destroyed has not been forgotten / Fie on the Spaniards who oppressed our country so sorely!"[5] Van de Velde designed, etched, and engraved a number of images of the Huis ter Kleef that indeed more soberly emphasize its significance as a relic of the war.[6] The most substantial of these is his large-scale panorama of Haarlem (411 x 1615 mm), engraved on three plates after a design by Pieter Molijn, which foregrounds the ruin as a symbol of the suffering and survival of the city.[7] He also supplied an illustration of the Huis ter Kleef for Ampzing's aforementioned book. In fact, Jan van de Velde made more drawings and prints of the ruin than any other artist of

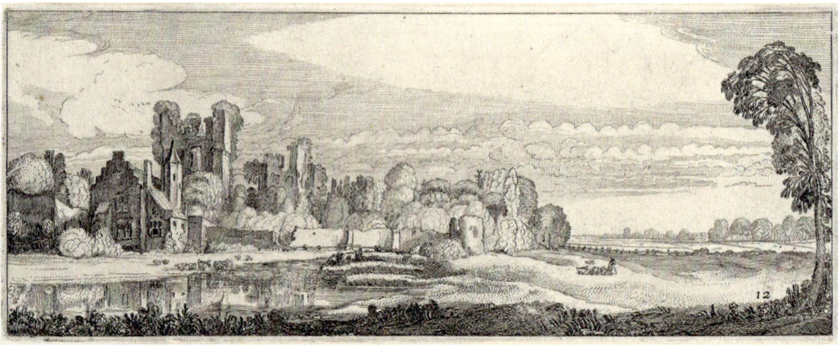

28.1 Jan van de Velde II, *Huis ter Kleef*, from the *Amoenissimae aliquot regiunculae*, 1615. Rijksprentenkabinet, Amsterdam.

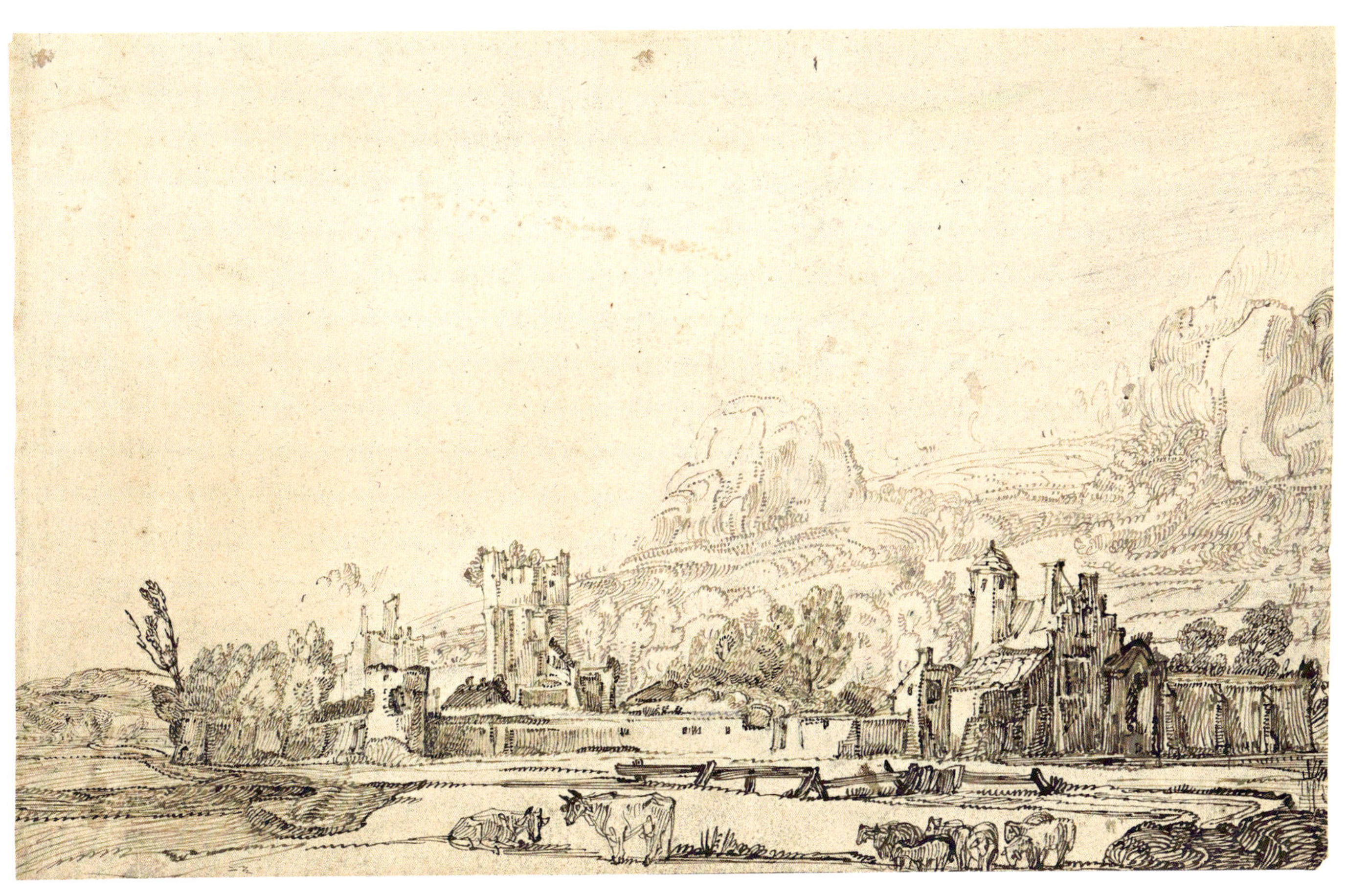

his generation. The same holds true for some of the other wartime ruins in the area, such as those of Brederode Castle.[8]

Van de Velde may have had a print in mind when he drew this image. This same view of the Huis ter Kleef appears in slightly modified form in his landmark series of etchings, the *Amoenissimae aliquot regiunculae et antiquorum momumentorum ruinae* (Some Most Pleasant Places and Ruins of Antique Monuments) published in 1615 (fig. 28.1).[9] The eighteen plates in this series imaginatively combine real and invented architectures, mostly set in prosaic and indeed visibly "pleasing" rural settings. The present drawing was not strictly preparatory for the plate showing the Huis ter Kleef, but a number of elements were adapted for the etching.[10] The span of the full enclosure, running from the stepped-gable house on the right to the short tower on the left appears cast in reverse on the plate, with various elements and the overall width quite close in scale to the Moore drawing, which has been trimmed slightly on either side (as revealed by the Berlin copy). He modified elements of the ruin within the enclosure, however, and encrusted it with additional foliage, suggesting a place further lost in time. Since the *Amoenissimae aliquot regiunculae* was Jan van de Velde's first major published work, this drawing is likewise probably one of his earliest to survive. With a date of creation around 1615, it also serves as one of our earliest extant images of this historically significant ruin. It was later dismantled, and today only parts of the foundation remain visible. **RF**

CORNELIS VAN POELENBURCH

Utrecht 1594/95–1667 Utrecht

29

Study of River and Rocks (recto) and *Study of a Statuette of Two Fighting Figures* (verso), ca. 1622–24

Pen and brown ink, with brown wash, over traces of black chalk or graphite (recto); red chalk and graphite (verso)
287 x 185 mm

INSCRIPTIONS Verso, lower left, signed, in red chalk: CP

PROVENANCE Christie's, Amsterdam, 21 November 1989, lot 84; private collection, Amsterdam; Haboldt and Co., Paris and New York, by 1991; private collection; Sotheby's, London, 6 July 2010, lot 60; where acquired by Clement C. Moore

SELECT REFERENCES Plomp 2020, 463; Mackelaitė 2022

Promised gift of Clement C. and Elizabeth Y. Moore

Cornelis van Poelenburch was concerned with the study of landscape and the investigation of the human form throughout his career.[1] The present sheet, which dates from the artist's early years, exemplifies this dual interest. Executed predominantly in brush, the recto depicts a large, rocky outcrop. The sun illuminates the left side of the boulder and is reflected off the curly foliage growing out of its crevices. With only a few touches of wash, Poelenburch transforms the foreground into a river or stream and describes the soft reflections of rocks on its gleaming surface. Visual affinities—low viewpoint, the reliance on loose, broadly applied passages of brown wash, and an interest in chiaroscuro effects—connect the study to works made between 1622 and 1624, towards the end of Poelenburch's Italian sojourn.[2] Similar large rocks executed in soft gray and brown tones were a recurrent feature in Poelenburch's painted landscapes from this time onward, providing rugged backdrops for his religious and mythological scenes.[3]

On the verso, a young male nude is depicted trampling a supine adversary, ready to strike him with a weapon held in his unfinished right hand. Using compact strokes of red chalk, Poelenburch painstakingly described the figure's complex musculature and twisting pose, conveying a palpable sense of three-dimensionality. While this exact configuration is not repeated in any of the artist's paintings, the standing man reappears in the guise of mythological figures, such as Mercury in *Mercury Holding Argus's Severed Head*, one of the painted panels that decorate the so-called Portland cabinet in the Welbeck Estate, Nottinghamshire (fig. 29.1).[4] In fact, the shading employed by Poelenburch for the painted Mercury follows the present drawing so closely that it seems likely that the Moore sheet served as a direct model for the painted figure.

A study in the Rijksprentenkabinet, Amsterdam, also combines a loosely drawn landscape on the recto with a red chalk figure on the verso (fig. 29.2).[5] Although the Amsterdam and the Moore nudes have been observed from different directions, the positions of their legs, their forward-thrusting torsos, and their left arms are identical, suggesting that the two sketches originated from the same model—either a small-scale bronze or a terracotta, with part of its round plinth visible underneath the trampled man in the Moore sheet.[6] Attempts to identify Poelenburch's sculptural model remain inconclusive. As observed by

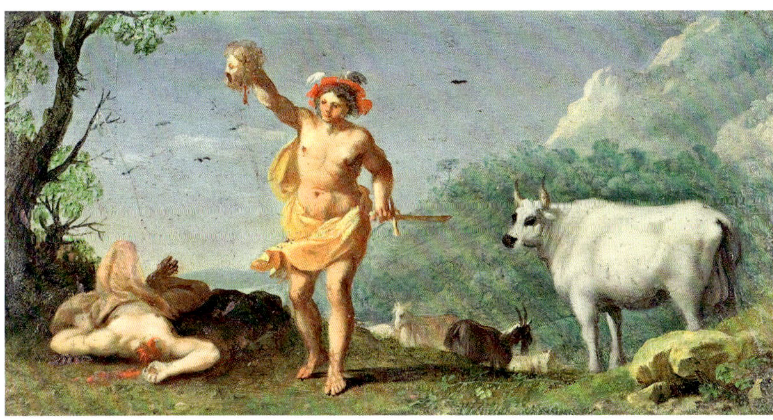

29.1 Cornelis van Poelenburch, *Mercury Holding Argus's Severed Head*, ca. 1625–36. Portland Collection, Welbeck Estate, Nottinghamshire.

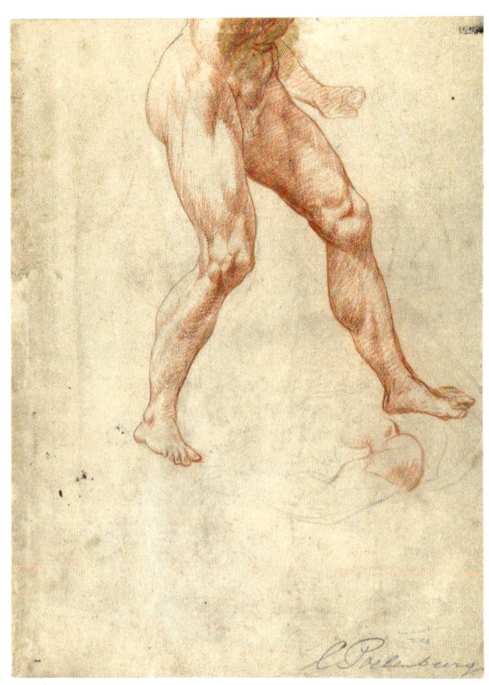

29.2 Cornelis van Poelenburch, *Study of the Lower Body of a Walking Male Nude*, ca. 1622–24. Rijksprentenkabinet, Amsterdam.

Frits Scholten, the standing figure's upper body is likely derived from the famous Hellenistic marble of a dancing faun in the Tribuna of the Uffizi, Florence.[7] Taken as a whole, however, the iconography of the statuette copied by Poelenburch seems far removed from this playful ancient work, instead bringing to mind small-scale sculpture groups depicting the Archangel Michael Vanquishing the Devil or Virtue Punishing Vice.

Crucially, Poelenburch's monogram "CP" appears in the lower left corner of the verso. The sheet thus belongs to an extremely small core group of works that can be attributed to the Utrecht master on grounds other than style. Even more significant is the fact that the Moore sheet is the only signed red chalk drawing by the artist. As such, it carries significant ramifications for how we understand an intriguing group of later works by Poelenburch—a small group of red chalk figure drawings that relate to paintings from the artist's years in Utrecht, including no. 30. Although Alan Chong accepted these drawings as autograph on the basis of style, questions regarding their attribution and function have continued to linger.[8] The monogrammed verso of the present sheet is a strong argument in favor of Poelenburch as the artist responsible for the group. While the drawing undoubtedly shows the artist at an earlier stage of his development, the overall graphic language—characterized by the methodical use of dense hatching and crosshatching, the close attention to the distribution of light and shade, and the careful delineation of contour—is highly consistent with what we see in the artist's later figure studies, solidifying their place in Poelenburch's oeuvre. AM

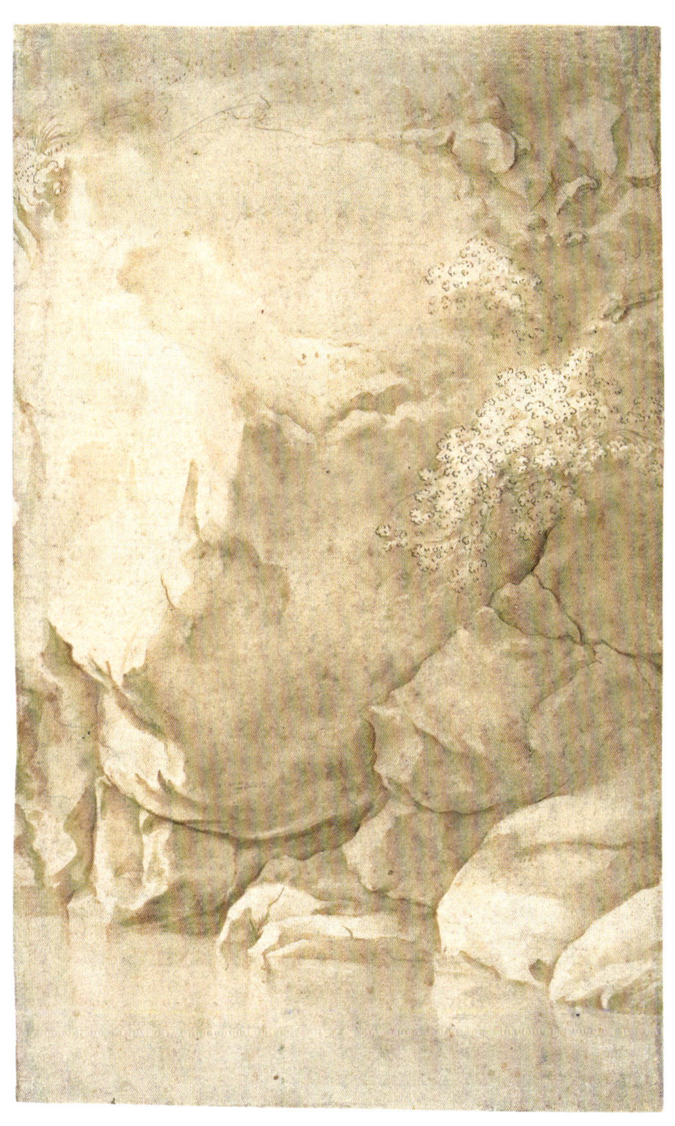

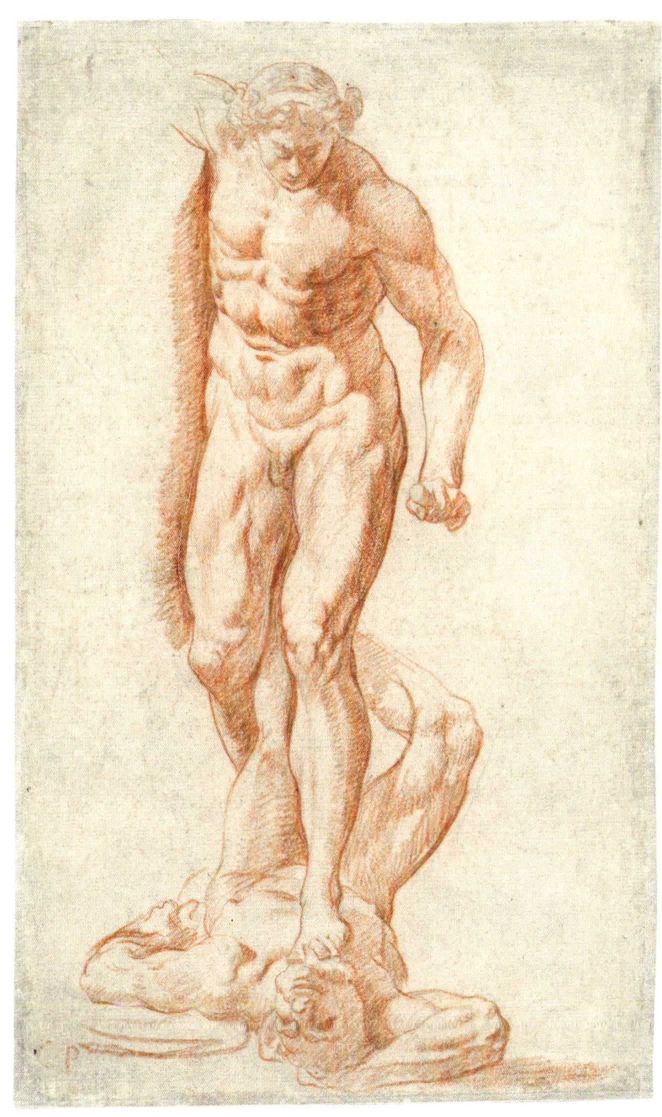

CORNELIS VAN POELENBURCH

Utrecht 1594/95–1667 Utrecht

30

Two Bathers, ca. 1635

Red chalk
186 x 287 mm

INSCRIPTIONS Verso, lower right, in pen and brown ink: N°. 401

PROVENANCE Fritz Hasselmann (d. 1894), Munich (L. 1012, verso, lower right); his sale, Hugo Helbing, Munich, 24–27 November 1892, lot 550 (as "Italienische Schule, 18. Jahrh."); private collection, Germany; Martin Grässle Kunsthandel, Munich; from whom acquired by Clement C. Moore, 2021

Promised gift of Clement C. and Elizabeth Y. Moore

This recently discovered sheet is a new addition to the sizable corpus of drawings by Cornelis van Poelenburch. Two women wrapped in folds of voluminous drapery sit side by side in a scantily rendered landscape. While the figures bring to mind mythological imagery—for instance, episodes of the goddess Diana and her entourage of bathing nymphs—the drawing is entirely devoid of narrative details or attributes. Instead, Poelenburch focuses on describing the soft and supple bodies of the two women. The impression of smooth, luminous flesh—one of the qualities that also distinguish female figures in his painted compositions—is created through meticulous and dense application of parallel- and crosshatching in red chalk. Typically for Poelenburch, the heavily worked and sharply outlined figures are set against the untouched background, creating a striking impression of relief.

The drawing belongs to a group of red chalk studies that bear close relationships to paintings that Poelenburch produced after his return from Italy to the Low Countries in 1625.[1] In the case of the present sheet, the seated woman at right is nearly identical to the nude bather included in a small painting that recently appeared on the German art market (fig. 30.1),[2] and she also shares many similarities with the figure seen in the far right corner of Poelenburch's most famous rendering of a literary subject—*Amaryllis Crowning Myrtillo* (1635) at the Gemäldegalerie, Berlin.[3]

While the drawing has a clear connection to the artist's painted oeuvre, the question of whether a work of this type was intended to serve as a preparatory study or as a *ricordo* of a completed composition is difficult to answer conclusively. The high degree of finish, a peculiarly fragmented approach to the visual field, a summary way of depicting limbs and faces, and a very close relationship with the finished pictures, which characterize many of the drawings in the

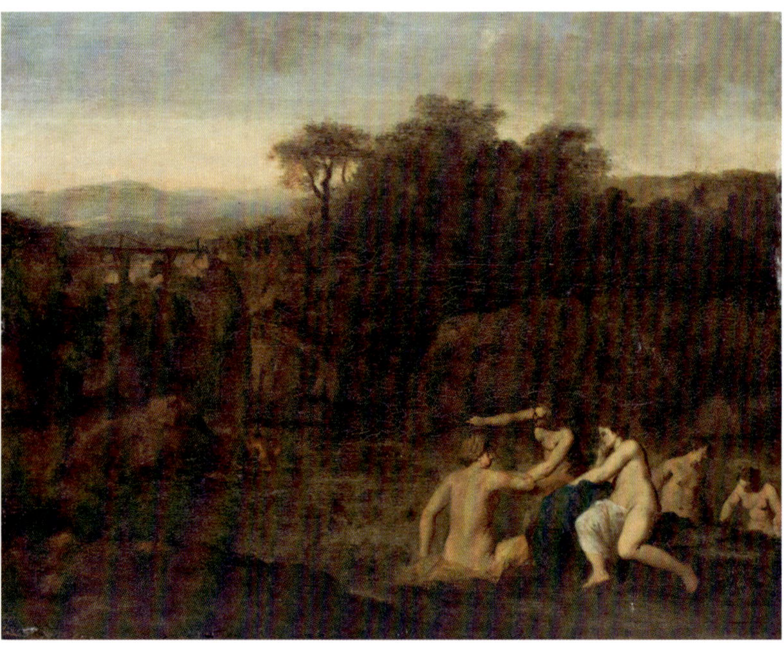

30.1 Cornelis van Poelenburch, *Bathing Women*, ca. 1635 (?). Present whereabouts unknown.

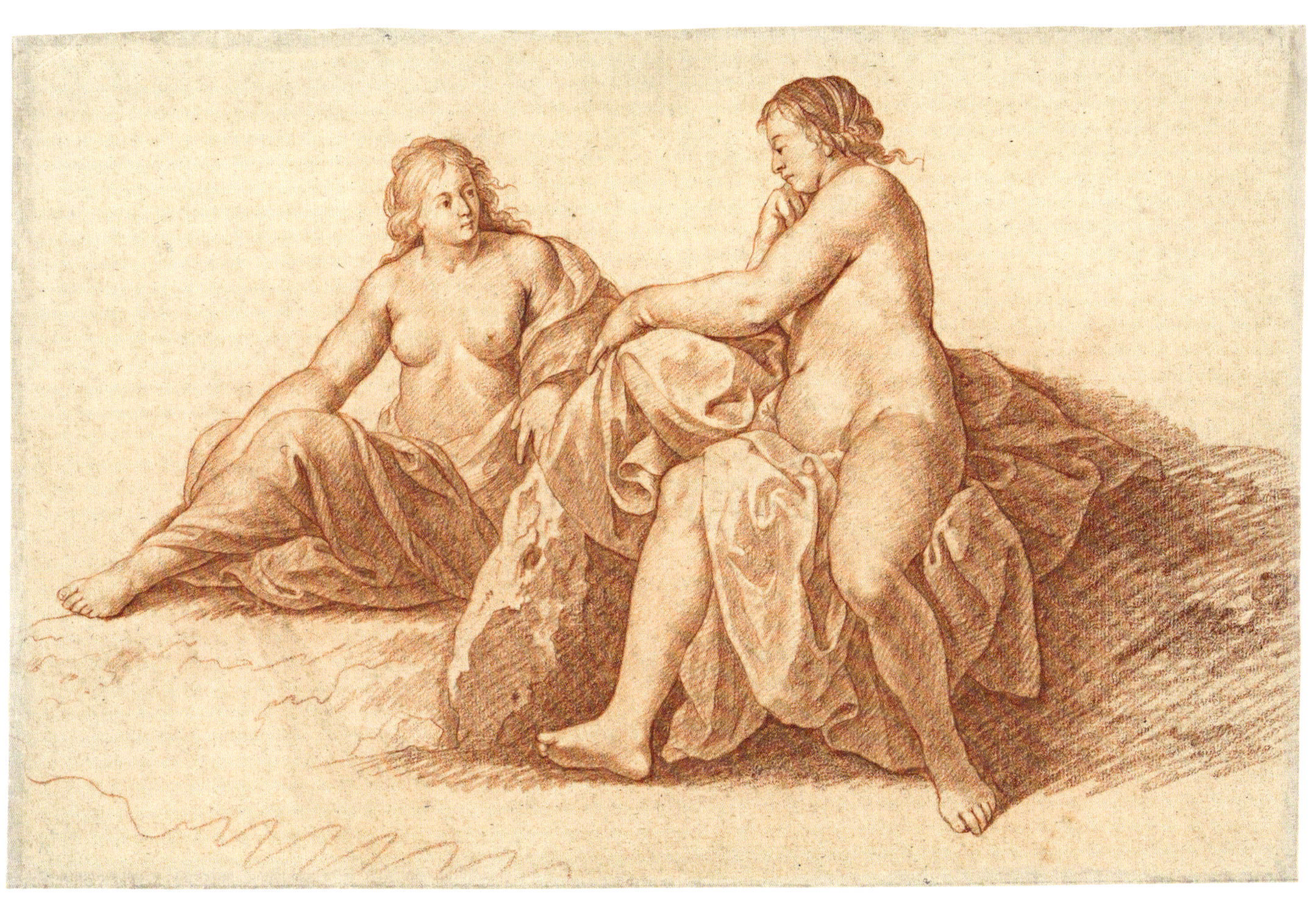

red chalk group, has led some scholars to suggest that they were all produced after Poelenburch's paintings, either by the artist himself or by members of his circle.[4] Alan Chong, in the meantime, has argued for a more nuanced and varied understanding of the group, suggesting that the sheets had a variety of functions in Poelenburch's creative process.[5]

Drawings that focus on a single figural group, like the present sheet, could indeed have been created as part of Poelenburch's preparatory process and then used in composing his paintings. A similar approach characterizes the luminous gray wash landscape drawings that Poelenburch was producing in Utrecht at around this time. Those compositions—just like the red chalk sheets—were incorporated verbatim in the artist's paintings, suggesting that he used a cut-and-paste approach to composing his painted work from various landscape and figural studies.[6] Finally, Chong's contention that the entire red chalk group should be attributed to Poelenburch himself is supported by the monogrammed red chalk verso of the other drawing by the artist in the Moore collection (no. 29). AM

BARTHOLOMEUS BREENBERGH

Deventer 1598–1657 Amsterdam

31

View of the Torre di Chia, ca. 1624 or after 1629

Pen and brown ink and wash, over black chalk, with later additions in gray wash
393 x 523 mm

WATERMARK Strasbourg lily in a crowned shield

INSCRIPTIONS Verso, upper left, in red pencil: B; verso, upper right, in red pencil (partially trimmed): 12; verso, lower center, in brown ink: *Bisshop*; verso, lower left, in graphite: *Jan de bisschop*; verso, lower right, in pencil: *NO clean. / ATTN only.*

PROVENANCE Christie's, London, 23 March 1982, lot 68; Baskett & Day, London, 1982; private collection, Kent; Day & Faber, London, 2004; from whom acquired by Clement C. Moore, 2006

SELECT REFERENCES Baskett & Day 1982, no. 22; Roethlisberger 1985, 66, n. 19 (as a copy by Jan de Bisschop, made in 1640); Day & Faber 2004, no. 8; Verdi 2004, no. 12; Fucci 2022b, 57, under no. 8, n. 20

Promised gift of Clement C. and Elizabeth Y. Moore

This is a connoisseur's drawing, posing one of the most challenging attributional issues faced by collectors and curators: how to distinguish a prime version, from an autograph replica, from a copy by another hand?[1] It is widely known that Breenbergh made second and third replicas of views drawn in Italy, where he was active for a decade from the age of twenty (1619–29). This is especially true of drawings carried out when he was apparently working for Paolo Giordano Orsini II, a major patron who in 1615 inherited the duchy of Bracciano, which included sites in the province of Viterbo, northwest of Rome, among them the gardens of Bomarzo and the thirteenth-century Torre di Chia.

The Moore sheet is one of three versions of the present composition.[2] The others are slightly smaller: one, in the Beaux-Arts de Paris (323 x 475 mm; fig. 31.1), is also on a sketchbook or album page with a central fold;[3] the other, signed and dated 1624, is in the Hermitage Museum, St. Petersburg (330 x 452 mm; fig. 31.2).[4] Similarly, there are three versions of the *Landscape with a Road below Cliffs, near Bracciano*: one in the Albertina (379 x 543 mm), also on a folded album page;[5] one in the Peck Collection, Ackland Art Museum (252 x 324 mm);[6] and a signed, but undated version in the J. Paul Getty Museum (409 x 562 mm).[7] Another instance of replicated compositions is the *View of Tivoli Downstream of the Great Waterfall*, recorded in a sheet in the Metropolitan Museum of Art (328 x 433 mm)[8] and in a signed and dated version (1626) in a private collection, also on a folded album page (346 x 511 mm).[9]

In all these cases, opinions vary as to which composition was the prototype and which were the autograph replicas. Richard Verdi believes the Moore drawing—characterized by delicate and nervous pen lines and subtle, transparent washes—to be the earliest version of the *Torre di Chia* composition, a conclusion shared by the late Egbert Haverkamp-Begemann, who considered the Paris sheet to be an elaboration of it, and the signed and dated Hermitage sheet to be a rather coarse simplification of the Paris composition.[10] This supposition is bolstered by the fact that only the Moore drawing features underdrawing in black chalk, as might be expected of a sketch made on the spot. This, of course, is not conclusive evidence.

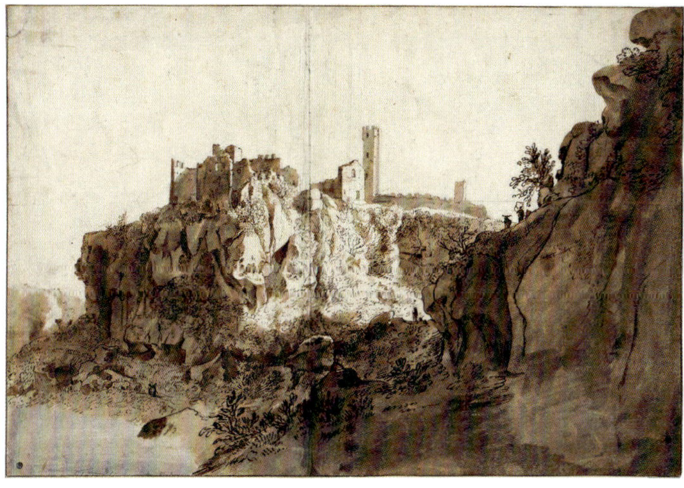

31.1 Bartholomeus Breenbergh, *View of the Torre di Chia*, ca. 1624. Beaux-Arts de Paris.

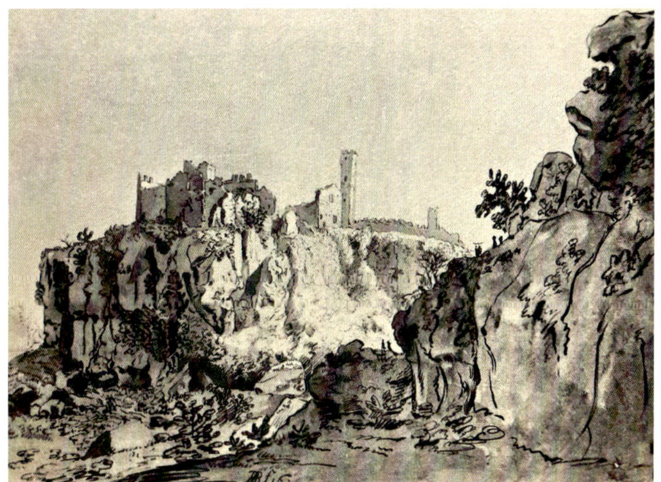

31.2 Bartholomeus Breenbergh, *View of the Torre di Chia*, 1624. State Hermitage Museum, St. Petersburg.

The Albertina and Getty versions of the *Bracciano* composition have black chalk, while the Peck sheet has none. In the case of the two abovementioned Tivoli views, both include traces of black chalk, but, as Stijn Alsteens noted, the paper of the private collection version of 1626 has an Italian watermark of a Strasbourg lily within a crowned circle;[11] the Metropolitan version and the Moore drawing, by contrast, have a later watermark, a crowned coat of arms with a Strasbourg lily, pointing to a date after Breenbergh's return to the Netherlands. Both the Beaux-Arts de Paris view of the *Torre di Chia* and the Peck drawing of *Bracciano* are on Italian paper with a different watermark, a six-pointed star above a crown.

The curious passages of gray wash at the lower left corner and the sky of the present drawing seem to be later additions. The corner was left blank in what Verdi and Haverkamp-Begemann assume to be the first replica in Paris, while it was filled in with imaginary foliage for the signed and dated Hermitage composition, presumably in order to make it into a more fully resolved scene intended for sale.

The question of the authorship of the Moore sheet is complicated by one further wrinkle. Owing to two inscriptions with the name of Jan de Bisschop on the verso, it was assumed by Marcel Roethlisberger to be a copy by De Bisschop after the Paris sheet. De Bisschop apparently never traveled to Italy and could never have visited the Torre di Chia. Yet his draftsmanship, with its broad, sometimes sharply defined areas of wash next to the blank areas of white paper, which create dramatic effects of light, so closely resembles that of Breenbergh that it is widely assumed that the younger artist trained with Breenbergh once he had returned to Amsterdam (see no. 62).[12] Learning by copying was standard practice for budding artists, and it is known that De Bisschop made two etchings after paintings by Breenbergh,[13] the lost *Joseph Selling Corn to the People*, formerly in Dresden (1644; destroyed), and the *Martyrdom of St. Lawrence* (1647) in the Städel Museum, Frankfurt am Main.[14] Two Italian sheets by De Bisschop in the Albertina—*Ripa Grande* and *SS. Giovanni e Paolo, Rome*, both previously attributed to Breenbergh—could record unknown models by Breenbergh.[15] None of these copies, however, is on Italian paper or on a sheet as large as the present work. **JST**

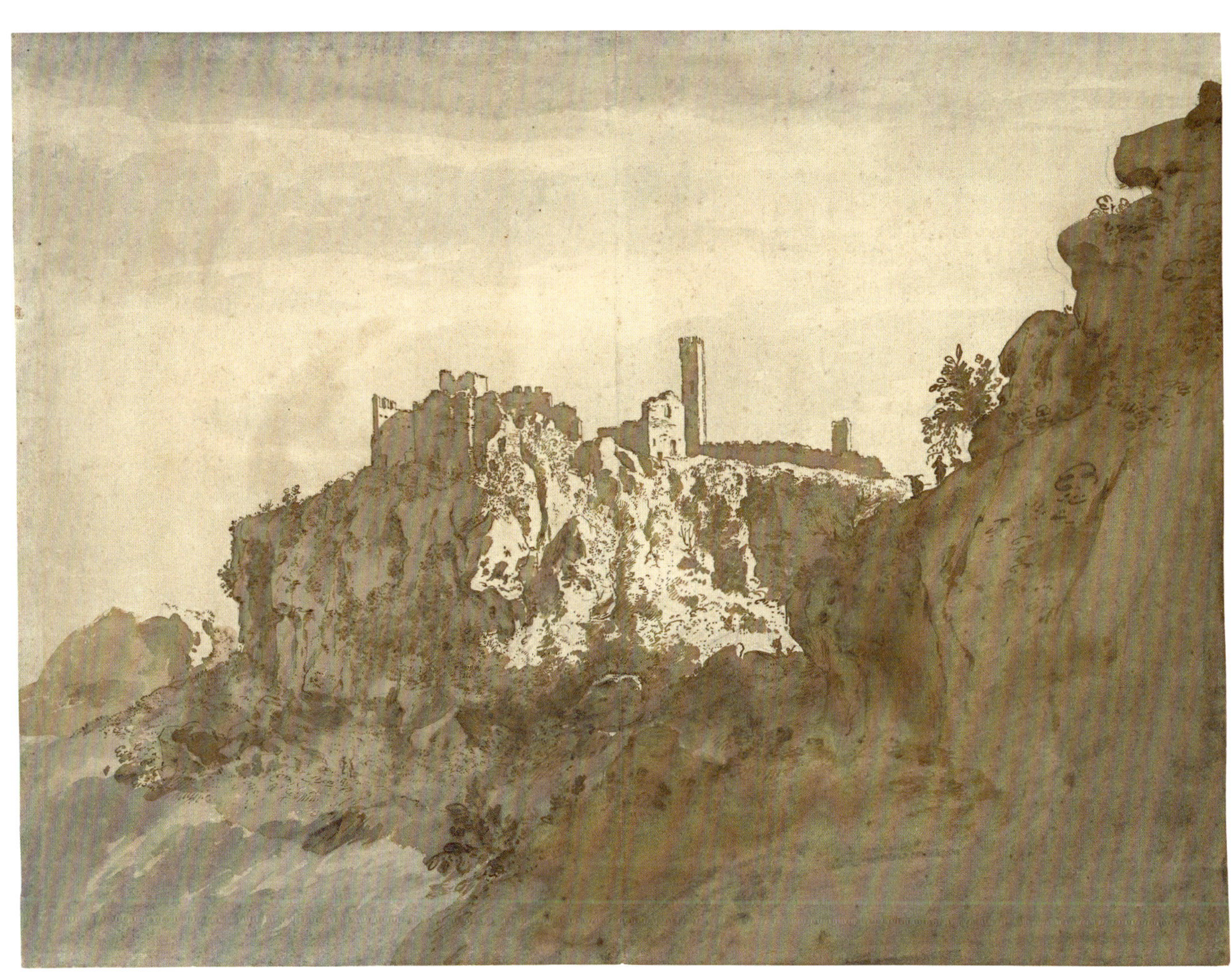

ANTHONY VAN DYCK

Antwerp 1599–1641 London

32

Study of Hands (recto) and *Figure Studies* (verso), ca. 1627–29

Black and white chalk on blue paper
227 x 237 mm

WATERMARK Quadruped in upper left quadrant

PROVENANCE Dr. Ludwig Burchard (1886–1960), Leipzig and London; his sale, Christie's, New York, 28 January 1999, lot 97; Thomas Williams Fine Arts, London; from whom acquired by Clement C. Moore, 2018

Promised gift of Clement C. and Elizabeth Y. Moore

The more than 300 surviving drawings by Anthony van Dyck offer a rich body of evidence with which to reconstruct his working method.[1] For his subject pictures, he began with compositional studies in pen and ink, often devising several possible compositions before settling on one and subsequently turning to studies of individual figures or details, usually in black chalk. For portraits, he often started directly with a chalk drawing. For all types of paintings, and from across his career, there are also detailed studies in chalk for the expressive hands that animate his compositions.[2] Rogier de Piles noted that Van Dyck employed his studio assistants as hand models, and on this basis Christopher Brown suggested that Van Dyck created a pattern book of hands.[3] And yet, although enough examples exist to imply that Van Dyck often made such hand studies, they are today surprisingly rare for an artist by whom so many drawings are known.[4] The Morgan is said to have the most comprehensive collection of Van Dyck's drawings in North America, for example, but hitherto, no drawing comparable to the present sheet.[5]

It is possible, however, that there are fewer hand studies than might be expected because Van Dyck may have used one drawing for multiple paintings. The hands studied on the recto of the Moore drawing, for example, were almost certainly originally drawn for the figure of St. Dominic in the *Christ on the Cross with St. Dominic and St. Catherine of Siena* (fig. 32.1).[6] Shortly before Van Dyck's father died in 1622, he expressed a wish that his son would paint an altarpiece for the Dominican convent of Sint-Catharina. Van Dyck presumably began the canvas soon after his return to Antwerp in 1627, and it was installed in 1629. The drawing matches the saint's hands in every detail of pose, highlight, and shadow. Yet, the drawn hands have also been compared to those of the *Virgin Mary as Intercessor* at the National Gallery of Art, Washington, and to those of the *St. Francis of Assisi* in the Musées Royaux des Beaux-Arts de Belgique, Brussels.[7] Both of these paintings were undertaken in the same period as the *Christ on the Cross*, and, although slight differences exist between the painted hands and those in the Moore drawing, one can easily imagine how Van Dyck might have repurposed the sheet.

The study of legs on the verso of the sheet, clearly a fragment of a larger drawing, cannot be definitively linked to any painting. Rather than a detailed study akin to the hands on the recto, however, the verso seems more like a compositional sketch, even if Van Dyck generally employed pen and ink for such drawings. Given his habit of making numerous sketches for a composition, this could perhaps be a variant idea for the angel at far right in the *Lamentation* now at the Alte Pinakothek, Munich, another painting from the same phase of Van Dyck's career.[8] JJM

32.1 Anthony van Dyck, *Christ on the Cross with St. Dominic and St. Catherine of Siena*, ca. 1627–29. Koninklijk Museum voor Schone Kunsten, Antwerp.

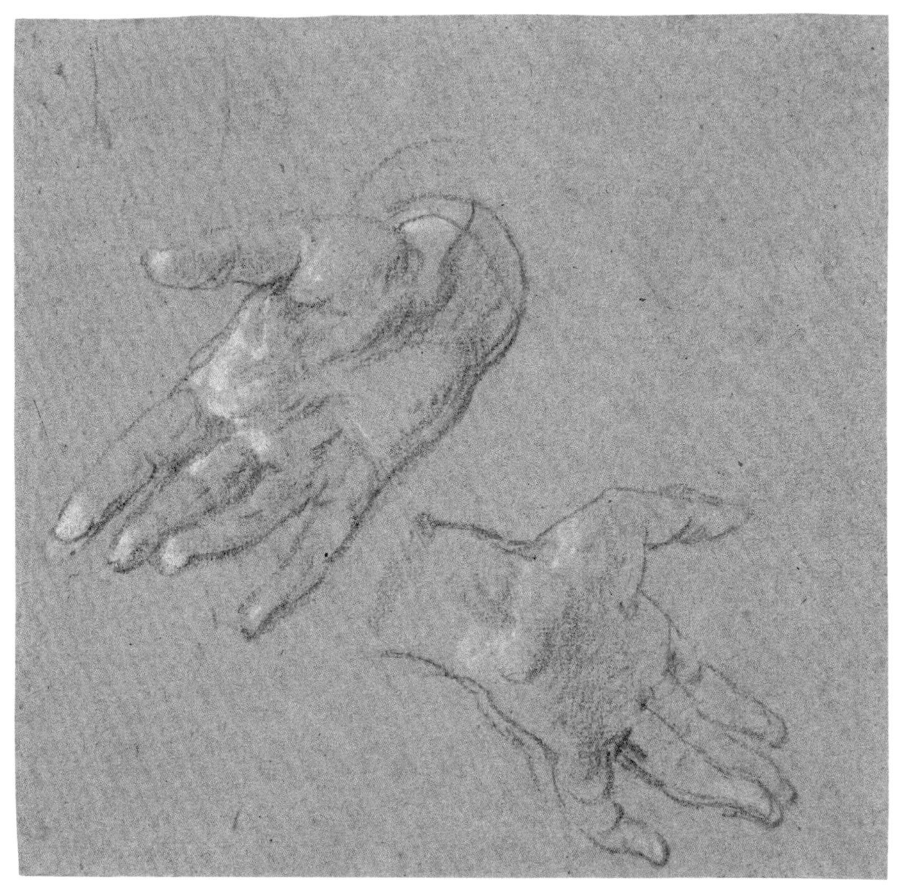

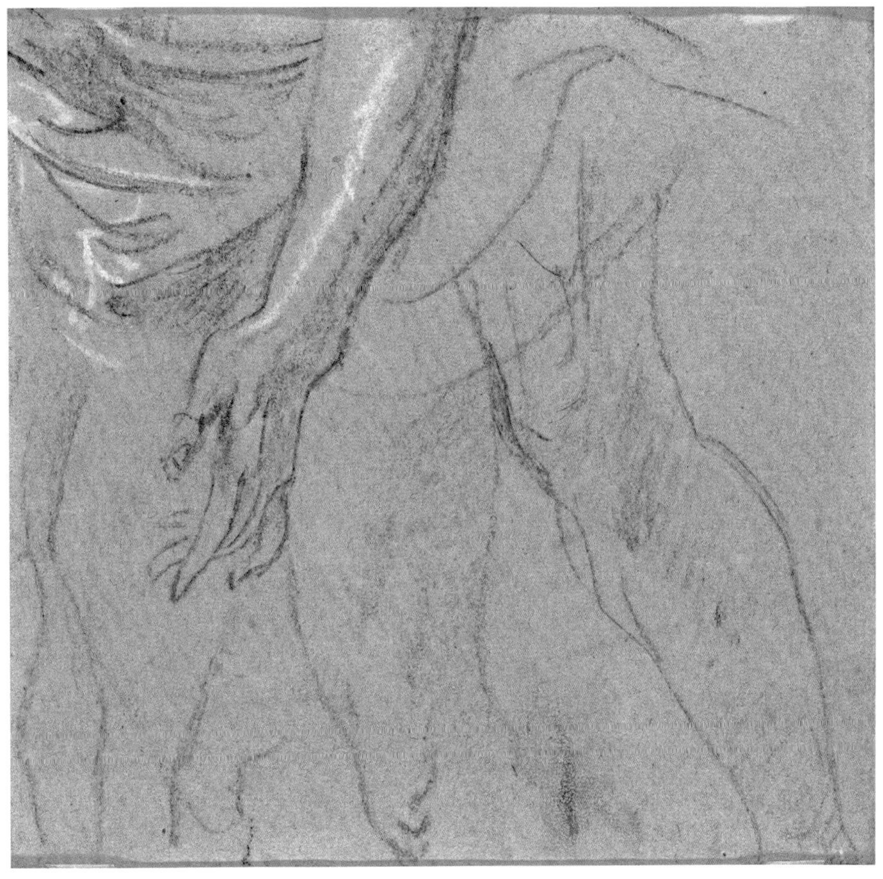

CLAUDE GELLÉE, *known as* CLAUDE LORRAIN

Chamagne (Lorraine) 1604/5–1682 Rome

33

Pastoral Landscape with a Figure by a Lake, ca. 1670–75

Black chalk and pen and brown ink, with brown, gray, and gray-brown wash; framing lines in brown ink
190 x 270 mm

INSCRIPTIONS Verso, in black chalk: *Designe facto per il^m Principe Don Gaspare*

PROVENANCE The artist's heirs; likely sold to Prince Don Livio Odescalchi (1652–1713), Rome (in an album of 81 drawings), between 1692 and 1713; by descent in the Odescalchi family to Maria Odescalchi (b. 1930) and Donato Sanminiatelli (1929–1979), Rome; album sold to Georges Wildenstein (1892–1963), Paris, 1960; acquired by Norton Simon (1907–1993), Pasadena, 1962, and dismembered, ca. 1978–80 (thereafter, as a single sheet); Artemis, London, 1980; Ladislaus von Hoffmann (1927–2014), Washington, 1989; thence by descent; W.M. Brady & Co., New York; from whom acquired by Clement C. Moore, 2018

SELECT REFERENCES Roethlisberger 1962, no. 26; Roethlisberger 1968, no. 1102; Roethlisberger 1971, no. 59; Brady 2017, no. 10; Roethlisberger 2018, 487–89

Promised gift of Clement C. and Elizabeth Y. Moore

For more than twenty years at the start of his career in Rome, Claude lived in modest circumstances in the city's quarter for foreign artists near the Piazza di Spagna. Among the artists that the young pastry chef found himself in contact with as he embarked on his effort to paint landscapes was the elder statesman of the Northern school, the Fleming Paul Bril, and a younger Dutch artist who studied under him, Bartholomeus Breenbergh (see nos. 6 and 31). Claude's early exposure to the practices of northern landscapists was critical to his development. By the 1630s he was established as a leading painter in the genre and produced a dozen paintings a year for an international aristocratic clientele.

By the 1670s, Claude's pace had slowed to around three pictures per year, though he maintained a regular drawing practice. As his biographer Filippo Baldinucci noted, by this time Claude's hands were affected by gout, causing him to limit his working hours and to leave traces of what Marcel Roethlisberger termed a "shaky, irregular duct of the pen and of the brush" in the present drawing.[1] Claude seems in his late drawings to be testing the means of creating a spacious landscape by varying the strength of his wash and the amount of penwork added. Thin veils of ink and the slightest contours make the trees and peaks in the distance seem remote, while the foreground, with its darker wash and bolder strokes, has the crisp focus of proximity. A rub of gray wash defines a small lake at center, swiftly expanding the depth of the view. The drawing has all the best elements of Claude's freshest drawings, free from overworking or the muddying effects of layered media. The open and airy quality is appealing to the modern eye but also was foundational to the history of plein air drawing.

Many of Claude's drawings come from large albums where they were grouped by theme. Twelve such albums were listed in a 1682 inventory, and Baldinucci recorded that the artist's heirs received five or six "great books of drawings of views from nature." The Moore sheet comes from an album containing drawings that Roethlisberger deemed "of the finest quality" from throughout the artist's career. Claude may have compiled the album between 1677 and 1682. If not his own creation, then the album must have been assembled in the decades following his death and before 1713, when it appears in the inventory of Prince Livio Odescalchi. It remained with the family, apparently intact, until the late 1950s, when Donato Sanminiatelli began selling at first a few sheets, then the entire album, a tale recounted by the art dealer Hans Calmann in his memoirs.[2]
The sheet remained in the album until the rapacious Californian collector Norton Simon, who had purchased the album from Wildenstein in 1962, decided around 1978–80 to dismember the volume and sell the sheets individually, thereby introducing to the market a cache of exceptionally well-preserved drawings from Claude's studio that had been kept together for nearly three hundred years.[3]

In his fundamental studies of Claude's drawings, Roethlisberger connected the present sheet with a series of studies more explicitly related to a pastoral scene produced in 1677 for Prince Lorenzo Onofrio Colonna. The painting, now in the Kimbell Art Museum, Fort Worth,[4] is recorded in the artist's *Liber Veritatis*, a book of drawings documenting the composition of paintings before they left the workshop.[5] Roethlisberger notes that another sheet from 1673, with the same frank

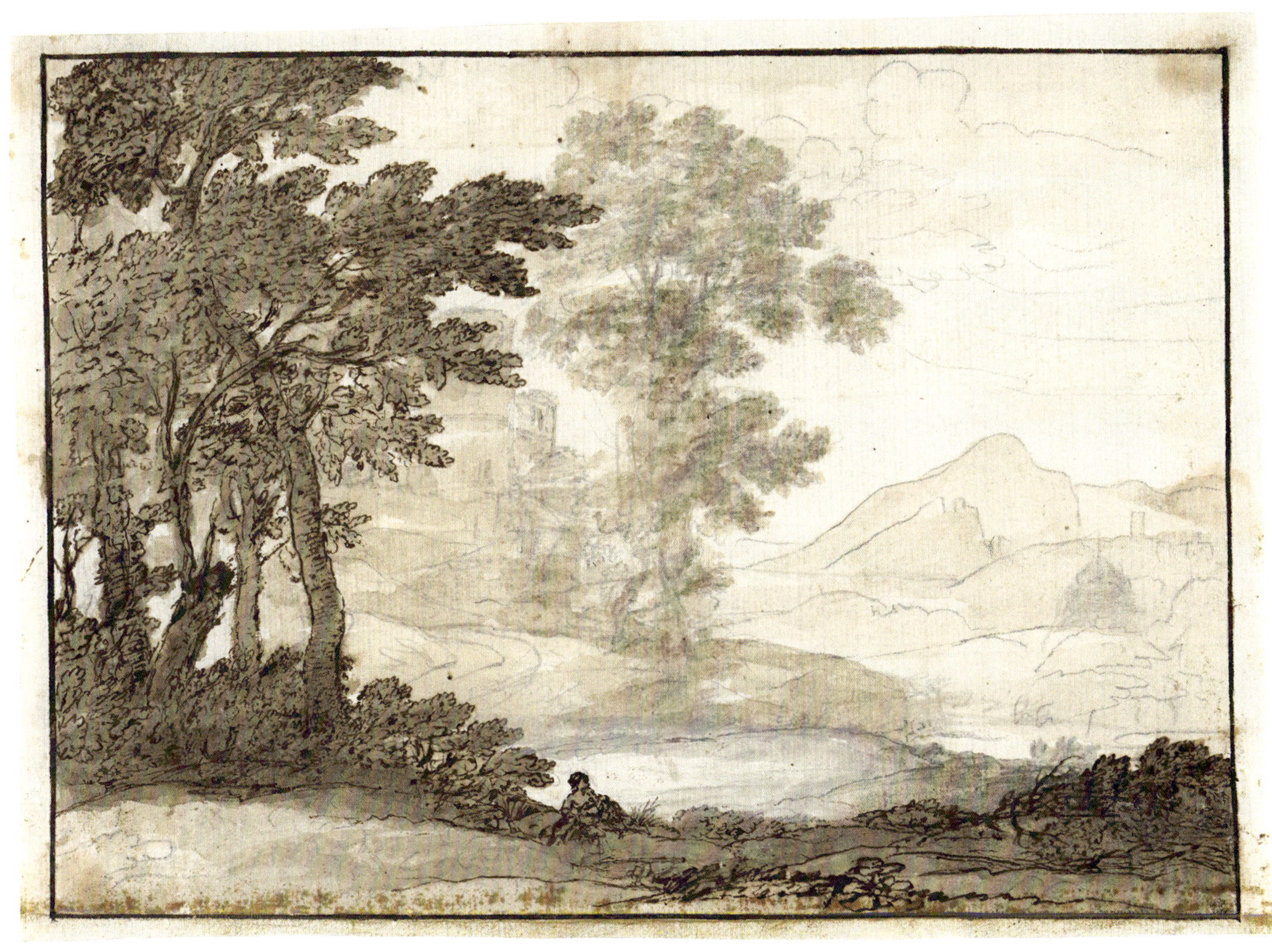

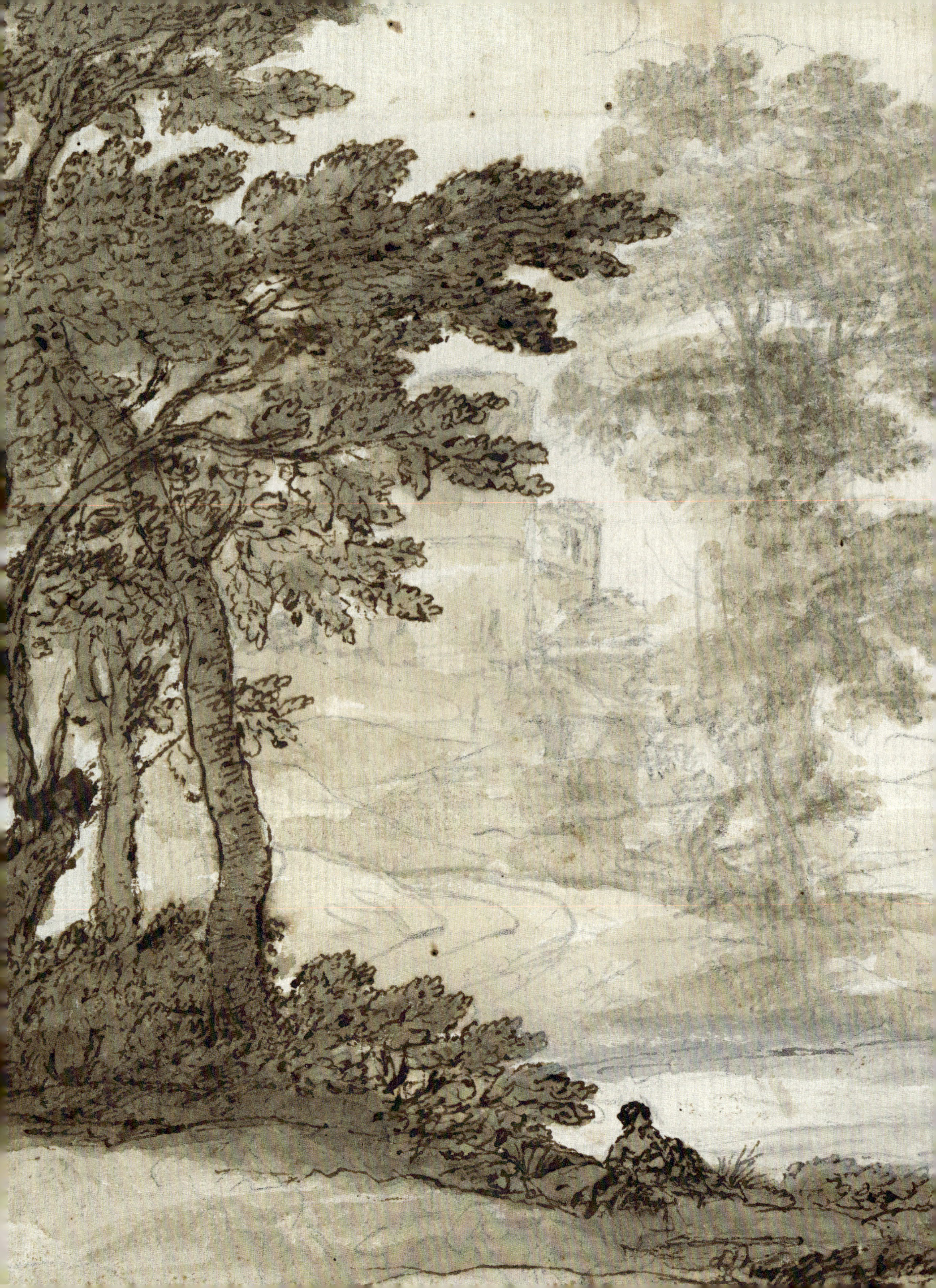

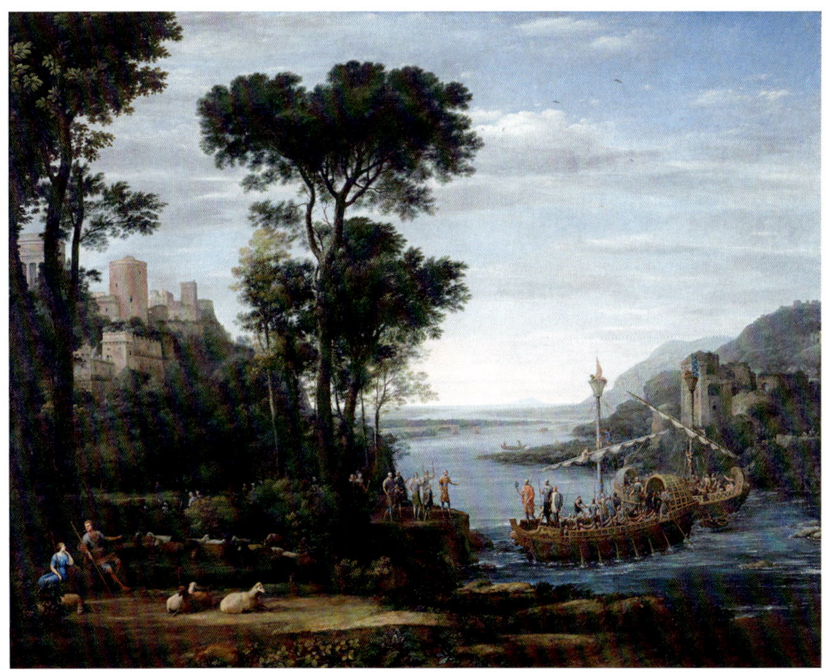

33.1 Claude Lorrain, *The Arrival of Aeneas at Pallanteum*, 1675. Anglesey Abbey, National Trust, Cambridgeshire.

quality as the present sheet and now in Nancy, also anticipates the ideation of the composition.[6]

In 2019, however, W.M. Brady deciphered a faint inscription on the verso of the sheet that indicates the design originally was intended for a slightly earlier project commissioned by "Don Gaspare," or Prince Gasparo Altieri, a Roman patron from one of the city's oldest families.[7] Brady observed that the composition bears similarities to *The Arrival of Aeneas at Pallanteum*, one of Claude's late works inspired by Virgil's *Aeneid*, painted for Altieri in 1675 (fig. 33.1).[8] The canvas may have been commissioned as early as 1670, and occasioned at least thirteen other drawings. The present sheet reveals Claude composing an idyllic scene, elements of which eventually would contribute to the broader, more structured and refined scenes of both the Altieri and Colonna pictures. JT

Attributed to SIMON DE VLIEGER

Rotterdam 1600/1–1653 Weesp

34

View of the Jeruzalemkapel and the Sint-Olofskapel, Amsterdam, ca. 1644

Black chalk, with gray wash, heightened with opaque white watercolor (partly oxidized), on paper prepared with a grayish-brown wash; framing line in gray wash
300 x 469 mm

INSCRIPTIONS Verso, upper left, in pencil: + 488 P. (partially effaced) and in brown ink: *Waaterloo =0102=*

PROVENANCE Clifford Duits (1909–1968), London;[1] his son Graham Charles Duits (1935–1979), London; thence by descent; acquired through Thomas Williams Fine Art, London as Jan Abrahamsz Beerstraten, by Clement C. Moore, 2014

Promised gift of Clement C. and Elizabeth Y. Moore

Built circa 1440, the Sint-Olofskapel (Chapel of St. Olaf) or Oudezijds Kapel (Old Side Chapel) is one of the oldest chapels in Amsterdam. It is situated near the Damrak, between the Zeedijk and the Nieuwebrugsteeg. In 1490, the chapel was enlarged by the adjacent octagonal Jeruzalemkapel (Chapel of Jerusalem), seen on the left. The drawing is one of the few depictions of the site, before the Jeruzalemkapel was torn down in 1644 in order to enlarge the Sint-Olofskapel in its current form with a three-aisled nave. Today, the chapel—dedicated to the Norwegian monarch venerated by the Dutch as the patron saint of dikes—is part of the Barbizon Hotel and is rented out as a party venue.

The same view of the site is represented in a drawing, cautiously attributed to Roelant Roghman, in the Rijksprentenkabinet, Amsterdam (fig. 34.1).[2] That sheet is inscribed on the verso with the date 1644, the year that the demolition of the chapel began. The present drawing, however, seems more monumental due to its elongated, slightly lower perspective. It also shows more detail, such as the structure of the brickwork and the beam construction in the interior of the dilapidated chapel. Moreover, the draftsman also depicted the houses to the right of the Sint-Olofskapel along the Zeedijk and, in the distance, the outline of the Nieuwe Brug, the bridge across the Damrak. There is, however, one striking similarity: in both drawings, the windows in the upper story of the chapel are open in exactly the same places, making it plausible that the two draftsmen drew the chapel around the same time.[3]

The old attribution of the drawing to Jan Abrahamsz Beerstraten is questionable,[4] and an alternative attribution to Simon de Vlieger has been proposed by several scholars.[5] The few drawings that can be securely attributed to Beerstraten, such as the signed *View of Kasteel Tongelaar at Gassel* in the Rijksprentenkabinet, Amsterdam,[6] are characterized by the loose yet delicate

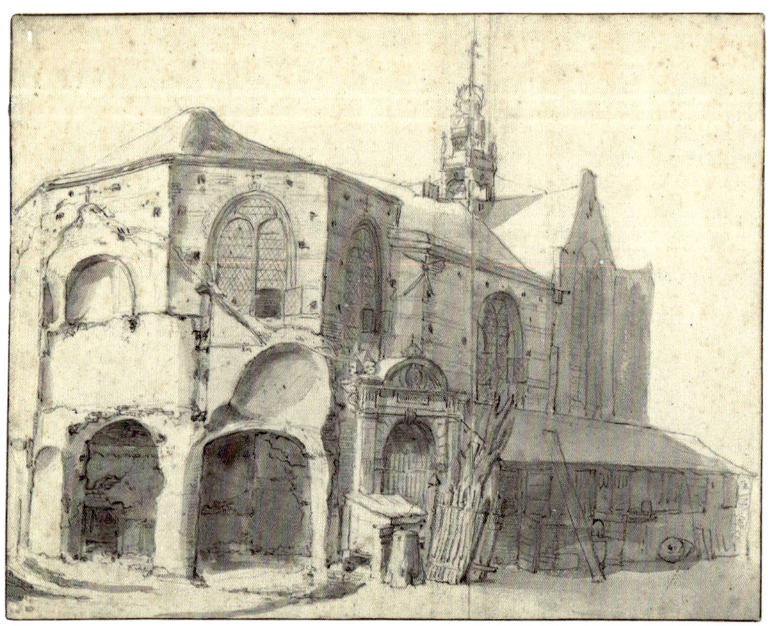

34.1 Attributed to Roelant Roghman, *View of the Jeruzalemkapel and the Sint-Olofskapel, Amsterdam, ca. 1644.* Rijksprentenkabinet, Amsterdam.

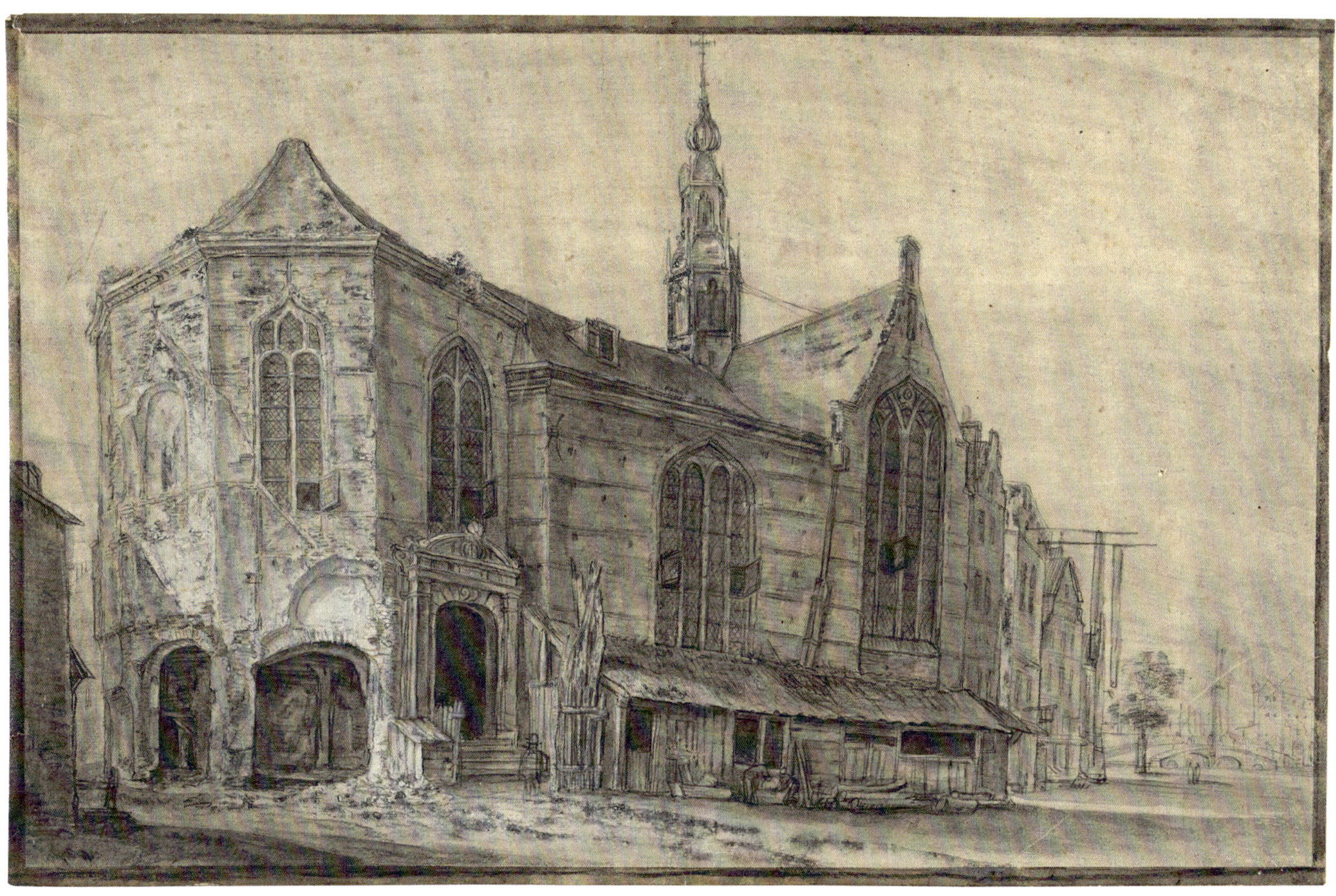

handling of black chalk, especially the way he outlines bricks in the wall with long horizontal and short vertical dashes. The black chalk lines in the present drawing, by contrast, are more coarsely drawn. The use of white opaque watercolor on washed paper is also uncharacteristic for Beerstraten, who seems to have drawn primarily in black chalk and brush and gray wash.

Although De Vlieger, as a landscape and marine artist, is best known for his drawn woodscapes on blue paper, works datable to the last decade of his life,[7] he also drew town walls, town gates, and dilapidated buildings in a style and technique comparable to the Moore view.[8] Characteristic of these drawings—and indeed the present sheet—is De Vlieger's dramatic distribution of light and dark, accentuated with heavy washes and sometimes also with white opaque watercolor.[9] The contrast between the brightly lit exterior wall of the dilapidated chapel and the dark alcoves, as well as the gloomy sky, give the scene an almost ghostly appearance. MR

HERMAN VAN SWANEVELT

Woerden 1603–1655 Paris

35

Landscape with the Prophet Elijah Awakened and Fed by an Angel on Mount Horeb, ca. 1633

Pen and brown ink, with brown wash; contours partially indented with a stylus
125 x 204 mm

INSCRIPTIONS Verso, lower right, in pen and brown ink: 40 [or 10?];[1] verso, upper left, in black chalk: *Lorain* (?); verso, lower center, in graphite: 244; verso, lower left and center, in pen and brown ink, in the hand of William Esdaile: 1835 *WE*$_x$ and *Swanefeldt*.

PROVENANCE Claude-Guillaume Debesse (d. before 1786), Paris (L. 729, verso, center); Jean-Baptiste-Florentin-Gabriel de Meyran, Marquis de Lagoy (1764–1829), Aix-en-Provence (L. 1710, lower right); William Esdaile (1758–1837), London (L. 2617, recto, lower left, and verso, lower left and center); Henry Scipio Reitlinger (1882–1950), London (no mark; see L. 2274a); his sale, Sotheby's, London, 22 June 1954, lot 720; Bolland & Marotz, Bremen, 4 July 2009, lot 592; private collection, New York, 2010; Day & Faber, London; from whom acquired by Clement C. Moore, 2010

SELECT REFERENCES Steland 2010, 2: 720, Nachtrag 4

Promised gift of Clement C. and Elizabeth Y. Moore

Added as a postscript in the 2010 monograph on Swanevelt by the late Anne Charlotte Steland, this is a preparatory study, in reverse, for the artist's etching of the subject (fig. 35.1).[2] The print is inscribed "H. Swaneüelt Fecit Rom / K. Audran excudit" and was published by Charles Audran, who was active in Rome from 1630 to 1634, coinciding with the first sojourn in Rome (1629–41) of this transitional Dutch Italianate artist. Swanevelt provides a link between the first generation of Bamboccianti in Italy (e.g., Cornelis van Poelenburch and Bartholomeus Breenbergh) and those of the second generation (e.g., Thomas Wijck and Nicolaes Berchem).

The present drawing was assigned a date by Steland of ca. 1633, on the basis of its similarity—especially the pose and dress of the angel--to the artist's etched *Landscape with Balaam and the Angel*;[3] to his preparatory drawing for that print, recently with Stephen Ongpin Fine Art, London;[4] and to the related dated painting of the subject in an English private collection.[5]

Not mentioned by Steland is another landscape drawing with the subject of Elijah and the angel, which, like the present work, was once in the collection of William Esdaile; it belonged also to Jacob de Vos Jbzn and later William Mayor.[6] As is known from the latter's posthumous catalogue of 1875,[7] however, this drawing, was of vertical rather than horizontal format (the dimensions of 8⅞ x 7⅞ inches are given); it was one of three in lot 20 of Mayor's 1909 sale.[8] In 2007 that drawing, which was on the London art market as by Swanevelt in 2003, was reattributed by Steland to the artist's pupil and brother-in-law Jacques Rousseau.[9] Either it or a lost prototype by Swanevelt may have been executed in connection with Swanevelt's signed and dated painting of the same theme (1649), which was on the London art market in 1995.[10]

Although many of Swanevelt's drawings and etchings include biblical and mythological subjects, these narrative elements usually occupy only a small

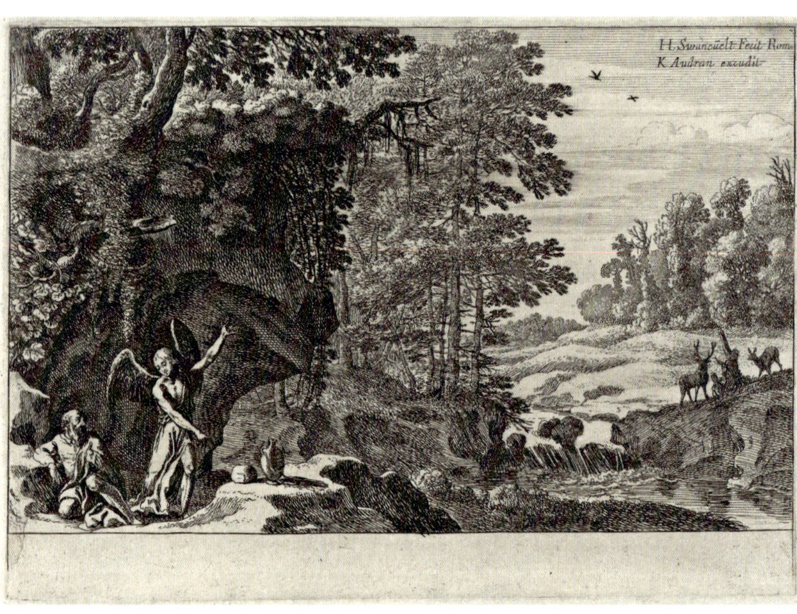

35.1 Herman van Swanevelt, *Landscape with the Prophet Elijah Awakened and Fed by an Angel on Mount Horeb*, ca. 1633. Rijksprentenkabinet, Amsterdam.

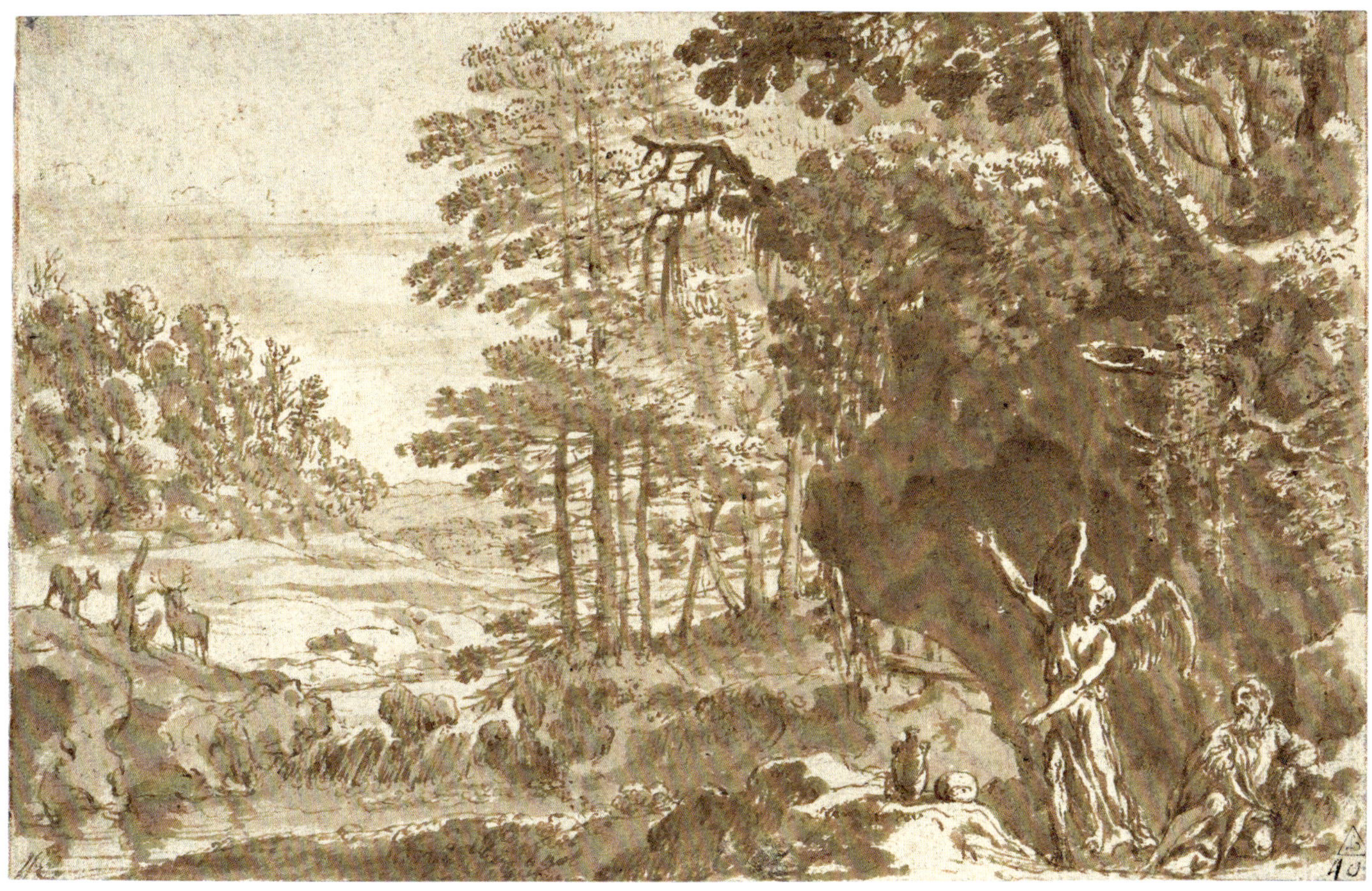

segment within a typical Italianate landscape setting—as, indeed, is the case here. Illustrating a passage from the Old Testament book of Kings (I Kings 19:5–6), an angel awakens the prophet Elijah, who has fallen asleep under a tree, overwhelmed by his circumstances and wishing to die. Encouraging him to "Get up and eat," the angel offers him a vessel with water and a large loaf of bread. With such biblical scenes, the artist often relied on a few set compositional formulas, with figures situated on one side of the foreground, a distant hilly vista bathed in hazy sunshine, and a large foreground tree extending beyond the frame. **JST**

PIETER JANSZ QUAST

Amsterdam 1605/6–1647 Amsterdam

36

The Mocking of the Spaniard, 1642

Black chalk and gray wash on parchment
222 x 300 mm

INSCRIPTIONS Recto, upper right, signed and dated by the artist: *PQuast 1642*

PROVENANCE Lionel Lucas (1822–1862), London (L. 1733a, recto, lower right); Charles Lucas (see his uncle's mark, L. 1733a); his sale, Christie's, London, 9 December 1949, part of lot 59; P. & D. Colnaghi & Co., London, 1950; Christie's, Amsterdam, 18 November 1985, lot 72; Sotheby's, New York, 14 January 1992, lot 136; Sotheby's, London, 9 July 2015, lot 89; where acquired by the Baymeath Art Trust and the Morgan Library & Museum

SELECT REFERENCES Stanton-Hirst 1982, 232, n. 27; Schwed 2020, under no. 11, n. 4

Morgan Library & Museum, Partial gift of the Baymeath Art Trust and partial purchase on the Charles Ryskamp Fund, inv. 2015.120

In his paintings, prints, and finished drawings, Pieter Quast offered a humorous, caricatural view of contemporary Dutch life. His works are populated with stock figures such as beggars, drinkers, quack doctors, dwarves, and the like, and while these would have been readily recognizable to Quast's audience (and familiar from the work of many of his contemporaries), Quast based many of his characters not on life observation, but rather on the work of earlier artists, especially Jacques Callot (see no. 24). The derivation from Callot's models, particularly the etchings of the *Balli di Sfessania* and *Varie figure di Gobbi* series of 1621–22, hints at the artificial and performative nature of Quast's characters; Callot's prints were themselves based on the theater: the *Balli di Sfessania* depicts fair performers,[1] and the *Gobbi* are caricatures of an actual troupe of dwarves whose performances Callot observed in Florence.[2]

Some of Quast's works not only derive from theatrical types, but are even based on actual theatrical productions.[3] These include several paintings in the Theatermuseum, Amsterdam,[4] as well as drawings like the present work, which is one of a group by Quast that seemingly reflect performances of *Spaanschen Brabander* (The Spanish Brabanter) by Gerbrand Adriaensz Bredero. Originally performed in 1617, the play remained popular through the seventeenth century. The drama consists of a series of picaresque episodes involving the fantasist Jerolimo, the eponymous "Brabanter," from the Brabant province in the Southern Netherlands. He has fled his debts in Antwerp and arrived in Amsterdam, where he pretends to be a rich man, adopting the elaborate costume of the Spanish, albeit a version that was long out of date, complete with the enormous millstone ruff; he repeatedly encounters commonfolk who see through his pompous disguise. Jerolimo's Spanish costume and braggadocio clearly derive from the

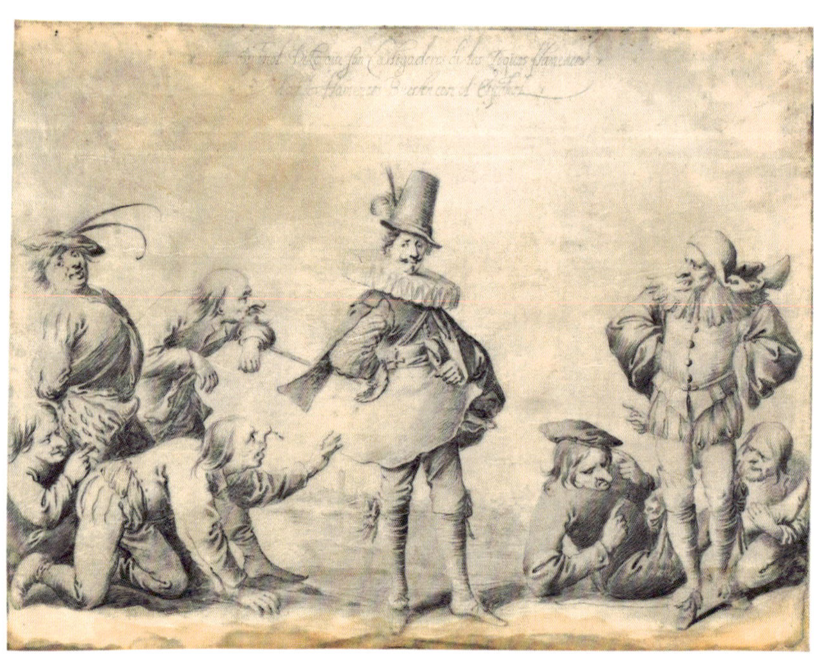

36.1 Pieter Quast, *Mockery of the Spaniard*, 1644. Rijksprentenkabinet, Amsterdam.

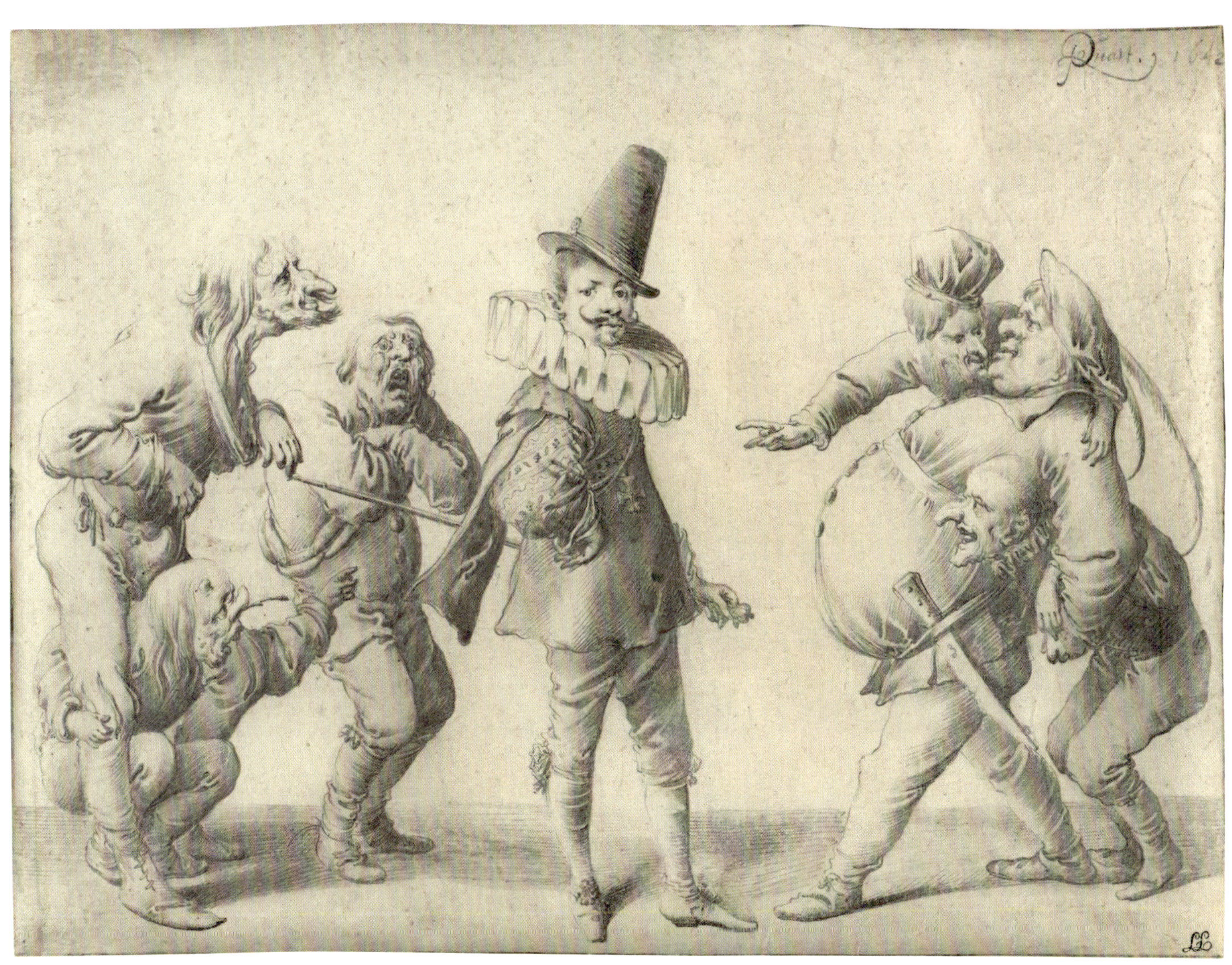
Quast. 1642

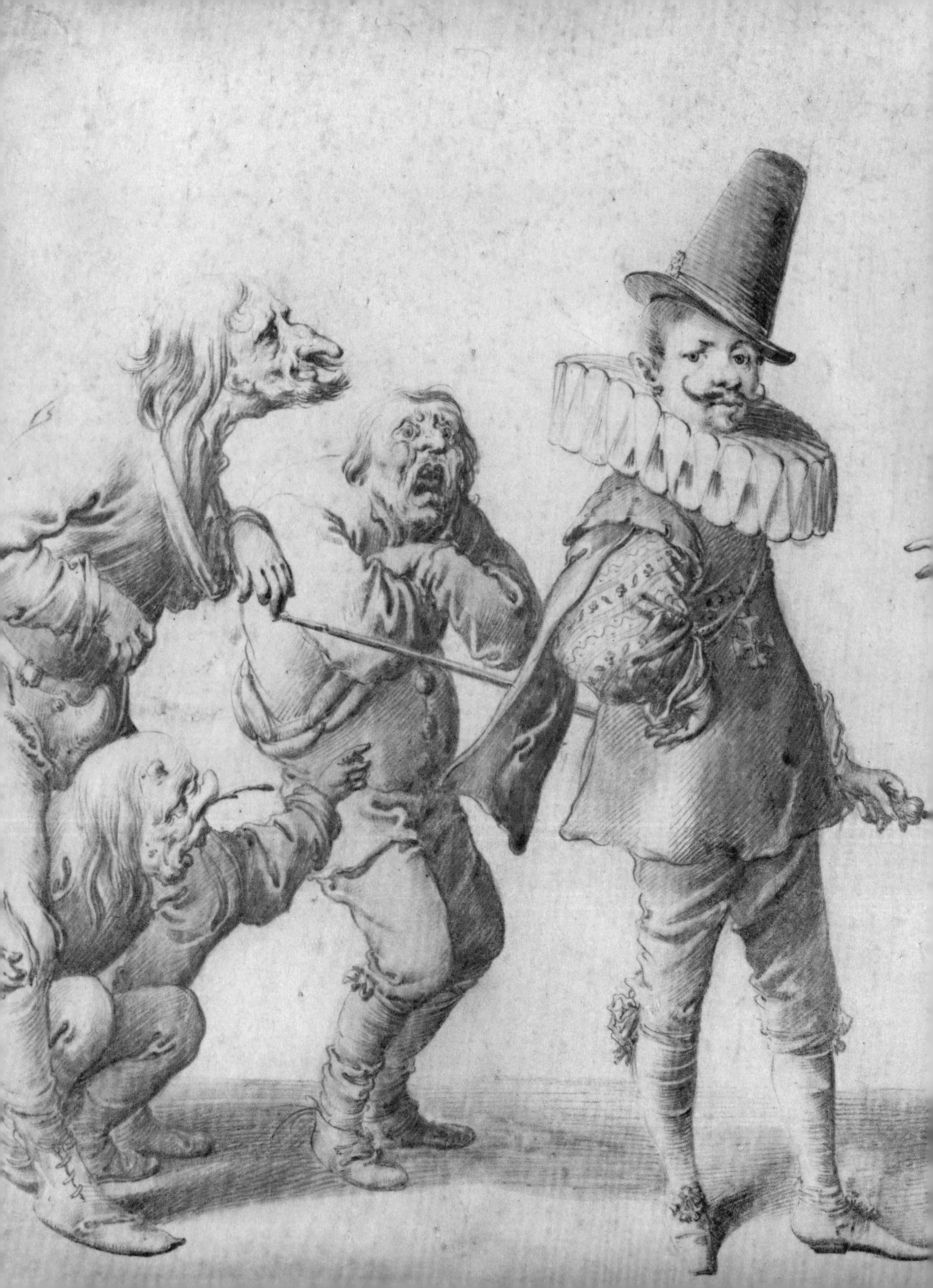

stock commedia dell'arte character of the Capitano. The play remained popular, however, not only for its amusing mockery of human nature, but also because of the prevailing sentiment against the Spanish (and against immigrants from the Spanish Southern Netherlands) during the Eighty Years' War: Jerolimo could stand in for both.[5]

This is one of a number of related drawings that contrast a central figure's outmoded Spanish elegance with earthy counterparts who are themselves caricatures and stock types. (Both Hanswurst, seen left of center with his garland of sausages, and the gluttonous figure at right reappear in the set of engravings of *Fools* designed by Quast.[6]) It is not always clear, however, whether the central figure in these drawings is meant to be the Spanish Brabanter of Bredero's drama, or an actual Spaniard. The closely related drawing in the Rijksprentenkabinet, for example (fig. 36.1),[7] bears the inscription "El Español disse que son Castigadores de los loquos flamencos, mas los flamencos buerlen con el Español" (The Spaniard says that they are punishers of the Flemish madmen, but the Flemish are fighting with the Spaniard) and thus seemingly draws a contrast between the foppish Spaniard and the coarse figures of Flanders who surround him.[8] The anti-Spanish message of the drawings remains the same either way.

Carefully finished, signed and dated, and drawn on parchment rather than paper, this is one of many drawings that Quast made as finished works in their own right, presumably for sale.[9] The proliferation of such works, and of Quast's paintings as well, would suggest that he enjoyed popular success. Documents published by Barbara Stanton-Hirst, however, reveal a life of debt and relative poverty.[10] JJM

REMBRANDT HARMENSZ VAN RIJN

Leiden 1606–1669 Amsterdam

37

A Beggar, Facing Left, Leaning on a Stick, ca. 1628–29

Pen and brown ink
112 x 88 mm

INSCRIPTIONS Verso of mount, upper left, in black chalk: *10 . . . L 28* (?); verso of mount, upper center, Richardson pressmarks in pen and brown ink: *B. 34. / Te 3.*; verso of mount, center, in graphite or black chalk: *Ry* (?) and lower left, in pen and brown ink: *. . .* [N?]*o 744*; above this, in graphite: *sr/* (?); and lower center, in pen and brown ink: *Pond* (similar but not identical to L. 2038)

PROVENANCE Jonathan Richardson, Sr. (1665–1745), London (L. 2983–84, verso, upper center);[1] Arthur Pond (1701–1758), London (according to inscription on verso); John Barnard (d. 1784), London (L. 1419, recto of mount, lower right, and verso, upper right); possibly his sale, Greenwood, London, 16 February 1787 sqq., one of a pair in lot 49; Nelson Goodman (1906–1998), Needham, MA; New Gallery [E.V. Thaw], New York, 1954; Edward Powis Jones (1919–1998) and Anne Keating Jones (1922–2014), New York; W.M. Brady & Co., New York; from whom acquired by Clement C. Moore, 2008

SELECT REFERENCES Poughkeepsie and New York 1961, no. 39; Sumowski 1962, 274–75; Sumowski 1964, 233–34; Benesch 1964, 106–7; Benesch 1970–73, 1: 248; Benesch 1973, 1: no. 23A; Bevers 2006, 30, under no. 3, n. 6; Shoaf Turner 2012, no. 29; Royalton-Kisch 2012–, under Benesch 0023A; Schatborn and Hinterding 2019, no. D202; Schrader 2022, 42

Promised gift of Clement C. and Elizabeth Y. Moore

The earliest of the Rembrandt drawings in the Moore collection, this sheet is exemplary of the first phase of the artist's career—his Leiden period of 1625–31. Rembrandt's preoccupation with the theme of beggars during that time bordered on fixation. Whether using a quill pen, black chalk, a brush, or an etching needle, he approached the subject with great sympathy.

In the present work and all Rembrandt's early drawn and etched studies of beggars, he used his media and tools with lightning speed to jot down the essence of the figure in a sequence of rapid, parallel strokes—testimony to his precocious talent. Specialists, including Otto Benesch, Werner Sumowski, and Peter Schatborn,[2] have been unanimous in assigning a date of ca. 1628–29 to this sheet. Other examples executed in pen from this period include *Young Man Leaning on a Stick, Full-Length, Turned to the Left*, formerly owned by Johan Quirijn van Regteren Altena and now in the J. Paul Getty Museum, Los Angeles;[3] among those in chalk are two sheets in the Rijksprentenkabinet, Amsterdam;[4] a good example in brush and wash is the *Beggar Woman Leaning on a Stick* in the National Gallery of Art, Washington;[5] while comparable etchings include B. 163 to B. 169.[6]

The standing figure in the present sheet, wearing a tall hat and large, ample cloak, is rendered with a few deft, mostly vertical pen lines. His stick is economically suggested by two quick strokes, which merge indistinguishably with the lines indicating drapery folds. The fall of light is conveyed by two means: first, by the areas of blank paper on the figure's hat, shoulders, and back and, second, by the shadows created by rapid parallel hatching in his face and left leg and on the ground at left. Rembrandt adjusted the pressure of his pen to vary the tones, thick for the darkest side of the hat, thin for the shading of the figure's face. The same delicate shading in the face is seen in a contemporary drawing, *Man in a Turban, Leaning on a Stick*, in the Kupferstichkabinett, Berlin,[7] a good demonstration of how a quick sketch from life, such as the present study, can be transformed into a character suitable for inclusion in a biblical or history scene.

Rembrandt was an avid art collector, which certainly contributed to his financial troubles.[8] As is well known from his two bankruptcy sales of 1657 and 1658, his collection included an enormous quantity of prints by earlier artists. His first documented purchase of prints was in Amsterdam in 1635.[9] Whether or not he owned some as early as the late 1620s—when he executed the present drawing—there can be no doubt, as has been noted by writers since the eighteenth century,[10] that his early work was profoundly influenced by the linear style and subject matter of prints by French artist Jacques Callot, especially Callot's series *Les Gueux* (The Beggars), which had appeared only in 1622.[11] Rembrandt's personal passion for Callot has apparently proven contagious to Chips Moore, who acquired a sheet with black chalk figure studies by Callot (see no. 24) of the sort that certainly would have inspired Rembrandt in the seventeenth century. JST

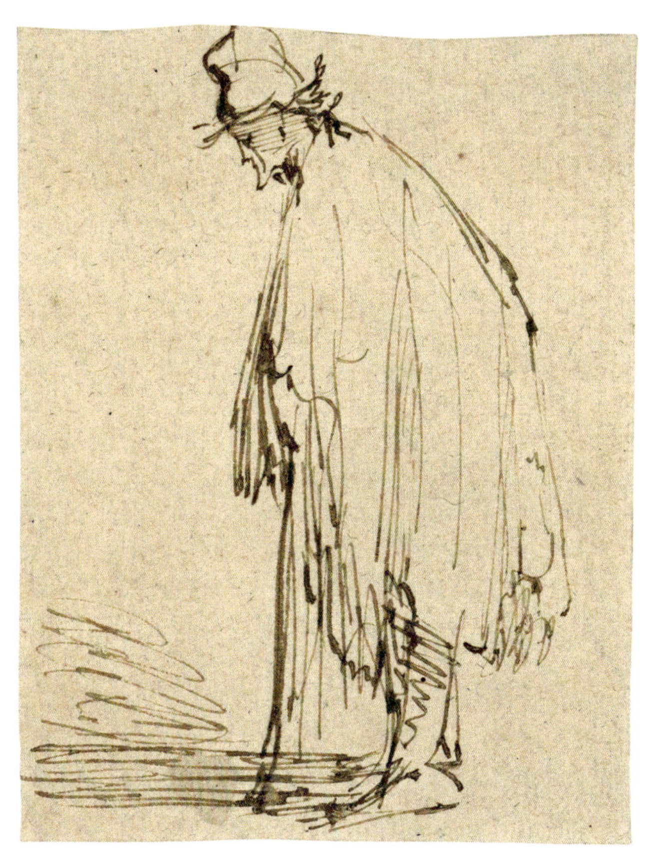

REMBRANDT HARMENSZ VAN RIJN

Leiden 1606–1669 Amsterdam

38

St. Peter Preaching (recto) and *Bust-Length Study of a Man Wearing a Tall Hat* (verso), ca. 1647

Black chalk
120 x 168 mm

INSCRIPTIONS Verso, upper left, in graphite: P11 (Duits probate inventory number); verso, center, in graphite: *Rembrandt*; verso, lower right, in black chalk: L

PROVENANCE Nathaniel Smith (1738–1809), London (L. 2296–98 and L. 3017, possible remnants of his code on verso, lower left, in black chalk); Duits Gallery, London;[1] F. Delius Giese, London; Charles E. Duits (1882–1969), London (L. 533a, verso, lower right); thence by descent; acquired through Thomas Williams Fine Art, London, by Clement C. Moore, 2006

SELECT REFERENCES Katz and Van Gelder 1948, no. 16; Benesch 1954–57, 3: no. 595; Benesch 1973, 3: 161, no. 595; Robinson 2000, 306, n. 2; Robinson 2002, 120, 256–57, under nos. 47a and 47b, n. 2; Shoaf Turner 2012, no. 32; Royalton-Kisch 2012–, under Benesch 595; Verdi 2014, 105; Schatborn and Hinterding 2019, 19 and nos. 85 (recto) and 399 (verso); Lee 2022, 37–38

Promised gift of Clement C. and Elizabeth Y. Moore

Rembrandt's characteristic economy and finesse of line are here exemplified: his extraordinary command of black chalk—from gauzy tracings to sharply defined contours—creates an array of spare but potent facial expressions and bodily gestures glimpsed among a crowd. The gathering horde surrounds a bearded man who stands slightly stooped from the hip, arms raised to mid-torso, palms downward. He appears to address the group with an air of serene confidence, or perhaps thinly disguised frailty. Despite, or in light of, such closely observed details, the precise subject of this drawing has long been debated. Otto Benesch tentatively identified the scene as *St. Peter Preaching*, though there are not enough details to unequivocally confirm this suggestion.[2] Other plausible proposals have included Christ and the twelve apostles, Jacob with his sons and Dinah, and St. Peter's Denial of Christ.[3] Jane Shoaf Turner ventured that this drawing, rather than depicting a biblical event, could be an elaborate figure study, for in the late 1640s and early 1650s, the artist normally used black chalk for figure studies, and not other purposes.[4] To this list of possibilities we might newly add one further hypothesis, that the sketch depicts Paul's miraculous healing of a disabled man at Lystra.[5] The Moore sheet may capture the moment the man jumped to his feet in front of a crowd and took his first steps. Such an action would explain the "slightly unsteady" posture of the central figure, previously noted by Shoaf Turner.[6] Alternatively, a red chalk drawing by Rembrandt of *Sts. Paul and Barnabas at Lystra*, now in the Musée Bonnat-Helleu, Bayonne, depicts a bearded, balding St. Paul in the same posture and dress seen in the Moore sheet.[7]

Another possibility, also here introduced, is that the sheet represents the story of Paul Preaching in Athens.[8] Raphael famously depicted this event in his *Acts of the Apostles* tapestry series, an enormously influential source of inspiration for artists (fig. 38.1).[9] Rembrandt, an admirer of Raphael, likely knew of the *Sermon of St. Paul*

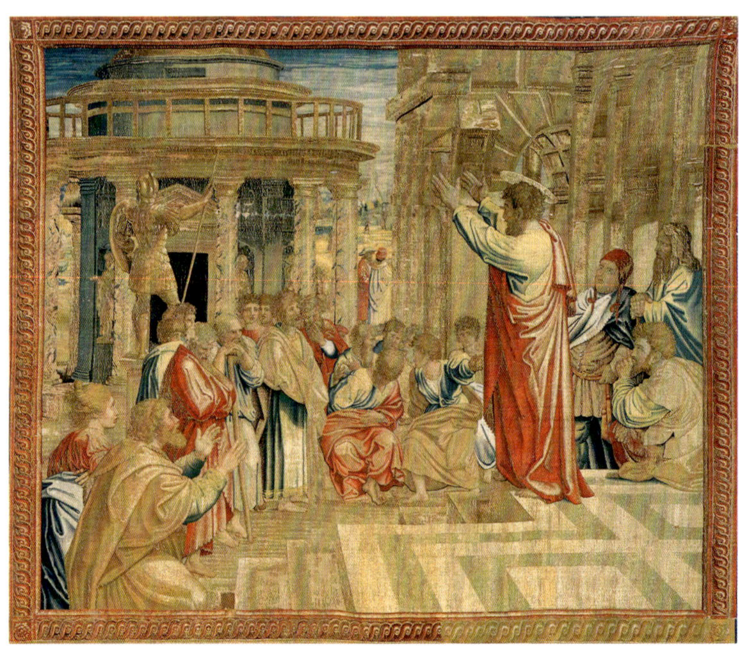

38.1 Designed by Raphael, woven in the workshop of Pieter van Aelst, *Acts of the Apostles: The Sermon of St. Paul in Athens*, 1515. Vatican Museums, Vatican City.

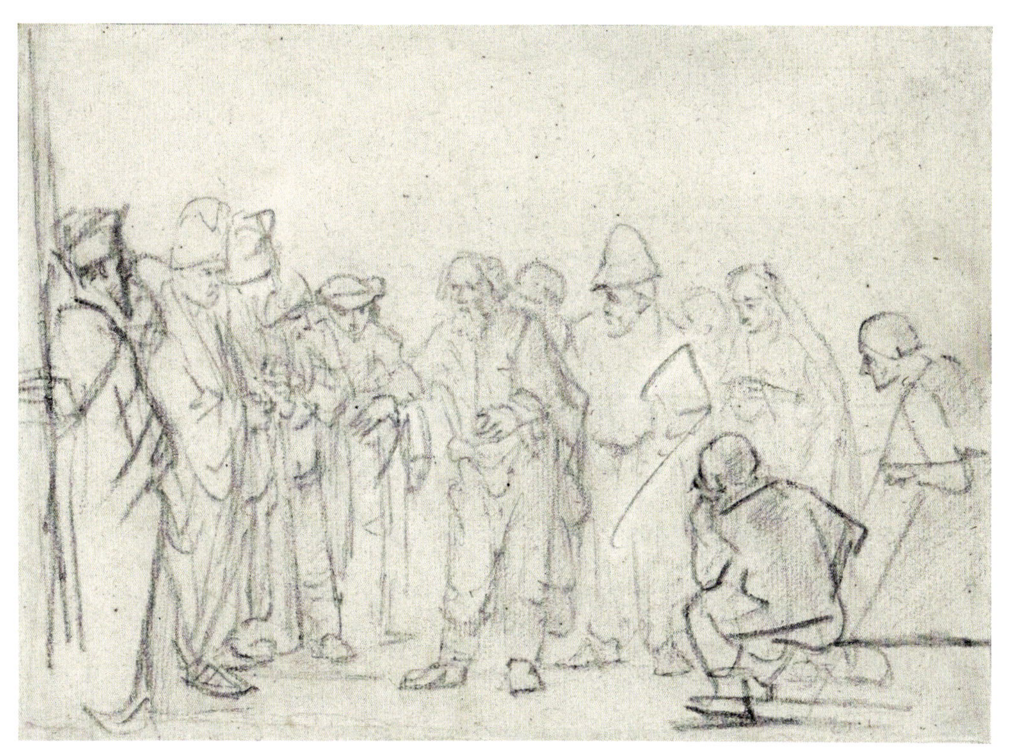

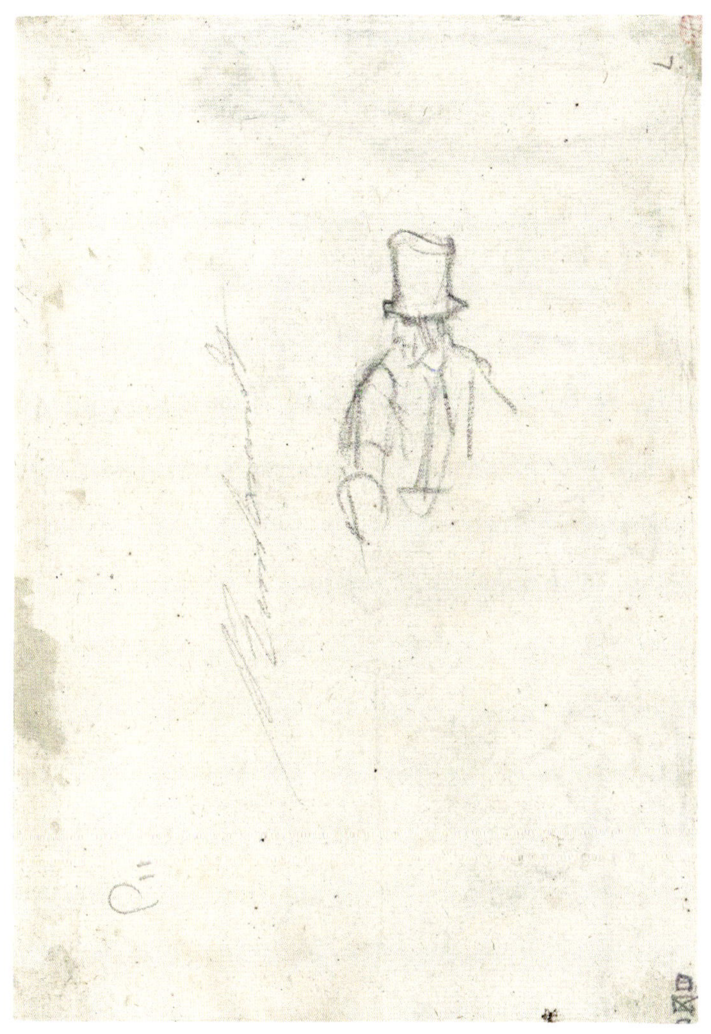

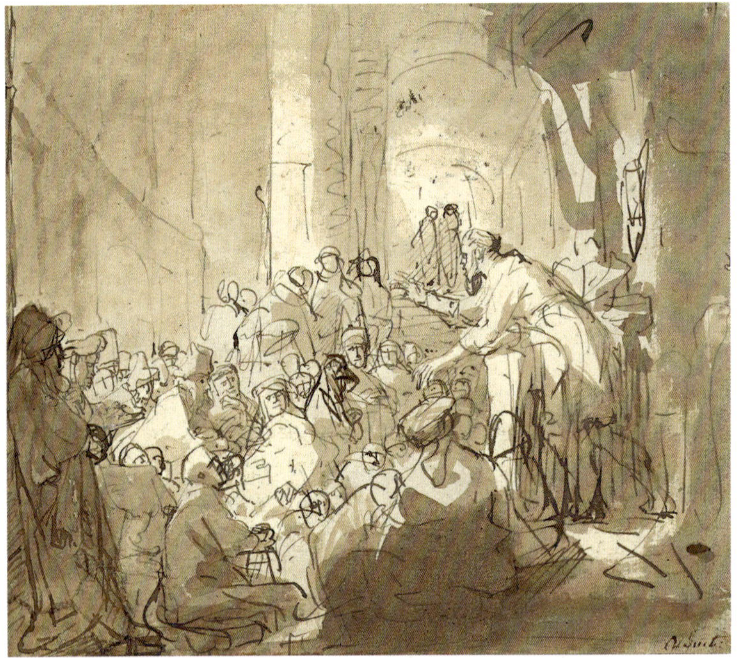

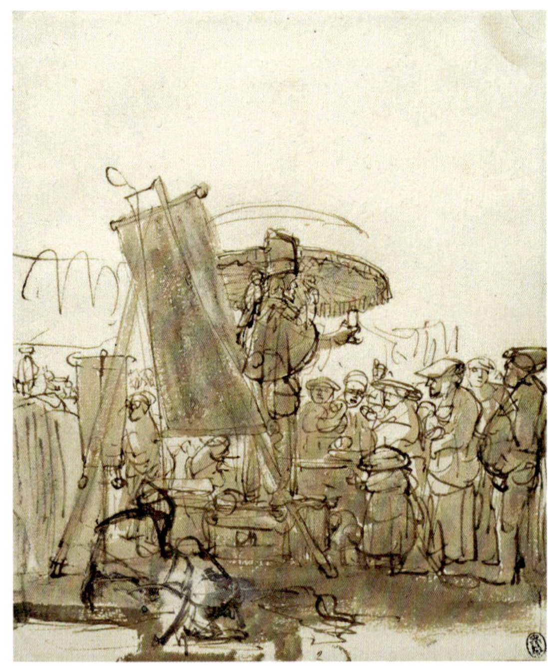

38.2 Gerbrand van den Eeckhout, *St. Paul Preaching at Athens*, ca. 1635–40. British Museum, London.

38.3 Gerbrand van den Eeckhout, *A Quack Addressing a Crowd*, ca. 1637. Courtauld Gallery, London.

tapestry through Marcantonio Raimondi's reproductive print.[10] Depictions of Paul appear throughout Rembrandt's oeuvre, and a pen-and-ink drawing identified as *Paul Preaching* and formerly attributed to Rembrandt is now thought to have been done ca. 1635–40 by his pupil Gerbrand van den Eeckhout while consulting materials in his master's workshop (fig. 38.2).[11] Van den Eeckhout's drawing bears some resemblance to Raphael's design, but Paul (at right) is pictured in a bent posture akin to the figure in the Moore sheet. Also strikingly similar in dress and physical appearance is the subject of a Louvre drawing attributed to Jan Lievens and believed to be a preparatory study for either Rembrandt's ca. 1629 engraving of Paul or his painting *Paul in Prison* now in Stuttgart.[12]

The verso of the Moore sketch features a man wearing a tall hat like the black beaver felt toppers so popular throughout Europe in the seventeenth century. This hat does not reappear among the crowd pictured on the sheet's recto, but the eponymous figure in the Courtauld Gallery drawing *A Quack Addressing a Crowd*, attributed to Van den Eeckhout, wears similar headgear (fig. 38.3).[13] Rembrandt's sketch might well depict a quack doctor, though it is unclear if this depiction should be viewed in correlation with or as alternate idea from the scene on the recto (notwithstanding that both sketches were done at the same time, around 1647).[14] Still, to enforce a strict dialectic between genre and biblical scenes serves neither the work of Rembrandt nor his pupils, who in their creative processes simultaneously explored diverse techniques and subjects while looking to similar sources. That the Van den Eeckhout and Rembrandt drawings depict a crouching figure in the foreground can but add to the intriguing continuities readily found among these sheets, and generally among the work of Rembrandt and his pupils.
SWM

REMBRANDT HARMENSZ VAN RIJN

Leiden 1606–1669 Amsterdam

39

Study of a Sick Woman for the "Hundred Guilder Print" and an Alternative Sketch of Her Head, ca. 1645–48

Pen and brown ink
80 x 109 mm

INSCRIPTIONS Verso, lower edge, in pen and brown ink: *Samuel de Festetits 1850.*; verso, upper center, in graphite: *f*; verso, lower left, in black chalk: *d*

PROVENANCE Samuel, Graf von Festetits (1806–1862), Vienna (L. 926, verso, lower edge), from 1850; from whom probably acquired by Philipp, Freiherr Drechsler [Dräxler] von Carin (1794–1874), Vienna, 1859; Josef Carl, Ritter von Klinkosch (1822–1888), Vienna, 1874 (no mark; see L. 577); his sale, Wawra, Vienna, 15 April 1889 sqq., lot 732; Elsa von Kuffner (d. 1938), Vienna; by descent to the Moriz und Elsa von Kuffner-Stiftung, Zurich; their sale, Sotheby's, London, 26 November 1970, lot 17; where acquired by Walter J. Johnson (1908–1996), New York; his sale, Christie's, London, 1 July 1997, lot 208; British Rail Pension Fund, 1999; private collection, New York; from which acquired by Clement C. Moore, 2005

SELECT REFERENCES Tietze 1908, 225, no. 6; Benesch 1935, 16; Münz 1952, 2: 101, under no. 217 (in reverse); Benesch 1954–57, 2: no. 388; Haverkamp-Begemann 1961, 15–16; Boon 1964, 87; Benesch 1964, 121; White 1969a, 1: 59–60, 2: fig. 69; White 1969b, 9, under no. 1; Benesch 1970, 256, 446; Benesch 1970–73, 16, 106, nn. 6–7; Vienna 1970, 112, under no. 186; Filedt Kok 1972 (and 1976), 67, under B. 74; Benesch 1973, 1: 50, under no. 183, 2: no. 388; Schatborn 1985a, 48–49, under no. 21, n. 3; Bevers, Schatborn, and Welzel 1991, 244–45, under no. 27 (entry by Barbara Welzel), n. 15; Royalton-Kisch 1993, 180, 191, n. 12; White 1999, 59; Hinterding, Luijten, and Royalton-Kisch 2000, 257, under no. 61 (entry by Martin Royalton-Kisch), fig. e; Schröder and Bisanz-Prakken 2004, 258, n. 4, fig. e; Bevers 2006, 142–43, under no. 40, n. 6; Van Tuyll van Serooskerken 2006, 205, n. 6; Slive 2009, 205; Schatborn 2011, 314, 316; Royalton-Kisch and Schatborn 2011, no. 62; Shoaf Turner 2012, no. 31; Royalton-Kisch 2012–, under Benesch 388; Hinterding and Rutgers 2013, 153, under no. 239; Schatborn 2015; Rumberg 2016, 50; Rutgers and Standring 2018, no. 91; Buck and Müller 2019, no. 50.5; Schatborn and Hinterding 2019, no. D89

Promised gift of Clement C. and Elizabeth Y. Moore

In the process of assembling a collection of seventeenth-century Dutch drawings over the course of three decades, few events can rival the early-morning telephone call from an unexpected source offering an opportunity to purchase the last study in private hands for Rembrandt's most celebrated etching, *Christ Healing the Sick*, universally known as the *Hundred Guilder Print* (B. 74; fig. 39.1), generally dated ca. 1648.[1] The present sketch, one of five or six probable studies for this monumental print, shows a rather haggard-looking, seated woman, her hands clasped in a gesture of entreaty, and a separate study for her head at upper right. In the print, this sick woman appears at the center of the composition, reclining on a straw mat at Christ's feet. The etching's long-standing nickname derives from the fact that there were complaints about its 100-guilder price tag from an Antwerp print dealer as early as 1654—within about six years of its completion.[2] Other prints routinely fetched no more than a few stuivers. The five other studies generally connected with the print, all datable ca. 1645–48,[3] consist of a double-sided sheet with alternative studies for the same sick woman, in the Rijksprentenkabinet, Amsterdam (figs. 39.2–3);[4] a more complex study showing the same reclining woman surrounded by some nine other figures, in the Kupferstichkabinett, Berlin (fig. 39.4);[5] a study in the Louvre, Paris, for the blind man leaning on a stick who stands alongside his wife (behind the wheelbarrow on the right of the print);[6] and a drawing in the Courtauld Gallery, London, possibly a study for the man with an outstretched arm between Christ and the blind man.[7] A drawing in the Pushkin Museum, Moscow, has been linked with the woman and child seen from behind at Christ's right hand, but the connection is more tenuous.[8]

The fortunate survival of four different studies for the sick woman—the present sketch, the two variants on the Amsterdam sheet, and the compositional vignette in the Berlin work—allows us to posit a possible progression as

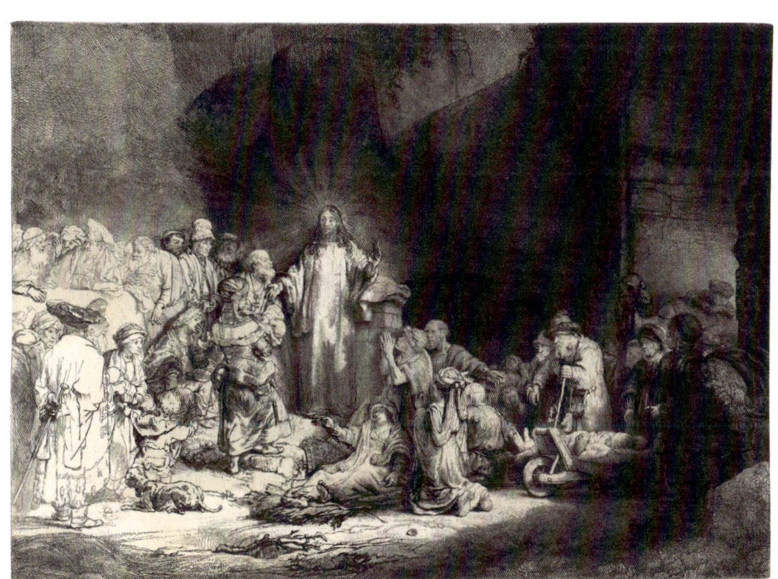

39.1 Rembrandt van Rijn, *Christ Healing the Sick* ("*Hundred Guilder Print*"), ca. 1648. Morgan Library & Museum, New York.

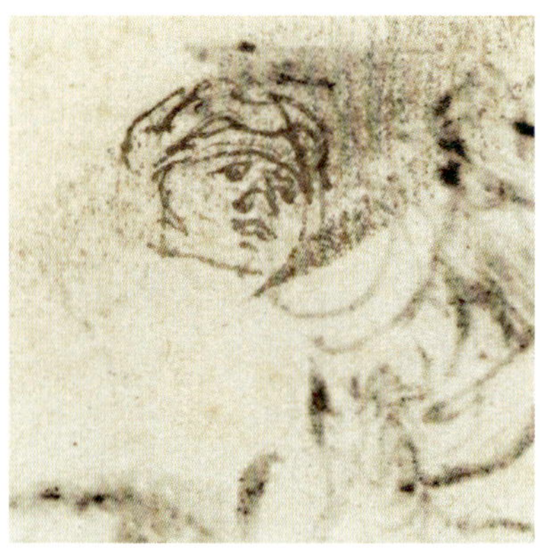

39.2 Rembrandt van Rijn, *Small Study of the Head of the Sick Woman* (detail of verso of fig. 39.3).

39.3 Rembrandt van Rijn, *Studies for the Sick Woman in the "Hundred Guilder Print,"* ca. 1645–48. Rijksprentenkabinet, Amsterdam.

39.4 Rembrandt van Rijn, *Study for the "Hundred Guilder Print,"* ca. 1645–48. Kupferstichkabinett, Berlin.

Rembrandt evolved and refined his thoughts about this central figure in the composition. Chronologically, the Moore sketch, in my opinion, probably came first. The figure, although infirm, still has the strength to sit upright and hold up her hands. Her illness is implied, above all, by her gaunt features—the obvious focus of Rembrandt's interest at this stage. From the quick, alternative sketch of her head on the right to the more complete study on the left, he exaggerated the single short pen line that economically but so convincingly suggests her sunken cheekbones. The separate head study on the verso of the Amsterdam drawing, which he rubbed out with his finger while the ink was still wet (fig. 39.2), reprises the basic position of the head of the Moore drawing, and this seems to have been the starting point for the study on the right side of the recto (fig. 39.3). In the study on the left of the recto, the figure is still seated upright, but both arms are now resting on her knees and her face is hidden in shadow. He must have begun to realize, however, that he needed to suggest her weakness through her whole body instead of just her face. Her posture is less erect in the right-hand study, a subtle shift that is further developed in the Berlin sketch (fig. 39.4), in which her torso and head are now supported by the figures behind her. Rembrandt concentrated at this point on the action of the hands and arms. As is evident from a pentimento in the right-hand study of the Amsterdam sheet, both hands were initially still in her lap (as in the left-hand study), but then he raised her left hand. This was a critical shift, a gesture meant to engage Christ's attention and integrate the figure into the narrative. But perhaps in order to accentuate her diminishing strength, in the Berlin drawing he lowered her hand and fingers. She is just barely able to hold her left arm aloft. Rembrandt also struggled with the figure's right arm, trying different positions until he arrived at the solution adopted in the print—in which the arm lies completely listless at her side.[9]

One of the former owners of the present sheet was Walter J. Johnson, a fifth-generation publisher who fled Nazi Germany. With his brother-in-law, he founded the Academic Press in New York, a major scientific publisher whose authors included Albert Einstein. Johnson put together one of the finest twentieth-century private collections of Rembrandt etchings. His impression of the coveted *Hundred Guilder Print* was not one of his best, but he was able to compensate with the purchase of this drawing in 1970, just a few years after it was definitively connected with the print by Egbert Haverkamp-Begemann.[10] **JST**

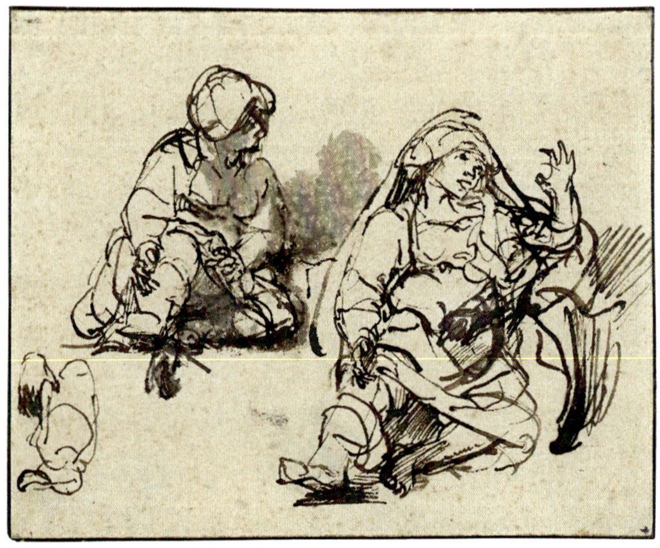

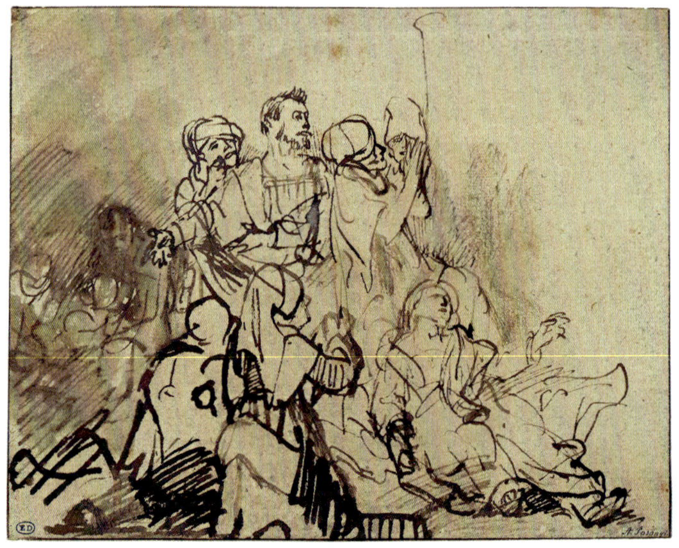

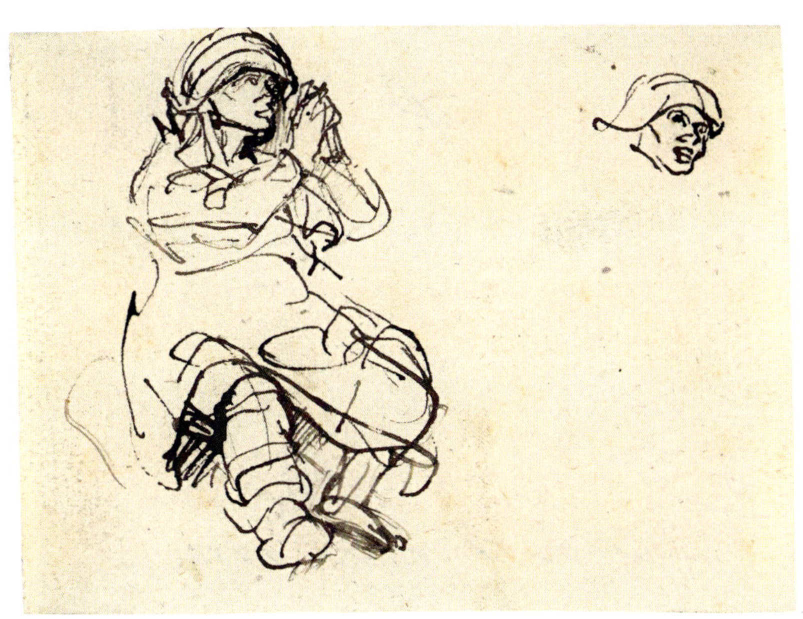

School of REMBRANDT HARMENSZ VAN RIJN

Leiden 1606–1669 Amsterdam

40

Three Figures Seated in a Landscape, ca. 1648–52

Pen and brown ink, with white opaque watercolor; arched framing lines in brown ink
198 x 180 mm

WATERMARK Strasbourg lily in crowned shield

INSCRIPTIONS Recto, lower left, in brown ink: *16*; recto of mount, lower center, in brown ink: *Rembrandt.*

PROVENANCE Possibly Richard Houlditch (d. 1736); Richard Houlditch, Jr. (before 1736–1759), London (L. 2214, recto, lower left); Sir Joshua Reynolds (1723–1792), London (L. 2364, recto, lower left); Nan Ino Cooper, Lady Lucas (1880–1958), Wrest Park (see her husband's mark, L. 1696); her sale, Sotheby's, London, 29 June 1926, lot 35; Wilhelm Reinhold Valentiner (1880–1958), Detroit; his sale, A.W.M. Mensing, Frederik Muller, Amsterdam, 25 October 1932, lot X; Eldridge R. Johnson (1867–1945), Moorestown, NJ; Thomas Williams Fine Art, London; from whom acquired by Clement C. Moore, 2012

SELECT REFERENCES Valentiner 1925–34, 2: no. 617 (as Rembrandt); Benesch 1973, no. 748 (as Rembrandt, 1646–47); Kettering 1977, 27–28; Kettering 1983, 96

Promised gift of Clement C. and Elizabeth Y. Moore

In a meadow beneath a precipitous mountainside, a shepherd reclines on his elbow and plays a transverse flute. Beside him a shepherdess wearing a broad-brimmed hat bedecked with flowers and ribbons sings from a sheet of paper held in her hands. A second shepherdess sits on the bank of a ditch or stream and raises the hem of her skirt to cool her legs over the water. She turns toward the singer and, moved by the music, presses her hand to her breast.[1] Two sheep drink from the stream below, and a sheep and a goat graze behind the piping herder.

In her comprehensive study of Dutch pastoral imagery, Alison Kettering located the Moore drawing in a broad category she defined as "nonnarrative multifigure scenes—or *concerts champêtres*."[2] Such works do not illustrate a specific text but combine familiar iconographic conventions of the pastoral literature that reached the height of its popularity in the Dutch Republic during the 1630s and 1640s.[3] Amorous shepherds, surrounded by their flocks, relax with music in an idyllic landscape. Innocent, arcadian love play is common to all these scenes, and in most their interactions are more demonstratively erotic than here. For example, in a slightly earlier drawing by an unidentified Rembrandt pupil, a piping shepherd is gently caressed by his two female companions (fig. 40.1).[4]

The inscription of Rembrandt's name on the eighteenth-century mount attests to the longevity of the attribution of this poetic sheet, which Otto Benesch retained in his 1973 catalogue of the artist's drawings. Yet shortcomings of the draftsmanship—tentative and superfluous contours and corrections in white opaque watercolor—betray the hand of a pupil, and the work was omitted from the oeuvre published in 2019 by Peter Schatborn.[5] To judge from its technique, the draftsman studied with Rembrandt around 1650.[6] The master trained several talented students during that time, including Willem Drost, Nicolaes Maes, Constantijn van Renesse, and Abraham van Dijk, but the Moore drawing cannot be assigned to any of these artists.

In several areas the unidentified draftsman used white opaque watercolor to delete lines or reduce their visibility.[7] He covered the shepherd's staff, perhaps because his feet rest rather awkwardly on top of it, as well as his facial features and lines on his forehead. Having initially drawn a plank over the ditch in front of the seated shepherdess at right, he changed his mind and whited out the board with opaque watercolor. The scrim of white over the trees and buildings to the left of the shepherd's head may have been intended to tone down their prominence rather than delete them completely. WWR

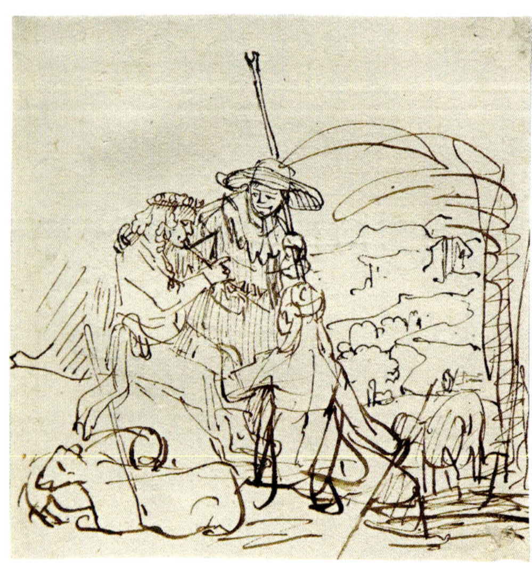

40.1 Rembrandt pupil, *Pastoral Scene: Flute Player and Two Figures with Sheep*, ca. 1638–40. Ossolineum, Wrocław.

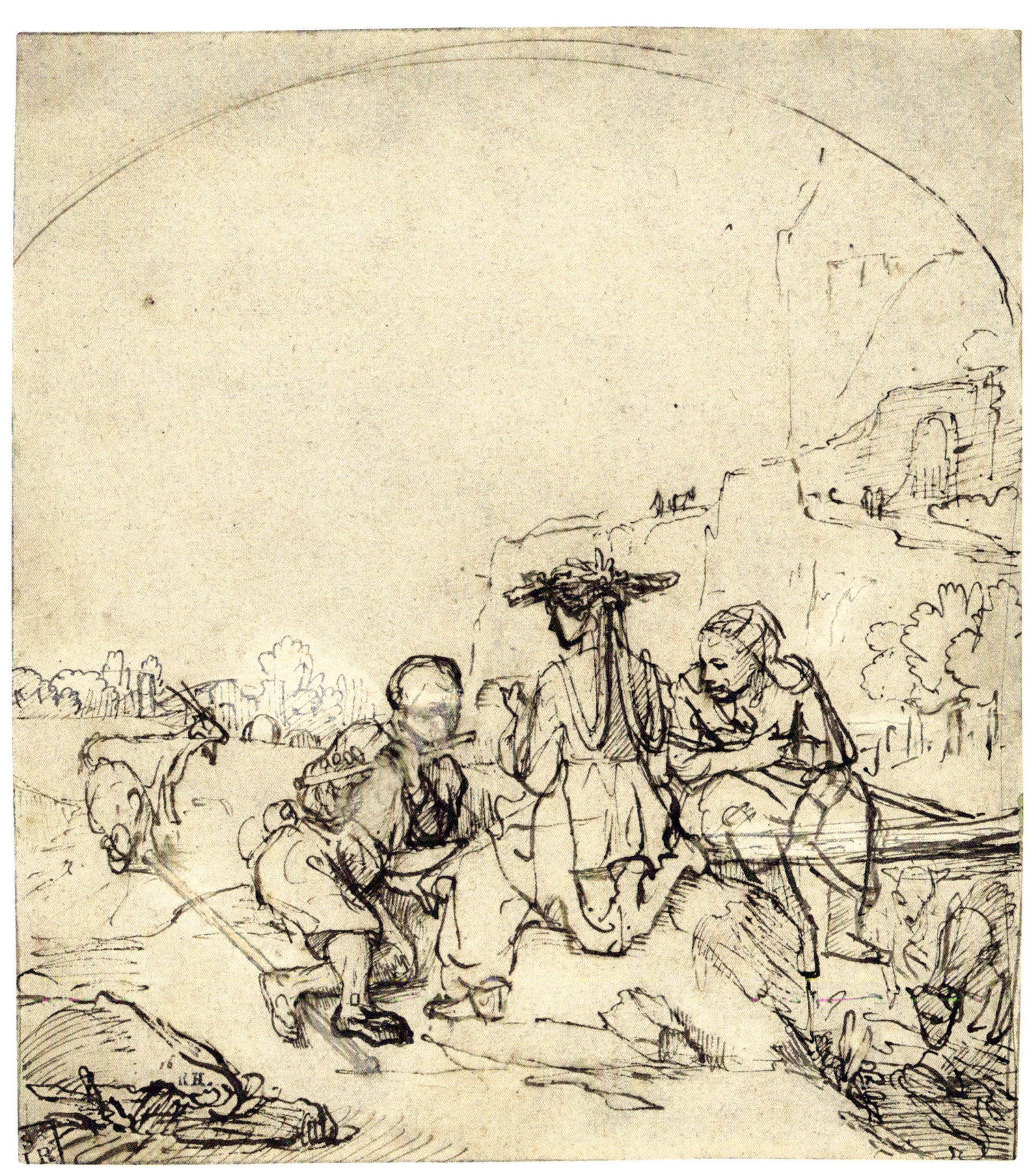

Attributed to REMBRANDT HARMENSZ VAN RIJN

Leiden 1606–1669 Amsterdam

41

View of Diemen, ca. 1650

Pen and brown ink and wash
144 x 278 mm

INSCRIPTIONS Recto of mount, lower center: *Rembrandt*; verso of mount, upper center, in pen and ink: R N°. 24

PROVENANCE John, Earl Spencer (1734–1783), Althorp (L. 1532, lower right); T. Philipe, London, 10–17 June 1811, lot 668; Sir Abraham Hume, 2nd Bt. (1749–1838), London; his grandson John Hume, Viscount Alford (1812–1851), London; by descent to the Rt. Hon. Adelbert Wellington, 3rd Earl Brownlow (1844–1921), London; by descent to the Rt. Hon. Adelbert Salusbury Cockayne Cust, 5th Baron Brownlow (1867–1927), London; Sotheby's, London, 29 June 1926, lot 27; Wilhelm Reinhold Valentiner (1880–1958), Detroit; his sale, A.W.M. Mensing, Frederik Muller, Amsterdam, 25 October 1932, lot XI; Duveen Brothers, New York, 1941–50; P. & D. Colnaghi and Co., London; Richard H. Zinser (1884–1984), Switzerland and Forest Hills, NY (no mark; see L. 5581); by descent to Suzanne Zinser Rosenborg (1928–2005) and her husband Rutger Rosenborg (1924–2007); N.G. Stogdon, Islip, Oxfordshire; from whom acquired by Clement C. Moore, 2016

SELECT REFERENCES Benesch 1954–57, 4: no. 839; Benesch 1973, no. 839; Stogdon and Artemis 1986, no. 11 (as Rembrandt); Bakker 1998, 239 (as "artist unknown"); Gnann 2021, fig. 123 (as Rembrandt)

Promised gift of Clement C. and Elizabeth Y. Moore

In the 1640s and early 1650s, Rembrandt and his pupils occasionally took long walks to sketch in the countryside, and most of their landscape drawings represent villages and farms in the immediate vicinity of Amsterdam. A favorite destination was Diemen, then an isolated rural settlement consisting of a church and some fifteen other buildings about four miles southeast of the city. Leaving by the Sint-Anthonispoort (Saint Anthony's Gate) near Rembrandt's house, they walked east on the Diemerdijk. The dike extended for miles, sheltering the low-lying fields east of the city from the floodwaters of the IJ, the bay at the south end of the Zuiderzee, Amsterdam's maritime outlet to the North Sea and Atlantic Ocean. At the Diemen turn-off (Diemer Afloop), they diverged from the dike and headed south about 700 yards to their destination. Several drawings and prints by Rembrandt and his followers have been identified as views along the Diemerdijk and of the village itself.[1]

The Moore drawing shows the approach to Diemen from the direction of the turn-off. A large farmstead, comprising a house, barn, haystack, and small shed, occupies the right half of the sheet and, at left, we see a small bridge over a ditch, another farmhouse and the tower of the late medieval church. Three other drawings attributed to Rembrandt include these same buildings from other viewpoints. At least two of them evidently originated on separate visits to the site. In one, the prominent haystack at the far right is full, its roof rising well above the farmhouse (fig. 41.1), while in the Moore drawing it is nearly depleted, and, in a third study, it does not appear at all.[2] Additionally, the fenestration of the brick extension to the farmhouse, just to the left of the haystack, differs in the Moore work from that in the other three sheets. Otto Benesch accounted for the missing haystack and discrepancies in the building's facade as artistic choices.[3] It is more likely, as proposed by specialists in Amsterdam's historical topography, that they reflect the partial demolition and reconstruction of the farmstead between visits by the artists.[4]

That Rembrandt was the author of this *View of Diemen* had never been questioned until 1998, when it was published by Boudewijn Bakker, without comment, as by an unknown draftsman, and the sheet does not appear in the complete oeuvre of the artist's drawings compiled in 2019 by Peter Schatborn.[5]

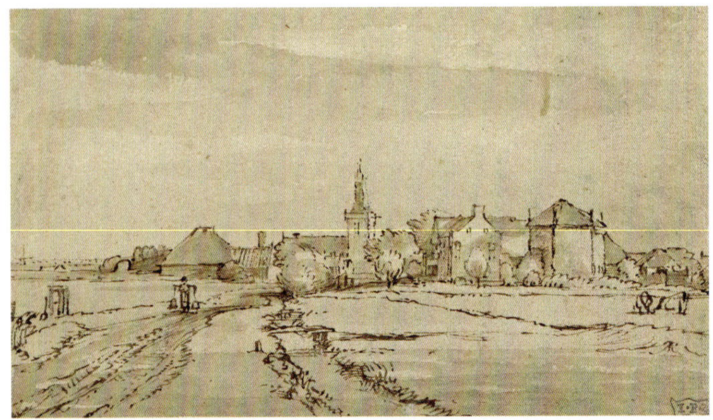

41.1 Attributed to Rembrandt van Rijn, *View of Diemen*, ca. 1650. Count Antoine Seilern Collection, Courtauld Gallery, London.

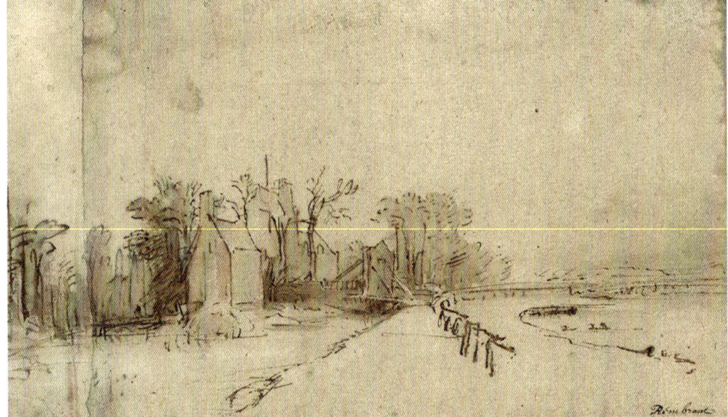

41.2 Rembrandt van Rijn, *Huis Kostverloren*, ca. 1650–52. Staatliche Kunstsammlungen, Kupferstich-Kabinett, Dresden.

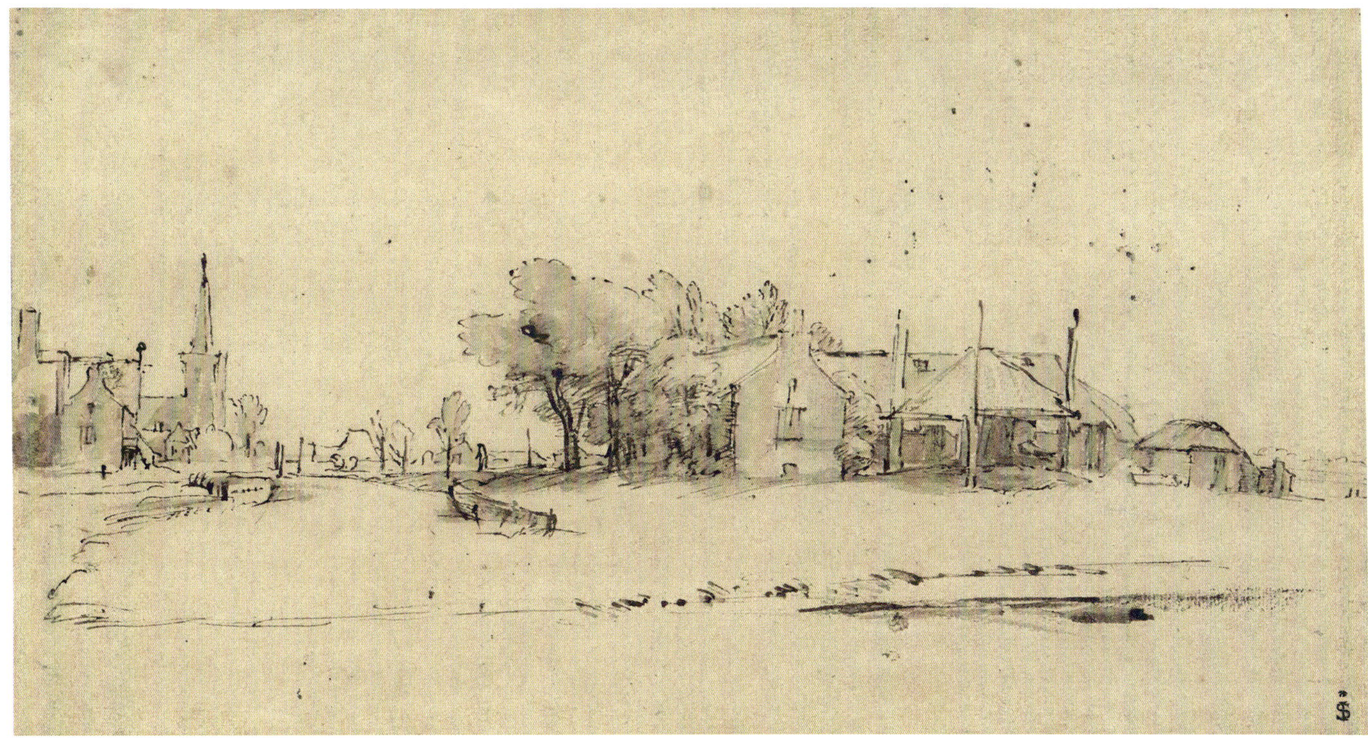

Subsequently, in a 2021 volume on Rembrandt's landscape drawings, Achim Gnann defended the traditional attribution.[6] On the one hand, it is hardly surprising that scholars have assigned this attractive and skillful study to the master's hand. As Gnann rightly pointed out, the loose, dark penwork of the foreground closely resembles the handling in a study of the same site that specialists, including Schatborn, unanimously attribute to Rembrandt.[7] On the other hand, when compared with a similar Rembrandt work of about the same date, a study of the country house Kostverloren (fig. 41.2), some technical shortcomings in the Moore drawing are evident.[8] The thin, undifferentiated pen lines in the left foreground and in the roofs and walls at far left do not effectively suggest form or evoke spatial recession as do the foreground strokes and contours of the buildings in the view of Kostverloren. In the study of Kostverloren, the finely modulated washes produce a varied and harmoniously integrated range of shadows. The washes on the farmhouse and haystack at the right of the Moore sheet are comparatively casually and uniformly applied, and it is especially the absence of variation and animation in the wash that casts doubt on Rembrandt's authorship of the drawing. WWR

WENCESLAUS HOLLAR

Prague 1607–1677 London

42

View of the Thames from the Head of Westminster Pier with Lambeth House in the Distance (recto) and *Sketch of a Landscape with a River* (verso), 1638

Pen and black ink, with gray wash, over black chalk; framing line in brown ink (recto); black chalk (verso)
65 x 137 mm

INSCRIPTIONS Recto, upper right, signed and dated, in black ink: *WH: 1638* (initials in ligature); recto, upper center, inscribed by the artist, in black ink: *Lambeth.* and center left, in the river (somewhat faded): *Thems flu*; verso, lower left, in black chalk (upside down, with the 1938 Sprinzels cat. rais. no.): N 330

PROVENANCE John Edmund Gardner (1819–1899), London; his son Edmund Thomas Gardner (d. before 1929), London; from whom purchased by Major Sir Edward Feetham Coates, 1st Bt. (1853–1921), London, 1909 (no mark; see L. 847); his sale, Sotheby's, London, 1–8 May 1924, probably one of a pair in lot 2299 ("Lambeth from the Horse-ferry, two small original drawings in pen and wash by W. Hollar, signed with his initials and dated 1628")[1] or one of seventeen in lot 2316 ("Lambeth Palace. Early Views of the Palace from the River, by W. Hollar, W. Lodge, J. Kipp and others, *some scarce*"); Henry William Hollebone (act. first half of twentieth century), London (no mark; see L. 1392a); his widow, Mrs. H. Hollebone, London; her sale, Sotheby's, London, 23 November 1955, one of a pair in lot 28; P. & D. Colnaghi and Co., London, 1956; Francis Springell [Franz Sprinzels] (1898–1974), Prague and later Portinscale, Northumberland (no mark; see L. 1049a); his widow, Gertrude Bertha Springell (1908–1985), Portinscale; her sale, Sotheby's, London, 30 June 1986, lot 22; Leger Galleries, London; Ladislaus von Hoffmann (1927–2014), Washington, 1989; his widow, Beatrix von Hoffmann; from whom acquired through Adrian Eeles, England, by Clement C. Moore, 2017

SELECT REFERENCES Sprinzels 1938, no. 330; London 1987, no. 9; Volrábová 2017, no. III/17

Promised gift of Clement C. and Elizabeth Y. Moore

Bohemian artist Wenceslaus Hollar left his native Prague in 1627, aged twenty, to escape the city's growing political and religious strife. For the next half century he led a peripatetic career that took him to Germany, Austria, the Northern Netherlands, Flanders, England, and Tangier, travels that provided endless source material for the landscape and topographical drawings and etchings for which he is now so renowned. Nearly two-thirds of his working life (thirty-two years) was spent in England, where he first arrived in December 1636 after earlier that year meeting the English diplomat and collector Thomas Howard, 2nd [14th] Earl of Arundel in Cologne. The previous two years (1634–35) Hollar had traveled in the Northern Netherlands, deriving inspiration from the Dutch landscape and producing some of his best early landscape drawings.[2]

Once in England, Hollar shifted his focus mainly to printmaking, with the notable exception of a coherent group of some forty-five drawings that can be dated to the late 1630s and early-to-mid-1640s, and a much smaller, more diverse group from his second English period (1652–77). The starting point for the dating of the earlier group is, in fact, the present monogrammed and dated sketch of 1638. Its view, from the north side of the River Thames looking upstream toward Lambeth Palace (the residence of the Archbishop of Canterbury), is one of several made along the banks of the river between Westminster and the area of London known as the City. A larger, more finished sheet in the Barber Institute, Birmingham (fig. 42.1),[3] drawn rather unusually in brown rather than black ink, shows the same pier from farther east and includes buildings annotated by the artist as *Parliament House* and *Westminster Hall*. The present sketch may have been made from a window in the upper story of one of the houses seen at the far right of the Barber drawing, just to the east of the pier. That pier was evidently where small, moored boats could be rented to cross the river, reminding one rather amusingly of an Oxford punts-for-hire service.

The faint sketch in black chalk on the verso does not include enough topographical information or landmarks to identify its precise location, but it is probably a view of the Thames Valley.

Although only a very few drawings that once belonged to Hollar's early English patrons and friends, such as the Earl of Arundel and John Evelyn, can be identified with certainty,[4] this sheet can be traced through the collections of several passionate nineteenth- and twentieth-century collectors of topographical

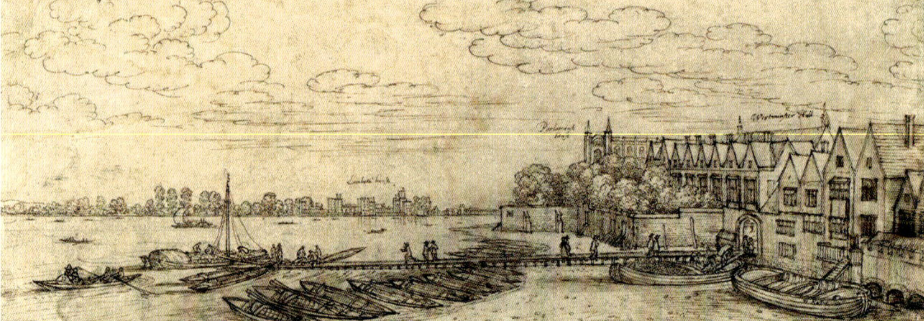

42.1 Wenceslaus Hollar, *View of the Thames below Westminster Pier*, ca. 1637. Barber Institute of Fine Arts, Birmingham.

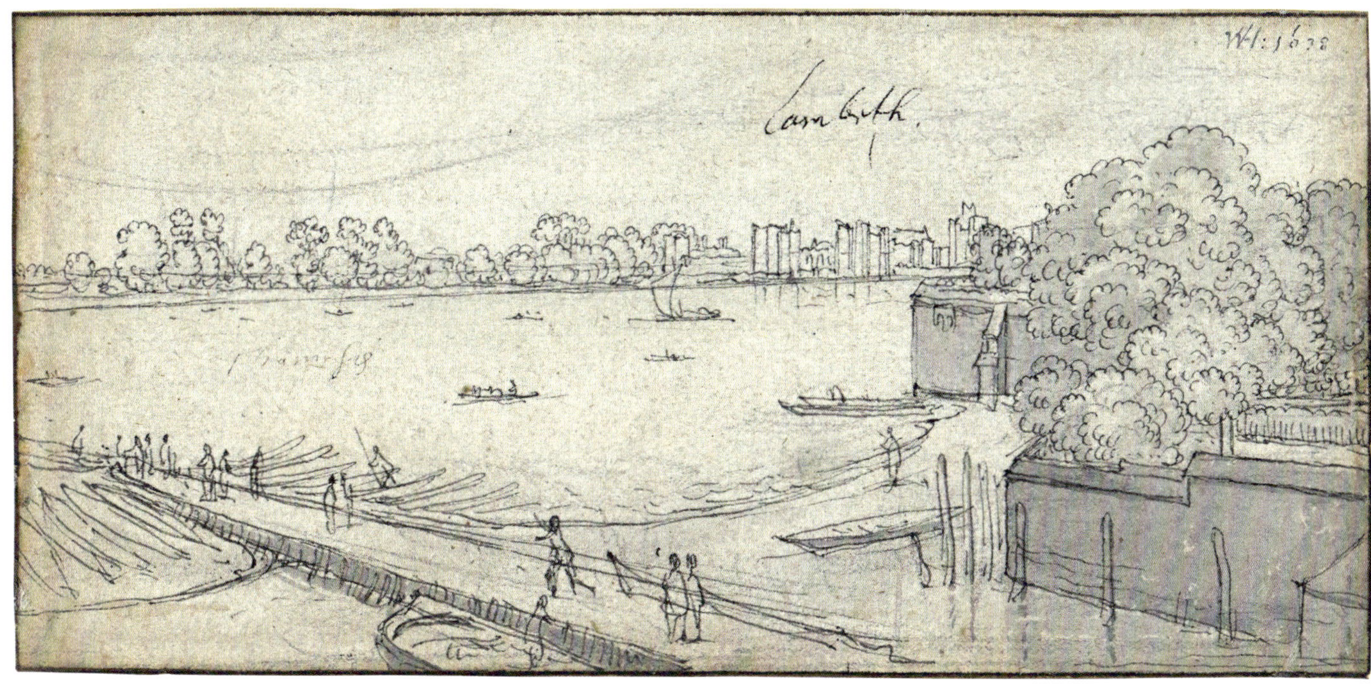

views of London. John Edmund Gardner assembled a collection of over 4,000 such drawings,[5] which was purchased en bloc from his son by the English politician and financier Sir Edward Feetham Coates, 1st Bt., who eventually owned over 100 portfolios of such views. Wine merchant Henry William Hollebone likewise formed a collection of topographical prints and drawings of London, including several works by Hollar that featured among the 283 lots in his widow's 1955 sale. The Moore drawing was then purchased at that sale by Colnaghi, perhaps on behalf of the first great scholar of Hollar's drawings, the Czech businessman and philanthropist Franz Sprinzels. He had fled the Nazi occupation of his country in 1939 and settled in England, where he anglicized his name to Francis Springell.

The holdings of these specialized English collections testify to the prominent role played by Hollar's work in the tradition of British topographical drawings that developed so strongly in the eighteenth and nineteenth centuries, a realm into which the Moore collection has now also naturally ventured. JST

JAN LIEVENS

Leiden 1607–1674 Amsterdam

43

Standing Man with a Cane, ca. 1632–35

Black chalk

339 x 179 mm

WATERMARK Small shield, lower center

INSCRIPTIONS Recto, lower right, in black ink: *Mister J. Liuense*

PROVENANCE Addison Francis Baker-Cresswell (1874–1921), Cresswell and Hadston, Northumberland; his gift to Dorothy Winkworth, mother of Mary Winkworth, later Mrs. G.W. Wrangham (ca. 1903–1933), London and Hatfield; by descent to Edward Addison Wrangham (1900–1986), Northumberland; James Faber, London; from whom acquired by Clement C. Moore, 2010

SELECT REFERENCES Parker 1928, 4, pl. 5 (as Van Dyck); Schneider 1932, 69; Van Hall 1963, 188, no. 11; Sumowski 1979–92, 7: 3676–77, no. 1649[x]

Promised gift of Clement C. and Elizabeth Y. Moore

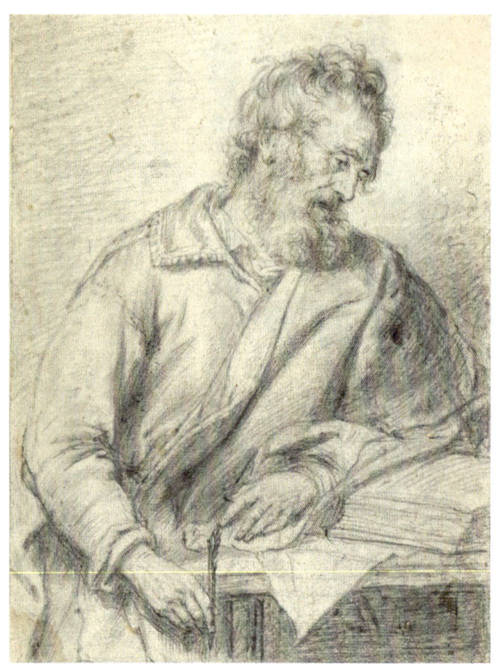

43.1 Jan Lievens, *St. Mark the Evangelist*, ca. 1635–43. Albertina, Vienna.

This swashbuckling, rapidly drawn depiction of a stylish gentleman, who eyes the viewer (or the artist) with a sympathetic but possibly slightly impatient look, encapsulates so many aspects of Jan Lievens's somewhat mercurial talents as a draftsman. It also seems to be one of extremely few drawings by Lievens that can be convincingly assigned to the period of his three-year stay in London, in 1632–35.

Something of a stylistic butterfly, Lievens was nonetheless one of the most original and accomplished draftsmen of the Dutch seventeenth century, with a rich and varied output that spans a number of different media, genres, and styles. From his early days in Leiden, when his art was so closely entwined with that of Rembrandt, through his more Van Dyckian Antwerp period, to his mature career as an ambitious history painter in Amsterdam, drawing always played an important part in his creative processes—and, as with Rembrandt, was not merely an adjunct to his painted work, but fulfilled its own independent artistic functions.

In no area of Lievens's work was this more true than in his portraits, and his magnificent black chalk portrait drawings—a few of them studies for prints but in most cases made as independent works of art—are without close parallels either in his own paintings or in the work of any of his contemporaries. The great majority of these, including all those that are actually dated, were executed during the last three decades of Lievens's life, after he established himself in Amsterdam.[1] There, especially in the later 1640s and the 1650s, he made a series of superbly intimate yet revealing studies of many of the leading figures in Amsterdam life, his subjects ranging from burgomasters and politicians, by way of clerics and scholars to the poets, playwrights, and actors with whom Lievens seems to have spent much of his time.

The most significant precedent for this series of portrait drawings is to be found in the work of Lievens's illustrious Flemish predecessor, Anthony van Dyck, with whose half- and three-quarter-length portrait drawings, made to be engraved in the famous *Iconographie* series, there are clear parallels, both stylistic and conceptual. Indeed, Van Dyck's impact on the course of Lievens's career was fundamental. The two artists seem first to have met in the winter of 1631–32, when the Flemish master, who was visiting the Northern Netherlands, made a drawing or painting, now lost, of the brilliant young Dutchman, which was engraved by Lucas Vorsterman for the *Iconographie*.[2] Not long afterwards, Lievens, who clearly aspired to the world of courtly elegance that Van Dyck so effortlessly embodied, followed his role model to England, where he seems to have worked in Van Dyck's studio for some three years, 1632–35. This devotion to things Flemish endured; after leaving London, Lievens settled in Antwerp, where he lived until 1643, when he finally moved north again, to Amsterdam.

Although no dated portrait drawing from earlier than 1649 survives, Lievens's Antwerp period does provide us with a couple of very Van Dyckian portraits, most notably that of the painter Adriaen Brouwer (the sitter's death in 1638 providing us with a *terminus ante quem* for the drawing's execution).[3] From the artist's previous, English period, however, astonishingly few drawings of any type are known: just a single, Van Dyckian landscape showing the view across the River Thames at Westminster,[4] another slight (and tenuously attributed) river view,[5] a pen-and-ink portrait sketch of King Charles I,[6] and a small handful of black chalk portrait

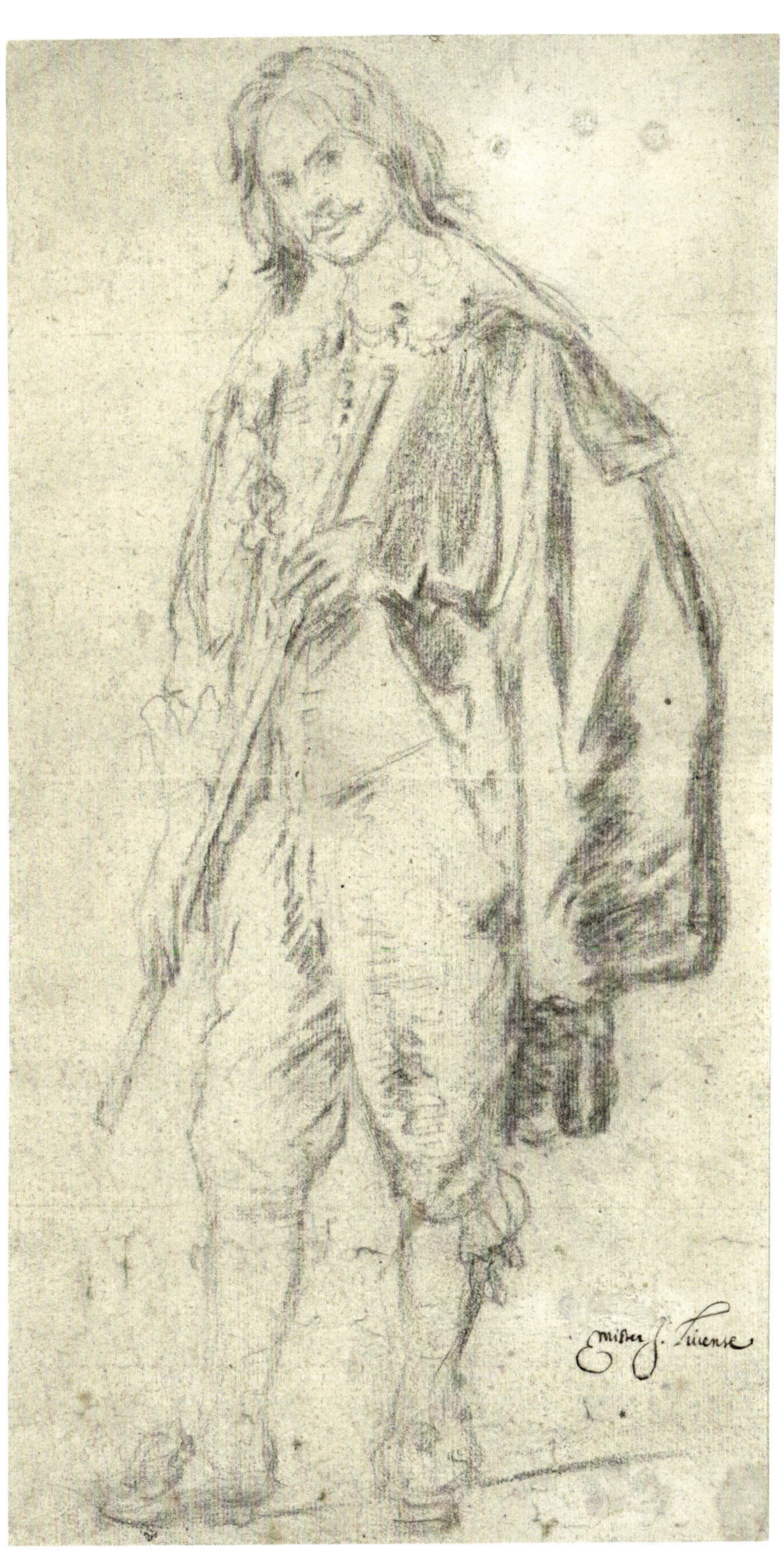

studies, including the present sheet, which seem in all probability to have been made in England, rather than afterwards.

Stylistically, the Moore drawing is indeed close to the portrait of Brouwer, and perhaps even closer to another drawing from the Antwerp period, the *St. Mark the Evangelist* in the Albertina, Vienna (fig. 43.1), which is a study for the artist's own etching.[7] Yet various factors, taken together, argue even more strongly for the assigning of the drawing to Lievens's preceding years in London. Not only is the stylistic debt to Van Dyck even more pronounced (indeed, the drawing was first published, by Karl Parker, as a portrait *of* Lievens, drawn by Van Dyck),[8] but the costume is also strongly reminiscent of those seen in Van Dyck's many portraits of English nobles and courtiers.[9] Also, though the distinctive facial features clearly indicate that this drawing was intended to be an image of a specific individual, Lievens has not taken the trouble to capture these features in the rather detailed way typical of his later drawn portraits, and the drawing, with its generally rather sketchy execution, seems as much a figure study as a portrait. But above all the English inscription, written in a hand that seems more or less contemporaneous, ties the drawing inescapably with England. It could, of course, have been made in the Low Countries at a later date and subsequently brought to England, but it seems far more likely that it was actually drawn there and never left.

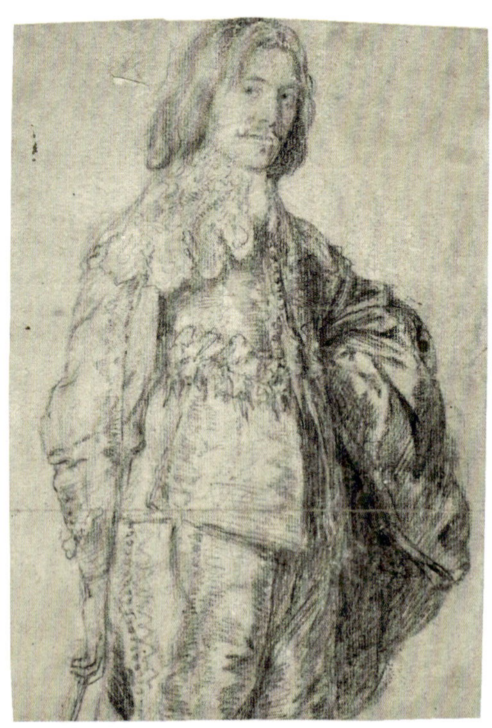

43.2 Jan Lievens, *A Young Man Standing in Three-Quarter Length, Facing Right*, ca. 1632–35. Kunstmuseum, Düsseldorf.

Just four other black chalk portrait drawings by Lievens, all now in Düsseldorf and very possibly depicting members of the same family, can reasonably be thought to date from the artist's stay in England. Of these, a drawing of a standing gentleman (fig. 43.2), though slightly smaller in scale, is the closest to the Moore portrait and may even represent the same man; the prominent mustache, heavy, descending eyebrows, strong jawline, and penetrating, dark eyes are strikingly similar in both drawings.[10]

Though documented in the literature for almost a century, this significant and original drawing, made at the watershed moment when Lievens largely turned his back on the Rembrandt-related drawing style of his early career, has never before been publicly exhibited. Seeing it at first hand, it is strikingly clear how profoundly Lievens had by this time come under Van Dyck's seductive spell, and how this influence merged with his earlier approach to figure drawing and portraiture, providing the basis for the distinctive and highly personal series of later portrait drawings that form such a central part of Lievens's artistic achievement and legacy. GMGR

JAN LIEVENS

Leiden 1607–1674 Amsterdam

44

A Wooded Landscape with a Herdsman and His Cattle near a Barn, ca. 1655–60

Pen and brown ink and wash

207 x 295 mm

WATERMARK Large shield in a circle

INSCRIPTIONS Verso, lower left, in pen and brown ink: *Jan Lievens*; verso, lower right, in graphite: *De Hochschild* and NH 6 (?); a number of other inscriptions at the lower edge have been erased

PROVENANCE Frederik Adama van Scheltema (1846–1899), Amsterdam; his sale, Frederik Muller, Amsterdam, 11 June 1912, lot 147 (to Gutekunst); Helbing, Munich, 8 June 1914, lot 946; Bernard Houthakker, Amsterdam, ca. 1929–32; private collection, the Netherlands; anonymous sale, Houthakker-Hollstein, Amsterdam, 21 February 1939, lot 39; Bernard Houthakker, Amsterdam, 1973; Frits Markus (1909–1996) and Rita Markus (1914–2005), New York; their sale, Christie's, New York, 24 January 2006, lot 77 (bought in); private collection, Europe; from which acquired through Johan Bosch van Rosenthal, Art Consult, Amsterdam, by Clement C. Moore, 2013

SELECT REFERENCES Amsterdam 1929, no. 234; Schneider 1932, no. Z292; Schneider and Ekkart 1973, 231, 370, no. Z292; Sumowski 1979–92, 7: 3814, under no. 1714[x]

Promised gift of Clement C. and Elizabeth Y. Moore

The landscape drawings of Jan Lievens comprise one of the most important and original aspects of this many-faceted artist's work. Often they are, like this example, substantial in scale and expansive in handling, and exude immense pastoral serenity. Though their subjects are various, including extremely dense woodland scenes, images like this one of farm buildings among trees, panoramic landscapes, and occasionally specific town views, all these sheets are united by their distinctive, energetic looping penwork and also by the fact that only in a couple of the earliest sheets is this penwork combined with any use of wash—something that distinguishes Lievens's landscape style from that of his great contemporary and fellow landscape draftsman, Rembrandt.

Another important respect in which the landscape drawings of the two artists differ is that many of Lievens's seem to have been made in the studio, as independent works for sale, rather than directly from nature. That said, Lievens surely based all his landscape compositions on real observations of nature, but even though a number of them exist in more than one version, differing only in minor details, it is rare to find a pairing in which it is totally clear which drawing came first, and there is only one known example of a large finished landscape drawing by the artist that is clearly based on a small, rapid sketchbook-type study.[1]

The existence of multiple, similarly sized versions of several compositions has led some to suggest that one or other version may have been drawn by Jan Lievens's son, Jan Andrea Lievens, but stylistic comparisons with the few signed drawings by Jan Andrea almost always contradict these attributions.[2]

No other version of the Moore collection drawing is known, but one of the most similar in character among the artist's other landscapes, a depiction of a homestead in a forest, exists in at least three autograph versions, and their comparison is particularly revealing regarding both Lievens's working method and the function of his various landscape drawings. The simplest of the three versions in terms of composition, in the Morgan Library & Museum (fig. 44.1), is also the

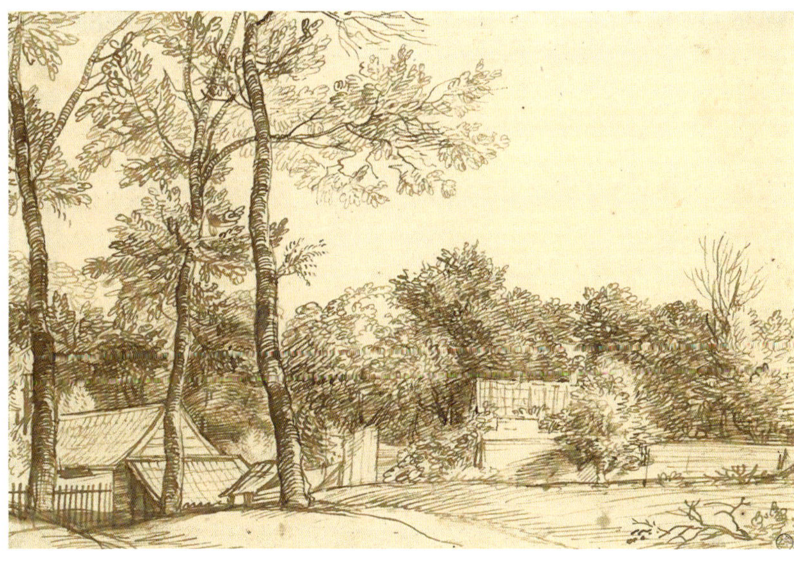

44.1 Jan Lievens, *Farm Buildings and Three Tall Trees*, late 1650s. Morgan Library & Museum, New York.

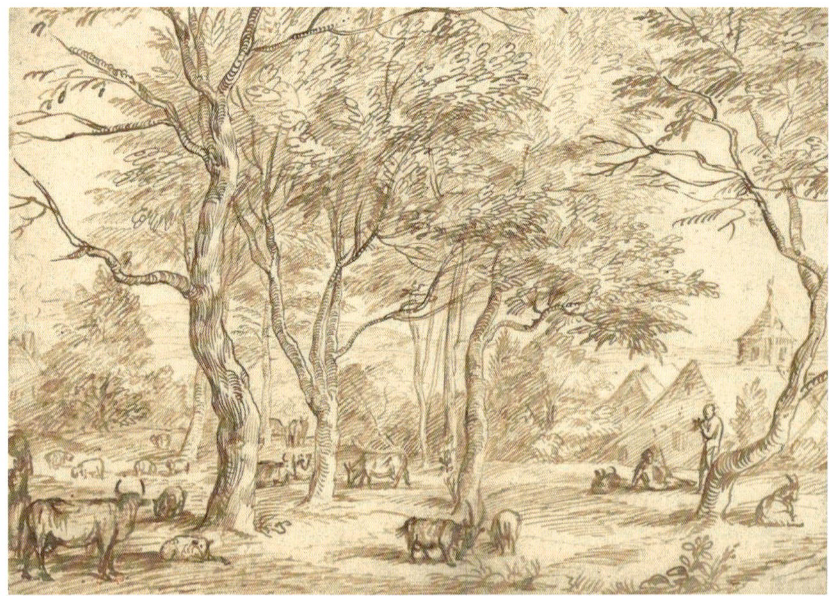

44.2 Jan Lievens, *Wooded Landscape with Shepherds, Flocks, and a Village*, late 1650s. John and Marine van Vlissingen Art Foundation.

smallest sheet, and is most likely the drawing from life that provided the basis for the other more elaborate versions—both, unusually, drawn on rather larger sheets of Asian paper.[3] (More frequently when two similar examples exist of "finished" landscapes by Lievens, one is on Asian paper, the other on European laid paper.[4]) In this case, the larger versions both expand the scene a little to the sides and include more trees, as well as a pair of resting figures, one playing the flute; furthermore, one of the drawings, in the Abrams collection, is signed with the artist's initials (the only known example of a signed landscape drawing by Lievens) and would appear to be the primary "finished" version, made for sale.[5] All the same, the other larger version of the composition, in the British Museum, is no less elaborate and only slightly less accomplished, so must also have been made to be sold.[6]

Pastoral motifs of shepherds and their animals, sometimes, as here, just resting, sometimes making music, recur in a number of Lievens's landscapes, giving these works an almost Claudian spirit. The most striking example of this approach to composition is the fine sheet in the John and Marine van Vlissingen Art Foundation (fig. 44.2), but the Moore drawing also belongs to this group of serene, rustic scenes, which constitute a particularly appealing subsection of Lievens's landscape drawings.[7] Though it is generally hard to date Lievens's landscapes with any certainty, it seems likely that most of these rather open, pastoral compositions date from the mid- to late 1650s.[8] **GMGR**

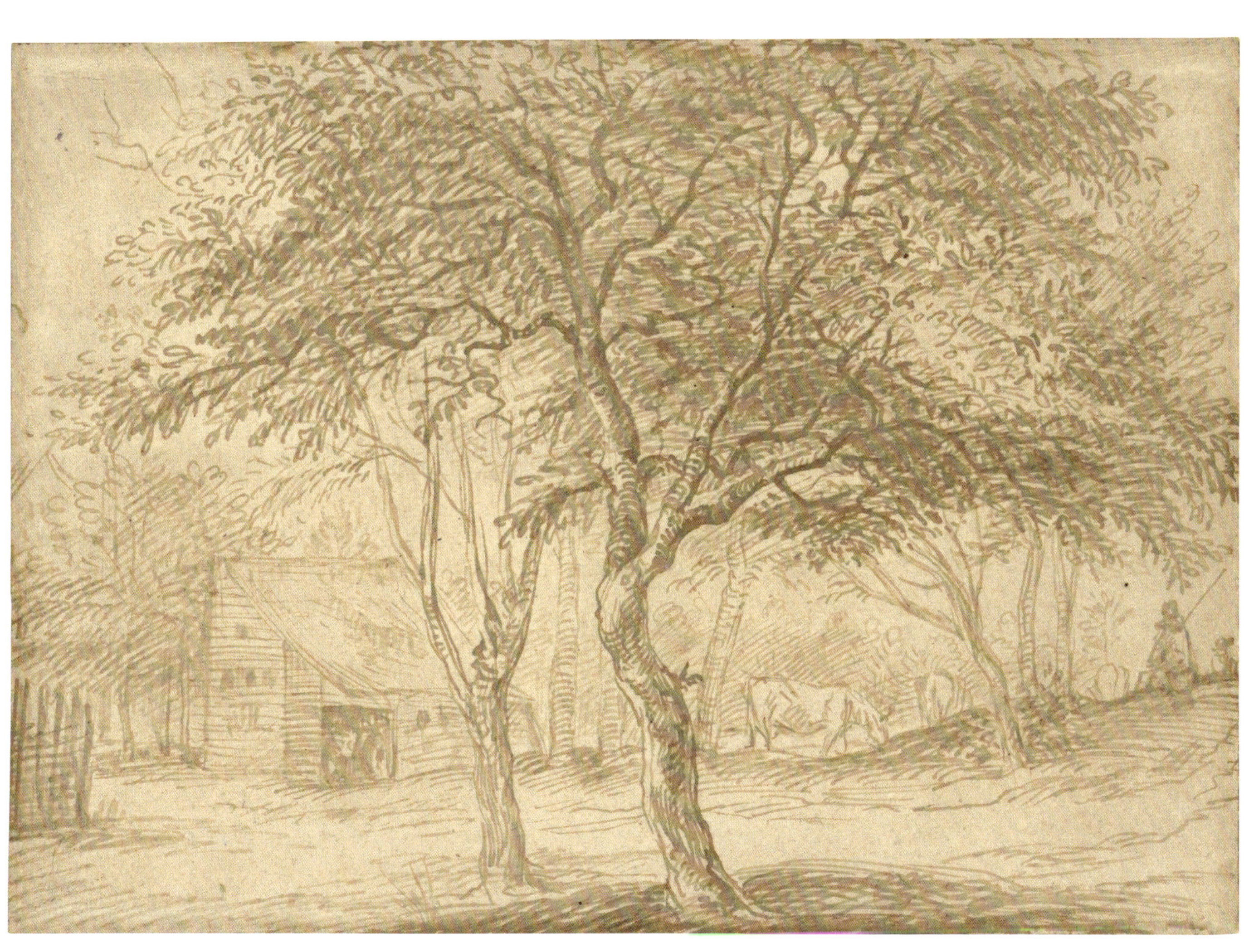

WILLEM VAN DE VELDE THE ELDER

Amsterdam 1628/29–1682 Amsterdam

45a,b

(a) *Portrait of the English Fourth-Rate Warship, "Tiger," as Rebuilt in 1681*, 1681

Brush and gray wash, over black chalk, with touches of pen and black ink, on two sheets of paper

311 x 565 mm

WATERMARK Two examples of the same motif (one upside down on the left-hand sheet, one near the center of the right sheet): three stacked circles, respectively containing a cross (this circle flanked by rampant lions), the letters AG and a triangle, surmounted by a crown, similar to Laurentius and Laurentius 2008, no. 35 (London, 1663)

INSCRIPTIONS Recto, lower right, in the artist's hand, in graphite: *de thijger*, and on the side of the ship, just below the top row of guns, *swart*; recto, lower right, in another hand, in brown ink, *Old Vandervelde*

PROVENANCE From an album of drawings primarily by Willem van de Velde the Elder and the Younger owned by the Dukes of Northumberland, Alnwick Castle, Alnwick, Northumberland; by descent to Ralph Percy (b. 1956), 12th Duke of Northumberland; by whom sold, Sotheby's, London, 9 July 2014, lot 39; where acquired by Clement C. Moore, 2014

SELECT REFERENCES Robinson 1958–74, 1: 172, under no. 596

Promised gift of Clement C. and Elizabeth Y. Moore

The son of a seaman and master of a military transport vessel, Van de Velde the Elder spent his entire life drawing boats and seascapes. Before he and his son Willem the Younger moved from the Netherlands to England, presumably to avoid the worsening political situation after the French invasion of the Dutch Republic in May 1672, Willem the Elder had served as an official artist for the Dutch fleet. To ensure the accuracy of his drawn and painted records, he usually observed the sea battles firsthand from a galliot. On their arrival in England, father and son "switched sides," so to speak, even though the Dutch Republic was still at war with England in the Third Anglo-Dutch War. The pair was immediately hired by King Charles II, himself a keen sailor who provided them with a house in Greenwich, and who early in 1674 granted them an annual salary of 100 pounds in addition to payments for commissioned works.[1]

As noted in the 2014 Sotheby's sale catalogue entry on the drawing, no. 45a is an excellent example of distinctive "ship portraits" uniquely made by Willem the Elder and the Younger. They are meticulous, accurate images of the vessels with which the Dutch fought the English during the 1660s and 1670s, during the Second and Third Anglo-Dutch Wars (1665–67 and 1672–74, respectively). Although drawn with a degree of liveliness, such "portraits" were intended to record every detail of the vessels in question, such as the stern decorations and the number of gun ports, so that the ships could later be incorporated accurately in the father and son's painted compositions.

The *Tiger*—the object of more individual "ship portraits" by Van de Velde the Elder than almost any other vessel—was built in 1647 (as a fourth-rate ship with forty-four guns) and rebuilt twice, in 1681 (with forty-eight guns) and 1702. It is seen here as it looked after the first rebuilding. Besides six studies of the ship in the National Maritime Museum, Greenwich, London,[2] and four in Museum Boijmans Van Beuningen, Rotterdam,[3] there is a detailed study of the ship seen from the starboard bow, made ca. 1675 (i.e., before the first rebuilding), which passed through the New York art market in 2005.[4] One of the Rotterdam sheets (inv. no. MB 1866/T 387, dated 1676) also shows the ship before its first rebuild, having been drawn shortly after the Van de Veldes moved from the Netherlands to England in the winter of 1672–73.

In his capacity as a retainer to the English king, Van de Velde the Elder was ultimately banned by the monarch at the age of sixty-two (1690) from risking his life on the open sea. Until then, however, he often accompanied Charles II on his journeys and kept a visual record of the trips. On 17–27 August 1681, for instance, the king sailed down the Thames to Woolwich to see the newly rebuilt *Tiger*, before she set sail for the Mediterranean, under Charles Berkeley, 2nd Baron Berkeley of Stratton, who was only nineteen when he was given command of the ship.[5] After dining aboard the *Tiger*, the king and his party sailed with her downstream as far as Sheerness and Chatham, before returning to London. During a period of only three days, Van de Velde made over eighty drawings of their voyage, many of which he numbered. Only some twenty-five drawings from the series are known: twenty-three in public collections, and two monumental works, no. 45b (numbered "7")—the largest of the surviving works—and another scene of the *Visit of Charles II to the Rebuilt "Tiger" at Woolwich, 17–27 August 1681* (numbered "3"), which were sold

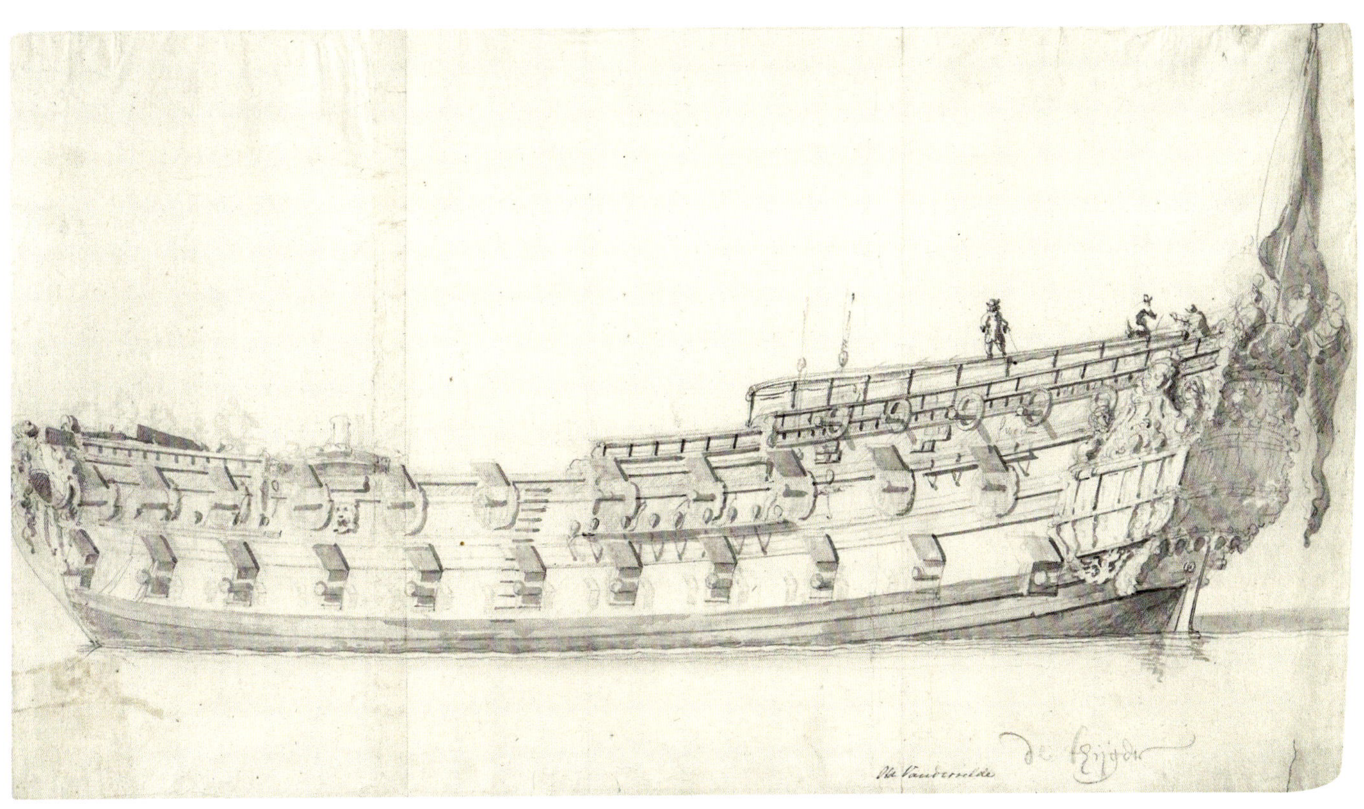

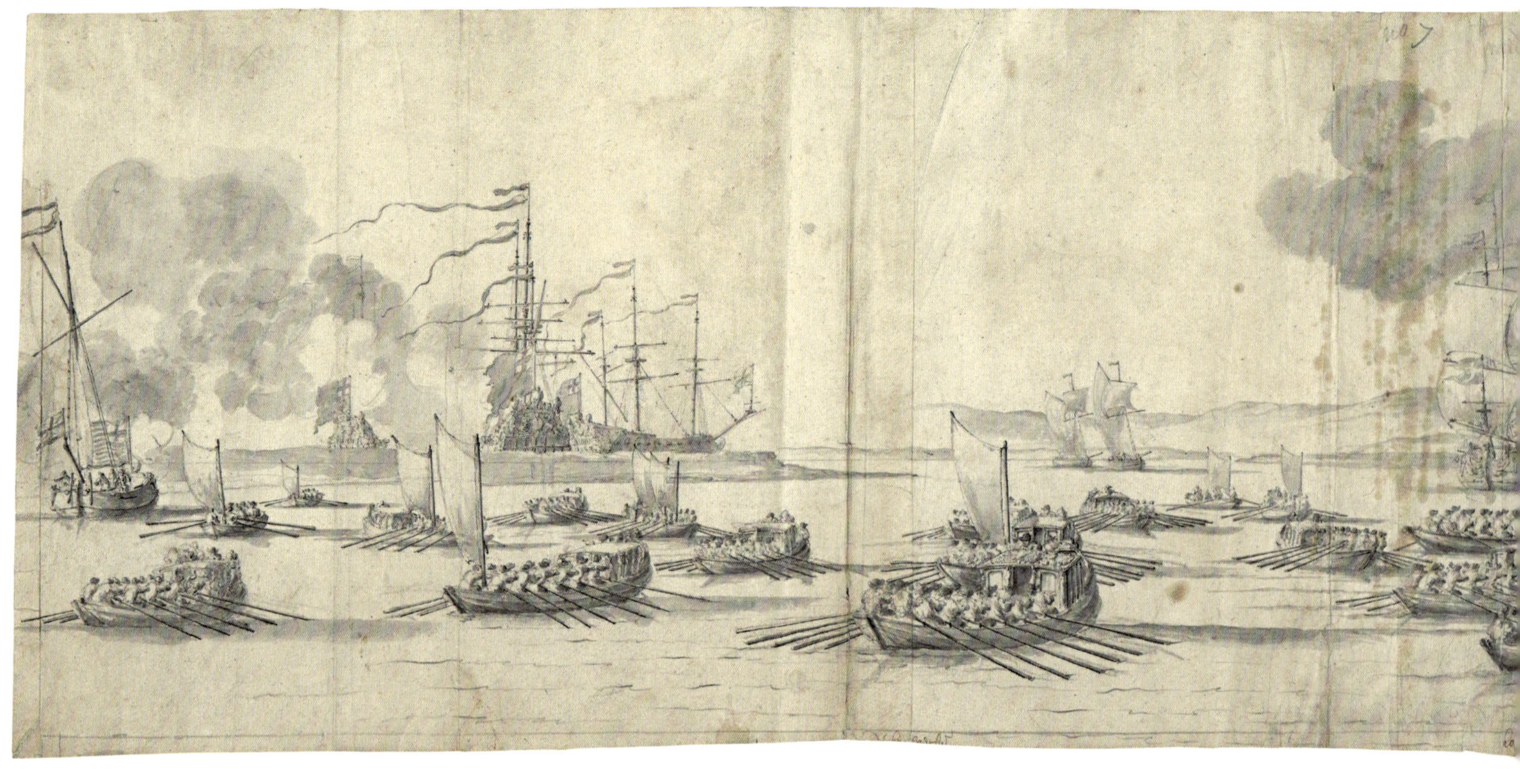

(b) *Visit of Charles II to the Rebuilt "Tiger" at Woolwich, 17–27 August 1681, and Several of the King's Ships*, 1681

Pen and black ink, with gray wash, over graphite, on four sheets of paper; ruled framing line along the lower edge
298 x 1263 mm

WATERMARK Grapes on an ornamental base between two pillars or posts, similar to Heawood 3514–15 (London, 1672)

INSCRIPTIONS Recto, upper center, in the artist's hand, in brown ink: *het paseren van wollits ende eenige konings schepen die daer inde / reviere laegen* ("the passing of Woolwich and several of the king's ships which lie there in the river"); underneath this, in another hand, in graphite: . . .*W de groote*; recto, lower edge, by the artist, in brown ink: *baersie* [trimmed at bottom] ("barge") and *konigs baersie* ("king's barge"); farther to the right, in another hand, in graphite: *de groote*. . . . ; recto, upper left center, by the artist, in graphite: *no 7*. . .; recto, upper right, in another hand: *9*; and above this, on an added sheet of paper, in a later hand: *9*

PROVENANCE Possibly Junius Spencer Morgan III (1892–1960); by descent to John Pierpont Morgan II (1918–2004), New York; his son, Junius Spencer Morgan IV (b. 1947), Locust Valley, NY; his sale, Sotheby's, New York, 25 January 2006, lot 9; where acquired by Clement C. Moore

Promised gift of Clement C. and Elizabeth Y. Moore

in 2006 as part of the major, rediscovered group of Van de Velde drawings from the collection of John Pierpont Morgan II, inherited by his son Junius Spencer Morgan IV.[6] They are assumed to have been purchased by John's father, Junius Spencer Morgan III, who, having served in the navy and later designed yachts, had a lifelong interest in marine subjects. Until the reappearance of these two drawings in 2006, the earliest known drawing from the sequence was *The "Tiger" with Sweeps Out* in Greenwich, which is numbered "11."[7]

The king's barge is in the center foreground of the *Visit of Charles II to the Rebuilt "Tiger"* (no. 45b, fig. 45.1), and behind it to the right are the warships from the Woolwich shipyard. Beyond is the Thames, looking downstream along the Woolwich Reach, with the higher ground of Kent in the background and farther to the right.

The *Portrait of the English Fourth-Rate Warship, "Tiger," as Rebuilt in 1681* is tangentially related to one of the sub-themes of the Moore collection—that is, Man vs. Nature—for it came from an album of drawings by Willem van de Velde the Elder and the Younger long owned by the Dukes of Northumberland. In 2014, the 12th Duke sold a large number of sheets from that album to raise £15 million to cover the costs of a flood of the River Tyne on 25 September 2012, when a culvert owned by the Northumberland Estates collapsed after heavy rains, leading to the demolition of several blocks of flats in the parish of Newburn near Newcastle upon Tyne. With the exception of Moore's purchase of this sheet at that sale (given its link to the *Visit of Charles II to the Rebuilt "Tiger,"* (no. 45b, fig. 45.1), with its ex-Morgan provenance, already in his collection), all the others from the album were acquired by the Rijksmuseum's Department of History. JST

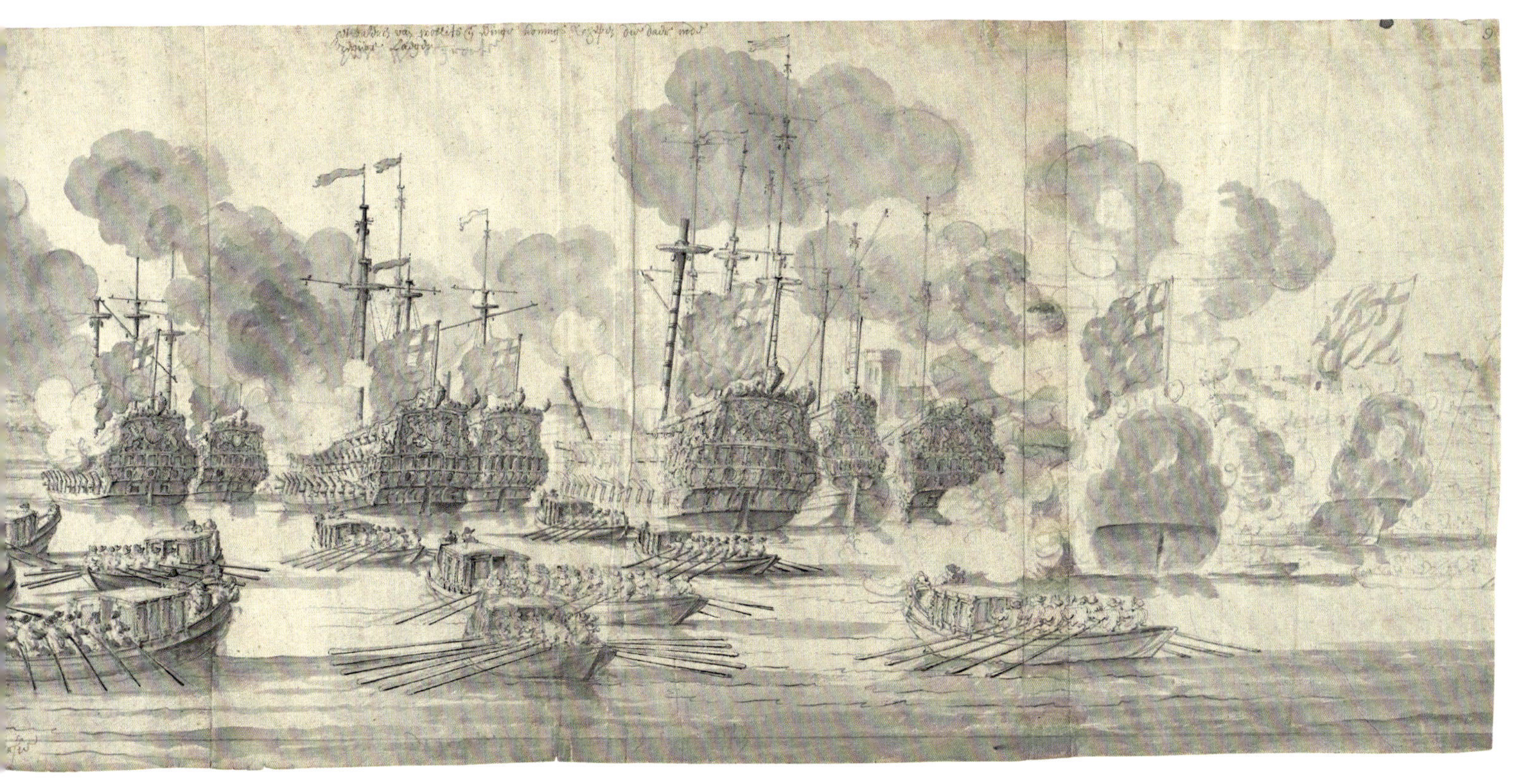

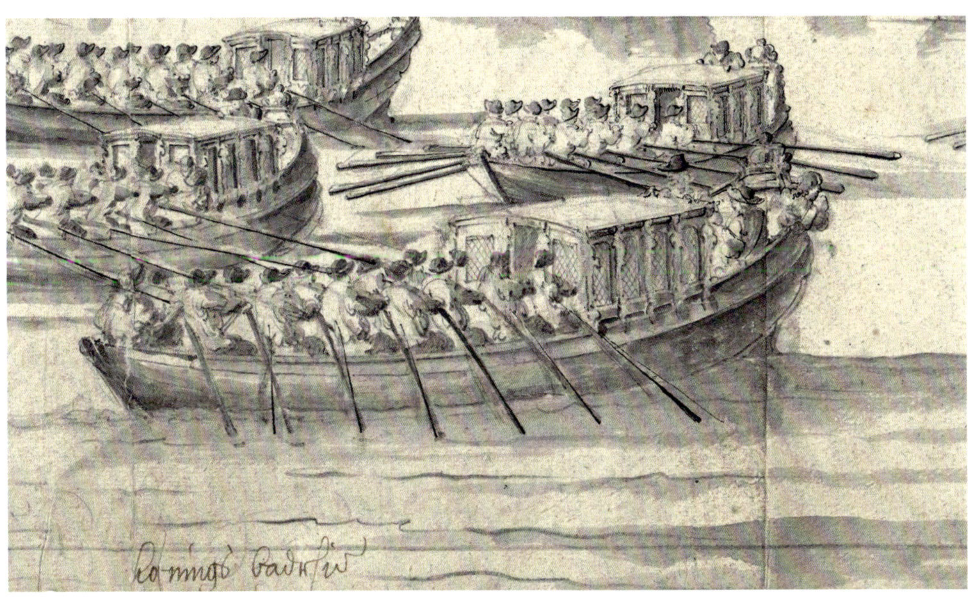

45.1 Detail of no. 45b showing the king's barge.

JACOB MARREL

Frankenthal 1613/14–1681 Frankfurt am Main

46

Two Stems of a Red and White Tulip: "Colombijn en wit van Poelenburg," ca. 1632–49

Watercolor and opaque watercolor, over black chalk
344 x 225 mm

WATERMARK Strasbourg lily, center

INSCRIPTIONS Recto, lower right, in brown ink: *Colombijn en wit van Poelenburg*; verso, upper right, in brown ink: N°19

PROVENANCE Sotheby Mak van Waay, Amsterdam, 3 May 1976, lot 118 (as on parchment); Sotheby's, London, 4 July 2012, lot 106; where acquired by Clement C. Moore

Promised gift of Clement C. and Elizabeth Y. Moore

Tulips, native to Central Asia, reached the Netherlands via the Ottoman court in the sixteenth century. By the second quarter of the seventeenth century, the flower's elegant form and almond-shaped petals, available in a vibrant array of colors and patterns, was a ubiquitous and conspicuous sign of the fledgling Dutch Republic's economic prowess. The tulip's appeal reached across various socioeconomic strata, though its popularity certainly reflected the interests of a powerful, newly monied class—the regents (*regenten*)—who, funded in part by colonial exploits, assembled collections of art, objects, plants, and *naturalia* from vast geographical territories. *Regenten* nursed their tulip obsession through often lavish expenditures on the newest or most exquisite cultivars. Yet more extreme is the case of Dr. Nicolaes Tulp, famously depicted by Rembrandt, who changed his surname from Pieterszoon to Tulp (Dutch for tulip), thus expressing his aspirations of social ascendancy—he would become a powerful politician—through a beguiling flower and all it entailed.[1]

Artists, too, helped sate this mania with artworks featuring the comely flower, though the tulip became just as much an emblem for beauty as for vainglorious pursuits. Dutch artist Hendrick Goltzius's 1614 *Federkunststuck* masterpiece *Young Man Holding a Skull and a Tulip* in the Morgan Library & Museum, with its inscription "QVIS EVADET / NEMO" ("Who escapes? No man"), alludes to the flower's perceived moral ambiguity (fig. 46.1).[2] Nevertheless, the graceful tulip proved for artists a willing and profitable subject across media, from printed books to natural history drawings, dazzling still-life paintings, textiles, and even diminutive blue and white tiles. Tulip books (*tulpenboeken*), albums containing detailed watercolor drawings of tulips, also emerged from this milieu. Such works—which presented fresh flowers in perpetuity—documented fantastic arrays of specimens to entice and inform bulb buyers or to inventory tulip collections. Painter and draftsman Jacob Marrel became one of the foremost practitioners of the genre, with a particular penchant for red and white tulips.[3] Having trained with still-life masters Georg Flegel and Jan Davidsz de Heem, Marrel was prepared to meet the demands of tulip lovers, and his well-timed 1632 arrival in Utrecht from Frankfurt was perhaps part of a plan to work also as a bulb dealer.[4] A tulip book done by Marrel, dated to 1642, would seem to express some regret for his choices, for the title page reads, "as a reminder of the senseless trade, conducted with them in the years 1635, 1636, and 1637."[5] Whatever his misfortunes, the artist continued to paint and draw the flower even after leaving Utrecht for Frankfurt in 1650. Moreover, he was a teacher (and stepfather) to celebrated artist and naturalist Maria Sibylla Merian (see no. 70), whose drawings and prints likewise feature tulips.

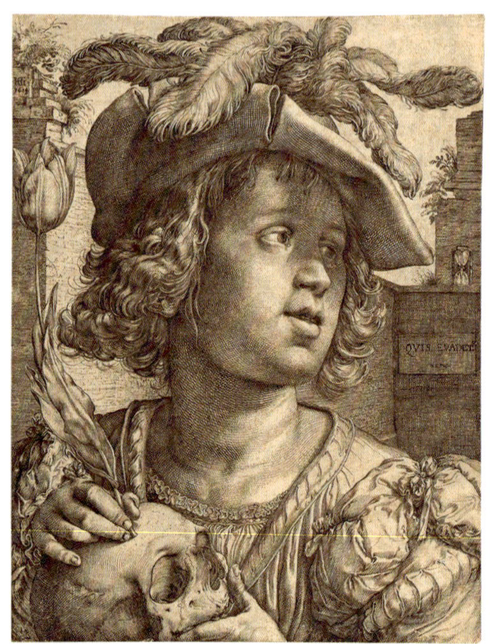

46.1 Hendrick Goltzius, *Young Man Holding a Skull and a Tulip*, 1614. Morgan Library & Museum, New York.

This finely drawn and colored sheet exemplifies Marrel's work, which was praised in his time and shortly thereafter by Arnold Houbraken and Joachim von Sandrart.[6] Here, Marrel pictures two gracefully entwined stems, a smaller, less mature bloom lilting to the left across the stem of the larger tulip. Strokes of crimson and white show off the flowers' elaborate variegated and speckled marks. Blue-gray wash forms a shadowy cast across satiny petals revealing the inner folds of flowers only just opening in warm light. The drawing is a superb example of Marrel's technique: faint chalk lines trace the tulips' silhouettes while passages of

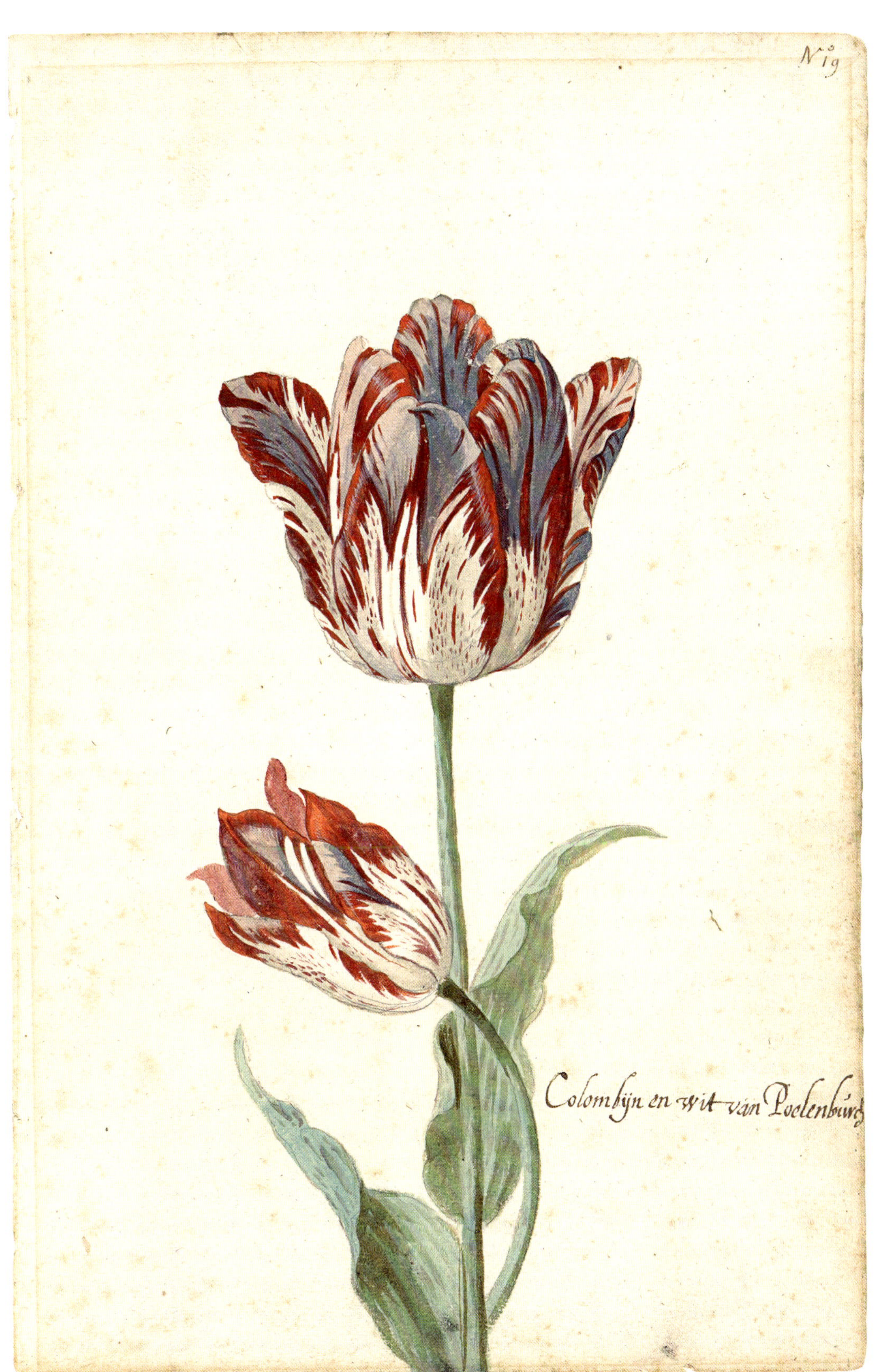
No 19
Colombijn en wit van Poelenburg

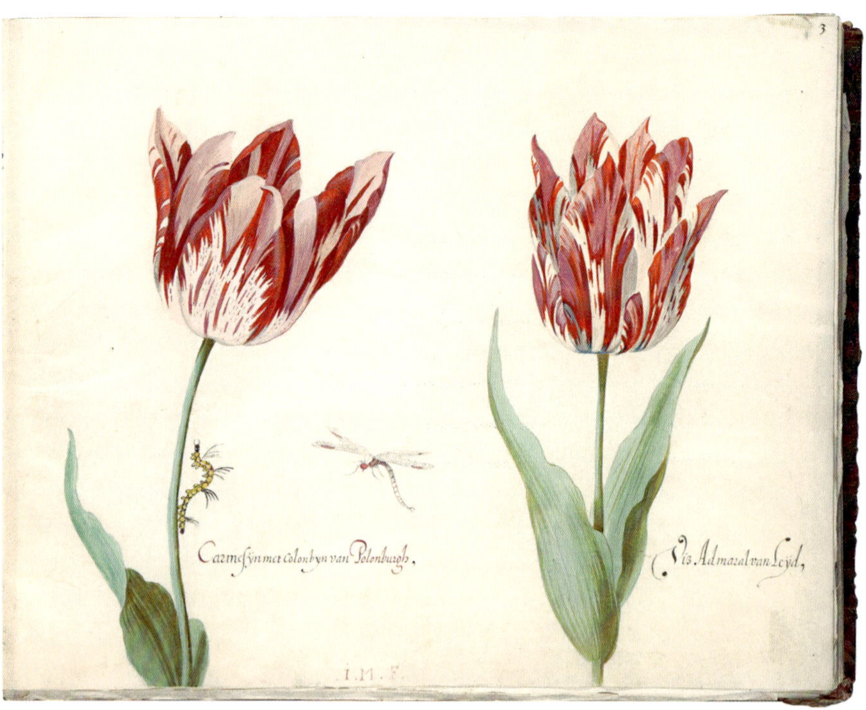

46.2 Jacob Marrel, Two Tulips (*Carmesijn met Colonbijn van Polonburgh / Viz Admaral van Leijd[en]*) *with a Caterpillar and Damselfly*, 1637. Rijksprentenkabinet, Amsterdam.

precisely applied opaque and translucent watercolor fill out the form and largely mask the underdrawing.

An inscription at right identifies the tulip as "Colombijn en wit van Poelenburg." The lengthy moniker has variously been understood as one or two names though likely refers to a single tulip pictured twice rather than two varieties shown concurrently.[7] The artist often depicted multiple varieties on a single sheet, though rarely (if ever) do these tulips and their names intermingle. For example, a drawing of a single red and white tulip, now in an album of Marrel drawings in the Rijksprentenkabinet, is similarly labeled "Carmesijn met Colonbijn van Polonburgh," this title referring unmistakably to but one variety of tulip (fig. 46.2).[8]

A number of *tulpenboeken* and various individual sheets, typically on parchment and occasionally on paper, are the only known drawings by Marrel.[9] Ingvar Bergström identified the (ostensibly) only known dispersed album on paper, the so-called Codex PAR, counting among its pages a drawing in a private collection of the red and white "Generalissimo del Costa" tulip.[10] To this list Stijn Alsteens added the Teylers Museum's drawing of the "Brandenborger" and the "Generael vander Eyck" tulips, which is numbered "17" at upper right.[11] The Moore sheet has several small stitching holes along the left edge and a page number inscribed in the upper right corner, suggesting it was once bound in an album. This, alongside its paper support, suggests it may be here newly identified as part of the Codex PAR. Moreover, the technique and size of the Moore sheet corresponds to the aforementioned PAR drawings.[12] SWM

PIETER HOLSTEYN THE YOUNGER

Haarlem 1614–1673 Amsterdam

47a,b

Common Blue Morpho (*Morpho helenor*), *Dorsal View* (a) and *Common Blue Morpho* (*Morpho helenor*), *Ventral View* (b), ca. 1640

Pen and black ink, with watercolor and opaque watercolor
(a) 161 x 209 mm; (b) 161 x 210 mm

INSCRIPTIONS (a) Recto, signed between wings, in black ink: *PH* (in ligature); (b) recto, between the insect's feet, in black ink: *PH* (in ligature)

PROVENANCE Private collection, Switzerland; Daxer & Marschall Kunsthandel, Munich, 2013; Mireille Mosler, New York; from whom acquired by Clement C. Moore, 2013

SELECT REFERENCES Vignau-Wilberg 2013, nos. 9 (a) and 3 (b)

Promised gift of Clement C. and Elizabeth Y. Moore

Pieter Holsteyn the Younger was a painter and prolific printmaker well known for his engraved portraits. Like his father, Pieter Holsteyn the Elder, the younger Pieter also made watercolor drawings of birds, plants, and insects, variously placing them in landscape settings or the pristine isolation of a blank page.[1] In the two Moore drawings, we see Holsteyn use his characteristically soft lines and subtle blending of colors to depict a common blue morpho, a species of butterfly native to the tropical forests of Mexico, Central, and South America.[2] One sheet (no. 47a) depicts the dorsal view of the butterfly, that is, with wings unfurled, the striking blue color for which it is known formed by the smooth application of opaque, azure-hued watercolor on paper. The velvety black edge of the butterfly's wing dissipates into the blue, Holsteyn having used a series of small black dots to create a hazy effect. The artist similarly employs small, engraved dots in his printed portraits to create nuanced tones and shading.

Holsteyn almost certainly drew the blue morpho's outer wings from a preserved specimen. Not so the lively ventral view in the second sheet (no. 47b), which seemingly captures a glimpse of the insect momentarily luxuriating in the bright warmth of the sun. The butterfly is shown in profile to the right. Its erect wings reveal a subdued palette—brown with a smattering of white, blue, and crimson markings. A pale gray shadow beneath the morpho's torso creates the illusion that it stands on a flat horizontal surface. The artist placed his interlaced "PH" monogram (conspicuously) beneath the butterfly's feet. The artist's mark, unlike the butterfly, is untethered from the page, seemingly floating on the surface of the paper. Its liminal position defies a carefully crafted depiction of perspectival space that ostensibly contains a living butterfly. Holsteyn's self-conscious acknowledgment of such visual trickery reflects period debates about the moral status of images meant to enthrall and deceive viewers. Butterflies were also a potent allegory for the beauty and brevity of life in early modern Europe. (Perhaps the artist knew of the blue morpho's limited lifespan, which averages four to five months.) When viewed as a pair, these sheets might be understood as a memento mori: the artist's animating touch can but reiterate the beautiful creature's inevitable death.

Holsteyn produced another pair of blue morpho drawings, both now in Copenhagen (figs. 47.1, 47.2).[3] The dorsal view in Copenhagen closely resembles the Moore sheet. The ventral view features the butterfly in profile to the left rather than the right, with taupe, crimson, and black markings on the wings. The refined workmanship of the Moore and the Copenhagen pairs suggests they were perhaps intended to be autonomous artworks, although they could have alternately been part of a larger series or studies for a painting or collector's album. In the Royal Horticultural Society, London, for instance, is an album of flower drawings, occasionally featuring a moth or butterfly (none of them morphos), done by Holsteyn, Anthony Claesz II, and an anonymous artist.[4]

The blue morpho was a popular subject for Holsteyn's near contemporaries, including Rachel Ruysch, Johanna Helena Herolt, and Maria Sibylla Merian, who not only twice featured the butterfly in her *Metamorphosis insectorum Surinamensium* (see no. 70) but also produced at least two more blue morpho drawings, now housed in the Sloane albums at the British Museum.[5] Unlike Merian and Herolt,

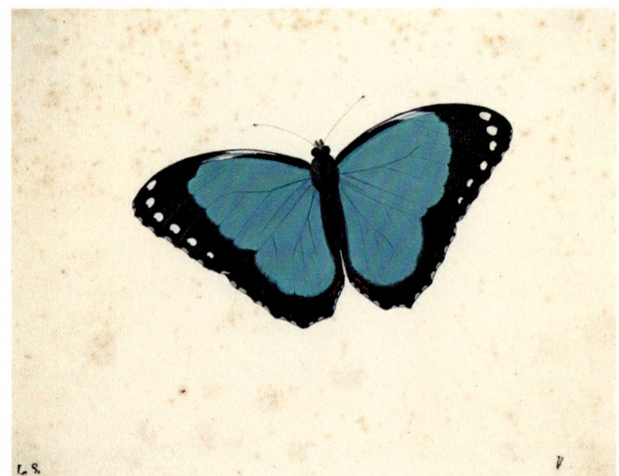

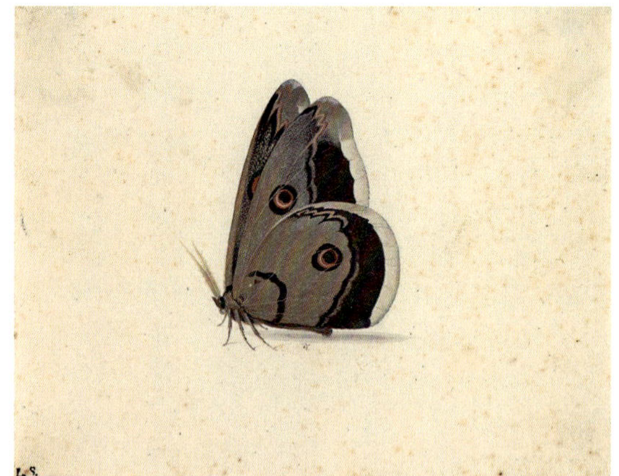

47.1 Pieter Holsteyn the Younger, *Common Blue Morpho, Dorsal View*, ca. 1640. Statens Museum for Kunst, Copenhagen.

47.2 Pieter Holsteyn the Younger, *Common Blue Morpho, Ventral View*, ca. 1640. Statens Museum for Kunst, Copenhagen.

Holsteyn never visited the Americas (indeed he rarely left the Netherlands). Blue morphos are similarly residential and do not migrate within the Americas, let alone Europe. The artist likely relied on images in printed sources, which in some cases were first drawn from live specimens, or on the close study of imported specimens, both living and preserved, to depict the butterfly.[6]

Holsteyn's superb drawings evidence the ever-increasing intellectual and cultural imbrication of the Netherlands and the Americas. Still, long before European transatlantic trade and travel, blue morphos—and butterflies in general—bore diverse meanings among myriad territories and peoples living in the Americas. For instance, some pre-Columbian Mesoamerican cosmologies closely associated birds, butterflies, and other winged creatures with deities, warriors, and deceased ancestors.[7] The blue morpho might not have been understood by Holsteyn through these paradigms; yet the enduring charisma of his encyclopedic attempts to record as many insects, birds, and animals as possible reminds us today of the vast temporal, geographical, and cultural history of the world's flora and fauna. The Moore sheets are also an important visual record of a species whose rarity within the Netherlands compelled Holsteyn to make art of a butterfly and a blank sheet of paper. His prescient pictures anticipate the insect's increasingly fugitive existence as a result of modern-day deforestation in the Americas. SWM

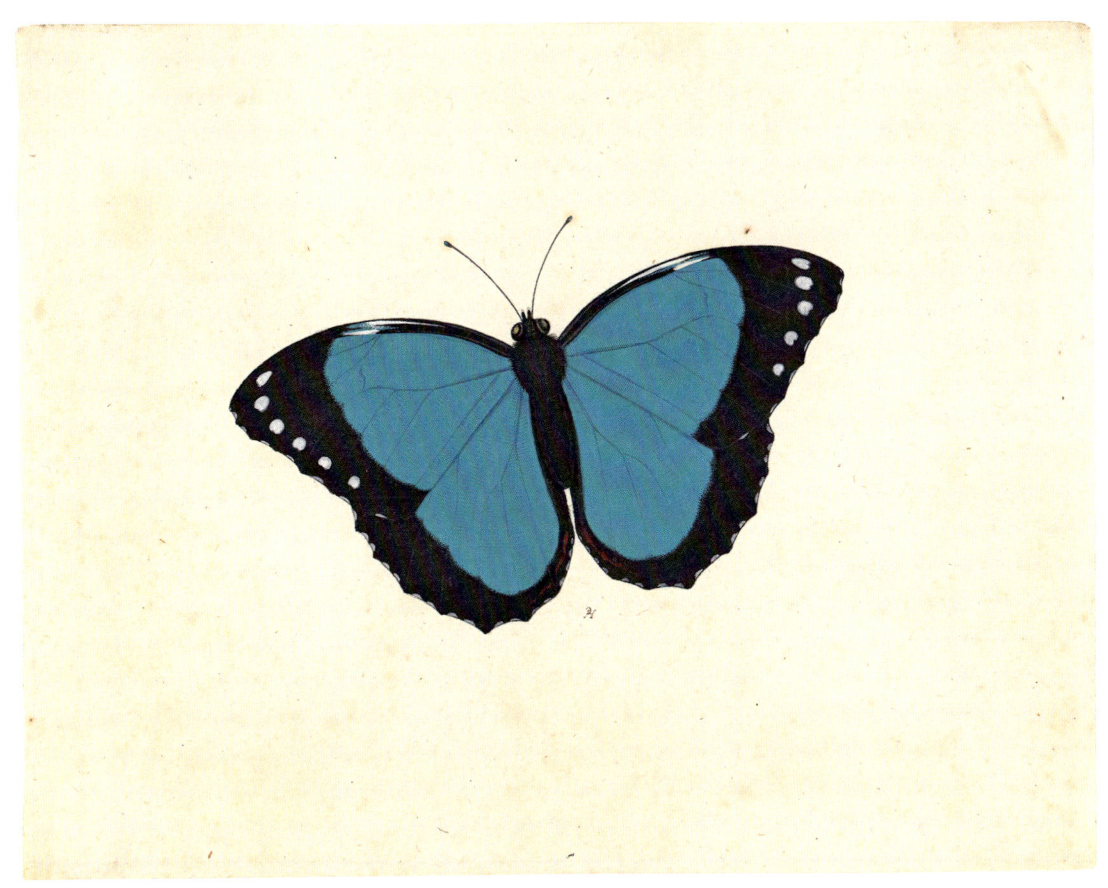

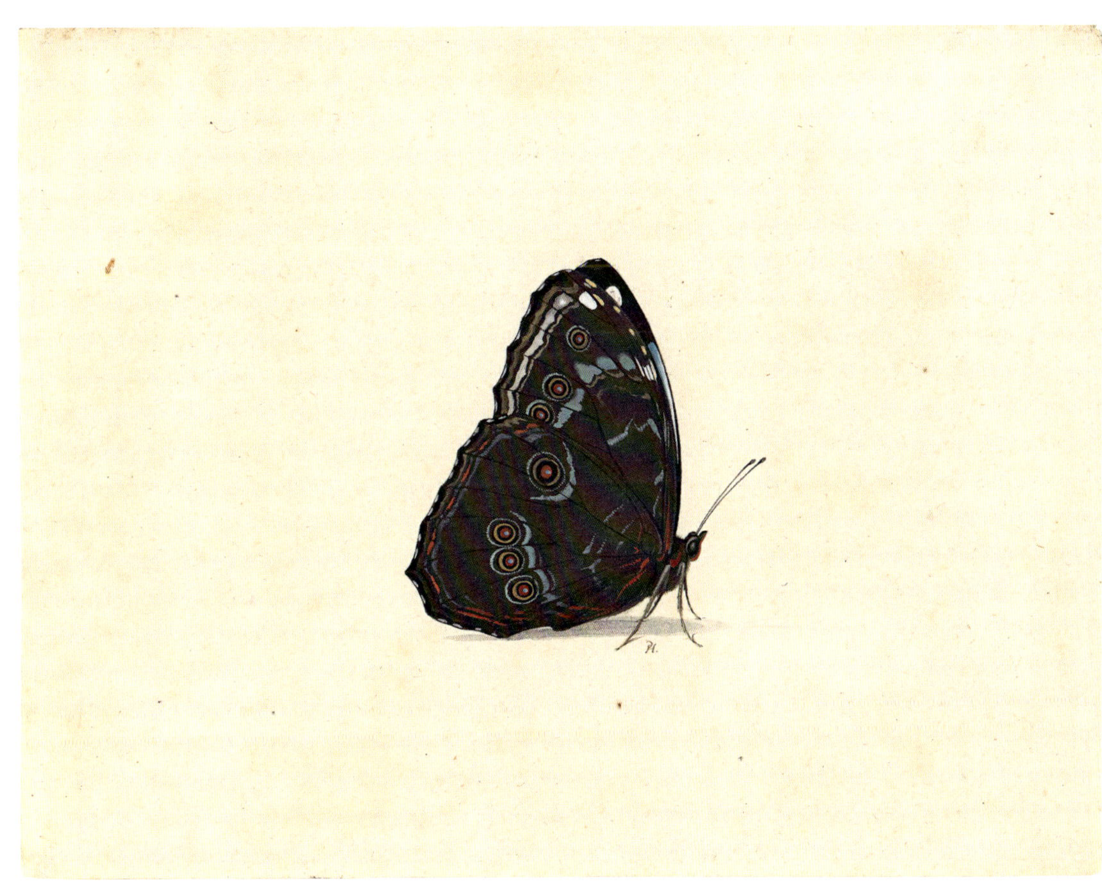

THOMAS WIJCK

Beverwijk ca. 1616–1677 Haarlem

48

View of the Palazzo Contarini del Bovolo from the Corte Coppo, Venice, ca. 1645–50

Point of brush and gray wash, over black chalk
371 x 286 mm

WATERMARK Strasbourg lily with "W"

PROVENANCE Leendert Dupper (1799–1870), Dordrecht; his sale, C.J. Roos et al., Dordrecht, 28–29 June 1870, lot 443: "Th. Wijck. 443. Monument antique, en ruines. A l'encre de Chine" to Carel Vosmaer (1826–1888), The Hague; possibly his sale, Martinus Nijhoff, The Hague, 30 April 1890, perhaps among the multiple lots 380, 381, 382, 383, or 384; possibly with J.H.J. Mellaart (1895–1972), London; from whom purchased by Johan Quirijn van Regteren Altena (1899–1980), Amsterdam (no mark; see L. 4617), April 1927 (according to his inventory book, no. 297); by descent to his heirs; their sale, Christie's, London, 10 July 2014, lot 64; where acquired by Clement C. Moore for the Baymeath Art Trust

SELECT REFERENCES Giltaij 1976, no. 159; Meijer 1991, no. 64; Oud, Jonker, and Schapelhouman 1995, no. 20

Promised gift of Clement C. and Elizabeth Y. Moore, through the Baymeath Art Trust

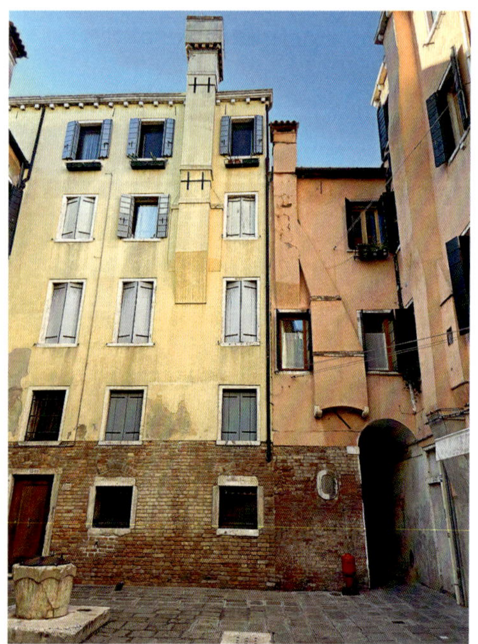

48.1 Current view of the Corte Coppo, Venice, matching Wijck's position on the square.

The strong fluctuations of the tide in the Lagoon of Venice and the resulting high water, especially during the winter months, often cause the city to flood. The culmination of this phenomenon is known as *acqua alta*, an impressive if also daunting experience. As early as 1560, Alvise Cornaro wrote about the city's high water levels in his *Trattato di acque* (Treatise on Waters), basing his measurements and predictions on his own observations, including the height of green algae against the facades of buildings and the walls of canals.[1] Early visual sources of the floods or their damage, on the other hand, are quite rare.[2]

It might not be a coincidence that it was not an Italian artist, but a Dutchman—accustomed to the widespread use of dikes to protect against rising water levels and floods—who depicted the consequences of this phenomenon on paper. Whether or not the Haarlem-born Thomas Wijck witnessed the height of the *acqua alta*, in this drawing he depicted a moment in which the water was either rising or subsiding. As Chips Moore was the first to point out, Wijck very subtly captured the reflection of the well in this flooded courtyard, using gray wash. Similarly, below the arched passageway a pool of water is delicately indicated in gray. In all likelihood, the situation would have been only casually noticed by local passersby, most probably considered to be a relatively normal occurrence by the city's residents—but not by Wijck.

It has not previously been noted that the artist was likely seated in the middle of the Corte Coppo, near the alley Ramo Coppo. At lower left is a typical *vera da pozzo* (wellhead)—one of many spread throughout Venice—characterized by its simple architectural decoration but corresponding to the one still present in this courtyard (fig. 48.1).[3] Looking west from here, Wijck's eye would have caught sight of the Palazzo Contarini del Bovolo, with its arcades and eccentric domed spiral staircase, added to the palace in 1499 by the architect Giovanni Spavento. Although situated less than 50 meters west of the square, the palazzo occupies a position in the background of the present drawing.[4]

That Wijck does not allow the well-known building to take center stage in his composition is typical of the artist. He seems to have preferred modest, everyday settings. His drawn oeuvre is dominated by courtyards, arches, wells, and staircases, as well as deserted interiors such as bedrooms and kitchens.[5] This sets Wijck's interests apart from those of many of his contemporaries who, especially in Italy, recorded antiquities and topographically recognizable places. Possibly, this approach was fostered by his apprenticeship under Adriaen van Ostade, whose work often focuses on dilapidated barns and domestic interiors. With that in mind, it is not surprising that Wijck in this sheet, too, drew attention to the heap of bricks and the plainer house facades. However, more than the cracks in the walls, it is the play of the Venetian light on the buildings that caught his eye.

Speculation concerning Thomas Wijck's stay in Italy persisted for a long time owing to the lack of concrete evidence: such a journey southward was supported only by many Italianate views and his absence from his hometown between 1644 and 1653.[6] Based on the topographical accuracy of the Moore sheet, it seems that this doubt should perhaps now be dispelled, and that Arnold Houbraken's statement in *De groote schouburgh* (1721) that Wijck's [pen works] were "drawn from life by himself in Italy" should thus very likely be taken as true.[7] **MvS**

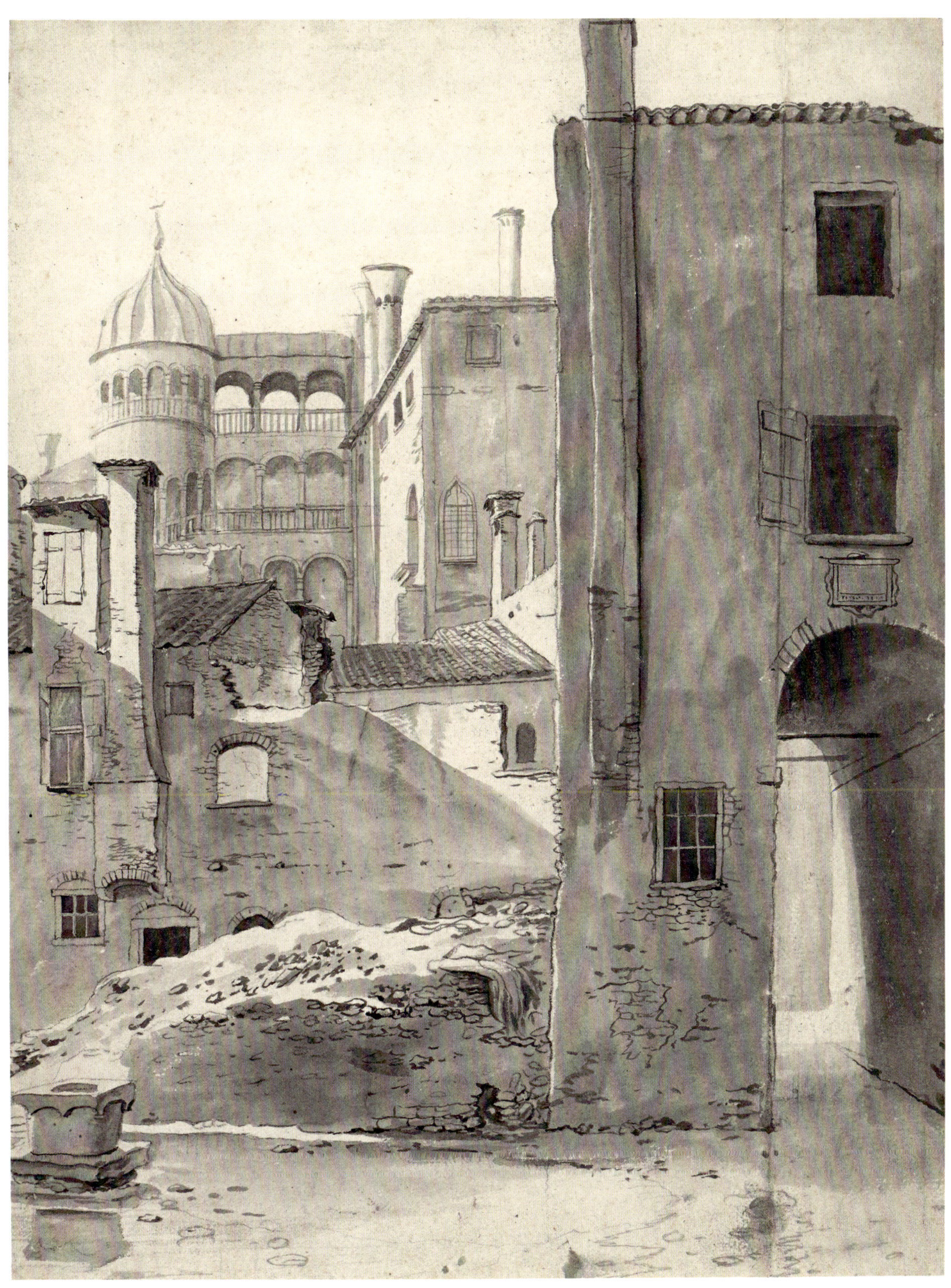

PETER LELY

Soest, Westphalia 1618–1680 London

49

Portrait of a Man, Possibly a Self-Portrait, ca. 1660

Black, white, and red chalk on brown paper
255 x 178 mm

INSCRIPTIONS Recto, center left, monogrammed in black chalk: PL (in ligature); verso, center, in a later hand, in graphite: *Lely Pierre Van der Faës / (dit le chevalier) / né à Hoets (Westphalie 1618 mort à Londres 1680 / Peintre de Charles I*[er]

PROVENANCE Private collection, France; from which acquired by James Faber, London, 2013; from whom acquired by Clement C. Moore for the Baymeath Art Trust, 2015

Promised gift of Clement C. and Elizabeth Y. Moore, through the Baymeath Art Trust

Born in Westphalia (where his father, a Dutch soldier, was stationed), Pieter van de Faes—Lely's birth name—was presumably raised in The Hague, where his family was based, and where they owned a house called In de Lelye because of the lily carved on its gable. From this, he adopted the name Pieter Lely, by which he was already known when in 1637 he was listed in the Guild of St. Luke at Haarlem as a pupil of Frans Pietersz de Grebber.[1] The circumstances behind his move to London are not known, but he was there by the early 1640s. After the deaths of Anthony van Dyck and William Dobson, Lely was the finest portrait painter in England, and he skillfully managed to work for both Oliver Cromwell during the Commonwealth and Charles II after the Restoration.[2]

To scholars of drawings, Lely is best known as one of the greatest collectors of his age, amassing perhaps 10,000 sheets by artists from across Europe (see no. 23, for example).[3] Drawing was also, however, central to his work as a painter. Writing in 1673, the painter William Gandry noted, "Mr. Lilly did often say . . . that painting was nothing else but draft [i.e. drawing]."[4] Although only 80 or so drawings by Lely survive, they make clear that he must have made them at every phase of his work: extant examples include rough sketches and more finished compositional drawings, such as the well-known figure studies for the Garter Procession,[5] as well as detailed studies of hands, arms, and drapery.[6] There are also more finished portraits, in mixed chalks, signed by the artist; in Lely's posthumous sale, several "Craions" [i.e., colored chalk drawings] are mentioned as having ebony frames, suggesting that these were works for display rather than preparatory studies.[7] In a 1663 letter Christiaan Huygens recounted that he discussed the technique of these drawings with Lely, and even visited the man who produced the pastels.[8]

The Moore drawing is among the finest of all these finished portraits on paper. More elaborately worked than examples such as the *Veiled Lady in Three-Quarter Length* or the *Portrait of John Greenhill* in the British Museum,[9] or the 1658 *Portrait of a Lady* at the Morgan,[10] the closest comparisons for the present work are Lely's *Portrait of Charles Cotterell* in the British Museum,[11] and especially the *Self-Portrait* long on display at the Fitzwilliam Museum prior to being sold at Sotheby's in 2016 (fig. 49.1).[12] All of these works are nonetheless seemingly contemporary. The Cotterell portrait shows the sitter wearing a gold chain and medal given to him only in 1661, while in the self-portrait Lely adopts a hairstyle and a pencil-thin mustache said to have been in fashion in the late 1650s and early 1660s.

It has been suggested that the present work is also a self-portrait of Lely. The sitters certainly have much in common: aquiline noses, high foreheads, hooded eyes, full eyebrows, and sharp lips, all characteristics also seen in the painted *Self-Portrait* in the National Portrait Gallery, London, dated ca. 1660.[13] While comparing physiognomy in this manner is an imprecise art, it does indeed seem possible that we are looking in the Moore drawing at Lely himself, and that the differences between it and the ex-Fitzwilliam drawing have to do with the rather different tone and expression of the two works: alert and engaging the viewer in one case, but dreamily melancholy, staring into the distance, in the other. Whoever it depicts, the Moore drawing is of the highest quality, and, in the soulful, parted-lip gaze of the sitter, is among the most compelling of seventeenth-century portrait drawings by Lely or any other artist. JJM

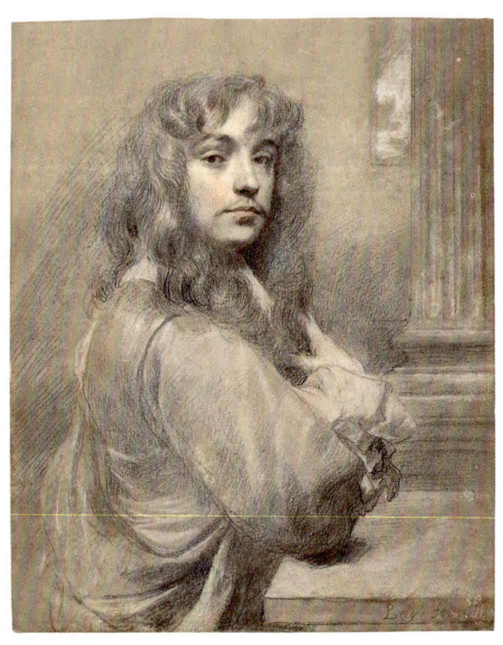

49.1 Peter Lely, *Self-Portrait*, ca. 1660. Present whereabouts unknown.

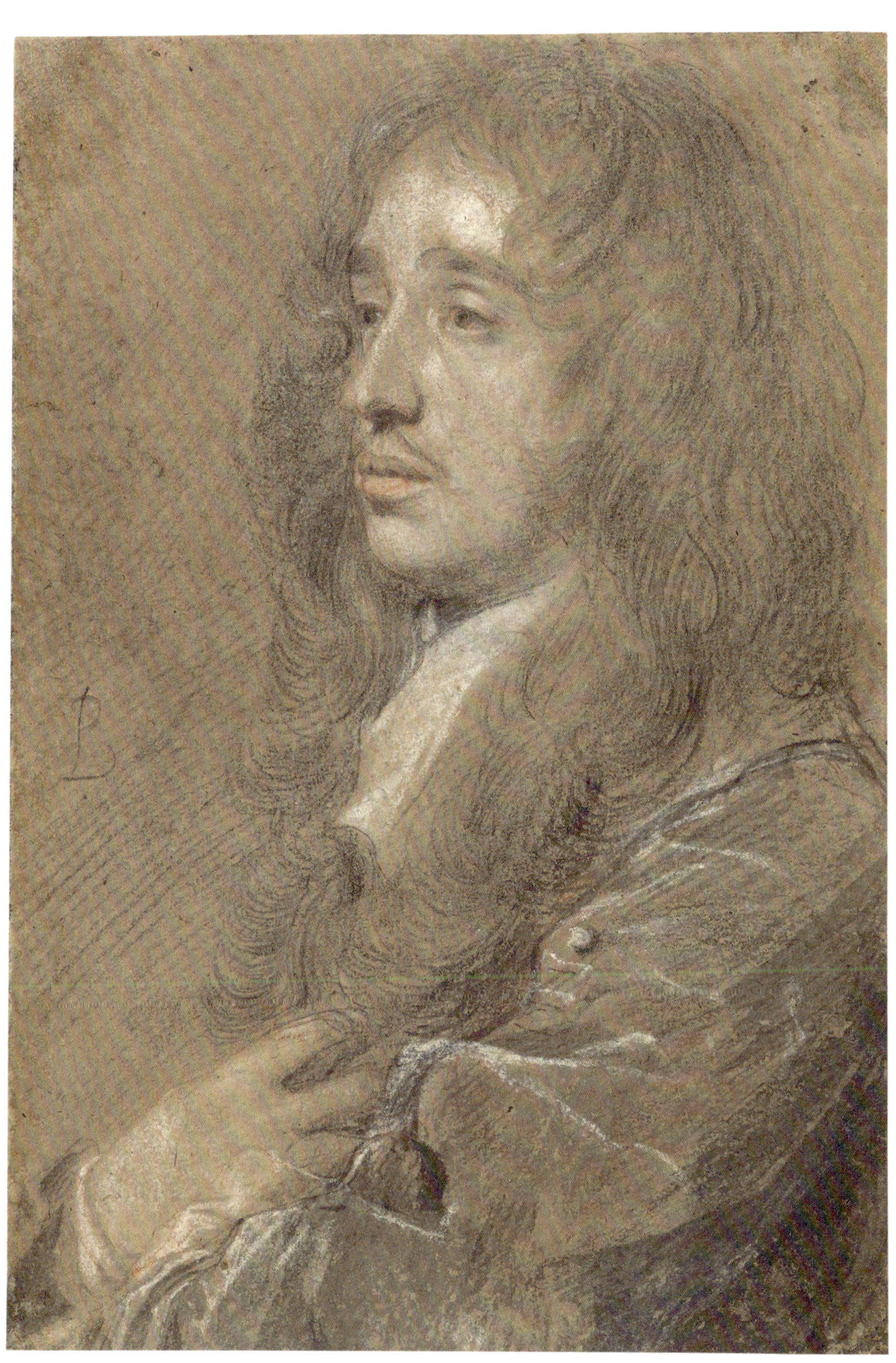

GILLIS NEYTS

Rijssel (now Lille) 1618–1686 Antwerp

50

Landscape with a Monumental Tree and an Amorous Couple, ca. 1640–65

Pen and brown and some black ink, with brown wash; framing line in brown ink
205 x 317 mm

WATERMARK Foolscap with seven points above three balls

INSCRIPTIONS Recto, lower right, signed, in brown ink: *Æ. neyts. f.*; verso, center, in graphite: *3300*; verso, lower center, in graphite: *Landscape by Neyts bought at Hamilton's auction £0.17*

PROVENANCE William Douglas-Hamilton, 12th Duke of Hamilton (1845–1895), Hamilton Palace, South Lanarkshire, Scotland, and Easton Park, Suffolk, by 1887;[1] probably with Nicolaas Beets, Amsterdam; from whom purchased by Johan Quirijn van Regteren Altena (1899–1980), Amsterdam (no mark; see L. 4617–18), 31 October 1925 (according to his inventory book, no. 132); by descent to his heirs; their sale, Christie's, London, 8–10 July 2014, lot 16 (to Day & Faber); Day & Faber, London; from whom acquired by Clement C. Moore, 2018

SELECT REFERENCES Bernt 1957–58, 2: no. 438; Van Puyvelde 1965, no. 339; Giltaij 1976, no. 93; Gustot 2008, 133 and 226, no. D. 235; Alsteens et al. 2009, 114–15, under no. 51, n. 14

Promised gift of Clement C. and Elizabeth Y. Moore

Flemish draftsman Gillis Neyts is known above all for his accurate topographical drawings and his imaginary landscapes. These include several wild and idiosyncratic views of trees and wooded scenes, such as the *Wooded Landscape* on the verso of an unsigned sheet in the National Gallery of Scotland, Edinburgh (fig. 50.1), formerly attributed to Albert Flamen,[2] and a signed drawing in the Klassik Stiftung, Weimar, of almost identical format to the present sheet (fig. 50.2).[3] The Weimar drawing features a remarkably similar gnarled and twisted, almost anthropomorphic tree occupying most of the right half of the composition. These three horizontal landscapes have been dated by Stijn Alsteens to the artist's mature period, before he moved to Namur in 1665. Unlike the Moore drawing, however, the Edinburgh and Weimar drawings are completely devoid of figures.

To judge from the slightly different shade of ink and overlapping lines, the three figures in the Moore drawing were added later, introducing an intriguing narrative element to this fantastical wooded scene. But what exactly is the story that the artist—either Neyts himself or a later hand (as tentatively postulated by Giltaij)—is trying to tell? A couple is seen at lower left, a seemingly well-dressed woman and a young man. Is she perhaps trying to evade his advances? Or are they dancing? Yet more curious is the motif of a figure up a ladder in the tree. He is looking down, but not spying on the couple. It has been suggested that he may be harvesting apples, but this is no apple tree, there is no evidence of fruit in the branches, and, in any case, he has no basket or container in which to gather apples. Immediately to his left are a pair of ambiguous oval shapes that may indicate where branches of the ancient tree have been pruned; those pen lines apparently existed before the addition of the figure on the ladder.

While it may not be possible to elucidate the intended narrative of this ambiguous scene, this drawing embodies the enjoyment that can be derived from "close looking" at such works together with owners, fellow curators, and students. There is always some new detail to fire the imagination, and it is stimulating to share thoughts and interpretations with colleagues, an activity in which Chips Moore has increasingly engaged as his collection has grown. JST

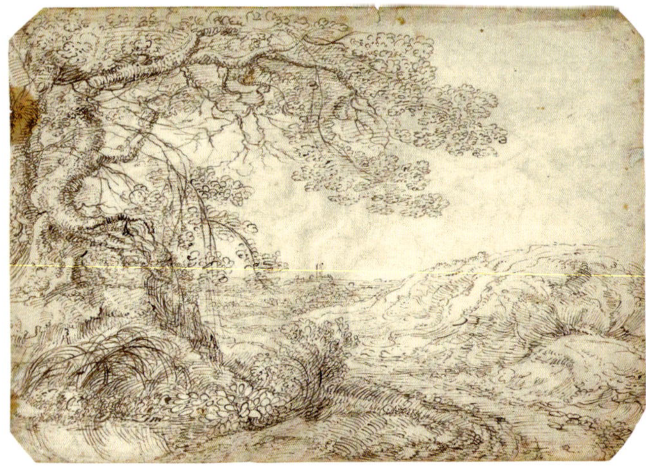

50.1 Gillis Neyts, *Wooded Landscape*, ca. 1640–65. National Gallery of Scotland, Edinburgh.

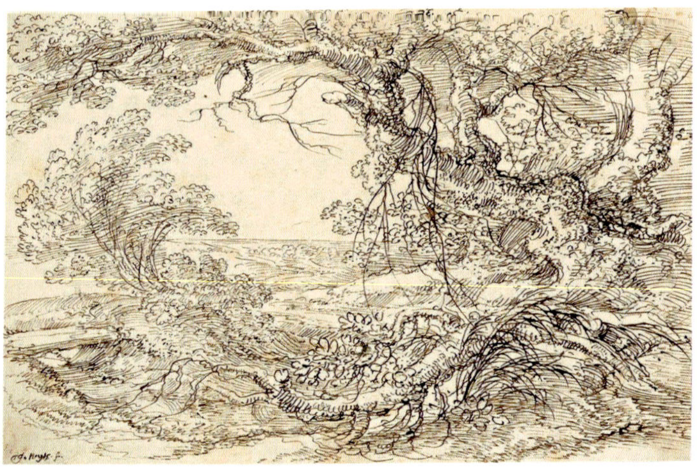

50.2 Gillis Neyts, *Study of a Tree*, ca. 1640–65. Klassik Stiftung, Weimar.

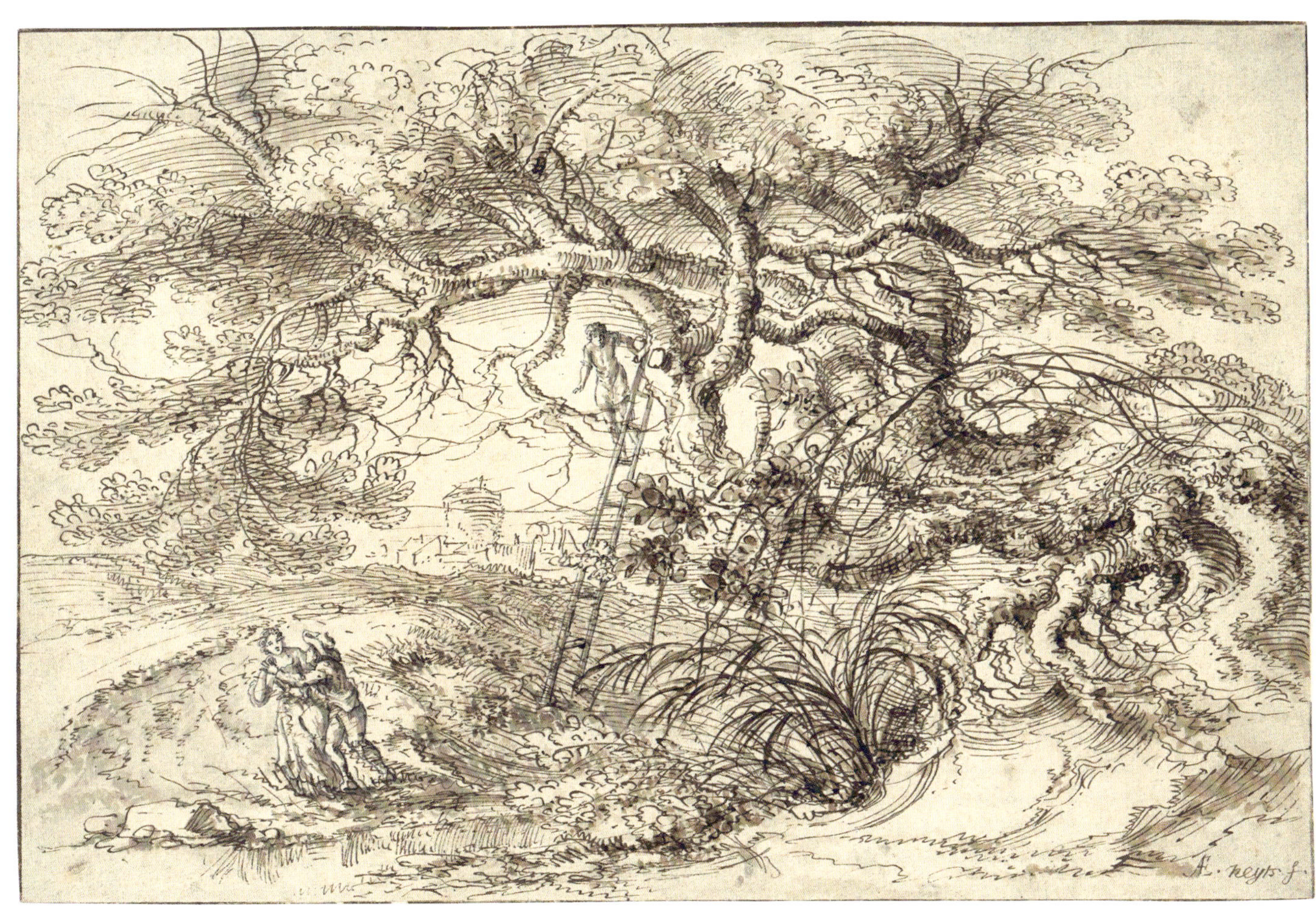
A. neyts f.

PHILIPS WOUWERMAN

Haarlem 1619–1668 Haarlem

51

A Rider about to Mount a Piebald Horse, a Boy Holding the Bridle, ca. 1640–46

Black chalk, graphite, gray wash, and touches of pen and brown ink
141 x 182 mm

WATERMARK Foolscap

INSCRIPTIONS Recto, upper left, signed in monogram, in black chalk: *PHW*

PROVENANCE Greffier François Fagel VI (1740–1773); by descent to his son Baron Hendrik Fagel III (1765–1838); his sale, Philipe, London, 24 May 1799, lot 535 (to "Clark"); Dr. Carl Robert Rudolf (1884–1974), London (no mark; see L. 2811b); his sale, Sotheby Mak van Waay, Amsterdam, 6 June 1977, lot 94 (to "A. Stein"); Henry H. Weldon (1905–2003) and June Weldon (1922–2014), New York; their sale, Sotheby's, London, 8 July 2015, lot 93; where acquired by Clement C. Moore

Promised gift of Clement C. and Elizabeth Y. Moore

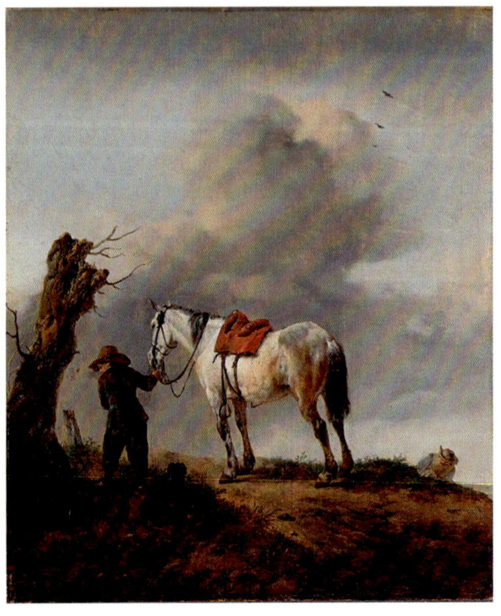

51.1 Philips Wouwerman, *The Gray Horse*, ca. 1646. Rijksmuseum, Amsterdam.

Philips Wouwerman occupies a special place in the history of Dutch art. He was, quite simply, the king of horse painters, and his ubiquitous depictions of all sorts of equestrian subjects—battle scenes, elegant hunting parties, horse fairs, blacksmiths' shops, and many more—are both instantly recognizable and unparalleled in quality. They are also numerous; even discounting the immense numbers of copies and imitations that pass under his name, probably more than 600 paintings survive, a number that is in stark contrast to the known corpus of the artist's drawings. Indeed, although early sale records refer to significant quantities of drawings by Wouwerman, only some twenty-five universally accepted sheets can be identified today, most of them in just three museum collections, in Haarlem (Teylers Museum), London (British Museum), and Amsterdam (Amsterdam Museum). Small wonder that the biographer Arnold Houbraken, writing in 1719, claimed that Wouwerman had ordered from his deathbed that all his drawings should be burned.[1]

The drawing in the Moore collection, depicting a fine piebald horse, its bridle held by a young boy as it stands patiently waiting for a gentleman to climb into the saddle, is a splendid example of one of Wouwerman's more contemplative and measured compositions. The motif is one that recurs throughout the artist's work, most frequently in the context of a scene of a visit to the blacksmith, or the rest of a hunting party. In almost every case, though, the horse in question is, in equestrian parlance, gray (actually meaning white). The strikingly marked piebald seen here appears only very rarely in Wouwerman's work, most conspicuously in a painting of *The Annunciation to the Shepherds*, in the collection of the Louvre, which Birgit Schumacher dates to the second half of the 1640s.[2]

Another painting by Wouwerman from the same period, the Rijksmuseum's famous *The Gray Horse* (fig. 51.1), in many ways provides the closest parallels of all to the Moore drawing, in terms of its compositional simplicity and serene rural setting.[3] *The Gray Horse* is signed with the same *PHW* monogram that we see on the drawing, which provides us with a *terminus ante quem* for the dating of both works, as it has been established by Frits Duparc that after 1646 the artist employed a more elaborate form of monogram incorporating the letters *PHILS W*.[4]

Generally, in the field of seventeenth-century Dutch drawings, the presence of a signature or monogram on a drawing signifies that it was made not as a sketch or preparatory study but rather as a finished work, intended for sale. This is not, however, the case for Wouwerman: almost all of the artist's rare drawings are signed, yet some do still seem to have served as preliminary explorations of ideas and motifs that were worked out more fully in the artist's paintings. The drawing of *The Gray Horse* in the Teylers Museum, for example, clearly relates to a larger, painted composition from the 1650s, *The Hayfield*, now in a German private collection.[5] Conversely, there are drawings of subjects that Wouwerman painted frequently, such as the Metropolitan Museum's *Mounted Gray Horse Being Schooled in Piaffe* (fig. 51.2), which, like the very similarly conceived Moore drawing, cannot be connected with a known painting.[6]

With so few examples to work from, it is hard to establish a meaningful picture either of the chronology of Wouwerman's drawings or of his working method as a draftsman, but in his paintings at least it is generally true that as time went by

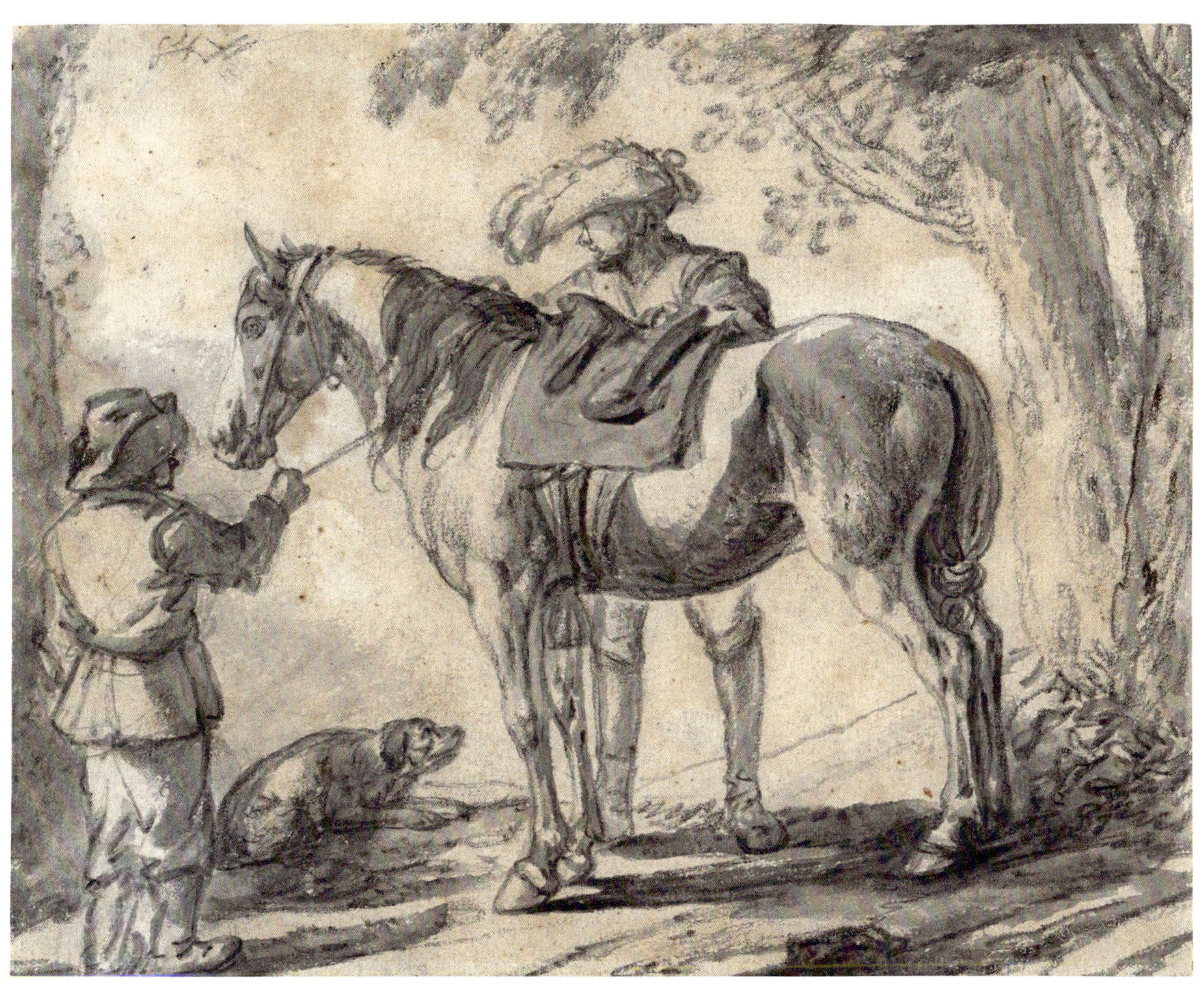

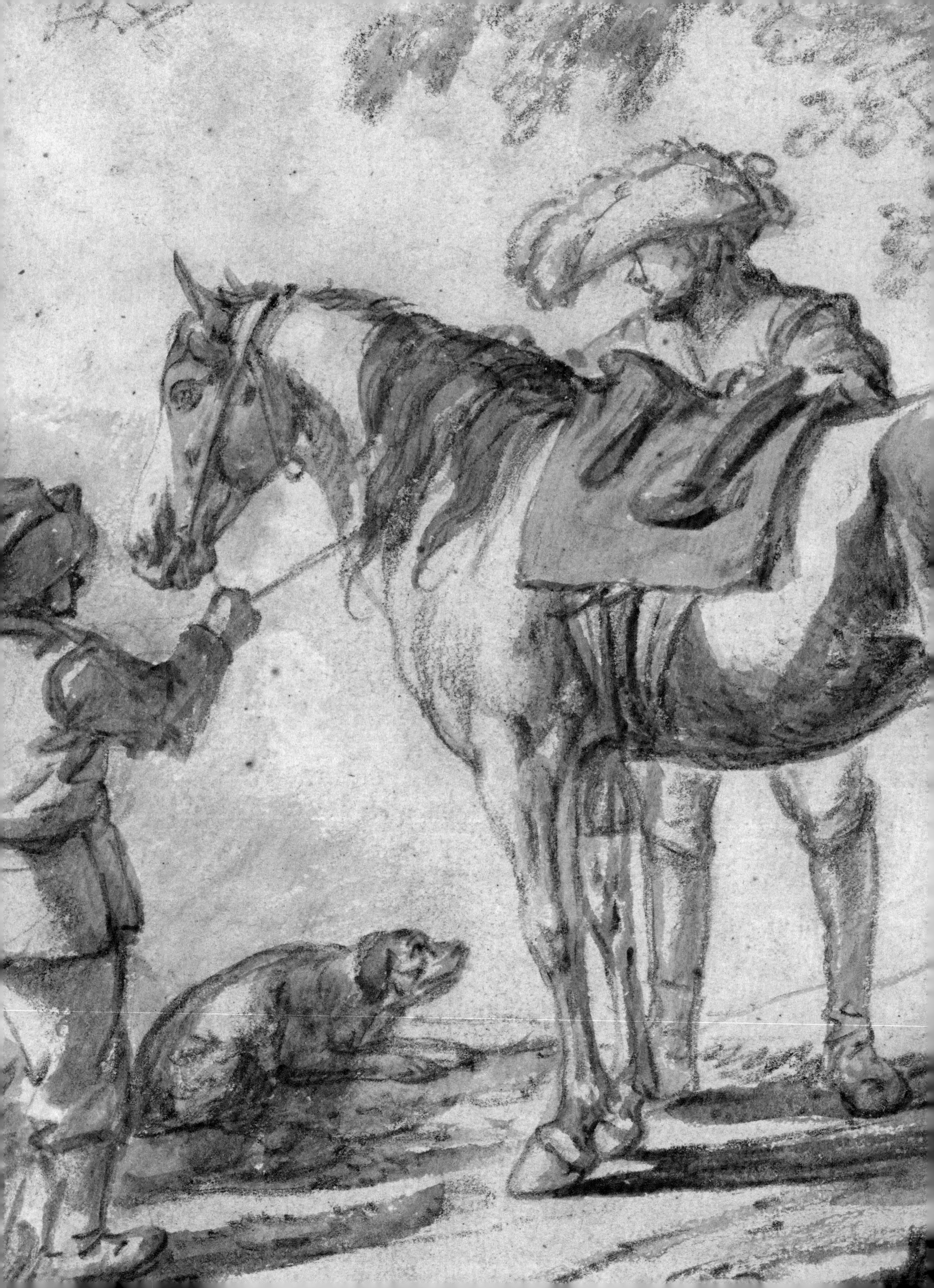

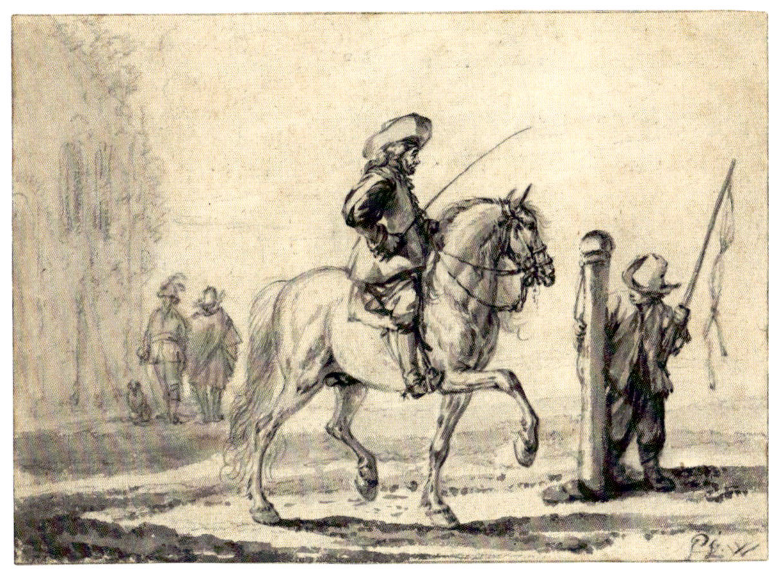

51.2 Philips Wouwerman, *A Mounted Gray Horse Being Schooled in Piaffe*, after 1646. Metropolitan Museum of Art, New York.

the compositions became increasingly elaborate and aristocratic in tone, moving steadily further from the more modest approach and subject matter of the artists such as Pieter van Laer and Adriaen van de Velde who inspired him in his earlier career. Though unquestionably elegant, the Moore drawing conveys a fundamental straightforwardness very different from the majority of the drawings by the artist in the Teylers Museum—all of which are, not perhaps surprisingly, signed with the later form of his monogram.

One of just two characteristic drawings by Wouwerman in American collections, this understated yet captivating sheet embodies his ambitions and talents at the golden moment in his career, when the growing quest for elegance was, it seems, in perfect harmony with the thoughtful and atmospheric imagery of his earliest works. GMGR

AELBERT CUYP

Dordrecht 1620–1691 Dordrecht

52

Windmill by a River, with a Jetty in the Foreground, ca. 1640

Black chalk, with gray and yellow wash, over graphite; in brown ink along the upper edge and black ink along right, lower, and left edges
126 x 187 mm

INSCRIPTIONS Verso, lower left, in pen and brown ink: 3

PROVENANCE John Rushout (1770–1859), 2nd Baron Northwick, Northwick Park, near London, and Cheltenham (no mark; see L. 2709a); his nephew George Rushout (1811–1887), 3rd Baron Northwick, Northwick Park; his step-grandson, Capt. Edward George Spencer-Churchill (1876–1964), Northwick Park; his sale, Sotheby's, London, 1–4 November 1920, lot 141 (to "Colnaghi"); A.W.M. Mensing, Amsterdam, 15–16 June 1926, lot 366 (to "Meyer Elte" for Hofstede de Groot);[1] Cornelis Hofstede de Groot (1863–1930), The Hague (no mark; see L. 561); his sale, C.G. Boerner, Leipzig, 4 November 1931, lot 50 (to "Beets" for Van Beuningen); Daniël George van Beuningen (1877–1955), Vierhouten (no mark; see L. 758); his third wife, Alberta Eveline ("Bep") van Beuningen-Charlouis (1896–1981), Vierhouten and Rotterdam; thence by descent; Bob P. Haboldt & Co., New York and Paris; from whom acquired by Clement C. Moore, 2001

SELECT REFERENCES The Hague 1930, no. 31; Hannema 1949, no. 156; Reiss 1975, 49; Dordrecht 1977, 122; Chong 1992, 175; Broos and Schapelhouman 1993, 70, under no. 7; Christie's, London, 13 December 1996, 31, under lot 13; Haverkamp-Begemann et al. 1999, 193–94; Haboldt 2001, no. 32; Wheelock 2001, 281, under no. 63, n. 2; Shoaf Turner 2012, no. 51; Christie's, New York, 19 April 2018, under lot 16 (as still in the D.G. van Beuningen collection, Vierhouten)

Promised gift of Clement C. and Elizabeth Y. Moore

Collecting is a journey of discovery, and it is only with time that the distinctions between "very good," "great," and "truly great" works of art can be understood. While the genius of someone like Rembrandt is immediately obvious, Cuyp is an artist whose exceptional talent requires a level of sophistication to be fully appreciated. During his lifetime, Cuyp's landscape art had little impact beyond his native Dordrecht, an important trading center but one slightly outside the artistic mainstream. By the eighteenth century, however, his popularity had escalated, especially in England, where collectors eagerly sought his paintings and drawings.[2] They were particularly attracted to his cattle and equestrian pieces as well as his idyllic views of the Dutch countryside, which, although northern in subject matter, are often bathed in a warm, southern light.

Cuyp's landscape drawings are invariably executed in black chalk, enhanced with gray wash, often combined with shades of watercolor, including a distinctive mustardy yellow color that anticipates the golden tonalities of his most sought-after paintings. His favorite subjects were rural scenery and river views in and around Dordrecht. After a terrible flood in 1421, which wiped out seventy-two villages, hamlets, and monasteries in the delta region of the Rhine, Meuse (Maas), and Scheldt rivers, Dordrecht was completely surrounded by water, cut off from land by the four great rivers of South Holland—the Oude Maas, Merwede (Waal), Dordtse Kil, and Hollands Diep. It may have been along one of these waterways that the present sketch was made, for there seems little doubt that the view, with its windmill and distant church tower, was based on an actual site. At the same time, Cuyp exercised a degree of artistic license to enhance its visual appeal. The blades of the windmill are not the same length, and the position of the jetty in the foreground was probably a pure construct from the artist's imagination, inserted as an audacious horizontal *repoussoir* to add depth to the composition. In dark, foreground passages such as this, Cuyp often moistened the black chalk or added gum arabic to intensify the blacks, while he used more delicate strokes to define

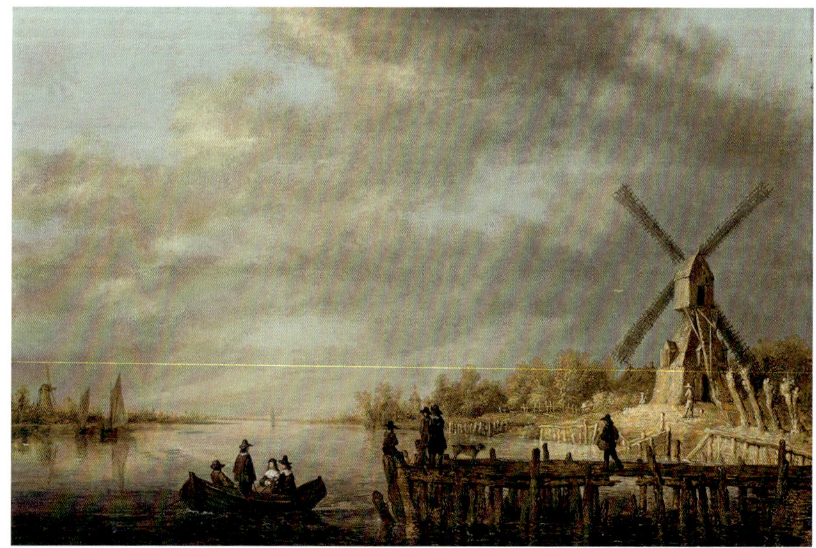

52.1 Aelbert Cuyp, *River Scene with Windmill*, ca. 1640–41. Present whereabouts unknown (formerly collection of Gerard Arnhold, São Paulo).

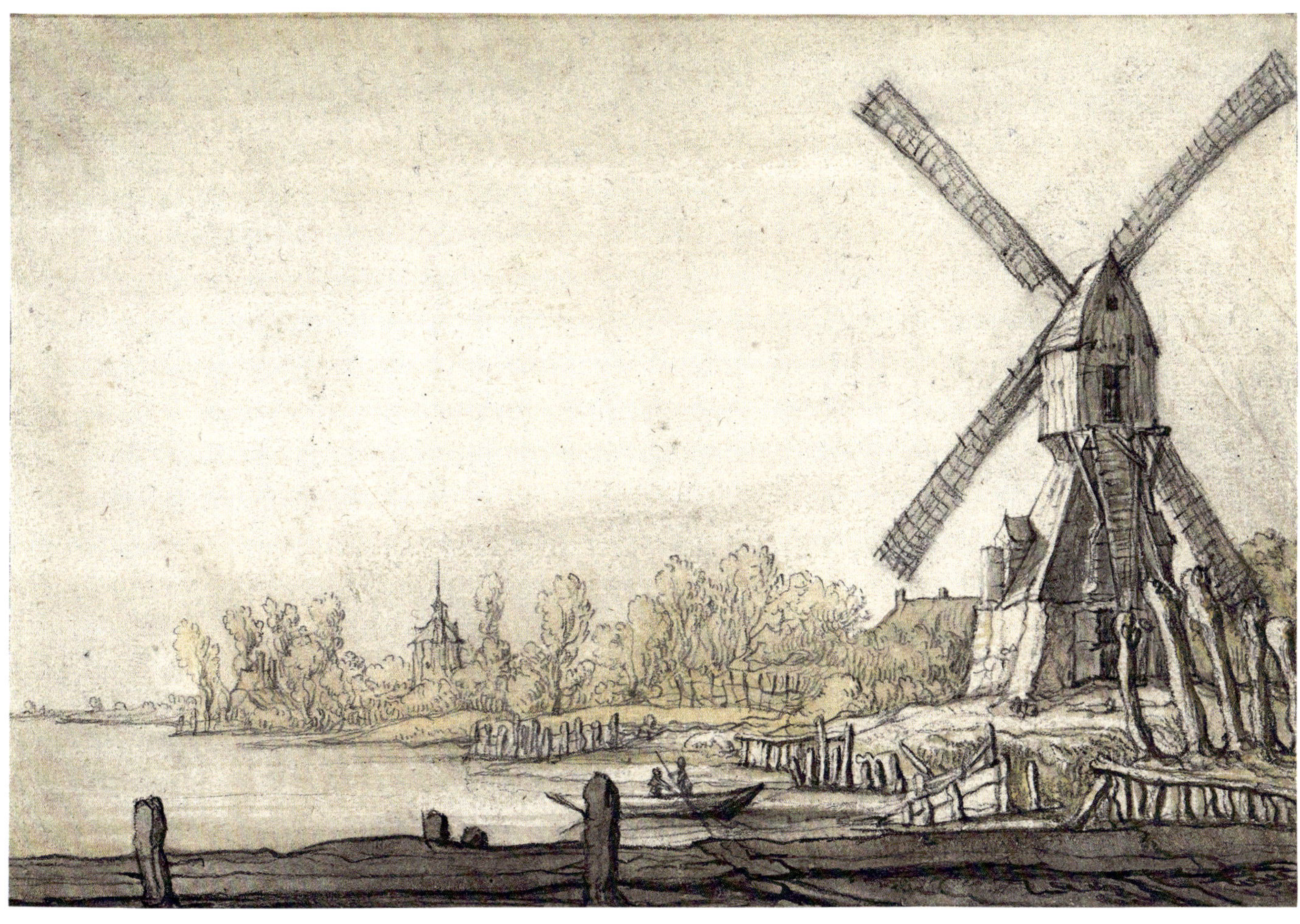

distant elements. With his heavy black contours, he also emphasized the rhythmic interplay of vertical elements—from the row of five tall mooring posts to the pilings that shore up the riverbank and provide structure to the pier. That these could be manipulated for artistic effect is further demonstrated in a painting of ca. 1640 or 1641 related to this drawing, which was sold in 2018 from the estate of the philanthropist and Chinese art collector Gerard Arnhold of São Paulo, who had acquired it in 1996 (fig. 52.1).[3] JST

AELBERT CUYP

Dordrecht 1620–1691 Dordrecht

53

The Hills near the Wylermeer between Nijmegen and Cleves, ca. 1651–52

Graphite, black chalk, and gray wash
165 x 248 mm

INSCRIPTIONS Recto, lower right, in pen and black ink: *A. Cuyp.*

PROVENANCE Charles E. Duits (1882–1969), London, before 1965 (no mark; see L. 533a); thence by descent; acquired through Thomas Williams Fine Art, London, by Clement C. Moore, 2013

SELECT REFERENCES De Bruyn Kops 1965, 164–65, 168; Burnett 1969, 378; Reiss 1975, 182; Chong 1992, 424; Wheelock 2001, 178, under no. 42 (entry by Axel Rüger); Kloek 2002, 37–393; De Groot 2022, n. 18

Promised gift of Clement C. and Elizabeth Y. Moore

In 1648, the signing of the Peace of Münster brought an end to the Dutch Revolt against Habsburg Spain, making travel in the border regions safer and easier. Situated in the picturesque Rhine Valley, along the present-day border between the Netherlands and Germany, the area surrounding the towns of Nijmegen and Cleves soon emerged as a major destination for itinerant artists. In the years and decades to come, Jan van Goyen, Jan Lievens, Anthonie Waterloo, and others went to the region, capturing its undulating hills, expansive waterways, and medieval townscapes in their paintings and drawings.[1]

A sizeable group of landscape studies by Aelbert Cuyp offers insights into that artist's travels to the vicinity of Nijmegen and Cleves around 1651–52.[2] The drawings, which include the present sheet, are united by their attention to topography, similar format and size, and their choice of drawing media, typically combining black chalk, graphite, and gray washes. As exemplified by the Moore sheet, Cuyp applied black chalk in his typical loops and zigzags, carefully modulating the pressure to produce lines of varying intensity, while the use of graphite was confined largely to the background of the composition. Its lighter tone helped the artist to successfully achieve tonal gradation without sacrificing the sharpness of individual details.

According to some scholars, the care with which Cuyp made these landscapes raises the possibility that he conceived them as autonomous works of art.[3] Yet many of the motifs and compositions in studies from the trip were later incorporated into his paintings, suggesting that, to Cuyp, this body of drawings functioned as a visual archive from which he could draw material as needed.[4] The Moore drawing exemplifies this practice. The sheet served as a preparatory study for the *River Landscape near Nijmegen with Riders Watering Their Horses*—a monumental sun-drenched canvas in the collection of the Rijksmuseum (fig. 53.1).[5] The painting faithfully follows the composition established in the drawing—from a sandy road that meanders along the Wylermeer, an old arm of the Rhine, to the ruin of Kranenburg Castle and the spire of the Sint-Johannes de Doperkerk, which rises in

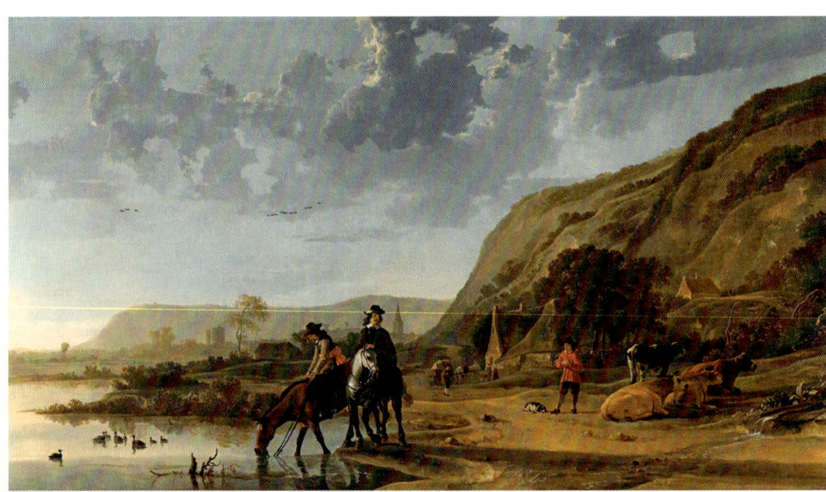

53.1 Aelbert Cuyp, *River Landscape near Nijmegen with Riders Watering Their Horses*, ca. 1653–57. Rijksmuseum, Amsterdam.

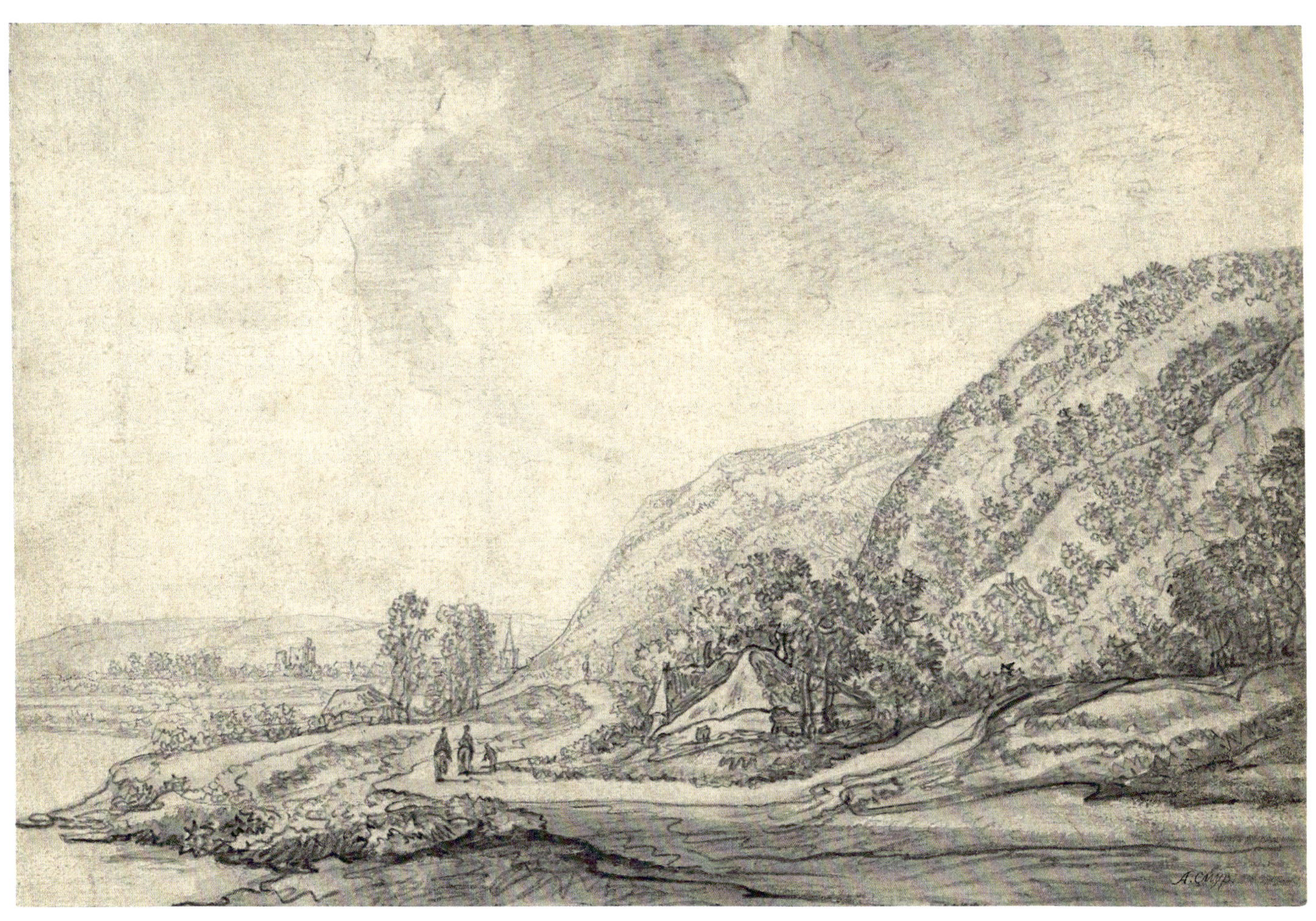
A.Cuyp.

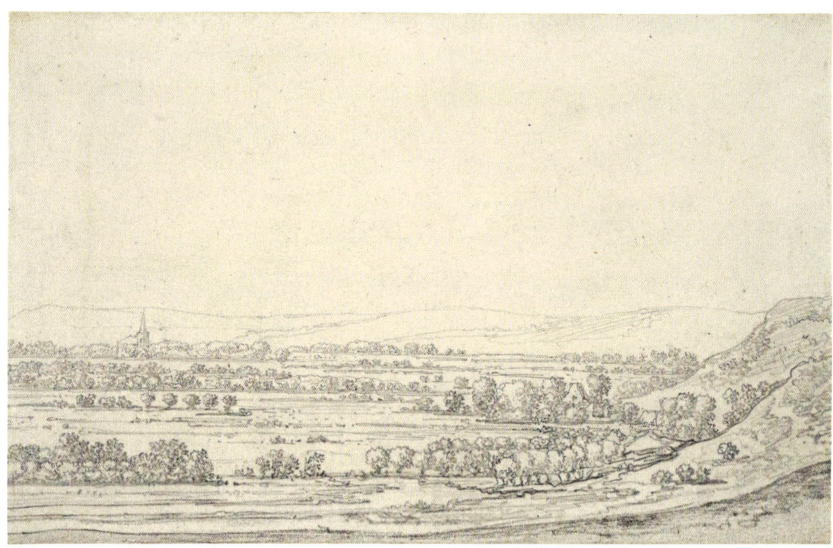

53.2 Aelbert Cuyp, *Wylermeer between Nijmegen and Cleves*, ca. 1651–52. British Museum, London.

the background.[6] As was typical for his creative process, Cuyp probably worked out the positions of the figures and the animals in separate sketches.[7]

The low vantage point and the carefully considered and fully resolved composition of the Moore sheet sets it slightly apart from the other drawings from Cuyp's stay in Nijmegen and Cleves, which either focus on individual motifs or, most commonly, depict panoramic views.[8] In the present work, the artist appears more concerned with the picturesque and the scenic, manipulating the natural landscape to bring different topographic elements closer together.[9] This raises the possibility that, rather than making the drawing in situ, as it has been generally assumed, Cuyp created the study back in his studio, relying on drawings done *naer het leven* (from life), such as a sheet in the British Museum (fig. 53.2), which offers a view of the same general area observed from a higher vantage point.[10]
AM

NICOLAES PIETERSZ BERCHEM

Haarlem 1621/22–1683 Amsterdam

54

Shepherd Playing a Pipe and Shepherdess with Her Flock, 1655

Black chalk, pen and brown ink and wash, with incised outlines; framing line in brown ink
187 x 147 mm

WATERMARK Fragment (upper third) of a foolscap, similar to Laurentius and Laurentius 2007, no. 549 (The Hague, 1649), and Laurentius and Laurentius 2008, no. 396 (The Hague, 1651)

INSCRIPTIONS Recto, lower right, signed, in pen and brown ink: *Berchem f.*; recto, lower left, in brown ink: *1655*; verso, lower center, in graphite: *A 2014*; verso, lower right, in graphite: *A 4800*.

PROVENANCE Jeronimus Tonneman (1687–1750), Amsterdam (no mark; see L. 2863a);[1] his sale, Hendrik de Leth, Amsterdam, 21 October 1754, portfolio O, lot 22 or 23;[2] Gerrit Braamcamp (1699–1771), Amsterdam; his sale, J. de Bosch, Amsterdam, 29 February 1768, Album A, lot 1;[3] Robert Daudet (1737–1824), Paris; Thomas Dimsdale (1758–1823), London (L. 2426, verso, lower left); Henry Scipio Reitlinger (1882–1950), London and Maidenhead (no mark; see L. 2274a); his sale, Sotheby's, London, 22–23 June 1954, part of lot 607; Carl Robert Rudolf (1884–1974), London (no mark; see L. 2811b); his sale, Sotheby Mak van Waay, Amsterdam, 6 June 1977, lot 139; Jacobus Adrianus Klaver (1928–1997), Amsterdam (L. 5353; recto of mount, lower right); his sale, Sotheby Mak van Waay, Amsterdam, 10 May 1994, lot 55; Adolphe Stein (1913–2002), Paris, Zurich, and Crans-sur-Sierre (Switzerland) (L. 5019; recto of mount, lower right); his sale, Christie's, London, 4 July 2000, lot 68 (bought in); his sale, Christie's, Paris, 22 March 2007, lot 283; where acquired by Clement C. Moore

SELECT REFERENCES *Rudolf Collection* 1962, no. 85; Hollstein, 41:35, under no. 43; Schapelhouman and Schatborn 1993, no. 61; Wuestman 1996, 39, n. 64; Stefes 1997, no. II/71

Promised gift of Clement C. and Elizabeth Y. Moore

A shepherd is playing a pipe, specifically a shawm. He is seen in profile, immersed in the shadows, his silhouette merging with the embankment. Only the top of his hat and the upper part of his back are touched by sunlight. As a *repoussoir* figure in shadow, he contrasts beautifully with the sun-drenched landscape. In a graceful, almost dance-like posture, a young woman leads her small herd to the water. Music is in the air—even the bleating sheep seem to catch the tune.

This paradigm of a southern pastorale was made by an artist who never visited Italy.[4] Nonetheless, broad washes contrasting with the white of the paper create a convincing illusion of southern light, making us forget that the animals are a Dutch domestic breed[5] and that the cypress-like trees in the background most likely are inspired by poplars found in the Netherlands.

Within Berchem's oeuvre, the drawing belongs to a group of large-figure pastorals in upright format, often showing music and singing. An early example is Berchem's etching *Shepherd Playing a Flute* of ca. 1648, its dimensions (183 x 140 mm) comparable to the present sheet.[6] Another flute player is found on a larger etching (262 x 209 mm), dated 1652,[7] for which Berchem made the washed chalk preparatory drawing now in Alençon (fig. 54.1).[8] Compared with the latter, the present drawing reveals the stylistic development Berchem underwent in the short period from 1652 and 1655. Though he had started only in 1654 to explore the potential of pen and ink,[9] the Moore sheet of 1655 is a brilliant example of his mastery of the technique. Berchem's vocabulary of line is rich and varied,

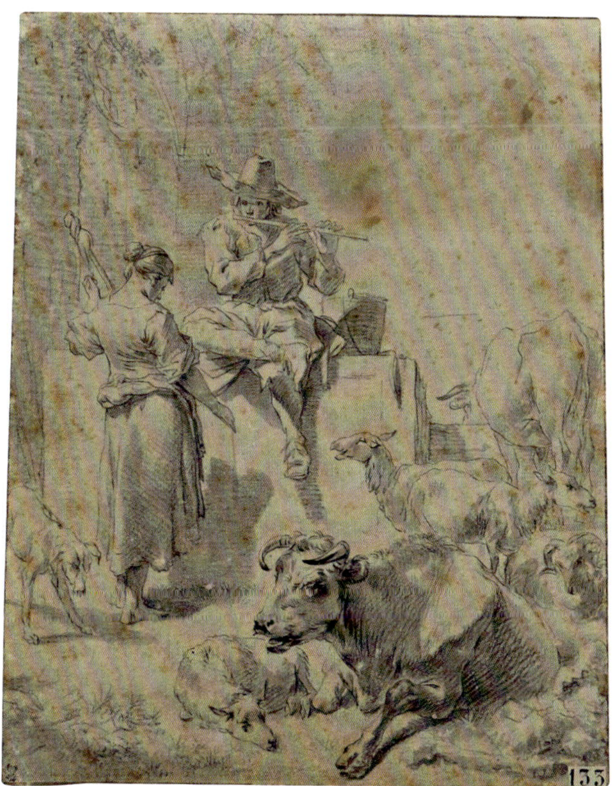

54.1 Nicolaes Pietersz Berchem, *Shepherd Seated on a Fountain and a Spinner*, ca. 1652. Musée des Beaux-Arts et de la Dentelle, Alençon.

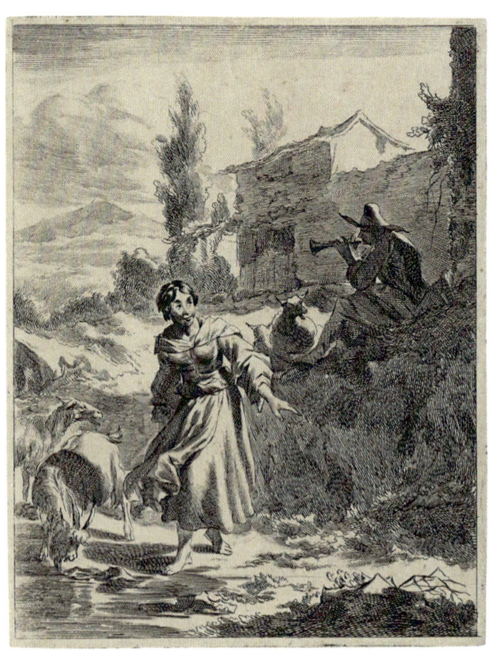

54.2 Johannes Visscher (after Nicolaes Pietersz Berchem), *Shepherd Playing the Pipe and Girl at a Ford*, ca. 1655. Rijksprentenkabinet, Amsterdam.

combining light-handed fluency with crisp shorthand, and with resolute pen strokes adding vigor and volume. There still is some black chalk found in the underlying sketch, but it functioned mainly as a visual aid, with the pen lines independently put to the paper.

Many of Berchem's pen drawings served as models for reproductive engravings, as was the case with the present sheet. It was engraved by Johannes Visscher (fig. 54.2).[10] To transfer the motif to the printing plate, the contours were incised with a stylus.[11]

Prints had the potential to make one's name better known. As a *peintre-graveur*, Berchem knew about this effect from early in his career.[12] Now, in the mid-1650s, he outsourced print production, with Johannes Visscher disseminating the lion's share of Berchem's motifs.[13] In the wake of this process, his drawn designs were no longer made exclusively as print templates.[14] The present sheet, for instance, is signed and thus marked as an independent work of art. Moreover, other than in the design for Berchem's own etching (fig. 54.1), there is no left-handedness found in the pipe player that would have anticipated the reversal of the image when printed.

Visscher's print made Berchem's drawing more widely known and in turn increased the sheet's market value. In the eighteenth century, it passed through the hands of prominent collectors, such as Jeronimus Tonneman and Robert Daudet,[15] and was reproduced by Jurriaan Cootwijck in the prestigious *Ploos-procédé*.[16] **AS**

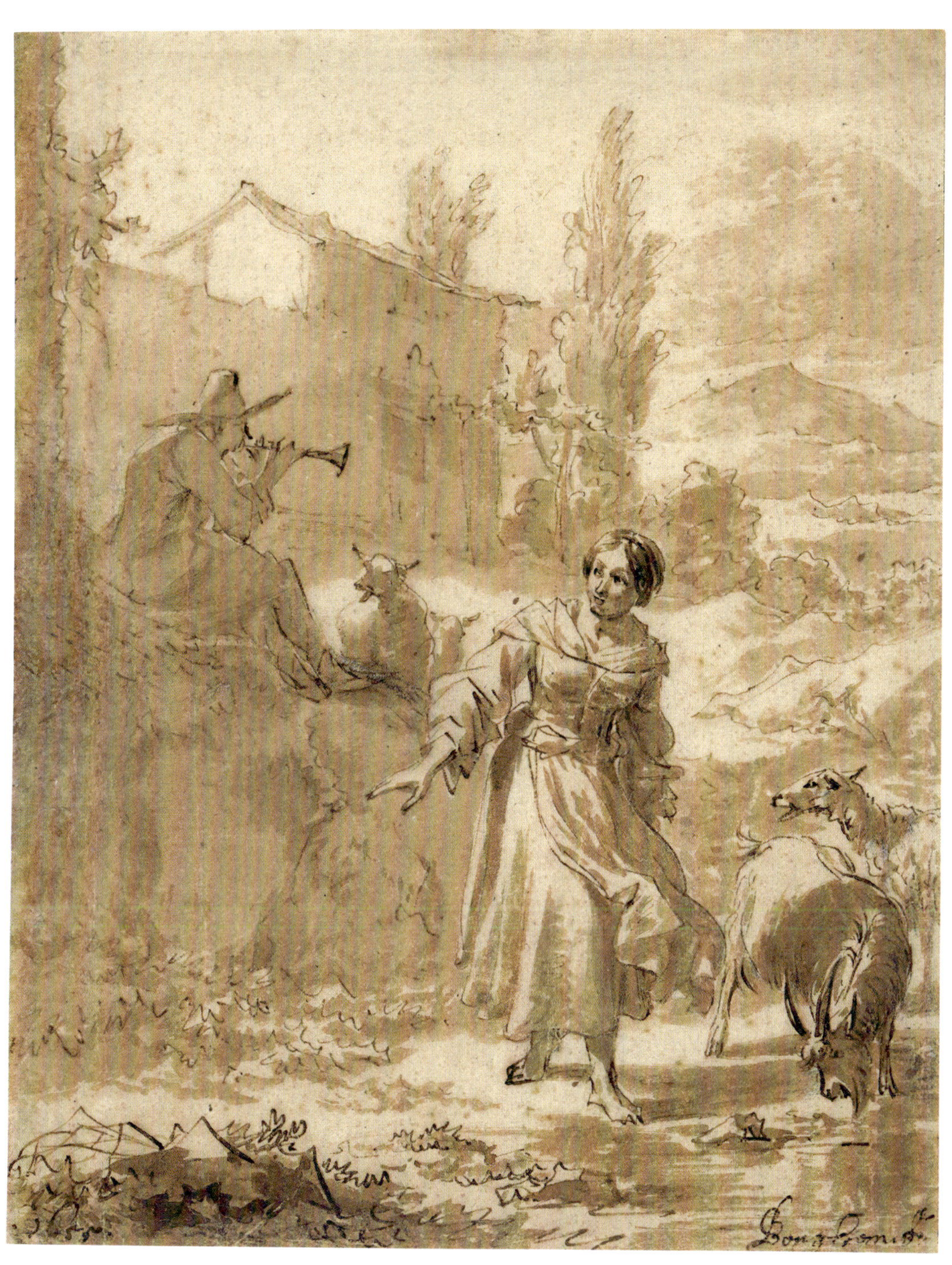

Attributed to JOHANNES JANSZ COLLAERT

Amsterdam ca. 1621/22–1679 Amsterdam

55

View from Neptune's Grotto in Tivoli, ca. 1660–70

Point of brush and gray and brown ink, with gray and brown wash, over black chalk; framing lines in dark brown ink

422 x 220 mm

WATERMARK Strasbourg lily, above "4" and "WR," and countermark "HIS"

INSCRIPTIONS Verso, lower right, in black chalk: 1340; verso, lower right, in graphite: *Paulus Bril geb 1554 overl. 1626.*; below that, in black chalk (effaced): C [. . .]. *g* [. . .]. *1675.*; below that, in graphite: *Paulus Bril.*

PROVENANCE Private collection, the Netherlands; Onno van Seggelen Fine Arts, Rotterdam; from whom acquired by Clement C. Moore, 2020

Promised gift of Clement C. and Elizabeth Y. Moore

Little is known about the landscape artist Johannes Collaert, not to be confused with his namesake Johannes Colaert, a near-contemporary history painter who was a pupil of Rembrandt in the early 1640s.[1] Like so many Dutch artists in the seventeenth century, Collaert traveled to Rome around 1646 or earlier.[2] The few drawings by him that survive depict the Roman countryside, especially the area near Tivoli with its famous waterfalls. Several landscape paintings by his hand have also been preserved.

New details of Collaert's life can now be provided, adding to the scant information previously available. For instance, Collaert combined his artistic activities with another profession: he was also a very busy wine merchant. Abraham Bredius found a dozen records of Collaert's wine business in the 1650s, 1660s, and 1670s, including a document relating to a trip to Bordeaux in 1656 to import wine.[3] The year in which he died, 1679, can now also be confirmed, a few years after he was admitted to the Amsterdam asylum for "sijne kranksinnigheyt" (his insanity).[4] He was buried on 4 March 1679 in the Oudezijds Kapel, also known as the Sint-Olofskapel (see no. 34).[5]

The present drawing can best be compared to a group of Roman landscape drawings attributed to Collaert in the Museum of Fine Arts, Budapest.[6] In particular, the way the somewhat stylized rock formations are depicted, with coarse washes and strong chiaroscuro contrasts, is similar. Like the Budapest drawings, it is questionable whether the present sheet was drawn after nature. In any case, it was not made during Collaert's trip in the 1640s, for the watermark in the paper indicates a later date, probably around 1660–70.[7] This dating corresponds to the almost illegible inscription on the verso, from which perhaps only the year 1675 can be deduced.

Collaert apparently continued to draw Italian landscapes for the art market after his trip to Rome. He may have used his travel sketches or drawings of other artists as models, as was a common practice among Dutch Italianate artists at that time.[8] The present drawing is likely to be a second version or a copy after such an earlier example, for the same view is also depicted in a painting attributed to Jan Asselijn in the Museo Nacional del Prado, Madrid (fig. 55.1).[9] MR

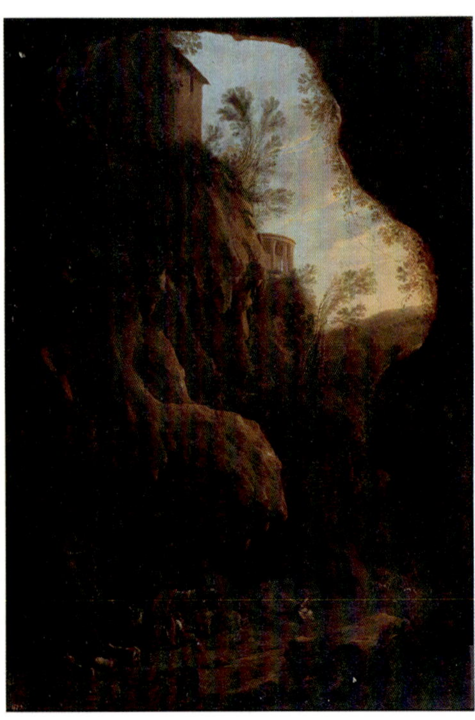

55.1 Attributed to Jan Asselijn, *View of Tivoli*, ca. 1639–41. Museo Nacional del Prado, Madrid.

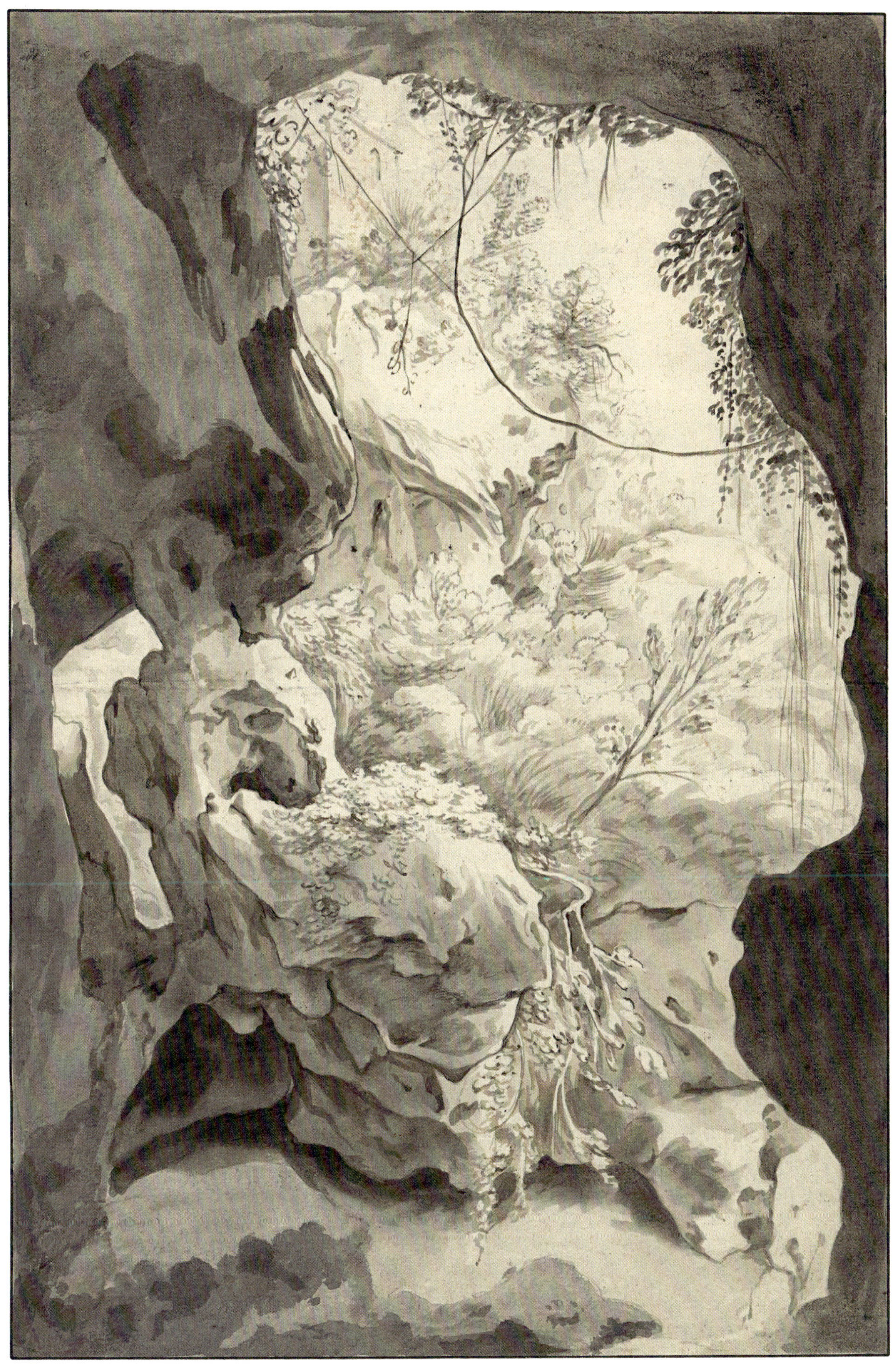

Attributed to GERBRAND VAN DEN EECKHOUT

Amsterdam 1621–1674 Amsterdam

56

Scene on the Stage of the Amsterdam Schouwburg, 1638–39

Pen and brown ink, with brown wash and white opaque watercolor
181 x 232 mm

INSCRIPTIONS Recto, lower right, in brown ink: *Rembrandt*

PROVENANCE Jean-Charles-Marie Jourdeuil (1811–1868), St. Petersburg and Lyon (L. 528, recto, lower right); his sale, Sotheby's, London, 12–13 June 1868, lot unknown (as Rembrandt); Marcus Kappel (1839–1919), Berlin; Wilhelm Reinhold Valentiner (1880–1958), Berlin; his sale, Frederik Muller, Amsterdam, 25 October 1932, lot 4 (as Rembrandt); Eldridge R. Johnson (1867–1945), Moorestown, NJ; by descent to his son George Fenimore Johnson (1928–2007), Chestertown, MD; his sale, Sotheby's, New York, 23 January 2008, lot 165; where acquired by Clement C. Moore

SELECT REFERENCES Bode 1914, 21 (as Rembrandt); Valentiner 1925–34, 1: 476, no. 208 (as Rembrandt); Kauffmann 1926, 174, n. 3 (as Rembrandt, ca. 1633–34); Hell 1930, 21 (as Rembrandt); Lugt 1929–33, 3: 44, under no. 1242 (as related to drawings characteristic of Bol or Flinck); Benesch 1935, 15 (as Rembrandt, ca. 1632–33); Van Guldener 1947, 48 (as Rembrandt); Benesch 1954–57, 1: no. 74 (as Rembrandt); Sumowski 1956–57, 259 (as Flinck); Albach 1972, pp. 114–15 (probably a school work of ca. 1638; according to K.G. Boon not by Rembrandt); Benesch 1973, 1: 24, no. 74 (as Rembrandt); Wegner 1973, 78, under no. 548 (cites Lugt's opinion as Van den Eeckhout [?]); Sumowski 1979–92, 3: no. 808 (as attributed to Van den Eeckhout); Schatborn 1985a, 97 (as Van den Eeckhout); Bevers 2006, 88, under no. 20 (as Van den Eeckhout); Bevers 2010, 50–51 (as Van den Eeckhout); Shoaf Turner 2012, no. 56 (as Van den Eeckhout); Royalton-Kisch 2012–, under Benesch 74 (as "Van den Eeckhout?"); Sluijter and Sluijter-Seiffert 2020, 292 (not Van den Eeckhout); Gnann 2021, 17 (as Rembrandt)

Promised gift of Clement C. and Elizabeth Y. Moore

This drawing offers a unique insight into the Amsterdam Schouwburg on Keizersgracht, in the late 1630s. The public theater opened its doors on 3 January 1638, and from then on visitors could attend performances, twice per week. The fact that we are looking at a scene on the stage of this specific theater is evident from the background: the typical architecture of the decor with columns, a balustrade—with people on it—and the more expensive public boxes, or loges, can be made out.[1] A painting that Hans Jurriaensz van Baden painted of the theater shows the same part of the interior (fig. 56.1).[2]

For a long time, this drawing was considered to be the work of Rembrandt himself, but there are several weaker passages that suggest a different hand, such as the hatching that obstructs the effect of three-dimensionality of the figures. Most scholars of the past generation accepted an alternate attribution of the drawing to Gerbrand van den Eeckhout, but this has recently been questioned, as has Van den Eeckhout's status as one of Rembrandt's pupils.[3] Arnold Houbraken, however, mentions Van den Eeckhout as both a friend and a student of Rembrandt, even one of his best. Moreover, the several Rembrandtesque drawings attributed to this artist clearly form a group and share stylistic characteristics with later, certain drawings by the artist. The question also arises as to which other artist from Rembrandt's circle could perhaps have been responsible for these works of art, but no satisfactory alternate idea has been proposed. In any case, it must have been an artist who was very close to Rembrandt's sphere of influence. The way of working with iron gall ink on prepared paper is typical for Rembrandt in the years 1638 and 1639 when this sheet must have been drawn.

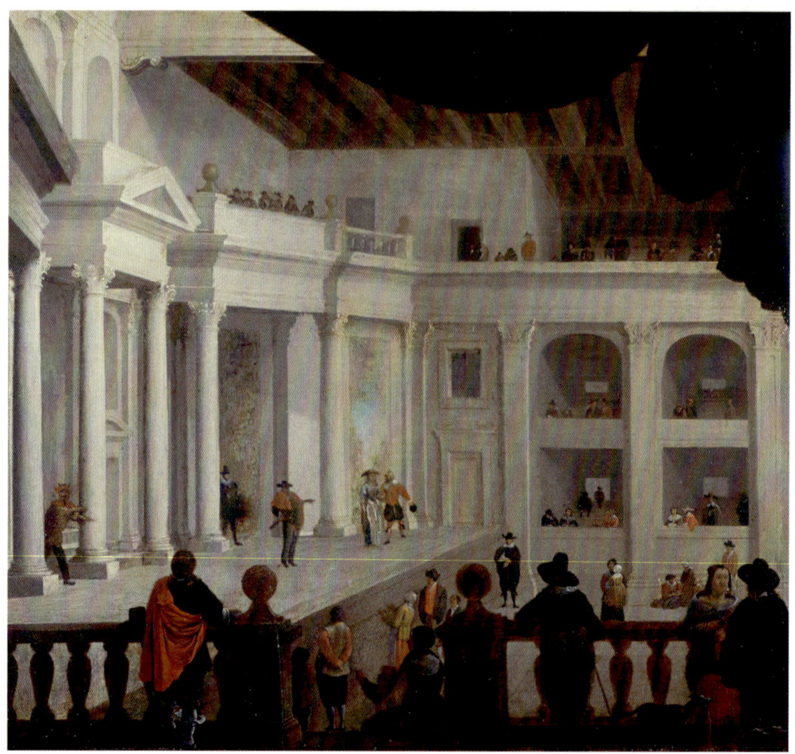

56.1 Hans Jurriaensz van Baden, *Interior of the Amsterdam Schouwburg, with a Scene from a Comedy*, 1653. John and Mable Ringling Museum of Art, Sarasota, Florida.

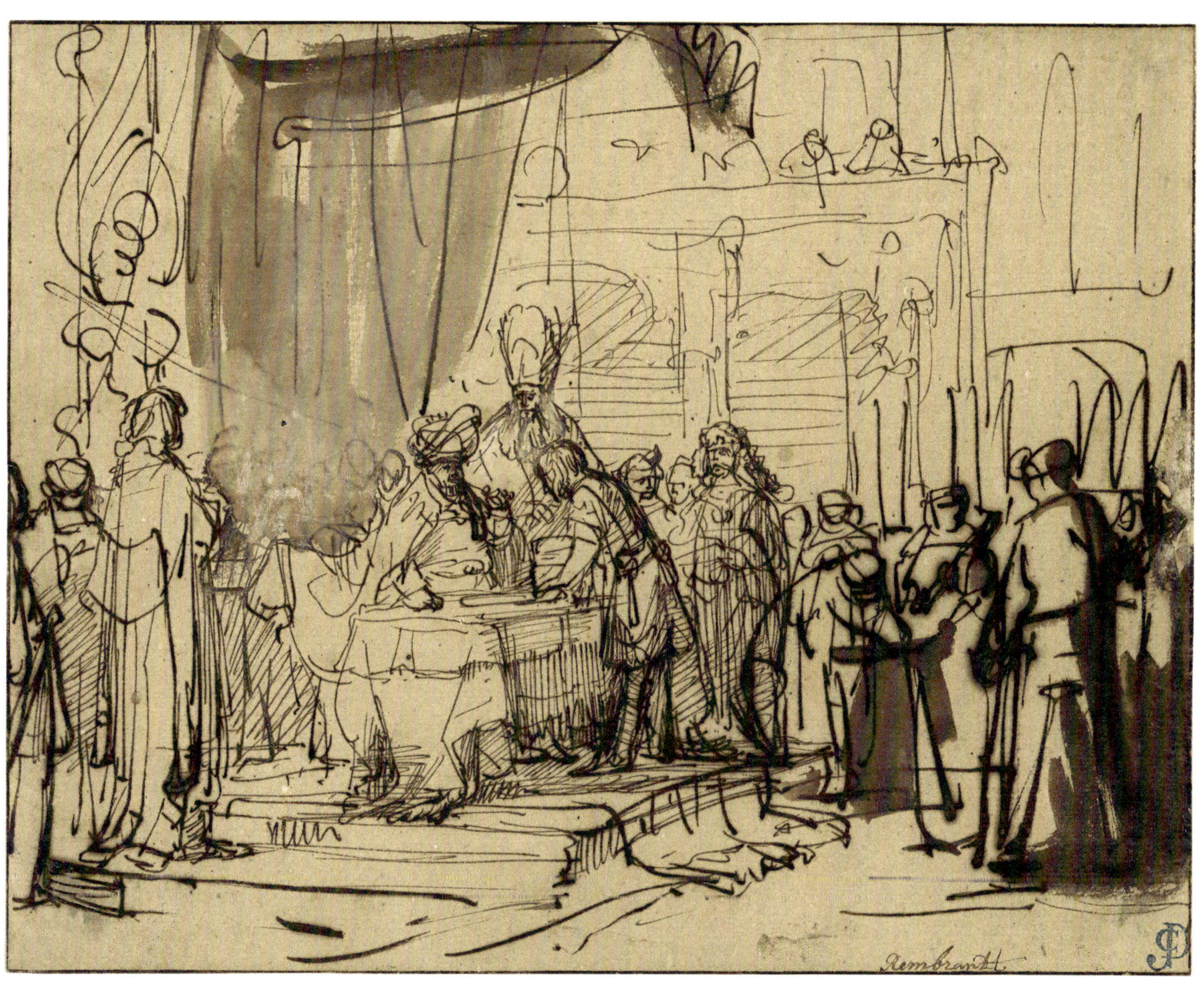
Rembrandt.

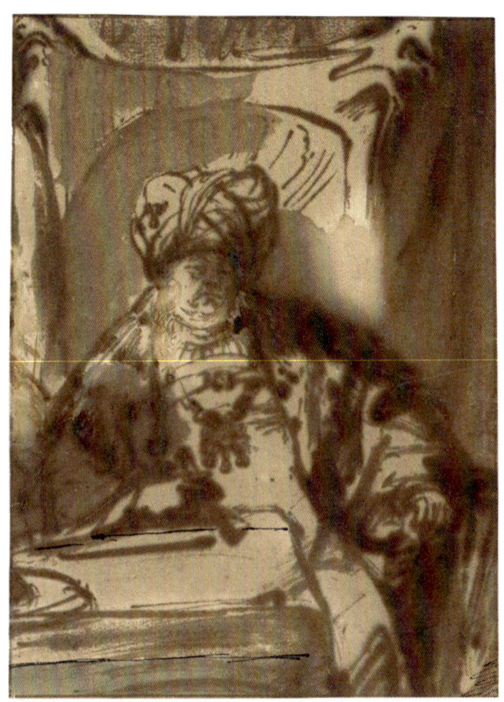

56.2 Rembrandt van Rijn, *Actor Willem Ruyter in the Role of an Eastern Monarch (Possibly Pharaoh in Vondel's Play "Josef of Sofompaneas")*, 1638–39. Rijksprentenkabinet, Amsterdam.

The drawing depicts a scene in which a specific actor, an acquaintance of Rembrandt, can be recognized: Willem Bartholsz Ruyter. Ruyter was a successful actor with great stage presence, who excelled in comic roles but also performed serious characters in tragedies. He played, for example, the role of Bishop Gozewijn in Joost van den Vondel's *Gysbreght van Aemstel*, the play Vondel wrote for the opening of the Amsterdam Schouwburg. Rembrandt must have met Ruyter more often, and he seems to have been fascinated by the actor's striking appearance. He drew the voluptuous Ruyter on several occasions, in varying roles.[4] One of these drawings—also done with iron gall ink on prepared paper—shows Ruyter dressed up with a turban, sitting on a throne (fig. 56.2).[5] This possibly shows the actor in the same role as in the drawing from the Moore collection. And while the pupil drew his scene from a distance, Rembrandt seems to have been allowed to get on stage—during or after a rehearsal?—to draw the actor up close.[6]

Ruyter's presence in combination with the architecture of the Schouwburg provides guidance for dating the creation of the drawing in the Moore collection quite precisely: between 25 October 1638 and 24 January 1639. For a play with such a scene that was performed in the Schouwburg, in which Ruyter could have appeared, almost only the play *Josef of Sofompaneas* qualifies. In this piece, which is a translation by Joost van den Vondel of a Latin text by Hugo de Groot, the later episodes in the history of the biblical hero Joseph are told.[7] After all his wanderings and misfortunes, Joseph has been given an important position at Pharaoh's court because he managed to interpret the monarch's dreams and thus saved the Egyptian people from starvation. The play premiered on 25 October 1638 and would be performed six times until 24 January 1639. Three more performances followed in September and October of 1639, but Ruyter had already died in April of that year.

We are probably looking at a scene in which Joseph is talking to Pharaoh.[8] That scene could have been performed in a "vertoning" (a tableau vivant). Such "living paintings" were performed on the streets in festive triumphal arches, on special occasions. They were also frequently inserted into the plays of the Schouwburg, as interruptions in a story. They confronted the audience with compelling events and continued for several minutes, much to the audience's delight. This perhaps also gave our artist time to capture the scene on paper with quick pen lines. Finally, as has already been mentioned by other authors, it should be noted that the figures in thicker lines—on the right in the composition—may have been added later by the draftsman and may not have appeared on stage, since they then would have blocked the view for the audience.[9] LvS

LAMBERT DOOMER

Amsterdam 1624–1700 Amsterdam

57

View of Paris as Seen from Montmartre, ca. 1671–73

Pen and brown ink, with gray, green, and rose wash, on account-book paper; framing line in brown ink
249 x 415 mm

INSCRIPTIONS Verso, lower edge, by the "pseudo-Ploos" hand, in pen and gray ink: *Aldús vertoont sigh Parijs van Mon Martere af te zien*

PROVENANCE Jeronimus Tonneman (1687–1750), Amsterdam; his mother, Maria Tonneman, born Van Breusegom (d. 1752), Amsterdam; her sale, Hendrik de Leth, Amsterdam, 21 October 1754, Album S, lot 29 (to "Van Son"); Karl Eduard von Liphart (1808–1891), Dorpat, Bonn, and Florence (L. 1687, recto, lower right, in red ink); his grandson Reinhold von Liphart (1864–1940), Dorpat and Munich-Grafeling (L. 1758, verso, lower left, upside down, and in black ink: 270); his sale, C.G. Boerner, Leipzig, 26 April 1898, lot 475 (as "S. van der Hoog"); Louis Deglatigny (1854–1936), Rouen, acquired around 1920 (L. 1768a, recto, lower right); his sale, Féral, Catroux, Huteau and M. Rousseau, Paris, 29 May 1937, lot 48 (as "J. Hoog"); possibly Bernard Houthakker Galerie, Amsterdam, 1955 (as Lambert Doomer);[1] Charles E. Duits (1882–1969), London (L. 533a, recto, lower right); thence by descent; acquired through Thomas Williams Fine Art, London, by Clement C. Moore, 2007

SELECT REFERENCES Van den Berg 1942, no. 71; Gerson 1942, 49 (as "J. Hoog"); Schulz 1972, 2: no. 201; Schulz 1974, no. 133; Sumowski 1979–92, 2: no. 36; Alsteens and Buijs 2008, no. 52

Promised gift of Clement C. and Elizabeth Y. Moore

At first glance, this rolling landscape dotted with windmills seems to be a view of the Dutch countryside, although suspiciously hilly. An inscription on the verso, "Aldús vertoont sigh Parijs van Mon Martere af te zien" (This presents Paris seen from Montmartre), reveals that it is a view of the French capital from the steep rise to the city's north.[2]

The twenty-two-year-old Doomer and his friend and fellow artist Willem Schellinks traveled to France in 1646 to visit Doomer's brothers in Nantes. On their voyage, Doomer and Schellinks made drawings in every town they visited. While sheets exist documenting most places on their itinerary, the present view is the sole example related to their visit to Paris, where Doomer and Schellinks sought out Dutch colleagues and stayed for almost a month. They made a brief sojourn in Lyon before returning to Rouen and parting company.[3] Back in the Netherlands, Doomer continued to travel and sketch sites throughout his native land, in Germany, and along the Rhine. Around 1670, Doomer put his many sketches from earlier voyages to good use. In the years 1671–73, he used informal on-the-spot studies as the basis for more finished drawings, often made on account-book paper in wash and watercolor. These finished sheets from the 1670s number over three hundred, and their wide distribution suggests they were highly saleable.

Frits Lugt was initially skeptical about the identification of the present sheet as a view of Paris, given some of the anomalies in the view. But, as Stijn Alsteens argues, Doomer combined accurate topographical elements with imagined ones in his finished drawings from the 1670s. Thus, the view is anchored by the distinctive form of Notre-Dame at center with the tall, square Temple donjon, a fortified monastery built in the thirteenth century by the Knights Templar, at left. The rest of the landscape is enlivened by the inclusion of bell towers and buildings that pepper the landscape. Alsteens proposes that Doomer may have been working in the 1670s from a 1646 sketch that lacked precise detail or that he was embellishing the view to produce a more picturesque scene in keeping with his late landscape style.

57.1 Matthäus Merian the Younger, *Map of Paris Seen from the Northeast*, 1654. Rijksprentenkabinet, Amsterdam.

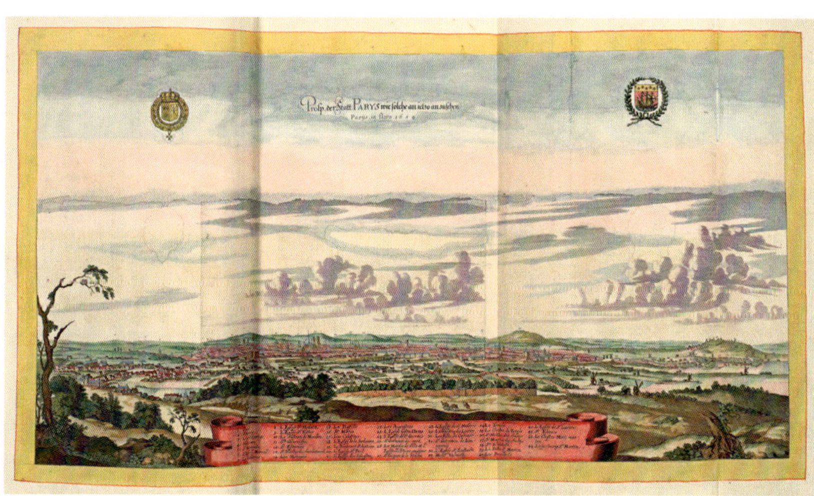

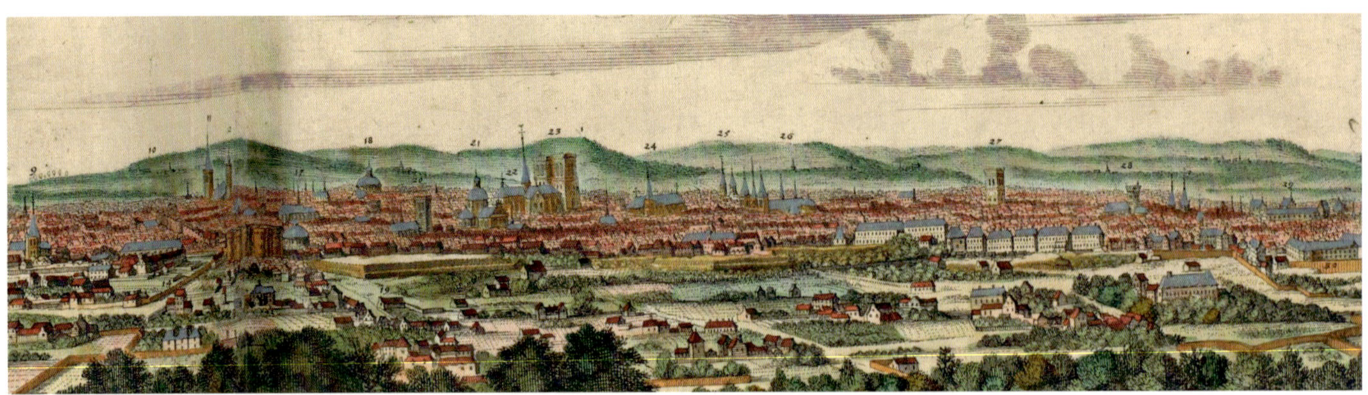

57.2 Matthäus Merian the Younger, *Map of Paris Seen from the Northeast* (detail), 1654. Rijksprentenkabinet, Amsterdam.

Although admirers of belle-epoque Paris are aware of the emblematic Moulin Rouge nightclub with its signature windmill, in the seventeenth century Montmartre was outside the city walls and not yet part of the urban fabric. The hill was the site of a village peopled by artisans and agriculture workers surrounding a medieval Benedictine abbey and church. It had long been a site for windmills: a 1550 map of Paris by Truschet and Hoyau shows a mill and the abbey among the hills and farmland.[4] As the seventeenth century progressed, the use of windmills expanded, and, by some estimates, there were up to thirty mills in the vicinity. In Matthäus Merian the Younger's rare 1654 map, which offers a panorama of Paris seen from the northeast at a distance of a few miles, multiple mills and towers are visible in the distance (figs. 57.1–57.2).[5] As Alsteens and Buijs noted, the topography is also close to several engraved views from the same decade, including a view in a cartouche on Jacques Gomboust's 1652 map. Doomer's view of a carriage heading to the city includes a few small mills at right to preserve this sense of place, which must have seemed familiar to the young Dutchman abroad. JT

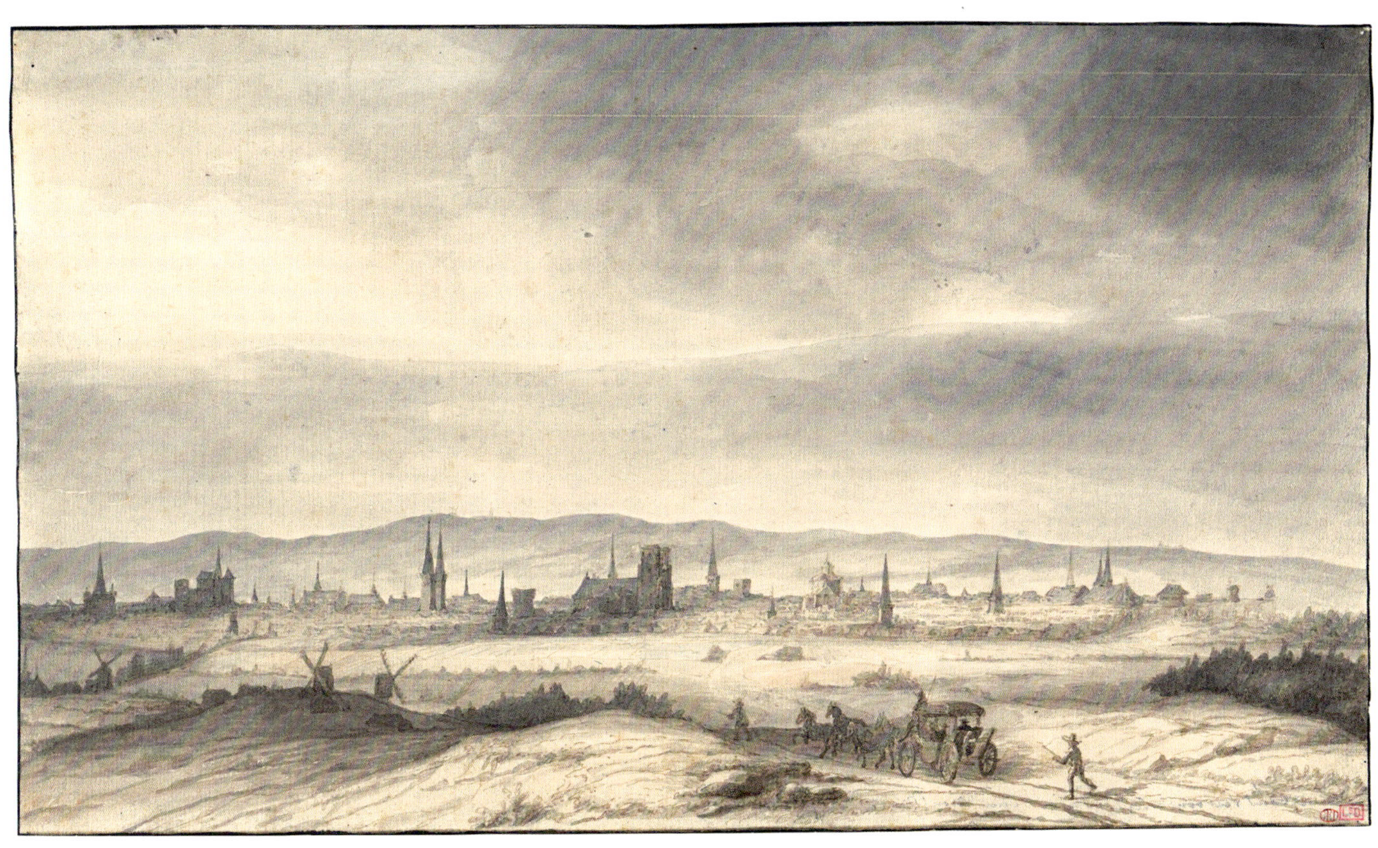

PAULUS POTTER

Enkhuizen 1625–1654 Amsterdam

58

Herdsmen and Their Animals Sheltering from a Storm, ca. 1647

Black and white chalk, on brownish-gray paper; framing line in brown ink

187 x 241 mm

INSCRIPTIONS Recto, lower right, falsely signed, presumably by a seventeenth-century hand, in brown ink: *Paulus. Potter. f.*[1]

PROVENANCE Sotheby's, London, 21 March 1973, lot 43; where acquired by Johan Quirijn van Regteren Altena (1899–1980), Amsterdam (L. 4617, verso, lower right); by descent to his heirs; their sale, Christie's, London, 8–10 July 2014, lot 54; where acquired by Clement C. Moore

SELECT REFERENCES Giltaij 1976, no. 101; Walsh, Buijsen, and Broos 1994, no. 37

Promised gift of Clement C. and Elizabeth Y. Moore

With parallel strokes of black chalk, Potter conveyed rain lashing down from the upper left. As depicted, the inclement weather—another manifestation of the theme of Man vs. Nature—causes not only the trees to bend over, but three figures to take refuge under a ramshackle farm shelter, open on all sides under a thatched roof, already damaged by the elements. The left-hand figure clings to an upright, while another at center, watched by a seated figure accompanied by a recumbent dog at right, grips something suspended from the top of the shelter. It has been suggested that he may be drawing water on a pulley from a well.[2] Despite the buffeting winds, the animals in the scene (cattle in the field in the left background, a steer and chickens at right, and even the seated dog), unlike their human counterparts, seem oblivious to the raging storm. The steer at right would have been based on one of Potter's numerous individual studies of animals, like the *Study of a Bull Standing*, seen from a similar angle, in the British Museum, London.[3]

In terms of style and technique, the Moore sheet has been compared with several works associated with the year 1647. These include two chalk drawings on tinted paper, both with genuine signatures: *Cow Calving in a Barn* in the Albertina, Vienna;[4] and *Figures and Cattle beside a River, with a Woman Washing out a Tub* in the Ashmolean Museum, Oxford (fig. 58.1).[5] The latter served as a preparatory study for a painting dated 1647, previously in a number of distinguished French collections, including that of Étienne François, Duc de Choiseul, and then long untraced until its appearance at auction in 2020.[6] The same date appears on a drawing, *Deer in a Wood*, in the Rijksprentenkabinet, Amsterdam.[7] Although that sheet is executed solely in black chalk, it is a variant of an unsigned drawing by Potter in the Crocker Art Museum, Sacramento,[8] carried out in the same technique as the Moore sheet. JST

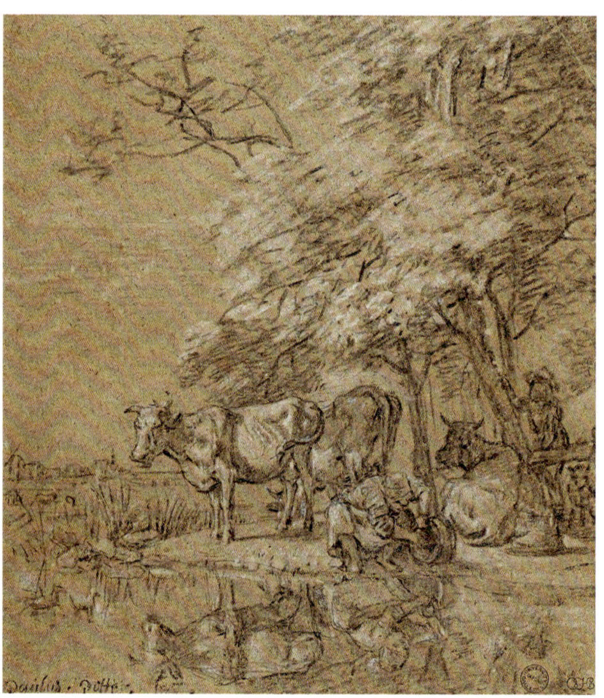

58.1 Paulus Potter, *Figures and Cattle beside a River, with a Woman Washing out a Tub*, ca. 1647. Ashmolean Museum, Oxford.

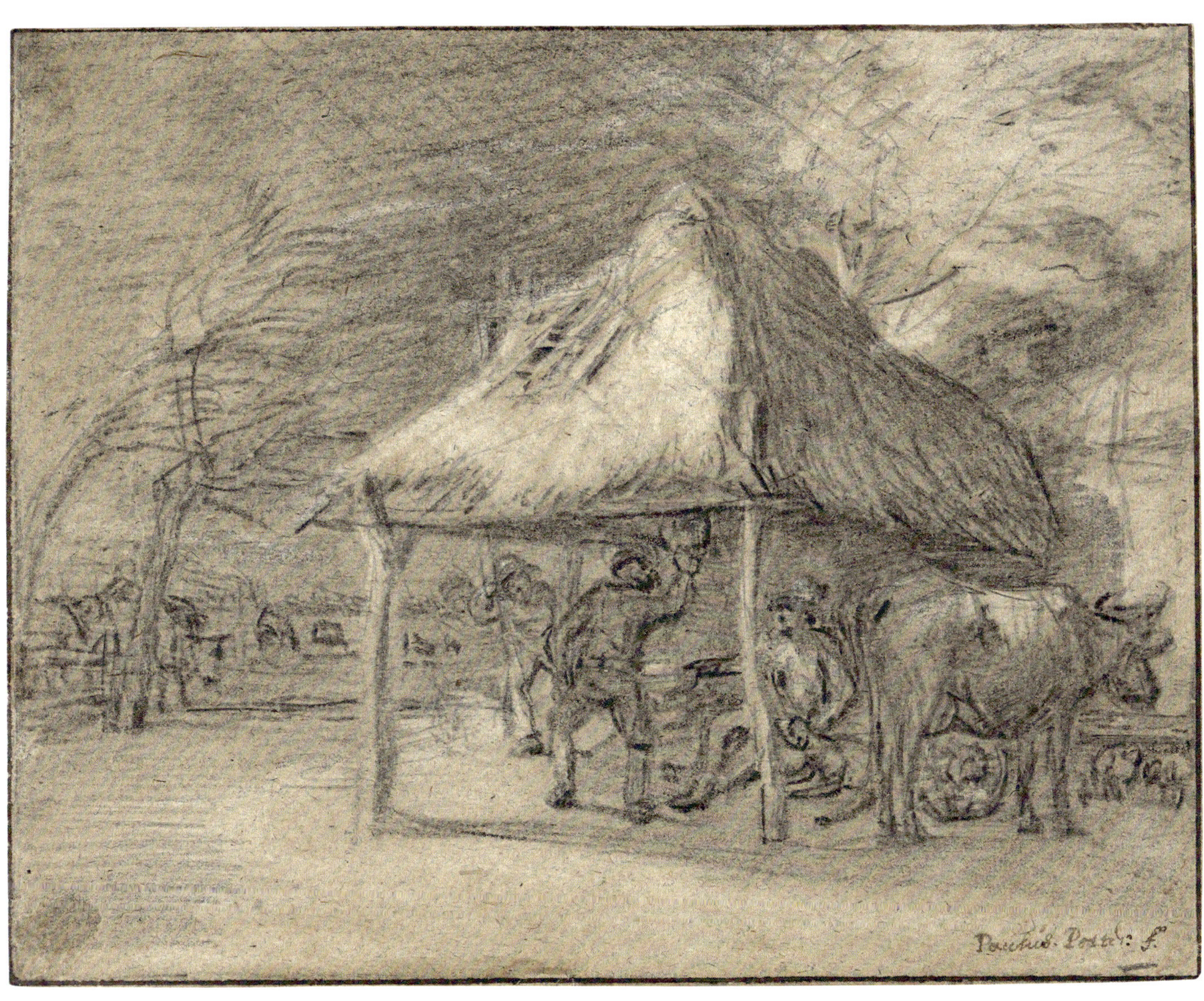

CLAES VAN BERESTEYN

Haarlem ca. 1627/29–1684 Haarlem

59

Study of a Truncated Willow Tree, ca. 1650–75

Pen and brown ink; framing line in brown ink
150 x 122 mm

PROVENANCE Private collection, the Netherlands; Onno van Seggelen Fine Arts, Rotterdam; from whom acquired by Clement C. Moore, 2016

SELECT REFERENCES Giltaij 2017, 322–23; Shoaf Turner 2018

Promised gift of Clement C. and Elizabeth Y. Moore

59.1 Claes van Beresteyn, *Study of a Truncated Willow*, ca. 1650–75. Present whereabouts unknown.

59.2 Claes van Beresteyn, *Landscape in an Oval*, ca. 1650–75. Rijksprentenkabinet, Amsterdam.

Drawings by this Dutch dilettante, son of a distinguished and wealthy Haarlem lawyer, are rare. Van Beresteyn's work has often been confused with that of Adriaen Hendriksz Verboom, a fellow Haarlemer or native of Rotterdam. Both artists are known for their delicate draftsmanship, with stellate-shaped clumps of leaves, trees, and grass rendered with fine, short pen strokes in a quasi-pointillist style, as if each leaf were drawn using an etching needle. Typical motifs in Van Beresteyn's landscapes are gnarled, twisted tree trunks. Of thirty-eight drawings given to the artist by Horst Gerson in 1940, only three are still considered to be autograph, two of which are signed with the artist's monogram: *Knotty Old Tree in the Dunes with a Fence*, recently with the dealer Mireille Mosler, New York,[1] and *Landscape with Gnarled Trees in the Foreground* in the Klassik Stiftung, Weimar.[2] A third signed sheet, *Landscape with Trees*, has since emerged in the collection of the P. & N. de Boer Foundation, Amsterdam.[3] Alongside this trio of monogrammed examples, Jeroen Giltaij in 2017 accepted as autograph only three other drawings, the present work and two sheets published by Gerson, *Dune Landscape with Gnarled Trees*, acquired by the Rijksprentenkabinet in 2014 from the second sale of the heirs of Johan Quirijn van Regteren Altena;[4] and, implicitly, a sixth drawing, *Study of Oak (?) Trees*, in the British Museum, London, which had earlier been assigned to Van Beresteyn by Frits Lugt.[5]

When Peter Schatborn confirmed Van Beresteyn's authorship of the present work in October 2015,[6] he described it as the only known example of a single tree as a subject.[7] Seven months later, another study of a solitary truncated willow tree emerged in a sale at Bassenge in Berlin (fig. 59.1).[8] That tree also shows evidence of having had a large vine of ivy growing up its trunk. While ivy was long misunderstood as a parasitic plant that would harm its host, it is now recognized that this occurs only when the vine takes over a host tree that is already weak,

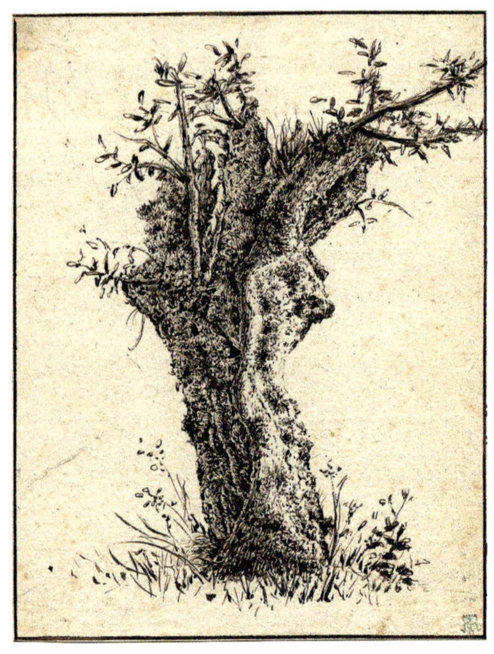

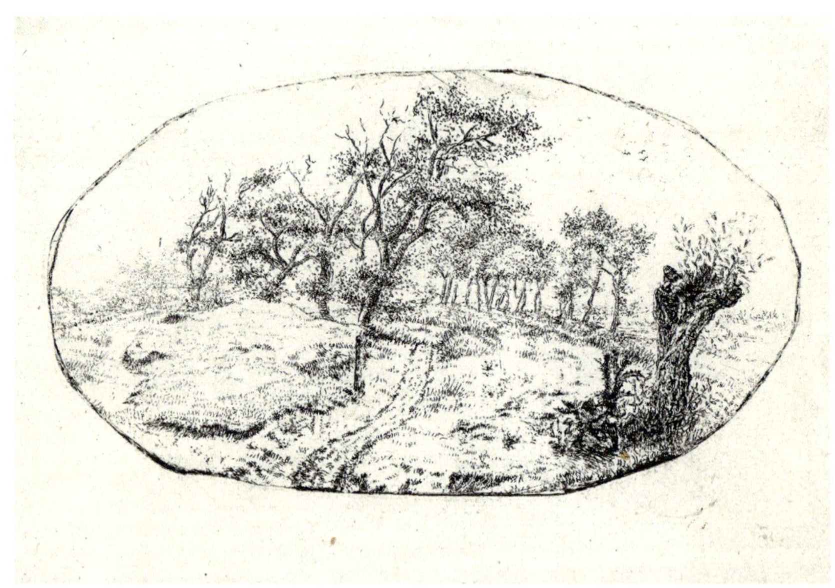

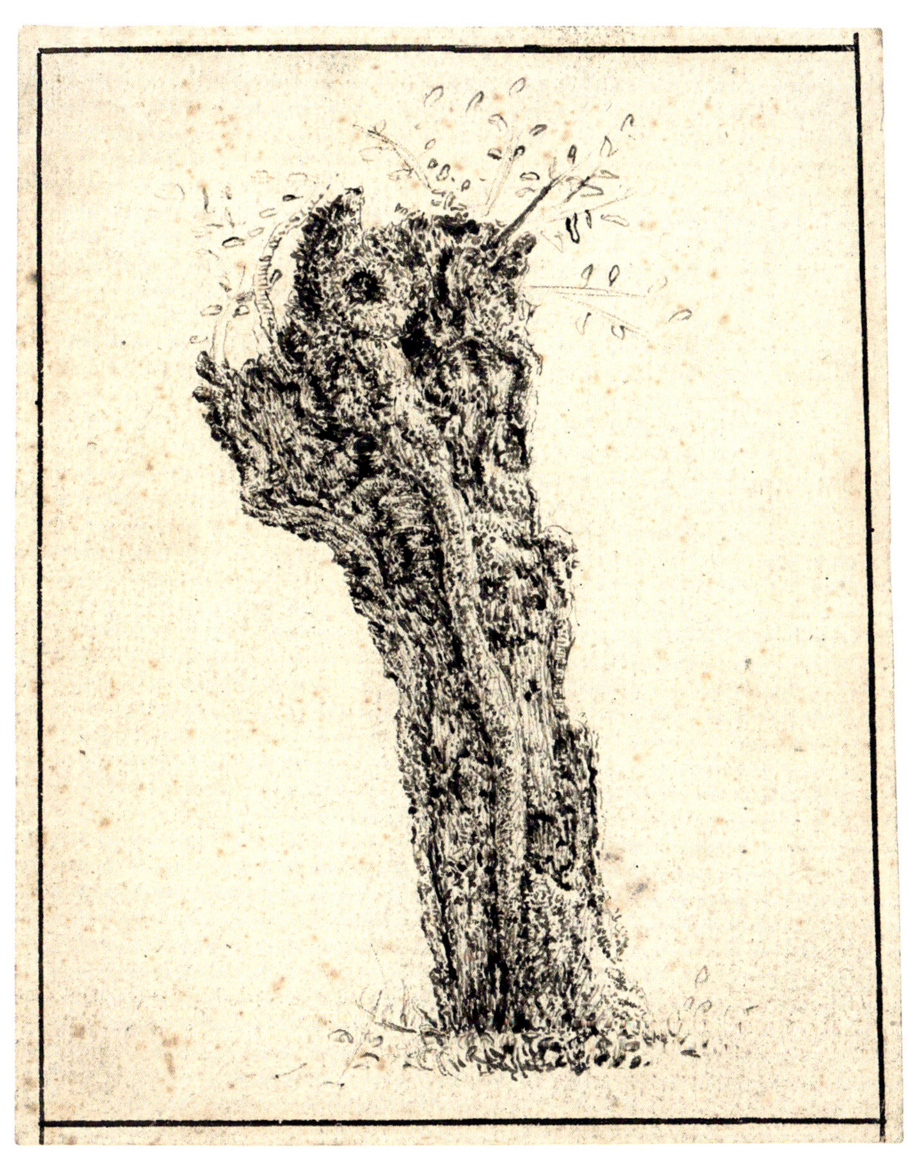

rotten, or damaged, as may be the case with the tree in the Moore drawing. The truncated trees studied in these two drawings resemble the pollarded willow at right in one of the artist's nine etchings, the undated *Landscape in an Oval* (fig. 59.2).[9] Aside from two etchings that are dated 1650, it is difficult to establish a chronology of Van Beresteyn's work. Mentioned as a pupil of Salomon de Braij in the 1644 records of the Haarlem Guild of St. Luke, he had probably stopped working as an amateur artist by the mid- to late 1670s, by which time he had founded the Hofje van Beresteyn in Haarlem, a family-funded almshouse for elderly Catholic women. JST

SAMUEL VAN HOOGSTRATEN

Dordrecht 1627–1678 Dordrecht

60

The Annunciation, ca. 1649–50

Pen and brown ink and wash, and black chalk, with white opaque watercolor
156 x 152 mm

WATERMARK "PB" below coat of arms with a bend and two quadrupeds

PROVENANCE Possibly Hendrik van Limborch (1681–1759), The Hague; his sale, Mattijas Hijmbach, The Hague, 17 September 1759, Album 7, part of lot 230; P. & D. Colnaghi and Co., London (according to inscription on the mount), by 30 November 1856; Marsden J. Perry (1851–1935), Providence and New York (no mark; see L. 1880); Duveen Gallery, New York, ca. 1919; Wilhelm Reinhold Valentiner (1880–1958), Berlin; his sale, A.W.M. Mensing, Frederik Muller, Amsterdam, 25 October 1932, lot XXI; Guy C. Tomme (1928–2010), Barto, PA; his sale, Christie's, Amsterdam, 21 November 1989, lot 38; Richard Day, Ltd., London, 1990; Sotheby's, New York, 29 January 2014, lot 142; where acquired by Clement C. Moore for the Baymeath Art Trust

SELECT REFERENCES Sumowski 1979–92, 5: no. 1186x; Shoaf Turner 2006, 83–84, under no. 106

Promised gift of Clement C. and Elizabeth Y. Moore, through the Baymeath Art Trust

Samuel van Hoogstraten was the only Rembrandt pupil who wrote extensively on the theory and practice of art. In his *Inleyding tot de hooge schoole der schilderkonst* (Introduction to the Illustrious School of Painting), 1678, he instructed young artists to develop narrative compositions by repeatedly sketching scenes from the Bible and other literary sources.[1] His recommendation reflects a pedagogical routine devised by Rembrandt, who had his students draw "histories," for which they could consult his own works and those in his extensive collection. When teaching his own students, Van Hoogstraten followed this practice, requiring his pupils to submit a new composition every week for his critique.[2]

The Annunciation belongs to a large group of similar drawings by Van Hoogstraten, most depicting subjects from Jewish and Christian history, that date from ca. 1649–50.[3] Having completed his training with Rembrandt, Van Hoogstraten returned, by early 1648, to his native Dordrecht. He operated a workshop there until May 1651, when he embarked on a five-year journey through Germany, Austria, and Italy. He would have taken on his first pupils at that time and probably made the drawings as models for their instruction.[4] Several works in this group are signed and a few are dated 1649 or 1650. *The Sacrifice of Manoah* in the Herzog Anton Ulrich-Museum, Braunschweig, signed and dated 1649 (fig. 60.1), is closely comparable to *The Annunciation*, which provides a date for the Moore drawing and should dispel any doubts about its attribution.[5] Like the Virgin and the angel Gabriel in the Moore *Annunciation*, the figures in these drawings are short and compact in proportion and their gestures restrained and unaffectedly expressive. The penwork combines emphatic, sometimes doubled, contours with fine, parallel strokes for shading.

60.1 Samuel van Hoogstraten, *The Sacrifice of Manoah*, 1649. Herzog Anton Ulrich-Museum, Braunschweig.

60.2 Unidentified artist (after Samuel van Hoogstraten), *The Annunciation*, eighteenth century. Morgan Library & Museum, New York.

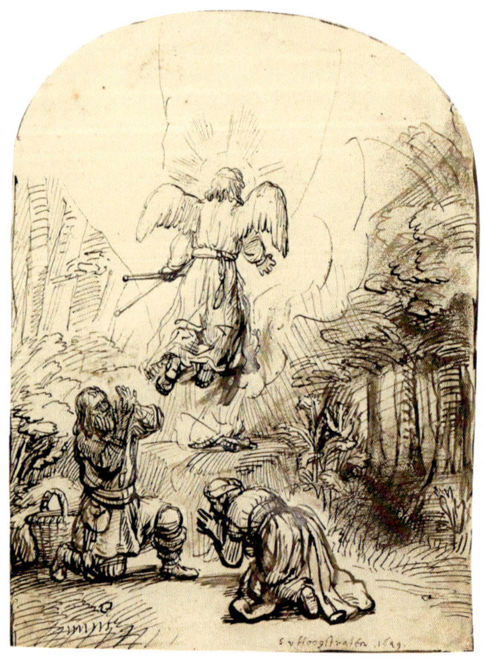

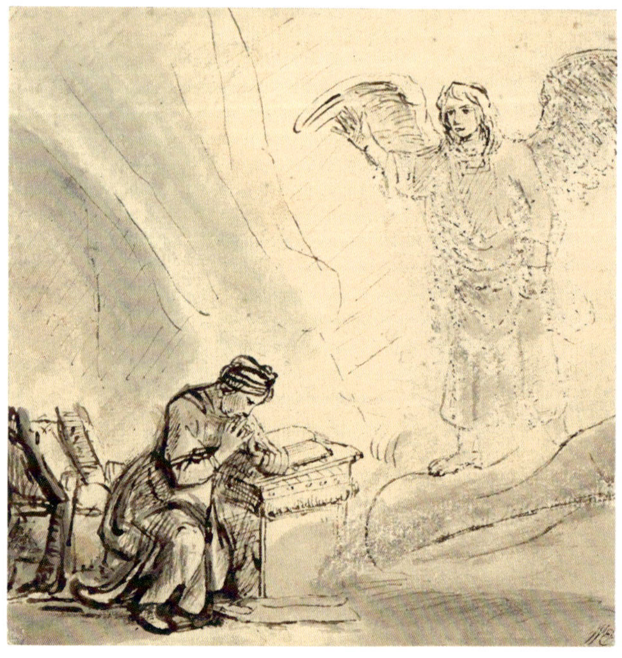

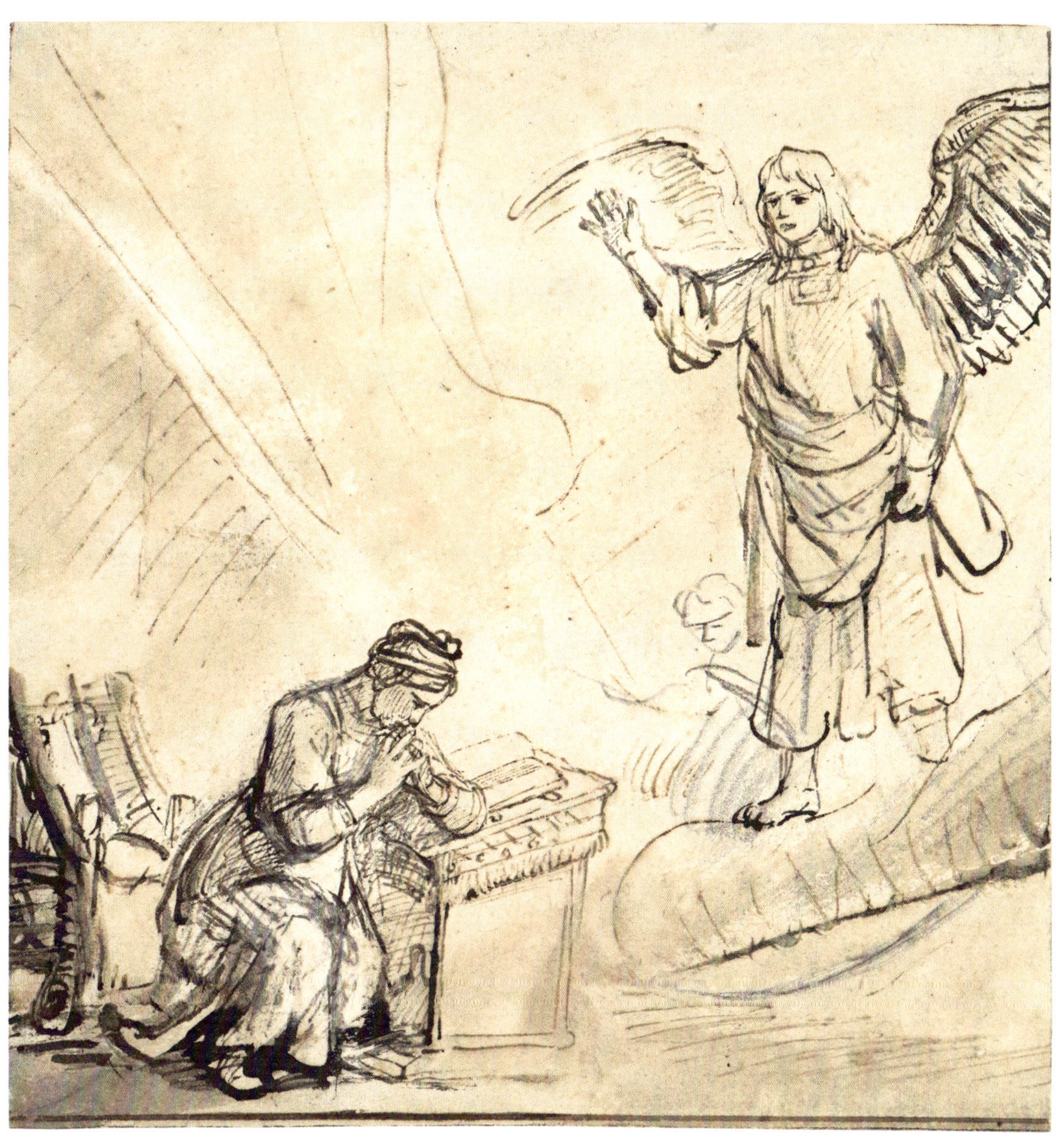

A copy after the Moore drawing is in the Morgan Library & Museum (fig. 60.2).[6] The unknown, probably eighteenth-century draftsman omitted the incidental head beside the angel's knee in the Moore drawing, which might be a false start or left over from a previous use of the sheet. The copyist scratched into the lines describing the angel's figure to emphasize the incorporeal nature of the heavenly messenger. WWR

JAN SIBERECHTS

Antwerp 1627–1703 London

61

River Landscape with a View of Oxford in the Distance (recto); *Horseman along a River in England* (verso), after 1672

Pen and brown ink, with watercolor and opaque watercolor, over black chalk (recto); watercolor and opaque watercolor, over black chalk (verso)

170 x 224 mm

PROVENANCE Alfred Brod Gallery, London; C.G. Boerner, Düsseldorf, 1962; private collection, Belgium; Bassenge, Berlin, 5 June 2009, lot 6249 (as "Niederländisch, 17. Jh."); Thomas Williams Fine Art, London (as Gillis Neyts); from whom acquired by Clement C. Moore, 2011

SELECT REFERENCES Boerner 1962, no. 147; Rubinstein 2012, 389–91, figs. 44, 45

Promised gift of Clement C. and Elizabeth Y. Moore

This intriguing sheet has on its two sides two attractive panoramic landscapes, each executed in a rather different technique, but nonetheless similar enough in palette, tonality, and general spirit for both to be attributed to the same artist.

The question of who this artist should be has, however, been debated; over the last half century or so, the drawing has been offered for sale as an anonymous seventeenth-century Netherlandish work, and also under the names of two different Flemish artists, Gillis Neyts and Jan Siberechts. The last of these attributions seems on balance the most convincing, not least because the view on the recto clearly depicts an English location: Oxford, seen from Iffley, a mile or two to the south of the ancient university city. A further 25 miles or so downstream lies the Oxfordshire town of Henley-on-Thames, depicted by Siberechts in no fewer than five majestic canvases.[1]

It is a well-known fact that almost all the significant early topographical views of British towns, whether drawn, painted, or engraved, were the work of foreign artists, mostly from the Low Countries, who were either visiting Great Britain or had settled there.[2] Oxford is no exception: other than Moore drawing, the three most significant sixteenth- and seventeenth-century prospects of Oxford were probably Joris Hoefnagel's drawing of ca. 1568, now in the Royal Collection in the Print Room at Windsor Castle,[3] the engraved view that Wenceslaus Hollar incorporated into his city map of around 1643,[4] and a distant view from the South West, drawn by Jan van der Vinne during a short visit to England in around 1686.[5]

Siberechts, a native of Antwerp, came to England in 1672 at the behest of the 2nd Duke of Buckingham and remained there for the rest of his life, almost single-handedly creating the genre of the country house view, works that depicted and celebrated the stately country seats of the aristocracy, many of which had been sadly neglected during the Civil War and Commonwealth but were, following the 1660 Restoration of the monarchy, being returned to their former glory. Siberechts's paintings of English country houses, seen both from ground level and in bird's-eye view, were original enough, but perhaps even more significant to the history

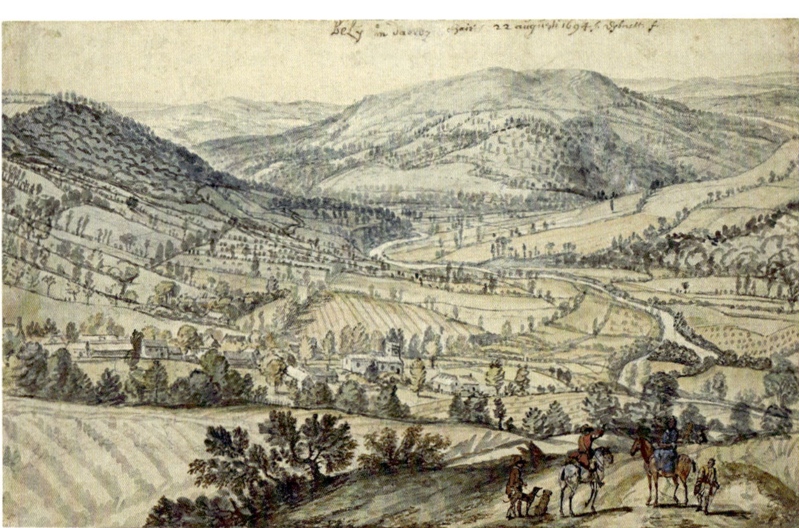

61.1 Jan Siberechts, *View of Beely, near Chatsworth, Derbyshire*, 1694. British Museum, London.

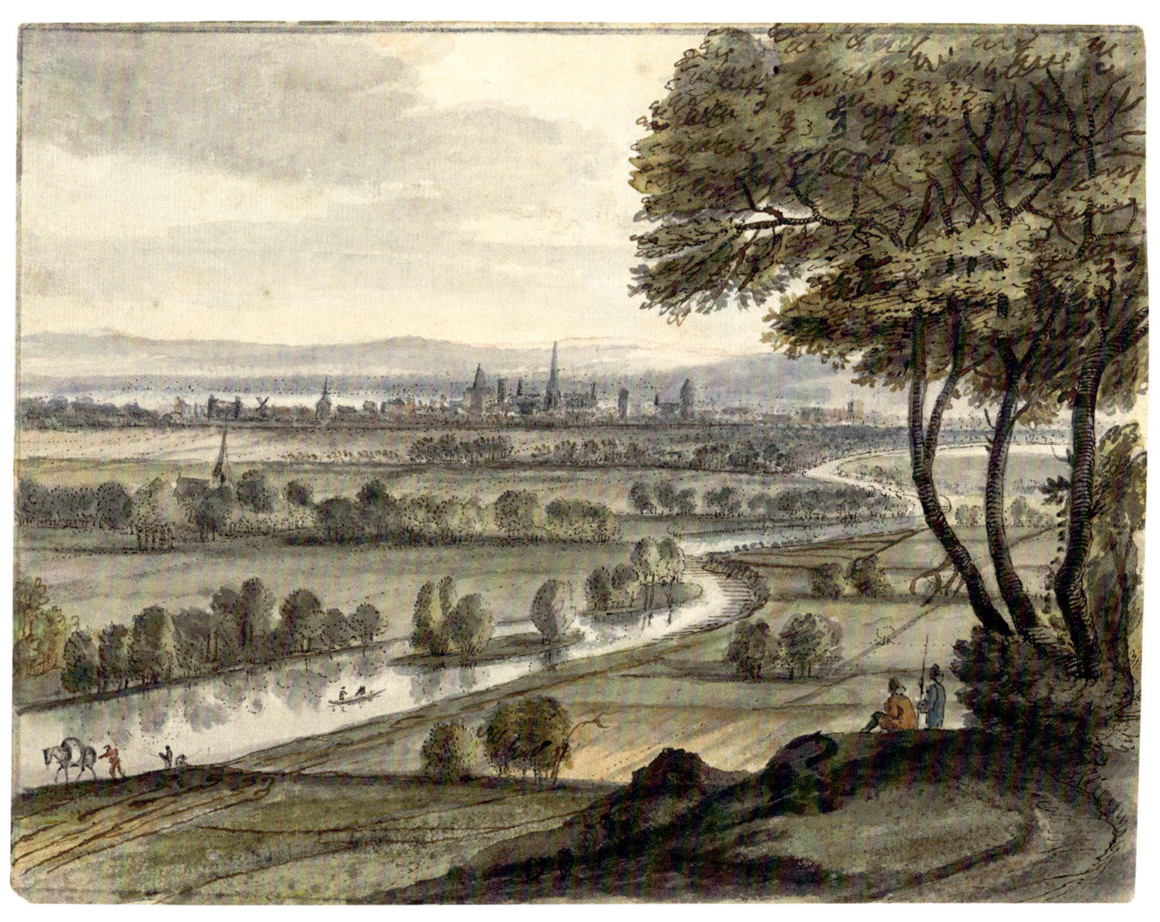

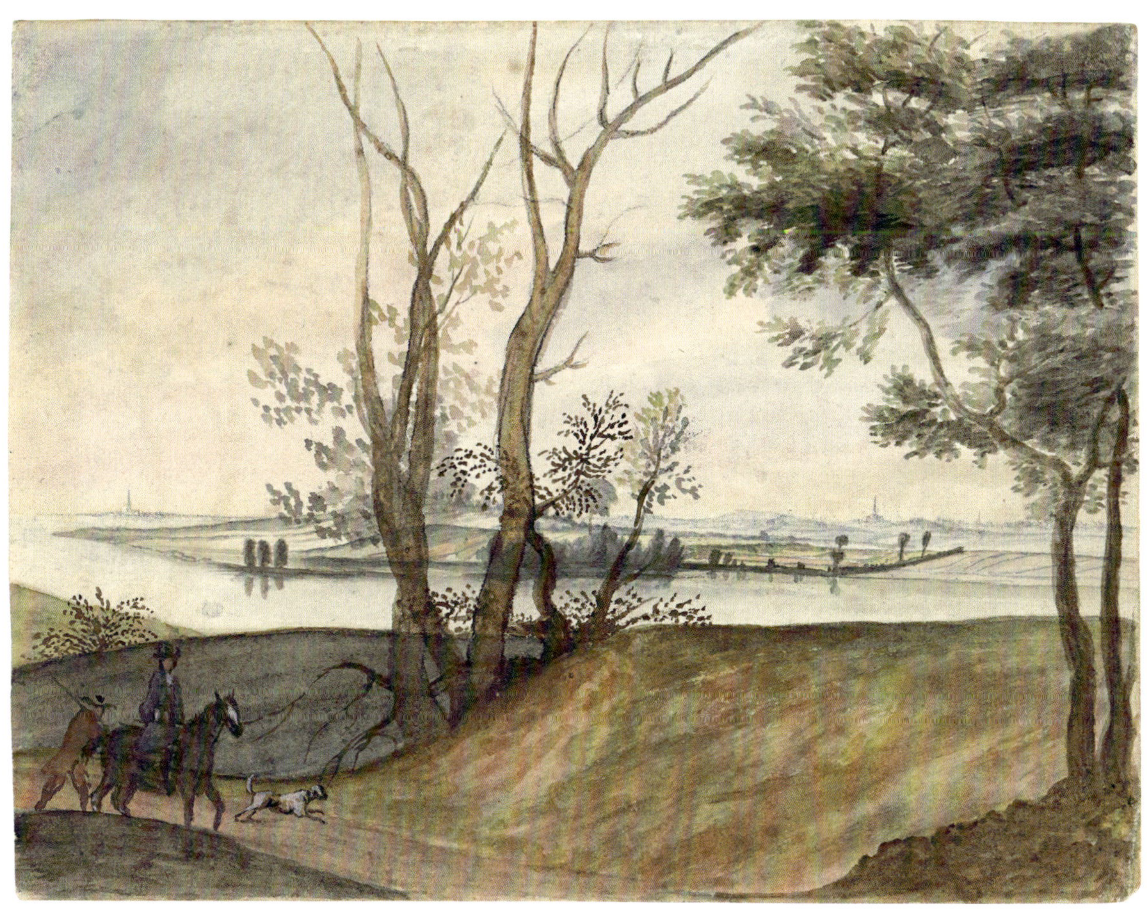

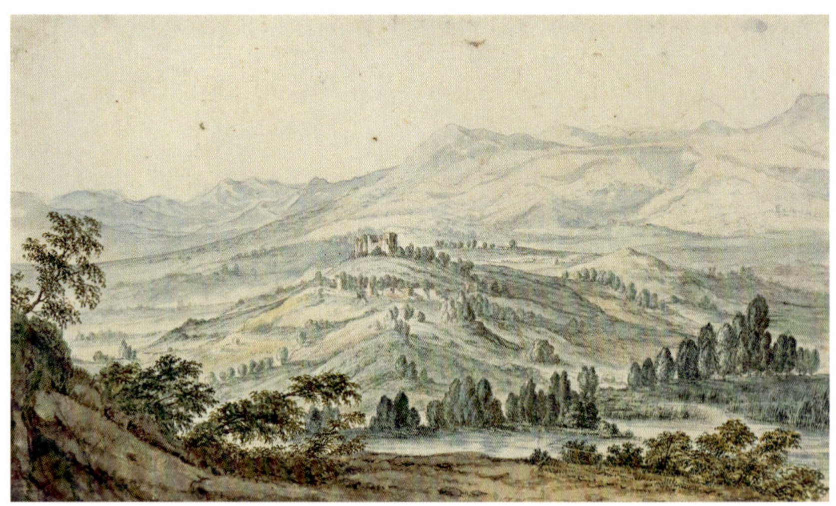

61.2 Attributed to Jan Siberechts, *Panoramic Mountain Landscape*, 1690s (?). Klassik Stiftung, Weimar.

of British art were his exceptional landscape watercolors, works with few real precedents, which provided a vital springboard for the emergence of watercolor as one of eighteenth-century England's preeminent art forms.

Particularly notable is the group of at least three watercolors depicting locations near Chatsworth, in Derbyshire, executed in the 1690s (fig. 61.1, for example), in which the approach to the landscape and the handling are very similar to what we see in the broad river landscape on the verso of the Moore collection drawing.[6] The rendering of aerial perspective, the color palette, the specific way in which the foliage is constructed with dabs of unmodulated color, and the figure types are all very comparable.

As already noted, the handling in the view of Oxford on the recto is rather different. Here, the forms of the different compositional elements are more clearly defined, using a structure of fine lines and dots in pen and ink—something that is not to be found in any of the small handful of drawings that can be attributed to Siberechts with total certainty, but is seen in a fine colored drawing in Weimar (fig. 61.2), also formerly attributed to Gillis Neyts, which can be tentatively given to Siberechts on the basis of compositional links with one of the artist's paintings.[7] The pen technique in the Oxford view is also in a certain way comparable to the dotted touches of chalk in the very distinctive group of black chalk sketchbook pages by Siberechts, which in turn relate to earlier Flemish traditions of landscape drawing, and the works of artists such as Jan Wildens and Lodewijk de Vadder.[8]

The relationship between the art of the Low Countries and that of the British Isles has always been of particular interest to Chips Moore. Through this appealing drawing we are able to travel back together, accompanying our Flemish visitor as he discovers the beauty of England's countryside and the grandeur of her cities.
GMGR

JAN DE BISSCHOP *after* FRANS VAN MIERIS

Amsterdam 1628–1671 The Hague / Leiden 1635–1681 Leiden

62

A Young Woman in a Feathered Beret, ca. 1660–65

Black chalk, pen and brown ink, and brown wash
210 x 160 mm

PROVENANCE Possibly Michiel Oudaan (ca. 1702–1766), Rotterdam; his sale, 3 November 1766, Album R, lot 6 (as Jan de Bisschop after Ter Borch), to Kock; Herbert E. Feist Gallery, New York, by 1967 (as by Frans van Mieris); Christian Humann (1929–1981), New York, by 1978; Sotheby's, New York, 20 January 1983, lot 685 (as after Frans van Mieris); Mr. and Mrs. Otto Naumann, New York; from whom acquired for the Baymeath Art Trust by Clement C. Moore, 2017

SELECT REFERENCES Naumann 1978, 34

Promised gift of Clement C. and Elizabeth Y. Moore through the Baymeath Art Trust, in honor of Eugene V. Thaw

62.1 Hendrik Bary, *A Young Woman in a Feathered Beret*, ca. 1660–65. British Museum, London.

Jan de Bisschop led a remarkable double life. Professionally, he enjoyed a successful career as a lawyer at the Court of Holland in The Hague. In his private time, he was an accomplished and widely admired draftsman. A supreme master of the brush, De Bisschop's several hundred extant drawings are characterized by their rich, luminous washes reminiscent of Bartholomeus Breenbergh (see no. 31), with whom De Bisschop is thought to have studied in Amsterdam between 1644 and 1648.[1]

Aside from a couple of hundred landscape drawings and a small group of figure and genre studies of his own invention, the largest part of De Bisschop's sizeable drawn oeuvre consists of copies after other artworks. Some of these he etched and published himself, such as his prints after classical sculptures in his *Signorum veterum icones* (The Hague, 1669), and his prints after drawings by earlier artists in his didactic *Paradigmata graphices* (The Hague, 1671). Arnold Houbraken famously noted in *De groote schouburgh* of 1718–21 that, despite his status as a dilettante draftsman (rather than a professional painter), De Bisschop merited attention not only for his pedagogical importance to young artists but also because his copies after paintings were drawn "so artfully that one could see already at first glance whether his drawing was after a painting by Tintoretto, Bassano, Carracci, Paolo Veronese, Rubens, Van Dyck and so on and [this is] why these same [copies] are highly esteemed by art lovers."[2]

The present drawing is one of these stunningly beautiful copies that earned De Bisschop fame. In this case, the identification of the prototype has been complicated by an inscription on a print after the drawing by the Gouda printmaker Hendrik Bary: "G. Ter Burg pinx. HBary sculp." (fig. 62.1).[3] On the basis of this print, the prototype was long thought to have been a lost painting by Gerard ter Borch the Younger.[4] When this drawing first came onto the market with the dealer Herbert E. Feist in New York in 1967, however, the print was unknown to them, and the Leiden painter Frans van Mieris was posited as the actual author of the drawing.[5] Otto Naumann subsequently rejected this attribution in 1978.[6] In his 1981 monograph on Van Mieris's paintings, however, Naumann argued convincingly that the lost prototype was more likely by Van Mieris from the early 1660s than by Ter Borch, an idea that has since been widely accepted, despite the inscription on the print.[7] As Naumann writes, "the hands, which are puffy and tapered, are uncharacteristic of Ter Borch, while they are typical for Van Mieris."[8] Additionally, a similar feathered beret can be found in several paintings by Van Mieris, and none by Ter Borch.[9] The curious inclusion of "G. Ter Burg pinx." on the Bary print, along with the fact that it was listed as "Vrouwtje, door Terburg" in the 1679–80 catalogue of Bary's publisher Nicolaus Visscher, in other words, during Van Mieris's lifetime,[10] can be explained, as Eddy de Jongh suggests, by the probability that Bary simply made a mistake.[11]

This is one of twelve drawings, of which seven are still extant, by De Bisschop that were engraved by Bary.[12] Most of them are portraits of distinguished men after paintings by artists such as Ferdinand Bol and Hendrick Martensz Sorgh, but this sheet and a drawing in Stockholm of an *Old Hag* both represent genre scenes by Van Mieris.[13] Interestingly, De Bisschop is credited only once on a print by Bary as the draftsman.[14] Several of the prints contain poems, in the case of the

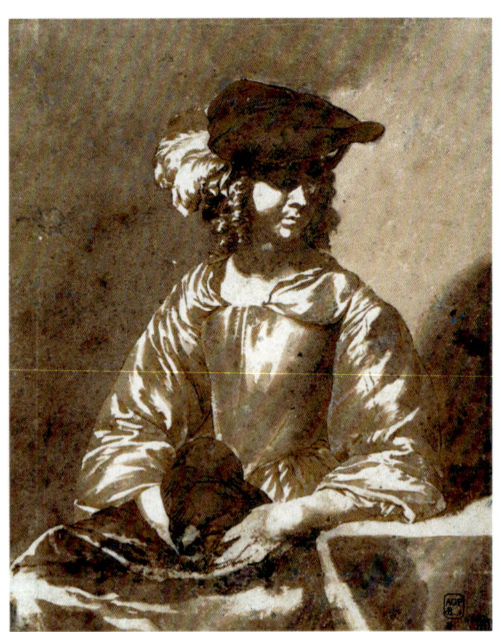

62.2 Jan de Bisschop, *A Young Woman in a Feathered Beret*, ca. 1660–65. Städtische Wessenberg-Galerie, Constance.

Young Woman in a Feathered Beret probably by De Bisschop's brother-in-law Casper Barlaeus the Younger. The Latin couplet reads "Me licet haud vincat Cytherea, Senecta colores / Quam cito, me febres et Libitina rapit" (Even if Venus does not win the crown for me, how swiftly age will steal my beauty, and fevers and death my very self).[15] Considering Barlaeus was in Lisbon between 1664 and 1672, the print and the drawing were probably made in the early 1660s, shortly after the lost painting.[16]

Unlike the other drawings in the group related to Bary's prints, there is another version of the present drawing in the Städtische Wessenberg-Galerie in Constance, Germany (fig. 62.2).[17] Although its condition has suffered and it is less legible, it clearly shows De Bisschop's characteristically masterful handling of the brush. Seen side by side, however, the two drawings are quite different. The washes in the German sheet are saturated and dramatic. Those in the present sheet are more subtle and applied in a palette of various hues of brown and dark yellow. A similar handling can be found in a few other drawings related to Bary's prints, including the *Old Hag* after Van Mieris. When comparing those drawings with the prints, it would seem that the more subtle ones would have been more useful and legible for Bary. It is interesting to consider that De Bisschop made multiple drawings of the same subject, perhaps with Bary's collaboration in view. A thorough study of their relationship remains a desideratum. **IvT**

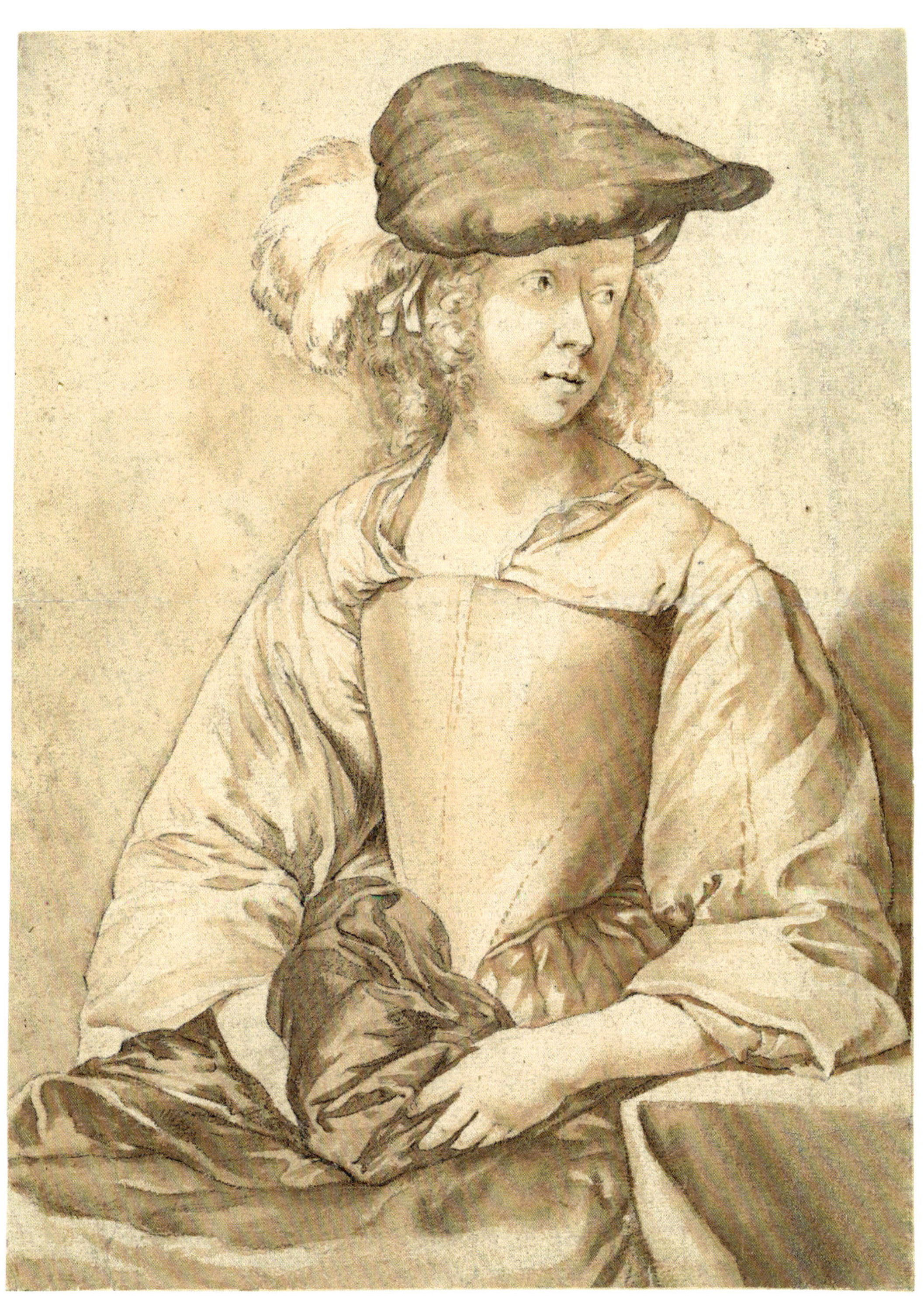

JACOB VAN RUISDAEL

Amsterdam 1628/29–1682 Amsterdam

63

Dune Landscape with a Bent-Over Pollarded Willow and Two Oak Trees, 1646

Black chalk, with pen and gray ink and gray wash; framing line in brown ink
143 x 205 mm

INSCRIPTIONS Recto, lower left, monogrammed and dated, in point of brush and gray ink: *R 1646*; verso, center right (turned 90° to the left), in graphite: *18*; verso, lower left, in black chalk: E.H. L. . . . / *vol* [?] / *d J* / *S. . .*; above this, in brown ink, in William Esdaile's hand: *1836 WE 160 x Jacob Ruysdael.*

PROVENANCE William Esdaile (1758–1837), London (L. 2617, lower left and center and verso, lower right); possibly his sale, Christie's, London, 18–25 June 1840, one of a pair (perhaps with no. 64) in lot 1087 (to "White"); John P. Heseltine (1843–1929), London (L. 1507, verso, lower left), together with no. 64, by 1910; Henry Oppenheimer (1859–1932), London (no mark; see L. 1351), together with no. 64, by 1928; his sale, Christie's, London, 10–14 July 1936, lot 321B (together with no. 64 [lot 321A] to "Cassirer"); Franz W. Koenigs (1881–1941), Haarlem (his second collection; no mark; see L. 1023a),[1] by 1941; private collection; acquired through Johan Bosch van Rosenthal, Art Consult, Amsterdam, by Clement C. Moore, 2014

SELECT REFERENCES Heseltine 1910, no. 27; Rosenberg 1928, no. Z52; Haverkamp-Begemann, Lawder, and Talbot 1964, 1: 21, under no. 16, n. 3 (as not by Ruisdael, probably Pieter de Molijn);[2] Giltay 1980, 142–43, 201, no. 105; Slive and Hoetink 1981, 168, under no. 63; Slive 2001, 509, 531, and no. D132; Giltaij 2001, 30–31; Slive 2005, 176, under no. 65

Promised gift of Clement C. and Elizabeth Y. Moore

When a collection has more than one example of the draftsmanship of an artist, it is stimulating to be able to chart the individual's artistic development through works from different periods. With its delicate, feathery handling of the chalk and its diagonal compositional formula inspired by landscapes from the late 1620s and 1630s by such artists as Jan van Goyen, the present work—the earlier of two drawings by Jacob van Ruisdael in this exhibition (see no. 64, dating from the 1660s)—is one of three known drawings and two etchings by Ruisdael dated 1646. This is the earliest date found on any of his surviving works on paper. According to Jeroen Giltaij, the first of this trio of drawings, carried out when the artist was only seventeen or eighteen years old, is likely to be the upright *Landscape with a Pollarded Willow and Other Trees near a Pond*, formerly in the collection of Prince Johann II of Liechtenstein, Feldsberg.[3] Giltaij posited that this would have been followed chronologically by the present work, which must have been executed in the summer of 1646 to judge by the foliage of the trees. The third dated sheet from that year is the *Hunter with Three Dogs Entering a Wood* preserved in the Kupferstichkabinett, Berlin, assumed by him to date from the autumn.[4]

Of Ruisdael's drawn oeuvre of more than 130 sheets, there are only three others that bear dates, all likewise from early in his career. One is from 1648, the *View of the Shore of the Zuider Zee with Three Anglers* in the British Museum, London,[5] and two are from 1649, *Landscape with a Grainfield and a Church with a Ruined Choir*, also in the British Museum,[6] and *Oak Trees on a Slope, with a Distant View on the Left*, formerly in the collection of Alfred Beurdeley, Paris.[7]

The original purpose of the centuries-old tradition of pollarding willow trees—like the specimen at lower right of the present sheet and at the center of the ex-Liechtenstein landscape—was to produce leafy new growth for animal fodder. Pieter Bruegel the Elder included a detail of a man cutting branches of a pollarded willow at the lower right of his painting *The Gloomy Day* (1565) in the Kunsthistorisches Museum, Vienna.[8] The practice has always been appreciated in the Netherlands, given its flat, open countryside: the process lowers a tree's center of gravity, greatly reducing the chance of damage from wind shear or torsional force. Further advantages came to light in 2018, when experiments at TU Delft successfully tested the capacity of Dutch pollarded willows to dampen waves during a storm surge.[9] The trees, subjected to waves up to 2.5 meters high, did not break, offering insights into how nature can be harnessed by the ever-enterprising Dutch to protect their countryside from flooding. **JST**

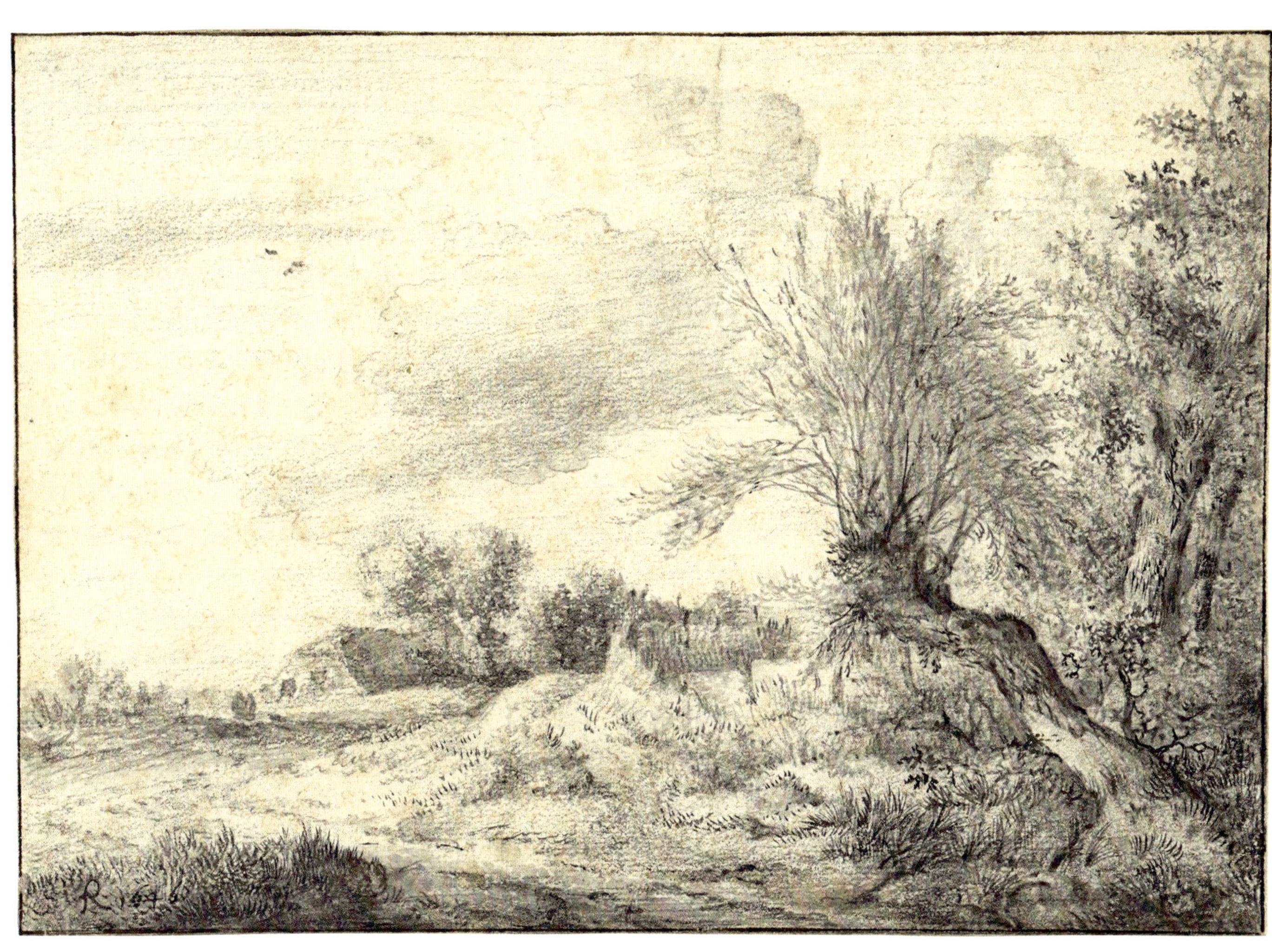

JACOB VAN RUISDAEL

Amsterdam 1628/29–1682 Amsterdam

64

View of the Bank of a Stream with Trees and a Road, 1660s

Black chalk, with gray wash; framing line in brown ink
150 x 192 mm

INSCRIPTIONS Verso, lower left, faint traces of a monogram or signature (?), in black chalk; verso, lower left, in black chalk: *n 310x*; below this, in pen and brown ink: *J. Rúysdaal*

PROVENANCE Pieter van der Dussen van Beeftingh (1794–1875), Rotterdam; his sale, Lamme, Rotterdam, 29–30 May 1876, lot 675; Ignatius Franciscus Ellinckhuysen (1814–1897), Rotterdam (no mark; see L. 3008); his sale, Frederik Muller, Amsterdam, 16–17 April 1879, lot 215 (to "Hogarth"); John P. Heseltine (1843–1929), London (L. 1507, verso, lower left), together with no. 63, by 1910; Henry Oppenheimer (1859–1932), London (no mark; see L. 1351), together with no. 63, by 1928; his sale, Christie's, London, 10–14 July 1936, lot 321A (together with no. 63 [lot 321B] to "Cassirer"); Franz W. Koenigs (1881–1941), Haarlem (his second collection; no mark; see L. 1023a),[1] by 1941; thence by descent; private collection, 1980; acquired through Johan Bosch van Rosenthal, Art Consult, Amsterdam, by Clement C. Moore, 2014

SELECT REFERENCES Heseltine 1910, no. 28; Rosenberg 1928, no. Z51; Haverkamp-Begemann, Lawder, and Talbot 1964, 1: 21, under no. 16, n. 3 (as not by Ruisdael, probably Pieter Molijn); Giltay 1980, no. 104; Slive 2001, no. D133

Promised gift of Clement C. and Elizabeth Y. Moore

The drawing—accurately assigned to Ruisdael in an old inscription on the verso—exemplifies the kind of art-historical vicissitudes to which drawings are sometimes subjected by modern connoisseurs. In 1964 Egbert Haverkamp-Begemann suggested that Pieter de Molijn was probably the author of this and six other sheets he believed to be by the same hand. At least two of these are signed and properly given to Molijn;[2] the status of one, which in 1928 was in the collection of Julian G. Lonsades, London, is uncertain;[3] and Begemann's proposal of Molijn as the author of the four that were once all together in the Heseltine collection—nos. 63, 64, *Yard of a Farmstead with a Man Working* (currently untraced),[4] and *Village Road*, now in the Clark Art Institute, Williamstown, MA[5]—was firmly rejected by leading Ruisdael specialists Jacob Rosenberg, Jeroen Giltaij, and Seymour Slive. Nos. 63 and 64 are universally considered to be autograph by these experts, although from very different phases of Ruisdael's career, the former being signed and dated 1646, the latter datable as much as two decades later, in the 1660s. In the opinion of Slive, *Yard of a Farmstead with a Man Working* is neither by Molijn, nor by Ruisdael. As for the *Village Road* in the Clark, Slive suggested that it might belong to a small group of drawings assigned by Giltaij in 1979 to Isaac Koene, a fellow pupil of Ruisdael's father, Isaac van Ruisdael.[6]

Many of Ruisdael's mature landscape drawings, especially examples among the dozen sheets once owned by the well-known Dutch collector Sybrand II Feitama and his family, are reputed to have had staffage figures, gray washes, and even signatures and monograms, added by later hands. This does not seem to have been the case with the figure of a farmer driving a cow (or ploughing with an ox) at far left, or the couple standing and seated at center right, near a wooden pen—motifs that seem to be integral elements of the composition. The darker wash accents, especially those with a slight brown tone, are harder to judge. We know from Sybrand's manuscript *Notitie der teekeningen* (1746–58) that both he and his father regularly commissioned artists to embellish drawings in their possession.[7] Such "creative" transformations of drawings were often proudly referred to in old sale catalogues and in verso inscriptions as "opgemaakt" (finished) or "verbeterd" (improved). Eighteenth-century collectors enjoyed a far more relaxed attitude to such interventions, for they valued anecdotal scenes to pure, unwashed landscapes, which they considered to be incomplete. This accounts for the kind of extensive gray washes occasionally applied to pen-and-ink drawings by Rembrandt, a once-accepted practice of "improvement" that horrifies modern curators and collectors.
JST

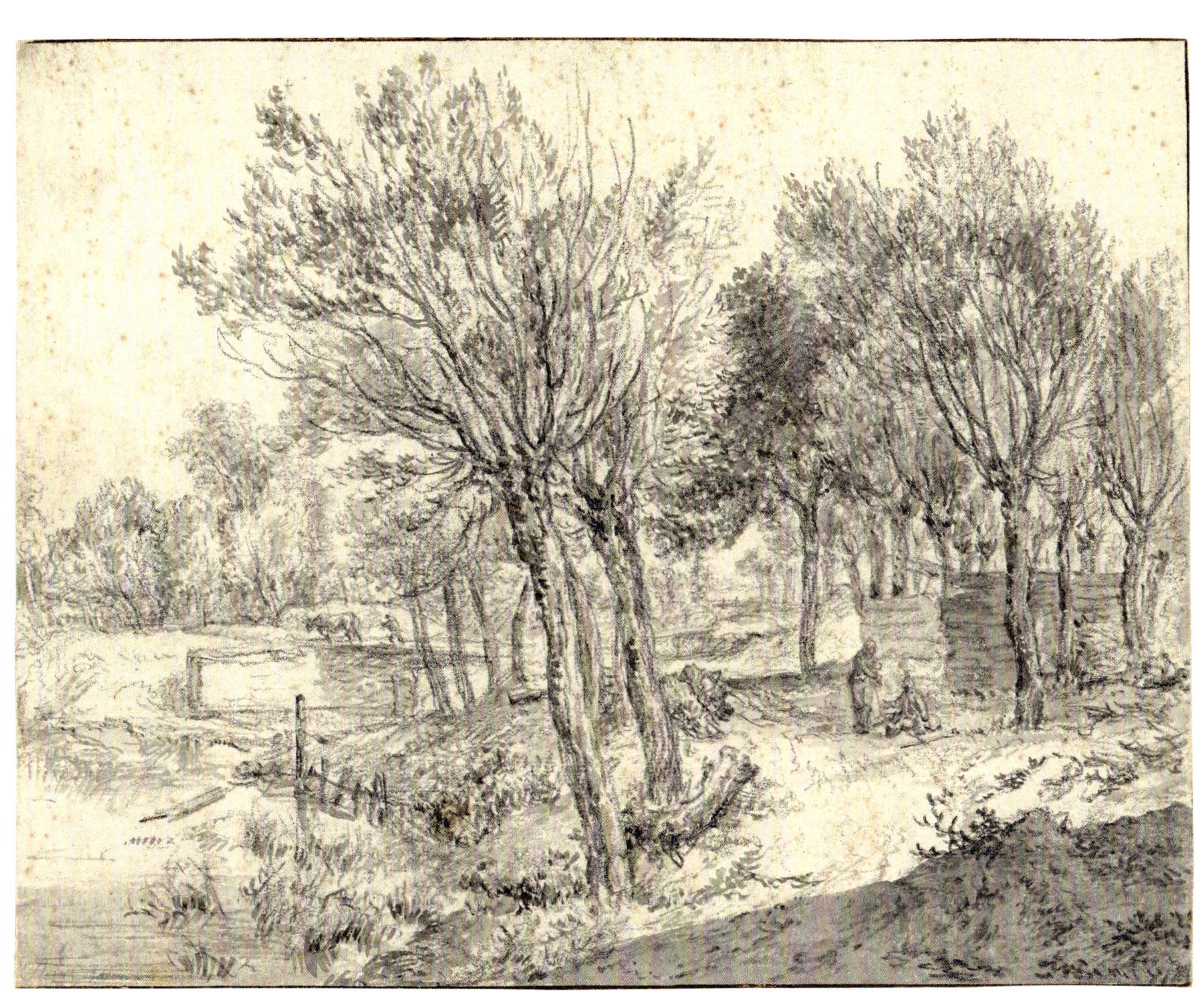

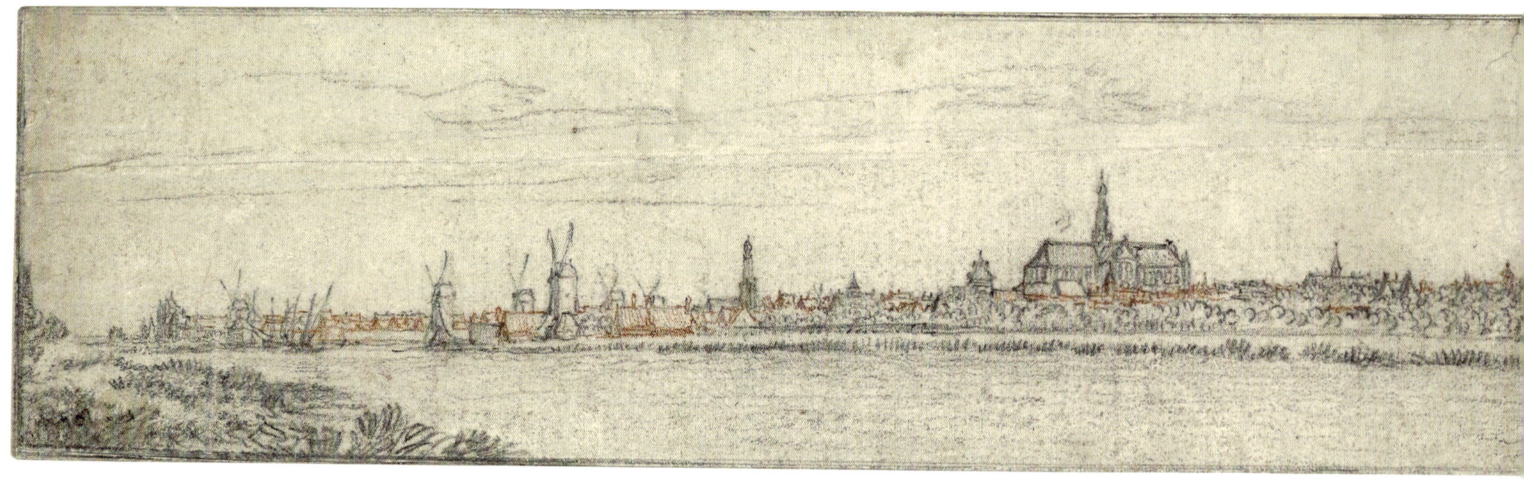

VINCENT LAURENSZ VAN DER VINNE

Haarlem 1628–1702 Haarlem

or

LAURENS VINCENTSZ VAN DER VINNE

Haarlem 1658–1729 Haarlem

65

View of Haarlem, seventeenth century

Red and black chalk
92 x 618 mm

PROVENANCE Charles E. Duits (1882–1969), London (no mark; see L. 533a); thence by descent; Thomas Williams Fine Art, London; from whom acquired for the Baymeath Art Trust by Clement C. Moore, 2014

Promised gift of Clement C. and Elizabeth Y. Moore, through the Baymeath Art Trust

The silhouette of Haarlem with its imposing Grote Kerk (or Sint-Bavokerk) was frequently drawn, painted, and etched in the seventeenth century, including by Allaert van Everdingen, Jan van Goyen, and Rembrandt. Best known are the painted views of the city by Jacob van Ruisdael, with the bleaching fields in the foreground and a grand cloudy sky above. These views of Haarlem, according to seventeenth-century inventories, even had a diminutive nickname: "Haarlempjes" (meaning "Little Haarlems").[1]

In the most famous of Ruisdael's Haarlem views, the city is usually a long way away on the horizon, and the landscape with bleaching fields or dunes still occupies an important place, but, in the present drawing, the view is reduced almost to a silhouette. We are looking at the city from the northeast across the River Spaarne. From left to right we can see, among other things, the Amsterdamse Poort, the mills "De Rietvink" and "De Halve Maen," the Bakenesserkerk, the Clockhouse, the Grote or Sint-Bavokerk, and the Janskerk.

Given some liberties, it is questionable whether the artist drew this work on the spot. For example, the choir of the Sint-Bavokerk is turned to the southeast (when it should have been to the southwest) and neither the towers to the right of center nor the farm and mill in the right foreground are easy to identify. Perhaps this is a drawing started on the spot and finished in the studio. Or is it a copy drawing after a partly imaginary example, perhaps after an otherwise unknown "Haarlempje" by Ruisdael? That famous artist did not always record things precisely.[2]

In the Noord-Hollands Archief in Haarlem is an almost equally sized variant of this drawing, also executed in red and black chalk, presumably made after the same prototype; the archives also possess a sheet, only in black chalk, which is largely similar to the left half.[3] Both sheets have been erroneously attributed to Aelbert Cuyp in the past (and still appear under that name on the Archief's website).[4] An attribution to a member of the Haarlem artist family Van der Vinne—the name under which Clement Moore purchased the present drawing—makes more sense. The traditional attribution to Vincent Laurensz van der Vinne, the best-known member of this great family of artists, is not certain, however. Some ten (male) members of the family were members of the local Guild of

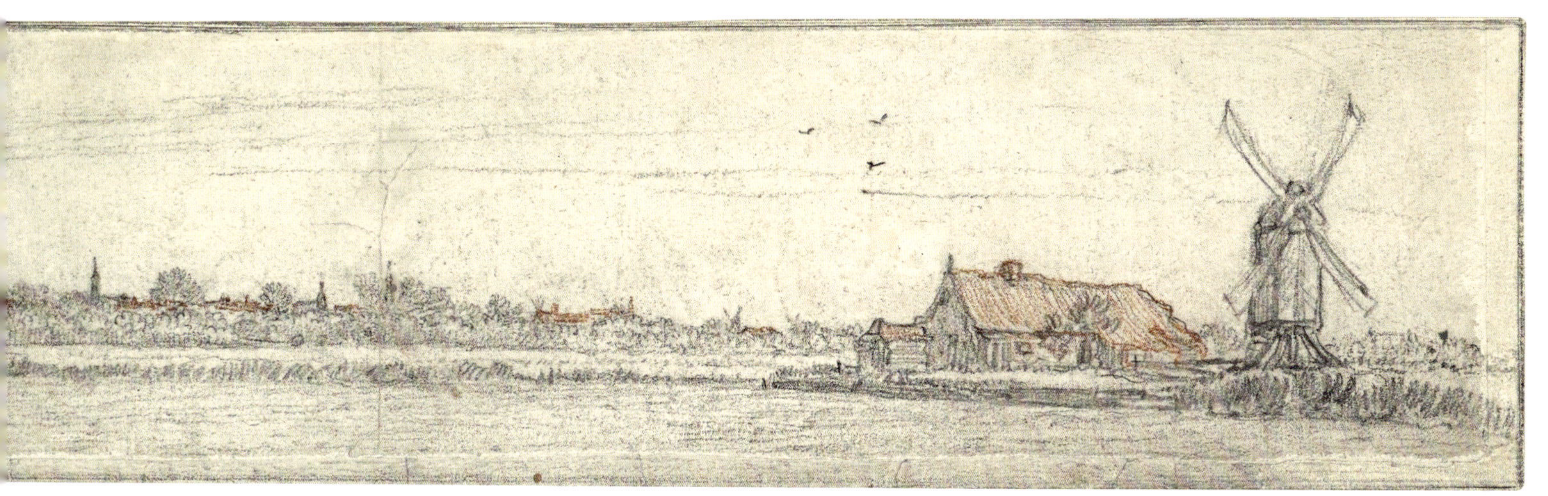

St. Luke in the seventeenth and eighteenth centuries. It is rather difficult to tell these often eponymous artists and their works apart: several members had a distinct individual style only in a limited sense, they barely signed their work, and they regularly copied drawings from each other or from their ancestors.[5]

The present sheet is an exception to this in that it can probably be classified in a group of drawings that all show, some more than others, the influence of the Haarlem artist Nicolaes Berchem. That influence manifests itself in the same drawing style and in the technique of black chalk, often combined with red chalk. Sheets from the group (e.g., figs. 65.1 and 65.2)[6] are associated with both Vincent Laurentsz and his eldest son, Laurens Vincentsz.[7] Both were in direct contact with their well-known fellow townsman: Vincent was friends with Berchem, and Laurens, according to an early nineteenth-century source, was apprenticed to him. Laurens's drawings would even deceptively resemble Berchem's, according to that same source.[8] However, the extremely rare signed drawings by Laurens, and for that matter also by the father, hardly show this affinity with Berchem we must thus leave it here an open question as to which of the two (or perhaps an entirely different member of the family?) was responsible for the fascinating group.[9] MCP

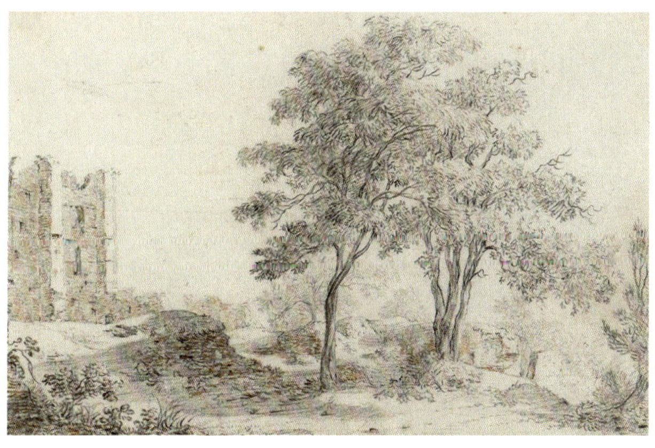

65.1 Vincent Laurensz van der Vinne or Laurens Vincentsz van der Vinne, *Ruins of Brederode Castle*, ca. 1650–1729. Teylers Museum, Haarlem.

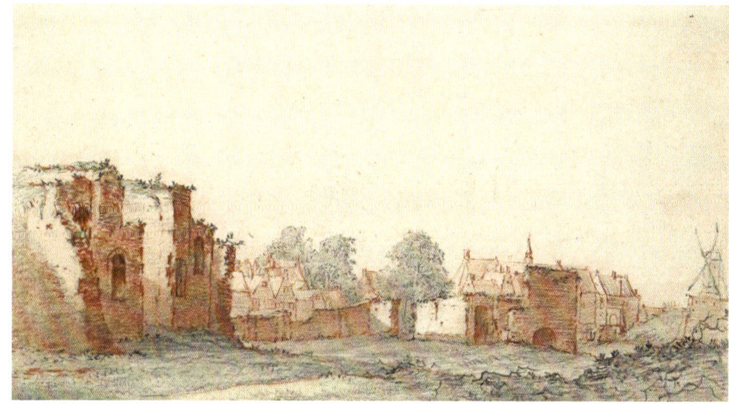

65.2 Vincent Laurensz van der Vinne or Laurens Vincentsz van der Vinne, *The Half-Demolished Kruyspoort and Northern City Wall of Haarlem*, ca. 1650–1729. Noord-Hollands Archief, Haarlem.

ABRAHAM RUTGERS

Amsterdam ca. 1632–1699 Amsterdam

66

View of the River Vecht, with Fishermen, Pollarded Willows, and a Boathouse on the Opposite Bank, late 1680s

Pen and brown ink, with brown wash, over black chalk
125 x 173 mm

INSCRIPTIONS Verso, upper left, unidentified perforated stamp, in black and blue ink; verso, upper center, stamped on tape (in reverse and upside down), in black (partially obscured by mounting hinges): *. . . ffardt's Boek- en Muziekhand. . .*; verso, upper center, in graphite: *Anglers fishing in a Lake / by Abraham Rutgers (1660–1690) / Coll. van Gogh, Schöller, Dr Kurt Otto*; verso, lower left, above Springell stamp, in graphite: *Lugt 2049a* [*sic*]; below this, in pen and brown ink: *n° 75.*; to the right of this, in graphite: *A.5634*; verso, lower center, in graphite: *N 6*; superimposed on top of this, next to Otto stamp: *Lugt 2007 d „non identifié"*;[1] below this, in graphite: *Leupenius*; to the right of this, in graphite: *L 2511*

PROVENANCE Vincent van Gogh (1866–1911), Amsterdam; his sale, R.W.P. de Vries, Amsterdam, 2 December 1913, lot 471 (as Johannes Leupenius; to "F. Muller"); Paul, Ritter von Schöller (1853–1920), Vienna; his sale, C.G. Boerner, Leipzig, 11–12 November 1921, lot 14 (as Leupenius; to "Otto"); Dr. Curt Otto (ca. 1880–1929), Leipzig (L. 611c, verso, lower center left), 1921; his sale, C.G. Boerner, Leipzig, 7 November 1929, lot 87 (as Leupenius; to "Colnaghi"); probably Seyffardt's Boek- en Muziekhandel, Amsterdam (their stamp, verso, upper center, not in Lugt);[2] Francis Springell [Franz Sprinzels] (1898–1974), Prague and later Portinscale, Northumberland (L. 1049a, verso, lower left); private collection, Switzerland; La Tâche Fine Art, Vaduz; from whom acquired by Clement C. Moore, 2012

Promised gift of Clement C. and Elizabeth Y. Moore

Abraham Rutgers came from a family of Mennonite textile merchants who fled religious persecution in Antwerp, settling first in Haarlem, and later in Amsterdam. Alongside his work as an Amsterdam silk merchant, he was an amateur draftsman, known for his views along the River Vecht, near Utrecht, where several family members owned properties. Abraham and his brother, David Rutgers III, who ran a mill weaving velvet and floral-patterned silk, were first cousins of the horticulturalist collector Agnes Block, who famously commissioned artists to record plants in the garden of her estate on the Vecht, called Vijverhof, located just north of David III's country house Groenevecht, near Breukelen, on the stretch of the river called the Zandpad. In 1682 Abraham Rutgers purchased his own property on the Zandpad, Hoogevecht (destroyed ca. 1830), near Maarssen. He bought it from Antonio Alvares Machado, a Portuguese Jewish merchant who made a fortune supplying bread to William III's army of 30,000 Dutch troops during the Forty Years' War with the French (1672–1712).

The present view employs Rutgers's idiosyncratic compositional approach, with a steeply receding perspective along a diagonal axis, and his typical bold, hatched pen technique. This resembles the draftsmanship of his friend Jacob Esselens, to whose children he was appointed guardian, as well as that of Johannes Leupenius. In fact, the drawing was attributed to Leupenius at least as far back as the sale of the dealer Vincent van Gogh, a cousin of his famous artist namesake.[3] Even though it again appeared under Leupenius's name in the 1929 Otto sale, as did the lot before and after it (lots 86 and 88), all three drawings had already been correctly recognized as by Rutgers by Alfred von Wurzbach.[4]

The country house with double gabled roofs, glimpsed at far left behind an attractive screen of pollarded trees, may well represent Kasteel Bolenstein in Maarssen.[5] In Rutgers's time, the house (rebuilt in the nineteenth century) was owned by Jacob Godi(j)n, Heer van Boelestein. This tentative identification is based on two inscribed drawings by Rutgers in an album of eighty-eight sketches preserved in Huis Van Gijn, Dordrecht (figs. 66.1–2).[6] Both those sketches of Bolenstein show the regularly placed platforms along the riverbank from which fishermen, such as the figure in the Moore drawing, could drop their lines.

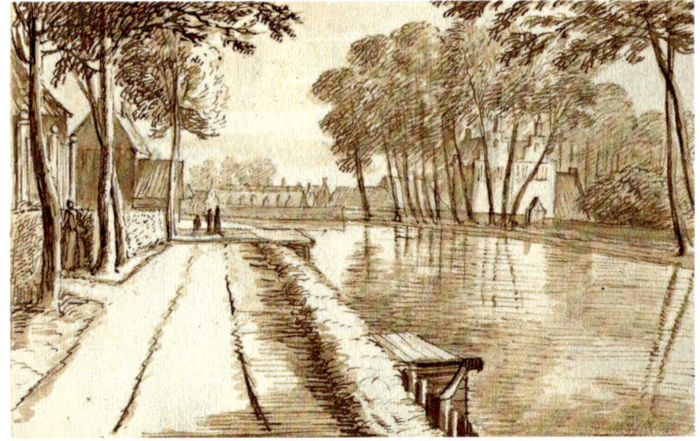

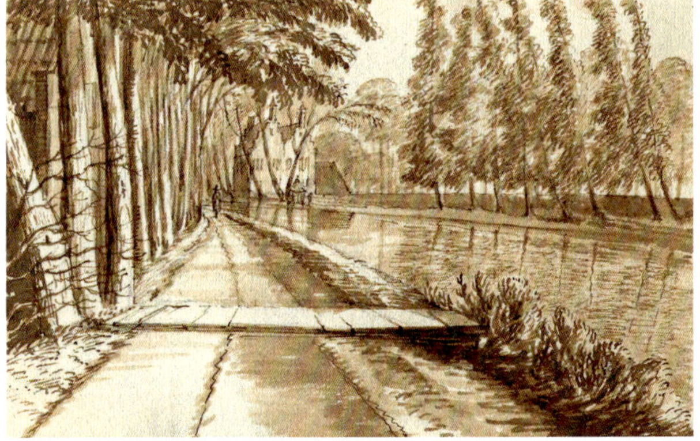

66.1–2 Abraham Rutgers, *Two Views of Kasteel Bolenstein on the River Vecht*, 1686/87. Huis Van Gijn, Dordrecht.

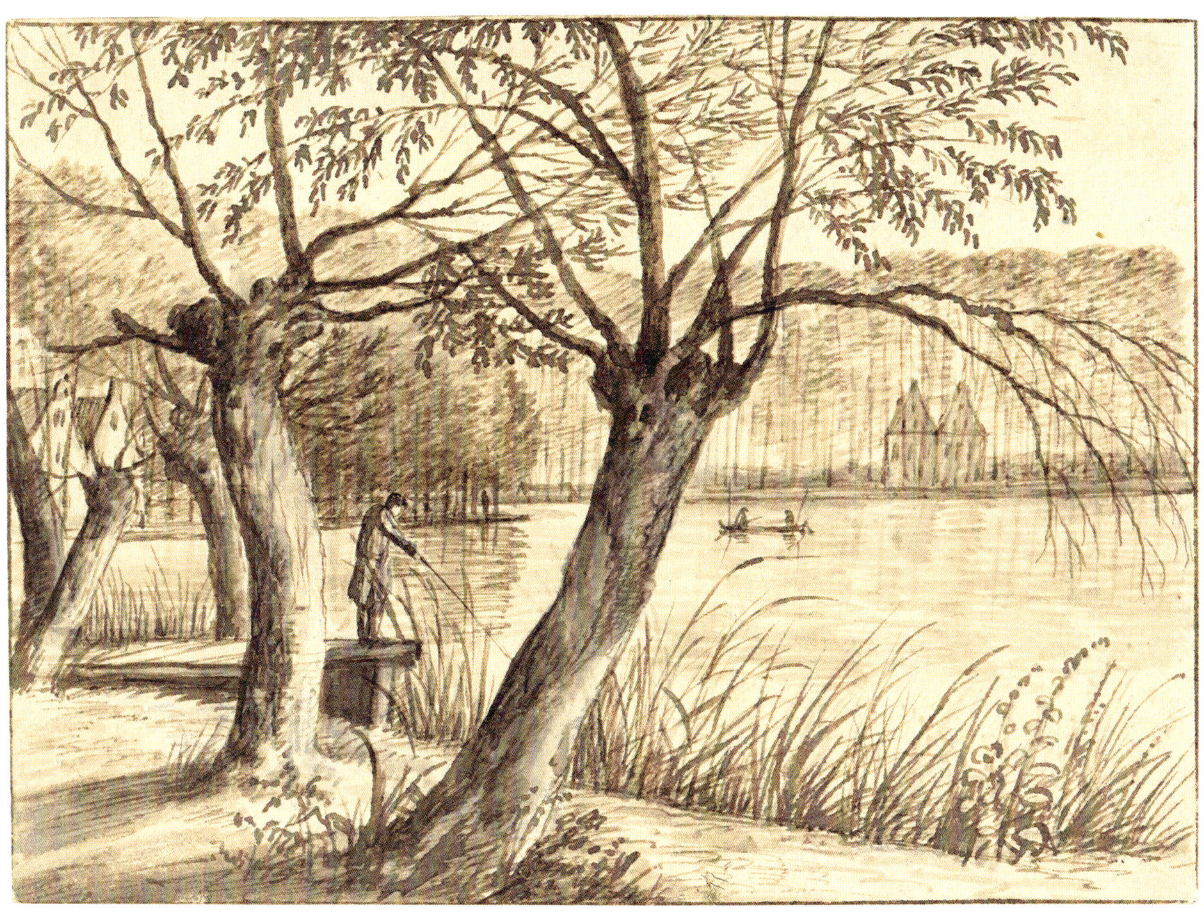

A similarly clad angler fishes from such a landing in a sheet formerly on the Paris art market, which perhaps also shows Bolenstein in the background.[7] Based on its location in relation to these presumed depictions of Bolenstein, the structure with twin hip roofs on the opposite riverbank in the present work may record the seventeenth-century brick boathouse of the country house Herteveld, owned from 1679 to 1704 by Jacob Scott.[8] **JST**

LIEVEN CRUYL

Ghent 1634–1720 Ghent

67

The Construction of the Pont Royal over the Seine, Paris, 1686

Pen and brown ink and wash, over traces of graphite; framing line in brown ink

178 x 279 mm

WATERMARK Possibly a church surmounted by a Latin cross

INSCRIPTIONS Recto, lower left, signed and dated, in brown ink: *LIVINUS CRUYL PBR fecit 1686.*

PROVENANCE Charles E. Duits (1882–1969), London, by the 1950s (no mark; see L. 533a);[1] thence by descent; Cheffins, Cambridge, 29 November 2012, lot 421; where acquired by Rafael Valls, London; W.M. Brady and Co., New York; from whom acquired by Clement C. Moore, 2020

SELECT REFERENCES Ongpin 2015, no. 9

Promised gift of Clement C. and Elizabeth Y. Moore

A priest from Ghent with a lively interest in architecture, Cruyl traveled to Italy, where he made numerous city views in Rome and elsewhere,[2] a number of which he also etched. On subsequent trips to France in the 1680s, Cruyl continued to chronicle urban building projects in sheets like the present work. Cruyl places us in the middle of a busy but orderly construction site, animated by the sound of horses plodding, men shouting, and carpentry tools banging amid the general bustle of the building trade. We are witnessing the erection of the Pont Royal, a stone bridge across Paris's Seine river (fig. 67.1). When a battered wooden bridge, built in 1642 and damaged repeatedly, collapsed during a storm in February 1684, the plans to replace it were shaped by the king's willingness to pay for its construction from the royal coffers. The new stone bridge would traverse the Seine between the Louvre and the Boulevard Saint-Germain, along a popular ferry route in the center of the bifurcated capital. The span was constructed between 1685 and 1689.

The bridge was part of Louis XIV's public works campaign spearheaded by his comptroller for finance, Jean-Baptiste Colbert. Early accounts record the royal architect Jules Hardouin Mansart as the designer (although his name does not appear in official documents before 1686) and François Romain, a Dominican friar from Ghent, as responsible for project drawings and oversight. State records make clear that the architect Jacques IV Gabriel played a critical role in the construction from March 1685 until he died in 1686. The bridge comprises five stone arches, with the central oval arch spanning 12 toises (roughly 75½ feet), supporting a wide roadway for horse-drawn carriages, and featuring one of the first sidewalks for pedestrians. The spectacle generated significant interest on the part of artists like Cruyl, who eagerly depicted the ambitious and swift-moving monument of modern engineering.

Cruyl casts the viewer as his companion on a visit to the construction site. We are positioned in the middle of the Seine looking west: the Tuileries gardens are along the riverbank at right, and what is now the Quai d'Orsay is lined with buildings at left. The challenge of the uneven banks is evident; this, combined with a strong current and a silty riverbed, made for a technically complex project. The engineers employed waterwheels and cofferdams to seal off the work area so

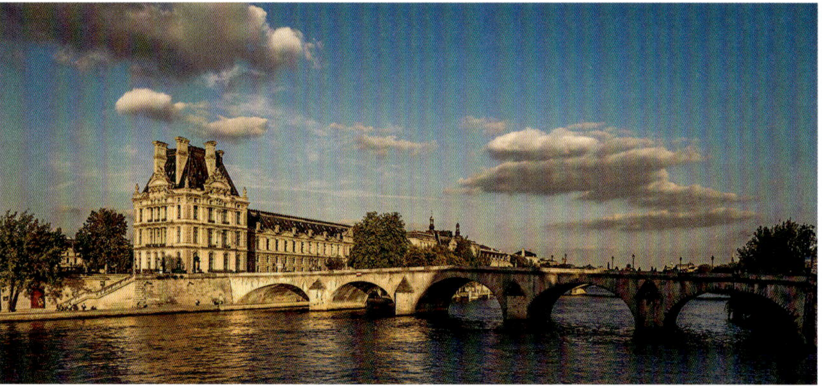

67.1 Pont Royal, Paris, looking east.

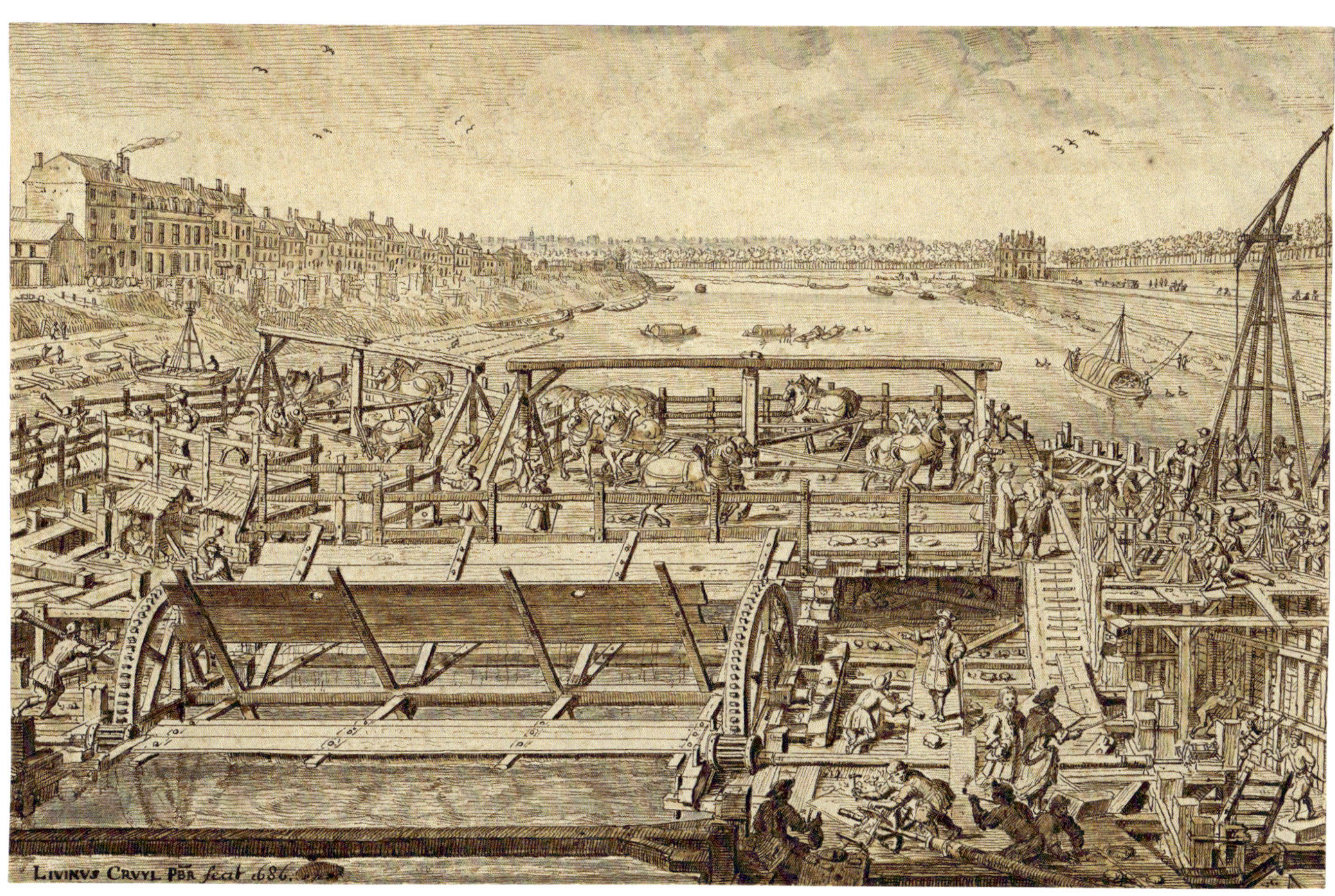
LIVINVS CRVYL PBR fecit 1686.

the foundation for the piers could be built. The artist's planning of the sheet is revealed in the fine graphite lines that trace the riverbank and roofs at left, and the quay at right. A pinhole at the center of the sheet just above the horizontal beam in the drilling structure suggests the artist used it to guide the perspective.

Of Cruyl's French subjects, it was the Pont Royal that generated the greatest number of drawings.[3] The Moore sheet is the newest addition to the seven known studies of the bridge: an additional five made during construction, between 1686 and 1687, and two views of the completed bridge made in 1689 (both in the Louvre).[4] Cruyl's drawings provide critical information about the bridge's construction, which in some details contradict written accounts. Germain Brice recorded that the construction began on the side of the Faubourg Saint-Germain, but Cruyl's drawing reveals that the work proceeded from the Louvre side of the river.[5] Along with a sheet in the Bibliothèque Nationale de France, the present drawing dates to 1686, when the foundations for three of the four pillars were installed in the riverbed.[6] Both sheets show the effort to establish the bridge's supports, which involved a drilling mechanism powered by horses circumambulating a wheel. Barbara Jatta identified the patron who likely commissioned the drawings as Michel Lepelletier de Souzy, *directeur général des Fortifications et du Génie*, the official who bore responsibility for the construction site. When this sheet first emerged from a private collection in 2012, it provided a new glimpse into activity at the Pont Royal site. Stephen Ongpin identified Gabriel, who oversaw the project, as the figure in the foreground to the right of center, who instructs the workers, and his assistant Romain, as the cleric directing laborers at lower right.[7]

Ultimately, only one printed view was produced, by an unknown engraver based on one of Cruyl's views of the finished bridge.[8] The construction crews have now become ferrymen, barge operators, small boat pilots, and carriage drivers along the quays and across the bridge, which is traversed by Parisians on foot. Cruyl's consistent interest in the site has left us a chronicle of this enduring construction that remains an indelible monument at the heart of the city. JT

ADRIAEN VAN DE VELDE

Amsterdam 1636–1672 Amsterdam

68

Study of a Seated Boy Leaning on a Flagon, ca. 1665

Red chalk, over traces of black chalk
193 x 254 mm

WATERMARK Shield surmounted by a crown, a bunch of grapes within the shield and the monogram "CP" below

INSCRIPTIONS Recto, lower left, in red chalk: *Carel Du Jardijn*

PROVENANCE Christie's, Amsterdam, 25 November 1991, lot 80a (as by Karel du Jardin); where acquired by Dr. Anton C.R. Dreesmann (1923–2000), Amsterdam; his sale, Christie's, London, 11 April 2002, lot 684; Christie's, New York, 26 January 2016, lot 41; where acquired by Clement C. Moore

SELECT REFERENCES Robinson 1993, 55–56

Promised gift of Clement C. and Elizabeth Y. Moore

Unlike his father and brother, Willem van de Velde the Elder (see no. 45) and Willem van de Velde the Younger, both marine artists, Adriaen van de Velde as a painter specialized in the depictions of the mainland. A few beach and winter scenes by him are known, and sporadically he seems to have depicted religious and mythological scenes, but the lion's share of his oeuvre comprises pastoral landscapes with reclining shepherds and shepherdesses accompanying their flocks. To compose these idyllic and sun-drenched landscapes, before taking up his brush, the Amsterdam artist undertook a thorough preparation on paper. This is attested by an exceptionally large number of surviving drawings—as many as fifty of which are directly related to his paintings.[1] The wide variety of this material makes it possible to follow Van de Velde's step-by-step working process.[2]

Van de Velde often began by collecting motifs while sketching from life outdoors. Both for landscape studies and those of animals, he set off into the countryside.[3] For his figures, however, he seems to have had models pose in his studio. On the one hand, he drew life studies of nude or barely dressed men and women, primarily to develop his skill in representing the human body. On the other, he drew clothed models, especially to explore a specific pose he had in mind for a painting.[4] The Moore drawing seems to represent yet a third, more final stage in the preparatory process, for which the model was no longer necessarily present; Van de Velde would have relied on previously made drawings from life to which he added further specific details.

The young man depicted is seen elegantly leaning forward against a large flagon, with his hands resting atop each other and his legs crossed, his back turned to the viewer. As pointed out by William W. Robinson, the figure reappears in this exact pose in a painting of a pastoral landscape, signed and dated 1665, also formerly in the collection of Dr. Anton C.R. Dreesmann (fig. 68.1).[5] There the lad is accompanied by a dog and a maid milking a cow. The striking similarities between

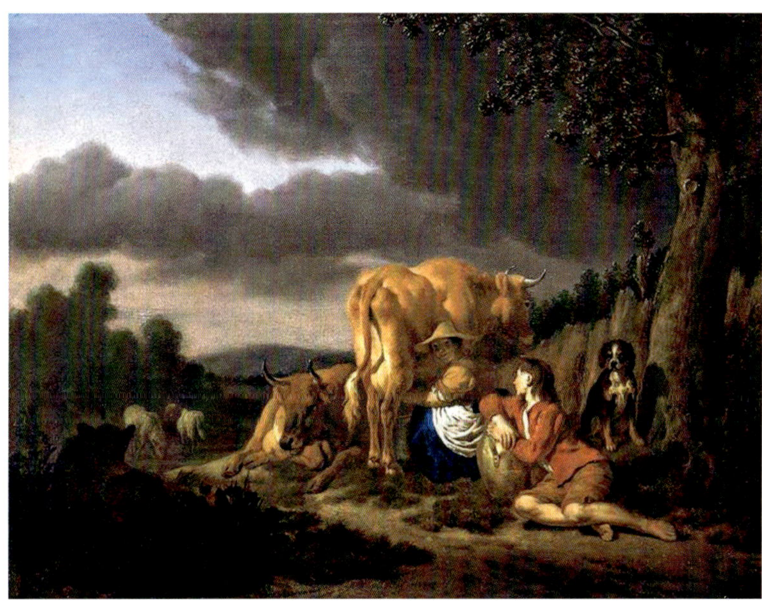

68.1 Adriaen van de Velde, *Pastoral Landscape with a Dairymaid Milking a Cow*, 1665. Present whereabouts unknown.

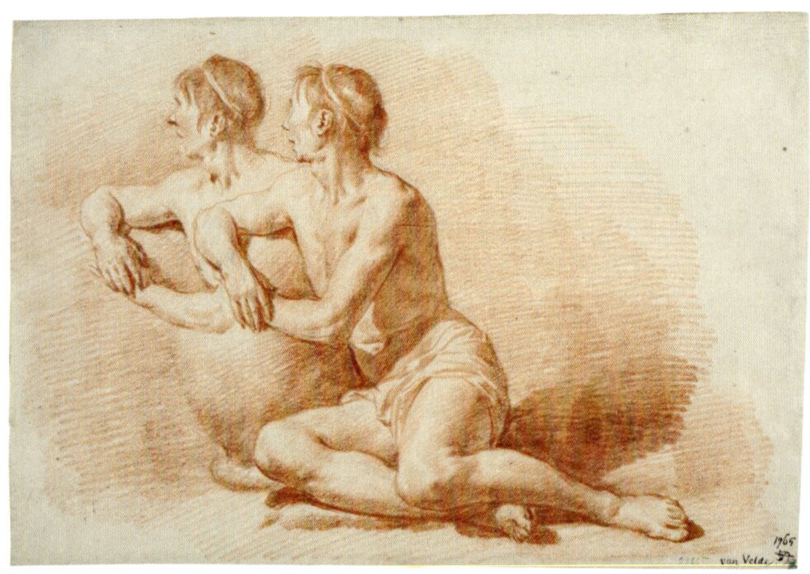

68.2 Adriaen van de Velde, *Study of a Male Nude Seated on the Ground*, ca. 1665. Nationalmuseum, Stockholm.

the drawn and painted shepherd, including his long hair, the specific pleating of the jacket and trousers, and the detailing of his flagon, indicate that Van de Velde in this drawing was at an advanced stage in the preparatory process and knew exactly which detailed elements he wanted to transfer onto the canvas.

For the Moore drawing, Van de Velde thus probably returned to life studies he had made earlier in his studio, including a nude study in the Nationalmuseum, Stockholm (fig. 68.2),[6] and possibly a now-lost version of a similarly posed figure, dressed but less fully resolved.[7] The soft modeling of the present figure in red chalk over minimal outlines in black chalk, without hesitant contours or pentimenti, underscores the idea that Van de Velde had little to explore at this stage and could shift his focus to the finer details of the figure. From the specific passages of light and shade to the carefully worked-out minor elements, everything corresponds to the final painting—although in the picture the form of the flagon is more tapered at the bottom—and are far removed from the nude figure study in Stockholm.

A similar method using a sequence of studies was seemingly followed by the artist in his preparations for the figure of Pomona in the painting *Vertumnus and Pomona* (1670) in the Kunsthistorisches Museum, Vienna.[8] After drawing the female model nude first,[9] and then in the same pose, but clothed,[10] it has been assumed by Robinson that Van de Velde made a definitive study on paper—corresponding, in terms of function, to the present sheet—incorporating the final changes to her appearance that appear in the painting.[11]

The inscription at the lower left in the present sheet, "Carel du Jardijn," could be easily explained as a mistaken conclusion about the authorship by a later collector.[12] Nonetheless, it highlights the strong stylistic overlap and shared iconographical interests between the two artists. As mentioned by Marijn Schapelhouman and Bart Cornelis, in at least one case the artists incorporated exactly the same motif in each of their paintings.[13] Thus far, however, this reclining young man has not been discovered in Du Jardin's oeuvre. **MvS**

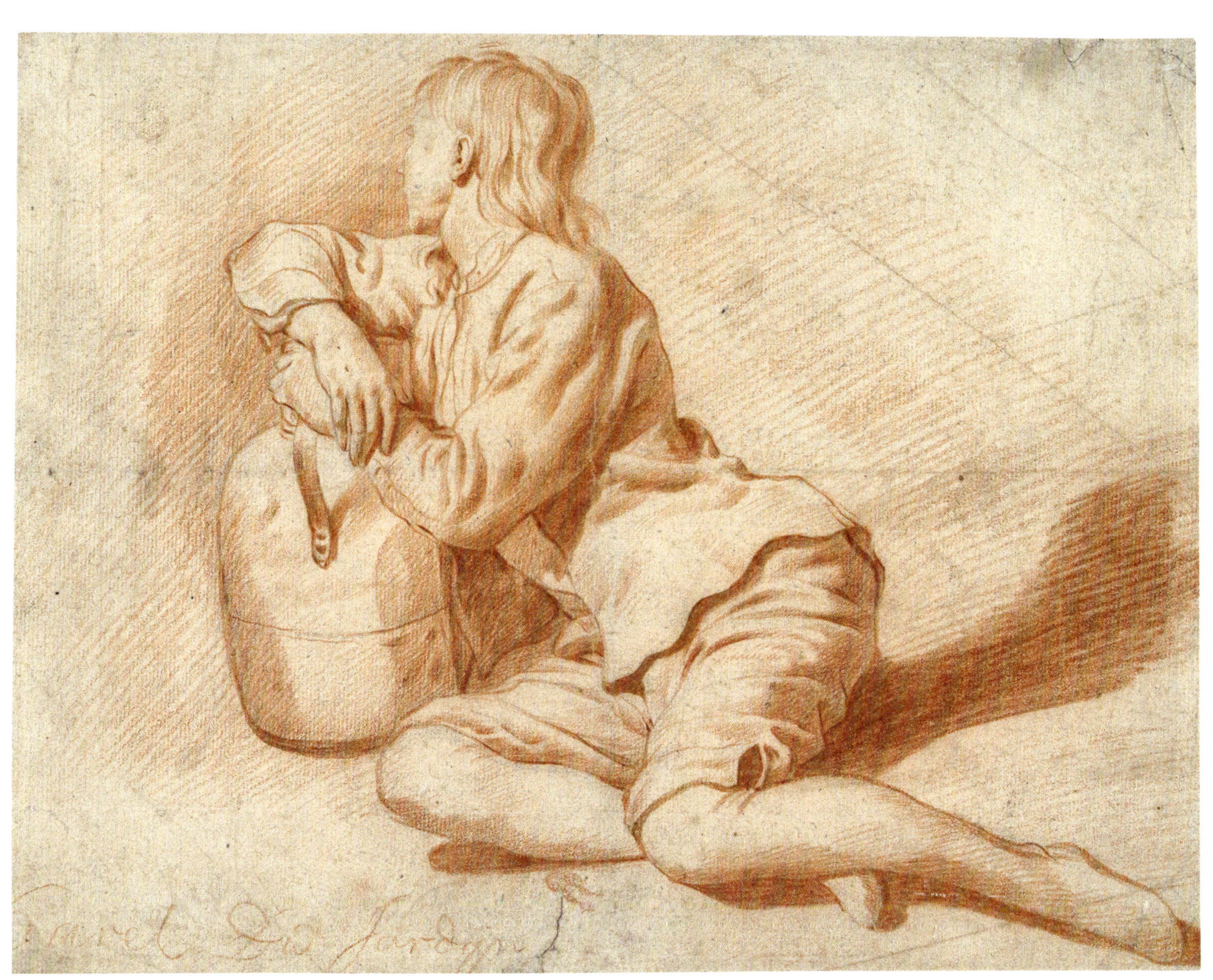

MOSES TER BORCH

Zwolle 1645–1667 Harwich

69

Study of a Seated Sailor, ca. 1660–65

Red chalk
195 x 143 mm

WATERMARK Letter "B" with crown, vertical orientation, center left

PROVENANCE Probably William Mayor (d. 1874), London (no mark; see L. 2799); perhaps Lady Sybil Grant (1879–1955); Sotheby's, London, 19 March 1947, lot 48 (as Frans van Mieris; to "Mattheim"); Sotheby's, New York, 30 January 2013, lot 288; where acquired by Clement C. Moore

Promised gift of Clement C. and Elizabeth Y. Moore

69.1 Moses ter Borch, *Self-Portrait*, 1661. Rijksprentenkabinet, Amsterdam.

69.2 Moses ter Borch, *Seated Young Man*, ca. 1660–65. Beaux-Arts de Paris.

The practice of drawing was a fundamental element of the education in the household of the Ter Borch family in the Hanseatic city of Zwolle. Not all the children of Gerard ter Borch the Elder would follow in his footsteps—only Gerard the Younger also succeeded in having a flourishing career—but certainly the siblings Anna, Jan, Gesina, Harmen, and Moses were well acquainted with their father's profession and had drawing tools at their disposal from a very young age.[1] Of Moses ter Borch we know of drawings from the age of only seven years old.[2] As part of his father's academic program, he copied many prints by Italian masters, Rembrandt, and Albrecht Dürer, among others, as well as casts of famous sculptures. In the meantime, he also drew many family members in their day-to-day activities and often practiced with his own reflection, as evidenced by an intriguing group of self-portraits in a variety of moods on blue paper (fig. 69.1).[3] These intimate drawn works by Moses, above all, reveal his skills as an observer and a rare degree of candor and zeal, qualities that can perhaps be explained only within the context of his in-house training and the fact that he never went on to be a professional artist.

In this drawing of a young sailor one recognizes the draftsman's same objective approach and the same lack of filter. Notable is the relaxed pose of the young man, comfortably leaning against an undrawn support. It is abundantly clear that he is very much at ease with Moses, unconcerned with the fact that he was being drawn, just as Moses and his siblings would not pay attention to each other when being

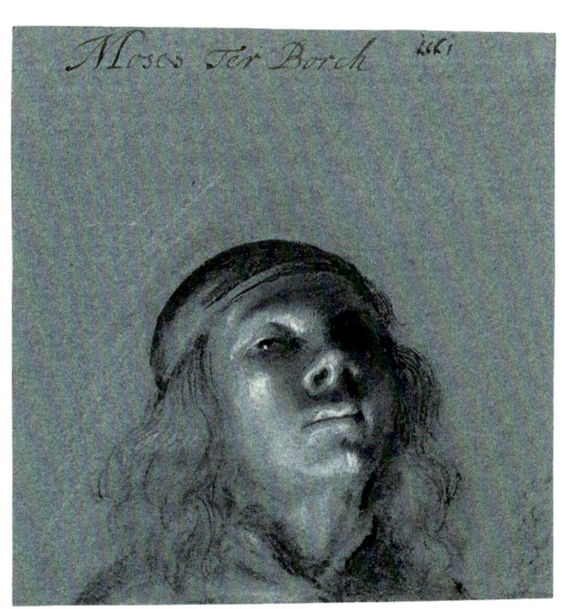

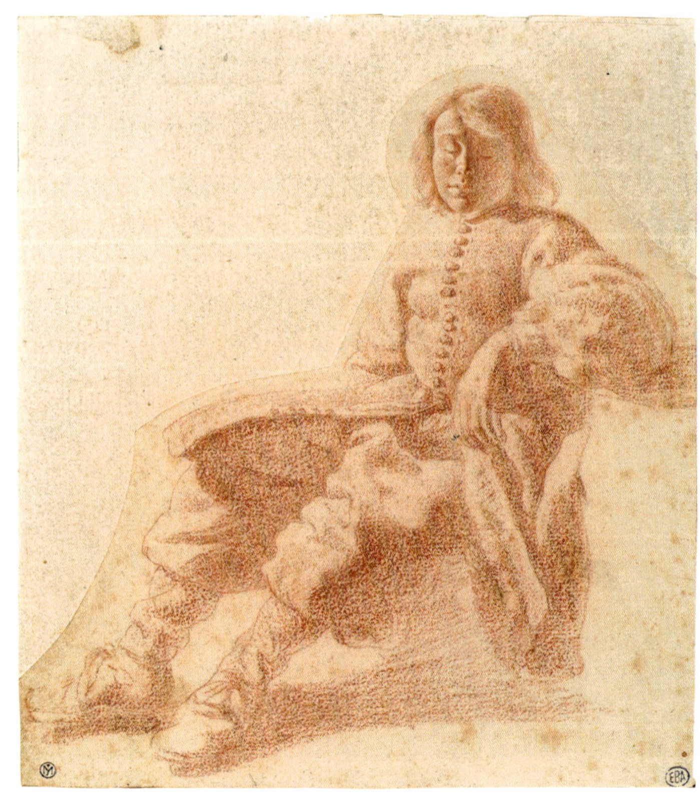

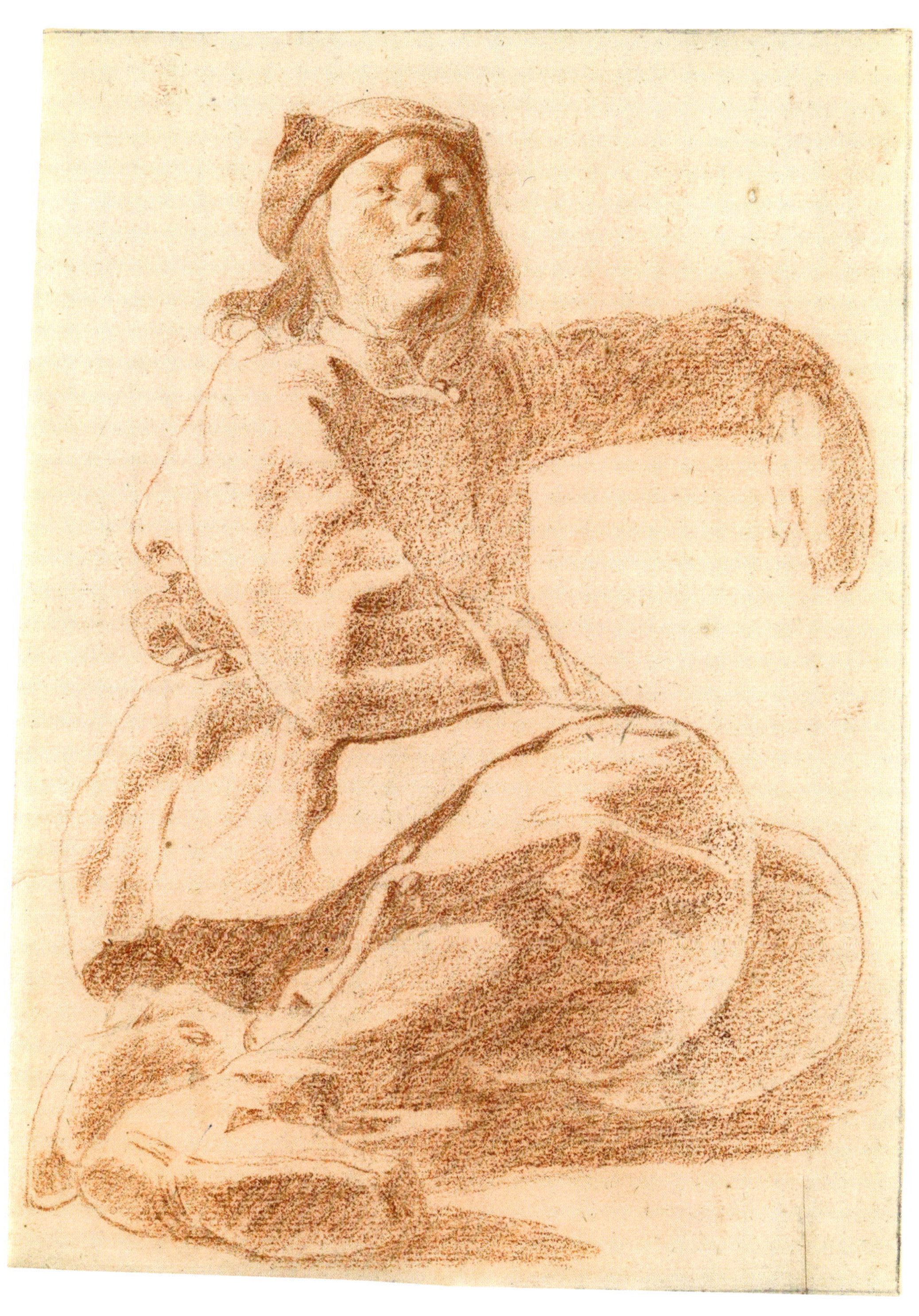

sketched by a family member. The proximity between the two young men—probably peers—is enhanced by the draftsman's low position, the same as that of his model.

The Moore drawing belongs to a larger group of approximately twenty figure studies of naval men and soldiers by Moses ter Borch,[4] most of which are drawn in red chalk (fig. 69.2) and some in black.[5] They generally appear to have been observed by Moses in situ, in their daily routines. The inscription "Mosus ter Borch - nae het leven geteijkent Januarij 1660" (Moses ter Borch - drawn from life January 1660), written by Gerard ter Borch the Elder on the drawing of a *Young Soldier* in the collection of the Baltimore Museum of Art, would attest to that theory.[6] However, a copy of the Baltimore study, drawn in a darker shade of red chalk and preserved in the Kupferstichkabinett, Berlin, led Alison McNeil Kettering to suggest that some figures were drawn later and used "as presentation sheets - handsome, elegantly executed drawings for giving away."[7] Based on that idea, there might have been another version of the Moore seated figure. Its subtle stumping of the red chalk and the pale transitions to the white of the paper clearly imply this depiction was made from life, possibly in a situation where Moses could not see the boy's left hand and therefore left that passage unresolved.

Moses's interest in these soldiers and sailors was shared with his older brothers. Not only do guardroom scenes comprise a significant portion of Gerard the Younger's painted oeuvre, but sketches of soldiers out in the streets and in taverns are also familiar in the work of Harmen. Moses's drawings of *Two Seated Soldiers* (ca. 1662) in the Rijksprentenkabinet, Amsterdam,[8] and the *Study of a Wrecked Field Gun* (1661) in the British Museum, London,[9] make it evident that he had already turned his attention to military subjects early on. The idea that Moses came into contact with this group of naval men only once on board ship and that he drew them while sailing thus seems farfetched.[10] More plausible is the possibility that Moses was intrigued by these military figures as a young man and was perhaps inspired by them to join the fleet. In the summer of 1666, he left Zwolle to enlist in the navy to fight in the Second Anglo-Dutch War (1665–67).[11] Only a year later, on 12 July 1667, he was killed at sea during the Battle of Harwich against the British.[12]
MvS

MARIA SIBYLLA MERIAN

Frankfurt am Main 1647–1717 Amsterdam

70

Metamorphosis insectorum Surinamensium (Amsterdam, Johannes Oosterwyk), 1719

Printed book, with hand-colored engraved plates
Folio (507 x 355 mm)

INSCRIPTIONS Inside cover page, upper left corner, in graphite: [?] / *Brown. 72 plates (coloured)* £25., center top, in pen and brown ink: *Stephen Cave / bequeathed to him by his father in law. / The Revd. William Smyth of Elkington. / Prebendary of Leicester. January 1873. / Given to W. H. Smyth by the widow of Sir Stephen Cave. in 1886*

PROVENANCE Rev. William Smyth (1761–1837), Great Linford, near Milton Keynes, Buckinghamshire; his eldest son, Rev. William Smyth (1791–1873), Elkington Hall, Lincolnshire; his son-in-law, Sir Stephen Cave (1820–1880), London, 1873; his widow, Emily (Emma) Jane (née Smyth) Cave (1822–1905); her brother, William Henry Smyth (1821–1912), Elkington Hall, 1886; his son Capt. William Grenville Smyth (1857–1940), Lincoln, Lincolnshire; possibly the bookseller William Brown, Eton; from whom possibly purchased by Henry Rogers Broughton, 2nd Baron Fairhaven (1900–1973), Anglesey Abbey, Cambridgeshire; his library sale, Sotheby's, London, 18 May 2022, lot 152; where acquired by Clement C. Moore

Promised gift of Clement C. and Elizabeth Y. Moore

Feathery spines bristle off the back of a bulbous green caterpillar that plods on furry feet along the sanguine petals of a flower. The tiny creature is in pursuit of a glorious crown of bananas—the telltale crescent form and exuberant yellow calling the insect like a moth to a flame.[1] Indeed, this hand-colored print shows us how the tenacious crawler will, in due time and with the fruit's nourishment, transform into a bullseye moth (*Automeris liberia*).

This scene unfolds on plate 12 of artist and naturalist Maria Sibylla Merian's groundbreaking volume *Dissertatio de generatione et metamorphosibus insectorum Surinamensium* (or, more commonly, *Metamorphosis insectorum Surinamensium*), which at the time of its first publication in 1705 newly documented life cycles of moths and butterflies in Suriname.[2] The volume, consisting of sixty engraved plates and explanatory texts, resulted from Merian's two-year residence (1699–1701) in Dutch colonial Suriname. Though her trip at the time would have been unconventional for most women, Merian's well-established entomological expertise—she was among the first to observe and document metamorphosis in butterflies and moths—was a more than sufficient reason for her journey.[3]

Merian was a skilled draftswoman and printmaker, though for this volume she worked with numerous engravers to translate her vision into prints.[4] She later endeavored to add another twelve plates to the set (for a total of seventy-two); her death in 1717 meant the expanded edition appeared posthumously, with the assistance of her daughters, Johanna Helena Graff Herolt (see no. 73) and Dorothea Maria Graff, both of whom had learned their mother's craft. Upon completing Merian's work, Johanna and Dorothea sold the plates to Amsterdam printer Johannes Oosterwyk, who from 1719 issued lavish editions with coloring and gilding throughout.[5]

The impression of *Banana and Bullseye Moth* pictured here is part of the Moore collection's exceptionally well-preserved and unique album. This album consists of plates from a 1719 Oosterwyck edition, including a dedication to Balthazar Scott, an Amsterdam alderman and art collector. Glinting gold touches appear throughout the Moore album, for example in plate 29 where the gilt veining of the butterflies (the *Urania leilus*) corresponds to Merian's description of the insect's colors as white and burnished silver and gold (fig. 70.1). Distinguishing the Moore album from a standard Oosterwyck copy of the book are handwritten English translations of Merian's Latin text, alongside two concordances and a handwritten title page, pasted on pages interleaved between hand-colored plates. The album's distinctive pagination begins with Merian's printed title page and Latin texts and is followed by a handwritten title page, then annotations and images. The order suggests that the album was made to suit the interests of a particular owner, possibly the author of the English translations. The exact date of the binding is unknown, though it likely corresponds to the annotations, which appear to be in an eighteenth-century hand. Further eliding the date of annotations with the binding is the scalloped border framing the handwritten title page, which mirrors the Chippendalesque gilded ornamental details embossed on the album's red morocco leather binding typical of the period.

The Moore album in binding, size, dedication to Scott, and use of gilding is comparable to a copy of the *Metamorphosis* in the Fagel Collection at Trinity

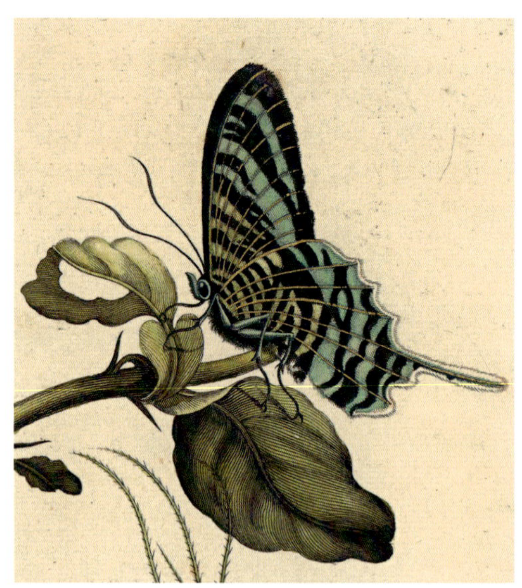

70.1 Maria Sibylla Merian, *Plate 29 from "Metamorphosis insectorum Surinamensium* (detail)," 1719 (cat. 70).

College, Dublin, dated to the eighteenth century.[6] A 1736 album in the John Carter Brown Library at Brown University, Providence, also bears a dedication to Scott as well as handwritten English translations similar in script and semantics: Natalie Zemon Davis has pointed out that the Carter Brown translation selectively foregoes the use of the word "slave" and instead uses "Indian Servant," though Merian writes of her reliance on enslaved and Indigenous labor in her studies.[7] The Moore album's translations follow those of the Carter Brown album, suggesting a possible connection between the two albums.[8] Merian herself would maintain, to modern eyes, a seemingly ambiguous attitude toward enslavement in Suriname—critiquing the institution and the attendant sugarcane monoculture while also making extensive use of Indigenous and enslaved labor to conduct research. Her stance might be indicative of the ways in which the English translators also selectively recognized the practice of slavery in daily life.

What is more certain, however, is an uncanny connection between Merian's work and one of the album's later owners, Sir Stephen Cave, who openly grappled with legacies of the western European colonial constructs evinced in *Metamorphosis*. Cave owned the album from 1873 until his death in 1880.[9] He was a politician, lawyer, and member of the Royal Geographic Society of London, the Zoological Society of London, the Philosophical Society of Great Britain, and Society of Antiquaries. He was also a well-known abolitionist.[10] In 1849, shortly after returning from a plantation tour throughout the Americas and Caribbean, Cave published a rebuke of British sugar tariffs that exacerbated reliance on enslaved labor among trading partners.[11] Perhaps, years later, through his inheritance of this album so full of Merian's stunningly observed plants and insects, Cave grasped the gossamer threads of metamorphosis, of oppression and transformation winding from the past to his present. The Moore album is a profoundly important artwork because it encapsulates enduring legacies of the Dutch Atlantic. **SWM**

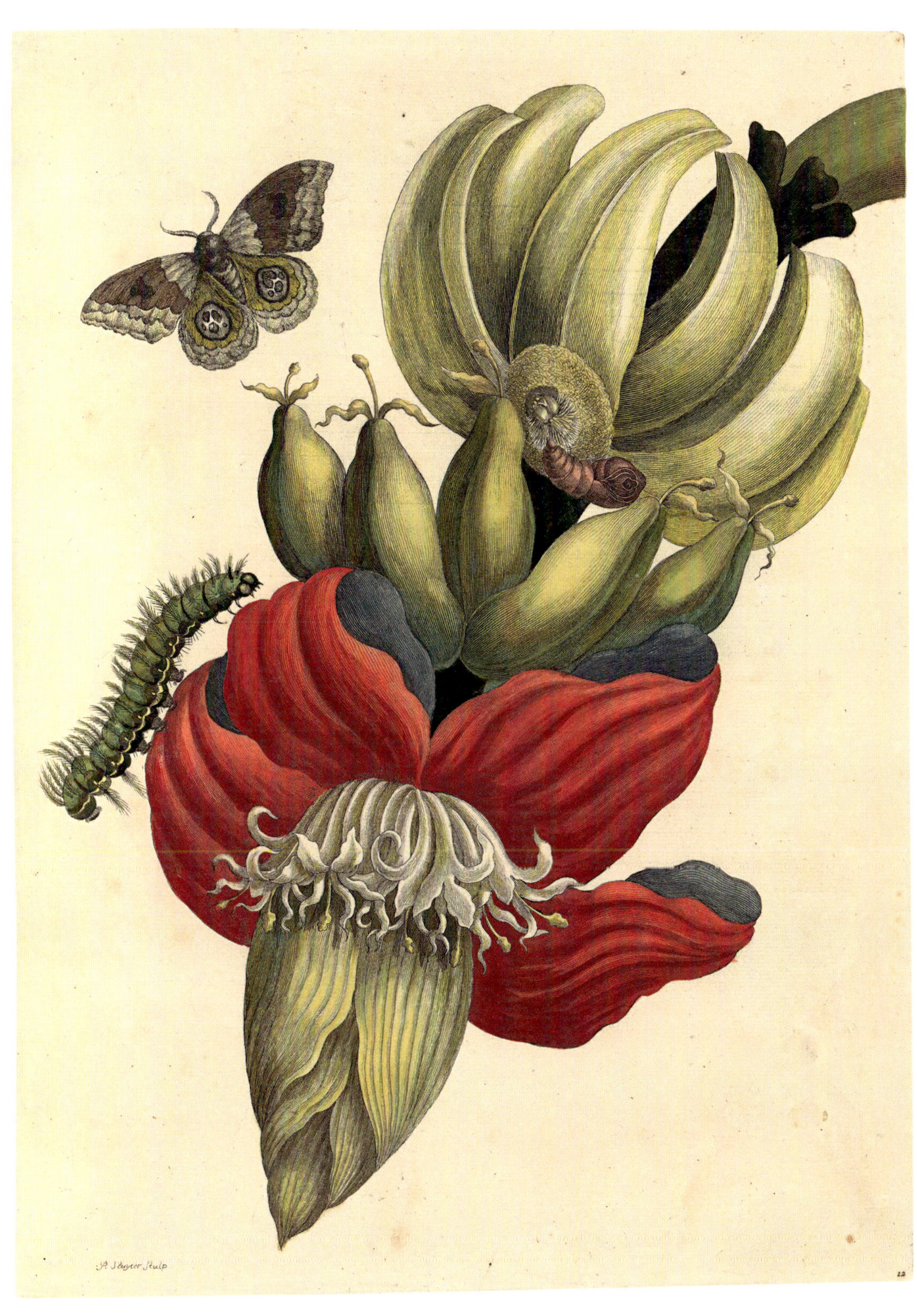

CORNELIS DUSART

Haarlem 1660–1704 Haarlem

71

Seated Man, Leaning on a Staff and Reading, 1688

Watercolor and black and red chalk on parchment
227 x 179 mm

INSCRIPTIONS Recto, lower right, signed and dated, in black ink: *Corn: Dusart. fe. 1688.*; recto, center, on paper, in pen and gray ink: *Extraordinaires Nouvelles uijt / Engelandt Londen*

PROVENANCE Frans van de Velde (d. 1774 or before), Amsterdam; his sale, Ploos van Amstel et al., Amsterdam, 16 January 1775, Album F, lot 315 (to "Metayer"); Louis Philipsz Metayer (1728–1799), Amsterdam; his sale, Philippus van der Schley, Amsterdam, Album E, lot 9; probably Judah Benjamin Senior Henriquez (1718–1782), Amsterdam; his sale, Smit, Amsterdam, 4 November 1782, Album B, lot 57; Dirk van Dijl (1742–1814), Amsterdam; his sale, Vinkeles, Amsterdam, 10 January 1814, Album D, lot 25; Charles de Valori (1820–1883), Marquis-Prince Rustichelli, Paris (no mark; see L. 2500); his sale, Lair-Dubreuil, Paris, 25–26 November 1907, lot 52 (to "Bredeliedre"); Émile Joseph-Rignault (1874–1962), Paris and Saint-Cirq-Lapopie (L. 2218, recto, lower right); his sale, Baudoin, Paris, 26 May 1937, lot 49; private collection; Sotheby's, Paris, 1 April 2015, lot 101; where acquired by Clement C. Moore

Promised gift of Clement C. and Elizabeth Y. Moore

Active toward the end of the seventeenth century, Cornelis Dusart brought chalk figure studies into the realm of finished compositions. Based on the practices of his Haarlem forebears, including Cornelis Bega, Gerrit Berckheyde, and his master, Adriaen van Ostade, Dusart often posed models in a variety of costumes and created chalk studies of them for later consultation. Very shortly after Adriaen's death in 1685, Dusart also began to incorporate colored chalk and watercolor into his figure studies, sometimes with a signature and date, transforming them into fully fledged independent works of art.[1] Within just a few years, he began to place these figures into settings with anecdotal elements, often choosing luxurious parchment as a support. Altogether, these drawings are a unique contribution to Dutch draftsmanship.

Signed and dated 1688, the *Seated Man, Leaning on a Staff and Reading* is a quintessential example of this practice. It is one of five known Dusart watercolors on parchment depicting a seated man reading in an interior, often accompanied by a table or barrel and holding items such as a pipe or bottle. Two others are also signed and dated 1688, one in Frankfurt and the other in Haarlem, whereas two more known through the trade date from 1690 and 1691.[2] Each man is based on a different model, and, while all are seated, the poses vary, as do the interiors. All hold a single sheet of paper, presumably a newspaper, typically bearing illegible or nondescript writing or printing.[3] The newspaper appearing in the present sheet includes at the top the decipherable words "Extraordinaires Nouvelles uijt / Engelandt Londen" (Extraordinary News from England London).[4] This headline likely references the Glorious Revolution, when William III of Orange, then stadtholder of the Dutch Republic and husband of Mary II, arrived in England with significant military support, successfully advancing to London on 5 November 1688 and overthrowing James II (Mary's father). The couple would become joint monarchs ruling over England, Ireland, and Scotland, while William remained stadtholder—an important political and military alliance.

Despite the preponderance of village scenes, tavern interiors, and laborers in Dusart's corpus, he was no stranger to political themes. On one extreme, he created many watercolor roundels of heavily caricatured members of the Catholic clergy that were used as preparatory designs for two anonymously published and scathing critiques of the Catholic Church and Louis XIV, *Renversement de la morale chrétienne* and *Les Héros de la Ligue* of 1691.[5] Adopting a more jovial tone, he issued a small series of mezzotints with publisher Jacob Gole in celebration of the Siege of Namur, a major victory by William III in 1695 as he recaptured the city from the French during the War of the Grand Alliance (1688–97, also known as the Nine Years' War).[6] In the present sheet, Dusart subtly alluded to pro-Orange sentiment, a tactic well suited to a man savoring a moment alone in a quiet corner, lost in thought as he reads the news before him. SA

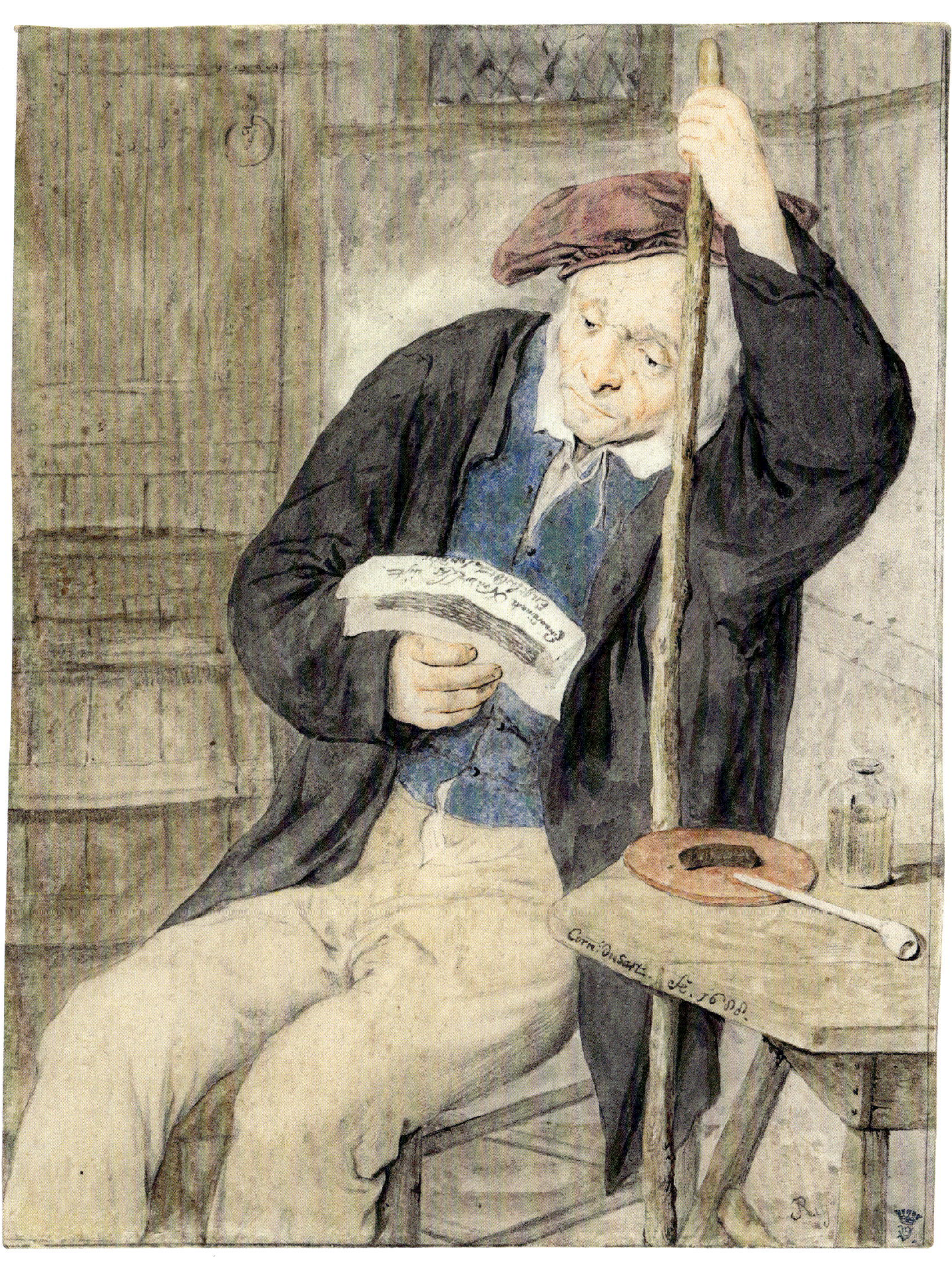

HERMAN HENSTENBURGH

Hoorn 1667–1726 Hoorn

72a,b

Four Moths, Including a Green-Banded Urania (*Urania leilus*) (a) *and Two Moths, a Butterfly, and a Flying Insect* (b), ca. 1686

(a) Watercolor and opaque watercolor, over black chalk; (b) watercolor and opaque watercolor
(a) 191 x 223 mm; (b) 164 x 191 mm

WATERMARK (a) Fragment of a Strasbourg lily, similar to Churchill 403 (produced by Pieter van der Ley, 1686)[1]

INSCRIPTIONS (a) Recto, lower right, monogrammed in pen and brown ink: *HHB. fē:*; recto, lower left, in brown ink: *4*; verso, upper right, in pen and brown ink: *263*; verso, upper right, in graphite: *10*; verso, lower right, in graphite: *153* (b) recto, lower right, signed, in pen and brown ink: *HHB. fe:*; recto, lower left, in brown ink: *9.*; verso, upper left, in pen and brown ink: *198*; verso, lower left, in graphite: *7/9*; verso, lower right, in graphite: *146*

PROVENANCE Private collection, the Netherlands, 1991; Sotheby's, London, 7 July 2011, lots 96 and 97; Mireille Mosler, New York, 2012; from whom acquired by Clement C. Moore, 2013

SELECT REFERENCES Zaal 1991a, 2: nos. A037 and A038; Zaal 1991b, no. 25

Promised gift of Clement C. and Elizabeth Y. Moore

Herman Henstenburgh spent his life in the harbor town of Hoorn, working as a baker, draftsman, and painter. He followed the professional trajectory of his teacher, Johannes Bronckhorst, also a pastry baker and artist. Both men—as well as Henstenburgh's baker and artist son Antony—garnered praise in their lifetimes (and beyond) for skillful depictions of flora and fauna. Hoorn was the headquarters of the Dutch East India Company (VOC), and the port from which all their ships came and went. Arriving with these ships was a constant supply of exotic birds, animals, and insects, some alive, but mostly stuffed or preserved as specimens. Arnold Houbraken and the poet and minister Joannes Vollenhove fervently praised Bronckhorst's lifelike watercolors; artist and biographer Johan van Gool, similarly enraptured with Henstenburgh, associated his work with a pantheon of exalted men.[2] Among Henstenburgh's other admirers was Cosimo III de' Medici, Grand Duke of Tuscany, who by 1700 had several of the artist's drawings in his collection.[3]

The two Moore sheets, monogrammed at lower right and numbered "4" and "9" at lower left, respectively, are superlative examples of Henstenburgh's draftsmanship. The artist, informed by oil painting techniques, built up delicate layers of watercolor over black chalk to delineate whisper-soft textures, subtle colors, and patterns indicative of insect wings.[4] We see an array of moths, a butterfly, and a flying insect gently scattered across two sheets of laid paper. The insects' crisp, shadowless silhouettes on the creamy white grounds are reminiscent of artfully arranged specimen boxes. In the center of sheet "9" (no. 72b) is a large brown moth, perhaps the tropical swallowtail moth (*Lyssa zampa*), native to Southeast Asia.[5] It sits alongside a male barred yellow butterfly (*Eurema daira*), found in the Americas from Argentina to the southern United States, as well as a smaller, unidentified moth and an ichneumon wasp. Though we might further speculate about the artist's specimen selections, undeniably

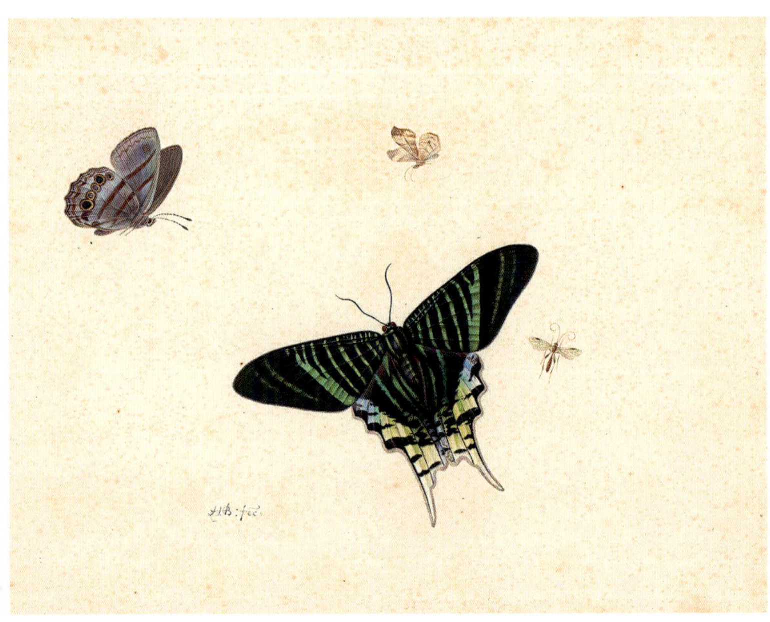

72.1 Herman Henstenburgh, *Two Moths, a Butterfly, and a Flying Insect*, ca. 1677–1726. Rijksprentenkabinet, Amsterdam.

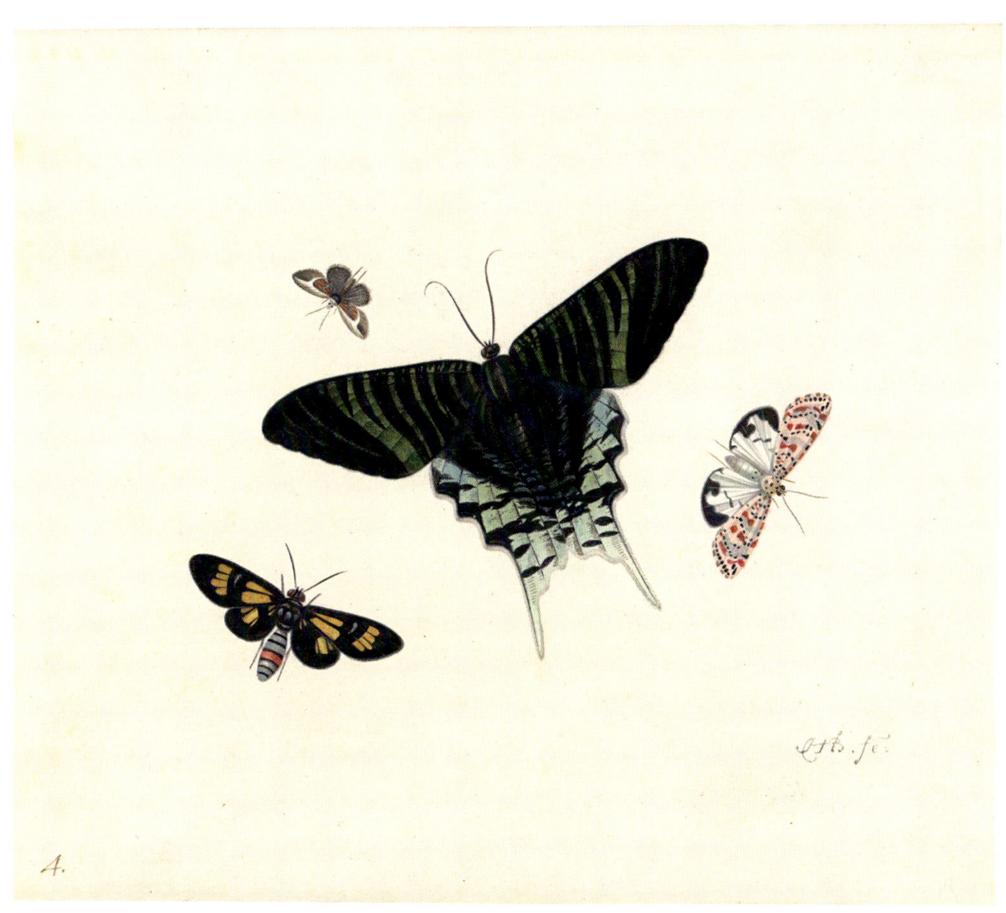

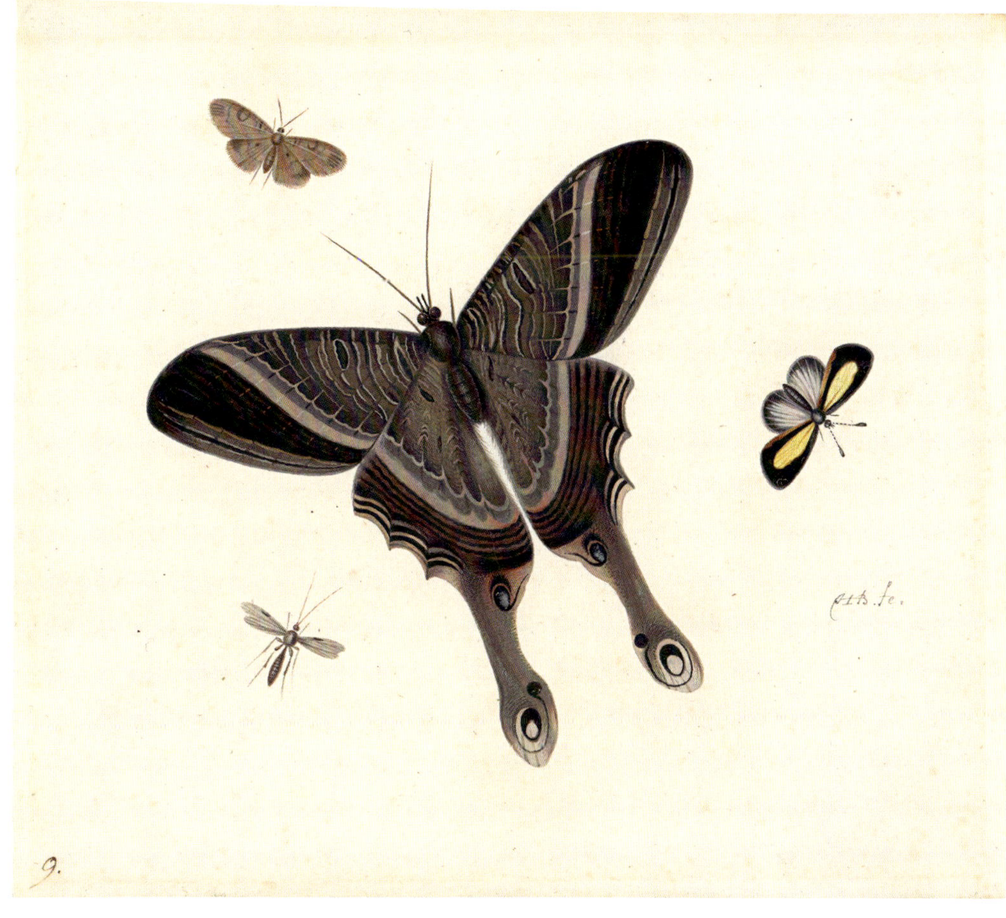

apparent is his placement of the largest insect in the center of the composition. Henstenburgh's clever use of scale both records the disparate size of his subjects and unites their forms into a harmonious picture.

Henstenburgh repeats this compositional formula throughout his oeuvre. In the other Moore drawing (no. 72a), a large, vibrant green-banded urania (*Urania leilus*), a day-flying moth typically found in South America, especially in the Amazon rainforest, occupies the page's center. To its right is the crimson-speckled footman moth (*Utetheisa pulchella*), native to Europe, North Africa, Western Asia, and Central Asia. To the left of the urania is another day-flying moth, possibly a wasp moth (*Euchromia folletii*), found throughout Africa. A smaller moth with gray and brown markings completes the quartet. The captivating *Urania leilus* draws the eye, this perhaps a reflection not simply of its size, but also of Henstenburgh's affinities and aptitudes: he depicted the moth in at least three more drawings, now in various private collections and the Rijksprentenkabinet (fig. 72.1).[6]

Bronckhorst also drew the *Urania leilus*, suggesting master and student worked after each other or from similar sources.[7] Henstenburgh never decamped from Hoorn but had ample opportunity to study flora and fauna via sprawling gardens and *naturalia* cabinets assembled by noted collectors, including Agnes Block, who commissioned works from the artist. The insects pictured on the Moore sheets do not coexist in nature, hailing as they do from habitats across the world, many within the Dutch colonial empire; still, in the realm of a collector's cabinet, geographically divergent objects commingled. Henstenburgh's drawings testify to the artist's remarkable talent, irrevocably shaped by the period's extractive collecting practices indicative of the Dutch relationship to places far and away. SWM

JOHANNA HELENA HEROLT

Frankfurt am Main 1668–ca. 1723/43 Suriname

73

Yellow and Purple Verbascum, with the Life Cycle of a Moth, ca. 1691–1711

Watercolor, over black chalk, on parchment
380 x 300 mm

INSCRIPTIONS Verso, upper left, in pen and black ink: 148; verso, lower right, unidentified collector stamp

PROVENANCE Possibly Agnes Block (1629–1704), Vijverhof, Loenen aan de Vecht, near Utrecht; possibly from whom acquired by Valerius Röver (1686–1739), Delft (no mark; see L. 2984a); Johan Pieter van den Brande or Pieter van den Brande (1707–1758), Middelburg; by descent to Baron Elbert Carsilius van Pallandt (1898–1964), Leiden; his sale, Mak van Waay, Amsterdam, 26 September 1972, part of lot 322b (as H. Henstenburgh); Johan Quirijn van Regteren Altena (1899–1980), Amsterdam (no mark; see L. 4617); by descent to his heirs; their sale, Christie's, Amsterdam, 13 May 2015, lot 247; where acquired by Clement C. Moore

SELECT REFERENCES Giltaij 1976, no. 75 (as Antony or Herman Henstenburgh)

Promised gift of Clement C. and Elizabeth Y. Moore

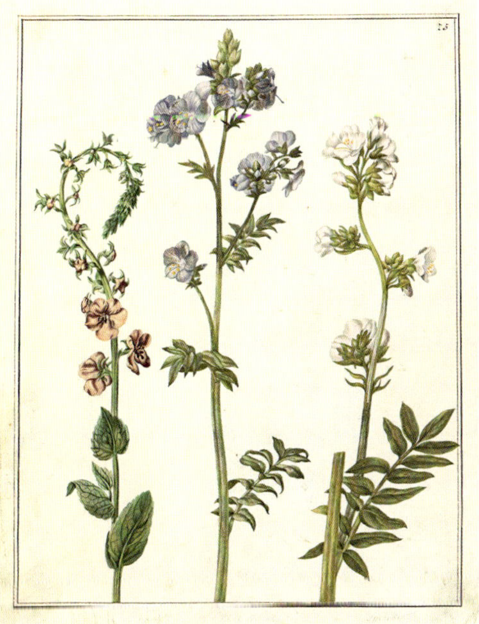

73.1 Johanna Helena Herolt, *Purple Mullein* (Verbascum phoeniceum) *and Two Stems of Jacob's Ladder* (Polemonium reptans), ca. 1698. Herzog Anton Ulrich-Museum, Braunschweig.

Johanna Helena Herolt (née Graff), alongside her sister Dorothea Maria Graff, trained at the knee of her parents, Maria Sybilla Merian and Johann Andreas Graff, who had themselves been apprenticed to Merian's stepfather, the eminent flower painter Jacob Marrel (see no. 46).[1] In this finely executed watercolor drawing of verbascum (perhaps moth mullein, or *Verbascum blattaria*) we see Herolt continue the natural history drawing tradition begun by the Merian lineage. Three stems with white, yellow, and purple flowers—each stem from a different plant—fill the page. Herolt drew their silhouettes in fine black chalk lines then elaborated color, volume, and texture using a multitude of small, smooth strokes of watercolor, typically letting each layer dry before applying the next. Though she was influenced by her mother's technique, more indicative of Herolt's style is the arabesque curvature of the verbascum's stems—a clever conceit to guide the eye up the cache of tiny blossoms amid which we see the life cycle of an owlet moth.[2] Proceeding from the lower right stem, a small brown caterpillar grows, then as a pupa spins itself inside a cocoon, and soon emerges delicate and flitting among soft mullein petals. The mature moth appears with wings fully splayed, this rigid position an indication Herolt drew the insect, if not the whole picture, using preserved specimens and her apt imagination. Indeed, the harmonious placement of moth and plant is an idealized vignette intended to show the subjects' superlative features throughout various developmental stages, a feat of synchronicity that would never transpire in nature.

Herolt likely produced this drawing while living in Amsterdam, from 1691 to 1711. In pursuit of professional opportunities, the artist moved from Friesland to Amsterdam with her husband, Jacob Hendrik Herolt, and her mother and sister. During this period, she collaborated with her mother and made flower books and drawings, recording, for instance, plants cultivated by notable collector Agnes Block at her estate Vijverhof on the River Vecht near Utrecht, and those growing in the Hortus Botanicus of Amsterdam.[3] Herolt would permanently relocate to Suriname in 1711, alongside her husband, returning only briefly to Amsterdam in 1714 to visit her ailing mother.[4]

Some uncertainty surrounds Herolt's oeuvre, with many of her works attributed to her mother or other artists.[5] The Moore sheet is one such example, having formerly been catalogued as by Herman Henstenburgh.[6] Though the express purpose of this sheet is yet unknown, it might well have been part of a (now disassembled) flower book or album. In the "Bloem Boek," an album of forty-nine Herolt watercolor drawings of flowers dated to ca. 1698, now in the collection of the Herzog Anton Ulrich-Museum, Braunschweig, the artist included a drawing of a verbascum alongside two stems of Jacob's ladder (fig. 73.1).[7] The Moore and Braunschweig sheets are both done on parchment and share similar dimensions and pictorial conceits, for example a dramatically cropped stem in the foreground, as if the artist trimmed away excess foliage to improve the composition.

Though Herolt depicted verbascum on at least two occasions, this plant, thought of as a useful sort of flowering weed, was not a common subject in florilegia, which more often featured the ornamental blossoms of irises, lilies, peonies, roses, and tulips. (In Merian's vast oeuvre we have yet to identify a mullein.) The plant was, however, a mainstay of herbals, including *De materia medica*, written in 50–70 CE by Greek physician Dioscorides, subsequently copied, illustrated, and circulated for millennia. The tome was among the most influential texts of its kind in the early modern period. Many of the earliest surviving illustrated copies, which feature verbascum, are on parchment; Herolt's drawing thus represents a profound link in the long chain of artistic tradition wrought from the study of nature.[8] So important was the verbascum as a treatment for an array of ailments—ulcers, inflammation, dysentery, barren wombs, pleurisy—European colonizers cultivated the plant in the Americas, where it set down roots and grew with abandon.[9] Herolt was familiar with various herbals and would have encountered mullein in her daily life: John Gerard's *The Herball; or, Generall Historie of Plantes* (1597), much inspired by *De materia* and Pliny the Elder's writings, notes that moth mullein had no obvious use except to attract bugs.[10] Herolt's drawing can but confirm and refute his assertion, for in her remarkable drawing of this workaday weed we experience the allure of reciprocity between insect, plant, and artist. SWM

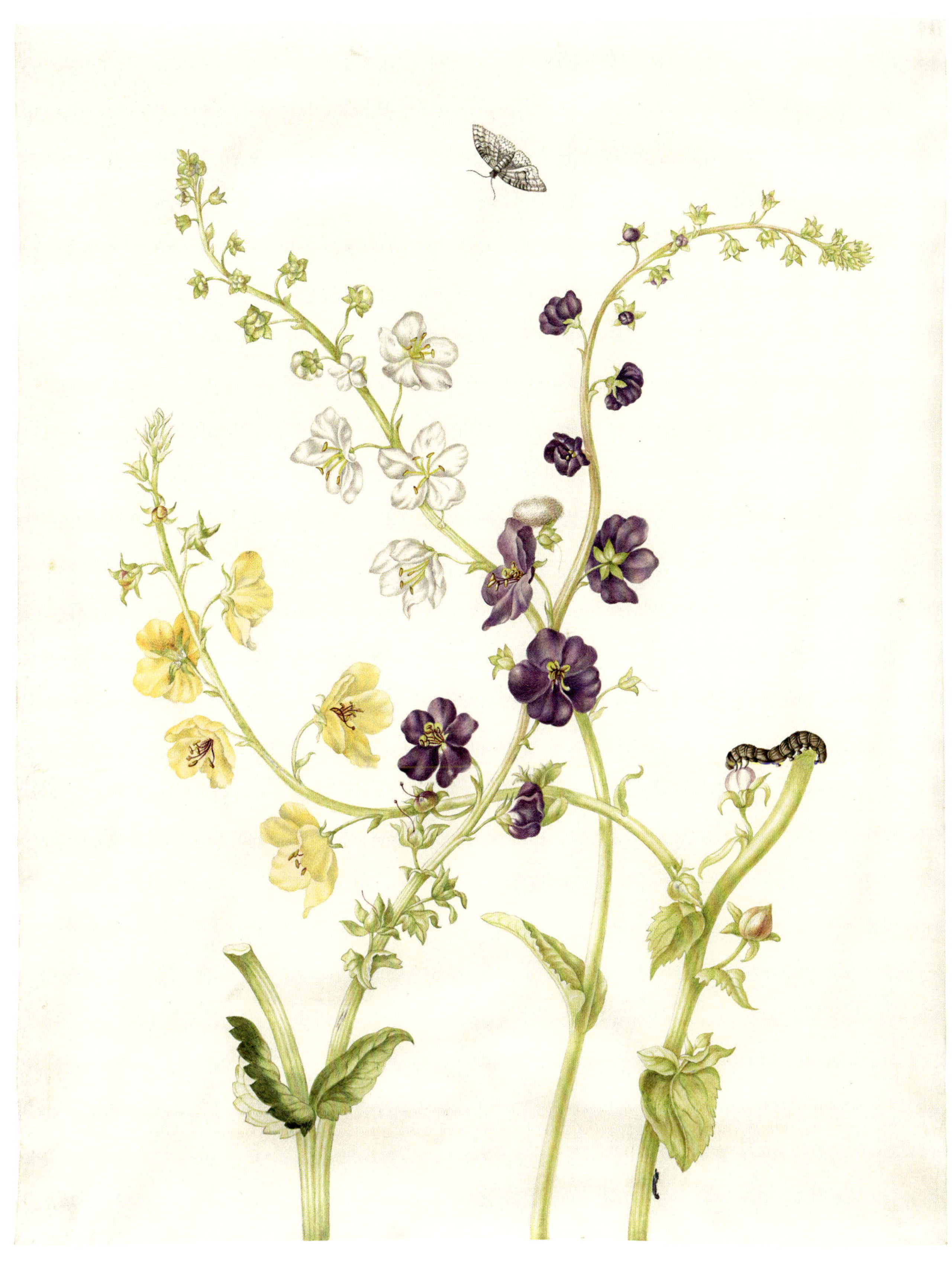

JAN AUGUSTIN VAN DER GOES

Antwerp 1671–after 1698

74

Still Life with Hazelnuts and Bread, ca. 1700

Opaque watercolor on parchment
84 x 109 mm

INSCRIPTIONS Recto, lower center, signed, in gold paint: *JAN AUG x V x GOES F*

PROVENANCE Jean-Luc Baroni & Marty de Cambiaire, Paris; from whom acquired by Clement C. Moore, 2023

SELECT REFERENCES Marty de Cambiaire 2024, no. 16

Promised gift of Clement C. and Elizabeth Y. Moore

Until recently, the relatively obscure artist Jan Augustin van der Goes—who was registered with the Guild of St. Luke in Antwerp as a painter and illuminator from 1694 to 1698[1]—was known mainly for a dozen miniatures of insects and crustaceans, even though old sale catalogues hinted at a wider range of still-life subject matter. Surviving examples of his work include a set of eight oval and round miniatures preserved since 1884 in the collection of the Rijksprentenkabinet, Amsterdam,[2] and four similar drawings recently acquired by the Fondation Custodia, Paris.[3] These miniatures feature motifs such as moths and beetles, a grasshopper, a spider, a shrimp, and a hermit crab, all executed in opaque watercolor on parchment.

With the newly discovered drawing in the Moore collection, a different side of the artist has reemerged. Here, Van der Goes carefully depicted a large hunk of bread and more than a dozen hazelnuts, some of which have had their hard shell cracked open to reveal their edible kernel. Although a seemingly random arrangement, the elements of the still life must have been deliberately composed: the soft inside of the torn-off piece of bread is clearly visible because of how it was placed on top of the nuts, scattered on a blue surface. As with his miniature depictions of tiny creatures, Van der Goes drew on parchment, in an oval format, and framed the composition with a golden border—albeit covered or trimmed, its traces are still visible and "replaced" with his signature in gold.

The simplicity of the composition, focusing on two ingredients set against a neutral dark background, is reminiscent of the intimate oil still lifes by another late seventeenth-century artist, Adriaen Coorte. Like the work of Coorte, the Moore miniature stands in complete contrast to the ornate, luxury still lifes known as *pronkstillevens*, popular works characterized by an abundance of precious items. Coorte also worked on a small scale, as is clear from his *Still Life with Two Walnuts* (1702) in the Museum of Fine Arts, Budapest—executed in oil on paper and the smallest work in his oeuvre (109 x 156 mm, just slightly larger in size than this miniature).[4]

That Van der Goes devoted himself to still lifes of edible foods was previously known mainly from documentary evidence.[5] From descriptions in old sale catalogues, miniatures by his hand are noted as depicting mussels, butter, sugar cakes, fruit, eggs, sausages, tripe, and so forth. Closely comparable to the Moore miniature is a rectangular *Still Life with Bread and Almond Biscuits* in the collection of the Kröller-Müller Museum, Otterlo (fig. 74.1), at present the only other known food rendering by Van der Goes.[6] Yet, as is evident from more recent auctions, more complex small-format still lifes on parchment, with spices, jugs, glassware, and dice, were also part of his repertoire.[7]

Although Van der Goes's work is rare today, his miniatures were cherished by early collectors. In the Southern Netherlands, the region in which he was active, his fellow townsman Petrus Franciscus van Schorel, as well as Philippe Lambert Joseph Spruyt, owned examples of his work. The insects and edibles also found their way up north, ending up in the collections of, among others, Willem van der Lely, Jan Tak, Jan van Dijk, Cornelis Ploos van Amstel, and even Lothar Franz von Schönborn. Presumably they were safely stored by their owners in collectors' albums, although it is also not inconceivable that these precious objects were framed and hung on the walls of art cabinets. **MvS**

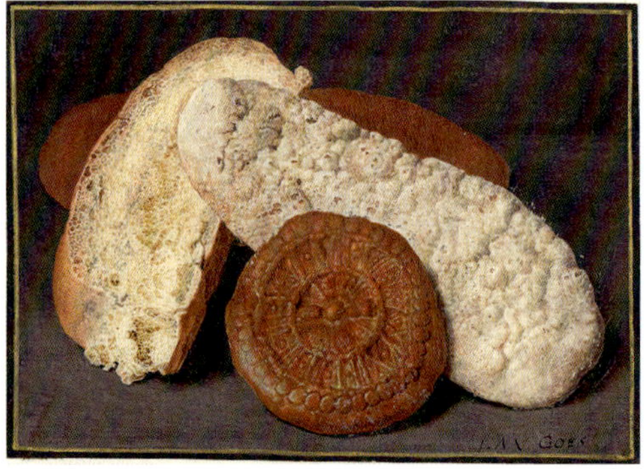

74.1 Jan Augustin van der Goes, *Still Life with Bread and Almond Biscuits*, ca. 1700. Kröller-Müller Museum, Otterlo.

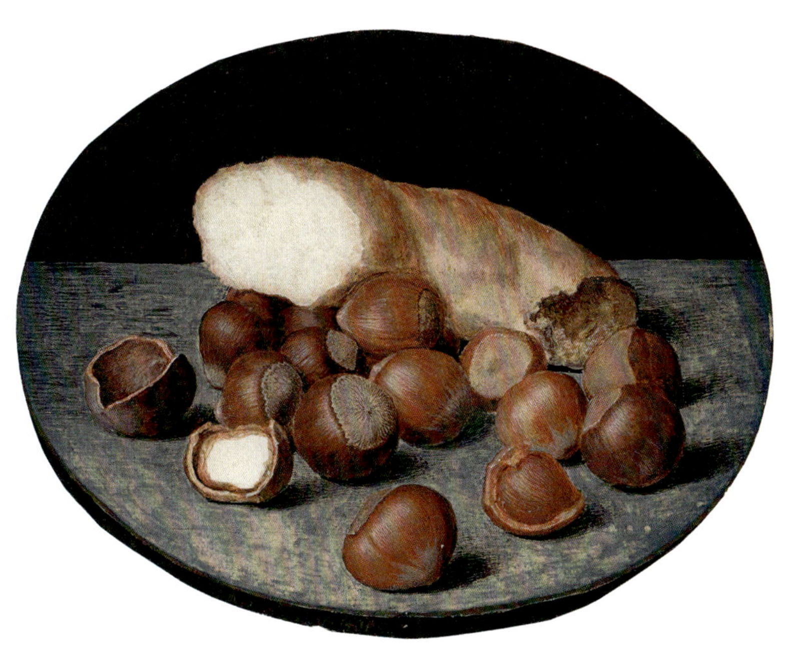

ALEXANDER COZENS

Kazan (Tatarstan) 1717–1786 London

75

The Small Lake, ca. 1763

Pen and black ink and gray wash; framing line in black ink
113 x 150 mm

INSCRIPTIONS Recto, lower left, signed with the artist's initial, in pen and brown ink: C; recto of mount, lower right, in graphite: *A. Cozens / exhibited at RA: 1772–1781*; verso of mount, lower edge, in pen and brown ink: *307 -o-Couzinis*[1]

PROVENANCE L.H. Gilbert (twentieth century; dates unknown), Lisbon; his sale, Christie's, London, 6 March 1973, lot 56; Thomas Agnew & Sons, London; private collection, UK, from 1974; thence by descent; Rosebery's, London, 19 July 2022, lot 82; Andrew Clayton-Payne, London; from whom acquired by Clement C. Moore, 2023

SELECT REFERENCES London 1974, no. 62

Promised gift of Clement C. and Elizabeth Y. Moore

Dutch artists' elevation of landscape drawings as independent and highly collectible works paved the way for the rise of finished landscape drawings as a specialty in Britain during the eighteenth century. In contrast to his Dutch predecessors, however, Cozens pursued an unconventional path less wedded to naturalism. Raised until age ten in St. Petersburg, Russia, he was sent to London in 1727 to learn the basics of painting and drawing. He refined these skills during a two-year stay in Italy before establishing himself in London in 1746. Drawing had not yet become as ubiquitous there as it would in the nineteenth century, when schools, societies, and instruction for amateurs were widespread. Still, the seeds for such institutions were being sown. Informal academies were established, and London's Society of Artists was founded in 1760, with the Royal Academy following in 1768.

Cozens parlayed his skill as a draftsman into a living as a drawing teacher. In 1750, using his experience as the well-traveled son of a naval family, he secured a position instructing students being trained as navigators and seamen at Christ's Hospital, a school founded in 1553 to educate fatherless and impoverished children. Frustrated with the indifferent pupils at the school and finding more motivated ones through private instruction, Cozens resigned in 1754. He eventually took another teaching post in 1763 at Eton College, where he would remain for five years. At the same time, as Grand Tourists returned home with their treasures, many sought to develop their drawing skills, providing Cozens with a lucrative career tutoring amateurs and the children of wealthy families.

Cozens devised a complicated and theoretical—perhaps even inscrutably so—set of guidelines for creating innovative blot drawings in a two-page *Essay to Facilitate the Inventing of Landskips*, published in 1759 between his tenures at Christ's Hospital and Eton. His blot technique involved a brush loaded with ink, daubed on a sheet of paper, and a second thin sheet on which he traced the outline of the resulting composition. Cozens employed this method in his pedagogical work, reserved for more advanced drawing students, with the intention of liberating their imagination and encouraging them to compose more expressively. In the 1760s, he began working on another text, *A Treatise on Perspective and Rules for Shading by Invention*, completed by 1765, although no trace survives today.

This compact landscape relates to a larger group of sheets by the artist produced following his 1759 treatise and likely as he was working on his rules for shading. In contrast to the blot and outline drawings, Cozens made a series of landscapes using short, tightly placed pen and ink strokes, varying the pressure to create a minutely textured surface that—like the present sheet—relied on a tonal structure.[2] Kim Sloan associates the larger group of these landscape drawings with Cozens's work on the 1765 *Treatise*, and several bear a date of 1763.[3] Using a wide vocabulary of marks in this sheet, he produced the foreground's thicker vegetation, the lake's glittering surface, and the faintness of the distant peaks, all beneath a dynamic sky. A human presence is indicated by two wandering figures whose silhouettes can be seen along the near edge of the lake. They are more refined than those in other sheets from this moment, and their presence swiftly conveys the monumentality of the mountain landscape.

Cozens made these landscapes at a time when he was actively exhibiting at the Society of Artists, which held its first show in 1760. Francesca Kaes convincingly

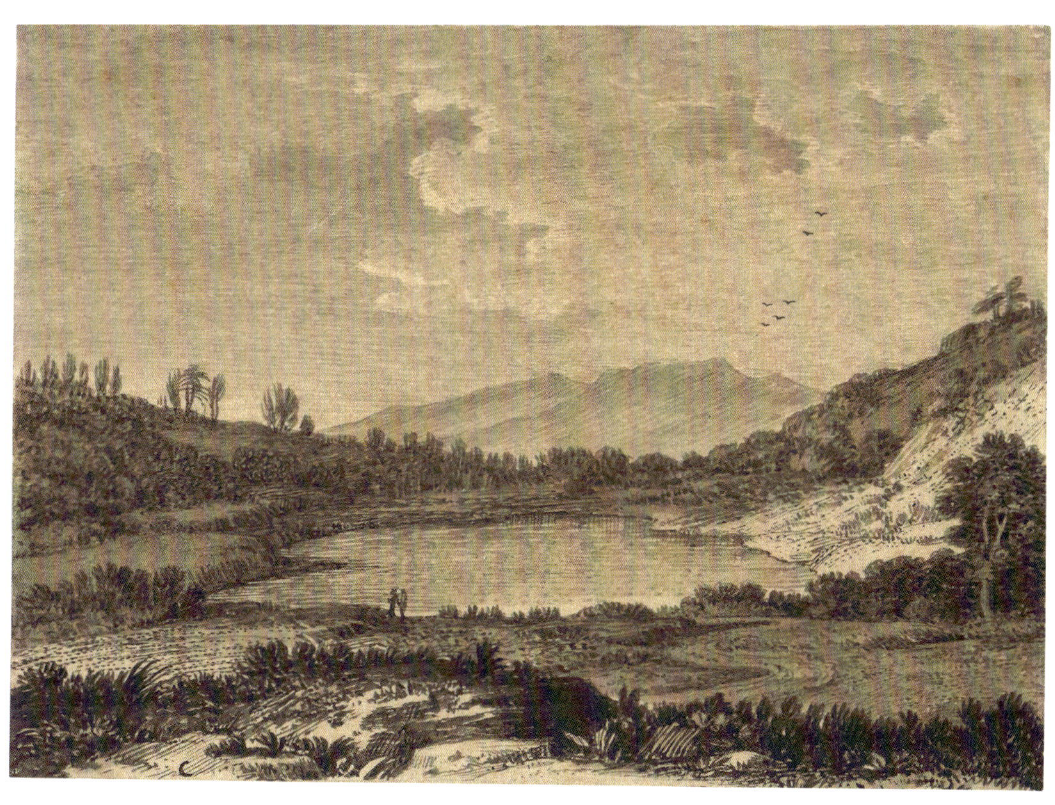

posits that Cozens created highly finished and signed works for exhibition, but that some of the smaller finished works were instead preparatory studies for larger drawings intended for display.[4] She observed that the artist's signature on two sheets at Tate Britain, London, although executed in the same technique as the Moore drawing, differs from the simple "C" inscribed on the present drawing;[5] the more formal signature of "Al. Cozens" on the Tate sheets could support the idea that they were intended for a wider audience, and, indeed, the Tate sheets compare to other larger sheets, such as *A View near Rome,* in the Victoria and Albert Museum, London.[6] Nonetheless, the unforgiving medium of ink would necessitate careful planning and execution, and Cozens's desire to make his name through publicly exhibiting his works must have inspired him to create smaller works that, though somewhat preparatory, have an ambition equal to that of sheets on a larger scale. JT

THOMAS GAINSBOROUGH

Sudbury, Suffolk 1727–1788 London

76

Wooded Landscape with Shepherds, Sheep, and Cottages, ca. 1760–63

Watercolor and opaque watercolor, over graphite, on tan paper
213 x 279 mm

PROVENANCE Given by the artist to Henry Temple, 2nd Viscount Palmerston (1739–1802), London and Broadlands, Hampshire; his son Henry John Temple, 3rd Viscount Palmerston (1784–1865), Broadlands; his widow, Emily Lamb, Countess Palmerston (1787–1869); her son, William Cowper-Temple, 1st Baron Mount Temple (1811–1888), Broadlands; his great-nephew Evelyn Ashley (1836–1907), Broadlands; his son Wilfrid Ashley, 1st Baron Mount Temple (1867–1939), Broadlands; his daughter Edwina Ashley, Countess Mountbatten (1901–1960), Broadlands, Hampshire; from whom acquired by Clifford Duits (1909–1968), London by 1960; thence by descent; acquired through Thomas Williams Fine Art, London, by Clement C. Moore, 2020

SELECT REFERENCES Parker and Byam Shaw 1953, no. 463; Hayes 1960, no. 17; Hayes 1971, 1: 172, no. 272 and under no. 27

Promised gift of Clement C. and Elizabeth Y. Moore

This beautiful watercolor dates from 1760–63, during the artist's residence in the fashionable spa city of Bath. Gainsborough had moved there in 1759, attracted by a richer clientele than could be found in his native county of Suffolk. Once there, he began almost immediately to employ a broader range of drawing materials than the graphite and black chalk he had relied upon before.[1] Opaque and transparent watercolors, ink washes, and colored paper all made an appearance in Gainsborough's Bath period, as we find here. Indeed, these experiments proved to be only the beginning of a restless exploration of graphic media that absorbed the artist for the rest of his working life.

The Moore drawing sits among Gainsborough's early watercolor essays in Bath, the first of which is dated 1759.[2] He has relied on pencil for the underlying structure of the design, and to describe the figures, buildings, and trees. Watercolor and light-colored opaque watercolor were then applied, and the composition expanded. Much of the woodland area to the left was drawn primarily using only these water-based media. Lastly, areas of detail were enlivened with staccato touches of opaque pigments. The muted coloring brings to mind the naturalistic style that the artist favored in the 1750s. The fallen tree trunk and the cottage half hidden by foliage, seen at the center right, are both recurring features in his paintings and drawings of the 1750s and 1760s. In the Moore drawing, the artist ingeniously made use of the paper color, leaving it exposed in places to act as a mid-tone, particularly evident in the trees at the upper right.[3] Two sheets that make use of the same technique can be found in the Ashmolean Museum, Oxford (figs. 76.1 and 76.2).[4] John Hayes further cites a drawing "identical in handling," which is in a private collection in England.[5] The use of such a colored support may reflect the practice, already begun by Gainsborough in Ipswich, of employing a warm, reddish-brown as the ground for his canvases.

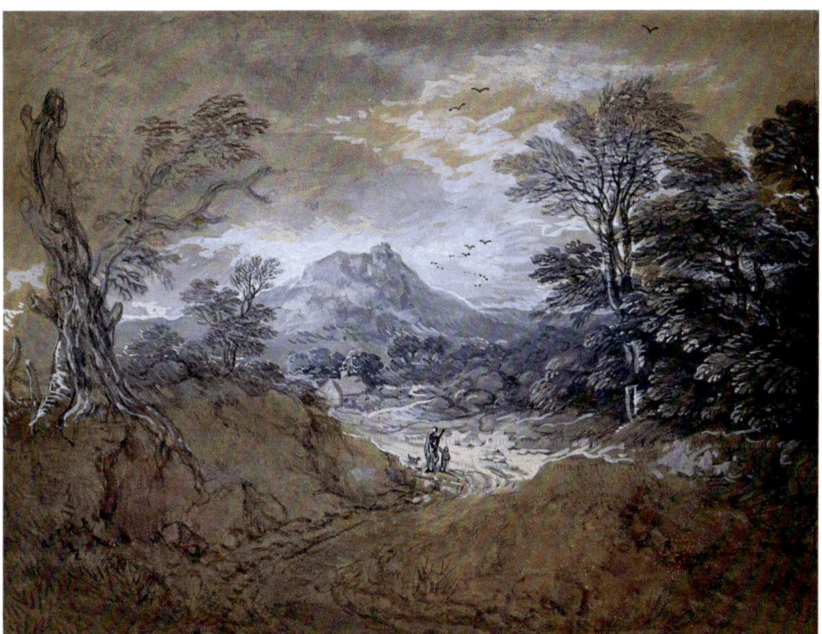

76.1 Thomas Gainsborough, *Wooded Landscape with Figures and Distant Mountain*, 1760–63. Ashmolean Museum, Oxford.

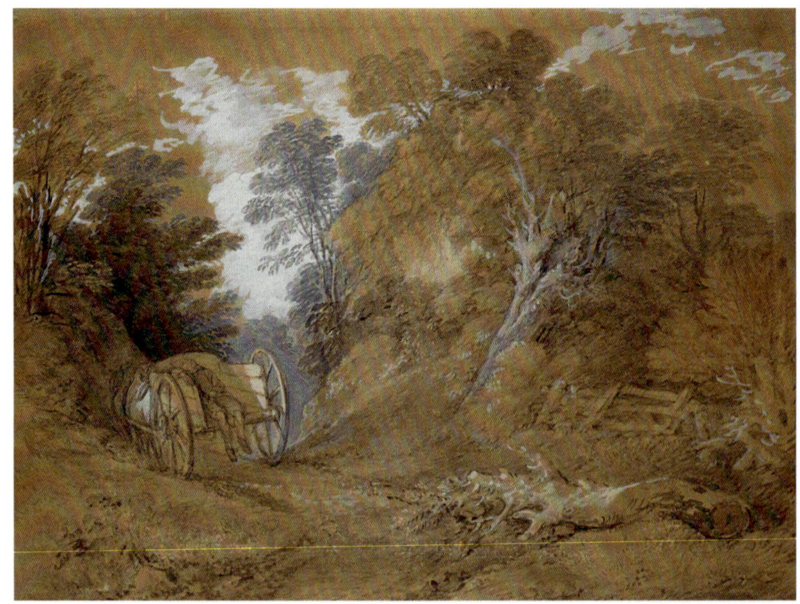

76.2 Thomas Gainsborough, *Wooded Landscape with a Peasant Asleep in a Cart*, 1760–63. Ashmolean Museum, Oxford.

Gainsborough's arrival in the west of England gave rise to significant changes in his outlook. Firstly, it introduced him to a landscape very different to the flat, coastal plains he was familiar with in Suffolk. Here, he was amongst the steep valleys and hillsides in which Bath was situated, perched above the River Avon. This allowed him to view the drama of nature at first hand, rather than through the lens of Ruisdael and the other seventeenth-century Dutch masters he emulated as a young man.[6] He began to make regular excursions on horseback through the tumescent countryside, "the circumjacent Scenery . . . picturesque, and beautiful in a high Degree."[7] The romance of his surroundings gave him not only the need to respond to it, but, more importantly, as Lindsay Stainton observed, to record his love of it.[8]

Furthermore, taking advantage of his new, aristocratic patronage in Bath, Gainsborough was able to see the noble collections of pictures at Wilton, Stourhead, and other great houses nearby, a revelatory introduction to Rubens, Van Dyck, and Claude Lorrain especially. It was through his study of these masters that he completed the transition toward a more grandiloquent, Rococo style, evident in the present sheet. It is also worth noting, given the choice of medium, that Gainsborough had recently become familiar with the work of Paul Sandby, whom he mentioned in a letter to Lord Hardwicke in the early 1760s. Of course, Sandby was a mere "view painter," whereas for Gainsborough nature was simply the starting point for creative genius; his landscapes were drawn, as he explained to Hardwicke, "of his own Brain."[9]

Although the artist is reported to have sold his drawings as a young man, from the time of his arrival in Bath he made them exclusively for his own pleasure or as gifts to friends and patrons. The Moore drawing thus remained in the artist's studio until his move to London in 1774, where he gave it to Henry Temple, 2nd Viscount Palmerston, who lived in Hanover Square, a short walk from the house that Gainsborough and his family had taken in Pall Mall. TW

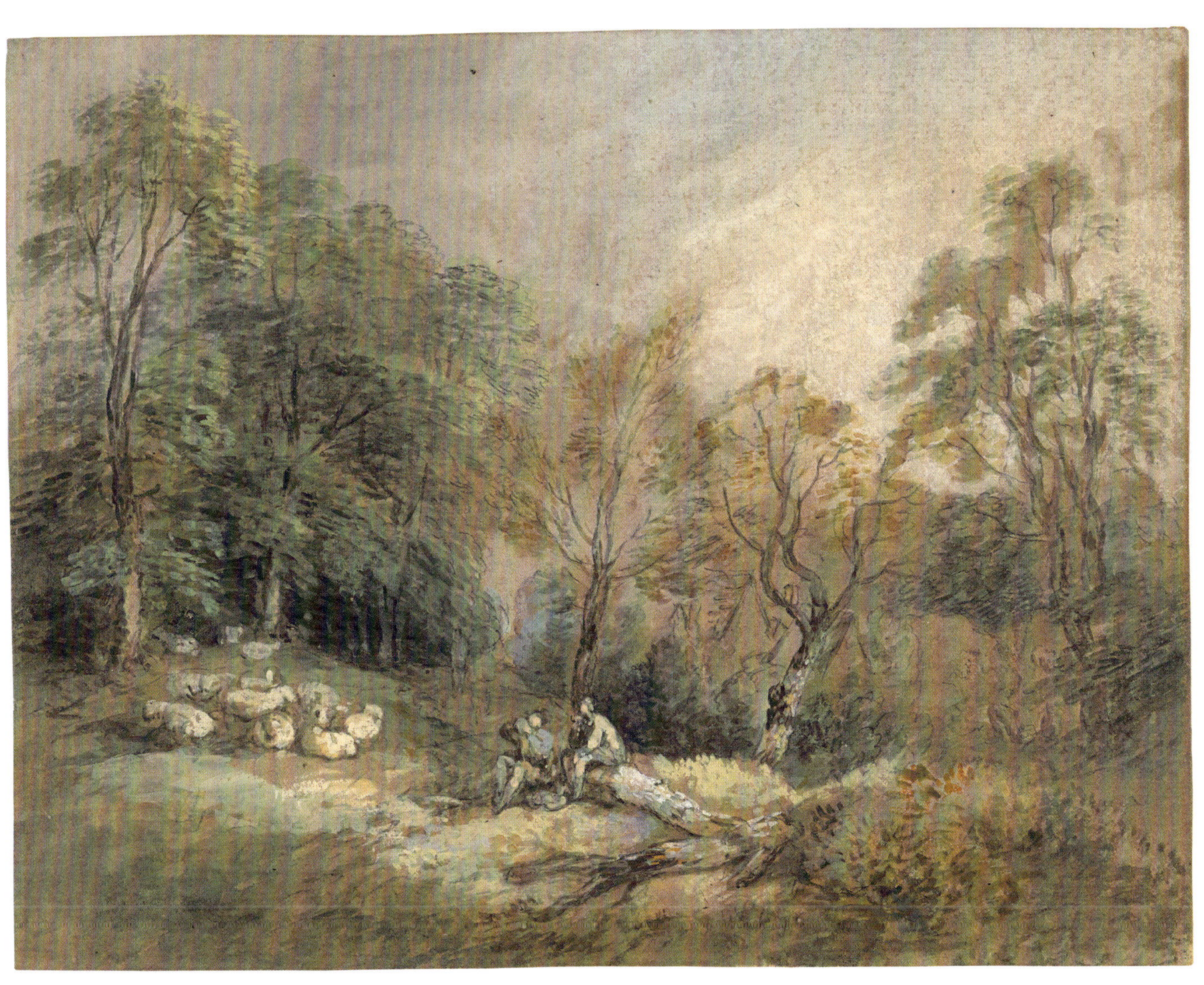

THOMAS GAINSBOROUGH

Sudbury, Suffolk 1727–1788 London

77

A Wooded Landscape with Roma Gathered around a Fire, ca. 1778–80

Pen and brown ink and wash, with white opaque watercolor, over black chalk, on brown paper
225 x 322 mm

PROVENANCE Ozias Humphry (1742–1810), London; by whom given to William Upcott (1779–1845), Islington, London, 1809; by whom given to Charles Hampden Turner (1772–1856), Rook's Nest, near Godstone, Surrey; his daughter Mary Wigram (née Turner) (d. 1883), Moor Place, Much Hadham, Hertfordshire; by descent to her grandson Alfred Money-Wigram, MP (1856–1899), Romford, Essex; his daughter Venetia Gladys Money-Wigram (1883–1963), London; thence by descent; Thomas Williams Fine Art, London; from whom acquired by Clement C. Moore, 2020

Promised gift of Clement C. and Elizabeth Y. Moore

The striking, romantic subject of this drawing, an encampment of Roma or foresters at the edge of a dark wood in the twilight, reflects the implicit narrative thread that underlies a great part of Gainsborough's work. The different elements are keenly observed: horses are being tethered for the night, a female figure stands in the firelight, and a church tower in the distant valley is picked out by the falling rays of the sun.

Gainsborough first addressed this theme in two small-scale paintings of 1753–54, one in the Fitzwilliam Museum, Cambridge;[1] the second, unfinished, at Tate Britain.[2] A third variant is known through an engraving by John Wood, dated 1764,[3] and a finished watercolor, of circa 1760–63, is in the Mellon Collection at the Yale Center for British Art, New Haven.[4] Nearly twenty years later, Gainsborough returned to the subject in a larger canvas, also at Tate Britain (fig. 77.1).[5] It is to this last work that the wonderfully preserved Moore drawing is most closely related. Its formal character supposes that Gainsborough had in mind a particular purpose for it, that of a presentation drawing. It is indeed quite different stylistically from an earlier, rapidly drawn working study for the same picture, to be found in the Mellon Collection at Yale.[6]

The elements in the Moore sheet were built up with a mixture of heavy black chalk, stump, dark gray and black inks, and his favorite "Bristol White" opaque watercolor. The figures, animals, foliage, and pond in the foreground were all fully resolved, and were executed with a degree of detail that Gainsborough reserved almost exclusively for drawings he made as gifts. In his treatment of the light, Gainsborough relied on his masterly control of the liquidity of the white pigment against brown paper to reveal differing tactile qualities. These range from staccato brilliance in the firelight, to the shimmering reflections in the leaves of the trees, to the hazy clouds catching the evening sun. The overall effect is painterly, and is

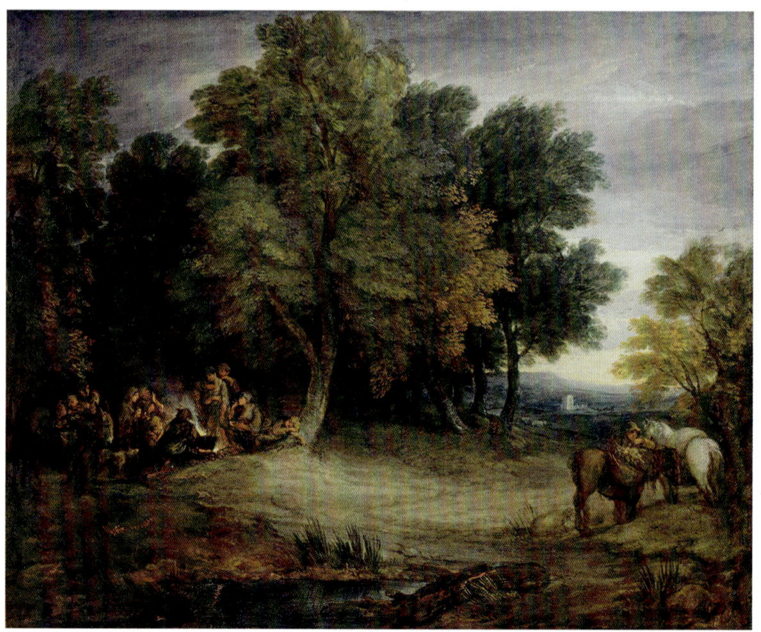

77.1 Thomas Gainsborough, *Encampment at Sunset*, 1778–80. Tate Britain, London.

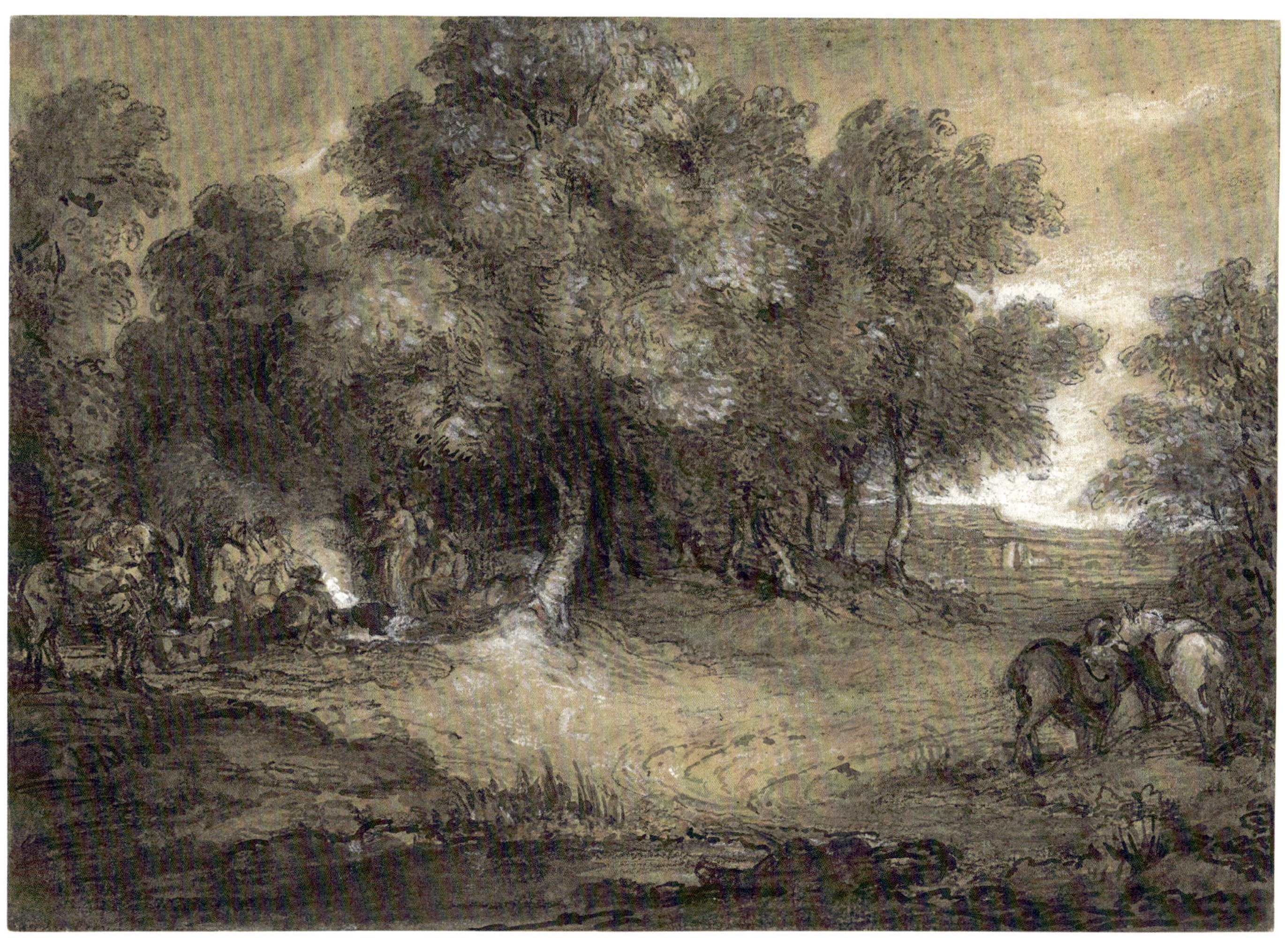

one of Gainsborough's most lyrical responses to Claude, "filled with beauty and a tender, brooding melancholy."[7]

The provenance of the Moore *Wooded Landscape* confirms its formal status. An account given by its former owner, William Upcott, states that it was made expressly for his father, Gainsborough's friend and fellow artist, Ozias Humphry.[8] Humphry was in London from 1777 to 1785, giving a precise timeframe for the execution of this work. TW

VINCENT JANSZ VAN DER VINNE

Haarlem 1736–1811 Haarlem

78

Interior of the Grote Kerk in Haarlem, Looking into the Nave toward the West, ca. 1780

Pen and black ink, with gray wash, over graphite; framing line in black ink

282 x 411 mm

INSCRIPTIONS Recto, lower right, signed, in pen and black ink (upside down): *V. V. Vinne*; verso, lower left, in pen and black ink: *Grote Kerk at Haarlem I Vincent van der Vinne*; verso, upper left, in graphite (Duits's probate inventory number[1]): Add C10/65

PROVENANCE Charles E. Duits (1882–1969), London (no mark; see L. 533a); thence by descent; acquired through Thomas Williams Fine Art, London (as Vincent Laurensz van der Vinne) by Clement C. Moore for the Baymeath Art Trust, 2013

Promised gift of Clement C. and Elizabeth Y. Moore, through the Baymeath Art Trust

The Grote Kerk (or Sint-Bavokerk), a medieval Gothic cruciform church on the Grote Markt in Haarlem, is one of the largest churches in the Netherlands. Built for Roman Catholic worship between 1370 and 1520, it was taken over by Protestants in 1578, following the Reformation. Well-known seventeenth-century masters such as Pieter Saenredam and the brothers Gerrit and Job Berckheyde drew and painted interiors and exteriors of the church.[2]

In the Moore drawing, we see the nave of the church, facing west, with wooden pews to the left and right. In the center left is the pulpit equipped with a beautiful canopy. At the end of the nave against the west wall is the large organ by the German-Dutch organ builder Christian Müller, placed in the church in 1738. At the time, it was the largest organ in Europe and was widely acclaimed. Georg Friedrich Handel came twice to Haarlem expressly for it, in 1740 and 1750. Mozart played on it extensively during his Grand Tour with his father and sister in 1766.

Most striking in this church interior is the huge number of memorial plaques, referred to as mourning boards in Dutch, affixed to the columns wherever there is room.[3] A mourning or crest board is a wooden board bearing the name, title, and coat of arms of a prominent deceased person, with the date of birth and death. Small, diamond-shaped mourning boards, as seen here at lower left, were carried in front of the coffin at burial and later placed in the church near the grave. Larger mourning boards were exclusively for hanging in the church. It was a privilege for which one had to pay handsomely. As early as the Middle Ages, coats of arms were given a place in the church, but in the period after the Reformation, until 1795, the custom became increasingly popular. For example, Job Berckheyde's 1668 painting of the *Interior of the Sint-Bavokerk* shows far fewer plaques than here.[4]

The extent to which these plaques were considered of documentary interest may be seen from a request by the well-known Amsterdam collector and printmaker

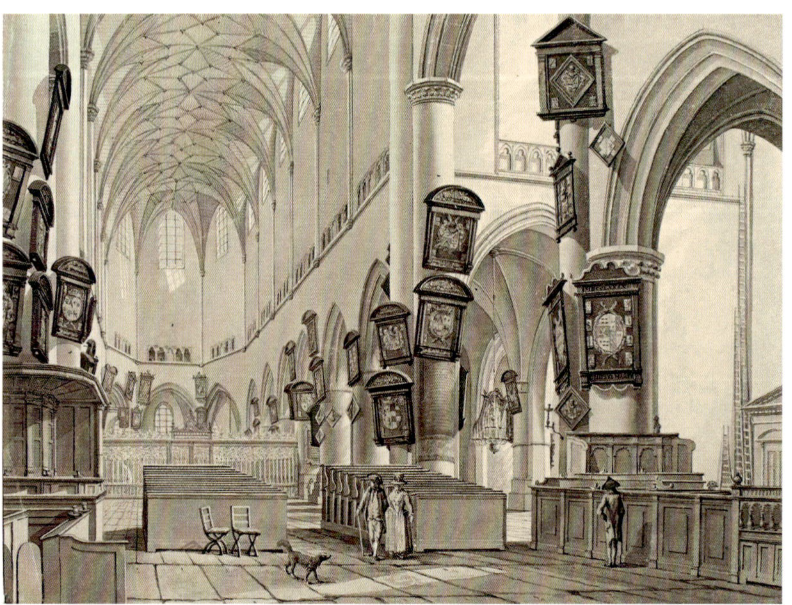

78.1 Vincent Jansz van der Vinne, *Interior of the Grote Kerk in Haarlem, Looking into the Choir*, 1789. Noord-Hollands Archief, Haarlem.

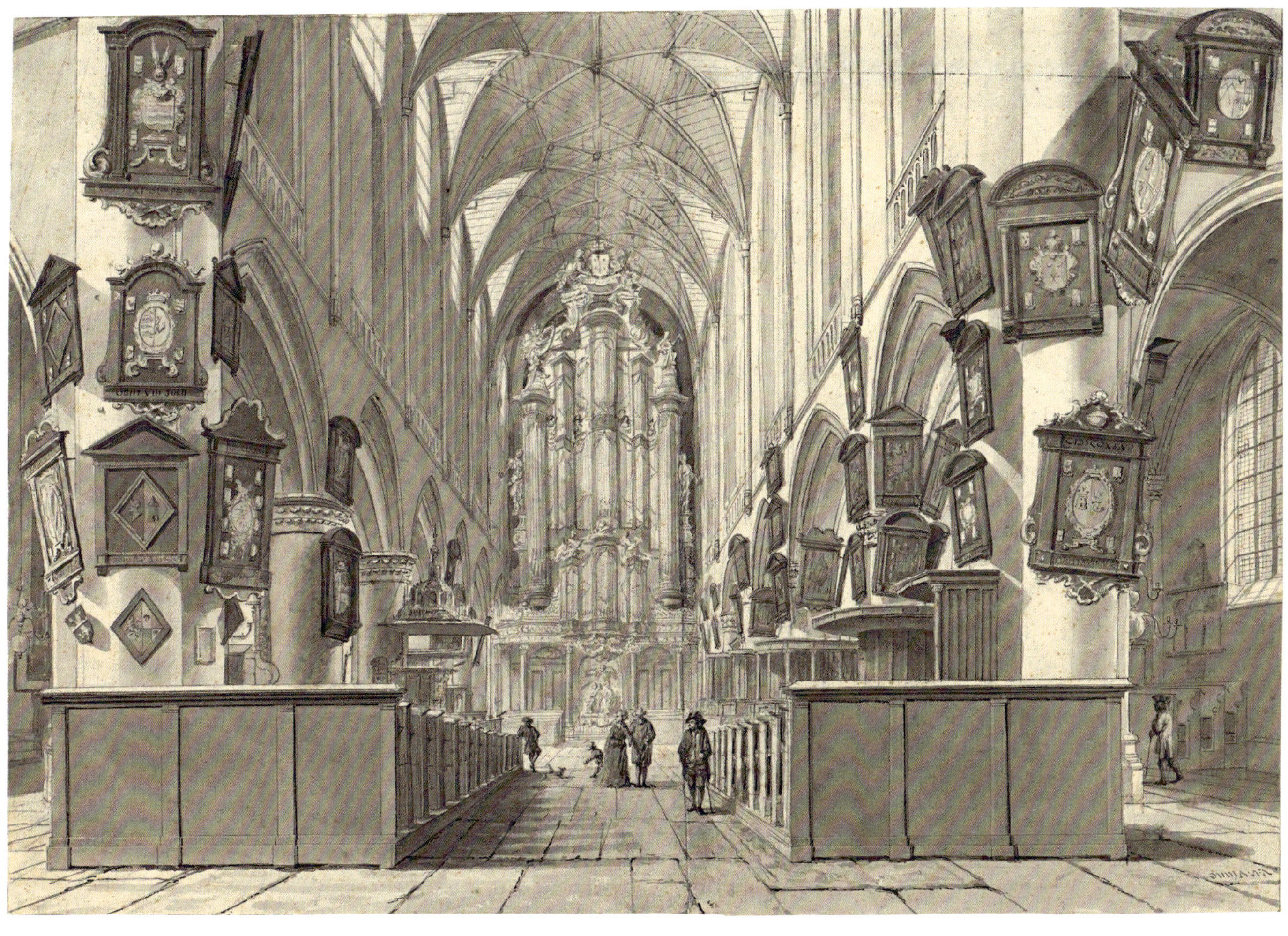

Cornelis Ploos van Amstel. Between 1793 and 1795, he asked the Utrecht artist Cornelis van Hardenbergh to record various Utrecht church interiors where funerary plaques of the Ploos van Amstel family could be found. He must have used this information to assemble his genealogical register or family tree.[5] Ploos completed the exercise just in time, because as of 1795 it was forbidden to hang funeral plaques and they were even removed. Under the notion of "Freedom, Equality, and Fraternity" in the French era, these kinds of distinctive signs and coats of arms had come to an end.

Because he occasionally signed and dated his drawings, Vincent Jansz is one of the figures with a relatively clear profile within the knotty attributions of the great Haarlem artist family Van der Vinne (see no. 65).[6] This drawing is also signed, and it joins two closely related signed interiors of the Grote Kerk by Vincent Jansz in the Noord-Hollands Archief in Haarlem, one of which is dated 1789 (fig. 78.1).[7] The Moore drawing must have been created around the same period, perhaps during the time when Vincent Jansz was *castellan* (governor) of the Teylers Foundation, which had been established in 1778. For that position, which he held from 1778 to 1785, he moved into Pieter Teyler's old residence on Damstraat, a stone's throw from the Grote Kerk; he was also responsible for Teyler's art collection in the museum and was allowed to expand it with purchases.[8] **MCP**

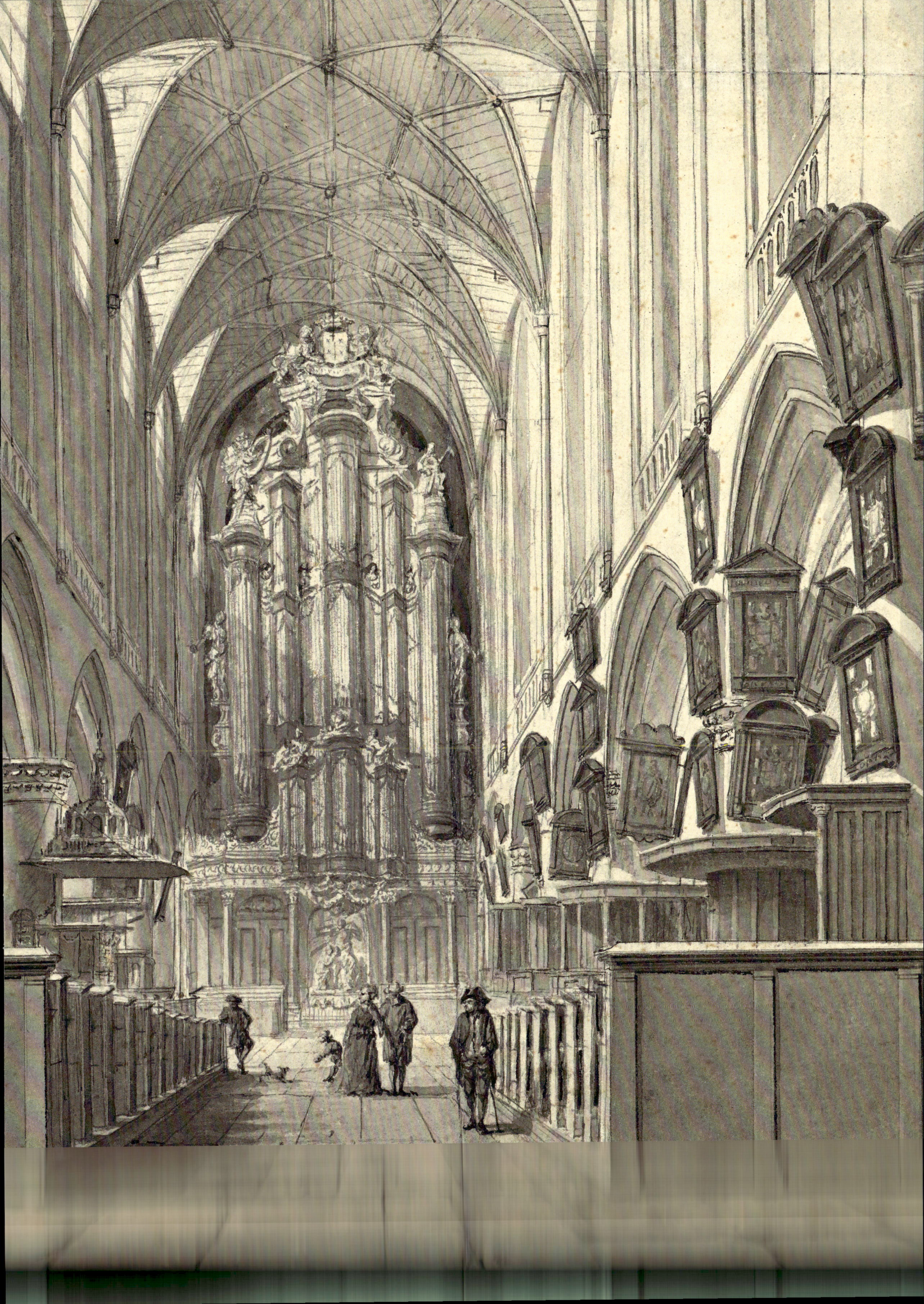

JOSEPH MALLORD WILLIAM TURNER

London 1775–1851 Chelsea

79

Study of a Mackerel, ca. 1845

Watercolor, over graphite, on hot-pressed paper
228 x 310 mm

INSCRIPTIONS Verso, center, in graphite: 12

PROVENANCE John Edward Taylor (1830–1905), Manchester; Christie's, London, 8 July 1912, lot 146; Gooden & Fox, London; Christie's, London, 4 June 1974, lot 179; where acquired by Joseph Goldyne (b. 1942), San Francisco; private collection, USA, to 2020; Lowell Libson and Jonny Yarker Ltd, London; from whom acquired by Clement C. Moore, 2020

SELECT REFERENCES London 1953, no. 134; London 1974, 98, under no. 269; Goldyne 1975, 110–11; Wilton 1979, no. 1400; Johnson and Goldyne 2006, 108–9

Promised gift of Clement C. and Elizabeth Y. Moore

This shimmering study of a single mackerel was painted by Turner toward the end of his life. It belongs to a sequence of exquisite late natural history watercolors that have long been celebrated. John Ruskin owned at least three watercolors of mackerel, seeing them as profoundly sophisticated essays on Turner's approach to the medium:

> [T]hese sketches . . . are all executed with a view mainly to colour, and, in colour, to its ultimate refinements, as in the grey down of the birds and the subdued iridescences of the fish. There is no execution in watercolour comparable to them for combined rapidity, delicacy, and precision—the artists of the world may be challenged to approach them.[1]

This study is the most successful of Turner's mackerels, capturing the qualities of speed, delicacy, and precision that Ruskin particularly admired.

Turner spent the last two decades of his life between London and Margate on the Kent coast, where he lived with the widowed Sophia Caroline Booth, who kept a lodging house facing the harbor. Margate had a profound impact on Turner's late work, providing him with pyrotechnic sunrises over water, ever-changing effects of weather, and a ready supply of fresh fish: one of Turner's depictions of mackerel is inscribed, "Sketched from Fish brought in for dinner / at Margate of which Fish Mr Turner partook for his dinner."[2] Ruskin's own notes on his drawings by Turner lists two of his mackerel studies: "study on his kitchen dresser at Margate, splendid . . . just a dash for three more. Cook impatient."[3] This gives a charming sense of the intensely personal nature of these studies.

Unlike Turner's other natural history studies, such as the ornithological drawings he made for his patron Walter Fawkes at Farnley, this watercolor of a mackerel was not a commission. This is the only study to depict a single mackerel. A similar sheet from Ruskin's collection, now in the Ashmolean Museum, Oxford (fig. 79.1),[4] shows three fish side by side, while others in the sequence show fish arranged with shrimp. As such, the present work is graphically the boldest of the group, showing one glistening fish on the page, without any extraneous details and no suggestion of the setting. This effectively transforms the study from still life to something more abstract, a pure expression of Turner's fascination with watercolor. This is an idea further underscored by Turner's choice of support, for, rather than using a sketchbook page, as in the Ashmolean study, Turner has worked directly on hot-pressed paper, which provides a less absorbent surface; on such paper, watercolor retains more of its body, producing an enameled effect. Turner sketched out the mackerel in pencil first and then applied vivid washes of green and turquoise, with dabs of pure color layered on the top to capture the iridescent quality of a freshly landed fish. **JY**

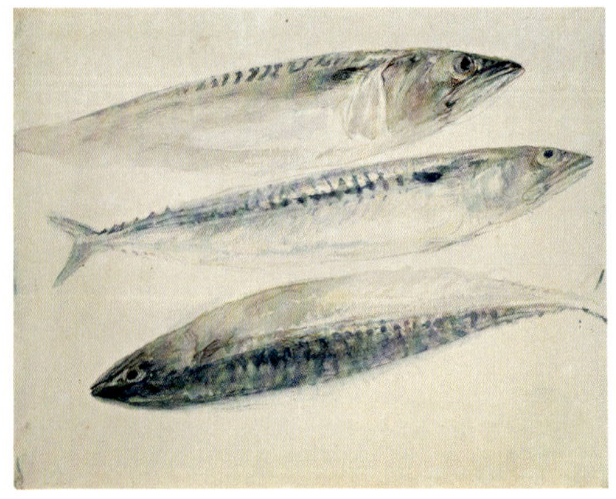

79.1 Joseph Mallord William Turner, *Sketch of Mackerel*, ca. 1835–40. Ashmolean Museum, Oxford.

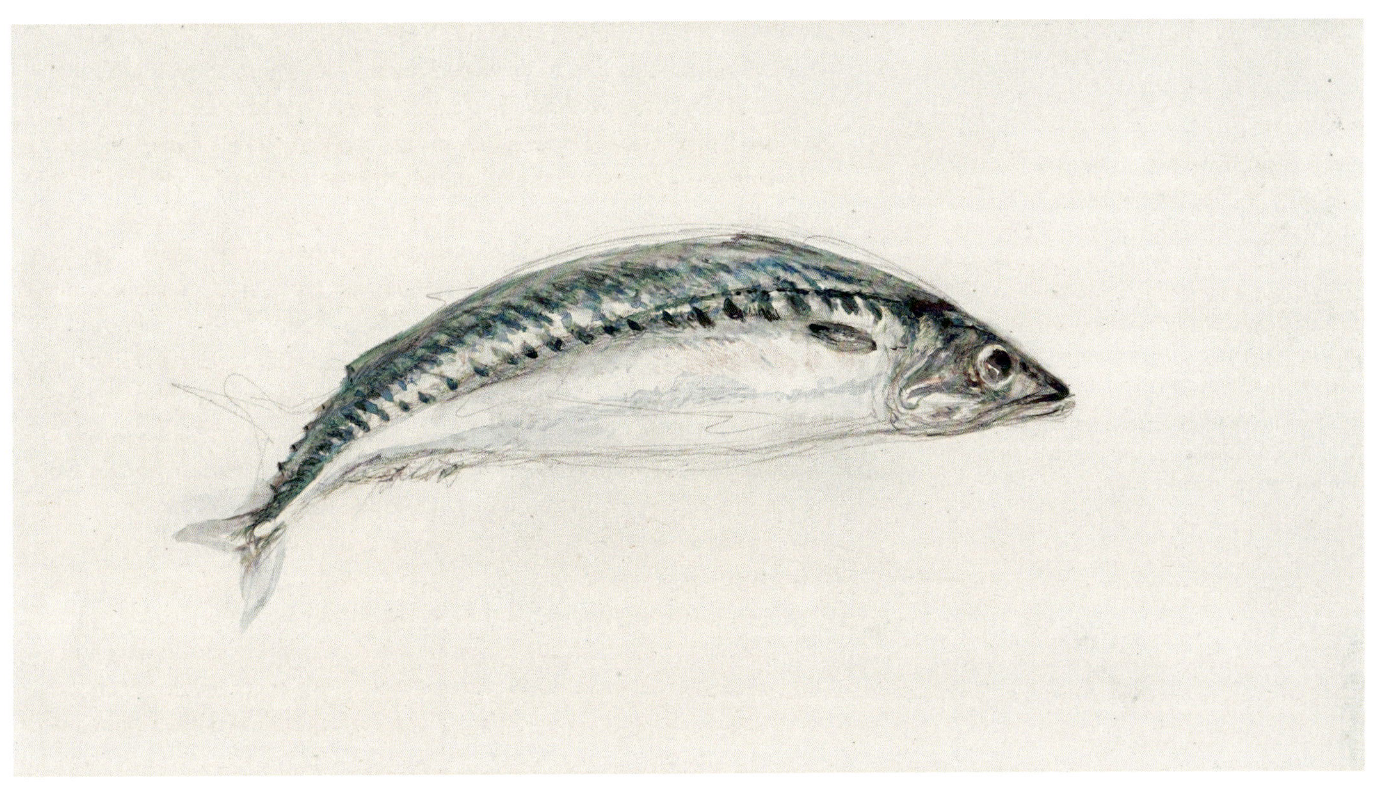

JOHN CONSTABLE *after* AERT DE GELDER

East Bergholt 1776–1837 London / Dordrecht 1645–1727 Dordrecht

80

Jacob's Dream, ca. 1830

Pen and brown ink and wash
172 x 146 mm

PROVENANCE Alan Charles Hobson (1942–2002), Kidderminster, Worcestershire; Andrew Wyld (W.S. Fine Art Ltd), London, 2010; his sale, Christie's, London, 10 July 2012, lot 83; private collection, to 2022; Lowell Libson and Jonny Yarker Ltd, London; from whom acquired by Clement C. Moore for the Baymeath Art Trust, 2022

SELECT REFERENCES Baker 2010, 625; Evans 2014, 114–15; Bergvelt and Jonker 2016, 94; Hadjinicolaou 2019, 172; Plomp 2020, 54; Bergvelt and Jonker 2021, under no. DPG126

Promised gift of Clement C. and Elizabeth Y. Moore, through the Baymeath Art Trust

In the nineteenth century, a small nocturnal composition depicting *Jacob's Dream* (fig. 80.1) was among the most beloved paintings thought to be by Rembrandt in British collections.[1] Writing in 1842, Victorian art historian and critic Anna Jameson marveled at the "wild, visionary and poetical" quality of the work, unparalleled "within the realm of creative art," while the American painter Washington Allston described it as "one of the sublimest pictures I know."[2] The work's popularity was further confirmed by its inclusion, alongside the Rijksmuseum's famous *Night Watch*, in an 1841 canvas depicting *Rembrandt in His Studio* by the English portraitist and landscapist John Scarlett Davis.[3] Even after 1880, when Jean Paul Richter and John Sparkes rejected the attribution to Rembrandt—the painting was eventually assigned to Aert de Gelder, the artist's last pupil—Edward Cook argued that "the design of the picture is intensively Rembrandtesque—in its sense of grandeur, and in its unconventional treatment of a biblical subject. Visitors who are not too much under the tyranny of names may well feel free still to study the picture carefully. None in the Gallery has been more admired by judges of repute."[4]

The "Gallery" in question was the Dulwich Picture Gallery—the oldest public art museum in England. Completed in 1815 and opened to a general audience in 1817, it was the first public institution to house a permanent collection of high-quality works of art and also served as a resource for training the new generation of painters. As part of an agreement between Dulwich and the Royal Academy, a group of six paintings was selected and sent to Somerset House each year between 1816 and 1937, for students to sketch and copy in oil.[5] A key element in the traditional academic curriculum, copying was meant to improve both the manual dexterity and the intellectual prowess of aspiring artists, thus enabling them to produce their own inventions.[6]

As a member of the Royal Academy Council in 1830 and 1831, John Constable participated in deliberations over which paintings should be borrowed from the Dulwich Picture Gallery. His own lifelong study of the old masters—from the highly faithful oil copies after Claude Lorrain's landscapes, to meticulous pen-and-ink reproductions of etchings by Jacob van Ruisdael—would have made the artist particularly well suited to the task at hand.[7] In all likelihood it was at this time that *Jacob's Dream*, then still attributed to Rembrandt, caught Constable's attention. Although the painting does not seem to have been part of the Royal Academy Council's official selection, the artist produced this small-scale rendition of the work using pen and ink and brown washes, perhaps drawing directly in front of the canvas in the gallery.[8]

Like his contemporaries, Constable fully embraced and even enhanced the visionary quality of *Jacob's Dream*. While he adhered to the overall compositional arrangement of the Dulwich original, the two angels were significantly enlarged, resulting in a greater emphasis on the relationship between Jacob and the heavenly creatures. Constable paid special attention to tonal contrasts and dramatic chiaroscuro—a feature that he particularly associated with Rembrandt's work.[9] To achieve the desired effect, the artist saturated most of the sheet with layers of wash, creating an intense contrast between the darker fields and the areas of paper left untouched, mostly around the figures. The shaft of light, which streams down

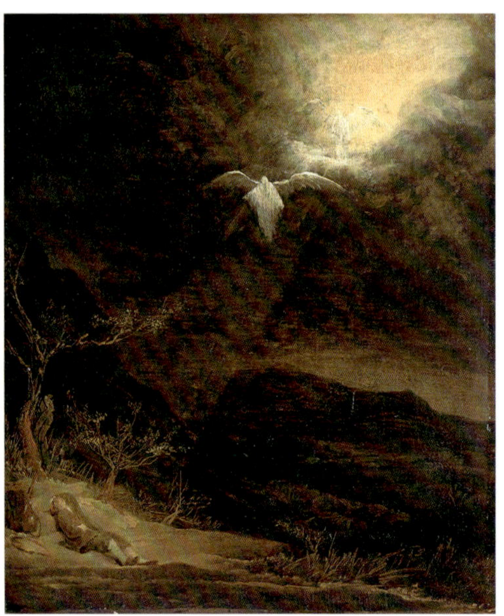

80.1 Aert de Gelder, *Jacob's Dream*, 1710–15. Dulwich Picture Gallery, London.

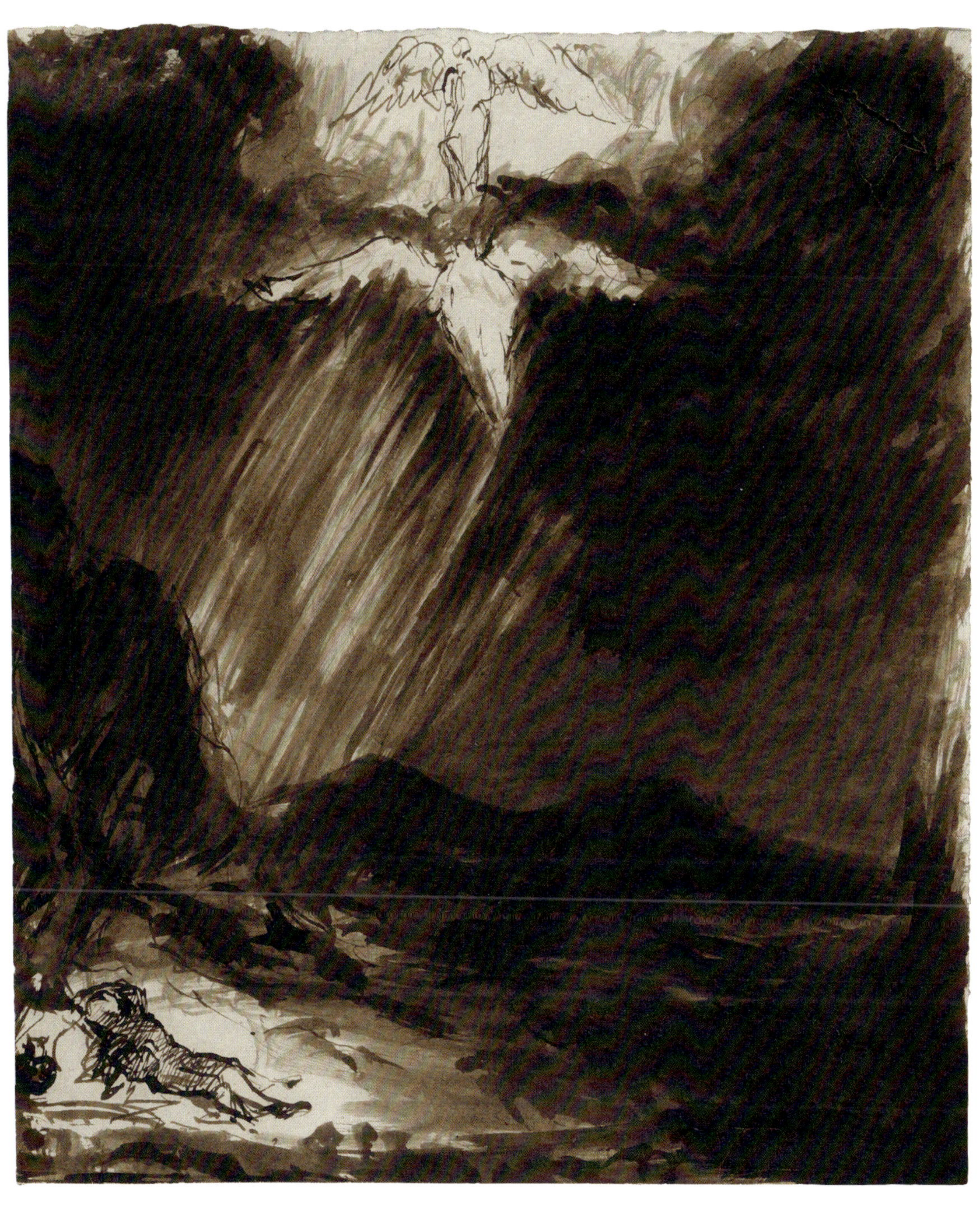

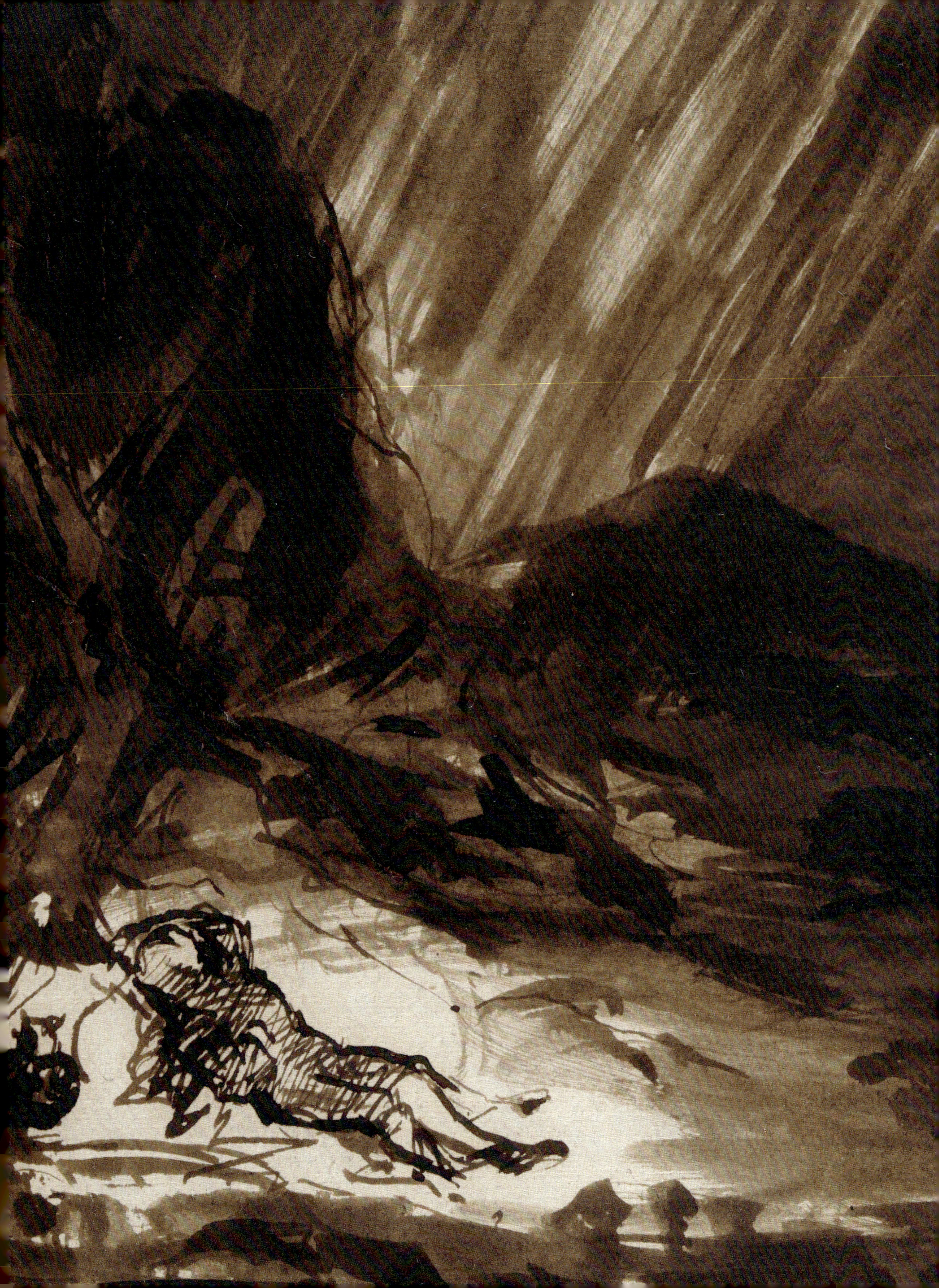

from the angels and illuminates the sleeping Jacob, was particularly masterfully rendered, with reserve paper shining through from underneath and between carefully modulated strokes of translucent wash.

As his writings suggest, Constable differentiated between a "sketch" or a "study"—a partial and more subjective record of a work of art—and a "facsimile," which was a faithful replica that could serve as a substitute for the original.[10] The present drawing clearly falls into the former category, filtering the Dutch original through the lens of Constable's late experiments in drawing. The dramatic use of tone, bold brushwork, and an almost abstract approach to landscape connect the sheet to a small group of brooding sheets from the 1830s—the final episode in Constable's long career as a draftsman.[11] AM

JOHN CONSTABLE

East Bergholt 1776–1837 London

81

A Watermill, ca. 1833–36

Pen and brown ink and watercolor, with white opaque watercolor and scratching out, over graphite
196 x 247 mm

PROVENANCE Mrs. A.F. Macfarlane; Sotheby's, London, 1 April 1993, lot 65; Sotheby's, London, 4 July 2018, lot 212; where acquired by Clement C. Moore

SELECT REFERENCES Reynolds 1996, no. 33.57

Promised gift of Clement C. and Elizabeth Y. Moore

Although watercolor is one of the techniques most closely associated with British landscape painting of the eighteenth and nineteenth centuries, it was not generally employed by John Constable, one of the greatest practitioners of British landscape. He had painted the occasional watercolor early in his career, and there is a notable set (now in the Victoria and Albert Museum) dating to his 1806 trip to the Lake District, when he was inspired by the Thomas Girtin watercolors in the collection of Sir George Beaumont.[1] The medium was not, however, one he often used until late in his career, when his practices began to shift. By 1830, he had largely given up oil paint for his plein-air sketches, and he began instead to employ watercolor both for casual sketching and in works produced for exhibition.

Many of Constable's late watercolors are based on sketches done years earlier. His watercolor of *Greenstead Mill* now in the Thompson collection, for example, was exhibited at the Royal Academy in 1833 but was based on a drawing from 1816.[2] Similarly, his watercolor of *Warwick Castle* from ca. 1830–32—recently promised to the Morgan by Jean-Marie and Elizabeth Eveillard—is based on a sketch made in 1809.[3] Yet, while the scene in the Moore drawing seems like a familiar setting in Constable's work, it does not correspond to any earlier drawing or a known place and is more likely a fantasy, a *capriccio* of the "Constable country" scenes from his beloved Suffolk, but drawn after the artist had settled in London.[4]

The building at the center of the scene has at least since 1993 been identified as a watermill, but there is something uncertain about the structure, with water issuing from a sluice in front of a house and forming a pool, but no visible mill wheel, race, or river behind. It is nonetheless difficult to imagine that Constable, after a lifetime of depicting mills, locks, and riverside cottages, would not have had some particular type of building in mind. Whether a real or imagined place, the scene is filled with anecdotal detail: a top-hatted angler (like that hidden in the bushes at the right side of the *Hay Wain*[5]), a dog lapping at the pool with its bright red tongue, birds skimming over the water, and a woman looking on from atop the sluice gate. Indeed, the drawing evokes the scene in one of the most often quoted of Constable's letters: "But the sound of water escaping the mill dams, &c., willows, old rotten planks, slimy posts, and brickwork. I love such things. . . . As long as I do paint, I shall never cease to paint such places. They have always been my delight."[6]

Depicting a bright, sunny scene, this watercolor is not as densely pigmented as some others from the 1830s, but this allows more of Constable's penwork, both underneath and atop the watercolor, to remain legible. The scraping used to create the highlights of the water, however, as well as the bright touches of red to grab and lead the eye around the scene, are familiar aspects of his later work in the medium.[7] JJM

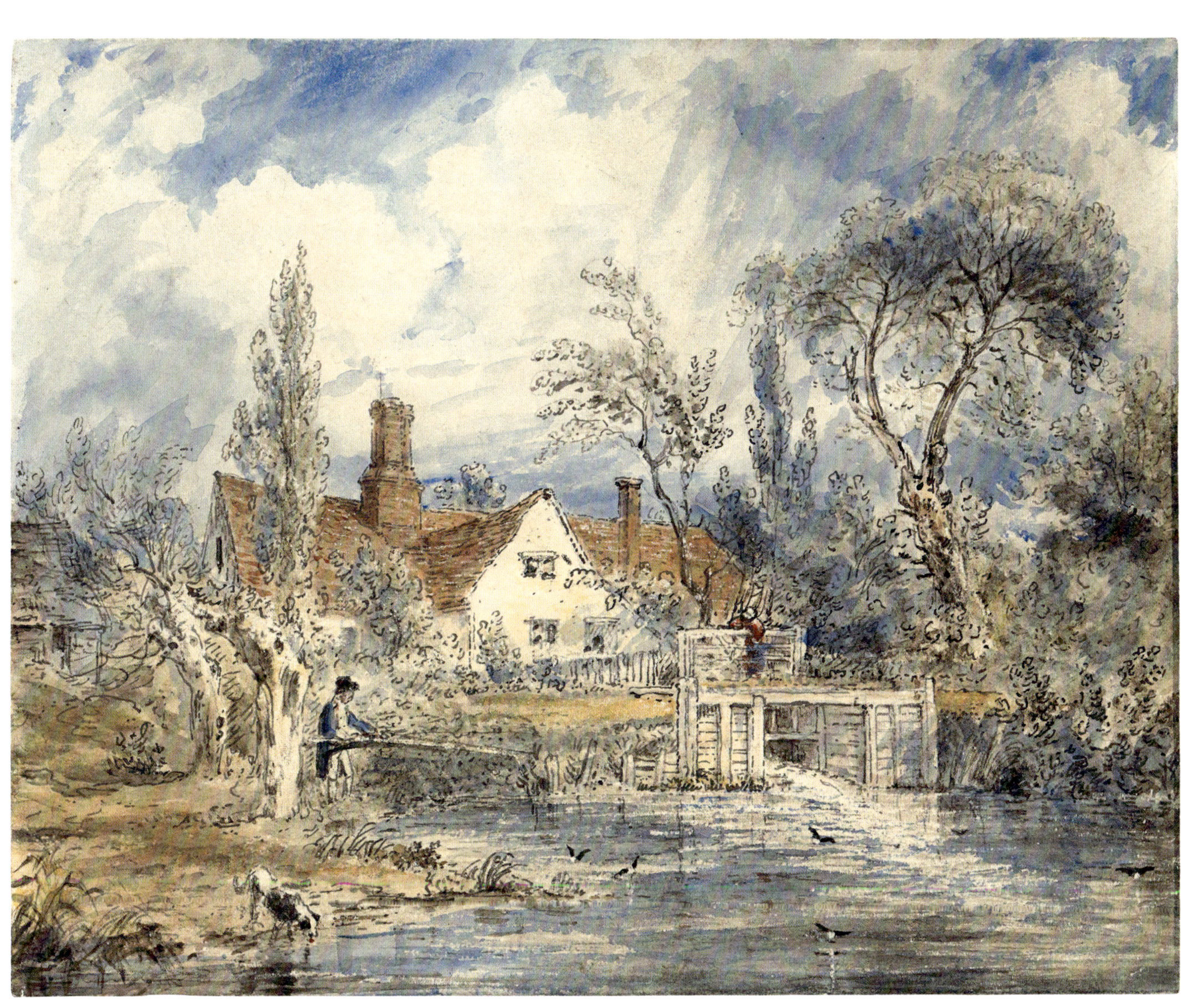

NOTES

cat. 1

1 Although the work has not been specifically identified in Crozat's sale, Py 2015, 397, n. 3, and Rosenberg 2019, no. I261, accept that it was owned by Crozat, whose drawings by Campagnola, like the present example, were those copied by Watteau.

2 On Lestevenon as the intermediate owner between Séroux d'Agincourt (who is cited as a previous owner in the Lagoy inventory) and the Marquis de Lagoy, see Moustier 2012.

3 Figure 1.1: Red chalk counterproof, 222 x 333 mm; Rijksprentenkabinet, Amsterdam, inv. RP-T-1948-141; see Rosenberg and Prat 1996, no. 252, with previous bibliography.

cat. 2

1 On Stradanus, see Baroni Vannucci 1997, Leesberg 2008, and Baroni Vannucci and Sellink 2012.

2 Figure 2.1: Pen and brown ink, with gray wash, 153 x 105 mm; Cooper Hewitt Smithsonian Design Museum, New York, inv. 1901-39-161.

3 Baroni Vannucci 1997, nos. 185 and 186.

4 Elen 2012.

5 Inv. 1901-39-146. As noted by Dorine van Sasse van Ysselt in Czére 2007, no. 31, the drawing depicts the story of Titus Sabinus as related in Pliny the Elder's *Natural History* (Book 8, Chapter 61): when Titus was imprisoned, murdered, and left on the Gemonian Steps, his dog remained faithfully by his master's side, even trying to bring food to his corpse. Cesare Ripa refers to the story in his discussion of Faithfulness in the *Iconologia*, referring back to Pliny, but mistakenly identifying the subject as Titus Labienus.

6 Dorine van Sasse van Ysselt in Czére 2007, under no. 31. The Cooper Hewitt eagle drawing is inv. 1901-39-144, and a finished version is in the Louvre, inv. 20517.

cat. 3

1 Van Mander 1604, fols. 259r–259v.

2 On Barendsz, see especially Judson 1970, although the oil sketches had not yet come to light at that date and are not accounted for there. On Barendsz and Italian art, see especially Meijer 1988.

3 Chennevières and Montaiglon, the editors of the first published edition of the *Abecedario*, recorded the offer to the Louvre, which evidently was rejected. Chennevières and Montaiglon 1851–60, 1: 66–68.

4 Foucart and Rosenberg 1978. They were able to account for seven of the drawings; further examples came to light and were discussed by Stampfle 1991, no. 28, an entry on the Morgan's other drawing from the set, *Christ Appearing to His Disciples on the Sea (Peter Sinking in the Waves)*, inv. 1985.52.

5 Many of the drawings retain their eighteenth-century French mounts, with numbers and inscriptions, but the mount of the *Ecce Homo* has been trimmed: the borders remain, but the inscriptions and numbers are gone. It might well have been number 19 in the series, following just after the *Pilate Washing His Hands as Christ Is Led Away* at the National Gallery of Art, Washington, inv. 1998.58.1, which is number 18.

6 Royalton-Kisch 1989, 15, notes that those which relate to prints have incised outlines. Hollstein, 21: nos. 201–5.

7 See, for example, Marciari 2018, 31–35.

8 Meijer 1988, 150.

9 Figure 3.1: Engraving, 234 x 199 mm; Philadelphia Museum of Art, inv. 1982-52-3265; see Hollstein, 21: no. 214 (part of a Passion of Christ series).

10 For other parallel designs by Barendsz and De Vos, see also Sadeler's engravings of *Jonah and the Whale*, after Barendsz (Hollstein, 21: no. 128, for which see Judson 1970, 36–38) and the remarkably similar drawings by De Vos (e.g. Yale University Art Gallery, New Haven, inv. 1961.65.51, for which see Boorsch and Marciari 2007, no. 21).

cat. 4

1 According to https://rkd.nl/explore/images/253955 and https://rkd.nl/explore/images/253959.

2 See Mielke 2015, nos. 277–324, and Diels and Leesberg 2005, nos. 1530–62. For other hunting prints produced or designed by Bol, see Mielke 2015, nos. 144–50, 225, 276, and 325–32. See also the drawings of hunting subjects by the artist in the Herzog Anton Ulrich-Museum, Braunschweig, inv. 167, Kl. 23; Bibliothèque Royale de Belgique, Brussels, inv. S.IV 25469; Nationalmuseum, Stockholm, inv. NMH 1880/1863; and those that appeared at auction at Christie's, New York, 24 January 2006, lot 59; Sotheby's, London, 7 July 2011, lot 10; and Sotheby's, New York, 29 January 2016, lot 452. On Bol as a draftsman, see Franz 1965.

3 Figure 4.1: Engraving, plate: 80 x 213 mm, sheet: 84 x 216 mm; Garrett Collection, Baltimore Museum of Art, inv. 1946.112.1847. Figure 4.2: Engraving, plate: 79 x 213 mm, sheet: 84 x 220 mm; Garrett Collection, Baltimore Museum of Art, inv. 1946.112.1842.

4 Mielke 2015, part 1, xciv. On hunting as a pastime and related laws in the Southern Netherlands, see Buylaert, De Clercq, and Dumolyn 2011, 403–4, and, more broadly, Liesenborghs 2005.

5 Mielke 2015, part 1, xcii.

6 Mielke 2015, part 1, xciv.

7 For this series, see Leesberg 2008, nos. 421–64. See also, with regard to Bol's emulation of Stradanus, Bok-van Kammen 1977, 71–73, and Mielke 2015, part 1, xcii.

8 Buylaert, De Clercq, and Dumolyn 2011, 403–4. See also Koslow 1996, 689.

9 Leesberg 2008, no. 479. This series is dated to ca. 1596. On Stradanus's other derivations from Bol, see Mielke 2015, part 1, xcii.

10 Mielke 2015, nos. 288 and 292; for Bol's drawing for the former, see Sotheby's, New York, 23 March 1972, lot 30.

11 For a discussion of gallows fields and their depiction in Netherlandish art, see Gobin 2021, 78–134.

12 The combination of the man lying on the ground and the figure in the tree above bears a curious resemblance to depictions of Aesop's fable about two travelers encountering a bear, one of whom climbs a tree, while the other, left to fend for himself, pretends to be dead. While the print's caption makes no reference to this story or to the notion of playing dead, it is possible that Bol's audience would have recognized the allusion.

13 Vinckboons's designs for the series are in the Berlin Kupferstichkabinett; for the wolf hunt, see KdZ 2221; for the bear hunt, see KdZ 2222. For the engravings, cut primarily by Pieter Serwouters, see Hollstein, 26: nos. 20–26.

cat. 5

1 Thanks to Nicolas Schwed for details of the provenance.

2 Orenstein 2001, 276–81.

3 The Oxford drawings represent November (inv. 199:311) and January (inv. 202:308), and the Paris sheet (inv. 6638; Boon 1992, 1: no. 167) represents June. The watermark of the Fondation Custodia sheet (Boon 1992, 2: fig. 167) is identical or nearly identical to that of the Moore drawing.

4 These seven drawings were consigned to the Paris art dealer Nicolas Schwed by a French private owner. The two acquired by the Getty Museum show the months of *March* (inv. 2016.14.1) and *August* (inv. 2016.14.2). *February* is in a private collection, London, *September* and *October* in a private collection, Amsterdam, and *December* in a Canadian private collection. Thanks to Stephanie Schrader and Nicolas Schwed for images and information about the privately held drawings.

5 Fig. 5.1: Brush and indigo ink, indigo wash, heightened with white opaque watercolor, brown ink framing lines, 212 x 310 mm; J. Paul Getty Museum, Los Angeles, inv. 2016.14.2.

6 Bleyerveld, Elen, and Niessen 2014, 102–15, no. 32, especially 108 (*May*).

7 Technical analysis of the Getty drawings, carried

out by the Getty Conservation Institute, confirmed that the pigment used is indigo. See the "Scientific Report" in the Getty curatorial files. Thanks to Michelle Sullivan and Stephanie Schrader for access to this report.

8 Ketelsen, Hahn, and Kuhlmann-Hodick 2011, 249–61. For drawings by Stradanus with extensive blue washes, see Bleyerveld, Elen, and Niessen 2014, no. 59.

cat. 6

1 Figure 6.1: Pen and brown ink, with brown and gray wash, over black chalk, 225 x 169 mm; Clement C. Moore Collection. Louisa Wood Ruby (1999, no. 22) lists the drawing as being of tentative attribution because she had not seen the work in person. When it reappeared on the art market in 2005, she confirmed the attribution, as noted in Le Claire 2005, no. 3.

2 On the paintings of the brothers Bril, with discussion of their legacy, see especially Hendriks 2003 and Cappelletti 2006.

3 Wood Ruby 1999, 43–49, and Wood Ruby 2012.

4 On Matthijs's drawings—which are often discussed in relation to those of his brother Paul—see especially Burnett 1978, Wood Ruby 1999, and Wood Ruby 2012.

5 Wood Ruby 1999, 8–9.

6 Wood Ruby 1999, 10, adopts an odd stance with regard to Muziano's influence. She writes first that "the significance of Muziano for the Brils cannot be underestimated" [given the context, this appears to be a mistaken word choice, for the sense implied is "overestimated"], but then, a few paragraphs later, she writes that "Muziano's graphic style seems to have had little effect on Paul's or Matthijs's drawings." This seems to protest matters too much, for while one can distinguish between the penwork of Muziano and Matthijs just as one can distinguish between Matthijs and Paul Bril, it is difficult to deny that Muziano was the primary reference for such landscape drawings in Rome.

7 On the Accademia under Muziano, see Marciari 2009. One of the primary concerns of the Accademia in this early period was to "care for the young artists who day after day arrive in Rome to study painting."

8 As evidence of Bril's close study of Muziano, one might cite—following Pijl 2000, 177—Matthijs's copy (British Museum, London, inv. 1895,0915.1373) after a drawing by Muziano. There are at least five versions of this drawing (also including Uffizi, Florence, inv. 831P and Morgan Library & Museum, New York, inv. 1984.54, both wrongly attributed to Remigio Cantagallina, and several in private collections). It could have been a work that Muziano allowed young artists to copy at the Accademia di San Luca, although it is also possible that the multiple copies were made later, from one of the drawings that Paul Bril allowed others to copy.

cat. 7

1 Van Mander 1604, 285v: "Ick acht niet, dat yemant so vast en veerdigh is, een beeldt, jae een gantsche Historie, uyt der handt, sonder yet te bootsen, te trecken ten eersten met de Pen, met sulcken volcomenheyt, en suyverlijck te voldoen, en met so grooten geest." Eng. trans. in Van Mander (ed. Miedema 1994–99), 1: 401.

2 Shoaf Turner 2012, no. 3.

3 See Sluijter 2000a, 22–69. For the *Metamorphoses* prints, see Leesberg 2012, 3: nos. 532–83.

4 See Sluijter 2000b, 28–30, 361–68. According to Sluijter, between 1591 and 1610 only one other episode—Perseus and Andromeda—was more frequently published in the Netherlands.

5 Owned jointly by the National Gallery, London (inv. NG 6616), and National Galleries of Scotland, Edinburgh (inv. NG 2844). See Wethey 1969–75, 3: no. 10; Wivel 2020, 158–65.

6 Figure 7.1: Engraving, 441 x 368 mm; Rijksprentenkabinet, Amsterdam, inv. RP-P-BI-6372; see Sellink 2000, 3: 75, no. 189. Cort's engraving closely follows a painted version from ca. 1566, now at the Kunsthistorisches Museum, Vienna (inv. 71); see Ferino-Pagden 2007, no. 2.3. For a further discussion of the relationship between the painting and the print, see Wivel 2020, 164–65.

7 Sluijter 2000a, 61.

8 Goltzius first used the figure of the undressing nymph at right in a print with the same subject published in 1590. See Leesberg 2012, no. 558.

9 Schatborn 1975, 142; Reznicek 1993, 236.

10 Figure 7.2: Oil on panel, 55 x 96 cm; present whereabouts unknown; see Van Thiel 1999, no. 127.

11 Inv. RP-T-00-563; see Reznicek 1961, 1: no. 111.

12 Inv. Z 2287; see Reznicek 1961, 1: no. 110.

cat. 8

1 Inv. 1963.9.73; see Van Regteren Altena 1983, 2: no. 112.

2 Figure 8.1: Pen and brown ink, 365 x 258 mm; Rijksprentenkabinet, Amsterdam, inv. RP-T-1897-A-3487; see Van Regteren Altena 1983, 2: no. 493.

3 Inv. 2006.101; previously at Sotheby's, London, 8 December 2005, lot 19.

4 Inv. 408; see Van Regteren Altena 1983, 2: no. 505.

5 Van Mander (ed. Miedema 1994–99), 1: 437, fol. 294v.

6 Van Regteren Altena 1983, 1: 101.

7 Bevers 2011, 59; Robinson and Anderson 2016, 148–50.

8 Boon 1992, 1: 159.

cat. 9

1 For the *Wapenhandelinghe, van roers, musquetten ende spiessen* (published in an English edition in 1607 with the title *The Exercise of Armes for Calivres, Muskettes, and Pikes*; see Kist 1971), Boon 1978, 1: 69–74; Van Regteren Altena 1983, 2: 64–67. For one of the preparatory drawings in the Moore collection, see Shoaf Turner 2012, no. 9.

2 Jacques de Gheyn II, *Envy*, ca. 1596, Hamburger Kunsthalle, inv. 52329; see Van Regteren Altena 1983, 2: no. 180.

3 Metropolitan Museum of Art, New York, inv. 1974.1; see Liedtke 2007, 1: no. 48.

4 Rijksprentenkabinet, Amsterdam, inv. RP-T-1898-A-3964; see Van Regteren Altena 1983, 2: no. 206.

5 Figure 9.1: Pen and brown ink, over black chalk, 190 x 181 mm; Metropolitan Museum of Art, New York, inv. 2013.645; previously at Ketterer Kunst, Munich, 23 November 2012, lot 43.

6 Examples are in the collections of the Teylers Museum, Haarlem, the Bibliothèque Royale de Belgique, Brussels, the Museum of Fine Arts, Boston, and the Staatliche Graphische Sammlung, Munich, among others. The artist's reasons for adopting this tiny format should be the subject of further research.

cat. 10

1 Elen 2011, 31–38.

2 Bolten 2017, 69; Roethlisberger 1993, 2: fig. 155.

3 For the Giroux album, see Bolten 2007, 1: 350–62, 2: nos. 1093–136. As noted by Bolten, the non-consecutive numbers indicate an "external" rather than "internal" numbering system, meant to be published in print.

4 The album in the Fitzwilliam Museum, Cambridge (inv. PD 166.1963), includes 160 drawings in an order similar but not identical to the printed first edition of the drawing book. See Bolten 2007, 1: 362–98, 2: nos. 1137–313. The present sheet includes forms seen in the Cambridge album, including nos. 13 and 18 (see Bolten 2007, 2: nos. 1162 and 1167).

5 See Roethlisberger 1993, 1: 389–420, 2: nos. T1–T174; Bolten 1993, 1–10; Fowler 2016, 17–18. For the hypothesis that Abraham's son Frederick Bloemaert was the driving force behind the drawing book, see Marquaille 2022, 182–86.

cat. 11

1 Figure 11.1: Engraving, 196 x 250 mm; British Museum, London, inv. D,7.111. B. 77; see Hollstein, 11, no. 198.

2 See www.themorgan.org/blog/drawing-print-abraham-bloemaerts-danaë-receiving-golden-rain.

3 Inv. H 260; see Unverfahrt 2000, no. 39 (as Gerrit Pietersz?); Roethlisberger 1993, 148, under no. 106 (as probably a copy); Bolten 2007, no. 492 (as Bloemaert).

4 Inv. PK-T-1894; see Roethlisberger 1993, 148, under no. 106 (as Bloemaert); Bolten 2007, fig. 492a (as a "less good" version of the Göttingen drawing).

5 Leeflang and Luijten 2003, 252.

6 Inv. M 84.191; see Leeflang and Luijten 2003, no. 103.

7 Figure 11.2: Red and black chalk, 251 x 380 mm; collection of Jean Bonna, Geneva; see Strasser 2013, no. 24.

cat. 12

1 Van Mander 1604, fols. 287r–288v. For more

information on Vroom's biography, see Keyes 1975, 1: 8–16; Alsteens and Buijs 2008, 227–32; T. van der Molen in Saur 1992–, 188–90.

2 Inv. RP-T-1903-A-4766 (pen and brown ink; 213 x 166 mm); see Keyes 1975, 1: 45–46, 129, n. 75; Boon 1978, no. 481.

3 Figure 12.1: Pen and brown ink, 137 x 210 mm; Frits Lugt Collection, Fondation Custodia, Paris, inv. 3662; see Keyes 1975, 1: 75, 130, n. 81; Boon 1992, no. 231. The connection to the Frits Lugt sheet was previously noted by Onno van Seggelen in his online entry on this drawing; see http://www.onnovanseggelen.com/.

4 Keyes 1975, 1: 47; Boon 1992, no. 231.

5 Inv. 1961.66.37; see Haverkamp-Begemann and Logan 1970, no. 443; Keyes 1975, 1: 45, 129, n. 73.

6 Boon 1992, no. 231.

7 Alsteens and Buijs 2008, 227–32. In these drawings, Vroom used the broader pen primarily for drawing the foreground, creating the illusion of depth by contrasting the thick, dark pen strokes with the finely drawn background.

8 This dating is also confirmed by the watermark in the paper, for the reference to which I thank Charles R. Johnson, Jr.

cat. 13

1 Figure 13.1: Etching, 450 x 830 mm; Rijksprentenkabinet, Amsterdam, inv. RP-P-OB-67.971; Hollstein, 14: no. 114.

2 Clement Moore informs me that, according to Jef Schaeps, a small pen-and-ink copy of this lost composition was mentioned in a letter from the Bibliothèque de la Ville d'Eaux to the Universiteitsbibliotheek Leiden, dated 4 January 1939; the copy was apparently inscribed "Copiez après le fameux Breugel qui l'avait deseignez l'an 1602 [sic, a mistake for 1612?] et qui a été gravé à Bruxelles," and described as belonging to the estate of the local Spa historian and archivist Albin Body (1836–1916).

3 Inv. 743; see London et al. 1972, 19–20, no. 14. Signed and dated *Spa Bruegel fec. adi 22 Agosto 1612.*

4 Loze and Vautier 2017, 130.

5 Figure 13.2: Pen and brown ink, with brown and gray wash, over black chalk, 139 x 212 mm; Special Collections, Universiteitsbibliotheek Leiden, inv. PK-T-AW-1006; see Gerszi and Wood Ruby 2019, no. 61. Inscribed in brown ink, at upper left, *Sauonir tot spa x 1612*; at lower center: *fonteyne om doogen te baden.*

6 Figure 13.3: Pen and two shades of brown ink, with gray wash, 108 x 158 mm; Bibliothèque Royale de Belgique, Brussels, inv. S.V. 85639; see Gerszi and Wood Ruby 2019, no. 59.

7 Figure 13.4: Oil on copper, 22.6 x 33.5 cm; Alte Pinakothek, Munich, inv. 1884/662; see Ertz 1979, no. 255; Gerszi and Wood Ruby 2019, 160.

8 Figure 13.5: Oil on panel, 52 x 90.5 cm; Kunsthistorisches Museum, Vienna, inv. Gemäldegalerie, 9102; see Ertz 1979, no. 278.

9 Oil on copper, 22.2 x 39.8 cm; see Ertz 1979, no. 307. An autograph replica of the painting appeared at Christie's, London, 7 December 2017, lot 6.

10 The same group appears in a finished compositional drawing for that painting, preserved in the Museum der Bildenden Künste, Leipzig (inv. NI.465a); see https://rkd.nl/explore/images/27003, another (signed) version of which is in the Städel Museum, Frankfurt am Main (inv. 3785 Z); see https://sammlung.staedelmuseum.de/en/work/strasse-in-einem-dorf-mit-vielen-figuren.

11 Inv. P001438; see Ertz 1979, no. 379; Gerszi and Wood Ruby 2019, 159.

cat. 14

1 I am grateful to Yvonne Bleyerveld for suggestions on the dating, provenance, and possible subject of this work. Thanks go as well to James Mundy for sharing his thoughts on this drawing.

2 The couple resembles Matham's engraving of *Venus and Adonis*, ca. 1599–1600; see Widerkehr 2007–8, pt. 2, no. 192. Other possible identities for this couple include Ceres and Iasion, as well as Paris and Oenone.

3 See Metzler 2014, 266–67.

4 See Filedt Kok 1991, 186, and Leeflang 2012, 31–33. The drawing by Zuccaro is now in the Rijksprentenkabinet, Amsterdam (inv. RP-T-1889-A-2188).

5 See Widerkehr 1999, 93–109.

6 Figure 14.1: Engraving, 224 x 299 mm; Ashmolean Museum, Oxford, inv. WA1863.5104. Carracci's print and the related painting (now in the Kunsthistoriches Museum, Vienna, inv. 2363) do not share an identical composition; Matham's drawing is closer to the former, for which see DeGrazia Bohlin 1979, no. 191. Samuel Vitali (2021, 47) suggests that Goltzius encouraged Matham to spend time in Venice, in part due to Goltzius's own exposure to Venetian art via the Carracci.

7 See Widerkehr 2007–8, pt. 1, xxxiv; pt. 2, no. 191. In the 1924 auction catalogue for the Ederheimer collection (see Provenance, above), this sheet was described as a preparatory drawing for the print.

8 Bleyerveld 2022, 31.

9 *Hunter with Animals near Brederode*, 1630, inv. D. 520; see Widerkehr 2007–8, pt. 1, xxxiv. For the dating of Matham's pen works, see Bleyerveld 2022, 31–34 (esp. 34, n. 6).

cat. 15

1 Two other drawings by Major bearing Thane's collector's mark are known: *A Mountainous Coastal Landscape with Ruins on a Cliff* (Sotheby's, Amsterdam, 18 November 1985, lot 15) and *A River Landscape with a House on a Rocky Island*, J. Paul Getty Museum, Los Angeles, inv. 88.GA.25 (Goldner and Hendrix 1992, no. 132); contrary to what was previously written about the latter drawing, the additions in watercolor are most likely made by a later hand.

2 Stockholm 1953, no. 80.

3 Spicer 1979, 289–90, n. 42b. This attribution was endorsed by DaCosta Kaufmann 1982, 178–79; and Freyda Spira in Alsteens and Spira 2012, 152–53, under no. 69.

4 Alsteens and Spira 2012, 152–53.

5 *A Woodland at the Edge of a River* (Sotheby's, Amsterdam, 2 November 2004, lot 36); *A Rugged Mountain Landscape with Figures by a Waterfall* (Sotheby's, New York, 29 January 2020, lot 3); *A Rocky Landscape with Fallen Trees in the Foreground*, previously in the collections of Walter and Hans-Ulrich Beck, Berlin (photo at the RKD); *A Rocky Landscape with an Arch*, previously with the dealer Jean Willems, Brussels (Willems 1991, no. 15); *A Hilly Landscape with a City in the Distance and A Landscape with a Waterfall and a Tower on a Cliff*, Museum Plantin-Moretus, Antwerp, inv. PK.OT.02196 and PR.OT.02192, respectively (Antwerp 1971, nos. 75–76 [as Jan Siberechts]); *A Rocky Landscape with a River and an Arch*, previously in the collection of Ludwig Baldass, Vienna (photo at the RKD); *A Rocky Landscape with Fallen Trees, A Rocky Landscape with an Arch*, and *A Rocky Landscape with a Hut on a Hillside*, Statens Museum for Kunst, Copenhagen, inv. KKSgb16503, KKSgb16504, and KKSgb16505. For most of these newly discovered drawings, I am greatly indebted to An van Zwollo, who transferred to Major photos of drawings previously catalogued at the RKD under the names of Joos de Momper, Jacob and Roelant Savery, and Jan Siberechts.

6 Only the Bremen drawing has a different size, measuring 111 x 163 mm; see Alsteens and Spira 2012, 152–53, under no. 69.

7 Hollstein, 33: nos. 8–16.

8 *A Rugged Mountain Landscape with Figures by a Waterfall* (Sotheby's, New York, 29 January 2020, lot 3) and *A Rocky Landscape with a Wooden Bridge Crossing a Waterfall*, Beaux-Arts de Paris, inv. F 355; see Hollstein, 33: nos. 8 and 14; Brugerolles and Guillet 1985, no. 125.

9 Goldner and Hendrix 1992, 298, under no. 132.

10 At least eight of the thirteen known larger drawings bear this old numbering system, including the present sheet, which is numbered "40" at the upper right corner.

11 De Jaegere 2010, 121; Spicer 1979, 52–54.

cat. 16

1 Matthew 21:8 and Mark 11:8 refer to people cutting branches. These passages describe them spreading the branches, in addition to clothing, on the ground rather than waving them. John 12:13 simply states that "they took palm branches and went out to greet him."

2 Figure 16.1: Engraving, 430 x 640 mm; Rijksprentenkabinet, Amsterdam, inv. RP-P-OB-67.525.

3 Ertz and Nitze-Ertz 2016, 260. A painting on copper that appeared at auction at Christie's East, New York, 25 November 1998, lot 83, corresponds closely to Bolswert's engraving, but this work, measuring only 24.5 x 35.5 cm and in the same orientation, is a later, reduced copy after the print.

4 Figure 16.2: Pen and brown ink, 110 x 81 mm; Teylers Museum, Haarlem, inv. KT 2008 014.

5 Bleyerveld and Veldman 2016, 237. For additional drawings related to this group that have come to light, see Bleyerveld and Veldman 2018, 32–35.

cat. 17

1 Paul Taylor, curator at the Warburg Institute, was credited with the identification in the Sotheby's catalogue.

2 Van Tuinen 2018, 21–22.

3 See, for instance. Lemeunier et al. 1980, no. G7 (a late fifteenth-century polychrome wooden sculpture of Lambert with book in left hand and crosier in right, preserved in the Musée d'Art Religieux et d'Art Mosan, Liège) and no. G10 (a late fifteenth-century polychrome wooden sculpture of Lambert with two killers at his feet, preserved at the Musée Curtius in Liège).

4 Figure 17.1: Oil on panel, 66.5 x 46 cm; private collection (previously Sotheby's, New York, 28 January 2016, lot 31); see Held 1980, no. 420.

5 The visual correspondence between the drawing and the oil sketch prompted the initial misidentification of the subject matter in the 1945 Galerie Fischer catalogue. For a discussion of Van Mildert's sculpture, executed to accompany Rubens's 1624 *Adoration of the Magi* in the church of the Sint-Michielsabdij in Antwerp, see also Sutton and Wieseman 2004, no. 13.

6 Figure 17.2: Oil on panel, 66.6 x 25 cm; Dulwich Picture Gallery, London, inv. DPG040a; see Held 1980, no. 350A. For a more recent discussion, see Lammertse and Vergara 2018, no. 9.

7 See, for example, Rubens's *Studies for a Kermis*, ca. 1630–32, British Museum, London, inv. 1885,0509.50; see Held 1986, nos. 193 and 194. With thanks to Reba Fishman Snyder, paper conservator at the Morgan's Thaw Conservation Center, for confirming that the black chalk in the *St. Lambert* is indeed applied over the pen and wash (email correspondence, October 2023).

8 Kupferstichkabinett, Berlin, KdZ 12 222; see Held 1986, no. 219; Logan 2005, no. 198. British Museum, London, inv. 1895,0915.1042; see Held 1986, no. 213.

9 I am grateful to Anne-Marie Logan who kindly shared with me that the *St. Lambert* will not be included in the third and final volume of her catalogue (see Logan 2021 and Logan and Belkin 2022 for the first two volumes), despite her previous endorsement of the attribution to Rubens (see Logan 2018). I would also like to thank Stijn Alsteens, who likewise shared his reservations and whose observations were helpful.

cat. 18

1 The artist's use of a lead white ground—which would have intensified the watercolor washes—was noted for the first time by Margaret Holben Ellis of the Morgan's Thaw Conservation Center (October 2007).

2 According to Welcker 1933. Most of the seven drawings by Hendrick Avercamp in the 1931 Huldschinsky sale came from the collection of Eduard Cichorius of Leipzig and Dresden, the friend and patron of German Nazarene artists. The Cichorius sale, scheduled to take place in Leipzig, under the supervision of C.G. Boerner, on 5–6 May 1908, was canceled (and most of the sale catalogues destroyed); a portion of the collection, including at least some of the Avercamp drawings, was purchased privately by Huldschinsky. The Cichorius provenance is not specifically mentioned for this drawing in the Huldschinsky sale catalogue, but it does not appear in any of the Boerner stock catalogues in which remnants of the Cichorius collection were later offered for sale. It is not known from what source Cichorius secured the group of Avercamp drawings. Some may have been among the 833 drawings from Avercamp's estate that were inherited by the marine painter Jan van de Cappelle.

3 Although most grasses and herbaceous plants are harvested for hay in the summer, the wagon, as the collector has observed, may have contained a native Dutch species similar to salt marsh hay or salt-meadow cordgrass (*Spartina patens*), which grows on the Atlantic coast of the United States, is harvested twice a year, is resistant to rot, and was widely used as cattle fodder in colonial times.

4 Inv. KK 4726; see Barth 1981, no. 9 (as Hendrick Avercamp); Welcker (ed. Hensbroeck-van der Poel 1989), no. T.xxxii.3 (as a copy).

5 Figure 18.1: Oil on panel, 24 x 39.2 cm; Frits Lugt Collection, Fondation Custodia, Paris, inv. 2689; see Buvelot and Buijs 2002, no. 2.

6 These differences in the fashion of men's hats were first noted by Saskia Nihom-Nijstad (1983).

7 Carlos van Hasselt (see Van Hasselt and Van Berge-Gerbaud 1989, 4, under no. 1) called attention to an individual study for this figure in the Print Room at Windsor Castle (RCIN 6489; see White and Crawley 1994, no. 263).

8 It has been suggested by Hans Buijs (see Buvelot and Buijs 2002) that the Lugt painting may have been conceived as a pair of summer/winter scenes with a painting of a *Winter Landscape with Two Men Transporting a Calf on a Sledge*, of identical format, formerly in the collection of Pieter and Olga Dreesmann, Brussels (inv. B1; see Roelofs et al. 2009, 63; their sale, Christie's, London, 3 July 2012, lot 19). Pieter Roelofs (Roelofs et al. 2009, 168, n. 121), however, has pointed out that they were painted on panels of different kinds of wood.

cat. 19

1 Clement C. Moore, "Preface," in Shoaf Turner 2012, p. x.

2 Figure 19.1: Watercolor and opaque watercolor, 183 x 293 mm; Kupferstichkabinett, Berlin, KdZ 5363; see Bevers 2002, no. 56.

3 Goldman 2012.

4 Giltaij 1976, 7, under no. 8; Leeflang and Luijten 2003, 183, under no. 65. See also Van der Grinten 1962.

5 Van Deinse 1918, 36–38.

6 Inv. N 080; see Leeflang and Luijten 2003, no. 65.1.

7 Leesberg 2012, no. 202.

8 KdZ 768; see Haverkamp-Begemann 1959, no. 35.

9 Hollstein, 4: no. 13.

10 Inv. 2001.100.4763; see Keyes 1984, no. 19 (as still in the Kendall Whaling Museum, Sharon, MA).

11 Hollstein, 23: no. 121.

cat. 20

1 Simon 1958, nos. 1, 3–4, 16, 21, 35, 36–41, 47, 49, 52, 63, and 70. See Robinson 2002, 34–35, 246, n. 3, and, for a recent discussion of the drawings in the context of working outdoors from direct observation, Yvonne Bleyerveld in Seidenstein and Anderson 2022, 39.

2 Hollstein, 38 and 39: nos. 149–60. On the series, see esp. Gibson 2000, 85–116.

3 Figure 20.1: Etching, 102 x 159 mm; Rijksprentenkabinet, Amsterdam, inv. RP-P-1879-A-3465. The primary print designs for these two etchings (neither of which features any figures) are found, respectively, in the Rijksprentenkabinet, Amsterdam, inv. RP-T-1902-A-4701E; and the Noord-Hollands Archief, Haarlem, inv. 42340.

4 Peter Schatborn in Luijten et al. 1993, 651, notes the common practice of leaving blank the foreground of print designs made from life. It is worth noting that the motif of the galloping horse in the empty middle ground features in the twelfth print in the Pleasant Places series.

5 See Koerner 2009.

6 As discussed in Peeters and Schmitz 1997, the letter A appears in a study of a farmhouse in the Gemeentearchief Amsterdam, while the same structure reappears, also accompanied by an A, in a more elaborate landscape drawing by Visscher in the Noord-Hollands Archief, Haarlem; the Haarlem drawing served as the direct model for a print, but the Amsterdam drawing seems to have informed, at least in part, the rendering of the structure in question in the print. See also a drawing in the Rijksprentenkabinet, Amsterdam, inv. RP-T-1913-6(V), in which the letter B appears at far right, directly over a structure. My thanks to Catherine Lammersen for her research into this topic.

7 See Robinson 2002, 34.

cat. 21

1 For an overview of this imagery, see Bruijnen et al. 2002.

2 The distinction with making hay, which generally takes place in July and requires longer scythes, is made clear by examining captioned prints of the theme from around the same time. See, for example, the difference represented in some of the etchings by Jan van de Velde II: Hollstein, 33–34: nos. 40–41 and 52–53.

3 Six of the drawings are in the Moore collection, for which see Shoaf Turner 2012, nos. 18a–18f. Of the remaining six, two can be found in the Rijksprentenkabinet, Amsterdam (inv. RP-T-1881-A-122 and RP-T-1881-A-123); see Keyes 1984, nos. D61 and D132; Schapelhouman and Schatborn 1998, nos. 323–24. Two others are in the British Museum, London (inv. 1895,0915.1321 and 1895,0915.1322); see Keyes 1984, nos. D110 and D167. One is in the Fitzwilliam Museum, Cambridge (inv. PD.776-1963); see Keyes 1984, no. D152. And the last, formerly in a private collection, Amsterdam,

is now in the J. Paul Getty Museum, Los Angeles (inv. 2020.13); see Keyes 1984, no. D139; Lee 2022, 39, n. 4. For illustrations of the complete set of twelve, see the aforementioned entry by Shoaf Turner 2012, 47–53, under no. 18.

4 Hollstein, 33–34: nos. 34–54 (dated 1618), 46–57 (dated 1616), and 58–70 (undated, but probably from the 1610s). For a discussion of Jan van de Velde's time-cycle imagery, see Fucci 2018, 161–98.

5 Figure 21.1: Black chalk, with brown wash and some accents in gray wash, 185 x 139 mm; Rijksprentenkabinet, Amsterdam, inv. RP-T-1881-A-122; see Keyes 1984, no. D132; Schapelhouman and Schatborn 1998, no. 324.

6 Hollstein, 33–34: no. 41: "Regnas diva Ceres, inclita, fructibus / Praefecta uberibus ab Jove caelico / Tu quae nos serimus, tu sata prosperas / En, spicas rutilo semine deprimis." My thanks to Martje de Vries and Siward Tacoma for their help with the translation.

7 See Keyes 1987 for a study of this shift in technique.

8 Figure 21.2: Black chalk, with brown and gray wash, 270 x 387 mm; Rijksprentenkabinet, Amsterdam, inv. RP-T-1880-A-95; see Keyes 1984, no. D36; Schapelhouman and Schatborn 1998, no. 321. My thanks to Charles (Rick) Johnson for confirming the precision of the watermark match using MAWI software (personal email, 5 September 2023).

cat. 22

1 See Keyes 1975, 2: 234.

2 Figure 22.1: Pen and brown ink, with brown wash, 199 x 303 mm; Victoria and Albert Museum, London, inv. D.977-1900; see Keyes 1975, no. D 22; Shoaf Turner and White 2014, no. 416.

3 Inv. RP-T-1922-15; see Keyes 1975, no. D 3; Schapelhouman and Schatborn 1998, no. 434.

4 Among those authors who have assumed that these works depict an English setting are George Keyes, Peter Schatborn, and Jeremy Wood.

5 See the detailed biography of the artist by Irene van Thiel-Stroman in Biesboer and Köhler 2006, 328–32. Her findings are misquoted in the biography of the artist on the RKD site (see https://rkd.nl/explore/artists/82219), which claims Cornelis *was* in England from 1627 to 1628.

6 This suggestion was made by Mark Broch (conversation with the author, The Hague, 15 March 2011).

cat. 23

1 Although Esdaile's inscription on the verso indicates that the drawing comes from Ottley's collection, it does not appear in the Ottley sale held at T. Philipe, London, 6 June 1814 (and following days).

2 For a brief summary of the disposition of Guercino's drawings in the seventeenth and eighteenth centuries, see Marciari 2019, 21–24; the other Morgan drawing from Peter Lely's collection (inv. IV, 168a) is no. 2 in that catalogue. For a fuller discussion of the sale of Guercino's drawings, especially those that made their way into English collections, see Turner and Plazzotta 1991, 19–27.

3 Turner 1991, no. 26.

4 For a general discussion of the problem, see Turner and Plazzotta 1991, 191.

5 The Moore drawing seems to be previously unpublished. Turner's suggestion was made to the dealer Didier Aaron. For the Uffizi landscape (inv. 421P), see Turner 2008, no. 45 (there dated to ca. 1620); for the Casa Pannini paintings of ca. 1615–17, see Benati 2019; Stone's suggestion was made in conversation with the author.

6 Gabinetto Disegni e Stampe degli Uffizi, Florence, inv. 590P; see Turner 2008, no. 46.

7 Figure 23.1: Pen and brown ink, 254 x 429 mm; Morgan Library & Museum, New York, inv. IV, 168; see Marciari 2019, no. 16.

8 See Bagni 1985.

cat. 24

1 See Ternois 1962, 251–304.

2 Figure 24.1 a,b,c: Etching, full sheet: 424 x 662 mm; Rijksprentenkabinet, Amsterdam, inv. RP-P-OB-56.826.

cat. 25

1 See Bréton, Jouslin de Noray, and Schwed 2014. In addition to the *Woman at an Embroidery Frame*, another drawing from that set (the *Pastoral Scene of a Man and a Woman, Presumed Portraits of Frederick V and Elizabeth Stuart of Bohemia*, no. 19 in the 2014 catalogue) is also at the Morgan, acquired as a joint purchase between the Morgan and Clement Moore's Baymeath Art Trust: see http://corsair.themorgan.org/vwebv/holdingsInfo?bibId=374659. A handful of drawings that were originally part of the same album or sketchbook have been sold separately over the years, including sheets in Paris (Louvre, inv. RF 54429), Berlin (Kupferstichkabinett, KdZ 2805), a private collection in Amsterdam (later donated to the Rijksprentenkabinet, Amsterdam), and two recently acquired by the British Museum, London (inv. 2023,7003.1-2) from Onno van Seggelen Fine Arts, Rotterdam. On Honthorst's drawings, see also Van der Sman 2015.

2 See Marciari 2020.

3 Nasjonalmuseet, Oslo, inv. NG.K&H.B.15597; see Van der Sman 2015, 106.

4 Kupferstich-Kabinett, Dresden, inv. C 1181; see Van der Sman 2015, 109.

5 Koldeweij 2017, 73. By contrast, another sheet from the same set of drawings, now at the Teylers Museum, Haarlem, inv. KT 2017 030 (illustrated in Koldeweij 2017, 72), does show two women sketching.

6 The *Aristotle and Phyllis* (inscribed "No. 18" at lower left) has left an offset on the verso of another drawing from the album, the *Elegant Woman at Her Toilette with Attendants* (Bréton, Jouslin de Noray, and Schwed 2014, no. 6, inscribed "No. 10" at lower left), indicating that the numbering does not reflect the original disposition of sheets in the album or sketchbook.

7 The only well-known example from the seventeenth century is Alessandro Turchi's painting in the Musée Fabre, Montpellier (inv. 806.1).

8 Honthorst's 1623 painting of Phryne and Xenocrates, now known as *The Steadfast Philosopher*, is in the Hohenbuchau Collection, on permanent loan to the Liechtenstein Princely Collections, Vaduz–Vienna; see Papi 2015, 49.

cat. 26

1 Figure 26.1: Ivory, 56.5 cm high; State Hermitage Museum, St. Petersburg, inv. 12262. The statuette (see Feuchtmayr and Schädler 1973, no. 140) has been attributed to the Antwerp sculptor Artus Quellinus the Elder and dated to the late 1630s, but, given its appearance in drawings datable to around 1620, the alternate attributions to Georg Petel and François Duquesnoy must be reconsidered.

2 Morgan Library & Museum, New York, inv. I, 232; see Van Tuinen 2018, no. 4; Logan and Belkin 2022, no. 265.

3 British Museum, London, inv. T,14.1 (Logan 2021, no. 111) and Musée des Beaux-Arts, Dijon, inv. Sup. 49D (Logan 2021, no. 112). See also Art Institute of Chicago, inv. 2019.863 (McCullagh 2010, no. 32), although Logan no longer accepts this drawing as by Rubens.

4 Musée du Louvre, Paris, inv. RF2028; see Feuchtmayr and Schädler 1973, no. 140.

5 Jordaens was admitted to the Antwerp painters' guild as a *waterschilder*, a painter in tempera and watercolor, probably reflecting some early training in those media before he worked with Rubens.

6 See, for example, the Morgan's *Portrait of a Young Woman*, ca. 1635–40, inv. 1977.42; Van Tuinen 2018, no. 17.

7 Figure 26.2: Red and black chalk, brown wash, red watercolor, and white and brown opaque watercolor, 471 x 278 mm; Harvard University Art Museums, Cambridge (MA), inv. 1932.335. This drawing has the same "C" in chalk at upper left as the Morgan study, but the drawings appear to have been separated by the end of the eighteenth century, when the now-Harvard sheet was already in the collection of Sir Charles Greville (his mark appears on the Harvard sheet, but not the present drawing).

8 Inv. VII, 7; see Feuchtmayr and Schädler 1973, no. 140.

9 Inv. P001677; see Duerloo and Smuts 2016, 248.

10 Sold Christie's, South Kensington, 7 December 2005, lot 27.

cat. 27

1 The drawing featured in C.G. Boerner's "Master Drawings and Sculpture Week" special exhibition *Old Master Drawings from the Foljambe Collection*, Trinity Fine Art, London, 28 June – 5 July 2013.

2 As noted in Moore's files and conveyed in

conversation with the present author in 2017; see Van Tuinen 2018, 23, n. 61.

3 The main difference being the presence of the figure of Zacharias in scenes of the birth of St. John the Baptist; see, for instance, Cornelis Galle the Elder after Stradanus, ca. 1603, engraving, 225 x 275 mm; Rijksprentenkabinet, Amsterdam, inv. RP-P-2005-322, in which he is seen writing in the background. In a print without Zacharias by Jacob de Weert after Maerten de Vos, ca. 1590, engraving, 108 x 93 mm; Rijksprentenkabinet, Amsterdam, inv. RP-P-OB-61.293, the inscription identifying the scene as the birth of St. John the Baptist is the only indication of the subject matter.

4 Figure 27.1: Engraving, 188 x 266 mm; Rijksprentenkabinet, Amsterdam, inv. RP-P-BI-5942; see Mielke 2011, no. 169-2(2).

5 Figure 27.2: Watercolor and opaque watercolor, red and black chalk, charcoal, red chalk with wet brush and pen and brown ink, 440 x 332 mm; Morgan Library & Museum, New York, inv. III, 170; see D'Hulst 1974, no. A396; Stampfle 1991, no. 288; Van Tuinen 2018, no. 16. The second drawing is at the Plantin-Moretus Museum in Antwerp, inv. PK.OT.00527 A.24.5. In the related painting, Jordaens eventually abandoned the oculus dome in favor of a more Baroque interior. For Jordaens's earlier experimentation with open domes in various shapes, though seen from below, see Nora de Poorter in D'Hulst, De Poorter, and Vandenven 1993, 1: nos. A84–A86.

6 My thanks to Reba Fishman Snyder, paper conservator at the Morgan's Thaw Conservation Center, for sharing her notes and UV light photos. The two strips of paper are joined at left, with the upper piece overlaid on the lower piece.

7 In the Morgan drawing discussed above, the different levels of finish between the main sheet and the additions at left and right show that Jordaens expanded the sheet during the work process.

cat. 28

1 KdZ 14125; see Bock and Rosenberg 1930, 1: 297 (as Jan van de Velde); Van Gelder 1933, no. 280 (under doubtful attributions); Van Gelder 1955, 29 (as Jan van de Velde); Fucci 2022a, 12 (as a copy after Jan van de Velde).

2 For a history of the Huis ter Kleef, see Temminck 1995 and Kuipers-Verbuijs et al. 1997, 236–39.

3 The subject of these different registers is treated more extensively in the author's PhD dissertation. See Fucci 2018, especially chap. 4, 121–60; and for the Huis ter Kleef in particular, ibid., 144–47.

4 Ampzing 1628. For the print, designed by Pieter Saenredam and engraved by Jan van de Velde, see Hollstein, 33–34: no. 423.

5 "Wie dattet heft gesicht, kan niemand seker weten / Maer hoe het is verwoest, en is noch niet vergeten / Foey Spanjaerd die ons land soo deerlyk hebt geprangd!" For an English translation of the full caption, see Schwartz and Bok 1990, 290, under no. 184, from which this fragment is also taken.

6 Fucci 2018, 144–47.

7 Hollstein, 33–34: no. 167.

8 For Jan van de Velde's many treatments of Brederode Castle, see Donkersloot 2006 and Fucci 2018, 137–44.

9 Figure 28.1: Etching, 122 x 315 mm; Rijksprentenkabinet, Amsterdam, inv. RP-P-OB-15.417; see Hollstein, 33–34: no. 189. For the series, see ibid., nos. 178–95.

10 Fucci 2022a, 14–15.

cat. 29

1 This entry is a condensed and slightly revised version of my *Master Drawings* article dedicated to the work; see Mackelaitė 2022.

2 See, in particular, two drawings in pen and brown ink, with brown wash, in the Louvre, Paris, inv. 22554 and 22552. For the development of Poelenburch's drawing style in Italy, see Chong 1987a, 4–11. (The Moore sheet first appeared on the art market in 1989, shortly after Chong's seminal study of Poelenburch's drawings was published in *Master Drawings*, and was thus not included in that article.)

3 See, for instance, *Landscape with Tobias and the Angel Raphael*, ca. 1625, Osterley Park and House, National Trust, London, inv. 773373; and *Landscape with Diana and Actaeon*, ca. 1624, Musée des Beaux-Arts, Nancy, inv. 1699. See Sluijter-Seijffert 2016, nos. 22 and 116.

4 Figure 29.1: Oil on copper, 64 x 128 mm; Portland Collection, Welbeck Estate, Nottinghamshire. For this panel, see Sluijter-Seijffert 2016, no. 97-5. For the whole cabinet, see Sluijter-Seijffert 2013.

5 Figure 29.2: Red chalk and graphite, 295 x 218 mm; Rijksprentenkabinet, Amsterdam, inv. RP-T-1954-186(V).

6 The similarities in pose were first observed when the Moore drawing was sold at Christie's, Amsterdam, in 1989.

7 Email to author, 8 November 2021. Inv. 220; see Haskell and Penny 1981, no. 34.

8 Chong 1987a, 13, and nos. 100–127, regards the red chalk drawings to be autograph and believes that they were used both as preparatory studies for paintings and *ricordi*. Sluijter-Seijffert, however, considers it more likely that the red chalk drawings "are copies after paintings, perhaps intended for use in the artist's studio," by Poelenburch and others. See Sluijter-Seijffert 2003 and Sluijter-Seijffert 2016, 190, n. 78. For a further discussion of this group, see no. 30.

cat. 30

1 Chong 1987a, 13.

2 Figure 30.1: Oil on panel, 26.5 x 34 cm; sold Auktionshaus Schwab, Mannheim, 18 April 2020, lot 400860.

3 Inv. 956; see Sluijter-Seijffert 2016, no. 149. The connections to the Mannheim and Berlin paintings were first suggested by Martin Grässle in correspondence with Clement C. Moore.

4 Sluijter-Seijffert 2003 and Sluijter-Seijffert 2016, 190, n. 78. A good example of a *ricordo* drawing is *The Rest on the Flight to Egypt*, ca. 1640; Hamburger Kunsthalle, inv. 22367, which faithfully reproduces fragments of a Poelenburch painting in a Scottish private collection. See Chong 1987a, no. 116, and Sluijter-Seijffert 2016, no. 43.

5 Chong 1987a, 13.

6 The authenticity of the landscape drawings, fully accepted by Chong, was once questioned by some scholars, such as Peter Schatborn (2001, 64–65). Three examples are in the Victoria and Albert Museum, London (inv. Dyce 424–426); see Shoaf Turner and White 2014, 195–200, nos. 147–49.

cat. 31

1 This is such a stimulating exercise that the Rijksmuseum held a conference devoted to the topic in a series of master classes for young curators of Dutch drawings, *"Second Best": Copies, Autograph Replicas, School Works, Pastiches and Fakes among 17th-Century Dutch Drawings* (9–10 September 2019), in which no fewer than eight authors of this catalogue participated.

2 A different landscape view of the Torre di Chia is preserved in a signed and dated drawing by Breenbergh (1627) in Museum Boijmans Van Beuningen, Rotterdam (inv. MB1979/T5; see Roethlisberger 1991, 93), and a painting on copper of that composition, dated by Roethlisberger ca. 1630 (Sotheby's, London, 12 December 1990, lot 41; see Roethlisberger 1991, no. 5).

3 Figure 31.1: Pen and brown ink, with brown wash, 323 x 475 mm; Beaux-Arts de Paris, inv. MAS.1576; see Roethlisberger 1969, no. 14; Schatborn 2001, 67.

4 Figure 31.2: Pen and brown ink, with gray wash, 330 x 452 mm, signed and dated, lower center, in brown ink: BB [interlaced] *f* 1624; State Hermitage Museum, St. Petersburg, inv. 18354; see Roethlisberger 1969, no. 13 (as the earliest date recorded on a drawing by Breenbergh); Brussels, Rotterdam, and Paris 1972, no. 14.

5 Inv. 9369; see Roethlisberger 1969, no. 34.

6 Inv. 2017.1.15; see Fucci 2022b, no. 8.

7 Inv. 2020.34; see Roethlisberger 1969, no. 35.

8 Inv. 63.2; see Roethlisberger 1969, no. 98; Alsteens 2015, 444.

9 Alsteens 2015, 445.

10 Communication from Clement Moore, 8 April 2023. Fucci (2022b, 57, under no. 8, n. 20), by contrast, doubted that the Moore sheet was the prototype; Roethlisberger (1969, no. 13) posited the Hermitage sheet as the earliest version, Schatborn (2001, 67) agreeing, though more cautiously.

11 Alsteens 2015, 447.

12 See Roethlisberger 1969, 18–19; Van Gelder 1971, 206.

13 Hollstein, 2: nos. 1–2 and 3.

14 Inv. 621; see https://sammlung.staedelmuseum.de/en/work/the-martyrdom-of-saint-lawrence.

15 Inv. 9363 (250 x 402 mm) and 10223 (253 x 365 mm); see Roethlisberger 1969, 18–19.

cat. 32

1 The standard catalogue of Van Dyck's drawings remains Vey 1962, although, as is often noted (see White 1960, Held 1964, or Jaffé 1991), Vey had a very conservative, restrictive view and rejected many works that others would accept. For more recent accounts of Van Dyck's creative practice, see Brown 1991, Haverkamp-Begemann 1990, and Eaker 2015.
2 Notable examples, roughly in chronological order, include the subsidiary studies on the Courtauld's *Man Reaching with Outstretched Arm* (Vey 1962, no. 14; Brown 1991, no. 5), the Chatsworth *Three Studies of Hands* for the Prado *Worship of the Brazen Serpent* (Vey 1962, no. 48); the study of a right hand holding a staff on the verso of the Ashmolean study for the *Mocking of Christ* (Vey 1962, no. 77; Brown 1991, no. 29); the detailed hand studies at the margin of the Metropolitan Museum of Art's *Study for a Portrait of a Lady* (Vey 1962, no. 188; Brown 1991, no. 78); and the powerful forearms studied on the verso of the National Gallery of Canada's *A Little Boy at His Mother's Knee* (Brown 1991, no. 82).
3 Brown 1991, 35.
4 Some mention should be made of a large group of hand studies in the Rijksprentenkabinet, sometimes attributed to Van Dyck, but rejected by Vey and largely ignored by recent scholars. This is not the place to take up the arguments for and against the attribution, but they do represent further examples of the kind of drawings that likely existed in the studio. Similarly, see the large group of hand studies by Peter Lely, Van Dyck's successor at the English court, at the Yale Center for British Art, New Haven, inv. B2016.28.1-13.
5 For the Morgan's drawings, see Stampfle 1991, nos. 267–74 and Van Tuinen 2018.
6 Figure 32.1: Oil on canvas, 314 x 245 cm; Koninklijk Museum voor Schone Kunsten, Antwerp, inv. 401; see Barnes et al. 2004, no. III.28.
7 Thomas Williams suggested the link to the Washington painting (inv. 684; see Barnes et al. 2004, no. III.37), and the 1999 Christie's sale catalogue proposed the link to the *St. Francis* (inv. 218; see Barnes et al. 2004, no. III.45).
8 Inv. 606; see Barnes et al. 2004, no. III.31.

cat. 33

1 Roethlisberger 1962, 21.
2 On Calmann, see Tonkovich 2021. In 1957, after buying at auction an album of animal studies by Claude Lorrain, Calmann learned the source for the album was an Italian art historian, Donato Sanminiatelli, who had married into the famed Odescalchi family in Rome. Calmann visited Sanminiatelli and was shown another album of Claude drawings he could not afford. The album may have contained eighty-one drawings, and Calmann acquired eight of them, which he cut from the album himself. Although Sanminiatelli assured Calmann that he would not sell the rest of the album, he must have sold separately around thirteen sheets. A few years later, Sanminiatelli sold the volume, which still contained at least sixty drawings, to Georges Wildenstein. The French dealer, in short order, sold the album to Norton Simon.
3 As Suzanne Muchnic recounts (2019, 212–13), Simon, with Eugene Thaw acting as an agent, made a deal with Agnew's in 1980 to sell for $4.42 million fifty-three sheets out of the sixty in the album that Simon had purchased in 1970 for $1 million. Simon was frustrated by not being able to show the drawings from the album easily, and in his opinion the drawings lacked broad public appeal.
4 Kimbell Art Museum, Fort Worth, inv. APx 1967.04. Roethlisberger 1968, 405, suggested that the drawing now in the Moore collection "probably represents a first study in view of the picture."
5 The *Liber Veritatis*, which entered the British Museum, London, in 1957, contains 195 drawings made between 1635 and 1682. It is now disbound and the sheets mounted individually (inv. 1957,1214.6–206). The 1677 Colonna painting is number 190 in the *Liber*.
6 Palais des Ducs de Lorraine – Musée Lorrain, Nancy, inv. 2006.0.3971; see Roethlisberger 1968, no. 1060.
7 Brady 2017, no. 10.
8 Roethlisberger 1962, no. 185, fig. 301. *The Arrival of Aeneas at Pallanteum* is number 185 in the *Liber*.

cat. 34

1 According to a note in the Duits Archive, Getty Research Institute, Los Angeles, inv. 860290. With special thanks to Casey Lee. William Clifford Duits, usually known as Clifford Duits, was the son of Charles E. Duits, the London-based art dealer and drawings collector (for whom see L. 533a and Lee 2022).
2 Figure 34.1: Black chalk, with gray wash and some pen and brown ink, 253 x 324 mm; Rijksprentenkabinet, Amsterdam, inv. RP-T-1899-A-4218; see Stefes 2018. A third drawing of the Jeruzalemkapel at the beginning of its demolition, attributed to Willem Schellinks, is in the Atlas Splitgerber Collection, Stadsarchief, Amsterdam, inv. 010001000162.
3 The details of the lean-to shanty temporarily erected alongside the chapel for its demolition slightly differ, arguing against the possibility of a joint sketching session.
4 This attribution probably comes from Clifford Duits, who owned the sheet in the previous century.
5 This attribution was suggested by Charles Dumas (annotation on a photo of the drawing at the RKD), by Stijn Alsteens (in an email to Clement Moore, 2015), and by Annemarie Stefes (in an email to the author, 24 June 2023).
6 Inv. RP-T-1893-A-2811; http://hdl.handle.net/10934/RM0001.COLLECT.64516.
7 Van Eeghen 2015.
8 Van Eeghen 2011, 194–99.
9 For example *View of the Ramparts of a Town* in the Hessisches Landesmuseum, Darmstadt (inv. AE 850) (see Van Eeghen 2011,199).

cat. 35

1 Lot 40 of the sale of Benjamin West, Christie's, London, 9 June 1820, included four unspecified landscape drawings.
2 Figure 35.1: Etching, 140 x 198 mm; Rijksprentenkabinet, Amsterdam, inv. RP-P-1902-A-22409; see Hollstein 29: no. 4.
3 Hollstein, 29: no. 5.
4 Steland 2010, 2: no. Z 1, 13.
5 Steland 2010, 1: no. G 1, 15.
6 https://rkd.nl/explore/excerpts/525290.
7 *Mayor Collection* 1875, no. 738 (pen and black ink, with brown wash, 225 x 200 mm; ex-collections "M. de Vos and William Esdaile").
8 Christie's, London, 19 April 1909, one of three in lot 20: *A Landscape, with Elijah and the Angel – from the Esdaile Collection*.
9 Sotheby's, New York, 21 January 2003, lot 64 (as Herman van Swanevelt); see Steland 2007, 167, fig. 1 (as Rousseau).
10 Christie's, London, 7 July 1995, lot 294.

cat. 36

1 See Posner 1977.
2 Gobbi 2008.
3 Stanton-Hirst 1982 provides a comprehensive discussion of this topic. A complete catalogue raisonné of the drawings of Quast is currently under preparation by Jochai Rosen of the University of Haifa, who presented an overview, "The Drawing Oeuvre of Pieter Quast (c. 1605–1647): An Assessment," at the Peck Drawings Symposium at the Rijksmuseum, Amsterdam (1–2 June 2023).
4 Stanton-Hirst 1982, 216–18.
5 On the cultural background of the *Spaanschen Brabander*, see Pollmann 2007; regarding attitudes toward the Brabant émigrés, see Janssen 2017.
6 Hollstein, 17: nos. 57–68; the Spanish Capitano himself appears as number 12 in the series.
7 Figure 36.1: Black chalk on parchment, 286 x 382 mm; Rijksprentenkabinet, Amsterdam, inv. RP-T-1898-A-3683.
8 My thanks to Laurien van der Werff and Maud van Suylen for helping to sort out the inscription.
9 A number of other examples have come to the market in recent years, including several iterations of the *Quack Doctor* of 1642 (Schwed 2020, no. 11; Christie's, New York, 29 January 2015, lot 47; Sotheby's, London, 4 July 2018, lot 138), and the *Merry Company, or Allegory of Seduction* recently sold by Onno van Seggelen to the Ackland Art Museum, Chapel Hill (inv. 2023.25).
10 Stanton-Hirst 1982, 234–36.

cat. 37

1 Before 2012 it had not been noted that the drawing's distinguished provenance also included Jonathan Richardson, Sr., and that it was laid down on one of his typical mounts of pale buff

card, surrounded by a painted gold border, double framing lines, and a thick outer line in brown ink. Although Richardson's inscription on the recto of the mount has been erased, his characteristic pressmarks appear on the verso, letters and numbers corresponding to the portfolio and location where the drawing was kept while in his collection. See James et al. 1997, 26–27.

2 Schatborn's opinion was quoted in the dealer description provided by W. Mark Brady. For the others, see the Select References above.

3 Inv. 2020.11; see Benesch 1973, 1: no. 27; Schatborn and Hinterding 2019, no. D204; Schrader 2022, 41.

4 Inv. RP-T-1889-A-2046 (see Benesch 1973, 1: no. 30; Schatborn and Hinterding 2019, no. D187); and RP-T-1889-A-2047 (see Benesch 1973, 1: no. 32; Schatborn and Hinterding 2019, no. D190).

5 Inv. 1943.3.7050; see Benesch 1973, 1: no. 24; Schatborn and Hinterding 2019, no. D212.

6 See White and Boon 1969–70 and Schwartz 1994. The beggars in Rembrandt's etchings were the subject of Schwartz 2006, an exhibition of 2006–13 based on etchings in the John Villarino collection, which was subsequently sold at Swann Auction Galleries, New York, 29 October 2019.

7 KdZ 3100; see Benesch 1973, 1: no. 10; Bevers 2006, no. 3; Schatborn and Hinterding 2019, no. D203.

8 On the role that Rembrandt's collecting played in his eventual bankruptcy in 1656, see Crenshaw 2006, chap. 5.

9 He purchased thirteen lots of prints and drawings at the sale of the portrait painter, innkeeper, actor, and art dealer Barent van Someren (1572–1632), Amsterdam, 22–29 February 1635; see Crenshaw 2006, p. 93, citing Strauss and Van der Meulen 1979, no. 1635/1; Bredius 1915–22, 3: 799; http://research.frick.org/montias, montias1#535.

10 See Gersaint 1751, 133–34.

11 See Lieure 1924–29, nos. 479–503.

cat. 38

1 The Duits notebook at the Getty Research Institute (for which see Lee 2022) indicates that this had been sold to the dealer Delius Giese by Duits, who then later reacquired the drawing.

2 Benesch 1954–57, no. 595. Sincerest thanks to John Marciari and Joanna Sheers Seidenstein for their contributions to this entry.

3 For further discussion of the possible subjects, see Royalton-Kisch 2012–, under Benesch 595 (posted 18 April 2023; accessed 7 September 2023), especially nn. 2, 3.

4 Shoaf Turner 2012, 82. See also note 14 below.

5 Acts 14:8–28.

6 Shoaf Turner 2012, 82. Rembrandt's teacher, Pieter Lastman, is known to have painted this subject at least twice, though only one canvas has been located, now in the Amsterdam Museum, inv. SA 31443.

7 Musée Bonnat-Helleu, Bayonne, inv. 1470. The drawing is a copy after Pieter Lastman's 1614 painting of the subject (whereabouts unknown), which itself draws upon Raphael's tapestry series.

8 See Acts 17:16–34.

9 Figure 38.1: Wool silk, gilt-metal-wrapped threads, 498/504 x 535 cm; Musei Vaticani, Vatican City, inv. MV.43876.0.0. For the history and import of Raphael's tapestry designs and panels, see Campbell 2002, 187–223.

10 Crenshaw 2006, 94–99, 102–104, notes that Rembrandt had numerous prints after Raphael, thought to be done by Raimondi, in his collection; and, that Rembrandt famously made a sketch and (likely) self-portrait after Raphael's *Portrait of Baldassare Castiglione*. Royalton-Kisch 2012–, also notes, "The central, bearded old man also seems persuasive as a then-current type, comparable to other street characters seen in Rembrandt's work from his Leiden period onwards (cf. Benesch 0031). Perhaps the cloak over his left arm in the manner of many a Renaissance apostle by Raphael and others gives him a historicizing accoutrement, though this is not certain."

11 Figure 38.2: Pen and ink, 180 x 207 mm; British Museum, London, inv. T,14.7; see Benesch 1973, 1: no. 138. See also Royalton-Kisch 2010 (Gerbrand van den Eeckhout, no. 1), who observed that Van den Eeckhout's drawing may have been inspired by Rembrandt's *St. John the Baptist Preaching* (Gemäldegalerie, Staatliche Museen, Berlin, inv. 828K), and related preparatory drawings (see Benesch 1973, 1: nos. 139A, 140, 141, 142, 142A, 143, and 2: no. 336). Sluijter 2015, 346–61, and Sluijter and Sluijter-Seijffert 2020, 281–99, dispute the attribution of the British Museum drawing and argue that Van den Eeckhout was not Rembrandt's pupil.

12 Musée du Louvre, Paris, inv. 22985; Staatsgalerie, Stuttgart, inv. 746; see Benesch 1973, 1: nos. 15 and 49. A similar depiction of Paul appears in the 1628 Rembrandt painting *Two Scholars Disputing*, National Gallery of Victoria, Melbourne, inv. 349-4.

13 Figure 38.3: Pen and brown ink and wash with white opaque watercolor, 189 x 167 mm; Courtauld Gallery, London, inv. D.1978.PG.186. Bevers 2010, 43, fig. 4 included this drawing in his important assessment of Van den Eeckhout's early drawings. Sluijter and Sluijter-Seijffert 2020, 291–92, dispute this attribution. Costume is another possible avenue of interpretation for this sheet. We might propose that the woman wearing a long veil (identified by Royalton-Kisch 2012–, under Benesch 595, as a *huik*, popular among Netherlandish women in the sixteenth and seventeenth centuries) could be Damaris, who upon hearing Paul's sermon converted to Christianity. Raphael included her (without veil) in the left foreground of his tapestry.

14 Bevers 2010, 43. Schatborn 1985a and Robinson 1998 discuss Rembrandt's black-chalk figure drawings from the late 1640s and early 1650s. This sheet shares qualities with those works and has been dated to around 1647. Royalton-Kisch 2012–, under Benesch 595 notes that "[a] date of around 1647 for this and many others is anchored by the closely comparable style of the documentary drawing, Benesch 0749. . . ."

cat. 39

1 Figure 39.1: Etching and drypoint on Japanese paper, 283 x 395 mm; Morgan Library & Museum, New York, inv. RvR 116 (B. 74); see Hinterding and Rutgers 2013, no. 239.

2 In a letter dated 9 February 1654, to Karel van den Bosch, bishop of Bruges, the Antwerp artist and print dealer Joannes Meyssens noted: "Vooder is alhier de raerste print van Rembrant dier wtgaet, daer Criistus de melatsche geneest, ende jck wete als datse jn Hollant diversche keeren vercocht syn 100 gul. ende meer; ende is soo groot als dit blad pampier, seer fray ende ardich, maer sy souden moeten 30 guldens costen, is seer schoon ende suyver" (Also here is the rarest [i.e., finest] print published by Rembrandt, in which Christ is healing the sick, and I know that in Holland [it] has been sold various times for 100 guilders and more; and it is as large as this sheet of [writing] paper [which was 310 x 210 mm], very fine and lovely, but ought to cost 30 guilders. It is very beautiful and pure). See Van den Bussche 1880, 358–59, and Hinterding, Luijten, and Royalton-Kisch 2000, 255–56, n. 3.

3 For a summary of the related drawings and their dating, see Bevers 2006, 140–43.

4 Figures 39.2–3: Pen and brown ink, with brown wash, 101 x 122 mm; Rijksprentenkabinet, Amsterdam, inv. RP-T-1964-127; see Benesch 1973, 1: no. 183; Schatborn 1985a, no. 21; Schatborn and Hinterding 2019, no. D86.

5 Figure 39.4: Pen and brown ink, with brown wash and some white opaque watercolor, 144 x 185 mm; Kupferstichkabinett, Berlin, KdZ 2695; see Benesch 1973, 1: no. 188; Bevers 2006, no. 40; Schatborn and Hinterding 2019, no. D87.

6 Inv. 22891; see Benesch 1973, 1: no. 185; Van Tuyll van Serooskerken 2006–7, no. 36; Schatborn and Hinterding 2019, no. D92.

7 Inv. D.1978.PG.188; see Benesch 1973, 1: no. 184; Schatborn and Hinterding 2019, no. D91. The drawing's connection with the print has been questioned by Martin Royalton-Kisch (Hinterding, Luijten, and Royalton-Kisch 2000, 78–79, under no. 61) and Holm Bevers (2006, 143, under no. 40).

8 Inv. 4713; see Benesch 1973, 5: no. 1071; Sadkov 2010, no. 321; Schatborn and Hinterding 2019, no. D90. Not all scholars, including Benesch and Schatborn, are unanimous in accepting this as a preparatory drawing for the print (see Hinterding, Luijten, and Royalton-Kisch 2000, 78–79, under no. 61).

9 Martin Royalton-Kisch, by contrast, believes that the Moore drawing comes between the Rijksprentenkabinet sheet and the Berlin drawing (see Royalton-Kisch 2012–, Benesch 0183 (posted 12 January 2015; accessed 1 August 2023), seeing a progression in the positioning of the figure's

right leg, which Rembrandt may have wished to emphasize as the "seat of her pain." In my view, the evolution of the hand gestures, and the raising of the woman's left arm in the study on the right of the Amsterdam study, are far more critical steps in the conceptualization of the woman's weakness as expressed in the final solution; he is right, however, to point out that the Moore figure's abandoned prayer gesture was recycled for the bearded man immediately above her in the etching.

10 The drawing's relationship to the print was long overlooked; a possible connection was suggested, but only tentatively, for the first time by Ludwig Münz (1952, 2: 101). That it is certainly a preparatory study for the print was first noted by Haverkamp-Begemann 1961, 15–16, in his review of the first two volumes of Benesch's corpus of Rembrandt drawings.

cat. 40

1 For a shepherdess's similar emotional reaction to a shepherd's piping, see the painting by Jacob Cuyp and Aelbert Cuyp, *Shepherd and Shepherdess in a Landscape*, ca. 1639–40, Musée Ingres, Montauban, inv. no. MI.855.10; Kettering 1983, fig. 118; Paarlberg 2002, no. 26.

2 Kettering 1983, 4, 96.

3 Kettering 1983, 20, 88–89.

4 Figure 40.1: Pen and brown ink, 125 x 124 mm; Ossolineum, Wrocław, inv. 8718; see Royalton-Kisch 2012–, Benesch 0424, as Rembrandt?/Gerbrand van den Eeckhout? (posted 17 April 2019; accessed 5 September 2023).

5 Schatborn and Hinterding 2019. Martin Royalton-Kisch (email correspondence with the author, 8 September 2023) agrees that the drawing is close to Rembrandt but not by him: "an 'almost' Rembrandt but the landscape and some other parts seem too wrong." He dates it in the mid- to late 1640s.

6 Compare Rembrandt's *Baptism of the Ethiopian Chamberlain*, *Susanna and the Elders*, and *Tobias and the Angel*, Schatborn and Hinterding 2019, nos. D118, D133, and D136, all dated by Schatborn ca. 1652.

7 Dietz and Penz 2018, 297–98, discuss the use of white opaque watercolor in drawings by Rembrandt and his pupils.

cat. 41

1 Bakker 1998, 206–44.

2 Bakker 1998, 236–38, figs. 1, 3, 4. Figure 41.1: Pen and brown ink and wash on paper; brown ink framing lines, prepared with a brown wash, 89 x 155 mm; Count Antoine Seilern Collection, Courtauld Gallery, London, inv. D.1978.PG.199; see Benesch 1973, 6: no. 1231. Not in Schatborn and Hinterding 2019.

3 Benesch 1973, 4: under no. 839. Gnann 2021, 139–40, repeats Benesch's explanation of the differences between the buildings.

4 Bakker 1998, 239.

5 Schatborn and Hinterding 2019.

6 Gnann 2021, 139.

7 Benesch 1973, 4: no. 838; Schatborn and Hinterding 2019, no. D549.

8 Figure 41.2: Pen and brown ink and brown wash, touched with white opaque watercolour and red wash, 133 x 228 mm; Staatliche Kunstsammlungen, Kupferstich-Kabinett, Dresden, inv. C1910-52; see Dittrich and Ketelsen 2004, no. 110; Schatborn and Hinterding 2019, no. D572; Royalton-Kisch 2012–, under "Not in Benesch" (posted March 2013, accessed 11 October 2023). Thanks to Martin Royalton-Kisch (emails to Armin Kunz, 20 April 2016, and to the author, 6 October 2023) for suggesting the comparison with the Dresden drawing.

cat. 42

1 The date in the auction catalogue is probably a typographical mistake; what is likely to be the companion drawing, now missing, was in a private London collection when published by Sprinzels 1938, no. 329, where it is described as "*The Horse Ferry in Westminster*, pen and black ink, 54 x 136.5 mm, signed *WH 1638*, inscribed *London* and *Lambeth*"; it later appeared on the London art market with Colnaghi in 1956 (see Colnaghi 1956, no. 1, and Volrábová 2017, no. A.III/27).

2 Turner 2010.

3 Figure 42.1: Pen and brown ink, over lead pencil, 146 x 401 mm; Barber Institute of Fine Arts, Birmingham, inv. 54.3; see Volrábová 2017, no. III/18.

4 Volrábová 2017, 29–30.

5 Garrod 1997.

cat. 43

1 Just five of the artist's surviving portrait drawings are actually dated, four executed in 1649–50, one in 1657; see Rubinstein 2008, 70.

2 Wheelock 2008, 10–11.

3 Frits Lugt Collection, Fondation Custodia, Paris, inv. 1203; see Wheelock 2008, 241.

4 Collection of the House of Lords, London; see Wheelock 2008, 239.

5 Städel Museum, Frankfurt, inv. 7150; see Rubinstein 2008, 72–73.

6 Biblioteca Reale, Turin, inv. 16365; see Rubinstein 2008, 72.

7 Figure 43.1: Black chalk with touches of pen and brown ink, 278 x 212 mm; Albertina, Vienna, inv. 8903 For the print, see Hollstein, 6: no. 10.

8 Parker 1928, 4, pl. 5 (as Van Dyck). A painted portrait, formerly in the collection of Angelica Kauffman, was twice offered for sale from the collection of Thimothée Francillon in 1816 and 1817, as a portrait of Lievens by Van Dyck. See Getty Provenance Index entry for Sale Catalog F-618. That painting cannot be identified today, and it is not possible to know if it was connected with the present drawing, the above-mentioned print by Vorsterman after Van Dyck, or neither.

9 Emilie Gordenker has observed that the costumes in these drawings are certainly consistent with English fashions of these years but are not different enough from contemporary costumes in Flanders to prove that the drawings were executed in England. Rubinstein 2008, 79, n. 10.

10 Figure 43.2: Black chalk, 234 x 162 mm; Kunstpalast, Sammlung der Kunstakademie Düsseldorf (NRW), inv. KA (FP) 5098; see Sumowski 1979–92, 7: 3668–69, no. 1645^{x}. The others in the group represent a woman who seems to be around the same age as the standing gentleman (inv. F.P. 4967; Sumowski 1979–92, 7: 3686–67, no. 1654^{x}), a younger man, standing, three-quarter length (inv. F.P. 5090; Sumowski 1979–92, 7: 3672–73, no. 1647^{x}) and a youth, depicted half-length (inv. F.P. 5087; Sumowski 1979–92, 7: 3670–71, 1646^{x}).

cat. 44

1 The finished drawing is in the Metropolitan Museum of Art, New York (inv. 61.137), the sketch in the Kupferstich-Kabinett, Dresden (inv. C 1453); see Rubinstein 2008, 75.

2 There are two signed drawings by Jan Andrea Lievens that incorporate significant landscape elements, both in the British Museum, London: *The Holy Family in a Landscape* (inv. 1836,0811.343) and *Sleeping Venus and Satyr in a Landscape* (inv. 1922,0410.3); see Rubinstein 2008, 74.

3 Figure 44.1: Pen and brown ink, 199 x 300 mm; Morgan Library & Museum, New York, inv. III, 186a. The other versions are in the British Museum, London (inv. 1847,0326.13; pen and brown ink and wash on Asian paper, 227 x 370 mm) and in the George and Maida Abrams Collection, promised gift to the Fogg Art Museum, Harvard University Art Museums, Cambridge (MA) (inv. 1.2018.101; pen and brown ink and wash on Asian paper, 223 x 370 mm); see Wheelock 2008, no. 126.

4 See, for example, the two versions of the same landscape in the British Museum and the Ames Collection; Wheelock 2008, 277–79, no. 138 (no. 138 fig. 1 erroneously reproduced as no. 137 fig. 1, on the previous page). On Lievens's use of Asian papers, see Rubinstein 2008, 75–76.

5 Robinson 2002, 144–45, no 59.

6 A further version of the composition, a copy after the drawing in the British Museum, is also in the Morgan Library & Museum, New York, inv. III, 186e.

7 Figure 44.2: Pen and brown ink, 255 x 365 mm; John and Marine van Vlissingen Art Foundation, Zeist, the Netherlands.

8 Rubinstein 2008, 75–76.

cat. 45

1 Robinson 1990, 1: xx.

2 Inv. PAG6229, PAG6250, PAG6251, PAH9366, PAI7280, and PAI7304; see Robinson 1958–74, 1: nos. 595–96, 2: nos. 1106 and 1219–21.

3 Inv. MB 1866/T 355 (PK), MB 1866/T 356 (PK), MB 1866/T 357 (PK), and MB 1866/T 387 (PK); see Robinson 1979a, 1: 120–21.

4 Christie's, New York, 25 January 2005, lot 203.
5 He died of smallpox aged only twenty while on duty in the Straits of Gibraltar on 6 March 1682.
6 For the other sheet, see Sotheby's, New York, 25 January 2006, lot 11.
7 Inv. PAH3921; Robinson 1958–74, 1: 99, no. 578.

cat. 46

1 Griffey 1997, 3–34; on the speculative mania over tulip bulbs (a phenomenon known as tulipomania), see also Krelage 1942, Dash 1999, and Goldgar 2007.
2 Figure 46.1: Pen and brown ink, 460 x 354 mm; Morgan Library & Museum, New York, inv. III, 145. Tulips became symbols, emblems for a variety of values and vices; see Segal and Roding 1994.
3 For Marrel and tulip books, see Tongiorgi Tomasi 1997, 268, 274, 276, 278–91; Bergström 1984; Alsteens and Spira 2012, 198–200.
4 Alsteens and Spira 2012, 200, n. 4.
5 Alsteens and Spira 2012, 199. This album is now in the collection of the Oak Spring Garden Library, Upperville, VA. Marrel's comments refer to tulipomania, which began in 1634 and peaked in February 1637; it is now recognized as the first economic bubble crash in market history.
6 Houbraken 1718–21, 81–82, 221, as Jakob Murel; Sandrart 1675–79, 1: 331, 339, 376, and 2: 76, 85, 88, as Moreel and Morell, among other variants.
7 In the Sotheby Mak van Waay catalogue, the lot is listed as "COLOMBYN EN WIT VAN POELENBURCH" and "A TULIP." The 2012 Sotheby's catalogue interprets this title and drawing as two types of tulips, "colombijn" and "wit van poelenburg." In my opinion, the drawing depicts one type of tulip, thus the title should be "Colombijn et wit van Poelenburg." The 2012 catalogue also suggests that the tulip might be named after Nicolaes Tulp's mother, Cornelia van Poelenburg.
8 Figure 46.2: Pencil and watercolor on parchment, 265 x 335 mm; Rijksprentenkabinet, Amsterdam, inv. RP-T-1950-266-3-2. Goldgar 2006, 184, notes, per Sam Segal, other "Poelenburg" tulip names in watercolor tulip books, including the "Poelenburg," the "Columbijn van Poelenburg," and "Columbijn met root en wit van Poelenburg."
9 Two such parchment sheets are in the collection of the Morgan Library & Museum, New York: inv. 2001.43 and 2001.44.
10 Bergström 1984, 41, 43.
11 Alsteens and Spira 2012, 200, n. 7. Teylers Museum, Haarlem, inv. T 083b.
12 My thanks to Reba Fishman Snyder, paper conservator at the Morgan's Thaw Conservation Center, for sharing with me her observations about the Moore sheet.

cat. 47

1 Houbraken 1718–21, 15 (possibly Pieter Holsteyn I), 105, 124, 309. The author would like to thank Mireille Mosler for sharing her thoughts on these drawings.
2 Morpho butterflies are a genus that comprises twenty-nine accepted species and 147 subspecies. The subspecies pictured here appears to be *Morpho helenor*.
3 Fig. 47.1: Watercolor, pen, and ink, 150 x 197 mm; Statens Museum for Kunst, Copenhagen, inv. KKSgb16520. Fig. 47.2: Watercolor, pen, and ink, 157 x 210 mm; Statens Museum for Kunst, Copenhagen, inv. KKSgb16521. Vignau-Wilberg 2013, 31, 39.
4 Lindley Library, Royal Horticultural Society, London, inv. 118. Holsteyn also produced work for Agnes Block.
5 For Ruysch, see LVR-LandesMuseum, Bonn, inv. 36.497. For Herolt, Herzog Anton Ulrich-Museum, Braunschweig, inv. D XVII H27. Drawings for the *Metamorphosis*, see plates 7 and 9. Two additional Merian drawings of morpho butterflies are in the British Museum, London, inv. Sloane 5275, fols. 7, 9, 53, 69, though Sam Segal gives fol. 69 to Dorothea Maria Henrietta Gsell. Another Merian study of a blue morpho was sold at Christie's, Amsterdam, 14 November 1994, lot 139; see also Russian Academy of Sciences, St. Petersburg, inv. 10-89-9; Print Room, Windsor Castle, Royal Collection Trust, RCIN 921162.
6 As noted by Ruud Vlek in the RKD profile for Pieter Holsteyn II, https://rkd.nl/artists/39285.
7 Nielsen 2016, 101–7.

cat. 48

1 Cornaro 1560.
2 The works of artists including Veronese (for example his *Adoration of the Virgin by the Coccina Family*, ca. 1571; Gemäldegalerie, Dresden, inv. 227), Canaletto, and Bellotto, with their depictions of the Venetian canals, are today used to compare the changing water levels over time.
3 Photograph by Dr. Camilla Pietrabissa.
4 Bert Meijer (1991, 144) was still under the assumption that Wijck might have allowed himself some creative freedom and had taken more distance as to the building than would have been possible in reality.
5 See Schatborn 2001, 117–23; Van Suylen 2020; Fucci 2022b, 202–4.
6 See Schatborn 2001, 117; in May 1644 Thomas Wijck married Trijntgen Adams in Haarlem and their son Jan was born on 29 October 1652, which might suggest that Wijck returned home earlier, prior to his sister's passing in 1653.
7 Houbraken 1718–21, 2: 16–17; "door hem zelf in Italien naar 't leven afgeteekent."

cat. 49

1 Lely's early works also show the influence of Cornelis van Poelenburch (see nos. 29 and 30). The two most likely came into contact in Utrecht, though it is also possible that Lely arrived in London during Poelenburch's time there around 1638–41.
2 At the time of its acquisition, the drawing by Lely was potentially an outlier in the Moore collection, for Lely spent relatively little of his mature career in the Netherlands, and his works had only a slight influence on those of his Dutch contemporaries. In the intervening decade, however, it has become clear not only that the Moore collection's horizons have broadened, but also that the work by Lely now anchors a strong group of works created in England by both Dutch and native English artists.
3 On Lely as a collector of drawings, see for example Dethloff 1996 and Dethloff 2018.
4 Quoted in Libson and Yarker 2018, 60.
5 Stainton and White 1987, nos. 129–37.
6 For a representative group of hand and arm studies, see the group of recently rediscovered drawings acquired by the Yale Center for British Art, New Haven, in 2016, inv. B2016.28.1-.13; discussed online at https://www.libson-yarker.com/news-and-events/news/2017-stock-catalogue-and-a-major-lely-discovery.
7 *Burlington Magazine* (1943), 188.
8 Huygens 1891, 370–71.
9 Inv. 1866,0714.34 and 1857,1114.213.
10 Inv. III, 201.
11 Inv. 1884,0726.25; see Stainton and White 1987, no. 91.
12 Figure 49.1: Black, white, and red chalk on brown paper, 386 x 311 mm; Sotheby's, London, 5 July 2016, lot 216; see Stainton and White 1987, no. 89.
13 Inv. NPG 3897.

cat. 50

1 Giltaij 1976 gives this date of 1887, but it is unclear what the basis is for Hamilton's ownership. The sheet is not included in *The Manuscripts of the Duke of Hamilton*, K.T., London, 1887.
2 Figure 50.1: Pen and brown ink, 208 x 301 mm; National Gallery of Scotland, Edinburgh, inv. RSA 478 verso; see Gustot 2008, no. D238.
3 Figure 50.2: Pen and brown ink, 201 x 314 mm; Klassik Stiftung, Weimar, inv. 5258; see Gustot 2008, no. D236.

cat. 51

1 Houbraken 1718–21, 2: 73.
2 Musée du Louvre, Paris, on loan to the Musée des Beaux-Arts, Bergues, inv. M.N.R. 586; see Schumacher 2006, 1: no. A551.
3 Figure 51.1: Oil on panel, 43.9 x 37.6 cm; Rijksmuseum, Amsterdam, inv. SK-A-1610; see Schumacher 2006, 1: no. A328.
4 Duparc and Buvelot 2009, 38–41.
5 The drawing is Teylers Museum, Haarlem, inv. P* -36; for the painting, see Schumacher 2006, 1: no. A449.
6 Figure 51.2: Black chalk, graphite, and gray wash, 143 x 202 mm; Metropolitan Museum of Art, New York, inv. 2013.144; see Buvelot and Alsteens 2013.

cat. 52

1 Previously published provenances for this drawing have listed an unnamed "Comte de Robiano, Brussels" as a former owner, but that is probably

a false conclusion based on some consignments to the 1926 sale having come from his descendants. The known collector counts in the family were Louis François de Robiano (1700–1765), François-Xavier de Robiano (1778–1836), Louis de Robiano (1781–1855), and Ludovic de Robiano (1807–1887); given the sheet's documented Northwick Park provenance in the nineteenth and early twentieth century, it is unlikely that any of these Robiano family members could have owned the sheet and passed it on to a descendant for sale in 1926.

2 On the popularity of Cuyp's work with British collectors, see Chong 2001.

3 Figure 52.1: Oil on panel, 42.2 x 63.3 cm; see Reiss 1975, no. 21 (as collection of A. Laan, Bloemendael); Chong 1992, no. 14; Christie's, London, 13 December 1996, lot 13; Christie's, New York, 19 April 2018, lot 16 [from the estate of Gerard Arnhold]. As noted by previous authors, the elements on the left side of a drawing in the Rijksprentenkabinet, Amsterdam (inv. RP-T-1967-90; see Wheelock 2001, no. 63), served as a basis for the skyline view on the left of this painting; the whole of that drawing was reused for *Evening in the Meadows*, a painting dating from shortly after 1650, now in the Norton Simon Museum, Pasadena (inv. F.1970.07.P; see Wheelock 2001, 231).

cat. 53

1 For an overview of Dutch artists in the Rhine region, see Gerson 2017, 1.3 and 1.4.

2 For the drawings that Cuyp produced during this trip, see Haverkamp-Begemann 2001, 82–83, and Kloek 2002, 34–36.

3 Haverkamp-Begemann 2001, 76.

4 For an example in the Morgan collection, see *View of the Valkhof at Nijmegen from the Southwest*, inv. I, 122, used for a painting at the National Galleries of Scotland, Edinburgh, inv. NG 2314.

5 Figure 53.1: Oil on canvas, 128.7 x 227.8 cm; Rijksmuseum, Amsterdam, inv. SK-A-4118; see Wheelock 2001, no. 42 (entry by Axel Rüger).

6 For an extensive discussion of the topography, see De Groot 2022.

7 Arthur K. Wheelock, Jr. in Luijten, Schatborn, and Wheelock 2017, 194–201.

8 For representative examples, see Wouter Kloek in Wheelock 2001, 256–59.

9 As argued in De Groot 2022, "In reality, Kranenburg, Wyler and the Cleves hills are much further apart and cannot be seen in such detail from this spot." See also Kloek 2002, 37.

10 Figure 53.2: Black chalk and graphite, 168 x 267 mm; British Museum, London, inv. 1910,0212.134; see Hind 1915–32, 3: no. 20. The connection between the present sheet and the British Museum drawing was first made in Burnett 1969, 377–78, who also raised the possibility that the Moore drawing was created in a studio context.

cat. 54

1 Mentioned by Josi 1821, 83.

2 Each described as "Een dito [fray Landschap], van denzelven [N. Berghem], hoog 7 1/2, breet 6 duim, fl. 92" to "Lamers."

3 "Een Bergagtig Landschap, op de Voorgrond een Herderinnetje, by dezelve een Schaapen een Bok, en op de tweede Grond een Herder, spelende op een Schalmy, zittende op een hoogte en by dezelve twee Schaapjes, verder een Gebouw, en in't Verschiet hoog Gebergte, met de Pen en Roet gewassen, door N. Berchem."

4 See Stefes 1997, 12, 14, 47–48: Berchem's drawn oeuvre lacks Italian sketches; instead, Dutch motifs were italianized. See also Stefes 2006, 102–3, 107. Biographical data confirm these findings: see Biesboer 2006, 21, 23–24. In recent literature, therefore, scholarly opinion has shifted against a supposed trip to Italy, a rare exception being the entry by Arthur K. Wheelock, Jr. in Luijten, Schatborn, and Wheelock 2017, 59.

5 See, for instance, Berchem's sketchbook of ca. 1644, British Museum, London, inv. 1920,0214.2; see Stefes 1997, no. I/7: fols. 64 or 55.

6 Hollstein, 1: no. 6; Biesboer 2006, no. P 78.

7 *Shepherd Seated on a Fountain and a Spinner*, Hollstein, 1: no. 8; Biesboer 2006, no. P 86.

8 Figure 54.1: Black chalk and gray wash, with incised outlines, 260 x 205 mm; Musée des Beaux-Arts et de la Dentelle, Alençon, inv. 09.64.1; see Stefes 1997, no. II/5. A companion piece in the same collection, inv. 09.65.1 (Stefes 1997, no. II/6), served as the model for Berchem's etching: Hollstein, 1: no. 12; Biesboer 2006, 124.

9 This was already stated by Schapelhouman and Schatborn 1993, 132.

10 Figure 54.2: Etching and engraving, 194 x 152 mm; Rijksprentenkabinet, Amsterdam, inv. RP-P-1904-69; see Hollstein, 1: no. 43.

11 As the verso was not rubbed with black or red chalk, we may assume that an intermediary sheet was used in the transferring process.

12 Wuestman 1996, 22; Stefes 1997, 24–25, 28.

13 Visscher made more than eighty prints after Berchem; see Wuestman 1996, 22, and Wuestman 2006a, 127.

14 It has been assumed that printed series after Berchem were composed by the engraver or the publisher from a range of motifs; see Wuestman 1996, 21–22, and Wuestman 2006a, 127. We do not know whether this applies to the present sheet that apparently was published without serial context.

15 As was mentioned by Josi 1821, 83.

16 Rijksprentenkabinet, Amsterdam, inv. RP-P-OB-31590; see Van Huffel 1921, no. 9.

cat. 55

1 For an overview of his biographical details and known work, see Schatborn 2001, 139.

2 This dating is based on a signed and dated drawing of 1646 representing the waterfalls at Tivoli in the Hamburger Kunsthalle, inv. 21807; see Schatborn 2001, 138, and Stefes 2011, no. 212. Presumably, Collaert traveled to Italy earlier, as he had his will made up on 28 September 1643 (Abraham Bredius Archive, RKD, inv. NL-HaRKD.0380.106—0009—01.C05). For the record of Collaert's will, see Stadsarchief, Amsterdam, acc. no. 56, inv. 1433, fols. 307–8.

3 Abraham Bredius Archive, RKD, inv. NL-HaRKD.0380. For Collaert's testimony of his trip to Bordeaux in 1656, see Stadsarchief, Amsterdam, acc. no. 56, inv. 14447b, fols. 1151–54.

4 Abraham Bredius Archive, RKD, inv. NL-HaRKD 0380.106—0013—01.C01. For the annotation of his admission to the asylum, see Stadsarchief, Amsterdam, acc. no. 5061, inv. 742, fol. 77.

5 Stadsarchief, Amsterdam, acc. no. 5001, inv. 1064. Collaert was buried in grave number 177, where at least four of his children had previously been interred. His wife, Petronella van der Kleij (1627–1681), a daughter, also called Petronella (1659–1689), and a son, Johannes (1667–1670), were buried in the grave beside it, number 176.

6 Inv. 58.843–47; see Gerszi 2005, nos. 52–56; Schatborn 2001, 139, 209, n. 7; Burke 1976, 384. The attribution of the present drawing to Collaert was confirmed by Peter Schatborn during firsthand inspection on 26 November 2019 (see https://www.onnovanseggelen.com/catalogue/johannes-jansz-collaert-amsterdam-c1622-1678-amsterdam-grotto-of-neptune-tivoli-c1646).

7 The watermark in the paper seems to be an exact match with a watermark found in a drawing by Jan Lievens, traditionally dated around 1665, in the Herzog Anton Ulrich-Museum, Braunschweig, inv. Z 103; see Döring 2006, no. 36; see also Schneider and Ekkart 1973, no. Z. 206; Sumowski 1979–92, 7: 3710–11. With thanks to Charles R. Johnson, Jr., who provided the overlay video of the two watermarks using a watermark imaging device (WImSy); see Johnson, Sethares, and Ellis 2021.

8 Schatborn 2001, 16–18.

9 Figure 55.1: Oil on canvas, 160 x 112 cm; Museo Nacional del Prado, Madrid, inv. P002059; see Posada Kubissa 2009, no. 99. In this painting, formerly attributed to Jan Both, the Temple of Sibyl is prominently visible against the sky at center.

cat. 56

1 Albach 1972, 114–15.

2 Figure 56.1: Oil on panel, 44.5 x 47 cm; John and Mable Ringling Museum of Art, Sarasota, inv. SN654. For more information on theater in Amsterdam, and the connection between Rembrandt and theater, see Van Sloten 2024.

3 See Bevers 2010, 50–51, for his attribution of this drawing to Gerbrand van den Eeckhout. See Sluijter and Sluijter-Seiffert 2020 for arguments against the attribution of this and other drawings to Van den Eeckhout.

4 For more on Willem Ruyter in Rembrandt's art, see Van Sloten 2024, passim.

5 Figure 56.2: Pen and brown ink, with brown wash and white opaque watercolor, on paper toned with a light brown wash, later additions in pen and

black ink, 177 x 131 mm; Rijksprentenkabinet, Amsterdam, inv. RP-T-1930-38; Benesch 1973, 1: no. 85.

6 The figure in this drawing has also been identified as a rabbi or King Ahasuerus; see Schatborn 2017. The object the figure holds in his hand is seen as a scepter or a knife, although it might as well be a short pen. How this can be connected to the role of Pharaoh is uncertain, but given the connection to Ruyter's activities on stage in 1638 and 1639, the plays that were performed, and the dating of Rembrandt's iron gall ink drawings to those years, the suggestion of Ruyter in the role of Pharaoh should be seriously considered.

7 *Josef of Sofompaneas: Treurspel*, Vondel's translation of Hugo de Groot's Latin text *Tragoedia Sophompaneas*, appeared in 1635. For a full overview of the performances of this play at the Schouwburg, see https://www.vondel.humanities.uva.nl/onstage/plays/96.

8 Albach 1972, 114–15; Bevers 2010 identified the subject as Daniel explaining the dreams of King Nebuchadnezzar. In this he follows Benesch and Valentiner, although Bevers did not mention the particular features of the architecture in the background. Nor did Jane Shoaf Turner in her entry from 2012, where the work is catalogued as an "Unidentified Historical scene." The present author follows observations already made by Albach.

9 Van Guldener 1947, 48; Albach 1972, 115.

cat. 57

1 Although this drawing was exhibited at Houthakker, the Duits notebooks at the Getty Research Institute suggest that it was already owned by Duits at the time.

2 The inscription on the verso is by an unknown hand, referred to as the "pseudo-Ploos" since the inscriptions on Doomer's drawings were once mistaken for those of collector Ploos van Amstel. Alsteens and Buijs made a compelling case that they are in the hand of the collector Jeronimus Tonneman, who first owned this sheet and many others based on the artist's 1646 travels.

3 See Jane Shoaf Turner's introductory essay, pp. 17–21, for further discussion of the journey made by Doomer and Schellinks.

4 Bibliothèque Nationale de France, Paris, Département Cartes et Plans, GE C-9034; see Boutier 2000, 86–88.

5 Figure 57.1: Engraving, with hand coloring, 534 x 920 mm; Rijksprentenkabinet, Amsterdam, inv. RP-P-1957-606-13; see Boutier 2007, no. 88.

cat. 58

1 The authenticity of the signature was doubted by Ben Broos (Walsh, Buijsen, and Broos 1994, 168).

2 Giltaij 1976, 59, under no. 101.

3 Inv. 1910,0212.174; see Hind 1915–32, 4: no. 3.

4 Inv. 9846; Walsh, Buijsen, and Broos 1994, 168.

5 Figure 58.1: Black and white chalk, on brown paper, 251 x 228 mm; Ashmolean Museum, Oxford, inv. WA1855.110; see Walsh, Buijsen, and Broos 1994, 51.

6 Oil on panel, 42.5 x 37.5 cm; Christie's, London, 15 December 2020, lot 15; see also Walsh, Buijsen, and Broos 1994, 95. Until its recent appearance on the London art market, the painting was last recorded in a sale, A.W.M. Mensing, Amsterdam, 16 October 1928, lot 36. Hofstede de Groot (1929, 145) incorrectly described the Ashmolean drawing as a copy after the painting. That the painting belonged in 1777 to "François Joseph, Duc de Caylus" (b. 1820), as suggested in the RKD entry, is incorrect. We know only that a "Duc de Caylus" was the buyer of the picture in the 1777 sale of Louis François de Bourbon, Prince de Conti, but in that year the Duc de Caylus would have been Achille Joseph Robert, Marquis de Lignerac and 2nd Duc de Caylus. (The information was corrected in the 2020 Christie's sale catalogue entry.)

7 Inv. RP-T-1931-179; see Walsh, Buijsen, and Broos 1994, no. 35.

8 Inv. 1871.178; see Walsh, Buijsen, and Broos 1994, 164.

cat. 59

1 See Gerson 1940, no. B 21; Giltaij 2017, fig. 2. In 1940 this drawing was in the collection of the artist's descendant (Gerson's co-author for genealogical details in the article), Jhr. Eltjo Aldegondus van Beresteyn, The Hague (who also owned the Moore collection's drawing by Cornelis Vroom; see no. 22).

2 Inv. KK 4760; see Gerson 1940, no. B 32; Giltaij 2017, fig. 3.

3 Inv. B 678 B; see Giltaij 2017, fig. 4.

4 Inv. RP-T-2016-96; Christie's, Amsterdam, 10 December 2014, lot 214; see Gerson 1940, no. B 5; Giltaij 1976, no. 13; Giltaij 2017, fig. 7.

5 Inv. 1836,0811.564; see Lugt 1929–33, 1: 11 (in biography of Beresteyn); Gerson 1940, no. B 24.

6 His opinion was based on first-hand inspection of the original in Rotterdam on 1 October 2015.

7 See https://www.onnovanseggelen.com/catalogue/claes-van-beresteyn-harlem-1629-1684-harlem-study-of-a-truncated-willow-tree-c-1650: "... de enige met het motief van een alleen staande boom."

8 Figure 59.1: Pen and brown ink, 160 x 124 mm; Bassenge, Berlin, 27 May 2016, lot 6528.

9 Figure 59.2: Etching, 88 x 161 mm; Rijksprentenkabinet, Amsterdam, inv. RP-P-BI-1054; see Gerson 1940, no. 3, pl. 11; Hollstein, 2: no. 38.

cat. 60

1 "Den wegh, om zeker en gewis in het ordineeren te worden, is, datmen zich geweene veel Schetsen te maken, en veel Historien op 't papier te teyckenen. ... Schets en herschets, en speel de histroyen, en yder personadie eerst in uw gedachten; ... en laet niet af voor gy een aerdige ordening hebt uitgevonden" (The way to become certain and assured in composition is that one should become accustomed to making many sketches and drawing many histories on paper.... Sketch and sketch again and play out the history first in your thoughts, and don't give up until you have invented a pleasing composition). Van Hoogstraten 1678, 191–92.

2 Arnold Houbraken, who was a pupil of Van Hoogstraten, wrote in his biography of his master: "'T is gebeurt dat een van zyn discipelen de schets van zyn ordonantie qelyk ieder alle week doen moest aan hem vertoonde..." (It happened that one of his [i.e., Van Hoogstraten's] pupils showed him the sketch of his composition [the type each of them had to do weekly]..."). Houbraken 1718–21, 2: 162.

3 Drawings in this group include Sumowski 1979–92, 5: nos. 1108–9, 1111–15, 1175x–1184x, 1187x–1191x, 1193x–1194x, 1196x–1198x, 1200x, 1202x, 1202ax–1204x, 1207x, and 1208x.

4 Van Hoogstraten's brother Jan was his pupil at this period, and it is possible that Nicolaes Maes and Jacobus Leveck also studied with him before they joined Rembrandt's workshop; Roscam-Abbing 1993, 10, 40–41.

5 Figure 60.1: Pen and brush and brown ink, white opaque watercolor; partial, arch-shaped framing line in pen and brush in brown ink; signed and dated, lower right, in light brown ink, "S v Hoogstraten 1649," 248 x 185 mm; Herzog Anton Ulrich-Museum, Braunschweig, inv. Z 335; see Sumowski 1979–92, 5: no. 1108; Döring 2006, no. 18.

6 Figure 60.2: Pen and brown ink, with gray wash, the outlines of the figure of the angel scraped, 158 x 155 mm; Morgan Library & Museum, New York, inv. I, 215; see Shoaf Turner 2006, no. 106 (text by Felice Stampfle, with the suggestion that the Moore drawing is possibly not by Van Hoogstraten but a copy after a lost original by him). Hofstede de Groot 1906a, no. 1079, describes an *Annunciation* by Van Hoogstraten in the Esdaile collection, which must be the Morgan copy, and not the Moore original as has been sometimes thought.

cat. 61

1 Though presented by C.G. Boerner in 1962 as by Siberechts, when the drawing was sold at auction in 2009, the attribution was not maintained. Shortly after this, when Thomas Williams acquired the drawing believing it to be by Siberechts, he showed it to the present author, whom he knew to have worked on the artist. At the time, I felt the similarities with two drawings then attributed to Gillis Neyts (in Weimar and London) outweighed the stylistic links with firmly attributed drawings by Siberechts. Subsequently, as a result of the deeper immersion that led to my 2012 article on the drawings of Siberechts, I have come to believe that it is to him that the Moore drawing (and the other two) can most plausibly be attributed.

2 Rubinstein 1994.

3 RCIN 913261; see White and Crawley 1994, no. 54.

4 Turner 2009, no. 436.

5 British Museum, London, inv. 1879,0308.1; see Stainton and White 1987, no. 180.
6 Figure 61.1: Watercolor and opaque watercolor, 285 x 455 mm; British Museum, London, inv. 1952,0405.10; see Rubinstein 2012, 384. The other two are in the Rijksprentenkabinet, Amsterdam, inv. RP-T-1913-58 and inv. RP-T-1952-1; see Rubinstein 2012, 385–86.
7 Figure 61.2: Black chalk and watercolor, 237 x 147 mm; Klassik Stiftung, Weimar, inv. KK 5450; see Rubinstein 2012, 391.
8 Rubinstein 2012, 378–82.

cat. 62

1 Van Gelder 1971, 205–6.
2 Houbraken 1718–21, 3: 212–13: "konstig wist na te bootsen, dat men straks met den eersten opslag van 't gezigt konde zien, of zyne Teekening gevolgt was naar een schildery van *Tintoret, Bassan, Karats, P. Veronees, Rubbens, van Dyk* en zoo voort: waarom de zelve ook by de konstminnaars in groote waarden gehouden worden." Translation my own. For De Bisschop's drawings after paintings, see also Jellema and Plomp 1992, 38–39.
3 Figure 62.1: Engraving, 253 x 182 mm; British Museum, London, inv. 1861,1109.367; Hollstein, 6: no. 13-2(2).
4 Smith 1829–42, 4: no. 64; Hofstede de Groot 1908–27, 5: 137, no. 453 ("the original is lost. Described from an engraving by H. Bary"). Gudlaugsson 1959–60, 101–2, no. 84.
5 Feist 1967, no. 23.
6 Naumann 1978, 34.
7 Naumann 1981, no. B18; Eddy de Jongh in De Jongh and Luijten 1991, no. 72; Buvelot 2005, 19–20. There is a proof impression of Bary's print in the Rijksprentenkabinet, Amsterdam, inv. RP-P-OB-26.510, with "G. ter Burg pinx." written in pencil in a later hand. In the literature it is sometimes stated that this hand-written inscription is the reason for the erroneous attribution of the prototype to Ter Borch. It was, in fact, more plausibly copied from the second state. There is also an inscription on the verso of the Amsterdam proof identifying the woman as the artist Anna Maria de Koker Monnickendam. See Van Tatenhove 2001 for a convincing refutation of this identification.
8 Naumann 1981, no. B18.
9 For instance, *A Woman with a Bird in a Small Coffer*, 1676, Rijksmuseum, Amsterdam, inv. SK-C-182 and *The Letter Writer*, 1670, private collection (see Buvelot 2005, no. 42). It is, however, likely that Van Mieris was also looking at Ter Borch. The woman's facial features and position of her head are strikingly similar to Ter Borch's painting *Two Shepherdesses* in the collection of Lady Baillie in London (see Gudlaugsson 1959–60, no. 85). This painting influenced other artists as well, among whom Eglon van der Neer (see Schavemaker 2010, no. 10).
10 Wuestman 2006b, 67.
11 Eddy de Jongh in De Jongh and Luijten 1991, no. 72.
12 See Van Gelder 1971, n. 62 for a list of drawings by De Bisschop that are directly related to Bary engravings. The engravings are Hollstein, 1: nos. 10, *The Old Hag* (corresponding drawing in the Nationalmuseum Stockholm, inv. NMH 110/1866); 13 (present drawing and a drawing in the Städtische Wessenberg-Galerie in Constance, Germany, inv. 33/72); 29, *Portrait of Lieuwe van Aitzema* (drawing lost); 40, *Portrait of Simon Episcopius* (drawing lost); 56, *Portrait of Thadeus de Lantman* (drawing lost); 66, *Portrait of Bartholomeus Praevostius* (drawing formerly Van Regteren Altena collection, sold Christie's, London, 13 May 2015, lot 258); 67, *Portrait of Michiel de Ruyter* (drawing lost); 69, *Portrait of Joannes Naeranus* (drawing in the Special Collections, Universiteitsbibliotheek Leiden, inv. PK-T-2434); 69, *Portrait of Johannes Schelhammer* (drawing lost); 72, *Portrait of Ruardus Tapper* (drawing in Rijksprentenkabinet, Amsterdam, inv. RP-T-00-45); 77, *Portrait of David Vlugh* (drawing in British Museum, London, inv. 1895,0915.1121); 81, *Portrait of Frederik Adriaensz Westphalen* (drawing in Rijksprentenkabinet, Amsterdam, inv. RP-T-1884-A-390).
13 *The Old Hag*, Nationalmuseum, Stockholm, inv. NMH 110/1866; see Magnusson 2018, no. 32, and also Van Tatenhove 1991.
14 *Portrait of Johannes Schelhammer Aged 51*, 1665. Engraving, 305 x 205 mm. Hollstein, 6: no. 69-1(2).
15 Translation taken from De Jongh and Luijten 1991, no. 72. In this context, the feathered cap is a well-worn motif highlighting the vanity of the model.
16 De Jongh and Luijten 1991, no. 72.
17 Figure 62.2: Black chalk, pen and brush and brown ink, 239 x 190 mm; Städtische Wessenberg-Galerie, Constance, inv. 33/72; see Bringmann 2000, no. 31. This, and not the present drawing, is the work mentioned in Gudlaugsson 1959–60, under no. 84; Van Gelder 1971, 216, n. 62. So far it has gone unnoticed that there are in fact two drawings. Thanks to Franziska Deinhammer at the Städtische Wessenberg-Galerie in Constance for sending me a photo of the recto and a snapshot of the watermark (email of December 2023). The watermark fragment shows a lily in a coat of arms with the letters "WR." It is somewhat close to Briquet nos. 7210, 7211, 7212, and 7165, all of which are late sixteenth-century watermarks, mostly German, but also to Laurentius and Laurentius 2007, nos. 450–53, more appropriately from The Hague, ca. 1614–43.

cat. 63

1 See Elen 1989, 13, for the history of Koenigs's second collection.
2 See no. 64 for a rejected reattribution to Pieter de Molijn, proposed by Egbert Haverkamp-Begemann in 1964.
3 Slive 2001, no. D55.
4 KdZ 2618; see Slive 2001, no. D21.
5 Inv. 1895,0915.1299; see Slive 2001, no. D80.
6 Inv. Oo,11.248; see Slive 2001, no. D81.
7 Slive 2001, no. D109.
8 Inv. Gemäldegalerie, 1837.
9 See https://www.tudelft.nl/en/2022/citg/pollard-willows-stop-waves.

cat. 64

1 See Elen 1989, 13, for the history of Koenigs's second collection.
2 The two fully autograph works by Molijn are the *Landscape with a Small Bridge* (signed and dated 1659), also once owned by Franz Koenigs, which is now in Russia but claimed by Museum Boijmans Van Beuningen, Rotterdam (inv. H 45; Beck 1998, no. 331), and the *Cottage with Farmers* (also signed), known to Haverkamp-Begemann only through a reproduction by Benno Geiger (1948, pl. 44) but now in the Museum of Fine Arts, Boston (inv. 21.2552; see Beck 1998, no. 441).
3 See Borenius 1928, pl. 36; the sheet, current whereabouts unknown, was excluded from Hans-Ulrich Beck's 1998 catalogue raisonné of Molijn's drawings.
4 Heseltine 1910, no. 26. The drawing was last documented and reproduced in a sale, Gutekunst & Klipstern, Bern, 21–22 June 1949, lot 666.
5 Inv. 1955.1874; see Heseltine 1910, no. 25. As noted by Slive (2001, 588, under no. D132, n. 1), the drawing was in the 1883 sale of Jacob de Vos Jbzn, *not* that of his ancestor Jacob de Vos, as stated by Haverkamp-Begemann (and still incorrectly noted on the museum's website).
6 Giltaij 1979; Slive proposed a comparison with a drawing of *Barnyard* in the Hamburger Kunsthalle, Hamburg (inv. 22457; see Stefes 2011, no. 552).
7 RKD, The Hague, Archieven OCLC: 920708347. On the subject of improving and finishing drawings, see Broos 1985.

cat. 65

1 For Ruisdael's views of Haarlem and for the term "Haarlempje," see Slive 2001, 51–61.
2 See Van Suchtelen and Wheelock 2008, 156.
3 The variant of the Moore drawing (inv. 45306) measures 102 x 568 mm. The variant of the left half (inv. 43424) measures 100 x 282 mm.
4 The sheets most likely stem from the collection of A. van der Willigen Pz.; see Plomp 1997, 121.
5 Van Hasselt 1968, 166–68; Van den Berg 1969; Plomp 1997, 424–25; Shoaf Turner 2006, 201–2.
6 Figure 65.1: Black and red chalk, 195 x 300 mm; Teylers Museum, Haarlem, inv. R* 94. Figure 65.2: Black and red chalk, 170 x 310 mm; Noord-Hollands Archief, Haarlem, inv. 43979.
7 Van Hasselt 1968, 166–67 (see both the short biography and the entry), citing several examples of the group, attributes them to Laurens Vincentsz van der Vinne. Shoaf Turner 2006, 202, on the contrary, leans toward an attribution to Vincent Laurensz van der Vinne.
8 Van Eynden and Van der Willigen 1816–40, 1: 437.
9 In the Noord-Hollands Archief in Haarlem are

three partially authentic and personally illustrated travel books and a sketchbook by the hand of Vincent Laurensz van der Vinne; see Alsteens and Buijs 2008, 271–77. For Laurens Vincentsz van der Vinne's signed and dated *View of Arnhem* (1690) in the Rijksprentenkabinet, Amsterdam (inv. RP-T-1895-A-3114), see Van den Berg 1969, 163.

cat. 66

1 Mark misread as "OO" rather than "CO" (for Curt Otto).
2 Identified by Sarah Mallory (19 May 2023); see http://rudolfotto.uitgeverijabraxas.nl/Rudolf%20Otto%20Inri/Seyffardt.html.
3 The younger Vincent took over the Amsterdam business established by his father, founder of Kunsthandel C.M. van Gogh; on Van Gogh the dealer, see La Fontaine-Verwey 1988.
4 Wurzbach 1906–11, 2: 524; and https://rkd.nl/explore/excerpts/276681.
5 http://www.kasteleninutrecht.eu/Bolenstein.htm.
6 Figures 66.1 and 66.2: Both pen and brown ink, with brown wash, over black chalk, 106 x 166 mm; Huis Van Gijn, Dordrecht, inv. SIK 10, fols. 77 and 78; see Niemeijer 1964, 128, 134. On 1 June 2018 another extensive album of drawings by Rutgers, this one containing 130 sheets, was sold at Bubb Kuyper, Haarlem, lot 68/5996.
7 Hôtel Drouot (Ader-Tajan), Paris, 28 October 1994, lot 50.
8 From a description of Herteveld dating from 1785 (https://www.buitenplaatseninnederland.nl/maarssen-herteveld.html), it had a boathouse on the river; this may have been built in the style of the surviving seventeenth-century brick garden house, which has a similarly pitched hip roof; see https://gallery.castlephoto.info/picture/Maarssen—Herteveld—2013—ASP—01/category/708-maarssen—herteveld; and https://rijksmonumenten.nl/monument/508206/herteveld-tuinmanswoning/maarssen/#&gid=1&pid=2.

cat. 67

1 Charles Duits's ownership is established by the appearance of the work in his inventory book and photographic negative in the Duits papers at the Getty Research Institute.
2 One of Cruyl's Italian cityscapes, a view of the Grand Canal and Rialto Bridge in Venice, has also been acquired by Clement Moore and is on deposit at the Morgan as part of the Baymeath Art Trust promised gift; see Jatta 1992, no. 87.
3 Cruyl also depicted the Machine de Marly (1684; see Jatta 1992, no. 35s, fig 144), which served as the hydraulic system for Versailles, and made bird's-eye views of the palace and gardens (Jatta 1992, nos. 16 and 17), as well as rendering the chateau at Chantilly (Jatta 1992, no. 9).
4 See Jatta 1992, nos. 11, 12, 14, 15, 108, 109, and 110.
5 See Isabelle Dérens's chronicle of the construction of the Pont Royal, 540–44, in Gady 2019.
6 The BNF drawing is inv. Ve 53 h fol. 31; see Jatta 1992, no. 11.
7 See Ongpin 2015. Also see the entry by Gregory Rubinstein in the catalogue for the sale, Sotheby's, London, 4 July 2018, lot 47, with another recently surfaced sheet (now in a private collection).
8 See Jatta 1992, no. 141 for the print (Musée Carnavalet, Paris), based on the Louvre drawing (inv. 19891; Jatta 1992, no. 15).

cat. 68

1 Robinson and Anderson 2016, 290.
2 Schapelhouman and Cornelis 2016, 30–32.
3 Houbraken 1718–21, 3: 90.
4 See Robinson 1979b; Robinson 1993, 59–60.
5 Figure 68.1: Oil on canvas, 32 x 42 cm; current location unknown, last recorded in the Dreesmann sale, Christie's, London, 11 April 2002, lot 549; see Robinson 1993, 54–57.
6 Figure 68.2: Red chalk, 209 x 308 mm; Nationalmuseum, Stockholm, inv. NMH 2166/1863; a counterproof of that drawing is preserved in the Musée des Beaux-Arts et d'Archéologie, Besançon, inv. D 651; see Robinson 1993, 55.
7 During the drawing session of this male figure, Adriaen might at some point have shifted his position in relation to his model, anticipating his need for a wider variety of figural motifs. He may have studied the same reclining pose from a different angle in the study sheet at the British Museum, London, inv. 1875,0612.14.
8 Inv. 6446; see Schapelhouman and Cornelis 2016, 30–31.
9 Present whereabouts unknown.
10 E.B. Crocker Collection, Crocker Art Museum, Sacramento, inv. 1871.186.
11 Robinson 1979b, 11–12.
12 The signature of Karel du Jardin does not match that of this inscription. For Du Jardin's signed drawings, see Gruijs 2003.
13 Schapelhouman and Cornelis 2016, 27–28.

cat. 69

1 The vast majority of their youthful expressions were carefully preserved, first by their father, who annotated their work indicating who was the maker and in what year, and later by Gesina. Through her efforts, the extensive Ter Borch archive remained together within the family until 1887, when it was sold to the Rijksmuseum.
2 Kettering 1988, 1: 290, nos. M1, M2, and M3.
3 Figure 69.1: Black chalk, heightened with white chalk, some brush and gray ink, on blue paper, 118 x 115 mm; Rijksprentenkabinet, Amsterdam, inv. BI-1887-1463-51B; see Kettering 1988, 2: 634, Folio 51. Recto; the similar upward gaze in this drawn self-portrait by Moses lends a remarkable facial resemblance to the young man depicted in the drawing under discussion.
4 Kettering 1988, 2: 840–53, nos. 50–51, 53–60, 63–66, 71–75, and 77.
5 Figure 69.2: Red chalk, 180 x 143 mm; Beaux-Arts de Paris, inv. Mas.2052; see Lugt 1950, no. 74A.
6 Inv. 1958.143; see Kettering 1988, 2: 840, no. 50.
7 Kettering 1988, 1: 287; second versions seem all to have been numbered, suggesting that they were probably kept together in a sketchbook or album.
8 Inv. RP-T-1887-A-1333(R); see Kettering 1988, 1: 348, no. M123.
9 Inv. 1895,0408.3; see Kettering 1988, 2: 848, no. 69.
10 If this were to be true, this theory would contradict the date of the drawing in Baltimore.
11 Luijten 2005, 41.
12 Gesina ter Borch and Gerard ter Borch the Younger, *Memorial Portrait of Moses ter Borch* (1645–1667), Rijksmuseum, Amsterdam, inv. SK-A-4908.

cat. 70

1 This banana is identified as the hybrid Musa x paradisiaca, commonly called "edible banana" or "French plantain."
2 For more on the *Metamorphosis insectorum Surinamensium*, see Reitsma 2008; Todd 2007; Davis 1995, 140–202; Wettengl 1998.
3 Previously, Merian published her studies in *Blumenbuch*, vol. 1, 1675; *Blumenbuch*, vol. 2, 1677; *Neues Blumenbuch*, vol. 3, 1680; *Der Raupen wunderbare Verwandlung und sonderbare Blumennahrung*, vol . 1, 1679; *Der Raupen wunderbare Verwandlung und sonderbare Blumennahrung*, vol. 2, 1683. Carl Linnaeus used her works to identify new species.
4 Merian also produced a number of counterproofs on parchment, which were then hand-colored and closely resemble watercolor drawings. For more on this process, see Schrader, Turner, and Yocco 2012. An example of a counterproof of *Banana and Bullseye Moth* is in the Print Room at Windsor Castle, Royal Collection Trust, RCIN 1085787. Merian also made luxurious counterproof watercolors of selected plates, likely to raise funds to defray the cost of printing her book. Examples are found at Windsor Castle and at the British Museum, London. A counterproof watercolor on parchment is in the collection of the Morgan Library & Museum, New York, inv. 2001.10.
5 Not all editions from 1705 onward were colored or gilded.
6 The Fagel *Metamorphosis* also has more gilding throughout. See the Library of Trinity College Dublin, Fagel Collection, Fag.GG.2.10. Arader Galleries auctioned a comparable album, which consisted of counterproof impressions; Arader, New York, 23 April 2022, lot 91.
7 John Carter Brown Library, Providence, inv. 3101.
8 Natalie Zemon Davis (1995, 324, n. 180) notes that James Petiver, who corresponded with Merian and endeavored to translate *Metamorphosis* into English, could not be the author of these translations as he died in 1718, one year before the Oosterwyck edition appeared.
9 The original owner of the album is as yet unknown; however, it is possible that Rev. William Smyth of Great Linford owned the book sometime

after 1761. He left the contents of his library to his eldest son, Rev. William Smyth of Elkington Hall. An inscription in the album explains that Smyth of Elkington then left the album to his son-in-law Sir Stephen Cave, whose widow Emma Jane then gave it to her brother W.H. Smyth. He then bequeathed the book to his son Capt. W.G. Smyth, who left Elkington Hall in the 1930s. The estate house was demolished in 1974. We cannot be sure that the album left the collection in the 1930s; however, it came to the collection of Henry Rogers Broughton, 2nd Baron Fairhaven, who, according to James Miller, formerly of Sotheby's, often purchased the books for his well-known library in London or through William Brown in Eton. Inscribed in graphite on the upper left corner of the album's first page is "Brown/ £25," suggesting this book was at one point in the possession of Brown.

10 Though in 1834 enslaved people were emancipated in the British West Indies, many other nations with whom the British did business were still heavily involved in the chattel slave trade.

11 Cave 1849.

cat. 71

1 For example, *Seated Youth, Facing Right, Reading a Book*, Rijksprentenkabinet, Amsterdam (inv. RP-T-1881-A-103; see Schatborn 1981, no. 44) and *Seated Man, Facing Left, Reading a Book*, Rijksprentenkabinet, Amsterdam (inv. RP-T-1899-A-4247; see Schatborn 1981, no. 43). For signed and dated figure studies without background elements, possibly part of a series of the Five Senses, see *Seated Man, Leaning on a Chair and Holding a Pipe*, 1686, Biblioteca Reale, Turin (inv. 16512; see Sciolla 1999, 335–36), *Seated Man, Leaning on a Chair and Holding a Pipe with his Eyes Closed*, 1686, Maida and George Abrams Collection, Boston (see Robinson 2002, no. 89), and *Seated Man Leaning on a Chair and Holding a Bottle*, 1686, Klassik Stiftung, Weimar (inv. KK 5048).

2 *Seated Man, Leaning over a Chair and Reading*, 1688, Städel Museum, Frankfurt am Main (inv. 3689; see Frankfurt 1906, no. 78), *Seated Man, Facing Left, Reading*, 1688, Teylers Museum, Haarlem (inv. S 20; see Scholten 1904, 300, portfolio S, no. 20), *Seated Man in Three-Quarter Length, Leaning over a Chair and Reading*, 1690 (Sotheby's, New York, 29 January 2020, lot 91), and *Seated Man Leaning over a Chair and Reading*, 1691 (C.G. Boerner, Leipzig, 9–10 May 1930, lot 133).

3 Although assessing literacy rates in the Dutch Republic remains difficult, newspaper consumption did pervade the various social classes. See Van Groesen 2016.

4 Many thanks to Jaap van der Veen for his help transcribing the inscription (email to the author, 22 August 2023).

5 The majority of these watercolors survive in two collections, the Special Collections of the Universiteitsbibliotheek Leiden and the Maida and George Abrams Collection, Boston.

6 Hollstein, 6: nos. 33–36. Two of the prints have surviving preparatory drawings, *Woman Lighting a Rocket*, Hamburger Kunsthalle, Hamburg (inv. 21876; see Stefes 2011, no. 272), and *Man Lighting a Rocket*, British Museum, London (inv. 1836,0811.134; see Hind 1915–32, 3: no. 19).

cat. 72

1 Many thanks to Jane Shoaf Turner for bringing the watermark information to my attention, which allows us to give a more specific date range.

2 Houbraken 1718–21, 242–44; Van Gool 1750, 1: 254–56; Zaal 1991b, 3.

3 Zaal 1991a, 12.

4 The artist often heightened his drawings with various glazes (including egg white), gum arabic, and metallic pigments to enhance the velvety scales or shimmery iridescence of insect wings. He used silver pigments and gum arabic, for example, to create iridescent wings in his drawing *Black Swallowtail and Small Moth*, Herzog Anton Ulrich-Museum, Braunschweig, inv. Z 1550.

5 The same moth was represented by the artist at the center of a sheet with two butterflies and a flying insect sold at Christie's, London, 15 December 1992, lot 218.

6 Figure 72.1: Black chalk and watercolor, 201 x 262 mm; Rijksprentenkabinet, Amsterdam, inv. RP-T-FM-58 (on loan from the City of Amsterdam). A drawing of the *Urania leilus*, now attributed to Antony Henstenburgh and formerly in the collection of Maida and George Abrams, Boston, sold at Sotheby's, London, 8–9 July 2015, lot 191; another sold at Bonhams, London, 20 April 2005, lot 139.

7 The Bronckhorst *Urania leilus* formerly in the collection of Charles Ryskamp sold at Sotheby's, New York, 25 January 2002, lot 200.

cat. 73

1 For more on Herolt's work, see Sam Segal in Wettengl 1998, 69–87; Davis 1995, 140–202; Houbraken 1718–21, 3: 224; Reitsma 2008, passim, especially 139–44.

2 Reitsma 2008, 115, observed that Herolt's style is more "sinuous" and "Baroque" than that of Merian.

3 Herolt also contributed two works to the so-called Moninckx Atlas compiled by Maria Moninckx and other female artists to document plants in the Hortus Botanicus: the *Bush Daisy* (*Jacobaea Africana frutescens foliis Absinthii*, part 4, fol. 17) and *Bush Tansy* (*Tanacetum Africanum*, part 5, fol. 28). Reitsma 2008, 141, speculates that the Herolt drawings in the 1972 Van Pallandt sale could have been part of Agnes Block's collection, which was then purchased in part by Valerius Röver, eventually coming to the collection of Van Pallandt.

4 Herolt's date of death is 1723 or 1743; she is thought to have died in Suriname. Davis 1995, 334, n. 237, notes that the artist's name does not appear on any travel lists for return trips to the Netherlands from Suriname before 1723, thus deducing she spent the rest of her life there.

5 Herolt's drawings often entered collections as the work of Merian, and many are still identified as possibly by her or either daughter, Johanna Herolt or Dorothea Graff. For example, Reitsma identified a cache of Herolt's works formerly given to Merian in the British Museum, London; several more possible Herolt works are in the Print Room at Windsor Castle. The Morgan Library & Museum has three sheets given to Herolt, all formerly attributed to Merian: inv. 1995.4, 1979.37, and 1973.3.

6 Segal attributed a group of drawings in the Van Pallandt sale, including the Moore sheet, to Herolt. See Sam Segal in Wettengl 1998, 86–87, n. 68.

7 Figure 73.1: Watercolor over black chalk and graphite on parchment, 376 x 298 mm; Herzog Anton Ulrich-Museum, Braunschweig, inv. D XVII H27.

8 Mullein is illustrated in some of the earliest extant *De medica* manuscripts. It appears three times in the Vienna Dioscorides (the Juliana Anicia Codex), perhaps the best-known and earliest surviving copy of the text, on fols. 043v, 360v, and 361r. The Morgan Library & Museum's tenth-century Dioscorides (MS M.652) contains depictions of verbascum on fols. 185r, 185v, and 186r. The seventh-century Codex Neapolitanus features verbascum on fols. 26 and 148.

9 Verbascum, or mullein, appears in an array of classical herbals or other varieties of medical texts. See Pliny, *Natural History*, I, 166–17, XXV, 216–17, 254–55, XXVI, 288–89, 296–97, 356–57, 360–61, 370–71, 374–75, XXVII, 408–9; Galen, *Method of Medicine*, IV, 428–29; Hippocrates XI, LCL 538: 276–77, Hippocrates VIII, LCL 482: 348–49, Hippocrates X, LCL 520: 384–85.

10 Gerard 1597, 634.

cat. 74

1 Rombouts and Van Lerius 1864–76, 2: 573, 576, 598, 607; during the first year, Van der Goes held the position of master, and later on had at least two pupils, both otherwise unknown artists: Franciscus van de Zande, who studied with him in 1696–97, and Jacobus Bockoe, who was a student in the following year, 1697–98.

2 Inv. RP-T-1884-A-330A– RP-T-1884-A-330H.

3 Inv. 2020-T.53–2020-T.56; see Teeuwisse 2019, no. 61.

4 Inv. 75.9; see Buvelot 2008, 54–57.

5 See the nineteen auction catalogue excerpts in the Hofstede de Groot files, RKD.

6 Figure 74.1: Opaque watercolor on parchment, 111 x 157 mm; Kröller-Müller Museum, Otterlo, inv. KM 106.890; see Hammacher 1959, no. 97.

7 Leo Spik, Berlin, 31 March 1971, a pair in lot 242 (opaque watercolor, 140 x 120 mm).

cat. 75

1 The Latinized form of Cozens's name is unusual. The -o- mark suggests an unidentified dealer's price code.

2 These sheets include examples in the Metropolitan Museum of Art, New York (ca. 1755–65; inv. 2017.347), Tate, London (1763; inv. T00980-81), The Whitworth, Manchester (inv. D.1933.10,11), Victoria and Albert Museum, London (1763; inv. Dyce 669), and Huntington Library, Art Museum, and Botanical Gardens, San Marino (no date; inv. 59.55.366).

3 Sloan 1986, 44.

4 Kaes, email to the author, May 2023.

5 *A Lake*, 1763 (inv. T00980); *Landscape*, 1763 (inv. T00981).

6 Inv. Dyce 669.

cat. 76

1 There are a small number of exceptions to this rule, such as the *Wooded Landscape*, now in the Victoria and Albert Museum, London, inv. Dyce 676; see Hayes and Stainton 1983, 50–51, no. 13.

2 The location of this watercolor is now unknown; it was recorded by Hayes as the property of Desmond Morris, Oxford. Hayes 1971, no. 243, and Hayes 1982, 1: 98. It is unusual for Gainsborough to date a watercolor, which in this instance provides a useful marker for the development of his style. It is perhaps because of his move to Bath that he wished to record the date.

3 Belsey (2008, 434) notes the artist's frequent use of these colored papers and suggests they were of French manufacture.

4 Figure 76.1: Watercolor and opaque watercolor over graphite on brown paper, 279 x 375 mm; Ashmolean Museum, Oxford, inv. WA1934.1; see Hayes 1971, no. 265. Figure 76.2: Watercolor and opaque watercolor, 281 x 380 mm; Ashmolean Museum, Oxford, inv.WA1934.3; see Hayes 1971, no. 266.

5 Hayes 1971, no. 273.

6 A drawing by Gainsborough, ca. 1746–48, in The Whitworth, Manchester (inv. D.2.1935; see Hayes 1971, no. 80; Hayes and Stainton 1983, no. 6), is a direct copy of a painting by Ruisdael, *The Forest*, known to the artist through a copy.

7 Humphry MS ca. 1802, n.p.

8 Stainton 1987, n.p.

9 Thomas Gainsborough, letter to Philip, 2nd Earl Hardwicke, ca. 1764. Gainsborough (ed. Hayes 2001), 30. In the letter, he clarified the important distinction he made between the two creative activities, i.e. that of "view painters" such as Sandby, and an artist of genius such as himself: "With regard to real Views from Nature in this Country, he has never seen any Place that affords a Subject equal to the poorest imitations of Gaspar (Dughet) or Claude (Lorraine). . . . if His Lordship wishes to have any thing tolerable of the name of G(ainsborough) the Subject altogether, as well as the figures &c must be of his own Brain."

cat. 77

1 Inv. 1654; see Hayes 1982, 2: no. 42. The painting was extensively damaged and restored.

2 Inv. 5845; see Hayes 1982, 2: no. 43.

3 The original painting (Hayes 1982, 2: no. 44) is now lost. An example of John Wood's 1764 engraving can be found in the British Museum, London, inv. 1866,1114.310.

4 Inv. B1975.4.1197; see Hayes 1971, no. 276.

5 Figure 77.1: Oil on canvas, 120.7 x 149.8 cm; Tate Britain, London, inv. 5803; Hayes 1982, 2: no. 122. The surface of the painting has suffered significantly, so that the Moore drawing provides something of a guide as to its original appearance.

6 Inv. B1975.4.1522; see Hayes 1971, 1: no. 436; Hayes 1982, 2, 476.

7 This description of the general character of Gainsborough's drawings is taken from a lecture written by an early biographer of the artist, Henry J. Pfungst, at the Society of Antiquaries, London, in 1908, preserved at Gainsborough's House, Sudbury, Suffolk (inv. 1996.016), 11. Quoted in Belsey 2008, 435.

8 I am grateful to Lindsay Stainton for providing the information concerning the Humphry-Upcott provenance. Humphry was Gainsborough's old friend and fellow artist, who had lived in Bath from 1760 until 1764, and was frequently Gainsborough's riding companion after the artist's near-fatal illness in 1763. A large label pasted to the original backboard is inscribed "Sketch by T. Gainsborough / made by him for Ozias Humphry Esq. RA / by whom it was presented to W. Upcott, 1809." William Upcott was the illegitimate son of Ozias Humphry, by one Delly Wickers, daughter of an Oxford shopkeeper. The "contemporary account" of Upcott's rooms being crammed with paintings and drawings by Gainsborough comes from an obituary notice written by one of Upcott's friends and patrons, the banker and collector Dawson Turner. It was published under the pseudonymous initials "A.B" in *The Gentleman's Magazine* (2nd series, vol. 26 [1846], 473). Upcott inherited his collections of Gainsborough's work from Humphry, his natural father. This is, remarkably, the only surviving drawing to share a Humphry-Upcott provenance.

1 Regarding the Duits probate, see Lee 2022.

cat. 78

2 Biesboer and Köhler 2006, 390–92, 394–95; Schwartz and Bok 1989, 105ff.

3 Temminck-van Dijkhuizen and Temminck 1997, 13.

4 Frans Halsmuseum, Haarlem, inv. OS I-13; see Biesboer and Köhler 2006, 394.

5 Ploos van Amstel 1980, 2.

6 Van den Berg 1969, 162.

7 Figure 78.1: Pen and black ink and gray wash, 304 x 420 mm; Noord-Hollands Archief, Haarlem, inv. 45883. The other sheet, *Interior of the Grote Kerk in Haarlem, Looking into the Nave, toward the West*, is signed on the verso at lower left (inv. 45232).

8 Plomp 1997, 3–4.

cat. 79

1 Ruskin (ed. Cook and Wedderburn 1903–12), 13: 370.

2 Wilton 1979, no. 1401.

3 Harrison 2015, no. 56.

4 Figure 79.1: Watercolor over graphite on Whatman Turkey Mill paper dated 1818, 224 x 287 mm; Ashmolean Museum, Oxford, inv. WA.RS.ED.182.

cat. 80

1 Figure 80.1: Oil on canvas, 66.7 x 56.9 cm; Dulwich Picture Gallery, London, inv. DPG126; see Bergvelt and Jonker 2021, no. DPG126.

2 Jameson 1842, 1: 471; Flagg 1893, 297. For an overview of the painting's early reception, see Bergvelt and Jonker 2021, no. DPG126, and Waterfield 1988, 20–21.

3 Hereford Museum and Art Gallery, inv. 1683. Davis probably studied *Jacob's Dream* in 1822, when he is mentioned among the Royal Academy students who were granted permission to copy works at the Dulwich Picture Gallery. See Waterfield 1988, 13–14.

4 Richter and Sparkes 1880, 127–28; Cook 1914, 74. The picture was attributed to Aert de Gelder in 1914. The artist's authorship was confirmed by the discovery of his signature during a cleaning in 1946. See Bergvelt and Jonker 2021, no. DPG126.

5 Waterfield 1988, 7–11.

6 Hoock 2004. For copying Rembrandt, see Yarker 2018.

7 Evans 2014, 107–29, 151–81; Plomp 2020.

8 I am grateful to Lucy West and Helen Hilliard for providing me with information from Dulwich Picture Gallery's curatorial files to confirm that the painting was not lent to the Royal Academy during Constable's lifetime.

9 In his "Lecture on the Dutch and Flemish Schools," Constable argued that "[c]hiaroscuro is the great feature that characterizes [Rembrandt's] art, and was carried farther by him than by any other painter, not excepting Correggio." See Constable (ed. Beckett 1970), 62

10 Evans 2014, 118.

11 See, for instance, *View on the Stour: Dedham Church in the Distance*, ca. 1832–36, Victoria and Albert Museum, London (inv. 249-1888), and *Trees and a Stretch of Water on the Stour*, ca. 1832–36, Victoria and Albert Museum, London (inv. 250-1888); see Reynolds 1984, nos. 36.27–28. For a discussion of Constable's late drawing style, see Hargraves 2021.

cat. 81

1 Fleming-Williams 1990, 70–95.

2 Fleming-Williams 1990, 252–61.

3 Bailey et al. 2024, no. 13.

4 Hargraves 2021, 53, alludes to the evolution of Constable's practice in his late years, when the artist no longer lived in his native landscape.

5 National Gallery, London, inv. NG1207.

6 Constable (ed. Beckett 1969), 76–78.

7 Compare, for example, the watercolor of Willy Lott's cottage, British Museum, London, inv. 1888,0215.33; see Reynolds 1984, no. 32.17.

BIBLIOGRAPHY

The following list includes all sources cited in the entries. Short title references have been kept deliberately brief: publications with more than three primary authors or editors are given by the name of the first author, with *et al.*; catalogues of exhibitions shown in more than one calendar year are cited by the first year alone, in which the catalogue is published. Issue numbers are not given for journals with continuous pagination across a multi-issue year.

Albach 1972
Ben Albach. "Een tekening van het Amsterdamse toneel in 1638." *Kroniek van het Rembrandthuis* 26 (1972): 111–25.

Alsteens 2015
Stijn Alsteens. "An Earlier Version of the Metropolitan's View of Tivoli by Bartholomeus Breenbergh." *Master Drawings* 53 (2015): 443–50.

Alsteens et al. 2009
Stijn Alsteens et al., eds. *Raphael to Renoir: Drawings from the Collection of Jean Bonna.* Exh. cat. New York: Metropolitan Museum of Art; Edinburgh: National Gallery of Scotland, 2009.

Alsteens and Buijs 2008
Stijn Alsteens and Hans Buijs, with Véronique Mathot. *Paysages de France dessinés par Lambert Doomer et les artistes hollandais et flamands des XVIe et XVIIe siècles.* Paris, 2008.

Alsteens and Spira 2012
Stijn Alsteens and Freyda Spira, with contributions by Maryan W. Ainsworth et al. *Dürer and Beyond: Central European Drawings in the Metropolitan Museum of Art, 1400–1700.* Exh. cat. New York: Metropolitan Museum of Art, 2012.

Ampzing 1628
Samuel Ampzing. *Beschryvinge ende lof der stad Haerlem in Holland.* Haarlem, 1628. Reprint, Amsterdam, 1974.

Amsterdam 1929
Catalogus van de tentoonstelling van oude kunst door de vereeniging van handelaren in oude kunst in Nederland in het Rijksmuseum te Amsterdam. Exh. cat. Amsterdam: Rijksmuseum, 1929.

Bagni 1985
Prisco Bagni. *Il Guercino e il suo falsario: I disegni di paesaggio.* Bologna, 1985.

Bailey et al. 2024
Colin B. Bailey et al. *Liberty to the Imagination: Drawings from the Eveillard Gift.* Exh. cat. New York: Morgan Library & Museum, 2024.

Baker 2010
Christopher Baker. "Master Drawings and Paintings: London." *Burlington Magazine* 152 (2010): 624–25.

Bakker 1998
Boudewijn Bakker. *Landscapes of Rembrandt: His Favourite Walks.* Exh. cat. Amsterdam: Gemeentearchief; Paris: Institut Néerlandais, 1998–99.

Barnes et al. 2004
Susan J. Barnes, Nora De Poorter, Oliver Millar, and Horst Vey. *Van Dyck: A Complete Catalogue of the Paintings.* New Haven and London, 2004.

Baroni Vannucci 1997
Alessandra Baroni Vannucci. *Jan Van der Straet detto Giovanni Stradano: Flandrus pictor et inventor.* Milan, 1997.

Baroni Vannucci and Sellink 2012
Alessandra Baroni Vannucci and Manfred Sellink, eds. *Stradanus (1523–1605): Court Artist of the Medici.* Turnhout, 2012.

Bartsch 1801–21
Adam von Bartsch. *Le peintre graveur.* 21 vols. Vienna, 1801–21.

Barth 1981
Renate Barth. *Rembrandt & seine Zeitgenossen: Handzeichnungen niederländischer und flämische Meister des 17. Jahrhunderts aus dem Besitz der Kunstsammlungen zu Weimar.* Exh. cat. Weimar: Kunsthalle am Theaterplatz, 1981.

Baskett & Day 1982
Old Master Drawings. Sale cat. London: Baskett & Day, 1982.

Bauch 1926
Kurt Bauch. *Jakob Adriaensz Backer: Ein Rembrandtschüler aus Friesland.* Berlin, 1926.

Beck 1998
Hans-Ulrich Beck. *Pieter Molyn: Katalog der Handzeichnungen.* Doornspijk, 1998.

Belsey 2008
Hugh Belsey. "A Second Supplement to John Hayes's *The Drawings of Thomas Gainsborough.*" *Master Drawings* 46 (2008): 427–541.

Benati 2019
Daniele Benati. *Emozione Barocca: Il Guercino a Cento.* Exh. cat. Cento: Pinacoteca San Lorenzo, 2019–20.

Benesch 1935
Otto Benesch. *Rembrandt: Werk und Forschung.* Vienna, 1935.

Benesch 1954–57
Otto Benesch. *The Drawings of Rembrandt: A Critical and Chronological Catalogue.* 6 vols. London, 1954–57.

Benesch 1964
Otto Benesch. "Neuentdeckte Zeichnungen von Rembrandt." *Jahrbuch der Berliner Museen* 6 (1964): 105–50.

Benesch 1970
Otto Benesch. *Rembrandt: Werk und Forschung*, revised by Eva Benesch. Lucerne, 1970.

Benesch 1970–73
Otto Benesch. *Collected Writings*, ed. Eva Benesch. 4 vols. New York, 1970–73.

Benesch 1973
Otto Benesch. *The Drawings of Rembrandt: Complete Edition in Six Volumes*, revised by Eva Benesch. 6 vols. London, 1973.

Bergstrüm 1984
Ingvar Bergstrüm. "Jacob Marrel's Earliest Tulip Book, Hitherto Unknown." *Tableau* (1984): 32–49.

Bergvelt and Jonker 2016
Ellinoor Bergvelt and Michiel Jonker. *Dutch and Flemish Paintings: Dulwich Picture Gallery.* London, 2016.

Bergvelt and Jonker 2021
Ellinoor Bergvelt and Michiel Jonker. *Catalogue of Dulwich Picture Gallery: Dutch, Flemish and German Schools, with Addenda to the British School.* 2 vols. The Hague, 2021.

Bernheimer 2001
The Pfeiffer Collection of Old Master Drawings. Sale cat. Munich: Bernheimer Gallery, 2001.

Bernt 1957–58
Walther Bernt. *Die niederländischen Zeichner des 17. Jahrhunderts.* 2 vols. Munich, 1957–58.

Bevers 2002
Holm Bevers. *Kunstsinn der Gründerzeit: Meisterzeichnungen der Sammlung Adolf von Beckerath.* Exh. cat. Berlin: Staatliche Museen, Kupferstichkabinett, 2002.

Bevers 2006
Holm Bevers. *Rembrandt: Die Zeichnungen im Berliner Kupferstichkabinett.* Exh. cat. Berlin: Staatliche Museen, Kupferstichkabinett, 2006.

Bevers 2010
Holm Bevers. "The Early, Rembrandtesque Drawings of Gerbrand van den Eeckhout." *Master Drawings* 48 (2010): 39–72.

Bevers 2011
Holm Bevers. *Kupferstichkabinett: Aus Rembrandts Zeit; Zeichenkunst in Hollands Goldenem Jahrhundert*. Exh. cat. Berlin: Staatliche Museen, Kupferstichkabinett, 2011–12.

Bevers 2018
Holm Bevers. *Zeichnungen der Rembrandtschule im Berliner Kupferstichkabinett*. Dresden, 2018.

Bevers, Schatborn, and Welzel 1991
Holm Bevers, Peter Schatborn, and Barbara Welzel. *Rembrandt: The Master and His Workshop: Drawings and Etchings*. Exh. cat. Berlin: Altes Museum; Amsterdam: Rijksmuseum; London: National Gallery, 1991–92.

Biesboer 2006
Pieter Biesboer, ed. *Nicolaes Berchem: In the Light of Italy*. Exh. cat. Haarlem: Frans Halsmuseum; Zurich: Kunsthaus Zürich; Schwerin: Staatliches Museum, 2006–7.

Biesboer and Köhler 2006
Pieter Biesboer and Neeltje Köhler, eds. *Painting in Haarlem, 1500–1850: The Collection of the Frans Hals Museum*. Ghent, 2006.

Bikker, Bruijnen, and Wuestman 2007
Jonathan Bikker, Yvette Bruijnen, and Gerdien Wuestman. *Dutch Paintings of the Seventeenth Century in the Rijksmuseum Amsterdam, I*. Amsterdam and New Haven, 2007.

Bleyerveld 2022
Yvonne Bleyerveld. “Two Seated Monkeys: The Earliest ‘Pen Works’ by Jacob Matham.” *Master Drawings* 60 (2022): 31–34.

Bleyerveld and Veldman 2016
Yvonne Bleyerveld and Ilja M. Veldman, with contributions by Michiel C. Plomp and Bert Schepers. *The Netherlandish Drawings of the 16th Century in Teylers Museum*. Leiden and Haarlem, 2016.

Bleyerveld and Veldman 2018
Yvonne Bleyerveld and Ilja M. Veldman. “Hoogtepunten uit Museum Catharijneconvent: Nederlandse tekeningen 1549–1806.” *Delineavit et Sculpsit* 43 (2018): 2–118.

Bleyerveld, Elen, and Niessen 2014
Yvonne Bleyerveld, Albert J. Elen, and Judith Niessen. *Bosch to Bloemaert: Early Netherlandish Drawings in Museum Boijmans Van Beuningen, Rotterdam*. Exh. cat. Paris: Fondation Custodia; Rotterdam: Museum Boijmans Van Beuningen; Washington: National Gallery of Art, 2014–15.

Bock and Rosenberg 1930
Elfried Bock and Jakob Rosenberg. *Die Zeichnungen alter Meister im Kupferstichkabinett: Die niederländischen Meister*. 2 vols. Berlin, 1930.

Bode 1914
Wilhelm von Bode. *Die Gemäldesammlung Marcus Kappel in Berlin*. Berlin, 1914.

Boerner 1962
Neue Lagerlist 34: Handzeichnungen alter und neuerer Meister. Sale cat. Düsseldorf: C.G. Boerner, 1962.

Bok-van Kammen 1977
Welmoet Bok-van Kammen. “Stradanus and the Hunt.” PhD thesis, Johns Hopkins University, Baltimore, 1977.

Bolten 1993
Jaap Bolten. “Abraham Bloemaert (1564–1651) and His *Tekenboek*.” *Delineavit et Sculpsit* 9 (1993): 1–10.

Bolten 2007
Jaap Bolten. *Abraham Bloemaert (c. 1565–1651): The Drawings*. 2 vols. Leiden, 2007.

Bolten 2017
Jaap Bolten. “The Drawings of Abraham Bloemaert: A Supplement.” *Master Drawings* 55 (2017): 3–120.

Boon 1964
Karel G. Boon. “Een vroege studie voor de Honderd Gulden Prent.” *Bulletin van het Rijksmuseum* 12 (1964): 85–90.

Boon 1978
Karel G. Boon. *Catalogue of Dutch and Flemish Drawings in the Rijksmuseum, II: Netherlandish Drawings of the Fifteenth and Sixteenth Centuries*. 2 vols. The Hague, 1978.

Boon 1992
Karel G. Boon. *The Netherlandish and German Drawings of the XVth and XVIth Centuries of the Frits Lugt Collection*. 3 vols. Paris, 1992.

Boorsch and Marciari 2007
Suzanne Boorsch and John Marciari. *Master Drawings from the Yale University Art Gallery*. Exh. cat. Sarasota: John and Mable Ringling Museum of Art; Austin: Blanton Museum of Art; New Haven: Yale University Art Gallery, 2007–8.

Borenius 1928
Tancred Borenius. “Pieter Molyn (1595[?]–1661)–Landscape with Figures.” *Old Master Drawings* 3 (1928): 44–45.

Boutier 2000
Jean Boutier, with Jean-Yves Sarazin and Marine Sibille. *Les plans de Paris des origines, 1493, à la fin du XVIIIe siècle: Étude, carto-bibliographie et catalogue collectif*. Paris, 2000.

Boutier 2007
Jean Boutier, with Jean-Yves Sarazin and Marine Sibille. *Les plans de Paris des origines, 1493, à la fin du XVIIIe siècle: Étude, carto-bibliographie et catalogue collectif*. 2nd ed. Paris, 2007.

Bradley 2006
James W. Bradley. *Before Albany: An Archaeology of Native-Dutch Relations in the Capital Region, 1600–1664*. New York, 2006.

Brady 2017
W.M. Brady and Co. *Master Drawings, Vasari to Bonnard*. Sale cat. New York, 2017.

Bredius 1915–22
Abraham Bredius. *Künstler-Inventare*. 8 vols. The Hague, 1915–22.

Bremen 1979
Meisterzeichnungen aus drei Jahrhunderten: Niederländische Handzeichnungen des 17. bis 19. Jahrhunderts aus der Sammlung Hans van Leeuwen. Exh. cat. Bremen: Kunsthalle, 1979.

Bréton, Jouslin de Noray, and Schwed 2014
Étienne Bréton, Renaud Jouslin de Noray, and Nicolas Schwed. *Vingt-sept dessins de Gerrit van Honthorst (1592–1656)*. Sale cat. Paris: Saint Honoré Art Consulting, 2014.

Bringmann 2000
Michael Bringmann. *Von Rembrandt bis Menzel: Meisterwerke der Zeichenkunst: Die Sammlung Brandes*. Heidelberg, 2000.

Briquet 1966
C.-M. Briquet. *Les filigranes: Dictionnaire historique des marques du papier dès leur apparition vers 1282 jusqu'en 1600*. 4 vols. New York, 1966.

Broos 1985
Ben Broos. “Improving and Finishing Old Master Drawings: An Art in Itself.” *Hoogsteder-Naumann Mercury* 8 (1985): 34–55.

Broos and Schapelhouman 1993
Ben Broos and Marijn Schapelhouman. *Oude tekeningen in het bezit van het Amsterdams Historisch Museum, waaronder de collectie Fodor, IV: Nederlandse tekenaars geboren tussen 1600 en 1660*. Amsterdam, 1993.

Brown 1991
Christopher Brown. *The Drawings of Anthony van Dyck*. Exh. cat. New York: Pierpont Morgan Library; Fort Worth: Kimbell Art Museum, 1991.

Brugerolles and Guillet 1985
Emmanuelle Brugerolles and David Guillet. *Renaissance et maniérisme dans les écoles du Nord: Dessins des collections de l'École des Beaux-Arts*. Exh. cat. Paris: École Nationale Supérieure des Beaux-Arts; Hamburg: Hamburger Kunsthalle, 1985–86.

Bruijnen et al. 2002
Yvette Bruijnen et al. *De vier jaargetijden in de kunst van de Nederlanden, 1500–1750*. Zwolle, 2002.

Brussels, Rotterdam, and Paris 1972
Dessins flamands et hollandais du dix-septième siècle: Collections de l'Ermitage, Leningrad et du Musée Pouchkine, Moscou. Exh. cat. Brussels: Bibliothèque Royale Albert 1er; Rotterdam: Museum Boymans-Van Beuningen; Paris: Institut Néerlandais, 1972–73.

Buck and Müller 2019
Stephanie Buck and Jürgen Müller, with Mailena Mallach, eds. *Rembrandt's Mark*. Exh. cat. Dresden: Staatliche Kunstsammlungen, Kupferstich-Kabinett, 2019.

Burke 1976
James D. Burke. “A Drawing by Johannes Collaert.” *Master Drawings* 14 (1976): 384–86.

Burnett 1969
D.G. Burnett. "Landscapes of Aelbert Cuyp." *Apollo* 89 (1969): 372–80.

Burnett 1978
David Burnett. "The Drawing Styles of Matthew Bril." *Konsthistorisk Tidskrift* 47 (1978): 103–10.

Burlington Magazine 1943
"Sir Peter Lely's Collection." Unsigned editorial. *Burlington Magazine for Connoisseurs* 82 (1943): 188.

Buvelot 2005
Quentin Buvelot, ed. *Frans van Mieris, 1635–1681*. Exh. cat. The Hague: Mauritshuis; Washington: National Gallery of Art, 2005–6.

Buvelot 2008
Quentin Buvelot. *De stillevens van Adriaen Coorte (werkzaam c. 1683–1707), met oeuvrecatalogus*. Exh. cat. The Hague: Mauritshuis, 2008.

Buvelot and Alsteens 2013
Quentin Buvelot and Stijn Alsteens. "A Rediscovered Drawing by Philips Wouwerman." *Master Drawings* 51 (2013): 445–50.

Buvelot and Buijs 2002
Quentin Buvelot and Hans Buijs, with Ella Reitsma. *A Choice Collection: Seventeenth-Century Dutch Paintings from the Frits Lugt Collection*. Exh. cat. The Hague: Mauritshuis, 2002.

Buylaert, De Clercq, and Dumolyn 2011
Frederik Buylaert, Wim de Clercq, and Jan Dumolyn. "Sumptuary Legislation, Material Culture and the Semiotics of 'Vivre Noblemen' in the County of Flanders (14th–16th Centuries)." *Social History* 36 (2011): 393–417.

Campbell 2002
Thomas P. Campbell, with contributions by Maryan W. Ainsworth et al. *Tapestry in the Renaissance: Art and Magnificence*. Exh. cat. New York: Metropolitan Museum of Art, 2002.

Cappelletti 2006
Francesca Cappelletti. *Paul Bril e la pittura di paesaggio a Roma, 1580–1630*. Rome, 2006.

Cassidy 2011–12
Brendan Cassidy. "Alexander Cozens and the Patronage of the Grant Family, with a Recipe for Varnish and a Treatise on Landscape." *The British Art Journal* 12 (2011–12): 32–41.

Cave 1849
Sir Stephen Cave. *A Few Words on the Encouragement Given to Slavery and the Slave Trade, by Recent Measures and Chiefly by the Sugar Bill of 1846*. London, 1849.

Chaldecott and Marty de Cambiare 2019
Alexandra Chaldecott and Laurie Marty de Cambiare. *Works on Paper*. Sale cat. London: Jean-Luc Baroni Ltd.; Paris: Marty de Cambiare, 2019.

Chantelou 1972
Chantelou. "Au fil des ventes: Comestibles et vénéneux." *Le Monde*, 8 March 1972, 17.

Chennevières and Montaiglon 1851–60
Charles-Philippe de Chennevières-Pointel and Anatole de Montaiglon, eds. *Abecedario de P.J. Mariette, et autres notes inédites de cet amateur sur les arts et les artistes*. 6 vols. Paris, 1851–60.

Chong 1987a
Alan Chong. "The Drawings of Cornelis van Poelenburch." *Master Drawings* 25 (1987): 3–62, 85–116.

Chong 1987b
Alan Chong. "The Market for Landscape Painting." In *Masters of 17th-Century Dutch Landscape Painting*, ed. Peter C. Sutton, 110–12. Exh. cat. Amsterdam: Rijksmuseum; Boston: Museum of Fine Arts; Philadelphia Museum of Art, 1987–88.

Chong 1992
Alan Chong. "Aelbert Cuyp and the Meanings of Landscape." PhD thesis, Institute of Fine Arts, New York University, 1992.

Chong 2001
Alan Chong. "Aristocratic Imaginings: Aelbert Cuyp's Patrons and Collectors." In Wheelock 2001, 34–51.

Churchill 1935
W.A. Churchill. *Watermarks in Paper in Holland, England, France, etc., in the XVII and XVIII Centuries and Their Inter-Connection*. Amsterdam, 1935.

Colnaghi 1956
Exhibition of Old Master Drawings. Sale cat. London: P. & D. Colnaghi and Co., 1956.

Constable (ed. Beckett 1969)
John Constable. *John Constable's Correspondence, VI: The Fishers*, ed. Ronald Brymer Beckett. Ipswich, 1969.

Constable (ed. Beckett 1970)
John Constable. *John Constable's Discourses*, ed. Ronald Brymer Beckett. Ipswich, 1970.

Cook 1914
Edward Cook. *Catalogue of the Pictures in the Gallery of Alleyn's College of God's Gift at Dulwich, with Biographical Notices of the Painters etc., etc.* London, 1914.

Cornaro 1560
Luigi [Alvise] Cornaro. *Trattato di acque*. Padua, 1560.

Crenshaw 2006
Paul Crenshaw. *Rembrandt's Bankruptcy: The Artist, His Patrons, and the Art Market in Seventeenth-Century Netherlands*. Cambridge, 2006.

Czére 2007
Andrea Czére, ed. *In Arte Venustas: Studies on Drawings in Honour of Teréz Gerszi*. Budapest, 2007.

D'Hulst 1974
Roger A. d'Hulst. *Jordaens Drawings*. 4 vols. New York, 1974.

D'Hulst 1980
Roger A. d'Hulst. "'Jordaens Drawings': Supplement I." *Master Drawings* 18 (1980): 360–70, 410–29.

D'Hulst, De Poorter, and Vandenven 1993
Roger A. d'Hulst, Nora de Poorter, and M. Vandenven. *Jacob Jordaens 1593–1678*. Exh. cat. 2 vols. Antwerp: Koninklijk Museum voor Schone Kunsten, 1993.

DaCosta Kaufmann 1982
Thomas DaCosta Kaufmann. *Drawings from the Holy Roman Empire, 1540–1680: A Selection from North American Collections*. Exh. cat. Princeton University Art Museum, 1982–83.

Dash 1999
Mike Dash. *Tulipomania: The Story of the World's Most Coveted Flower and the Extraordinary Passions it Aroused*. New York, 1999.

Davis 1995
Natalie Zemon Davis. *Women on the Margins: Three Seventeenth-Century Lives*. Cambridge (MA), 1995.

Day & Faber 2004
Works on Paper. Sale cat. London: Day & Faber, 2004.

De Bruyn Kops 1965
C.J. de Bruyn Kops. "Kanttekeningen bij het nieuw verworven landschap van Aelbert Cuyp: En enige bijzonderheden over de waardering en export van zijn werk in het verleden." *Bulletin van het Rijksmuseum* 13 (1965): 161–76.

De Groot 2022
Erlend de Groot. "Aelbert Cuyp, *River Landscape near Nijmegen with Riders Watering their Horses*, c. 1653–1657." In *Dutch Paintings of the Seventeenth Century in the Rijksmuseum*, ed. Jonathan Bikker, 2022, hdl.handle.net/10934/RM0001.COLLECT.8331.

De Hond and Mostert 2013
Jan de Hond and Tristan Mostert. *Nova Zembla*. Amsterdam, 2013.

De Jaegere 2010
Isabelle De Jaegere et al. *Roelandt Savery: A Painter in the Services of Emperor Rudolf II*. Exh. cat. Prague: Národní Galerie; Kortrijk: Broelmuseum, 2010–11.

De Jongh and Luijten 1991
Eddy de Jongh and Ger Luijten. *Mirror of Everyday Life: Genre Prints in the Netherlands*. Exh. cat. Amsterdam: Rijksmuseum, 1991.

DeGrazia Bohlin 1979
Diane DeGrazia Bohlin. *Prints and Related Drawings by the Carracci Family: A Catalogue Raisonné*. Washington, 1979.

Dethloff 1996
Diana Dethloff. "The Executors' Account Book and the Dispersal of Sir Peter Lely's Collection." *Journal of the History of Collections* 8 (1996): 15–51.

Dethloff 2018
Diana Dethloff. "From the Cabinet to the Studio: Peter Lely and Drawing Collecting in Seventeenth-Century England." In *A Demand for Drawings: Five Centuries of Collectors and Collecting Drawings*, ed. John Marciari, 56–69. New York, 2018.

Diels and Leesberg 2005
Ann Diels and Marjolein Leesberg. *The New Hollstein: Dutch and Flemish Etchings, Engravings and Woodcuts, 1450–1700, 14: The Collaert Dynasty*, ed. Marjolein Leesberg and Arnout Balis. 8 parts. Ouderkerk aan den IJssel, 2005.

Dietz and Penz 2018
Georg Josef Dietz and Antje Penz. "Zeichnen mit Rembrandt: Material and Technik in Rembrandts Werkstatt." In Bevers 2018, 292–303.

Dittrich and Ketelsen 2004
Christian Dittrich and Thomas Ketelsen. *Rembrandt: Die Dresdener Zeichnungen*. Exh. cat. Dresden: Staatliche Kunstsammlungen, Kupferstich-Kabinett, 2004.

Dobson 2008
David Dobson. *Transatlantic Voyages, 1600–1699*. 2nd ed. Baltimore, 2008.

Donkersloot 2006
Wietske Donkersloot. "Brederode verbeeld: Tekeningen, prenten, schilderijen en kaarten van de ruïne van Brederode, 1537–1750." MA thesis, Universiteit Leiden, 2006.

Dordrecht 1977
Aelbert Cuyp en zijn familie, schilders te Dordrecht: Gerrit Gerritz. Cuyp (ca. 1565–1644), Jacob Gerritsz. Cuyp (1594–1651/52), Benjamin Gerritsz. Cuyp (1612–1652), Aelbert Cuyp (1620–1691). Schilderijen, tekeningen. Exh. cat. Dordrecht: Dordrechts Museum, 1977–78.

Döring 2006
Thomas Döring, with Gisela Bungarten and Christiane Pagel. *Aus Rembrandts Kreis: Die Zeichnungen des Braunschweiger Kupferstichkabinetts*. Exh. cat. Braunschweig: Herzog Anton Ulrich-Museum, 2006.

Duerloo and Smuts 2016
Luc Duerloo and R. Malcolm Smuts, eds. *The Age of Rubens: Diplomacy, Dynastic Politics, and the Visual Arts in Early Seventeenth-Century Europe*. Turnhout, 2016.

Duparc and Buvelot 2009
Frederik Duparc and Quentin Buvelot. *Philips Wouwerman (1619–1668)*. Exh. cat. Kassel: Gemäldegalerie Alter Meister; The Hague: Mauritshuis, 2009–10.

Durlacher 1937
Old Master Drawings. Sale cat. New York: Durlacher Brothers, 1937.

Eaker 2015
Adam Eaker. "Van Dyck between Master and Model." *Art Bulletin* 97 (2015): 173–91.

Eidelberg 1995
Martin Eidelberg. "Watteau's Italian Reveries." *Gazette des Beaux Arts* 126 (1995): 111–38.

Elen 1989
Albert J. Elen. *Missing Old Master Drawings from the Franz Koenigs Collection Claimed by the State of The Netherlands*. The Hague, 1989.

Elen 2011
Albert J. Elen. "A Gifted and Practical Draughtsman: Creativity and Utility in the Working Process." In *The Bloemaert Effect: Colour and Composition in the Golden Age*, ed. Liesbeth Helmus and Gero Seelig, 31–38. Exh. cat. Utrecht: Centraal Museum; Schwerin: Staatliches Museum, 2011–12.

Elen 2012
Albert J. Elen. "Johannes Stradanus: Four Drawings from the *Odyssey* Series." In Baroni Vannucci and Sellink 2012, 331–35.

Ertz 1979
Klaus Ertz. *Jan Brueghel der Ältere (1568–1625): Die Gemälde, mit kritischem Oeuvrekatalog*. Cologne, 1979.

Ertz and Nitze-Ertz 2016
Klaus Ertz and Christa Nitze-Ertz. *David Vinckboons (1576–1632): Monographie mit kritischem Katalog der Zeichnungen und Gemälde*. Lingen, 2016.

Evans 2014
Mark Evans. *John Constable: The Making of a Master*. Exh. cat. London: Victoria and Albert Museum, 2014–15.

Feist 1967
Master Drawings: Face and Figure through the Centuries. Sale cat. New York: Herbert E. Feist Gallery, 1967.

Ferino-Pagden 2007
Sylvia Ferino-Pagden, ed. *Der späte Tizian und die Sinnlichkeit der Malerei*. Exh. cat. Vienna: Kunsthistorisches Museum; Venice: Gallerie dell'Accademia, 2007–8.

Feuchtmayr and Schädler 1973
Karl Feuchtmayr and Alfred Schädler. *Georg Petel (1601/2–1634)*. Berlin, 1973.

Filedt Kok 1972
Jan Piet Filedt Kok. *Rembrandt Etchings & Drawings in the Rembrandt House*. Amsterdam, 1972.

Filedt Kok 1976
Jan Piet Filedt Kok. *Rembrandt Etchings & Drawings in the Rembrandt House*. 2nd ed. Amsterdam, 1976.

Filedt Kok 1991
Jan Piet Filedt Kok. "Hendrick Goltzius–Engraver, Designer and Publisher, 1582–1600." *Nederlands Kunsthistorisch Jaarboek* 42/43 (1991): 159–218.

Flagg 1893
Jared B. Flagg. *The Life and Letters of Washington Allston*. London, 1893.

Fleming-Williams 1990
Ian Fleming-Williams. *Constable and His Drawings*. London, 1990.

Foucart and Rosenberg 1978
Jacques Foucart and Pierre Rosenberg. "Some 'Modelli' of Religious Scenes by Dirck Barendsz." *Burlington Magazine* 120 (1978): 198–205.

Fowler 2016
Caroline O. Fowler. *Drawing and the Senses: An Early Modern History*. Turnhout, 2016.

Frankfurt 1906
Das holländische Sittenbild, I: Die Maler des Bauernstücks: Ostade und sein Kreis. Jan Steen. Exh. cat. Frankfurt: Städelsches Kunstinstitut, Kupferstichkabinett, 1906–7.

Franz 1965
Heinrich Gerhard Franz. "Hans Bol als Landschaftszeichner." *Jahrbuch des Kunsthistorischen Institutes der Universität Graz* 1 (1965): 19–67.

Frerichs and Schatborn 1975
L.C.J. Frerichs and Peter Schatborn. *De verzameling van Hans van Leeuwen*. Exh. cat. Amsterdam: Rijksmuseum, 1975–76.

Fribourg et al. 1982
Niederländische Meisterzeichnungen des 17. bis 19. Jahrhunderts aus der Sammlung Hans van Leeuwen. Exh. cat. Fribourg: Museum für Kunst und Geschichte; Passau: Oberhausmuseum; Trier: Städtisches Museum; Aachen: Suermondt-Ludwig-Museum, 1982–84.

Fucci 2018
Robert Fucci. "Landscape into History: The Early Printed Landscape Series by Jan van de Velde II (1593–1641)." PhD thesis, Columbia University, New York, 2018.

Fucci 2022a
Robert Fucci. "Reflecting on Ruins: The Earliest Landscape Drawings by Jan van de Velde II." *Master Drawings* 60 (2022): 7–26.

Fucci 2022b
Robert Fucci. *Drawn to Life: Master Drawings from the Age of Rembrandt in the Peck Collection at the Ackland Art Museum*. Exh. cat. Chapel Hill: Ackland Art Museum; Amsterdam: Rembrandthuis, 2022–23.

Gady 2019
Alexandre Gady, ed. *Jules Hardouin-Mansart: Le Chantier infini. Actes du colloque international Jules Hardouin-Mansart (Paris et Versailles, 12 et 13 décembre 2008) à l'occasion du tricentenaire de la mort de Jules Hardouin-Mansart*. Paris, 2019.

Gainsborough (ed. Hayes 2001)
Thomas Gainsborough. *The Letters of Thomas Gainsborough*, ed. John Hayes. New Haven, 2001.

Garrod 1997
J.H. Garrod. *John Edmund Gardner, 1819–1899: Print and Drawing Collector*. n.p., 1997.

Geiger 1948
Benno Geiger. *Handzeichnungen alter Meister*. Zurich, Leipzig, and Vienna, 1948.

Gerard 1597
John Gerard. *The Herball; or, Generall Historie of Plantes*. London, 1597.

Gersaint 1751
E.F. Gersaint. *Catalogue raisonné de toutes les pièces qui forment l'œuvre de Rembrandt composé par feu M. Gersaint, & mis au jour, avec augmentations nécessaires, par les sieurs Helle & Glomy*. Paris, 1751.

Gerson 1940
Horst Gerson. "Leven en werken van Claes v. Beresteyn." In *Genealogie van het geslacht van Beresteyn*, ed. A. van Beresteyn, 2: 143–74. The Hague, 1940.

Gerson 1942
Horst Gerson. *Ausbreitung und Nachwirkung der holländischen Malerei des 17. Jahrhunderts*. Haarlem, 1942.

Gerson 2017
Horst Gerson. *Gerson Digital: Germany I*, ed. Rieke van Leeuwen, Thomas Fusenig, and Juliette Roding, 2017, https://gersongermany.rkdstudies.nl/.

Gerszi 2005
Teréz Gerszi. *17th-Century Dutch and Flemish Drawings in the Budapest Museum of Fine Arts: A Complete Catalogue*. Budapest, 2005.

Gerszi and Wood Ruby 2019
Teréz Gerszi and Louisa Wood Ruby. *Jan Brueghel: A Magnificent Draughtsman*. Exh. cat. Antwerp: Snijders Rockox Huis, 2019–20.

Gibson 2000
Walter S. Gibson. *Pleasant Places: The Rustic Landscape from Bruegel to Ruisdael*. Berkeley, Los Angeles, and London, 2000.

Giltaij 1976
Jeroen Giltaij. *Le cabinet d'un amateur: Dessins flamands et hollandais des XVIe et XVIIe siècles d'une collection privée d'Amsterdam*. Exh. cat. Rotterdam: Museum Boymans-Van Beuningen; Paris: Institut Néerlandais; Brussels: Bibliothèque Royale Albert Ier, 1976–77.

Giltaij 1979
Jeroen Giltaij. "Tekeningen van Isaac Koene (1637/40–1713)." *Bulletin van het Rijksmuseum* 27 (1979): 129–33.

Giltaij 2001
Jeroen Giltaij. "Jacob van Ruisdael–het revolutionaire wonderkind." In Sitt and Biesboer 2001, 29–36.

Giltaij 2017
Jeroen Giltaij. "The Drawings of Claes van Beresteyn and Adriaen Verboom." *Master Drawings* 55 (2017): 317–32.

Giltay 1980
Jeroen Giltay. "De tekeningen van Jacob van Ruisdael." *Oud Holland* 94 (1980): 141–208.

Gnann 2021
Achim Gnann. *Rembrandt: Landschaftszeichnungen (Landscape Drawings)*. Petersberg, 2021.

Gobbi 2008
Christine Gobbi. "Jacques Callot *Varie Figure Gobbi*." MA thesis, Universität Wien, 2008.

Gobin 2021
Anuradha Gobin. *Picturing Punishment: The Spectacle and Material Afterlife of the Criminal Body in the Dutch Republic*. Toronto and London, 2021.

Godefroy 1928
Louis Godefroy. *Dessins anciens et modernes*. Sale cat. Paris: Galerie Simonson, 1928.

Goldgar 2006
Anne Goldgar. "Poelenburch's Garden: Art, Flowers, Networks and Knowledge in Seventeenth-Century Holland." In *In His Milieu: Essays on Netherlandish Art in Memory of John Michael Montias*, ed. Amy Golahny, Mia M. Mochizuki, and Lisa Vergara, 183–92. Amsterdam, 2006.

Goldgar 2007
Anne Goldgar. *Tulipmania: Money, Honor, and Knowledge in the Dutch Golden Age*. Chicago, 2007.

Goldman 2012
Victoria Sears Goldman. "Omen and Oracle: Dutch Images of Beached Whales," *Victoria's Blog*, 22 August 2012, http://www.victoriasearsgoldman.com/16th-17th-century-dutch-images-beached-whales/./.

Goldner and Hendrix 1992
George R. Goldner and Lee Hendrix, with Kelly Pask. *European Drawings, 2: Catalogue of the Collections, J. Paul Getty Museum*. Malibu, 1992.

Goldyne 1975
Joseph R. Goldyne. *J.M.W. Turner: Works on Paper from American Collections*. Exh. cat. Berkeley: University Art Museum, 1975.

Göpel 1931
Erhard Göpel. "Huldschinsky-Versteigerung ein Erfolg." *Vossische Zeitung*, 4 November 1931, 6.

Griffey 1997
Erin Griffey. "What's in a Name? Forging an Identity: Portraits of Nicolaes Tulp (1593–1674)." *Dutch Crossing* 21, no. 2 (1997): 3–53.

Griswold et al. 2011
William Griswold et al. *Mannerism and Modernism: The Kasper Collection of Drawings and Photographs*. Exh. cat. New York: Morgan Library & Museum, 2011.

Gruijs 2003
Marit Gruijs. "De tekeningen van Karel Dujardin (1626–1678)." PhD thesis, Universiteit Utrecht, 2003.

Gudlaugsson 1959–60
Sturla Gudlaugsson. *Gerard ter Borch*. 2 vols. The Hague, 1959–60.

Gustot 2008
Pierre Gustot, with Sabine van Sprang. *Gillis Neyts: Un paysagiste brabançon en vallée mosane au XVIIe siècle*. Exh. cat. Namur: Musée Provincial des Arts Anciens du Namurois, 2008.

Haboldt 2001
Northern European Old Master Drawings and Oil Sketches. Sale cat. New York and Paris: Bob P. Haboldt & Co., 2001–2.

Hadjinicolaou 2019
Yannis Hadjinicolaou. *Thinking Bodies – Shaping Hands: "Handeling" in Art and Theory of the Late Rembrandtists*. Leiden, 2019.

The Hague 1930
Verzameling Dr. C. Hofstede de Groot: Schilderijen, tekeningen en kunstnijverheid. Exh. cat. The Hague: Gemeentemuseum, 1930.

Hammacher 1959
Abraham Marie W.J. Hammacher. *Catalogus van schilderijen uit de Xve tot en met de XVIIIe eeuw benevens een keuze uit de tekeningen van die periode: Rijksmuseum Kröller-Müller, Otterlo*. Otterlo, 1959.

Hannema 1949
Dirk Hannema. *Catalogue of the D.G. van Beuningen Collection*. Rotterdam, 1949.

Hargraves 2021
Matthew Hargraves. "Majestic Darkness: Constable's Late Drawings." In *Late Constable*, 53–64. Exh. cat. London: Royal Academy of Arts, 2021–22.

Harrison 2015
Colin Harrison. *Great British Drawings*. Exh. cat. Oxford: Ashmolean Museum, 2015.

Haskell and Penny 1981
Francis Haskell and Nicholas Penny. *Taste and the Antique: The Lure of Classical Sculpture, 1500–1900*. New Haven and London, 1981.

Haverkamp-Begemann 1959
Egbert Haverkamp-Begemann. *Willem Buytewech*. Amsterdam, 1959.

Haverkamp-Begemann 1961
Egbert Haverkamp-Begemann. Review of Benesch 1954–57. *Kunstchronik* 14 (1961): 10–28, 50–57, 85–91.

Haverkamp-Begemann 1990
Egbert Haverkamp-Begemann. "Van Dyck and *The Brazen Serpent*." *Master Drawings* 28 (1990): 296–302.

Haverkamp-Begemann 2001
Egbert Haverkamp-Begemann. "The Beauty of Holland: Aelbert Cuyp as Landscape Draftsman." In Wheelock 2001, 74–85.

Haverkamp-Begemann, Lawder, and Talbot 1964
Egbert Haverkamp-Begemann, Standish D. Lawder, and Charles W. Talbot, Jr. *Drawings from the Clark Art Institute*. 2 vols. New Haven, 1964.

Haverkamp-Begemann and Logan 1970
Egbert Haverkamp-Begemann and Anne Marie Logan. *European Drawings and Watercolors in the Yale University Art Gallery*. 2 vols. New Haven, 1970.

Hayes 1960
John Hayes. *Gainsborough Drawings*. Exh. cat. York City Art Gallery; Bristol City Art Gallery; Liverpool: Walker Art Gallery; Edinburgh: National Gallery of Scotland; Cardiff: National Museum of Wales, 1960–61.

Hayes 1971
John Hayes. *The Drawings of Thomas Gainsborough.* 2 vols. New Haven, 1971.

Hayes 1982
John Hayes. *The Landscape Paintings of Thomas Gainsborough.* 2 vols. London, 1982.

Hayes and Stainton 1983
John Hayes and Lindsay Stainton. *Gainsborough Drawings.* Exh. cat. Washington: National Gallery of Art; Fort Worth: Kimbell Art Museum; New Haven: Yale Center for British Art, 1983.

Heawood 1950
Edward Heawood. *Watermarks Mainly of the 17th and 18th Centuries.* Hilversum, 1950.

Held 1964
Julius Held. Review of Vey 1962. *Art Bulletin* 46 (1964): 565–68.

Held 1978
Julius Held. Review of D'Hulst 1974. *Art Bulletin* 60 (1978): 717–32.

Held 1980
Julius Held. *The Oil Sketches of Peter Paul Rubens: A Critical Catalogue.* 2 vols. Princeton, 1980.

Held 1986
Julius Held. *Rubens: Selected Drawings.* 2 vols. Mt. Kisco, 1986.

Hell 1930
Hans Hell. "Die späten Handzeichnungen Rembrandts." *Repertorium für Kunstwissenschaft* 51 (1930): 4–43, 92–136.

Hendriks 2003
Carla Hendriks. *Northern Landscapes on Roman Walls: The Frescoes of Matthijs and Paul Bril.* Florence, 2003.

Heseltine 1910
J.P. Heseltine. *Original Drawings by Old Masters of the Dutch School in the Collection of J.P.H.* London, 1910.

Hildebrand (ed. Van den Berg et al. 1998)
Hildebrand. *Camera obscura*, ed. Willem van den Berg et al. 2 vols. Amsterdam, 1998.

Hind 1915–32
Arthur M. Hind. *Catalogue of Drawings by Dutch and Flemish Artists Preserved in the Department of Prints and Drawings in the British Museum.* 3 vols. London, 1915–32.

Hinterding 2006
Erik Hinterding. *Rembrandt as an Etcher.* 3 vols. Ouderkerk aan den IJssel, 2006.

Hinterding and Rutgers 2013
Erik Hinterding and Jaco Rutgers. *The New Hollstein: Dutch and Flemish Etchings, Engravings and Woodcuts 1450–1700, 24: Rembrandt*, ed. Ger Luijten. 7 parts. Ouderkerk aan den IJssel, 2013.

Hinterding, Luijten, and Royalton-Kisch 2000
Erik Hinterding, Ger Luijten, and Martin Royalton-Kisch. *Rembrandt the Printmaker.* Exh. cat. Amsterdam: Rijksmuseum; London: British Museum, 2000–1.

Hofstede de Groot 1906a
Cornelis Hofstede de Groot. *Die Handzeichnungen Rembrandts: Versuch eines beschreibenden und kritischen Katalogs.* Haarlem, 1906.

Hofstede de Groot 1906b
Cornelis Hofstede de Groot. *Die Urkunden über Rembrandt.* The Hague, 1906.

Hofstede de Groot 1908–27
Cornelis Hofstede de Groot. *A Catalogue Raisonné of the Works of the Most Eminent Dutch, Flemish and French Painters.* 8 vols. London, 1908–27.

Hofstede de Groot 1929
Cornelis Hofstede de Groot. "Einige Betrachtungen über die Ausstellung holländischer Kunst in London." *Repertorium für Kunstwissenschaft* 50 (1929): 134–46.

Hollstein 1949–2010
F.W.H. Hollstein et al. *Dutch and Flemish Etchings, Engravings, and Woodcuts, ca. 1450–1700.* 72 vols. Amsterdam and elsewhere, 1949–2010.

Hoock 2004
Holger Hoock. "Old Masters and the English School: The Royal Academy of Arts and the Notion of a National Gallery at the Turn of the Nineteenth Century." *Journal of the History of Collections* 16 (2004): 1–18.

Houbraken 1718–21
Arnold Houbraken. *De groote schouburgh der Nederlantsche konstschilders en schilderessen: waar van 'er vele met hunne beeltenissen ten tooneel een verschynen, en hun levensgedrag en konstwerken beschreven worden: zynde een vervolg op Het Schilderboek van K. v. Mander.* 3 vols. Amsterdam, 1718–21.

Humphry MS ca. 1802
Ozias Humphry, "Original Correspondence of Ozias Humphry, R.A.," unpublished autobiographical MS, vol. 1, ca. 1802. Royal Academy Library, London.

Huygens 1891
Christiaan Huygens. *Œuvres complètes de Christiaan Huygens, IV: Correspondance, 1662–1663.* The Hague, 1891.

Jaffé 1991
Michael Jaffé. Review of Brown 1991. *Burlington Magazine* 133 (1991): 341–44.

James et al. 1997
Carlo James et al. *Old Master Prints and Drawings: A Guide to Preservation and Conservation.* Amsterdam, 1997.

Jameson 1842
Anna Jameson. *Handbook to the Public Galleries of Art in and near London, with Catalogues of the Pictures.* 2 vols. London, 1842.

Janssen 2017
Geert H. Janssen. "The Republic of the Refugees: Early Modern Migrations and the Dutch Experience." *The Historical Journal* 60 (2017): 233–52.

Jatta 1992
Barbara Jatta. *Lievin Cruyl e la sua opera grafica: Un artista fiammingo nell'Italia del Seicento.* Brussels, 1992.

Jellema and Plomp 1992
Renske E. Jellema and Michiel Plomp. *Episcopius: Jan de Bisschop, Lawyer and Draughtsman.* Exh. cat. Amsterdam: Museum Het Rembrandthuis, 1992.

Jeudwine 1963
Exhibition of Old Master Drawings. Sale cat. London: W.R. Jeudwine at the Alpine Club, 1963.

Johnson and Goldyne 2006
Robert Flynn Johnson and Joseph R. Goldyne. *Judging by Appearance: Master Drawings from the Collection of Joseph and Deborah Goldyne.* Exh. cat. San Francisco: Legion of Honor, 2006.

Johnson, Sethares, and Ellis 2021
C. Richard Johnson, Jr., William A. Sethares, and Margaret Holben Ellis. "Overlay Videos for Quick and Accurate Watermark Identification, Comparison, and Matching." *Journal of Historians of Netherlandish Art* 13, no. 2 (2021), https://jhna.org/articles/automated-watermark-identification/0.5092/jhna.2021.13.2.1.

Josi 1821
Christiaan Josi. *Collection d'imitations des dessins d'après les principaux maîtres hollandais et flamands, commencée par C. Ploos van Amstel ... précédés d'un discours sur l'état ancien et moderne des arts dans les Pays Bas.* London, 1821.

Judson 1970
Richard Judson. *Dirck Barendsz. (1534–1592).* Amsterdam, 1970.

Kassel 1930
Meisterliche Handzeichnungen aus Privatbesitz: Sammlung Deiker. Exh. cat. Kassel: Hessisches Landesmuseum, 1930–31.

Katz and Van Gelder 1948
N. Katz and J.G. van Gelder. *Rembrandt-Ausstellung zu Ehren Ihrer Majestät Königin Wilhelmine der Niederlande.* Exh. cat. Basel: Katz Gallery, 1948.

Kauffmann 1926
Hans Kauffmann. "Zur Kritik der Rembrandtzeichnungen." *Repertorium für Kunstwissenschaft* 47 (1926): 157–78.

Ketelsen, Hahn, and Kuhlmann-Hodick 2011
Thomas Ketelsen, Oliver Hahn, and Petra Kuhlmann-Hodick, eds. *Zeichnen im Zeitalter Bruegels: Die niederländischen Zeichnungen des 16. Jahrhunderts im Dresdner Kupferstich-Kabinett. Beiträge zu einer Typologie.* Dresden, 2011.

Kettering 1977
Alison McNeil Kettering. "Rembrandt's *Flute Player*: A Unique Treatment of Pastoral." *Simiolus* 9 (1977): 19–44.

Kettering 1983
Alison McNeil Kettering. *The Dutch Arcadia: Pastoral Art and Its Audience in the Golden Age.* Montclair, 1983.

Kettering 1988
Alison McNeil Kettering. *Drawings from the Ter Borch Studio Estate in the Rijksmuseum.* 2 vols. The Hague, 1988.

Keyes 1975
George S. Keyes. *Cornelis Vroom: Marine and Landscape Artist.* 2 vols. Alphen aan den Rijn, 1975.

Keyes 1984
George S. Keyes. *Esaias van den Velde (1587–1630).* Doornspijk, 1984.

Keyes 1987
George S. Keyes. "Esaias van de Velde and the Chalk Sketch." *Nederlands Kunsthistorisch Jaarboek* 38 (1987): 136–45.

Kist 1971
J.B. Kist. *The Exercise of Armes: A Commentary.* Lochem, Netherlands, 1971.

Klinge 2005
Margret Klinge. *David Teniers der Jüngere (1610–1690): Alltag und Vergnügen in Flandern.* Exh. cat. Karlsruhe: Staatliche Kunsthalle, 2005.

Kloek 2002
Wouter Th. Kloek. *Aelbert Cuyp: Land, water, licht.* Amsterdam, 2002.

Koerner 2009
Joseph Leo Koerner. *Caspar David Friedrich and the Subject of Landscape.* 2nd ed. London, 2009.

Koldeweij 2017
Anna Cecilia Koldeweij. "Koninklijke verbeelders verbeeld? Twee recent ontdekte tekeningen van Gerard van Honthorst in perspectief." In *De verbeelder verbeeld(t): Boekillustratie en beeldende kunst*, ed. Anna Cecilia Koldeweij and Jos Koldeweij, 68–76. Nijmegen, 2017.

Koslow 1996
Susan Koslow. "Law and Order in Rubens's *Wolf and Fox Hunt.*" *Art Bulletin* 78 (1996): 680–706.

Krelage 1942
E.H. Krelage. *Bloemenspeculatie in Nederland.* Amsterdam, 1942.

Kuipers-Verbuijs et al. 1997
M.J. Kuipers-Verbuijs et al. *Ruïnes in Nederland.* Zwolle, 1997.

La Fontaine-Verwey 1988
Herman de La Fontaine-Verwey. "Vincent van Gogh (1866–1922): Art Dealer and Bibliophile." *Quaerendo* 18 (1988): 3–16.

Lammertse and Vergara 2018
Friso Lammertse and Alejandro Vergara. *Rubens: Painter of Sketches.* Exh. cat. Madrid: Museo Nacional del Prado; Rotterdam: Museum Boijmans Van Beuningen, 2018–19.

Laurentius and Laurentius 2007
Theo and Frans Laurentius. *Watermarks, 1600–1650, Found in the Zeeland Archives.* Houten, 2007.

Laurentius and Laurentius 2008
Theo and Frans Laurentius. *Watermarks, 1650–1700, Found in the Zeeland Archives.* Houten, 2008.

Le Claire 2005
Master Drawings: Recent Acquisitions. Sale cat. Hamburg: Thomas Le Claire Kunsthandel, 2005.

Lee 2022
Casey Lee. "A Note on Charles Emil Duits and His Collection of Drawings." *Master Drawings* 60 (2022): 37–39.

Leeflang 2012
Huigen Leeflang. "The Roman Experiences of Hendrick Goltzius and Jacob Matham: A Comparison." In *Ein privilegiertes Medium und die Bildkulturen Europas: Deutsche, französische und niederländische Kupferstecher und Graphikverleger in Rom von 1590 bis 1630. Akten des Internationalen Studientages der Bibliotheca Hertziana, Rom, 10.-11. November 2008*, ed. Eckhard Leuschner, 21–38. Munich, 2012.

Leeflang and Luijten 2003
Huigen Leeflang and Ger Luijten, eds. *Hendrick Goltzius (1558–1617), Dutch Master: Drawings, Prints, and Paintings.* Exh. cat. Amsterdam: Rijksmuseum; New York: Metropolitan Museum of Art; Toledo Museum of Art, 2003–4.

Leesberg 2008
Marjolein Leesberg. *The New Hollstein: Dutch and Flemish Etchings, Engravings and Woodcuts, 1450–1700, 18: Johannes Stradanus*, ed. Ger Luijten. 3 parts. Ouderkerk aan den IJssel, 2008.

Leesberg 2012
Marjolein Leesberg. *The New Hollstein: Dutch and Flemish Etchings, Engravings and Woodcuts, 1450–1700, 23: Hendrick Goltzius*, ed. Huigen Leeflang. 4 parts. Ouderkerk aan den IJssel, 2012.

Lemeunier et al. 1980
Albert Lemeunier et al. *Œuvres maîtresses du Musée d'art religieux et d'art mosan.* Exh. cat. Liège: Basilique Saint-Martin, 1980.

Libson and Yarker 2018
The Spirit & Force of Art: Drawing in Britain, 1600–1750. Sale cat. London: Lowell Libson & Jonny Yarker Ltd., 2018.

Liedtke 2007
Walter Liedtke. *Dutch Paintings in the Metropolitan Museum of Art.* 2 vols. New York and New Haven, 2007.

Liesenborghs 2005
Philippe Liesenborghs. "Het edele vermaak: De jacht in de Spaanse Nederlanden onder de Aartshertogen." MA thesis, Katholieke Universiteit, Leuven, 2005.

Lieure 1924–29
J. Lieure. *Jacques Callot.* 8 vols. Paris, 1924–29.

Logan 2005
Anne-Marie Logan, in collaboration with Michiel C. Plomp. *Peter Paul Rubens: The Drawings.* Exh. cat. New York: Metropolitan Museum of Art, 2005.

Logan 2018
Anne-Marie Logan. Review of Van Tuinen 2018. https://hnanews.org/hnar/reviews/power-and-grace-drawings-by-rubens-van-dyck-and-jordaens/.

Logan 2021
Anne-Marie Logan. *The Drawings of Peter Paul Rubens: A Critical Catalogue, I: 1590–1608.* Turnhout, 2021.

Logan and Belkin 2022
Anne-Marie Logan and Kristin Lohse Belkin. *The Drawings of Peter Paul Rubens: A Critical Catalogue, II: 1609–1620.* Turnhout, 2022.

London 1953
J.M.W. Turner R.A. (1775–1851): An Exhibition of Pictures from Public and Private Collections in Great Britain. Exh. cat. London: Whitechapel Art Gallery, 1953.

London 1974
Turner (1775–1851). Exh. cat. London: Royal Academy of Arts and the Tate Gallery, 1974–75.

London 1987
The Image of London: Views by Travellers and Emigrés, 1550–1920. Exh. cat. London: Barbican Art Gallery, 1987.

London et al. 1972
Flemish Drawings of the Seventeenth Century from the Collection of Frits Lugt, Institut Néerlandais. Exh. cat. London: Victoria and Albert Museum; Paris: Institut Néerlandais; Bern: Kunstmuseum; Brussels: Bibliothèque Royale de Belgique, 1972.

Loze and Vautier 2017
Pierre Loze and Dominique Vautier, eds. *Remigio Cantagallina (Borgo San Sepolcro 1575–Florence 1656): Il viaggio delle Fiandre/Le Voyage d'un artiste florentin dans les Pays-Bas méridionaux.* Ghent, 2017.

Lugt 1921
Frits Lugt. *Les marques de collections de dessins et d'estampes.* Amsterdam, 1921.

Lugt 1929–33
Frits Lugt. *Musée du Louvre. Inventaire général des dessins des écoles du Nord: École hollandaise.* 3 vols. Paris, 1929–33.

Lugt 1950
Frits Lugt. *École Nationale Supérieure des Beaux-Arts: Inventaire général des dessins des écoles du Nord.* Paris, 1950.

Lugt 1956
Frits Lugt. *Les Marques de collections de dessins et d'estampes: Supplément.* The Hague, 1956.

Luijten 2005
Ger Luijten. "Moses ter Borch leert tekenen." *Kunstschrift* 49 (2005): 36–41.

Luijten, Schatborn, and Wheelock 2017
Ger Luijten, Peter Schatborn, and Arthur K. Wheelock, Jr., eds. *Drawings for Paintings in the Age of Rembrandt.* Exh. cat. Washington: National Gallery of Art; Paris: Fondation Custodia, 2017.

Luijten et al. 1993
Ger Luijten et al. *Dawn of the Golden Age: Northern Netherlandish Art, 1580–1620.* Exh. cat. Amsterdam: Rijksmuseum, 1993–94.

Mackelaitė 2022
Austėja Mackelaitė. “A Double-Sided Drawing by Cornelis van Poelenburch in the Moore Collection.” *Master Drawings* 60 (2022): 43–46.

Magnusson 2018
Börje Magnusson. *Dutch Drawings in Swedish Public Collections.* Berlin, 2018.

Marciari 2009
John Marciari. “Artistic Practice in Later Cinquecento Rome and Girolamo Muziano’s Accademia di San Luca.” In *The Accademia Seminars: The Accademia di San Luca in Rome, c. 1590–1635*, ed. Peter Lukehart, 197–224. CASVA Seminar Papers 2. Washington, 2009.

Marciari 2018
John Marciari. *Drawing in Tintoretto’s Venice.* Exh. cat. New York: Morgan Library & Museum; Washington: National Gallery of Art, 2018.

Marciari 2019
John Marciari. *Guercino: Virtuoso Draftsman.* Exh. cat. New York: Morgan Library & Museum, 2019–20.

Marciari 2020
John Marciari. “Caravaggio Did Not Draw–But Are There Caravaggesque Drawings?” In *La scintilla divina: Il disegno a Roma tra Cinque e Seicento*, ed. Stefan Albl and Marco Simone Bolzoni, 346–67. Rome, 2020.

Marquaille 2022
Léonie Marquaille. “Printmaking in Bloemaert’s Workshop in Utrecht: Reconsidering Abraham’s Collaboration with His Sons Cornelis II and Frederick.” In *New Perspectives on Abraham Bloemaert and His Workshop*, ed. Léonie Marquaille, 167–86. Gouden Eeuw: New Perspectives in Dutch Seventeenth-Century Art 3. Turnhout, 2022.

Marty de Cambiaire 2024
Laurie Marty de Cambiaire. *Drawings and Oil Sketches.* Sale cat. Paris and New York: Marty de Cambiaire, 2024.

Mayor Collection 1875
A Brief Chronological Description of a Collection of Original Drawings and Sketches by the Old Masters of the Different Schools of Europe, from the Revival of Art in Italy in the XIIIth to the XIXth Century, Formed by the Late Mr. William Mayor, of Bayswater Hill, London, the Result of upwards of Fifty Years’ Experience and Research. London, 1875.

McCullagh 2010
Suzanne Folds McCullagh, ed. *Gray Collection: Seven Centuries of Art.* Exh. cat. Art Institute of Chicago, 2010.

Meadows 1998
Anne Meadows. “Collecting Seventeenth-Century Dutch Painting in England, 1689–1760.” PhD thesis, University College, London, 1998.

Meijer 1988
Bert Meijer. “On Dirck Barendsz and Venice.” *Oud Holland* 102 (1988): 141–54.

Meijer 1991
Bert Meijer. *Rondom Rembrandt en Titiaan: Artistieke relaties tussen Amsterdam en Venetië in prent en tekening.* Exh. cat. Amsterdam: Rembrandthuis, 1991.

Metzler 2014
Sally Metzler. *Bartholomeus Spranger: Splendor and Eroticism in Imperial Prague. The Complete Works.* Exh. cat. New York: Metropolitan Museum of Art, 2014.

Michel 1892
Émile Michel. *Les Brueghel.* Paris, 1892.

Mielke 2011
Ursula Mielke. *The New Hollstein: Dutch and Flemish Etchings, Engravings and Woodcuts, 1450–1700, 23: Crispijn van den Broeck*, ed. Ger Luijten. 2 parts. Ouderkerk aan den IJssel, 2011.

Mielke 2015
Ursula Mielke. *The New Hollstein: Dutch and Flemish Etchings, Engravings and Woodcuts, 1450–1700, 27: Hans Bol*, ed. Ger Luijten. 2 parts. Ouderkerk aan den IJssel, 2015.

Moustier 2012
Béatrice de Moustier. “La collection de dessins de l’école italienne du marquis de Lagoy (1764–1829).” PhD thesis, École du Louvre, Paris, 2012.

Muchnic 2019
Suzanne Muchnic. *Odd Man In: Norton Simon and the Pursuit of Culture.* Pasadena, 2019.

Münz 1952
Ludwig Münz. *Rembrandt’s Etchings: Reproductions of the Whole Original Etched Work.* 2 vols. London, 1952.

Naumann 1978
Otto Naumann. “Frans van Mieris as a Draughtsman.” *Master Drawings* 16 (1978): 3–34; 71–96.

Naumann 1981
Otto Naumann. *Frans van Mieris (1635–1681) the Elder.* 2 vols. Doornspijk, 1981.

New York 1973
Abraham Bloemaert (1564–1651). Exh. cat. New York: Metropolitan Museum of Art, 1973.

Nichols 2013
Lawrence W. Nichols. *The Paintings of Hendrick Goltzius (1558–1617): A Monograph and Catalogue Raisonné.* Doornspijk, 2013.

Nickel 2017
Tobias Benjamin Nickel. “Die Landschaftszeichnungen von Domenico Campagnola (1500–1564).” 3 vols. PhD thesis, Universität Wien, 2017.

Nielsen 2016
Jesper Nielsen. “The Cave and the Butterfly: Thoughts on Death and Rebirth in Ancient Mesoamerica.” *Contributions in New World Archaeology* 10 (2016): 101–12.

Niemeijer 1964
J.W. Niemeijer. “Varia Topografica, IV: Een album met Utrechtse gezichten door Abraham Rutgers.” *Oud Holland* 79 (1964): 127–30, 134.

Niemeyer 1958
J.W. Niemeyer. “Het oudste gezicht op Rijnsaterwoude.” *Zuid-Holland* 4 (December 1958): 74–79.

Nihom-Nijstad 1983
Saskia Nihom-Nijstad. *Reflets du siècle d’or: Tableaux hollandais du dix-septième siècle.* Exh. cat. Paris: Institut Néerlandais, 1983.

Ongpin 2006
Stephen Ongpin. *Master Drawings and Oil Sketches: New York and London 2006.* Sale cat. New York: Adam Williams Fine Art; London: Jean-Luc Baroni Gallery, 2006.

Ongpin 2015
Stephen Ongpin. *Master Drawings 2015.* Sale cat. New York: Dickinson Roundell, 2015.

Orenstein 2001
Nadine M. Orenstein, ed. *Peter Bruegel the Elder: Drawings and Prints.* Exh. cat. New York: Metropolitan Museum of Art; Rotterdam: Museum Boijmans Van Beuningen, 2001.

Oud, Jonker, and Schapelhouman 1995
Ingrid Oud, Michiel Jonker, and Marijn Schapelhouman. *In de ban van Italië: Tekeningen uit een Amsterdamse verzameling.* Exh. cat. Amsterdam: Amsterdams Historisch Museum, 1995.

Oursel 1981
Hervé Oursel. *Donation d’Antoine Brasseur.* Exh. cat. Lille: Musée des Beaux-Arts, 1981.

Paarlberg 2002
Sander Paarlberg, ed. *Jacob Gerritsz. Cuyp, 1594–1652.* Dordrecht, 2002.

Papi 2015
Gianni Papi, ed. *Gherardo delle Notti: Quadri bizzarrissimi e cene allegre.* Exh. cat. Florence: Galleria degli Uffizi, 2015.

Parker 1928
K.T. Parker. “Some Drawings by Rubens and His School in the Collection of Mrs. G.W. Wrangham.” *Old Master Drawings* 3 (1928): 1–6.

Parker and Byam Shaw 1953
K.T. Parker and James Byam Shaw. *Drawings by Old Masters.* Exh. cat. London: Royal Academy, 1953.

Paris 1967
Le cabinet d’un grand amateur, P.-J. Mariette (1694–1774): Dessins du XVe siècle au XVIIIe siècle. Exh. cat. Paris: Musée du Louvre, 1967.

Peeters and Schmitz 1997
Jan Peeters and Erik Schmitz. “Belangrijke aanwinst voor Gemeentearchief: Een blad met twee onbekende tekeningen van Claes Jansz Vischer.” *Amstelodamum* 84 (1997): 33–44.

Perman 1962
E. Perman. *Oude tekeningen uit de Nederlanden: Verzemeling Prof. E. Perman, Stockholm.* Exh. cat. Laren: Singer Museum, 1962.

Piccard 1961–97
Gerhard Piccard. *Die Wasserzeichenkartei Piccard im Hauptstaatsarchiv Stuttgart.* Veröffentlichungen der Staatlichen Archivverwaltung Baden-Württemberg, Sonderreihe. 25 vols. Stuttgart, 1961–97.

Pijl 2000
Luke Pijl. Review of Wood Ruby 1999. *Burlington Magazine* 142 (2000): 176–78.

Plomp 1997
Michiel C. Plomp. *The Dutch Drawings in the Teyler Museum: Artists Born between 1575 and 1630.* Haarlem, Ghent, and Doornspijk, 1997.

Plomp 2020
Michiel Plomp. “John Constable and the Old Masters.” In *John Constable*, ed. Conal Shields et al., 45–75. Exh. cat. Haarlem: Teylers Museum, 2020.

Plomp and Sonnabend 2016
Michiel Plomp and Martin Sonnabend. *Watteau: Der Zeichner.* Exh. cat. Frankfurt: Städel Museum; Haarlem: Teylers Museum, 2016.

Ploos van Amstel 1980
G. Ploos van Amstel. *Portret van een koopman en uitvinder Cornelis Ploos van Amstel: Maatschappelijk, cultureel en familieleven van een achttiende-eeuwer.* Assen, 1980.

Ploos van Amstel 2003
J.K. Ploos van Amstel. “De archiefschat van J.K. Ploos van Amstel.” *Archievenblad* 107, no. 7 (2003): 3.

Pollmann 2007
Judith Pollmann. “‘Brabanters Do Fairly Resemble Spaniards After All’: Memory, Propaganda, and Identity in the Twelve Years’ Truce.” In *Public Opinion and Changing Identities in the Early Modern Netherlands: Essays in Honour of Alastair Duke*, ed. Judith Pollmann and Andrew Spicer, 211–27. Leiden, 2007.

Posada Kubissa 2009
Teresa Posada Kubissa. *Pintura holandesa en el Museo Nacional del Prado: Catálogo razonado.* Madrid, 2009.

Posner 1977
Donald Posner. “Jacques Callot and the Dances Called Sfessania.” *Art Bulletin* 59 (1977): 203–16.

Poughkeepsie and New York 1961
Centennial Loan Exhibition: Drawings and Watercolors from Alumnae and Their Families. Exh. cat. Poughkeepsie: Vassar College Art Gallery; New York: Wildenstein & Co., Inc., 1961.

Py 2015
Bernadette Py. *La collection de dessins italiens de Pierre Crozat (1665–1740): L’œil de Mariette.* Paris, 2015.

Reiss 1975
Stephen Reiss. *Aelbert Cuyp.* London, 1975.

Reitsma 2008
Ella Reitsma. *Maria Sibylla Merian & Daughters: Women of Art and Science.* Exh. cat. Amsterdam: Rembrandthuis; Los Angeles: J. Paul Getty Museum, 2008.

Reynolds 1984
Graham Reynolds. *The Later Paintings and Drawings of John Constable.* 2 vols. New Haven and London, 1984.

Reynolds 1996
Graham Reynolds. *The Early Paintings and Drawings of John Constable.* 2 vols. New Haven, 1996.

Reznicek 1961
E.K.J. Reznicek. *Die Zeichnungen von Hendrick Goltzius.* 2 vols. Utrecht, 1961.

Reznicek 1993
E.K.J. Reznicek. “Drawings by Hendrick Goltzius: Thirty Years Later.” *Master Drawings* 31 (1993): 215–78.

Richter and Sparkes 1880
Jean Paul Richter and John C.L. Sparkes. *Catalogue of the Pictures in the Dulwich College Gallery with Biographical Notices of the Painters.* London, 1880.

Robinson 1958–74
Michael S. Robinson. *Van de Velde Drawings: A Catalogue of Drawings in the National Maritime Museum Made by the Elder and the Younger Willem Van de Velde.* 2 vols. Cambridge, 1958–74.

Robinson 1979a
Michael S. Robinson. *The Willem van de Velde Drawings in the Boymans-Van Beuningen Museum, Rotterdam.* 3 vols. Rotterdam, 1979.

Robinson 1979b
William W. Robinson. “Preparatory Drawings by Adriaen van de Velde.” *Master Drawings* 18 (1979): 3–23.

Robinson 1990
Michael S. Robinson. *Van de Velde: A Catalogue of the Paintings of the Elder and the Younger Willem van de Velde.* 2 vols. Greenwich, 1990.

Robinson 1993
William W. Robinson. “Some Studies of Nude Models by Adriaen van de Velde.” In *Donum Amicorum: Essays in Honor of Per Bjurström*, ed. Magnus Olausson and Ulf Cederlöf, 53–66. Stockholm, 1993.

Robinson 1998
William W. Robinson. “Five Black Chalk Figure Studies by Rembrandt.” *Master Drawings* 36 (1998): 36–45.

Robinson 2000
William W. Robinson. “A Black Chalk Drawing by Rembrandt.” In *Festschrift für Konrad Oberhuber*, ed. Achim Gnann and Heinz Widauer, 303–6. Milan, 2000.

Robinson 2002
William W. Robinson. *Bruegel to Rembrandt: Dutch and Flemish Drawings from the Maida and George Abrams Collection.* Exh. cat. London: British Museum; Paris: Institut Néerlandais; Cambridge (MA): Fogg Art Museum, 2002.

Robinson and Anderson 2016
William W. Robinson and Susan Anderson. *Drawings from the Age of Bruegel, Rubens, and Rembrandt: Highlights from the Collection of the Harvard Art Museums.* Cambridge (MA), 2016.

Roelofs et al. 2009
Pieter Roelofs et al. *Hendrick Avercamp: Master of the Ice Scene.* Exh. cat. Amsterdam: Rijksmuseum; Washington: National Gallery of Art, 2009–10.

Roethlisberger 1962
Marcel Roethlisberger. *Claude Lorrain: The Wildenstein Album.* Paris, 1962.

Roethlisberger 1968
Marcel Roethlisberger. *Claude Lorrain: The Drawings.* 2 vols. Berkeley, 1968.

Roethlisberger 1969
Marcel Roethlisberger. *Bartholomäus Breenbergh: Handzeichnungen.* Berlin, 1969.

Roethlisberger 1971
Marcel Roethlisberger. *The Claude Lorrain Album in the Norton Simon, Inc. Museum of Art.* Los Angeles, 1971.

Roethlisberger 1985
Marcel Roethlisberger. “New Works by Bartholomeus Breenbergh.” *Oud Holland* 99 (1985): 57–66.

Roethlisberger 1991
Marcel Roethlisberger. *Bartholomeus Breenbergh.* New York, 1991.

Roethlisberger 1993
Marcel Roethlisberger. *Abraham Bloemaert and His Sons: Paintings and Prints.* 2 vols. Doornspijk, 1993.

Roethlisberger 2018
Marcel Roethlisberger. “Drawings by Claude Lorrain.” *Master Drawings* 56 (2018): 486–516.

Rombouts and Van Lerius 1864–76
Philippe Rombouts and Théodore Van Lerius. *De liggeren en andere historische archieven der Antwerpsche Sint Lucasgilde, onder zinspreuk “Wt jonsten versaemt.”* 2 vols. The Hague, 1864–76.

Roscam-Abbing 1993
Michiel Roscam-Abbing. *De schilder & schrijver Samuel van Hoogstraten 1627–1678: Eigentijdse bronnen en oeuvre van gesigneerde schilderijen.* Leiden, 1993.

Rosenberg 1928
Jakob Rosenberg. *Jacob van Ruisdael.* Berlin, 1928.

Rosenberg 2019
Pierre Rosenberg. *Les dessins de la collection Mariette: Écoles italienne et espagnole.* 3 vols. Paris, 2019.

Rosenberg and Prat 1996
Pierre Rosenberg and Louis-Antoine Prat. *Antoine Watteau (1684–1721): Catalogue raisonné des dessins*. 2 vols. Milan, 1996.

Royalton-Kisch 1989
Martin Royalton-Kisch. “Dirck Barendsz. and Hendrick Goltzius.” *Bulletin van het Rijksmuseum* 37 (1989): 14–26.

Royalton-Kisch 1993
Martin Royalton-Kisch. “Rembrandt’s Drawings for His Prints: Some Observations.” In *Rembrandt and His Pupils: Papers Given at a Symposium in Nationalmuseum Stockholm, 2–3 October 1992*, ed. Görel Cavalli-Björkmann, 173–92. Stockholm, 1993.

Royalton-Kisch 2010
Martin Royalton-Kisch. *Catalogue of Drawings by Rembrandt and His School in the British Museum*, 2010, https://webarchive.nationalarchives.gov.uk/ukgwa/20190801111917/https://www.britishmuseum.org/research/publications/online—research—catalogues/rembrandt—drawings/drawings—by—rembrandt.aspx.

Royalton-Kisch and Schatborn 2011
Martin Royalton-Kisch and Peter Schatborn. “The Core Group of Rembrandt Drawings, II: The List.” *Master Drawings* 49 (2011): 323–46.

Royalton-Kisch 2012–
Martin Royalton-Kisch. *The Drawings of Rembrandt: A Revision of Otto Benesch’s Catalogue Raisonné*, 2012–, https://rembrandtcatalogue.net/.

Rubinstein 1994
Gregory M.G. Rubinstein. “Artists from the Netherlands in Seventeenth-Century Britain: An Overview of Their Landscape Works.” In *The Exchange of Ideas: Religion, Scholarship and Art in Anglo-Dutch Relations in the Seventeenth Century*, ed. Simon Groenveld and Michael J. Whintle, 163–91. Zutphen, 1994.

Rubinstein 2008
Gregory M.G. Rubinstein. “The Drawings of Jan Lievens.” In *Jan Lievens. A Dutch Master Rediscovered*, ed. Arthur K. Wheelock, Jr., 68–81. Exh. cat. Washington: National Gallery of Art; Milwaukee Art Museum; Amsterdam: Rembrandthuis, 2008–9.

Rubinstein 2012
Gregory Rubinstein. “The Drawings of Jan Siberechts.” *Master Drawings* 50 (2012): 365–96.

Rudolf Collection 1962
Old Master Drawings from the Collection of Mr. C.R. Rudolf. Exh. cat. London: Arts Council Gallery; Birmingham City Museum and Art Gallery; Leeds City Art Gallery, 1962.

Rumberg 2016
Per Rumberg, with Holm Bevers. *Rembrandt’s First Masterpiece*. Exh. cat. New York: Morgan Library & Museum, 2016.

Ruskin (ed. Cook and Wedderburn 1903–12)
John Ruskin. *The Works of John Ruskin*, ed. Edward T. Cook and Alexander Wedderburn. 39 vols. London, 1903–12.

Rutgers and Standring 2018
Jaco Rutgers and Timothy J. Standring. *Rembrandt: Painter as Printmaker*. Exh. cat. Denver Art Museum, 2018.

Sadkov 2010
Vadim Sadkov, with contributions by Charles Dumas, Thera Folmer-von Oven, and Bernard Vermet. *Netherlandish, Flemish, and Dutch Drawings of the XVI–XVIII Centuries, Belgian and Dutch Drawings of the XIX–XX Centuries*. Amsterdam, 2010 (translated and revised edition of a work originally published in Russian by the Pushkin State Museum of Fine Arts, Moscow, 2001).

Sandrart 1675–79
Joachim von Sandrart. *Teutsche Academie der Bau-, Bild- und Mahlerey-Künste*. 2 vols. Nuremberg, 1675–79.

Saur 1992–
Allgemeines Künstlerlexikon: Die bildenden Künstler aller Zeiten und Völker. 119 vols. Munich and Berlin, 1992–.

Savile 1930
Drawings by Old Masters. Sale cat. London: Savile Gallery, 1930.

Schapelhouman 2006
Marijn Schapelhouman. *Rembrandt and the Art of Drawing*. Zwolle, 2006.

Schapelhouman 2015
Marijn Schapelhouman. “A Note on the Pleasures of Traveling in Former Times.” In Shoaf Turner and Te Rijdt 2015, 8–14.

Schapelhouman and Cornelis 2016
Marijn Schapelhouman and Bart Cornelis. *Adriaen van de Velde: Dutch Master of Landscape*. Exh. cat. Amsterdam: Rijksmuseum; London: Dulwich Picture Gallery, 2016–17.

Schapelhouman and Schatborn 1993
Marijn Schapelhouman and Peter Schatborn. *Tekeningen van oude meesters: De verzameling Jacobus A. Klaver*. Exh. cat. Amsterdam: Rijksmuseum, 1993.

Schapelhouman and Schatborn 1998
Marijn Schapelhouman and Peter Schatborn. *Dutch Drawings of the Seventeenth Century in the Rijksmuseum, Amsterdam: Artists Born between 1580 and 1600*. 2 vols. Amsterdam, 1998.

Schatborn 1975
Peter Schatborn. “*Diana and Callisto* by Hendrick Goltzius.” *Master Drawings* 13 (1975): 142–44, 188.

Schatborn 1981
Peter Schatborn. *Dutch Figure Drawings from the Seventeenth Century*. Exh. cat. Amsterdam: Rijksmuseum; Washington: National Gallery of Art, 1981–82.

Schatborn 1985a
Peter Schatborn. *Catalogue of the Dutch and Flemish Drawings in the Rijksprentenkabinet, Rijksmuseum, Amsterdam, IV: Drawings by Rembrandt, His Anonymous Pupils and Followers*. Amsterdam, 1985.

Schatborn 1985b
Peter Schatborn. “Tekeningen van Rembrandts leerlingen.” *Bulletin van het Rijksmuseum* 33 (1985): 93–109.

Schatborn 2001
Peter Schatborn, with Judith Verberne. *Drawn to Warmth: Seventeenth-Century Dutch Artists in Italy*. Exh. cat. Amsterdam: Rijksmuseum, 2001.

Schatborn 2010
Peter Schatborn. *Rembrandt and His Circle: Drawings from the Frits Lugt Collection*. 2 vols. Bussum and Paris, 2010.

Schatborn 2011
Peter Schatborn. “The Core Group of Rembrandt Drawings, I: Overview.” *Master Drawings* 49 (2011): 293–322.

Schatborn 2015
Peter Schatborn. “Studies for the Sick Woman in the “Hundred Guilder Print,’ Rembrandt van Rijn, c. 1648.” *Dutch Drawings of the Seventeenth Century in the Rijksmuseum*, ed. Jane Shoaf Turner, 2015, hdl.handle.net/10934/RM0001.COLLECT.28144.

Schatborn 2017
Peter Schatborn. “Rembrandt van Rijn, Ahasuerus on his Throne, Amsterdam, c. 1635 – c. 1640.” In *Dutch Drawings of the Seventeenth Century in the Rijksmuseum*, ed. Jane Shoaf Turner, 2017, hdl.handle.net/10934/RM0001.COLLECT.28130.

Schatborn and Hinterding 2019
Peter Schatborn and Erik Hinterding. *Rembrandt: The Complete Drawings and Etchings*. Cologne, 2019.

Schavemaker 2010
Eddy Schavemaker. *Eglon van der Neer (1635/36–1703): His Life and His Work*. Doornspijk, 2010.

Schellinks (ed. Exwood and Lehmann 1993)
Willem Schellinks. *The Journal of William Schellinks’ Travels in England, 1661–1663*, trans. and ed. Maurice Exwood and H.L. Lehmann. London, 1993.

Schneider 1932
Hans Schneider. *Jan Lievens: Sein Leben und seine Werke*. Haarlem, 1932.

Schneider and Ekkart 1973
Hans Schneider. *Jan Lievens: Sein Leben und seine Werke*. With a supplement by R.E.O. Ekkart. Amsterdam, 1973.

Scholten 1904
H.J. Scholten. *Musée Teyler à Haarlem: Catalogue raisonné des dessins des écoles française et hollandaise*. Haarlem, 1904.

Schrader 2022
Stephanie Schrader. "Acquisition Affinities: Following the Lead of the Chips Moore Collection." *Master Drawings* 60 (2022): 40–42.

Schrader, Turner, and Yocco 2012
Stephanie Schrader, Nancy Turner, and Nancy Yocco. "Naturalism under the Microscope: A Technical Study of Maria Sibylla Merian's *Metamorphosis of the Insects of Surinam*." *Getty Research Journal* 4 (2012): 161–72.

Schröder and Bisanz-Prakken 2004
Klaus A. Schröder and Marian Bisanz-Prakken, eds. *Rembrandt*. Exh. cat. Vienna: Albertina, 2004.

Schulz 1972
Wolfgang Schulz. *Lambert Doomer, 1624–1700: Leben und Werke*. 2 vols. Berlin, 1972.

Schulz 1974
Wolfgang Schulz. *Lambert Doomer: Sämtliche Zeichnungen*. Berlin, 1974.

Schumacher 2006
Birgit Schumacher. *Philips Wouwerman (1619–1668): The Horse Painter of the Golden Age*. 2 vols. Doornspijk, 2006.

Schwartz 1994
Gary Schwartz. *The Complete Etchings of Rembrandt, Reproduced in Original Size*. New York, 1994.

Schwartz 2006
Gary Schwartz. *Rembrandt van Rijn, Sordid and Sacred: The Beggars in Rembrandt's Etchings. Selections from the John Villarino Collection*. Exh. cat. Raleigh: North Carolina Museum of Art, and elsewhere, 2006–13.

Schwartz and Bok 1989
Gary Schwartz and Marten Jan Bok. *Pieter Saenredam: The Painter and His Time*. The Hague, 1989.

Schwed 2020
Nicolas Schwed. *Dessins anciens et du XIXème siècle*. Sale cat. Paris: Nicolas Schwed, 2020.

Sciolla 1999
Gianni Carlo Sciolla. "Disegni di Cornelis Dusart nella Biblioteca Reale di Torino." In *Scritti di storia dell'arte in onore di Jürgen Winkelmann*, ed. Piero Narcisi, 335–39. Naples, 1999.

Segal and Roding 1994
Sam Segal and Michiel Roding. *De tulp in de kunst: Verhaal van een symbool*. Exh. cat. Amsterdam: Nieuwe Kerk, 1994.

Seidenstein and Anderson 2022
Joanna Sheers Seidenstein and Susan Anderson, eds. *Crossroads: Drawing the Dutch Landscape*. Exh. cat. Cambridge (MA): Harvard Art Museums, 2022.

Sellink 2000
Manfred Sellink. *The New Hollstein: Dutch and Flemish Etchings, Engravings and Woodcuts, 1450–1700, 17: Cornelis Cort*, ed. Huigen Leeflang. 3 parts. Rotterdam, 2000.

Shoaf Turner 2006
Jane Shoaf Turner, with contributions by Felice Stampfle. *Dutch Drawings in the Pierpont Morgan Library: Seventeenth to Nineteenth Centuries*. 2 vols. New York, 2006.

Shoaf Turner 2012
Jane Shoaf Turner. *Rembrandt's World: Dutch Drawings from the Clement C. Moore Collection*. Exh. cat. New York: Morgan Library & Museum; Haarlem: Teylers Museum, 2012–13.

Shoaf Turner 2018
Jane Shoaf Turner. "Claes van Beresteyn, *Dune Landscape with Gnarled Trees, Haarlem, c. 1670*." In *Dutch Drawings of the Seventeenth Century in the Rijksmuseum*, ed. Jane Shoaf Turner, 2018, hdl.handle.net/10934/RM0001.COLLECT.637426.

Shoaf Turner and Te Rijdt 2015
Jane Shoaf Turner and Robert-Jan te Rijdt, eds. *Home and Abroad: Dutch and Flemish Landscape Drawings from the John and Marine van Vlissingen Art Foundation*. Exh. cat. Amsterdam: Rijksmuseum; Paris: Fondation Custodia, 2015–16.

Shoaf Turner and White 2014
Jane Shoaf Turner and Christopher White. *Dutch & Flemish Drawings in the Victoria and Albert Museum*. 2 vols. London, 2014.

Simon 1958
Maria Simon. *Claes Jansz. Visscher*. Freiburg im Breisgau, 1958.

Sitt and Biesboer 2001
Martina Sitt and Pieter Biesboer, eds. *Jacob van Ruisdael: Het revolutie van het Hollandse landschap*. Exh. cat. Haarlem: Frans Halsmuseum; Hamburg: Hamburger Kunsthalle, 2001–2.

Slive 2001
Seymour Slive. *Jacob van Ruisdael: A Complete Catalogue of His Paintings, Drawings, and Etchings*. New Haven, 2001.

Slive 2005
Seymour Slive. *Jacob van Ruisdael: Master of Landscape*. Exh. cat. Los Angeles County Museum of Art; Philadelphia Museum of Art; London: Royal Academy of Arts, 2005–6.

Slive 2009
Seymour Slive. *Rembrandt Drawings*. Los Angeles, 2009.

Slive and Hoetink 1981
Seymour Slive and H.R. Hoetink. *Jacob van Ruisdael*. Exh. cat. The Hague: Mauritshuis; Cambridge (MA): Harvard University, Fogg Art Museum, 1981–82.

Sloan 1986
Kim Sloan. *Alexander and John Robert Cozens: The Poetry of Landscape*. New Haven, 1986.

Sluijter 2000a
Eric Jan Sluijter. *Seductress of Sight: Studies in Dutch Art of the Golden Age*. Zwolle, 2000.

Sluijter 2000b
Eric Jan Sluijter. *De "heydensche fabulen" in de schilderkunst van de Gouden Eeuw: Schilderijen met verhalende onderwerpen uit de klassieke mythologie in de Noordelijke Nederlanden, circa 1590–1670*. Leiden, 2000.

Sluijter 2015
Eric Jan Sluijter. *Rembrandt's Rivals: History Painting in Amsterdam (1630–1650)*. Philadelphia, 2015.

Sluijter and Sluijter-Seiffert 2020
Eric Jan Sluijter and Nicolette Sluijter-Seijffert. "Rembrandt's Pupils? The Attribution of Early Drawings to Gerbrand van den Eeckhout and Jan Victors." In *Connoisseurship: Essays in Honour of Fred G. Meijer*, ed. Charles Dumas, Rudi Ekkart, and Carla van de Puttelaar, 281–99. Leiden, 2020.

Sluijter-Seijffert 2003
Nicolette Sluijter-Seijffert. "Poelenburch [Poelenburg; Poelenburgh], Cornelis van." *Grove Art Online*, 2003, https://www.oxfordartonline.com/groveart/view/10.1093/gao/9781884446054.001.0001/oao-9781884446054-e-7000068232.

Sluijter-Seijffert 2013
Nicolette Sluijter-Seijffert. "'Un bellissima cabinetto': An Art Cabinet with Paintings by Cornelis van Poelenburch and Bartholomeus van Bassen." In *Liber Amicorum Marijke de Kinkelder: Collegiale bijdragen over landschappen, marines en architectuur*, ed. Charles Dumas et al., 359–68. The Hague, 2013.

Sluijter-Seijffert 2016
Nicolette Sluijter-Seijffert. *Cornelis van Poelenburch (1594/5–1667): The Paintings*. Amsterdam, 2016.

Smith 1829–42
John Smith. *A Catalogue Raisonné of the Works of the Most Eminent Dutch, Flemish and French Painters*. 9 vols. London, 1829–42.

Spicer 1979
Joaneath Spicer. "The Drawings of Roelandt Savery." PhD thesis, Yale University, New Haven, 1979.

Sprinzels 1938
Franz Sprinzels. *Wenceslaus Hollar and His Drawings/Hollar: Zeichnungen*. Vienna, 1938.

Stainton 1987
Lindsay Stainton. *Drawings by Thomas Gainsborough (1727–1788): A Loan Exhibition*. Exh. cat. New York: Davis & Langdale, 1987.

Stainton and White 1987
Lindsay Stainton and Christopher White. *Drawing in England from Hilliard to Hogarth*. Exh. cat. London: British Museum; New Haven: Yale Center for British Art, 1987.

Stampfle 1991
Felice Stampfle, with the assistance of Ruth S. Kraemer and Jane Shoaf Turner. *Netherlandish Drawings of the Fifteenth and Sixteenth Centuries and Flemish Drawings of the Seventeenth and Eighteenth Centuries in the Pierpont Morgan Library*. New York, 1991.

Stanton-Hirst 1982
Barbara Anne Stanton-Hirst. "Pieter Quast and the Theatre." *Oud Holland* 96 (1982): 213–37.

Stefes 1997
Annemarie Stefes, "Nicolaes Pietersz. Berchem: Die Zeichnungen." 3 vols. PhD thesis, University of Bern, 1997.

Stefes 2006
Annemarie Stefes. "Nicolaes Berchem as a Draughtsman." In Biesboer 2006, 97–115.

Stefes 2011
Annemarie Stefes. *Die Sammlungen der Hamburger Kunsthalle, 3: Niederländische Zeichnungen, 1450–1850*. 3 vols. Cologne, 2011.

Stefes 2018
Annemarie Stefes, 'Attributed to Roelant Roghman, *View of the Jeruzalemkapel and the Sint Olofskapel, Amsterdam*, c. 1644', in *Dutch Drawings of the Seventeenth Century in the Rijksmuseum*, ed. Jane Shoaf Turner, 2018, hdl.handle.net/10934/RM0001.COLLECT.60389.

Steland 2007
Anne Charlotte Steland. "Early Drawings by Jacques Rousseau in the Manner of Herman van Swanevelt." *Master Drawings* 45 (2007): 167–86.

Steland 2010
Anne Charlotte Steland. *Herman van Swanevelt (um 1603–1655): Gemälde und Zeichnungen*. 2 vols. Petersburg, 2010.

Stockholm 1953
Dutch and Flemish Drawings in the Nationalmuseum and Other Swedish Collections. Exh. cat. Stockholm: Nationalmuseum, 1953.

Stogdon and Artemis 1986
Drawings from the 15th to the 20th century. Sale cat. New York: N.G. Stogdon, Inc; London: Artemis Fine Arts, 1986.

Strasser 2013
Nathalie Strasser. *Dessins des écoles du Nord du XVe au XVIIIe siècle: Collection Jean Bonna*. Geneva, 2013.

Strauss and Van der Meulen 1979
Walter L. Strauss and Marjon van der Meulen, eds., with the assistance of S.A.C. Dudok van Heel and P.I.M. de Baar. *The Rembrandt Documents*. New York, 1979.

Sumowski 1956–57
Werner Sumowski. "Bemerkungen zu Otto Beneschs Corpus der Rembrandt-Zeichnungen, I." *Wissenschaftliche Zeitschrift der Humboldt-Universität* 6 (1956–57): 255–81.

Sumowski 1962
Werner Sumowski. "Unbekannte Rembrandtzeichnungen." *Kunstchronik* 15 (1962): 274–76.

Sumowski 1964
Werner Sumowski. "Rembrandtzeichnungen." *Pantheon* 22 (1964): 233–48.

Sumowski 1979–92
Werner Sumowski. *Drawings of the Rembrandt School*. 10 vols. New York, 1979–92.

Sutton 1992
Peter C. Sutton. *Dutch and Flemish Seventeenth-Century Paintings: The Harold Samuel Collection*. Exh. cat. London: Mansion House, 1992.

Sutton and Wieseman 2004
Peter C. Sutton and Marjorie E. Wieseman, with Nico van Hout. *Drawn by the Brush: Oil Sketches by Peter Paul Rubens*. Exh. cat. Greenwich: Bruce Museum of Arts and Science; Berkeley: Berkeley Art Museum and Pacific Film Archive; Cincinnati Art Museum, 2004-5.

Teeuwisse 2008
Ausgewählte Handzeichnungen (Selected Drawings) VI. Sale cat. Berlin: Nicolaas Teeuwisse, 2008.

Teeuwisse 2019
Selected Works: TEFAF 2019. Sale cat. Berlin: Nicolaas Teeuwisse, 2019.

Temminck 1995
J.J. Temminck, ed. *Huis ter Kleef: Het enige kasteel van Haarlem*. Haarlem, 1995.

Temminck-van Dijkhuizen and Temminck 1997
M.H.G.B. Temminck-van Dijkhuizen and J.J. Temminck. *De naamborden, rouwborden en tekstborden in de Grote Kerk te Haarlem*. Haarlem, 1997.

Te Rijdt 2003
R.J.A. te Rijdt. *De Watteau à Ingres: Dessins français du XVIIIe siècle du Rijksmuseum Amsterdam*. Exh. cat. Amsterdam: Rijksmuseum; Paris: Institut Néerlandais, 2003.

Ternois 1962
Daniel Ternois. *Jacques Callot: Catalogue complet de son œuvre dessiné*. Paris, 1962.

Ternois 1999
Daniel Ternois. *Jacques Callot: Catalogue de son oeuvre dessiné. Supplément, 1962–1998*. Paris, 1999.

Tietze 1908
Hans Tietze. *Die Denkmale der Stadt Wien*. Österreichische Kunsttopographie 2. Vienna, 1908.

Todd 2007
Kim Todd. *Chrysalis: Maria Sibylla Merian and the Secrets of Metamorphosis*. Orlando, 2007.

Tongiorgi Tomasi 1997
Lucia Tongiorgi Tomasi. *An Oak Spring Flora: Flower Illustration from the Fifteenth Century to the Present Time. A Selection of the Rare Books, Manuscripts and Works of Art in the Collections of Rachel Lambert Mellon*. Upperville, 1997.

Tonkovich 2021
Jennifer Tonkovich. "Hans Calmann and the American Market for Old Master Drawings, 1937–73." *Master Drawings* 59 (2021), 49–72.

Tschudin 1958
Walter F. Tschudin. *The Ancient Paper-Mills of Basle and Their Marks*. Monumenta Chartae Papyraceae Historiam Illustrantia 7. Hilversum, 1958.

Turner 1991
Nicholas Turner. *Guercino: Drawings from Windsor Castle*. Exh. cat. Fort Worth: Kimbell Art Museum; Washington: National Gallery of Art; New York: The Drawing Center, 1991–92.

Turner 2008
Nicholas Turner. *Guercino, la scuola, la maniera: I disegni agli Uffizi*. Exh. cat. Florence: Gabinetto di Disegni e Stampe degli Uffizi, 2008.

Turner 2009
Simon Turner. *The New Hollstein: German Engravings, Etchings, and Woodcuts, 10: Wenceslaus Hollar*, ed. Giulia Bartrum. 9 parts. Ouderkerk aan den IJssel, 2009.

Turner 2010
Simon Turner. "Hollar in Holland: Drawings from the Artist's Visit to the Dutch Republic in 1634." *Master Drawings* 48 (2010): 73–104.

Turner and Plazzotta 1991
Nicholas Turner and Carol Plazzotta. *Drawings by Guercino in British Collections*. Exh. cat. London: British Museum, 1991.

Unverfahrt 2000
Gerd Unverfahrt. *Zeichnungen von Meisterhand: Die Sammlung Uffenbach aus der Kunstsammlung der Universitäts Göttingen*. Exh. cat. Koblenz: Mittelrhein-Museum; Göttingen: Kunstsammlung der Universitäts; Oldenburg: Landesmuseum für Kunst und Kunstgeschichte, 2000.

Utrecht 1978
Nederlandse tekeningen uit drie eeuwen. Exh. cat. Utrecht: Centraal Museum, 1978.

Valentiner 1925–34
Wilhelm R. Valentiner. *Rembrandt: Des Meisters Handzeichnungen*. 2 vols. Stuttgart, Berlin, and Leipzig, 1925–34.

Van Beresteyn and Del Campo Hartman 1941
Eltjo Aldegondus van Beresteyn and W.F. del Campo Hartman. *Genealogie van het geslacht Van Beresteyn*. The Hague, 1941.

Van Deinse 1918
A.B. van Deinse. "Over de potvisschen in Nederland gestrand tusschen de jaren 1531–1788." *Zoölogische Medelingen* 4 (1918): 22–50.

Van den Berg 1942
Herma M. van den Berg. "Willem Schellinks en Lambert Doomer in Frankrijk." *Oudheidkundig Jaarboek* 4 (1942): 1–33.

Van den Berg 1969
Ellen van den Berg. "Haarlemse stadspoorten: Een serie tekeningen van Vincent Jansz. van der Vinne." In *Miscellanea I.Q. van Regteren Altena*, 162–63. Amsterdam, 1969.

Van den Bussche 1880
Emilie van den Bussche. "Un évèque bibliophile: Notes sur la bibliothèque et le cabinet de gravures de Charles Vanden Bosch, neuvième évèque de Bruges, ses relations avec Elzévirs, Meyssens, etc." *La Flandre: Revue des Monuments d'Histoire et d'Antiquités* 13 (1880): 345–63.

Van der Grinten 1962
E.F. van der Grinten. "Le Cachalot et le mannequin: Deux facettes de la réalité dans l'art hollandais du seizième et du dix-septième siècles." *Nederlands Kunsthistorisch Jaarboek* 13 (1962): 149–80.

Van der Sman 2015
Gert Jan van der Sman. "I disegni di Gerrit van Honthorst." In Papi 2015, 103–19.

Van der Vinne (ed. Sliggers 1979)
Vincent Laurensz van der Vinne. *Dagelijckse aentekeninge van Vincent Laurensz van der Vinne*, ed. Bert Sliggers, Jr. Haarlem, 1979.

Van Eeghen 2011
Christiaan P. van Eeghen. "Simon de Vlieger as a Draftsman, II: Chalk Drawings Other than Pure Landscapes." *Master Drawings* 49 (2011): 179–221.

Van Eeghen 2015
Christiaan P. van Eeghen. "Simon de Vlieger as a Draftsman, III: His Chalk Landscapes and Their Connections with Works by Anthonie Waterloo and Others." *Master Drawings* 53 (2015): 313–42.

Van Eynden and Van der Willigen 1816–40
Roeland van Eynden and Adriaan van der Willigen. *Geschiedenis der Vaderlandsche schilderkunst sedert de helft der XVIIIde eeuw*. 4 vols. Haarlem, 1816–40.

Van Gelder 1933
J.G. van Gelder. *Jan van de Velde (1593–1641): Teekenaar-schilder*. The Hague, 1933.

Van Gelder 1955
J.G. van Gelder. "Jan van de Velde (1593–1641): Teekenaar-schilder: Addenda I." *Oud Holland* 70 (1955): 21–40.

Van Gelder 1971
J.G. van Gelder. "Jan de Bisschop 1628–1671." *Oud Holland* 86 (1971): 201–59; 261–88.

Van Gool 1750
Jan van Gool. *De Nieuwe Schouburg der Nederlantsche kunstschilders en schilderessen: Waer in de levens- en kunstbedryven der tans levende en reets overleedene schilders, die van Houbraken, noch eenig ander schryver, zyn aengeteekend, verhaelt worden*. 2 parts. The Hague, 1750.

Van Guldener 1947
H.T. van Guldener. "Het Jozefsverhaal bij Rembrandt en Zijn School." PhD thesis, Rijksuniversiteit te Utrecht, 1947.

Van Groesen 2016
Michiel van Groesen. "Reading Newspapers in the Dutch Golden Age." *Media History* 22 (2016): 334–52.

Van Hall 1963
Hermine van Hall. *Portretten van Nederlandse beeldende kunstenaar*. Amsterdam, 1963.

Van Hasselt 1968
Carlos van Hasselt. *Dessins de paysagistes hollandais du XVIIe siècle*. Exh. cat. Brussels: Bibliothèque Albert Ier; Rotterdam: Museum Boymans-Van Beuningen; Paris: Institut Néerlandais; Bern: Kunstmuseum, 1968–69.

Van Hasselt and Van Berge-Gerbaud 1989
Carlos van Hasselt and Mària van Berge-Gerbaud. *Éloge de la navigation hollandaise au XVIIe siècle: Tableaux, dessins et gravures de la mer et de ses rivages dans la collection Frits Lugt*. Exh. cat. Paris: Institut Néerlandais, 1989.

Van Hasselt and De Gorter 1974
Carlos van Hasselt and Sadi de Gorter. *Willem Buytewech*. Exh. cat. Paris: Institut Néerlandais, 1974–75.

Van Hoogstraten 1678
Samuel van Hoogstraten. *Inleyding tot de hooge schoole der schilderkonst: Anders de zichtbaere werelt*. Rotterdam 1678.

Van Huffel 1921
Nicolaas Gerhard van Huffel. *Cornelis Ploos van Amstel, Jacob Corneliszoon en zijne medewerkers en tijdgenooten: Historische schets van de techniek der Hollandsche prentteekeningen gemaakt in de 2e helft der 18e eeuw*. Utrecht, 1921.

Van Mander 1604
Karel van Mander. *Het schilder-boeck, waer in voor eerst de leerlustighe iueght den grondt der edel vry schilderconst in verscheyden deelen wort voorghedraghen*. Haarlem, 1604.

Van Mander (ed. Miedema 1994–99)
Karel van Mander. *The Lives of the Illustrious Netherlandish and German Painters*, ed. Hessel Miedema. 6 vols. Doornspijk, 1994–99.

Van Puyvelde 1965
Léo van Puyvelde. *Le Siècle de Rubens*. Exh. cat. Brussels: Musées Royaux des Beaux-Arts de Belgique, 1965.

Van Regteren Altena 1983
J.Q. van Regteren Altena. *Jacques de Gheyn: Three Generations*. 3 vols. The Hague, 1983.

Van Sloten 2024
Leonore van Sloten, ed. *Directed by Rembrandt*. Exh. cat. Amsterdam: Museum Rembrandthuis, 2024.

Van Suchtelen and Wheelock 2008
Ariane van Suchtelen and Arthur K. Wheelock, Jr. *Hollandse stadsgezichten uit de Gouden Eeuw*. Exh. cat. The Hague: Mauritshuis; Washington: National Gallery of Art, 2008.

Van Suylen 2020
Maud van Suylen. "Drawings of Interiors by Thomas Wijck." *Master Drawings* 58 (2020): 195–206.

Van Tatenhove 1991
Janno van Tatenhove. "Miscellanea." *Delineavit & Sculpsit* 6 (1991): 30–31.

Van Tatenhove 2001
Janno van Tatenhove. "Miscellanea. Pieter Schenk." *Delineavit & Sculpsit* 23 (2001): 31–32.

Van Thiel 1999
Pieter J.J. van Thiel. *Cornelis Cornelisz van Haarlem (1562–1638): A Monograph and Catalogue Raisonné*. Doornspijk, 1999.

Van Tuinen 2018
Ilona van Tuinen. *Power and Grace: Drawings by Rubens, Van Dyck, and Jordaens*. Exh. cat. New York: Morgan Library & Museum, 2018.

Van Tuyll van Serooskerken 2006
Carel van Tuyll van Serooskerken. *Rembrandt dessinateur: Chefs-d'œuvre des collections en France*. Exh. cat. Paris: Musée du Louvre, 2006–7.

Verdi 2004
Richard Verdi. *Bartholomeus Breenbergh (1598–1657): Joseph Distributing Corn in Egypt*. Exh. cat. Birmingham: Barber Institute of Fine Arts; The Hague: Bredius Museum, 2004–5.

Verdi 2014
Richard Verdi. *Rembrandt's Themes: Life into Art*. New Haven, 2014.

Verhagen, Van Heusden, and Kolks 1987
Jorie Verhagen, Noël van Heusden, and Zeno Kolks. *Van schaamte ontbloot: Het naakt in de Nederlandse kunst*. Exh. cat. Enschede: Rijksmuseum Twenthe, 1987–88.

Vey 1962
Horst Vey. *Die Zeichnungen Anton van Dycks*. 2 vols. Brussels, 1962.

Vienna 1970
Rembrandt: Radierungen aus dem Besitz der Albertina. Exh. cat. Vienna: Albertina, 1970–71.

Vignau-Wilberg 2013
Thea Vignau-Wilberg. *Pieter Holsteijn the Younger (1614–1673): Alderhande kruypende en vliegende gedierten (Diverse Crawling and Flying Animals)*. Exh. cat. Munich: Daxter and Marschall Kunsthandel, 2013.

Vitali 2021
Samuel Vitali. "Dialogue at a Distance: The Artistic Exchange between Hendrick Goltzius and Agostino Carracci." In *Crossing Parallels: Agostino Carracci, Hendrick Goltzius*, ed. Susanne Pollack and Samuel Vitali, 31–52. Exh. cat. Zurich: Graphische Sammlung ETH, 2021.

Volrábová 2017
Alena Volrábová. *Wenceslaus Hollar (1607–1677): Drawings: A Catalogue Raisonné*. Prague, 2017.

Walker 1941
Robert Walker. "Domenico Campagnola: Venetian Landscape Draughtsman of the Sixteenth Century." PhD thesis, Harvard University, Cambridge (MA), 1941.

Walsh, Buijsen, and Broos 1994
Amy Walsh, Edwin Buijsen, and Ben Broos. *Paulus Potter: Paintings, Drawings, and Etchings*. Exh. cat. The Hague: Mauritshuis, 1994–95.

Waterfield 1988
Giles Waterfield. *Rich Summer of Art: A Regency Picture Collection Seen through Victorian Eyes*. London, 1988.

Wegner 1973
Wolfgang Wegner. *Kataloge der Staatlichen Graphischen Sammlung München, I: Die niederländischen Handzeichnungen des 15.–18. Jahrhunderts*. 2 vols. Berlin, 1973.

Welcker 1933
Clara J. Welcker. *Hendrick Avercamp (1585–1634), bijgenaamd "De Stomme van Campen," en Barent Avercamp (1612–1679): "Schilders tot Campen."* Zwolle, 1933.

Welcker (ed. Hensbroek-van der Poel 1979)
Clara J. Welcker. *Hendrick Avercamp (1585–1634), bijgenaamd "De Stomme van Campen," en Barent Avercamp (1612–1679): "Schilders tot Campen."* Annotated and revised by D.B. Hensbroek-van der Poel, Doornspijk, 1979.

Wethey 1969–75
Harold E. Wethey. *The Paintings of Titian: Complete Edition*. 3 vols. London, 1969–75.

Wettengl 1998
Kurt Wettengl, ed. *Maria Sibylla Merian (1647–1717): Artist and Naturalist*. Ostfildern, 1998.

Wheelock 2001
Arthur K. Wheelock, Jr., ed. *Aelbert Cuyp*. Exh. cat. Washington: National Gallery of Art; London: National Gallery; Amsterdam: Rijksmuseum, 2001.

Wheelock 2008
Arthur K. Wheelock, Jr., ed. *Jan Lievens: A Dutch Master Rediscovered*. Exh. cat. Washington: National Gallery of Art; Milwaukee Art Museum; Amsterdam: Rembrandthuis, 2008–9.

Wheelock 2014
Arthur K. Wheelock, Jr. "Rembrandt van Rijn/A Polish Nobleman/1637." In *Dutch Paintings of the Seventeenth Century*, NGA Online Editions, https://purl.org/nga/collection/artobject/85.

White 1960
Christopher White. "Van Dyck Drawings and Sketches." *Burlington Magazine* 102 (1960): 510–16.

White 1969a
Christopher White. *Rembrandt as an Etcher*. 2 vols. London, 1969.

White 1969b
Christopher White. *The Late Etchings of Rembrandt: A Study in the Development of a Print*. Exh. cat. London: British Museum, 1969.

White 1999
Christopher White. *Rembrandt as an Etcher: A Study of the Artist at Work*. New Haven, 1999.

White and Boon 1969–70
Christopher White and Karel G. Boon. *Rembrandt's Etchings: An Illustrated Critical Catalogue*. 2 vols. Amsterdam, 1969–70.

White and Crawley 1994
Christopher White and Charlotte Crawley. *The Dutch and Flemish Drawings of the Fifteenth to the Early Nineteenth Centuries in the Collection of Her Majesty the Queen at Windsor Castle*. Cambridge, 1994.

Widerkehr 1999
Léna Widerkehr. "Jacob Matham and the Diffusion of Recent Developments in Roman Art in Northern Europe." In *Fiamminghi a Roma, 1508–1608*, ed. Sabine Eiche, 93–109. Florence, 1999.

Widerkehr 2007–8
Léna Widerkehr. *The New Hollstein: Dutch and Flemish Etchings, Engravings and Woodcuts, 1450–1700, 16: Jacob Matham*, ed. Huigen Leeflang. 3 parts. Rotterdam, 2007–8.

Willems 1991
Jean Willems. *Master Drawings*. Brussels, 1991.

Williams 2008
Old Master Drawings. Sale cat. London: Thomas Williams Fine Art, Ltd., 2008.

Wilton 1979
Andrew Wilton. *J.M.W. Turner: His Art and Life*. Milan, 1979.

Wivel 2020
Matthias Wivel, ed. *Titian: Love, Desire, Death*. Exh. cat. London: National Gallery; Edinburgh: Scottish National Gallery; Boston: Isabella Stewart Gardner Museum, 2020–21.

Wood Ruby 1999
Louisa Wood Ruby. *Paul Bril: The Drawings*. Turnhout, 1999.

Wood Ruby 2003
Louisa Wood Ruby. "Before the Frescoes: The Drawings." In *Northern Landscapes on Roman Walls: The Frescoes of Matthijs and Paul Bril*, ed. Carla Hendriks, 73–85. Florence, 2003.

Wood Ruby 2012
Louisa Wood Ruby. "Bruegel/Breughel/Bril: The 'Lugt Group' Revisited." *Master Drawings* 50 (2012): 357–64.

Wuestman 1996
Gerdien Wuestman. "Nicolaes Berchem in Print: Fluctuations in the Function and Significance of Reproductive Engraving." *Simiolus* 24 (1996): 19–53.

Wuestman 2006a
Gerdien Wuestman. "Berchem as an Etcher: Effortless, Accomplished, and Peerless." In Biesboer 2006, 119–31.

Wuestman 2006b
Gerdien Wuestman. "Withered Nell or Rembrandt's Aunt? Prints of 'Tronies' and Their Titles." *Simiolus* 32 (2006): 58–77.

Wurzbach 1906–11
Alfred von Wurzbach. *Niederländisches Künstler-Lexikon*. 3 vols. Vienna, 1906–11.

Yarker 2018
Jonathan Yarker. "Copying Rembrandt in Eighteenth-Century Britain." In *Rembrandt: Britain's Discovery of the Master*, ed. Christian Tico Seifert, 81–91. Exh. cat. Edinburgh: National Galleries of Scotland, 2018.

Zaal 1991a
Anne M. Zaal. "Herman Henstenburgh 1667–1726." 2 vols. PhD thesis, Vrije Universiteit, Amsterdam, 1991.

Zaal 1991b
Anne M. Zaal. *Herman Henstenburgh (1667–1726)*. Exh. cat. Hoorn: Westfries Museum. 1991.

INDEX

Page numbers in bold indicate a catalogue entry on a drawing by the artist in question.

THE MORGAN LIBRARY & MUSEUM STAFF AND VOLUNTEERS

ADMINISTRATION

Colin B. Bailey
Katherine Delaney
Sarah Lees
Jessica Ludwig
Lydia Shaw
Kristina W. Stillman

COLLECTION INFORMATION SYSTEMS

Sandra Carpenter
Robert Decandido
Lenge Hong
Maria Oldal

COMMUNICATIONS AND MARKETING

Noreen Khalid Ahmad
Christina Ludgood
Chie Xu

DEVELOPMENT

Mirabelle Cohen
Eileen Curran
Annie Gamez
Molly Hermes
Hannah Lowe
Caroline Mierins
Hadassah Penn
Lauren Stakias
Kirsten Teasdale
Stacy Welkowitz

DRAWINGS AND PRINTS

Esther Levy
Sarah Mallory
John Marciari
Jennifer Tonkovich
Daniel Tsai

EDUCATION

Mary Hogan Camp
Esme Hurlburt
Jennifer Kalter
Kat Kiernan
Nicole Leist
Jessica Pastore

EXHIBITION AND COLLECTION MANAGEMENT

Elizabeth Abbarno
Sholto Ainslie
Nicholas Bastis
Alex Félix
Walsh Hansen
Erika Hernandez Lomas
Anne Reilly-Manalo

FACILITIES

Esperanza Ayala
Monica Barker-Browne
Jean-Luc Bigord
Beverly Bonnick
Ricardo Browne
Glenvet Cassaberry
Josean Colon
Gerard Dengel
Wilson Gonzalez
Melbourne Green
Eric Grimes
Rodney Grimes
Cortez Hackett
Raheem Johnson
Andrew LeeLam
James McCollough
Marina Mugnano
Gilbert Parrilla
Sonny Patrick
Vernon Pulliam
Javier Rivera
Lidia Rodriguez
Jonathan Scales
David Shim
Bromley Synmoie
Janeth Tenempaguay
Pedro Tejada
Noel Thomas
Catherine Torres
Benjamin Ubiera
Francis White
Cory Williams

FINANCE SERVICES

Nicholas Danisi
Carmen Mui
Faiyad Islam
Thomas Mercurio
Natalie Molloy
Mary Schlitzer

HUMAN RESOURCES

Niekeda Bourgeois
Dorian Lewis-Hood
Eden Solomon

IMAGING AND RIGHTS

Janny Chiu
Carmen González Fraile
Kaitlyn Krieg
Marilyn Palmeri
Eva Soos
Min Tian

LITERARY AND HISTORICAL MANUSCRIPTS

Erica Ciallela
Jathan Martin
Philip Palmer
Sarah Robinson

MANAGEMENT INFORMATION SYSTEMS

Josh Feldman
Dani Frank
Daniel Friedman
Adrian Giannini

MEDIEVAL AND RENAISSANCE MANUSCRIPTS

Deirdre Jackson
Emerald Lucas
Joshua O'Driscoll
Roger Wieck

MERCHANDISING SERVICES

Sherifa Ali-Daniel
Pedro Anlas
Samantha Eberhardt
Aubrey Herr
Alana Hollins
Mahogany Johnson
Michelle Macias
Maya Manaligod
Emily Pritykin
Heloise Robertson
Layla Williams
Stephany Zuleta

MODERN AND CONTEMPORARY DRAWINGS

Emily Roz

MUSIC MANUSCRIPTS AND PRINTED MUSIC

Robinson McClellan

PHOTOGRAPHY

Olivia McCall
Joel Smith

PRINTED BOOKS AND BINDINGS

Sheelagh Bevan
Jesse Erickson
John McQuillen
Samantha Mohite

PUBLICATIONS

Karen Banks
Yuri Chong
Michael Ferut
Ryan Newbanks

READING ROOM

Katherine Graves
Sylvie Merian
María Isabel Molestina
Victoria Stratis

REFERENCE COLLECTION

Peter Gammie
Alaina Poppiti
Sima Prutkovsky

THAW CONSERVATION CENTER

Michael Caines
Maria Fredericks
Elizabeth Gralton
Jonathan Johansen
Rebecca Pollak
Yungjin Shin
Reba Fishman Snyder
Francisco Trujillo
Ian Umlauf

VISITOR SERVICES

Afra Annan
Aidan Carroll
Simon Cooper
Mae Cote
Laura Fowler
Britney Franco
Tendajie Leon
Leah Marangos
Yvette Mugnano
Elliot Nuss
William Pardoe
Sabrina Rivera
Michelle Volpe

PART-TIME EDUCATORS

Gema Alava-Crisostomo
William Ambler
Azadeh Amiri Sahameh
Lauren Ball
Dina Gerasia
Nadja Hansen
Rukhshan Haque
Sarah Harris Weiss
Catherine Hernandez
Helen Lee
Mary-Linda Lipsett
Emily Long
Deborah Lutz
Belbelin Mojica
Benjamin Moore
Luned Palmer
Klara Seddon
Walter Srebnick
Maria Yoon

TEMPORARY ART HANDLERS AND REGISTRARS

Fidel Alleyne
Batja Bell
Lauren Clark
James Cullinane
Storm Harper
Junichiro Ishida
Thomas Kotik
Christopher Lesnewski
Meghan Magee
Dustin McBride
Kate McKenzie
Travis Molkenbur
Carolyn Morris
Gary Olson
Yoshinari Oshiro
Beverly Parsons
David Peterson
Anibal Rodriguez
James Sheehan

VOLUNTEERS

Sidney Babcock
Grace Brodsky
Mitchell Cohn
Deb Freeman
Judith Hill
Lois Hoffman
Cynthia Johnson
Liz Kaufman
Dede Kessler
Richard Kutner
Sara Lishinsky
Wendy Luftig
Fanette Pollack
Rick Mathews
Cathleen McLoughlin
Joseph Mendez
Carissa Montgomery
Dominique Picon
Pat Pilkonis
Susan Price
Leili Saber
Jacqueline Topche
Jean Vezeris
William Voelkle
Miryam Wasserman
Christie Yang

Current as of 1 January 2024

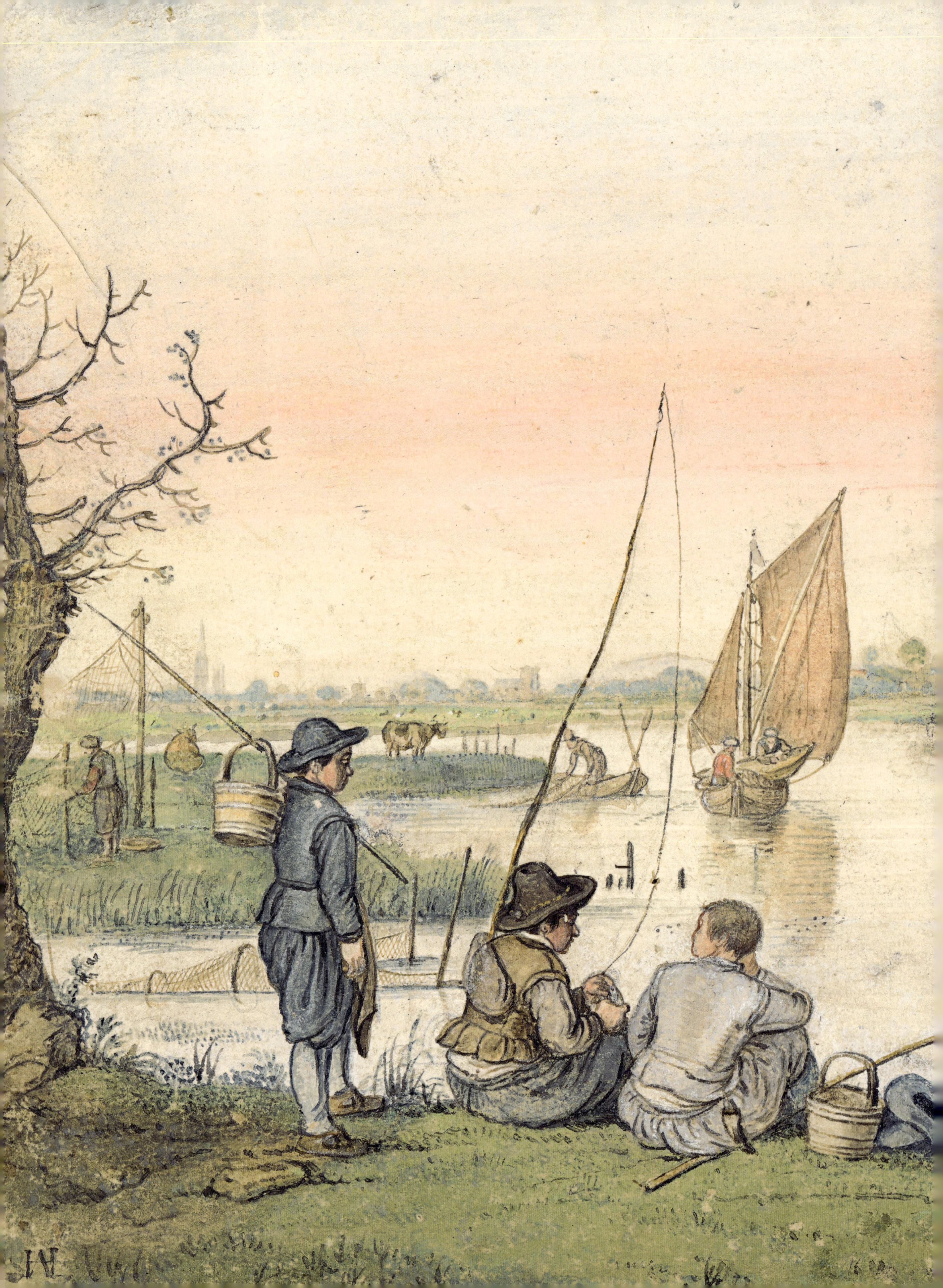